CAMBRIDGE

Official Cambridge Exam Preparation

CB082253

PREPARE

TEACHER'S BOOK WITH DIGITAL PACK

B2

LEVEL 7

Rod Fricker

Second Edition

Cambridge University Press
www.cambridge.org/elt

Cambridge Assessment English
www.cambridgeenglish.org

Information on this title: www.cambridge.org/9781009032490

First published 2015
Second Edition 2020
Second Edition update 2021

20 19 18 17 16 15 14 13 12 11 10 9 8 7 6 5

Printed in Malaysia by Vivar Printing

A catalogue record for this publication is available from the British Library

ISBN 978-1-00-903249-0 Teacher's Book with Digital Pack
ISBN 978-1-00-903247-6 Student's Book with eBook
ISBN 978-1-00-903248-3 Workbook with Digital Pack

CONTENTS

Cambridge One Digital Pa

Cambridge One hosts all your teaching tools and gives learners access to grammar, vocabulary, exam practice and tests across a range of digital devices.

Digital Packs on Cambridge One:

- Test & Train
- Practice Extra
- eBook
- Presentation Plus
- Teacher's Resources
- Class Audio

Learn more about the Prepare digital packs

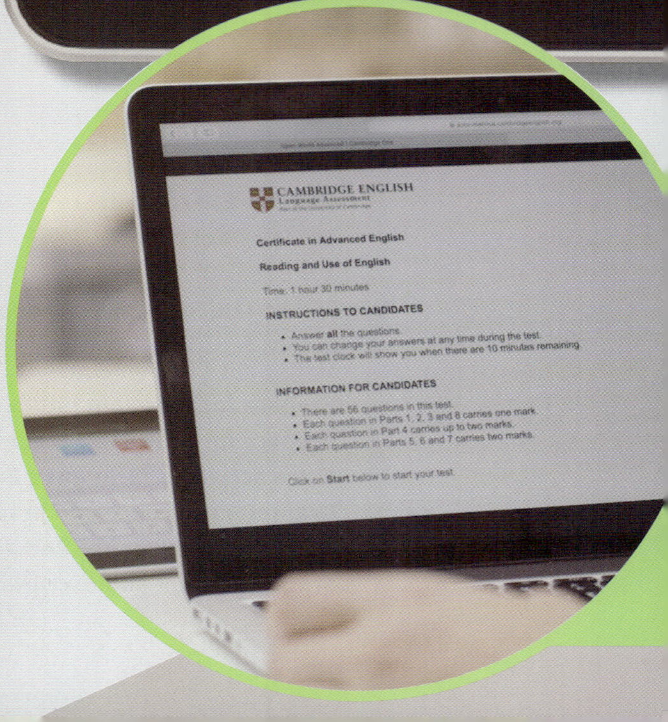

Digital resources all in one place

All the resources you and your students need are in one place: audio, video, worksheets and more.

Practice Extra

Practice Extra makes grammar and vocabulary practice more dynamic with games and exercises your students can use whenever and wherever they want.

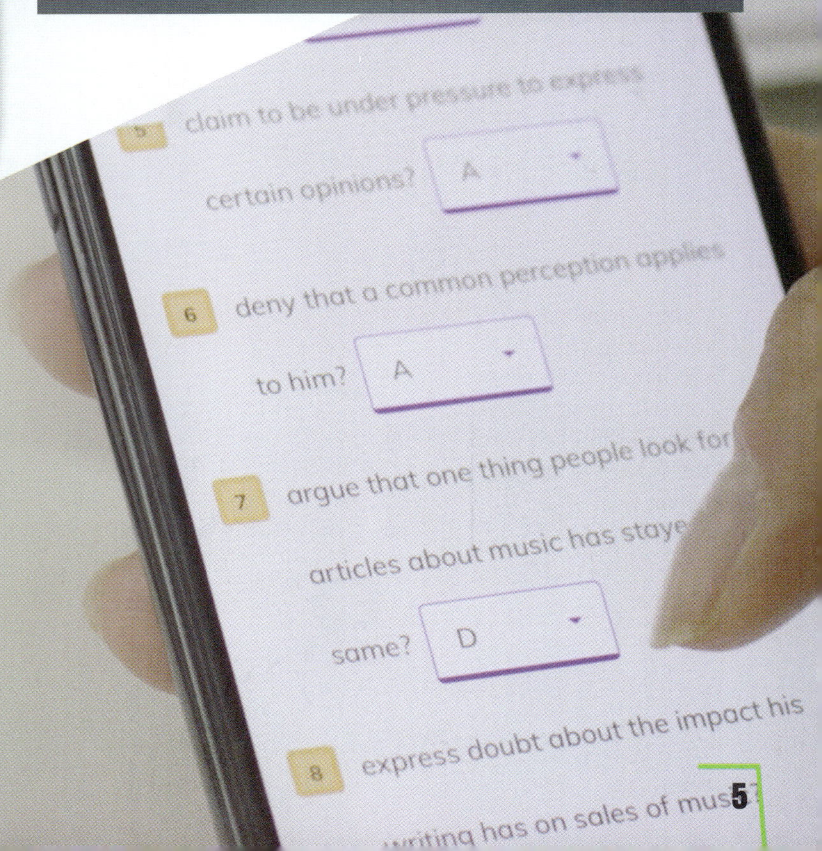

est & Train

xam Practice and **Practice Test** ets students ready for exam day.

WELCOME TO PREPARE

STUDENT'S BOOK OVERVIEW

All reading texts are recorded, giving the option to listen and read or listen and check answers where appropriate.

Each unit begins with **About you**, where students can talk about themselves and their lives.

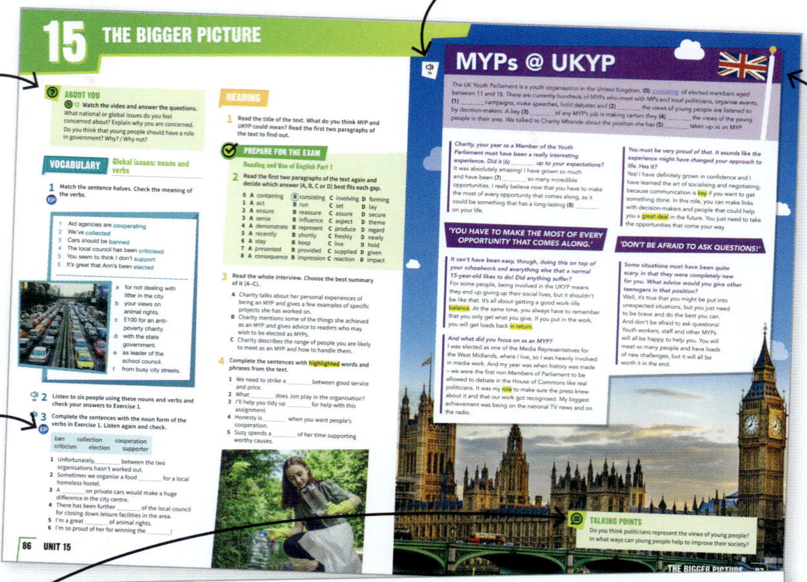

Motivating, topic-based **texts** specifically chosen to engage and inform students.

EP **Vocabulary sets** are informed by English Vocabulary Profile to ensure they are appropriate for the level.

Useful tips in **Prepare to write** help students learn to prepare, plan and check their writing.

Talking points provides opportunities to personalise language and encourage students to say what they think about the topic of the unit.

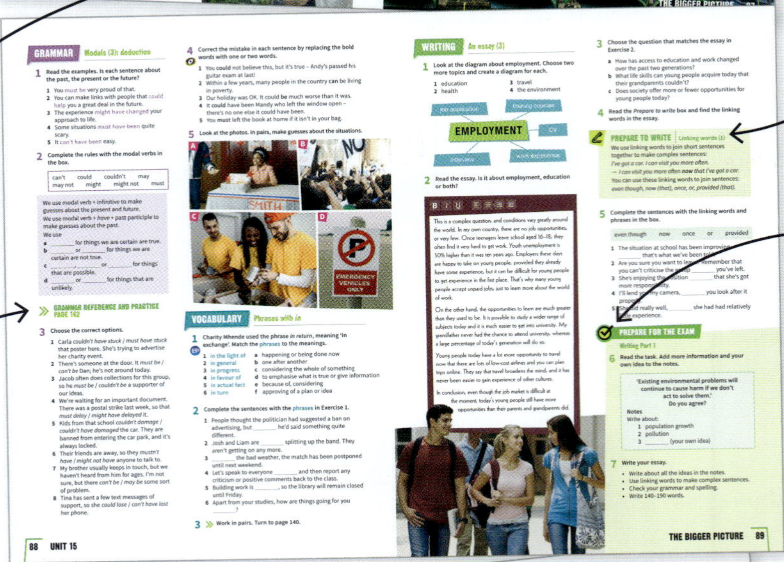

Prepare for the exam provides practice of every part of the *B2 First for Schools* exam.

Clear **grammar presentation and practice** is extended in the Grammar reference and practice section at the back of the book.

In **Prepare to speak**, students learn useful words and phrases for effective communication.

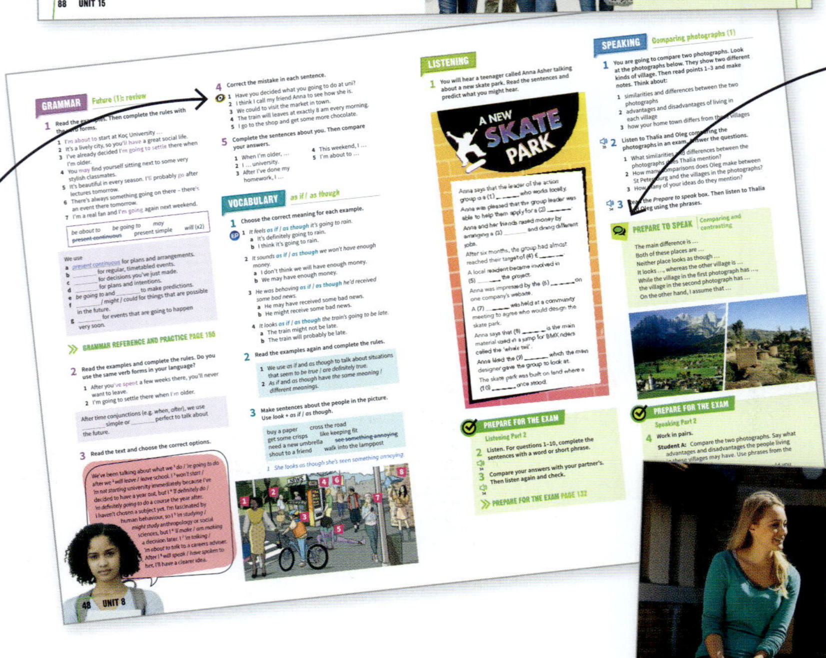

Common mistakes relevant to your students' level are identified in grammar activities marked with the **Cambridge Learner Corpus icon**.

Video interviews show real teens giving their opinion on the topic of the unit. Each video comes with a worksheet containing comprehension and discussion questions.

There is a **Life Skills** or **Culture** lesson after every two units. The **Life Skills** lessons help students develop important skills for their everyday lives.

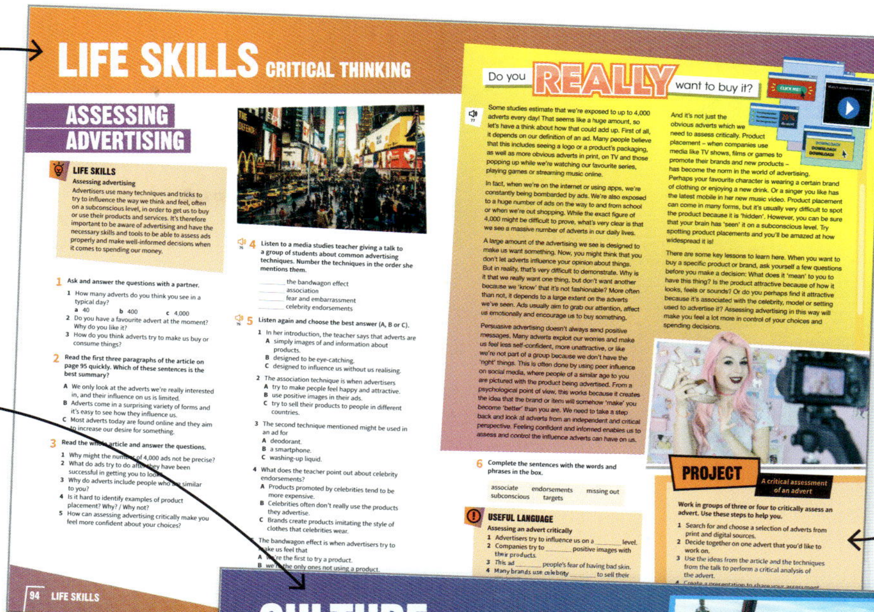

Culture lessons highlight interesting aspects of culture in English-speaking countries.

Projects in the Life Skills and Culture lessons encourage students to work together to create something fun and expand their learning.

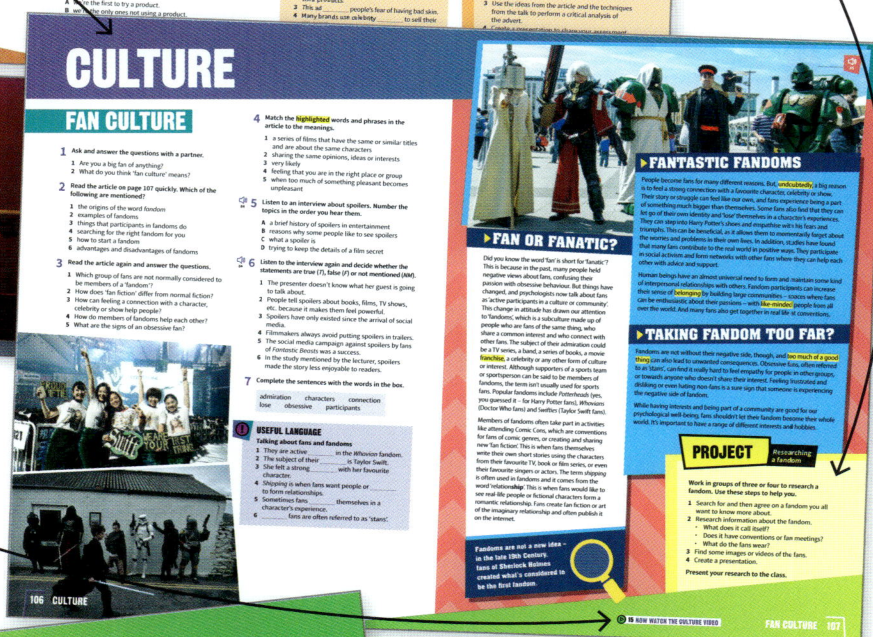

In the **videos** found in each Culture lesson, students can watch interesting documentaries about the Culture topics. Each video comes with a worksheet for students to complete as they watch.

The **Prepare for the exam** section at the end of the Student's Book contains useful tips and teaches techniques for the *B2 First for Schools* exam, as well as providing practice of exam tasks.

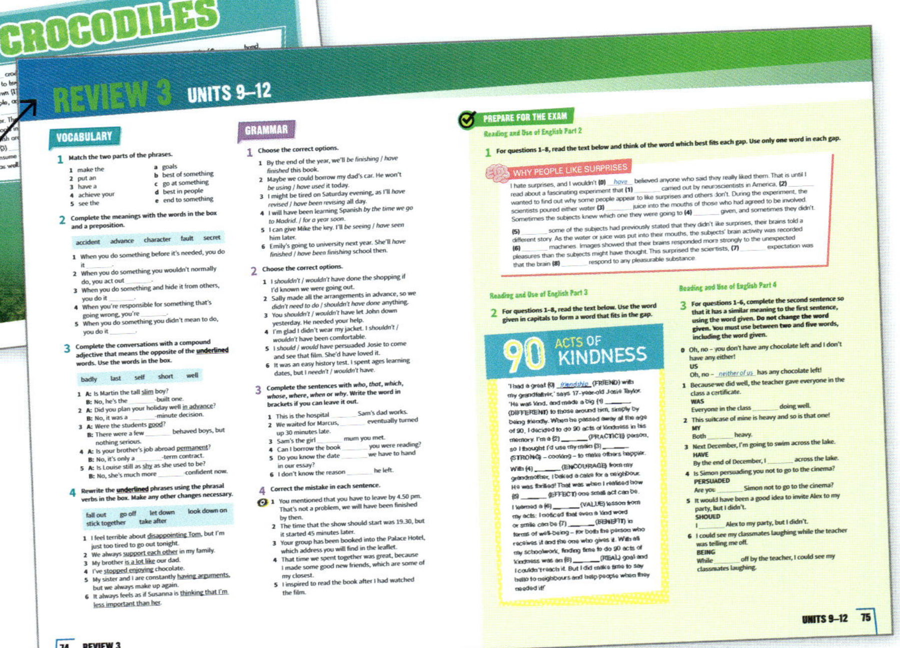

Review pages after every four units give further practice of language, skills and exam tasks.

COMPONENT LINE-UP

Student's Book with eBook

The Student's Book combines teen-appeal topics with preparation for the B2 First for Schools exam. With twenty lively core units, Reviews, Culture and Life Skills sections, a Vocabulary list, and a Grammar reference and practice section, the Student's Book has all the material you need to create interactive, personalised lessons. Full audio and extensive video to accompany the Student's Book is available for teachers online.

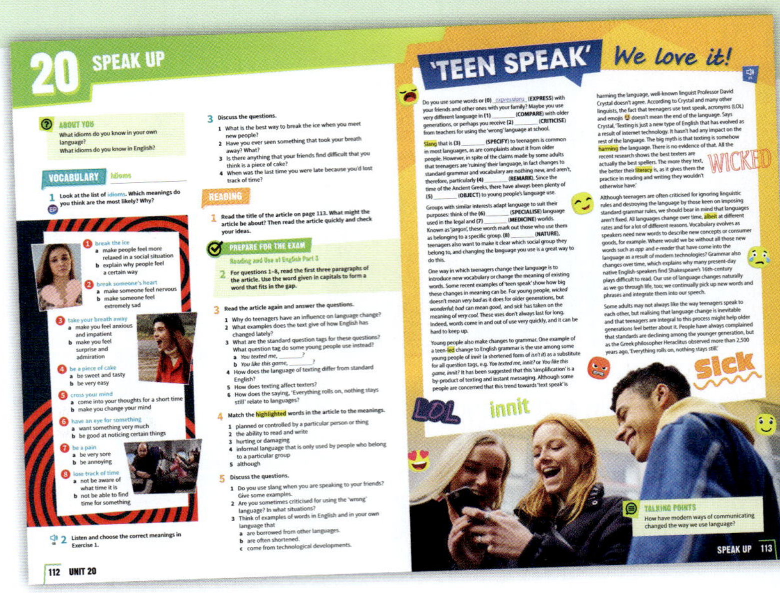

Workbook with Digital Pack

The Workbook gives additional practice of all the language from the Student's Book. It also provides students with comprehensive skills development work and further exposure to exam tasks. The Workbook is suitable for use both in the classroom and for homework.

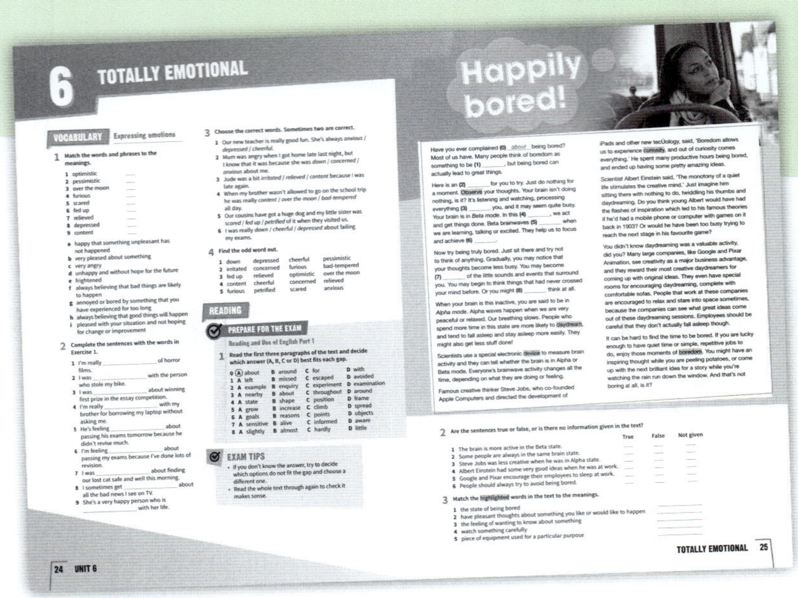

Teacher's Book with Digital Pack

The interleaved Teacher's Book contains complete teaching notes for all of the Student's Book tasks, in addition to answer keys and audioscripts. With a wealth of lesson ideas, warmers, coolers and extension tasks, the Teacher's Book helps you manage mixed-ability classes and work with fast finishers. Information panels include background information about themes, topics and cultural events. Prepare for the exam information boxes provide detailed descriptions of each task found in the B2 First for Schools exam, as well as useful tips on how to approach the tasks. Clear indications direct you to additional resources which support and extend learning.

The Teacher's Book provides access to a wide range of printable worksheets for use in class, including:

- Grammar worksheets (available at two levels of challenge: standard and plus)
- Vocabulary worksheets (available at two levels of challenge: standard and plus)
- Review Games
- Literature worksheets
- Speaking worksheets
- Writing worksheets
- Video worksheets

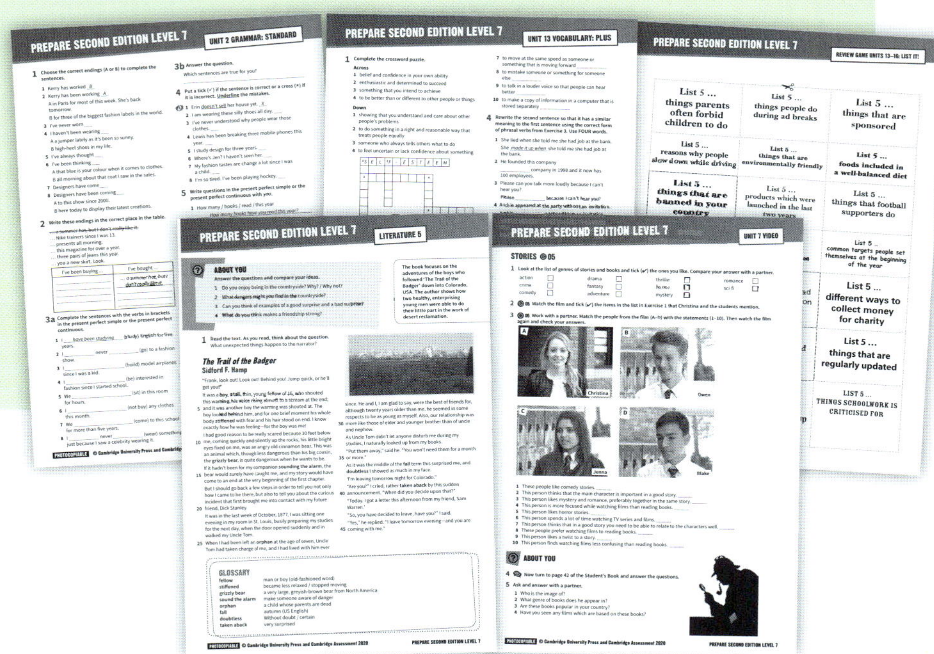

Learn more about the Prepare Digital Packs

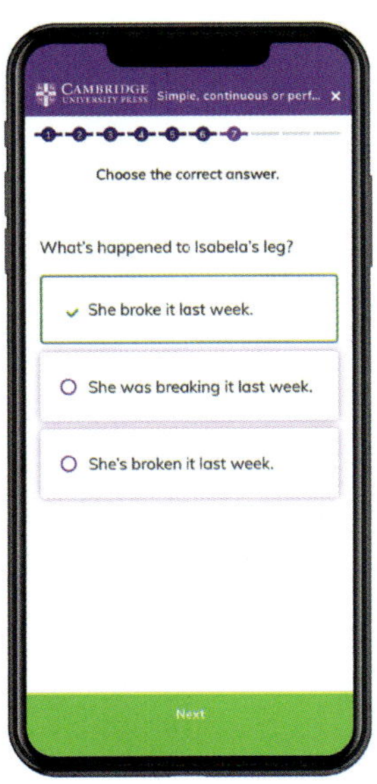

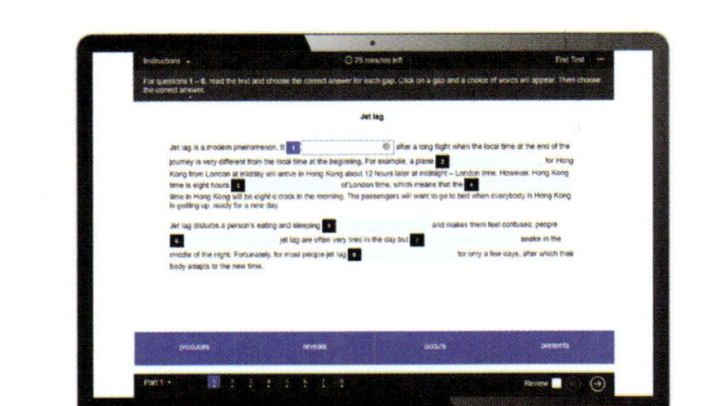

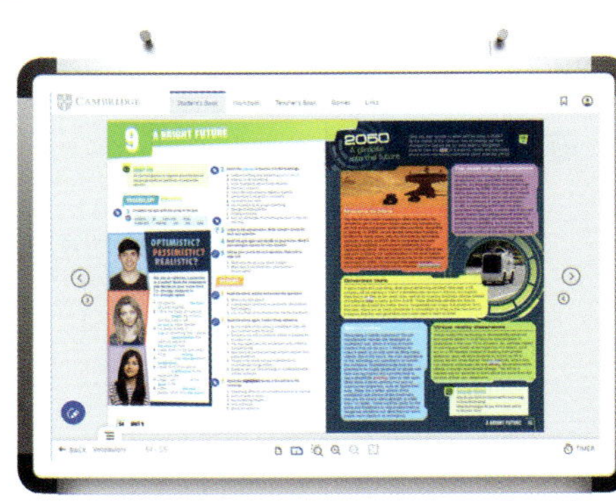

THE PREPARE EXAM JOURNEY

The *Prepare* Exam Journey combines teen-appeal topics with extensive preparation for Cambridge English Qualifications. Levels 6 and 7 of *Prepare* Second Edition take students on a two-year journey towards the *B2 First for Schools* exam. This approach builds confidence every step of the way from the first experiences of exam tasks to skills development; from language discovery to understanding how English works in the real world.

LEVEL 6

Prepare Level 6 gradually introduces authentic *B2 First for Schools* exam tasks, ensuring students become familiar with every part of the exam.

- Exam tasks are discreetly labelled with the exam icon in **Level 6 Student's Book**.

2 **Complete the second sentence so that it has a similar meaning to the first sentence, using the word given. Do not change the word given. You must use between two and five words, including the word given.**

1 My brother isn't like either of my parents. **TAKE**
My brother ______ either of my parents.

2 Lucy isn't talking to her brother because he lost her phone. **FALLEN**

- **Level 6 Workbook** offers further exposure to each part of the exam.

1 **Complete the second sentence so that it has a similar meaning to the first sentence, using the word given. Do not change the word given. You must use between two and five words, including the word given.**

1 My brother and I had an argument and now we're not talking.
FELL
I ______ my brother, and now we're not talking.

2 She never understood or shared the feelings of her older sister.
IDENTIFY
She couldn't ______ her older sister.

- Information about each part of the exam is included in **Level 6 Teacher's Book**.

2 B2 First for Schools Reading and Use of English Part 4

In this part, there are six questions plus an example. In each question, there is a sentence, a key word and a second sentence in which only the beginning and ending are given. Students have to complete the second sentence using two to five words, including the key word. They cannot change the form of the key word in any way. The task tests both grammatical and lexical items. There are two marks for each part, so the students can gain a mark even if a part of their answer is incorrect.

LEVEL 7

Prepare Level 7 provides complete coverage of the *B2 First for Schools* exam, driving students to exam success.

- Each exam task is highlighted clearly in the *Prepare for the exam* features in **Level 7 Student's Book**.

PREPARE FOR THE EXAM
Writing Part 1

6 **Write your essay.**
- Use your answers to the questions in Exercise 5.
- Organise your essay into the paragraph plan in the *Prepare to write* box.
- Use the expressions in Exercise 4.
- Check your spelling and grammar.
- Write 140–190 words.

» PREPARE FOR THE EXAM PAGE 130

- The *Prepare for the exam* section at the end of **Level 7 Student's Book** includes further guidance and support with practice tasks.

PREPARE FOR THE EXAM
B2 FIRST FOR SCHOOLS

Reading and Use of English Part 5 Multiple choice
(Unit 7, Unit 12, Unit 18)

EXAM INFORMATION
- You will read a fiction or non-fiction text.
- There are six four-option multiple-choice questions.
- The questions are in the same order as the information in the text.
- You should read the text carefully and choose only one option per question.

1 **Read the article on page 125 quickly. What is *Southfields*?**
A A documentary about old skateboarding movies
B A document about the award-winning skateboarder Stuart Laker
C A documentary about skaters in an area of London

2 **Read question 1 below. Then look at the highlighted part of the first paragraph, which confirms the answer. Why are A, B and D wrong?**

3 **Now read the exam instructions and complete the task.**

You are going to read an article about a film-maker called Stewart Laker and a skateboarding film he has made. For questions 1–6, choose the answer (A, B, C or D), which you think fits best according to the text.

1 What made the writer want to watch the film *Southfields*?
A the fact that it was made for younger audiences
B the reputation of the person who directed it
C the location where the film is set
D the publicity she had read about it

EXAM TIPS
Read the relevant paragraph and underline where you think the answer is. Check that the other three options are wrong.

2 Stewart Laker tells the writer that his main aim in making *Southfields* was

- **Level 7 Workbook** consolidates each exam task and includes Exam Tips.

PREPARE FOR THE EXAM
Writing Part 1

5 **Now complete the essay, using the plan and all your notes from Exercise 4, and give reasons for your point of view. Try to use the following expressions in your paragraphs: *to sum up*, *in contrast*. Write about 140–190 words.**

EXAM TIPS
- Make a plan for your essay before you write it.
- Give each paragraph a clear function – for example, an introduction with your opinion, ideas for the statement in the question, ideas against the statement and a conclusion.
- Be sure to address both prompts in the question and introduce your own idea.
- Use linking words to join your ideas.

- **Level 7 Teacher's Book** details each part of the exam and suggests teaching tips for the classroom.

PREPARE FOR THE EXAM

B2 FIRST FOR SCHOOLS
Writing Part 1
In this part, students write an essay in response to a statement or question with prompts. This task is compulsory. The functions tested will include agreeing and disagreeing, giving opinions with reasons and examples, giving information and/or explanations, comparing and contrasting, and drawing conclusions. Students must also add a third separate 'own idea', which should not overlap with the given prompts and must not be a conclusion. Students are expected to write 140–190 words in a neutral or formal register.

Tips Ask students to read the task carefully, underlining the key information. They should make a plan before they start writing and organise their essay into paragraphs as well as noting down useful vocabulary that they can use in their essay. When they have finished writing, they should check their work to make sure there are no obvious errors and that the essay is clear and easy to understand and answers the question.

B2 FIRST FOR SCHOOLS EXAM OVERVIEW

PAPER / TIMING	PART	FORMAT AND FOCUS	PRACTICE IN LEVEL 7
Reading and Use of English 1 hour 15 minutes	**Part 1** Eight 4-option multiple-choice cloze questions (8 marks)	A modified cloze test with eight gaps. The main focus is on vocabulary, e.g. idioms, collocation, phrasal verbs.	Student's Book pages 14–15, 31, 36–37, 53, 86–87, 97, 119, 120 Workbook pages 8–9, 24–25, 60–61
	Part 2 Eight open cloze questions (8 marks)	A modified cloze test with eight gaps. The main focus is on awareness and control of grammar with some focus on vocabulary.	Student's Book pages 31, 32–33, 53, 64–65, 75, 90–91, 97, 121 Workbook pages 20–21, 44–45, 64–65
	Part 3 Eight word formation questions (8 marks)	A text with eight gaps, each of which corresponds to a word. The stem of the missing word is given and must be changed to form the missing word. The main focus is on vocabulary.	Student's Book pages 53, 56, 75, 98–99, 112–113, 119, 122 Workbook page 38, 68–69, 80–81
	Part 4 Six key word transformation questions (12 marks)	Six separate items, each with a lead-in sentence and a gapped second sentence to be completed in two to five words, one of which is a given 'key' word. The focus is on grammar, vocabulary and collocation.	Student's Book pages 26, 31, 60, 75, 82, 97, 119, 123 Workbook pages 18, 42, 59
	Part 5 Six 4-option multiple-choice questions (12 marks)	A text followed by six multiple-choice questions. The focus is on detail, opinion, attitude, tone, purpose, main idea, gist, meaning from context, implication and text organisation features.	Student's Book pages 42–43, 68–69, 102–103, 124–125 Workbook pages 28–29, 48–49, 72–73
	Part 6 Six gapped text questions (12 marks)	A text from which sentences have been removed and placed in jumbled order after the text. Candidates must decide from which part of the text the sentences have been removed. The focus is on cohesion, coherence and text structure.	Student's Book pages 20–21, 58–59, 108–109, 126–127 Workbook pages 12–13, 40–41, 76–77
	Part 7 Ten multiple matching questions (10 marks)	A text or several short texts, preceded by multiple-matching questions. Candidates must match a prompt to elements in the text. The focus is on detail, opinion, specific information and implication.	Student's Book pages 10–11, 46–47, 76–77, 128–129 Workbook pages 4–5, 32–33, 52–53
Writing 1 hour 20 minutes	**Part 1** An essay (one compulsory task) 140–190 words	Candidates are required to deal with input of up to 120 words. There is an opening rubric to set the scene, and then an essay question with two given prompts, plus a prompt requiring candidates to write about their own additional idea. The focus is on giving opinions, reasons, conclusions, etc.	Student's Book pages 13, 57, 89, 111, 130 Workbook pages 7, 39, 63, 79
	Part 2 Choice of four options 140–190 words	A situationally based writing task specified in no more than 70 words. Writing one of the following: an article, an email, a letter, a review or a story. Question 5 is always based on a set reading text and students should not attempt this unless they have read the set text.	Student's Book pages 23, 35, 45, 67, 79, 101, 130 Workbook page 15, 23, 31, 47, 55, 71
Listening 40 minutes approximately	**Part 1** Eight 3-option multiple-choice questions	A series of short unrelated extracts from monologues or exchanges between speakers. There is one multiple-choice question per text. The focus is on genre, identifying speaker feeling, attitude, topic, opinion, purpose, agreement between speakers, gist and detail.	Student's Book pages 39, 115, 131 Workbook pages 27, 83
	Part 2 Ten sentence completion questions	A monologue lasting 3–4 minutes. Candidates are required to complete sentences with information heard on the recording. The focus is on detail, identifying specific information and stated opinion.	Student's Book pages 49, 71, 93, 132 Workbook pages 35, 51, 67
	Part 3 Five multiple matching questions	Five short related monologues. There are five questions, which require the selection of the correct option from a list of eight. The focus is on identifying speaker feeling, attitude, detail, gist and opinion.	Student's Book pages 17, 27, 83, 132 Workbook pages 11, 19, 59
	Part 4 Seven 3-option multiple-choice questions	An interview or exchange between two speakers lasting 3–4 minutes. The focus is on identifying opinion, attitude, detail, gist, main idea and specific information.	Student's Book pages 61, 105, 133 Workbook pages 43, 75
Speaking 14 minutes Part 1: 2 minutes Part 2: 4 minutes Part 3: 4 minutes Part 4: 4 minutes	**Part 1** A conversation between the interlocutor and each candidate	Spoken questions. The focus is on general interactional and social language.	Student's Book pages 17, 83, 134
	Part 2 Individual 'long turn'	In turn, the candidates are given a pair of photographs to talk about. The focus is on organising a larger unit of discourse; comparing, describing and expressing opinions.	Student's Book pages 49/138, 115/141, 134–135
	Part 3 Discussion task followed by decision-making task	A two-way conversation between the candidates, who are given spoken instructions with written stimuli. The focus is on sustaining an interaction, reaching a decision, etc.	Student's Book pages 71, 93, 136
	Part 4 Discussion task	A discussion on topics related to the previous collaborative task (spoken questions). The focus is on expressing and justifying opinions, agreeing and/or disagreeing and speculating.	Student's Book pages 71, 93, 137

Key to symbols:
✔ *B2 First for Schools* exam task ▶ Video

LISTENING	SPEAKING	WRITING	VIDEO
		An essay (1) ✔ Writing Part 1	▶ Creative minds
Five opinions about wearing a school uniform ✔ Listening Part 3	Talking about yourself ✔ Speaking Part 1		▶ Fashion
			▶ Influencers
		An informal letter or email ✔ Writing Part 2	
Five opinions about stress ✔ Listening Part 3	Offering help		
		An article (1) ✔ Writing Part 2	
Eight short conversations ✔ Listening Part 1	Generalising		
			▶ The meaning of colours
		A story ✔ Writing Part 2	▶ Stories
A talk about a new skate park ✔ Listening Part 2	Comparing photographs (1) ✔ Speaking Part 2		▶ Where we live
		An essay (2) ✔ Writing Part 1	
A radio interview about a surprise ✔ Listening Part 4	Expressing surprise		▶ Surprises!
			▶ Sensing language

Key to symbols:
✓ *B2 First for Schools* exam task ▶ Video

1 CREATIVE MINDS

ABOUT YOU

01 **Watch the video and answer the questions.**

What do you spend most of your time doing?
Have you ever been in a play?
Have you ever composed a piece of music?
Do you think people are naturally talented and creative or can they learn to be?

VOCABULARY Arts and media

EP **1** **Read the quiz. Check the meaning of the words.**

MEDIA QUIZ

1. Does your favourite TV show have an all-star **cast** or unknown actors?
2. Do you ever learn the lyrics to songs that are in **the charts**?
3. Do you read modern **bestsellers**, or do you prefer the **classics**?
4. What's your favourite **series** of books?
5. Have you ever seen a film being **shot**?
6. Do you have a favourite **piece** of art?
7. Have you ever seen someone famous make a public **appearance**?
8. Which channel **broadcasts** the best shows in your country?
9. What **track** do you listen to most on your favourite album?
10. Which app or website do you use to **stream** music?

2 **Do the quiz with your partner.**

Do you read modern bestsellers, or do you prefer the classics?

I like to read modern bestsellers. I'm reading a crime novel at the moment. I don't read classics very often.

READING

PREPARE FOR THE EXAM

Reading and Use of English Part 7

1 **Read the questions. Then read text A about a talented young person. Which two questions relate to text A?**

Which person

1. rapidly learned something they were interested in?
2. developed an interest after experiencing the work of others?
3. took up a new hobby so that they would understand something better?
4. has a clear idea of what they will do in the future?
5. became popular for sharing their everyday experiences?
6. felt confident that they would do well?
7. has a parent who was initially unsure about their child's ideas?
8. has a talent which was recognised in the media?
9. enjoys trying to help other people?
10. achieved an online record with their activity?

2 **Read the whole article. For the remaining questions in Exercise 1, choose from the people (B–D). The people may be chosen more than once.**

» PREPARE FOR THE EXAM PAGE 128

3 **Complete the sentences with the highlighted words and phrases from the article.**

1. I'm ________ the main character in my book ________ my sister, Charlie.
2. Lucy is ________ she can sing, but her voice is awful!
3. What ________ of novels do you like best? I love science fiction.
4. Have you sent in your ________ to the publisher yet?
5. Sonya's got a real ________ composing. She'll be famous one day.

1 CREATIVE MINDS

Unit Overview

TOPIC	Being creative
VOCABULARY	Arts and media
READING	The ones to watch
GRAMMAR	Simple, continuous or perfect
VOCABULARY	Creative jobs
WRITING	An essay (1)
EXAM TASKS	Reading and Use of English Part 7; Writing Part 1

Resources

GRAMMAR REFERENCE AND PRACTICE: SB page 148; TB page 267
PREPARE FOR THE EXAM: SB pages on TB pages 244–246; TB pages 257–258
WORKBOOK: pages 4–7
VIDEO AND VIDEO WORKSHEET: Creative minds
PHOTOCOPIABLE WORKSHEETS: Grammar worksheet Unit 1; Vocabulary worksheet Unit 1
TEST GENERATOR: Diagnostic test; Unit test 1
PRACTICE EXTRA: Unit 1

WARMER

On the board, draw a quick, random, wiggly line. Look at this with the students and elicit anything they think it looks like. Choose one of the options offered by the students and draw a picture of it using the line as part of the picture (or ask a student to do this on the board).

Students now work in pairs. Each student draws their own line and passes it to their partner who decides what it looks like and uses their imagination to make it into a picture. Set a time limit of one minute and then ask students to look at each other's pictures and ask who thinks their partner is very imaginative and creative.

ABOUT YOU

01 You can begin the class and introduce the topic of the unit by showing the video and asking students to complete the video worksheet. Then, read the questions in the *About you* box with the class. Put students into groups of three or four to discuss the four questions. Set a time limit of two minutes and elicit ideas. Ask what other activities can show that someone is creative, for example, *art*, *photography*, *website design*.

VOCABULARY Arts and media

1 Students work in pairs to see which of the words in blue they understand. Students then change partners and share their ideas with a different student. Students go back to their original partners and tell each other what they found out. Elicit the meanings of all the words and which words can be used with other forms of entertainment, for example, *a cast can be in a TV show, a film or a play, a series can also refer to a television series, you can also stream films and TV shows*. Ask students to write two new questions using the elicited forms of entertainment.

Answers
Students' own answers

2 Look at the example with the class. Elicit what else the person answering could say, for example, they could give reasons for not reading classics very often: *I don't read classics very often because I find the language in old books quite difficult to understand at times.* Encourage students to give similar answers when they are doing the exercise to practise their speaking skills. If students wrote new questions at the end of Exercise 1, they can also ask their partner those questions. Monitor and note interesting answers and invite students to share their answer to one of the questions with the class.

Answers
Students' own answers

READING

PREPARE FOR THE EXAM

B2 FIRST FOR SCHOOLS
Reading and Use of English Part 7

In this part, students have one long text or a number of short texts preceded by ten questions. They have to match the questions to the correct text or section of the text. Each text or section of the text can match more than one question.

Tips Ask students to read the text(s) first to understand the general idea. They should also note any important information in each text. This could be factual details, attitudes or opinions. When they then look at the ten questions, they should already know which texts some of them match. It is important to check the text again before deciding as, sometimes, students may see the same word in one text as in one of the questions but, when reading carefully, discover that the question doesn't match this text.

1 Look at the first question with the students and elicit what the key words are, for example, *rapidly learned*. Elicit synonyms for this phrase, for example, *quickly picked up*. Students underline the key words in the other questions in pairs. Then, they find the two questions for text A. Elicit the answers and the information in the text which matches them. 3 *trained in martial arts in order to write the fight scenes more accurately* 6 *believed in her ability to succeed*

Answers
3 and 6

CONTINUED ON PAGE 18

BACKGROUND INFORMATION

Nancy Yi Fan's books are *Swordbird*, *Sword Quest*, a prequel set 100 years before the events of the first book, and *Sword Mountain*. Nancy started writing after having a very vivid dream about birds at war after learning about the war on terror at school. In 2011, Nancy went to Harvard University to study.

Sigrid Solbakk Raabe has now appeared at Glastonbury Festival, so the newspaper critic was right. Her first album, *Sucker Punch*, came out in March 2019 and she went on tour with American band Maroon 5 and British singer George Ezra. She also had a track on the soundtrack album from the film *Justice League*.

Tom Cassell was influenced by a friend who made videos of himself playing *Call of Duty* and then cutting up the video and editing it to make a montage. Tom then thought it would be a good idea to upload videos of himself actually playing games and commenting on them. When he had reached about 300,000 views, he received an email offering to pay him if he allowed adverts on his videos. Tom now tries to post a video every day at 6 pm, as it is very easy for YouTubers to quickly lose followers if they don't keep putting out new content.

Tenith Adithyaa is from the Tamil Nadu area of India. He jokes that he was an outstanding student. He said that he stayed up so late every night doing experiments that he was never on time for school and so was always left standing outside the classroom.

2 Give the students a few minutes to read the other texts and note down what they think the key information in each is. When they have finished, they cover the texts and tell each other in pairs what they remember about each person. Students then look at the questions and match as many to the texts as they can. Finally, they read the texts again to check their answers or complete the matching if necessary. Elicit the answers and the extracts from the texts which match each question.

MIXED ABILITY

Put weaker students into groups of three. They read one of the remaining texts (B–D) each and make notes of the most important information about their person. They then tell each other what they found out and try to match as many questions as possible to their text. If there are some questions that none of them have chosen, or that more than one student has chosen, they work together to see which texts the questions should match.

Answers

1 D (mastering nine of them in no time)
2 B (was inspired at an early age by artists such as Joni Mitchell and Adele)
3 A
4 D (plans to spend the coming years making the site a success)
5 C (he vlogs about what he gets up to in his daily life … had over 2.5 million subscribers and 390 million views)
6 A
7 C (His father wasn't convinced it would be successful)
8 B (popular with critics … one national newspaper suggested she could be headlining at the UK's most famous music festival)
9 D (wants nothing more than to improve people's lives through his work)
10 C (he became the first person in the website's history to reach a million followers)

» PREPARE FOR THE EXAM TEACHING NOTES AND ANSWER KEY TB PAGE 257

01 The Reading text is recorded for students to listen, read and check their answers.

3 Tell students that the form of the words they use to complete the sentences may be different to those in the text, for example, a different tense, a plural instead of a singular form, etc. When students have finished, allow them to check their answers in pairs. Elicit the answers and the meanings of the words.

FAST FINISHERS

Ask fast finishers to try to think of their own sentences using some of the words and phrases from the exercise, for example *My cat is called Hulk. I named him after the film character.* When you have elicited the answers, invite fast finishers to share their sentences with the class.

Answers

1 naming … after 2 convinced 3 genre 4 proposal 5 passion for

TALKING POINTS

Put the students into groups of three or four and ask them to look at the first question. Say, 'One person in the group should imagine that they are uncreative. They'd like to be able to write, compose, paint or do some other kind of creative activity. The other students should give them suggestions about how they could become more creative.' Tell the student being given the advice that they need to remember this for later so may need to make notes. Set a time limit of two minutes and then ask the 'uncreative' student to tell the class the best piece of advice they were given.

Now look at the second question. Ask students how many vlogs or Instagram pages there are and how many people become famous from these things. Students then discuss why they think some people become successful while others don't. Set a time limit of two minutes and invite students to share their ideas with the class.

COOLER

Talk to students about different talents and abilities that people have. Give them an example about yourself, for example, you are good at English but you can't play a musical instrument. Write a sentence on the board: *I'll teach you English, if you teach me how to play the guitar.*

Ask students to think of similar sentences about themselves. They offer something they are good at and ask to be taught something they would like to be good at. Students then mingle to try to find someone who can help them or who they can help. Set a time limit of two or three minutes then ask the class if they found anyone who would be useful for them.

THE ONES TO WATCH

01

A Nancy Yi Fan

When Nancy Yi Fan moved to the US from China, aged seven, she spoke hardly any English. Already an enthusiastic reader and writer in her native Chinese, she learned English by reading the classics, she says. It took her two years to write her first novel, *Swordbird*. When she had finished it, she emailed a copy to several leading publishers in the USA. Without an agent, book proposals are rarely read, but Nancy believed in her ability to succeed. And she did – a year later, at the age of 12, she was a published novelist with a bestseller. Now, Nancy has not only completed all three books in the *Swordbird* series, but also translated them into Chinese herself. The story is about a world full of birds, at war over a lack of food. Nancy even trained in martial arts in order to write the fight scenes more accurately. Hopefully they'll shoot a film version of the series in the future!

B Sigrid

Sigrid, a young singer-songwriter from Norway, has always loved music, and was inspired at an early age by artists such as Joni Mitchell and Adele. When she was 17, Sigrid, whose full name is Sigrid Solbakk Raabe, started a band, called Sala Says Mhyp, with her sister, Johanne, naming it after a pet cat called Sala they'd had as youngsters. Sigrid wrote the lyrics of her debut track *Sun*, which was released in 2013, and just three years later, in 2016, she signed with Island Records. Soon her music had reached the top of the charts in Norway, Australia and the UK, where she was so popular with critics that one national newspaper suggested she could be headlining at the UK's most famous music festival, Glastonbury, in the near future. Sigrid has won several music awards and is fulfilling her dream of touring the world.

C Tom Cassell

Tom Cassell, better known as Syndicate, is an entrepreneur who turned a hobby into a living. A massive fan of gaming, Tom had the idea of filming a game and commenting on the action while he was playing. He started uploading his videos to his YouTube channel *TheSyndicateProject*, and the genre became a huge hit. Tom also operates a second YouTube channel called *Life of Tom*, in which he vlogs about what he gets up to in his daily life. His father wasn't convinced it would be successful, but by 2017, *Life of Tom* had over 2.5 million subscribers and 390 million views. Tom also runs a Twitch channel, and he became the first person in the website's history to reach a million followers. In 2017, *TheSyndicateProject* reached 10 million subscribers. He now travels widely, promoting his videos, and is a well-known figure in the video-gaming world.

D Tenith Adithyaa

At the age of eight, Tenith Adithyaa started to study software languages, mastering nine of them in no time. As he grew up, Tenith discovered a passion for finding solutions to problems, coming up with the adjustable electricity extension board (which allows multiple plugs to be connected to the same point) and banana leaf preservation technology (which preserves banana leaves for a year without using any chemicals and allows environmentally friendly cups and plates to be made from them rather than plastic). These are just a few of his many successes, and, by the age of 15, he had already produced 17 useful innovations, not to mention winning several prestigious awards. Tenith wants nothing more than to improve people's lives through his work. He is currently running Altruu, the social network he founded, and plans to spend the coming years making the site a success. He also makes appearances as a motivational speaker and as a judge for invention competitions.

TALKING POINTS

How do you think people could become more creative?

What other qualities do young people need in order to succeed?

GRAMMAR Simple, continuous or perfect

1 Match the examples to the meanings.

1 Sigrid **has** always **loved** music.
2 By the age of 15, he **had** already **produced** 17 useful innovations.
3 He **is** currently **running** Altruu, the social network he founded.
4 He now **travels** widely, promoting his videos.
5 Tom had the idea of commenting on the action while he **was playing**.
6 She **emailed** a copy to several leading publishers.

a an action in progress in the present
b an action in progress in the past
c an action that started in the past and continues into the present
d a fact or state in the present
e a single completed action in the past
f an action that took place before another time in the past

2 Complete the rules with *continuous*, *perfect* or *simple*.

We use the
a present or past ________ for permanent states and for regular or completed actions.
b present or past ________ for actions or states that are/were in progress or unfinished.
c present or past ________ for actions or states that connect two time periods.

» GRAMMAR REFERENCE AND PRACTICE PAGE 148

3 Choose the correct sentence or response. Can you explain your choices?

1 We didn't have time to speak to Jack for long.
  a When we arrived, he had left.
  b When we arrived, he was leaving.
2 I did nothing yesterday.
  a I spent the entire day sleeping.
  b I've spent the entire day sleeping.
3 What are you up to at the moment?
  a I often review films online.
  b I'm reviewing a film online.
4 I'm looking forward to the next book in the series.
  a I read all the others.
  b I've read all the others.
5 This actor is often in police thrillers.
  a Yes, he's playing lots of characters like this.
  b Yes, he plays lots of characters like this.

4 Choose the correct options.

1 Tonight, I *am going* / *go* to a concert with my friends.
2 They often *shoot* / *are shooting* films in our town because it's so beautiful.
3 Krishan *has written* / *writes* a bestseller about his childhood in India.
4 My dad *is having* / *has* a job at a recording studio.
5 What *are you reading* / *do you read* at the moment?
6 I *don't decide* / *haven't decided* what I want to do when I finish my studies.

5 Complete the sentences with your own ideas.

1 I have always listened to …
2 By the age of four, I had learned to …
3 I'm currently reading …
4 I often stream …

VOCABULARY Creative jobs

1 Match the creative jobs to the definitions.

EP

comedian	critic	editor	novelist
producer	programmer	TV presenter	

Someone who
1 gives their opinion of a book, play, film, etc.
2 corrects and changes text or film, or someone in charge of a newspaper.
3 is in charge of making a film, show or musical recording.
4 writes fictional books.
5 introduces a show.
6 produces apps or computer software.
7 entertains people by telling jokes.

02 **2 Listen to five people talking about their jobs. Match each speaker to a job in Exercise 1.**

02 **3 Listen again and make notes about each job. Then discuss the questions.**

1 Which job do you think is the easiest/hardest? Why?
2 Which job do you think is the most interesting? Why?

GRAMMAR Simple, continuous or perfect

WARMER

Write on the board:

Start this book: two weeks ago

Read: five pages a day

Read: 80 pages so far

At the moment: not reading

Elicit sentences about the information on the board and the tenses used, for example: *I started this book two weeks ago (past simple), I read 5 pages a day (present simple), I have read 80 pages so far (present perfect)* and *I'm not reading at the moment (present continuous)*.

Students work in pairs and write their own four pieces of information that they can then turn into four sentences, using a variety of tenses in the simple, perfect and continuous. When finished, invite pairs to share their sentences with the class.

1 Students work in pairs to do the matching. Elicit the answers and more information that the students can give about each sentence, for example, *1c: When did the action start? (A long time ago, for as long as Sigrid can remember.)*.

Answers

1 c 2 f 3 a 4 d 5 b 6 e

2 When the students have completed the rules, elicit more sentences which illustrate them. For example, Simple: *I like fish. (A permanent state – it is always true.) I went to Madrid last summer. (a completed, single action)* Continuous: *I am teaching (an action in progress) I was watching TV at 8 pm last night. (an action in progress at a specific time in the past)* Perfect: *I have been to India. (It connects the present to the past. This happened at some point between my birth and the present.) When I got to school, I realised I had forgotten the exam papers. (This connects arriving at school with an earlier time when I forgot the exam papers.)*

Answers

a simple b continuous c perfect

» **GRAMMAR REFERENCE AND PRACTICE ANSWER KEY TB PAGE 267**

3 Students work alone to think about this, then get together in pairs to share ideas and explanations. Elicit the answers and what the alternative choice would mean, for example: *1 a We didn't see Jack at all because he wasn't there when we arrived. 2 b The time period is unfinished so this can only be talking about today. 3 a This is what the person does regularly, but doesn't tell us what they are doing now. 4 a is not correct because time period is not mentioned. Unless the time period is clear – even if unstated – we should use the present perfect. 5 a This is grammatically incorrect. It would mean that he is playing all the characters at the moment.*

Answers

1 b They spoke to Jack, so Jack hadn't left when they arrived.
2 a *Yesterday* is a finished past time period.
3 b The question is asking about a current activity.
4 b He hasn't finished reading the series. The present perfect is used to connect two time periods (past and present) and here links the past reading with the present feeling.
5 b This happens regularly.

4 Look at the first sentence with the class. Elicit the correct answer and ask what this is an example of (*future arrangements using the present continuous*). Remind students that it is important to use the future time period in a sentence like this or it will sound as if the action is happening now. Students do the rest of the exercise alone. Elicit the answers.

FAST FINISHERS

Ask fast finishers to think of how they could explain which verb form is correct, in case any students give the wrong answers. When eliciting the answers, if someone does give a wrong answer, or doesn't know an answer, invite fast finishers to explain which answer is correct.

Answers

1 am going 2 shoot 3 has written 4 has 5 are you reading
6 haven't decided

5 You could give the class some examples about yourself before students do the activity. Set a time limit of two minutes for them to think of ideas and then put them into pairs or small groups to discuss their sentences. Invite students to share something interesting they learned about their partners with the class. Students give their own answers.

» **GRAMMAR WORKSHEET UNIT 1**

VOCABULARY Creative jobs

1 Before students look at the definitions, write four stress patterns on the board:

Oo *Ooo* *oOo* *oOoo*

Model the pronunciation of the words and ask students to listen carefully and say which stress pattern each one matches (*Oo – critic; Ooo – editor, novelist, programmer; oOo – producer, presenter; oOoo comedian*). Drill all the words and then ask students to do the matching. Elicit the answers and make sure students say each word correctly.

Answers

1 critic 2 editor 3 producer 4 novelist 5 TV presenter
6 programmer 7 comedian

02 **2** Divide the class into seven groups. Give each group one of the jobs in Exercise 1 to think about. Look at the task in Exercise 2 and ask each group to think of five key words or phrases they think someone in their job might use, for example *a comedian – laugh*. Elicit ideas from each group and write their words on the board. When students have listened to the recording, elicit any key words they heard.

Elicit the two unused jobs (*comedian* and *programmer*). Put students into pairs and ask them to choose one of these two jobs. Then set a time limit of three or four minutes for students to write a similar description of this job. Both students should write the description. Monitor and help where necessary. Students then change partners. They take it in turns to read their description for their new partner to guess the job. Invite one or two students to read out their descriptions to the class.

Answers

Speaker 1 novelist Speaker 2 critic Speaker 3 producer
Speaker 4 editor Speaker 5 TV presenter

02 **3** When students have listened for a second time, put them into groups of three or four to discuss what they noted down and the questions. Set a time limit of three or four minutes and then invite each group to share their ideas with the class. Students give their own answers.

» **AUDIOSCRIPT TB PAGE 286**

» **VOCABULARY WORKSHEET UNIT 1**

WRITING An essay (1)

1 Put the students into pairs to discuss the two questions. Set a time limit of three minutes and have a class discussion on whether the students think they should spend more or less time on creative subjects and why. Follow up by asking students if academic subjects can be creative and, if so, how? For example, *English can be creative when students prepare and present projects.*

Answers
Students' own answers

2 Look at the task with the class. Elicit the answer and re-elicit the ideas they had in the discussion in Exercise 1. Look at the third point with the class. Students work in groups of three or four to think of another point they could answer in their essay. You could follow this up by asking students about how they prepare themselves for writing an essay. Give an example of your own, for example, write *1, 2, 3* on the board, representing the notes in the task and related vocabulary and ideas next to each number: *1 Maths, English – exams aged 18; 2 foreign language – work abroad*, etc. Students then work in their groups to think of other ways to plan their ideas. Monitor and help where necessary and invite students to present their ideas to the class on the board.

Answers
Students' own answers, but they have to say whether or not they agree with the statement that subjects such as drama and music are just as important as maths and languages.

3 Look at the *Prepare to write* box with the class. If you used the idea about planning an essay in the previous exercise, point out that planning individual paragraphs is another way of preparing. After looking at each paragraph elicit an example statement about the current situation at school (*At the moment, we only have three hours a week of creative subjects.*). Students then do the matching activity.

Answers
Paragraph 1: B Paragraph 2: D Paragraph 3: C Paragraph 4: A

4 Students match the expressions to their uses. Then, in pairs, they compare and discuss any other expressions they know with the same meanings. Elicit these and write them on the board for the class to make a note of.

Answers
a Most people agree that (The majority of people agree that)
b Furthermore (Moreover, In addition)
c In contrast (Conversely, On the other hand)
d For instance (For example, such as)
e To sum up (In conclusion, In summary)

5 Students work alone. Set a time limit of five minutes for students to think of some ideas, then put them in pairs or small groups to compare ideas. Invite groups to share their ideas with the class when they have finished.

MIXED ABILITY
Put weaker students into pairs with stronger students to discuss the questions together. They then swap partners so that, even if the weaker student didn't contribute many ideas initially, they will now be able to compare ideas with a different student and add any new ideas to their own notes.

Answers
Students' own answers

PREPARE FOR THE EXAM

B2 FIRST FOR SCHOOLS
Writing Part 1: An essay
In this part, students write an essay in response to a statement or question with prompts. This task is compulsory. The functions tested will include agreeing and disagreeing, giving reasons and/or examples, giving information and/or explanations, comparing and contrasting, and drawing conclusions. Students must also add a third separate 'own idea' which should not overlap with the given prompts and must not just be a conclusion. Students are expected to write 140–190 words in a neutral or formal register.

Tips Ask students to read the task carefully, underlining the key information. They should make a plan before they start writing and organise their essay into paragraphs, as well as noting down useful vocabulary that they can use in their essay. When they have finished writing, they should check their work to make sure there are no obvious errors and that the essay is clear and easy to understand and answers the question.

6 In the exam, the students have 100 minutes for the two writing tasks, about 35 minutes for each part once they have made a plan. If you can't allow them a reasonable amount of time during the lesson, it would be better for them to do this at home so that the essay isn't too hurried. One way to do this would be to extend Exercise 5 and allow students to write a very rough version of the essay together, which they then write properly alone at home.

Model answer
This is a complex issue, and the balance of subjects will depend on the type of school and the aims of its students. However, it is certainly true that most teenagers would benefit from learning some practical skills.
Academic subjects such as science, maths and history are clearly important for any students intending to study at university, and there may not be much free time left for other aspects of education.
On the other hand, students do need basic skills to survive in the wider world. For instance, they should be able to set a spending budget and save money. Furthermore, when young people leave home, they will need to know how to change a plug or a light bulb!
Another thing to consider, in my opinion, is the continuing need for creative subjects in school, such as art and drama. Even if a student is not planning to have a career in these areas, they are enjoyable subjects and will make that individual a more interesting person.
To sum up, having a wider choice of subjects is good in theory. However, it may not always be achievable.

» PREPARE FOR THE EXAM TEACHING NOTES AND ANSWER KEY TB PAGE 258

COOLER
Elicit all the practical skills that a school could teach students suggested in Exercises 5 and 6 and write these on the board. Put students into groups of three or four. Tell the groups that the school has agreed that they can find time to teach three of these skills in the students' timetable. They work together to try to decide on the best three and reasons why they are important. Invite each group to present their ideas and reasons to the class.

WRITING An essay (1)

1 **Discuss the questions.**

1 What creative subjects do you do at school?
2 Do you spend as much time on creative subjects as academic subjects?

2 **Read the task. What question do you have to answer?**

In your English class you have been talking about different school subjects. Now your English teacher has asked you to write an essay for homework.
Write your essay using **all** the notes and giving reasons for your point of view.

> **'Subjects such as drama and music are just as important as maths and languages.'**
> **Do you agree?**
> **Notes**
> Write about:
> 1 which subjects are important in your country
> 2 which subjects are useful for a career
> 3 .... (your own idea)

3 **Read the** ***Prepare to write*** **box and the paragraphs of the essay (A–D). Match the paragraphs to the plan.**

PREPARE TO WRITE | Organising essays

You can use four paragraphs to write an opinion essay about a statement or question.

- **Paragraph 1**: an introduction, possibly a statement about the current situation
- **Paragraph 2**: one or more arguments for or against the statement, possibly with an example from your own knowledge or experience
- **Paragraph 3**: one or more contrasting arguments, possibly with an example from your own knowledge or experience
- **Paragraph 4**: a conclusion, your opinion of the statement

A To sum up, it is clearly necessary for everyone to study academic subjects, but, at the same time, creative subjects are often ignored by schools. They deserve a more significant role in children's education.

B This is an interesting question which many people hold strong opinions about. In most schools in my country, students have far more lessons in subjects like maths and languages than creative subjects such as drama and music. Furthermore, many students study no creative subjects after the age of 15.

C However, others feel that without music and drama, students may never get to express their creative sides. They might never discover their talent for singing, playing musical instruments or acting. Many of the highest academic achievers have a creative side. For instance, Einstein loved music as much as he loved physics.

D Most people agree that academic subjects are important. Almost everyone will need maths and foreign language skills in their future working life. In contrast, few people will be lucky or talented enough to earn a living as a professional musician or an actor.

4 **Which of the highlighted expressions in the essay introduces the following ideas? Give examples of more expressions that you could use.**

a a general opinion
b an additional idea
c a different idea
d an example
e the conclusion

5 **Read the task and answer the questions.**

In your English class you have been talking about the role of education. Now your English teacher has asked you to write an essay for homework.
Write your essay using **all** the notes and giving reasons for your point of view.

> **'Schools should teach a range of skills, such as how to manage money and apply for jobs, as well as academic subjects like science and history.'**
> **Do you agree?**
> **Notes**
> Write about:
> 1 academic subjects
> 2 practical skills
> 3 .... (your own idea)

1 Do you agree or disagree with the statement?
2 What arguments support the statement?
3 What arguments can be used against the statement?
4 What is your own idea for note 3?

PREPARE FOR THE EXAM

Writing Part 1

6 **Write your essay.**

- Use your answers to the questions in Exercise 5.
- Organise your essay into the paragraph plan in the *Prepare to write* box.
- Use the expressions in Exercise 4.
- Check your spelling and grammar.
- Write 140–190 words.

» PREPARE FOR THE EXAM PAGE 130

2 ADDICTED TO FASHION

ABOUT YOU

02 Watch the video and answer the questions.

What do you take into account when you buy clothes?

Do you think that clothing affects people's moods?

Why do you think some people are so concerned about fashion?

Do you think people will judge you according to what you wear?

VOCABULARY Personality: adjective + preposition

03 EP **1** **Read what four young people say about fashion. Match the sentence halves from the extracts. Listen and check.**

EMMA

1 I'm **aware of** what's in fashion
2 I'm easily **impressed by**
3 I'm pretty **adventurous with**

a my taste in clothes, but I'd never wear fur.
b designer labels. My favourite is Prada.
c because I read fashion blogs.

AHMED

4 I'm **addicted to** shopping
5 I do need to be **cautious about** spending
6 I'm absolutely **hopeless at** making

a decisions about clothes.
b for clothes. I just can't stop!
c too much, though.

DAN

7 I'm not all that **bothered about** what
8 You shouldn't be **critical of** the way
9 I've never been **mean about** a friend's

a dress sense. People can be very sensitive about their appearance.
b others think of my dress sense. I just wear whatever I like.
c others dress. It's up to individuals to choose how they want to look.

SARA

10 There's no point in being **loyal to** a
11 I certainly wouldn't be **jealous of** a friend
12 I'm fairly **decisive about**

a what to buy. I don't waste time worrying about what else might be available.
b just because they had an expensive brand of trainers.
c particular brand. You should feel free to wear anything that looks good.

03 **2** **Answer the questions. Listen again and check.**

1 Where does Emma buy most of her clothes?
2 What did Ahmed have to do when he accidentally spent too much?
3 Why does Dan like wearing conventional clothes?
4 What does Sara think of brands and labels?

3 **Which statements in Exercise 1 are true for you? Discuss your answers.**

READING

1 **Do you enjoy shopping for clothes in a market? Why? / Why not?**

2 **Read the article quickly. Which 'big question' are all the people answering?**

A Do people worry too much about fashion?
B Does fashion actually matter?
C Are you aware of the latest fashions?

PREPARE FOR THE EXAM

Reading and Use of English Part 1

3 **Read the first paragraph of the article again and decide which answer (A, B, C or D) best fits each gap.**

	A	B	C	D
0	select	agree	(C) settle	establish
1	disturbed	bothered	troubled	stressed
2	constant	immediate	latest	current
3	smoother	calmer	easier	plainer
4	hunting	viewing	looking	exploring
5	extended	extreme	expanded	extensive
6	deliver	present	supply	provide
7	budget	limit	economy	bargain
8	hope	passion	desire	feeling

» PREPARE FOR THE EXAM PAGE 120

2 ADDICTED TO FASHION

Unit Overview

TOPIC	Clothes and fashion
VOCABULARY	Personality: adjective + preposition
READING	The big question
GRAMMAR	Present perfect simple and continuous
VOCABULARY	Verb + preposition
LISTENING	Five opinions about wearing a school uniform
SPEAKING	Talking about yourself
EXAM TASKS	Reading and Use of English Part 1; Listening Part 3; Speaking Part 1

Resources

GRAMMAR REFERENCE AND PRACTICE: SB page 149; TB page 267
PREPARE FOR THE EXAM: SB pages on TB pages 236, 248 and 250; TB pages 254 and 260–261
WORKBOOK: pages 8–11
VIDEO AND VIDEO WORKSHEET: Fashion
PHOTOCOPIABLE WORKSHEETS: Grammar worksheet Unit 2; Vocabulary worksheet Unit 2
TEST GENERATOR: Unit test 2
PRACTICE EXTRA: Unit 2

WARMER

Put students into groups of four or five. Tell them to choose one student from their group. They then work together to write down what that person is wearing, including colours and styles as well as just the clothes items themselves. Set a time limit of two minutes. When they have finished, ask the students in the class to close their eyes. Choose one group to read out their description to see if the other groups can guess who it is. Repeat for the other groups. If students wear a uniform, groups can describe their favourite outfits instead.

ABOUT YOU

02 You can begin the class and introduce the topic of the unit by showing the video and asking students to complete the video worksheet. Then, read the questions in the *About you* box. Allow students to think alone for two minutes about the four questions and then get into groups of three or four to share their ideas. Invite groups to share their ideas with the class. Then carry out a class survey to find out how many students are interested in fashion.

VOCABULARY Personality: adjective + preposition

03 **1** Look at Emma's three sentences with the class and elicit the correct matches, but don't elicit the meanings of the vocabulary yet. Students then do the same for the other three speakers. When they have listened to the recording, elicit the answers.

Answers
1 c 2 b 3 a 4 b 5 c 6 a 7 b 8 c 9 a 10 c 11 b 12 a

03 **2** Before students look at the four questions, ask them to work in pairs to tell each other anything they can remember about the four people. They then look at the questions together to see if they answered any of the questions in their summaries. Elicit the answers when the students have listened again.

Answers
1 in department stores or online 2 He had to return a lot of clothes. 3 He believes in keeping things simple. 4 She thinks there's no point being loyal to brands.

» AUDIOSCRIPT TB PAGE 286

3 Before students discuss the statements, ask them to work in groups of three or four to see if they can explain what the highlighted words mean. Allow them to use dictionaries or phones to look up words they are unsure of. After they have discussed the sentences, elicit alternative ways of saying them and then ask students which are true for them. For example, Emma: *I know about what's in fashion. I really like designer labels and think they are great. I take a lot of chances with what I wear.*

Answers
Students' own answers

READING

1 Elicit a description of what kind of clothes the girl in the photo on page 25 of the Student's Book is wearing. Invite students to share their opinions and then ask the class if they know of any good markets to buy clothes in their own town or area.

Answers
Students' own answers

2 Set a time limit of two minutes so that students have to read quickly for overall understanding rather than for detailed understanding. When they have finished, ask students just to look at the answers in the text in bold and to give the correct answer based on these (*It must be question B, as it is the only one that makes sense for Natalia's answer: Does fashion…? I think it does.*).

Answer
B Does fashion actually matter?

CONTINUED ON PAGE 26

BACKGROUND INFORMATION

A *catwalk* in English originally referred to any narrow walkway, usually high above the ground, for example, along the side of a bridge or around the edge of a building to allow access for workers. The names comes from the fact that cats have no problems walking along narrow, exposed paths. By the early 20th century, the term was also used for the walkway used by models which tended to be narrower than they are now.

The term *fast fashion* has two meanings. It was originally used to describe how quickly cheap clothes could be produced and distributed to high street shops for sale after being seen on the catwalk. This has been helped by cheaper production of clothes, often in developing world countries, cheaper materials and the demand for new fashions to be immediately available because of the internet. Fast fashion has helped to increase sales as the regular introduction of new styles attracts customers to shops more often to see what is available. Although fast fashion is advantageous for both suppliers and customers, it has now acquired a new meaning. Rather than applying to the speed at which clothes are supplied, the adjective 'fast' in fast fashion is often used to describe how quickly new clothes are discarded nowadays. Critics say that fast fashion is now a leading contributor to pollution and poor working conditions for employees whose wages are often low because of the need to keep costs down.

PREPARE FOR THE EXAM

B2 FIRST FOR SCHOOLS

Reading and Use of English Part 1

In this part, students have a text with eight gaps and an example gap. For each gap, there are four multiple-choice options. Part 1 tests the students' lexical knowledge and understanding of the text. Some questions test at a phrasal level, such as collocations and set phrases. Other questions test meaning at sentence level or beyond. This part may test a lexico-grammatical element, such as when candidates have to choose the option which fits correctly with a following preposition or verb form.

Tips Ask students to look at the example (0). Elicit which words are definitely not followed by the preposition *on*. If the students can be sure that, for example, *select* and *establish* aren't followed by *on*, they are only left with a choice of two words. Ask them to think why *agree* might not be correct (*there is no reference to agreeing with anyone*). So, even if they don't know the phrase *settle on*, meaning to decide or choose, they can select it by eliminating the other choices.

3 Tell the students that, in the exam, this part will feature a standalone text, not one that is part of a longer text. When students have finished, allow them to compare answers in pairs and then elicit the correct answers.

Answers

1 B 2 D 3 C 4 D 5 D 6 B 7 A 8 C

» PREPARE FOR THE EXAM TEACHING NOTES AND ANSWER KEY TB PAGE 254

4 Set a time limit of ten minutes and ask students to note down the information in the text which helped them decide the correct answer. When they have finished, allow them to compare in pairs and, if they disagree with each other, they try to decide who is correct.

MIXED ABILITY

Put the students into mixed ability pairs and tell them to read two texts each: Arslan and Olivia or Camila and Natalia. When they have finished, they can tell each other the answers and show each other the information in the text which helped them to decide.

Answers

1 False. The traditional colours associated with boys and girls were the opposite 100 years ago.
2 False. Cheaper ones are really no different!
3 False. They may be jealous of you.
4 True
5 False. They can look just as good.
6 True

04 The Reading text is recorded for students to listen, read and check their answers.

5 Tell stronger students to cover the meanings in Exercise 5 and to look at the sentences in which the highlighted words appear. In pairs, they try to rephrase the highlighted words. Elicit ideas and then ask them to uncover the meanings and do the matching. You could help weaker students by writing a choice of word for each meaning on the board, for example, *1 up to a point, badges; 2 badge, catwalk; 3 dress, dress sense; 4 dress, up to a point; 5 dress sense, catwalk*. Elicit the answers and ask how the students rephrased the words to check if their ideas were correct.

Note that *a dress* is an item of clothing that women wear and, *dress*, without an article, refers to clothes in general. There can be a *dress code*, which means rules about what kind of clothes are acceptable, for example at work.

FAST FINISHERS

Ask fast finishers to select three or four new words from the text, for example, *the mainstream*. Tell them to give a definition of the word and write an example sentence using it. They can use their dictionaries to help. Ask one or two of the students to present their words to the class once everyone has finished.

Answers

1 up to a point 2 badges 3 dress sense 4 dress 5 catwalk(s)

TALKING POINTS

In pairs, students discuss the questions. If your students are preparing for the *B2 First for Schools* exam, ask them to speak about one question each for at least one minute as a monologue. The second student can then give their own views about the question as well. Monitor and help with ideas if necessary. Ask two or three students to tell the class about their partner's views.

COOLER

Ask the students to work in small groups to think of different situations they might find themselves in, for example, a first date, a job interview, a class trip to the mountains. They then swap lists with a different group and now give advice about what the students should wear in each of their situations. They can give general advice, such as comfortable walking boots for the class trip, or go into detail about styles and colours if they want to. Set a time limit of three minutes and then the groups swap their advice. Invite groups to share a good or bad piece of advice they were given.

THE BIG QUESTION: ____________?

04

However you answer the question, you still have to **(0)** *settle* on something to wear each day. But what do you base your choices on? Perhaps you're someone who isn't particularly **(1)** ________ about keeping up to date with **(2)** ________ trends, but you wear what's in fashion because it's **(3)** ________ to do so, and you aren't especially interested in **(4)** ________ alternatives. Maybe you're a 'quality not quantity' kind of person, preferring to spend your cash on a few great designer pieces than own an **(5)** ________ collection of cheaper items. Or perhaps you do your best *not* to follow fashion because you're keen to **(6)** ________ an image as far from the mainstream as possible: in other words, you don't want to do what everyone else is doing and would rather stand out from the crowd. It might also be your **(7)** ________ that determines your choices, or a strong **(8)** ________ to fit in with your friends.

Here's how some of our readers answered the question …

4 REPLIES 9 LIKES 2 SHARES

Of course, and I like to be adventurous with what I wear, but I'm more worried about other people's terrible dress sense! I've been reading an article about the history of fashion. It made some interesting points, like who says blue is for boys and pink is for girls? In fact, 100 years ago, pink was a boys' colour and blue was for girls! And what about skirts for men? They're comfortable and functional, but men in the West rarely wear them.

We tend to think of fashion as fast-moving, but it actually changes really slowly. Men have been wearing shirts, ties and suits for centuries. Similarly, women's dress has changed very little during the past few hundred years, except for the introduction of trousers in the 1950s. You see some weird stuff on the catwalks, but in real life, clothes are boring. I reckon it's time for a fashion revolution!

Arslan, 17 Ankara

Not really. I can't stand designer labels. Everyone at my school seems to be impressed by them, but I can't understand why people are willing to pay a fortune for top brands when cheaper ones are really no different! It's hard to know what to do at school! If you have cheap clothes, people might be mean about it, but if you have really expensive clothes, there's always the worry that someone might be jealous of them. The point is, logos and brands cause all kinds of problems.

Olivia, 16 Glasgow

Yes. Clothes actually make me happy – up to a point! I have clothes to suit every mood, occasion and season. Fashion is important because it helps people to express their individuality and identity. 'High' fashion – the clothing supermodels wear on the catwalk – is associated with Paris, Milan, New York and London, but every country has developed its own fashion industry and its own look. I'm cautious about spending loads of money on fashion – there's no point. Most good malls sell clothes that are inspired by the catwalk, so you can still buy clothes that look stunning but cost ten times less. With fashion, there's something for everyone.

Camila, 16 Madrid

I think it does, actually. Some people aren't interested in how they look, but everyone wears *some* form of clothing and their clothes make a statement. I think clothes matter because your choice of clothes influences how others think of you. Take me, for example. I'm really into 'alternative' clothing. I avoid chain stores in malls. I'm loyal to a few small, independent shops in my town and get second-hand clothes from markets. I collect badges. I've been looking for some 1950s American badges, but they're all much too expensive. So what do my clothes say about me? They say I'm an individual. I think independently. I'm original. I have my own style.

Natalia, 17 León

What do YOUR clothes say about YOU?

REPLY

4 **Are the sentences true or false? Correct the false sentences.**

1 One particular colour has always been associated with girls. (Arslan)
2 It is worth paying more for a good brand. (Olivia)
3 People might make fun of you for wearing fashionable items. (Olivia)
4 Your clothes can change the way you feel. (Camila)
5 Cheap clothes don't look as good as more expensive items. (Camila)
6 Clothes can tell other people about the wearer. (Natalia)

5 **Match the highlighted words and phrases in the article to the meanings.**

1 partly
2 pieces of metal or plastic with words or a picture on them that you wear on your clothing
3 ability to dress well
4 a particular style of clothes
5 long, narrow stage which models walk on in a fashion show

TALKING POINTS

Why do you think some people enjoy having designer clothes?
In what ways do you think the clothes someone wears show their personality?

GRAMMAR Present perfect simple and continuous

1 **Match the examples to the rules.**

1 Men **have been wearing** shirts, ties and suits for centuries.
2 Every country **has developed** its own fashion industry and its own look.
3 Women's dress **has changed** very little during the past few hundred years.
4 **I've been relaxing** at home, so I'm wearing something casual.

We use the present perfect simple for
a a past action with a present result.
b an action that happened in a time period that continues until now.

We use the present perfect continuous for
c an action that started in the past and is still continuing.
d an action (still continuing or just completed) that explains a present situation.

» GRAMMAR REFERENCE AND PRACTICE PAGE 149

2 **Choose the correct ending for each sentence.**

1 *Vogue* magazine has published …
2 *Vogue* magazine has been publishing …
  a only one super-long magazine. It was 916 pages long!
  b fashion magazines since 1892.

3 My wardrobe's almost empty. I've been getting rid …
4 I used to have loads of jackets, but I've got rid …
  a of them all, sorry.
  b of lots of old clothes recently. It's a nice feeling!

5 Anna works for Gucci. She's been designing …
6 Anna works for Gucci. She's designed …
  a handbags for 15 years.
  b hundreds of beautiful bags.

3 **Correct the mistake in each sentence.**

1 We're sitting outside without jackets all evening and I'm really cold now.
2 Stella McCartney produces some really interesting designs during her career.
3 I haven't been hanging your clothes outside yet. It looks like it might rain.
4 Look! Jen buys some new shoes! They're gorgeous.
5 I'm reading your blog all week. It's brilliant and I can't wait for tomorrow's update!
6 I've never been seeing such long queues in a clothes shop.

4 **Make five sentences with the present perfect simple or continuous form of the verbs in the box. Compare your sentences with your partner's.**

blog	buy	chill out (with)	learn
live (in)	play	watch	wear

I haven't been blogging for long. I think I wrote my first post about three months ago.

VOCABULARY Verb + preposition

1 **Complete the sentences with the correct form of the phrases in the box.**

EP

apologise for	compare with	cope with	
depend on	do without	~~heard of~~	laugh at

0 I haven't *heard of* *Teen Vogue*. What is it?
1 You still haven't ______ losing my scarf.
2 I hate it when people ______ my uniform.
3 Clothes these days are very comfortable ______ a century ago.
4 I hate ______ my parents for money to buy clothes.
5 Marta can't ______ going to crowded shopping centres.
6 I haven't got much money left this month, so I'll have to ______ that new pair of jeans I wanted.

2 **In pairs, ask and answer the questions using verb + preposition phrases.**

0 Is there anything that you can't do without?

Is there anything that you can't do without?

I definitely can't do without my sunglasses.

1 Could you cope with not having the latest fashions?
2 When was the last time you apologised for something you did?
3 What's the strangest fashion trend you've seen or heard of?
4 How stylish are you compared with your friends?
5 Who do you depend on for advice about fashion?
6 Would you ever laugh at someone because of what they were wearing?

16 UNIT 2

GRAMMAR Present perfect simple and continuous

WARMER

Write a few gapped sentences on the board about yourself:

I have been teaching for ______ years.

I have taught ______ different subjects.

I have taught about ______ students.

Put students into groups of three or four and ask them to guess the missing numbers. Elicit ideas and tell them the correct answers, at least for the first two sentences. Elicit the two tenses used (*present perfect continuous and present perfect simple*).

Follow up by asking students to write similar sentences about studying English and other languages. Students work alone. Monitor and help where necessary and then invite students to share their sentences with the class.

1 Put the students into pairs to discuss the sentences and do the matching. Elicit the answers and tell students that, if we talk about a general activity that is still continuing, we generally use the present perfect continuous but if we talk about specific numbers or other details, we generally use the present perfect simple. Elicit that we can't use the continuous form with state verbs, such as *like* or *know*.

You could mention that there are some verbs which can be used in the continuous or simple form with *for* or *since*, for example *work* or *live,* with little difference in meaning. However, this doesn't work for all verbs, so students should use the continuous form where possible.

Answers

1 c 2 a 3 b 4 d

» GRAMMAR REFERENCE AND PRACTICE ANSWER KEY TB PAGE 267

2 Look at the first two sentences with the whole class. Elicit the correct endings and reasons for them, i.e. a *is a single, specific event so we use the simple form. If we said when it happened, we would use the past simple.* b *is a general activity that is still continuing so we use the continuous form*.

Answers

1 a 2 b 3 b 4 a 5 a 6 b

3 Look at the first sentence with the students. Tell them to imagine that the sentence finishes at the word *jackets*. Ask them what this would mean (*this is what is happening now*) and what it doesn't tell us (*when the activity started or how long it has been going on for*). Now tell students to look at the next two words and say how they change the meaning of the sentence (*they tell us how long the activity has been going on, so it links the past to the present*). Ask what change students need to make to the sentence (*change the verb form to present perfect continuous*). Students then do the rest of the exercise alone and compare answers in pairs.

FAST FINISHERS

Ask fast finishers to identify what tenses are used in the original sentences and what we use those tenses for. They then decide why each one is wrong, as in the example above. When you elicit the answers, invite the fast finishers to explain what is wrong with each sentence and why. (*For example, 2 uses present simple but should use present perfect simple because it gives a time from the past to the present. 3 uses present perfect continuous but should use the simple form. We don't use the present perfect continuous with* yet. *4 uses present simple but should use the present perfect simple. 5 uses the present continuous but should use the present perfect continuous as it tells you how long for. 6 uses the present perfect continuous but* see *is a state verb so we need the present perfect simple.*)

Answers

1 We **'ve/have been sitting** outside without jackets all evening and I'm really cold now.
2 Stella McCartney **'s/has produced** some really interesting designs during her career.
3 I **haven't** / **have not hung** your clothes outside yet. It looks like it might rain.
4 Look! Jen **'s/has bought** some new shoes! They're gorgeous.
5 I **'ve/have been** reading your blog all week. It's brilliant and I can't wait for tomorrow's update.
6 I **'ve/have** never **seen** such long queues in a clothes shop.

4 Look at the example sentences with the class and ask them to think of a present perfect simple sentence to talk about blogs, for example, *I have written ten blogs so far*. Set a time limit of three minutes and elicit sentences from different students. Students give their own answers.

MIXED ABILITY

Allow weaker students to work in pairs to write their sentences. Monitor and give them prompts, for example: *I've been buying … what? Something in general?* Elicit an idea such as *food*: *I've bought … what? Something specific?* Elicit an idea such as *some bread*.

» GRAMMAR WORKSHEET UNIT 2

VOCABULARY Verb + preposition

1 Look at the phrases in the box and check that students know them all. *Do without* and *cope with* might be new to some of them. Ask students to finish the phrases in some way, for example *apologise for being late*. They then compare ideas with a partner. Students then complete the activity alone and compare answers in pairs. Elicit the answers and what they mean, for example, *I didn't know what* Teen Vogue *was. You haven't said sorry for losing my scarf.*

Answers

1 apologised for 2 laugh at 3 compared with 4 depending on 5 cope with 6 do without

2 Look at sentences 1 and 5 from Exercise 1. Ask what form the verbs following the verb + prepositions take (*the -ing form*). You could put stronger and weaker students into pairs so that the stronger ones can help if the weaker students have problems answering the questions with full sentences. Monitor and correct students if they use the wrong verb forms in their answers. When students have finished, invite pairs to ask and answer one question each in front of the class. Students give their own answers.

» VOCABULARY WORKSHEET UNIT 2

LISTENING

05 **1** Look at the first sentence with the class and elicit a synonym for *equal* that the girl might use, for example *the same*. Students work in pairs to identify the key words in each sentence and to think of possible synonyms. Elicit ideas to help the students when they do the listening. When they have listened, elicit key words from the text which helped them identify the correct answer, for example *helps focus – there's nothing to distract us*.

Answer
C

» AUDIOSCRIPT TB PAGE 286

2 Allow the students to discuss their ideas in pairs and then play the recording again for them to check or complete their answers. Elicit what is wrong with each one.

Answers
E is not true because although she says her collar is uncomfortable, this is not related to damage.
F is not true because she does not refer to making decisions about what to wear.
G is not true because she says the school blouse 'is not exactly the most comfortable thing to wear'.
H is not true because she does not refer to life outside school.

PREPARE FOR THE EXAM

B2 FIRST FOR SCHOOLS
Listening Part 3

In this part, students listen to five speakers talking about the same general topic. They have to match each speaker to one of eight sentences. Three of the sentences do not match any of the speakers. The task tests the understanding of general gist, details, attitudes, opinions, etc.

Tips Ask students to identify key words (as pupils did in Exercise 1) in the sentences and to think about how the speaker may say the same thing but using different words and phrases. There may also be distractors and it is important to use the second listening to check that the choices are correct.

06 **3** Before students listen, ask them to look through the sentences again. Play the recording a second time for students to check their answers and then allow them to compare in pairs. Elicit the answers and any words that helped the students to do the matching.

Answers
Speaker 2 G
Speaker 3 A
Speaker 4 H
Speaker 5 F

» AUDIOSCRIPT TB PAGES 286–287

» PREPARE FOR THE EXAM TEACHING NOTES AND ANSWER KEY TB PAGE 260

4 Put the students into groups of three or four to discuss the questions and set a time limit of about three minutes. Invite students to share their ideas with the class and ask them about other things that some schools might ban, such as make-up or unusual haircuts.

Answers
Students' own answers

SPEAKING Talking about yourself

07 **1** Encourage students to note key words only as they listen. Give them an example. If the question is *What's your name?* they can write *name*, and, when the recording has finished, they will be able to recreate the question. Play the recording then allow students to work in pairs to write the questions from the key words they wrote. Elicit the questions.

Answers
What's your name and where are you from? How long have you lived there/here? What do you like most about your school? Do you like shopping? What else do you like doing in your free time?

07 **2** Elicit the answers and ask students if they can remember what the two people said:

To be honest, I probably spend too much time in front of my computer. To tell the truth, I probably spend too much time shopping! Well, I guess I spend quite a lot of time online. Personally speaking, I'm not that bothered about clothes shopping. I would say one of the best things is the extracurricular programme. Elicit that we often use the first two phrases to admit a fault or to disagree with someone.

Answers
To be honest (V) To tell the truth (M) I guess (M)
Personally speaking (V) I would say (M)

» AUDIOSCRIPT TB PAGE 287

3 Tell students that these are just notes. They shouldn't write full sentences but note ideas they might mention. Set a time limit of two minutes. Monitor and help where necessary. Students give their own answers.

PREPARE FOR THE EXAM

B2 FIRST FOR SCHOOLS
Speaking Part 1

In this part, the examiner asks the students questions about their lives. The questions will be on a variety of subjects such as family, hobbies, school, future plans, holidays, etc. The candidates don't talk together but are expected to listen to each other. This part aims to give candidates time to settle in before dealing with the more specific tasks in Parts 2, 3 and 4.

Tips Tell students to focus on giving full and developed answers. Encourage them to give more information as well as answering the questions they are asked. Their answers should be relevant to the question asked.

4 Before students start the activity, write a question on the board, for example *How old are you?* Elicit an answer, for example *I'm 15*. Elicit more information, for example *I was born in … My birthday is on …* . Encourage the class to give longer answers like this in their interviews. When students have finished, invite two students to volunteer to be examinees and one student to act as an interviewer. They carry out the interview in front of the class. Students give their own answers.

» PREPARE FOR THE EXAM TEACHING NOTES AND ANSWER KEY TB PAGE 261

COOLER

Put students into pairs. Each pair thinks of five more questions that could be asked in this part of the exam. Both students write the questions. Students then change partners and ask and answer the questions. When students have finished, elicit some of the questions asked and ask students how well their partners answered them.

LISTENING

05 **1** **You will hear a girl talking about wearing a school uniform. Read the sentences carefully. Then listen and decide which of the sentences (A–H) expresses her opinion about wearing a school uniform.**

A It makes everyone feel equal.
B It gives me a sense of belonging.
C It helps students focus on their work.
D It isn't as expensive as other clothing.
E I don't need to worry about damaging my clothes.
F I don't have to think about what to wear every day.
G It's more comfortable than some of the other clothes I wear.
H It has a positive effect on how students behave outside school.

2 **Read the reasons why A–D in Exercise 1 are true or not true for the girl. Work in pairs and decide why E–H are not true.**

A Not true. She says, 'Not that I'm saying it makes us all the same – far from it.'
B Not true. She does not refer to a sense of belonging.
C True. She says, 'If there's nothing to distract us in class, … we can all get on with what we're meant to be doing.'
D Not true. She does not refer to expense.

PREPARE FOR THE EXAM

Listening Part 3

3 06 **You will hear four more teenagers talking about wearing a school uniform. For speakers 2–5, choose from the list (A–H) what opinion each speaker expresses about school uniform. Use the letters only once. There are three extra letters which you do not need to use.**

Speaker 1 C
Speaker 2 ....
Speaker 3 ....
Speaker 4 ....
Speaker 5 ....

» PREPARE FOR THE EXAM PAGE 132

4 **Discuss the questions.**

1 Do you think schools and colleges are right to ban some items of clothing or accessories, such as jewellery? Why? / Why not?
2 What are the good and bad points about uniforms at work?

SPEAKING Talking about yourself

07 **1** **Listen to an interview with Miguel and Vika. Write the questions which they are asked.**

07 **2** **Read the *Prepare to speak* box. Then listen again. Who uses each phrase? Write M (Miguel) or V (Vika).**

PREPARE TO SPEAK | Introducing an opinion

To be honest, …
To tell the truth, …
I guess …
Personally speaking …
I would say …

3 **Prepare for a short conversation about yourself.**

- Make notes on your answers to the questions in Exercise 1.
- Review your answers. Think about what tenses and relevant vocabulary you can use for each answer.

PREPARE FOR THE EXAM

Speaking Part 1

4 **Work in pairs. Ask each other questions.**

- Ask the questions from Exercise 1.
- Answer using phrases from the *Prepare to speak* box.

» PREPARE FOR THE EXAM PAGE 134

CULTURE

THE BRITISH FASHION SCENE

1 **Ask and answer the questions with a partner.**

1 Do you know what a fashion influencer is? Can you name any?
2 What other jobs and professions are related to the world of fashion?

2 **Read the article on page 19 quickly. Choose the best alternative title for the article.**

A The growing French influence on the London fashion scene
B The French influencer bringing her unique style to the British capital
C British influencer makes her mark on the French fashion scene

3 **Read the article again and answer the questions.**

1 Why does the writer consider Freddie to be a London fashion influencer rather than a Paris fashion influencer?
2 What qualities does the writer admire about Freddie?
3 How did Freddie feel when she wore clothes that other people would like?
4 What recognition has Freddie received for her work?
5 Apart from her writing and videos, how else does Freddie interact with people?
6 According to the writer, what does Freddie's success demonstrate?

4 **Match the highlighted words and phrases in the article to the meanings.**

1 meetings where people learn about a subject
2 caused a person to notice something
3 uncertain and having little confidence
4 all the people and things connected with an activity
5 belief and confidence in your own ability

08 **5** **Look at the photos. Do you know how these people are connected to fashion? Listen and check your ideas.**

Victoria and David Beckham

Katharine Hamnett

Kim Jones

Cara Delevingne

08 **6** **Listen again and choose the correct options.**

1 The British Fashion Council gave out *one award* / *two awards* / *five awards* in 1984.
2 The Fashion Awards began in *1984* / *1989* / *2018*.
3 Kim Jones has won the *Best Menswear* / *Trailblazer* / *Shaping Fashion* award once.
4 *David* / *Victoria* Beckham's fashion brand is named after *himself* / *herself*.
5 Clare Waight Keller has won the *Outstanding Achievement* / *Designer of the Year* / *Luxury Fashion* award.
6 Kate Moss and Cara Delevingne have both won the *Best Fashion Model* / *Emerging Talent* / *Designer of the Year* award.

7 **Complete the sentences with the words in the box.**

clients	look	made	modelling	names

USEFUL LANGUAGE

Talking about people in the world of fashion

1 She ________ a name for herself in modelling.
2 His ________ can be described as 'expensive luxury meets street style'.
3 Her ________ include Selena Gomez and Meghan Markle.
4 He is one of the up-and-coming ________ in fashion.
5 Her ________ career began when she was ten.

CULTURE

Learning Objectives

- The students learn about the British fashion industry and an important fashion influencer.
- In the project stage, the students write a profile of a fashion designer or influencer and present it to the class.

Vocabulary

caught her eye   insecure   scene   self-esteem   workshops

Resources

CULTURE VIDEO AND CULTURE VIDEO WORKSHEET: Influencers

WARMER

With books closed, write the word *fashion* on the board. Put students into groups of four and set a time limit of three minutes for them to write as many related words as they can think of. They can write the real names of people or places, other related nouns, adjectives or verbs. When they have finished, invite each group to share their words with the class and explain any that aren't immediately obvious.

1 Ask students to discuss the first question. Follow up by asking if they follow any influencers on social media. If they do, ask what kinds of influencers they follow, for example, beauty influencers, travel influencers, etc. If they don't, ask them why not. Then set a time limit of one minute for students to discuss the second question and, when they finish, ask them how influencers influence people. Invite students to share their ideas with the class.

Answers

Students' own answers

2 Set a time limit and ask students to read the article quickly. When they have finished, ask them to compare answers in pairs and to give each other reasons for their choices. Elicit the answers and reasons why the other two answers are wrong (*A the article is about one person, not the French in general; C Freddie lives and works in London, but she was born in France*).

Answer

B

3 Set a time limit of eight minutes for students to read the text more carefully. Decide how you want the students to answer the questions, for example, they could answer using full sentences or in note form in their notebooks. Make sure all the students do the same thing so that some don't finish much more quickly than others. Allow students to compare in pairs and then elicit the answers.

FAST FINISHERS

Ask fast finishers to think of another question they could ask about information in the text. When you have elicited the answers to the exercise, invite fast finishers to ask the class their questions and see who can find the correct answer first.

Answers

1 She has lived and worked in London for almost a decade.
2 The writer likes Freddie's honesty and openness.
3 It made her feel insecure about her appearance.
4 She has won several awards and been named fashion influencer of the year by *Cosmopolitan* magazine.
5 She runs workshops about style and self-confidence.
6 It demonstrates that a fashion influencer can have a positive impact on people's lives in many ways apart from fashion.

09 The Reading text is recorded for students to listen, read and check their answers.

4 Ask students to cover up the meanings in the exercise and to read the sentences with highlighted words in the article. Students work in pairs to try to guess the meaning from context and then do the matching. Elicit the answers and ask students follow-up questions to check their knowledge, for example, *What does the music scene consist of?; What's the opposite of low self-esteem? (high self-esteem); What was the last thing that caught your eye in a shop?; What kind of workshops does a teacher go to?.*

Answers

1 workshops   2 caught her eye   3 insecure   4 scene   5 self-esteem

08 **5** If you did the Warmer, re-elicit the names of any models or fashion designers that the students came up with. If not, ask them to close their books and brainstorm any people they know in the fashion industry. Set a time limit of one minute and then elicit ideas. With open books, students work in groups of three or four to discuss the people in the photos. Ask the groups how many of the people they know and what they do. When the students have listened to the recording, elicit the answers and ask if they heard anything surprising. Students may mention that David Beckham has modelled clothes and that Cara Delevingne is an actress.

Answers

Victoria and David Beckham both have their own fashion labels / brands.
Katharine Hamnett is famous for creating T-shirts with controversial slogans.
Kim Jones is a well-known British designer and has won several awards for his menswear.
Cara Delevingne is a famous model/supermodel.

CONTINUED ON PAGE 34

BACKGROUND INFORMATION

The British Fashion awards were established in 1989 by the British Fashion Council to showcase the talents of British designers. As a result of the work of the British Fashion Council, including the establishment of London Fashion Week in 1984, London is now considered one of the four most important fashion capitals, alongside Paris, Milan and New York.

Victoria Beckham first came to fame in the mid-1990s as a member of the pop group the Spice Girls. Her stage name was Posh Spice. She married footballer David Beckham in 1999 when he played for the British club Manchester United. She appeared as a guest model at London Fashion Week in 2000 and launched her fashion label in 2008. David Beckham played football for Manchester United, Real Madrid, Milan, LA Galaxy and Paris Saint-Germain. He was the first English player to win league championships in four different countries (England, Spain, the USA, France). He also played 115 times for the England football team. He has modelled clothes for a number of brands as well his own brand.

Katharine Hamnett started her clothes label in 1979. She is said to have invented the slogan T-shirt, with simple two- or three-word slogans in large, easy to read letters, often publicising important issues, for example, Stop Acid Rain or, more recently, Cancel Brexit. These have been popular amongst pop stars and models since the 1980s and she is still creating them today. She is also concerned about the environment and changed how she produced clothes in the 1980s to make them less damaging to the environment. She won the first ever British Designer of the Year award in 1984.

Kim Jones launched his label in 2003. He designed the suit that David Beckham wore to Prince Harry's wedding to Meghan Markle in 2019. He has worked with many fashion brands, including Louis Vuitton, Mulberry, Alexander McQueen and Hugo Boss.

Cara Delevingne is a British model. She began modelling at the age of ten with a photo shoot for *Vogue Italia* and first appeared on the catwalk in 2011. She won Model of the Year at the British Fashion Awards in 2012 and 2014. She has also acted in several films since her debut in a small role in *Anna Karenina* in 2012 and in the series, *Carnival Row*. In addition, she is a musician and has written a novel.

08

6 Ask students to read the sentences before they listen and discuss any answers they think they remember. When they have listened again, elicit the answers and ask the students which person they think sounds the most interesting and why.

Answers

1 one award
2 1989
3 Trailblazer
4 Victoria, herself
5 Designer of the Year
6 Best Fashion Model

» **AUDIOSCRIPT TB PAGES 287–288**

7 Students complete the phrases in pairs and then discuss what they mean. Elicit ideas and ask students to use the phrases in different sentences, for example, *I would like to make a name for myself in politics.*

MIXED ABILITY

Instead of asking weaker students to try to complete the sentences, give them the answers and then ask them to discuss in pairs or small groups what the sentences mean. If they don't know, they can look up the phrases in a dictionary or online. Stronger students could try to complete the sentences without looking at the word pool first.

Answers

1 made 2 look 3 clients 4 names 5 modelling

PROJECT *A fashion profile*

Put the students into groups of three where possible. Read the instructions with the students. Elicit how they could present their profile, for example, as a poster or a multimedia presentation. Tell the students that they should think of a fashion designer or influencer that they all know and then choose two questions each to research and present. They should agree on who will design the profile, but every student should present their part of it to the class.

When the groups have presented their projects, ask them which person from all the presentations they found the most interesting and why.

PROJECT EXTENSION

After the students have presented their projects, put them in new groups of three or four so that all of the new group members were originally in different groups for the project. Tell them to think about the people they researched and presented and imagine that they have now become a similar fashion influencer or designer. They have to think about the sort of fashions they are famous for, how they became famous and what makes them different from other designers and influencers. Set a time limit of about ten minutes to think of ideas and then invite the groups to present themselves and their ideas to the class. Ask the class to vote for the best ideas, apart from their own.

CULTURE VIDEO: Influencers

03

When students have completed the lesson, they can watch the video and complete the worksheet.

COOLER

Write a sentence on the board about fashion which it would be possible to agree or disagree with, for example, *Most clothes you see in fashion shows are ridiculous.* Ask students whether they agree or disagree with the statement and elicit reasons why. Students then work in pairs to write their own sentence about fashion, influencers or clothes in general. When they are ready, put the students into groups of five or six. They shouldn't be in the same group as their original partner. The groups now discuss each statement in turn, giving their opinions and reasons. When they have finished, invite each group to tell the class about which statement they found the most interesting to discuss and why.

LONDON FASHION WITH A FRENCH ACCENT

09

Freddie Harrel is one of our favourite London fashion influencers. Well, actually, she was born in Paris, but after nearly a decade in London, she's completely in love with the British capital and its fashion **scene**! She began her career in the marketing department of the popular online fashion retailer ASOS. She then became a personal stylist, helping people decide on every aspect of their appearance, from hair to clothes to make-up, and later started her own fashion blog.

What we really like about Freddie, apart from her amazing style, is her honesty and openness. She has often talked about her low **self-esteem**, the difficulties she has faced in life, and how these have helped her become the person she is today. There is so much more to her than just fashion and stylish clothes. But it is through fashion that she has chosen to develop her self-confidence and to demonstrate it to the world.

At the start of her career in fashion, Freddie often dressed in clothes that she thought other people would like, following a traditional idea of what is considered beautiful and attractive. But she found that dressing in that way only made her feel **insecure** about her appearance. It was then that she decided to start to dress in clothes that were bright, bold and that **caught her eye**. Freddie realised how curious and creative she was, and that she could use clothes to reflect different aspects of her personality and feelings.

Freddie regularly writes for a range of fashion magazines, has her own blog and also creates videos about her unique style. She's got hundreds of thousands of followers on social media, and that number will only continue to grow as more and more people discover her. She's also attracted the attention of fashion-industry experts, winning several awards, including being named fashion influencer of the year by the well-known fashion magazine *Cosmopolitan*.

Freddie Harrel

Apart from her online presence as an influencer, Freddie also has her own company making hair products, and she runs **workshops** about style and self-confidence. During the workshops, she shares her personal experiences and tips to fight worries and insecurities. She also talks about how clothes and style are an excellent way to show your true personality. We think it's great that the world is listening to influencers like Freddie, as it shows that being a fashion influencer doesn't just have to be about fashion and that influencers can have a positive impact on people's lives in many different ways.

PROJECT *A fashion profile*

Write a profile of a fashion designer or influencer. Use the questions below to help you.

1. Where is the designer from?
2. What do his/her designs look like?
3. When did he/she start in fashion?
4. Does he/she have a particular look?
5. Has he/she won any awards?
6. Is he/she involved in any other activities?

Present your profile to the class.

03 NOW WATCH THE CULTURE VIDEO

THE BRITISH FASHION SCENE 19

3 ALL IN THE MIND

ABOUT YOU

What things are you naturally good at?
What things have you learned to be good at?
Do you think people can learn to be good at anything?

VOCABULARY Abstract nouns

10 EP **1 Read the paragraph about a podcast called *The debate*. Choose the correct words. Listen and check.**

THE DEBATE

Is there finally [1] ***agreement*** / ***problem-solving*** in the debate over nature v nurture? Here's what the experts have to say.

One [2] ***success*** / ***belief*** is that we are born with a personality that never changes, with a fixed amount of intelligence and skills, such as being good at [3] ***development*** / ***problem-solving*** or communication. In other words, our [4] ***success*** / ***agreement*** in life is dictated by our genes: this is the 'nature' argument.

The other idea is that we start life as a blank sheet, and that our social and intellectual [5] ***development*** / ***success*** comes from our life experiences: this is the 'nurture' view.

New research appears to suggest that both sides in the debate are right to a certain extent.

11 **2 Listen to Clara and Yusuf talking about *The debate*. Are the sentences true or false?**

1 Yusuf has already listened to *The debate*.
2 According to the podcast, everyone has the genes to become a professional footballer.
3 You need the right genes and the right environment to be successful.
4 According to the podcast, people can become more intelligent by working hard.

11 **3 Complete the sentences with the abstract nouns in the box. Listen again and check.**

ambition	drive	luck	thought

1 You need the ________ to be born with the right genes.
2 You need more than just ________ to become a professional footballer.
3 Students who have the ________ to study hard can actually become more intelligent.
4 Maybe the same is true for your sporting ability. I'll give that some ________!

4 Complete the sentences with the correct abstract nouns from Exercises 1 and 3.

1 Have you got the necessary ________ to work hard and be successful?
2 I'm sure you'll win. I wish you good ________!
3 Are we in ________ that you can't be successful if you don't work hard?
4 Some people think ________ means having a big house and a fancy car.
5 It's important to give your future some ________ so you can prepare well for it.
6 I'm not very good at ________. I usually ask someone else what to do.
7 Chico's not very confident and he doesn't have a lot of ________ in himself.
8 I think personal ________ is really important – we should keep improving ourselves.
9 Katya's ________ is to become a physicist, but first she'll need to improve her maths.

5 Discuss the questions.

1 What is your opinion of the nature v nurture debate?
2 What do you think are signs of success?

READING

1 Look at the photos and read the title of the article. In what ways do you think that humans are smarter than other species? Read the article quickly and check your ideas.

PREPARE FOR THE EXAM

Reading and Use of English Part 6

2 Six sentences have been removed from the article. Read sentences A–G and notice the underlined words. What do you think they might refer to?

A Some psychologists have trained <u>one</u> to recognise over 1,000 words for things such as this.
B However, research suggests that <u>they</u> can't put individual words together to form complex sentences.
C <u>It</u> was using a rock to crack open a shell containing one of its favourite foods.
D It is the moment when <u>they</u> realise that the image they see is actually of themselves.
E <u>It</u> has got a bigger brain, but brain size doesn't equal intelligence.
F This happens whether or not <u>they</u> belong to the same family, and they will even help outsiders.
G <u>This</u> involves being able to imagine what it must be like to be in someone else's situation.

3 ALL IN THE MIND

Unit Overview

TOPIC	Intelligence and the mind
VOCABULARY	Abstract nouns
READING	Humans: the smartest species?
GRAMMAR	The grammar of phrasal verbs
VOCABULARY	Phrasal verbs: learning and thinking
WRITING	An informal letter or email
EXAM TASKS	Reading and Use of English Part 6; Writing Part 2

Resources

GRAMMAR REFERENCE AND PRACTICE: SB page 150; TB page 267
PREPARE FOR THE EXAM: SB pages on TB pages 242–243 and 246; TB pages 256 and 258
WORKBOOK: pages 12–15
PHOTOCOPIABLE WORKSHEETS: Grammar worksheet Unit 3; Vocabulary worksheet Unit 3
TEST GENERATOR: Unit test 3
PRACTICE EXTRA: Unit 3

WARMER

Tell the class you are going to give them a mathematical problem that needs no mathematical skills at all. Say: *You have four letters and four envelopes with addresses on them. You put the letters into the envelopes without looking. What is the probability of getting exactly three letters in the correct envelopes?* Put students into groups of three or four and tell them to discuss the problem and put their hands up when they think they have the correct answer. When they are ready, elicit the answer (*the answer is zero as, logically, if three are correct, so is the fourth*).

ABOUT YOU

Read the questions in the *About you* box and put the students into groups of three or four to tell each other the answers to the first two questions for them. Also, ask students to say why they think they are naturally good at some things and how they have learned to be good at others. Invite groups to share the most interesting answers with the class. Then ask them to discuss the third question. Set a time limit of one minute and elicit answers.

VOCABULARY Abstract nouns

1 Before students read the text, write: *nature v nurture* on the board and elicit or tell the students what it means (*It is the question about whether some people are born with certain skills and abilities or develop these as part of their upbringing.*). Students then read the text and choose the words alone before comparing in pairs. Elicit the words and the meanings.

10
Answers
The answers are recorded for students to listen and check.
1 agreement 2 belief 3 problem-solving 4 success
5 development

11
2 Ask students to look at sentences 1–4 and discuss in pairs whether they think they are true or false. Elicit ideas and reasons and then play the recording. Elicit the answers and anything the students can remember the two people saying which supports the answers.

Answers
1 False 2 False 3 True 4 True

11
3 Students work in pairs to think about which words go in which gaps. When they have listened, elicit the answers. You could follow this up by asking stronger students to work in pairs to form adjectives from the nouns (*ambitious, driven, lucky, thoughtful*).

Answers
1 luck 2 ambition 3 drive 4 thought

» AUDIOSCRIPT TB PAGE 288

4 Look at the first sentence with students. Ask them what sort of person is able to work hard and be successful (*someone who is motivated and has the mental strength to achieve what they want*). Elicit that the word which sums this up best is *drive*. Students work alone or in pairs to complete the sentences. Elicit the answers.

Answers
1 drive 2 luck 3 agreement 4 success 5 thought
6 problem-solving 7 belief 8 development 9 ambition

5 Ask the class whether they think nature or nurture is more important in determining someone's success. Put the students into groups of four and set a time limit of two minutes to discuss the first question. Invite each group to share their opinions and reasons with the class. Students then discuss the second question in their groups for two minutes. Invite groups to share their ideas with the class.

Answers
Students' own answers

READING

1 Allow students to discuss the question in pairs for one minute. Elicit ideas and then set a time limit of three minutes for students to read the text. Students discuss what they found out in pairs. Invite students to share what they read with the class.

Possible answers
Humans can use tools, problem-solve, communicate and use complex language, be self-aware and empathise with others. Some animals also have some of these abilities but not as well-developed as humans.

CONTINUED ON PAGE 38

BACKGROUND INFORMATION

As well as learning to take the lid off a jar, octopi have also shown many other abilities. An octopus called Inky, in New Zealand, escaped from its aquarium through a drainage tube which led back to the sea. An octopus in Boston was also caught climbing out of its tank and climbing into a neighbouring one to dine on the fish which lived there. Another octopus in Germany, called Otto, discovered that it could cause the lights to go off by squirting a jet of water at them. It then continued doing the same trick again and again. Octopi can also use coconuts and other shells as tools.

Interestingly, octopi not only have a central brain but also have neurons in their tentacles. These mean that each tentacle can make individual decisions without any information from the central brain.

PREPARE FOR THE EXAM

B2 FIRST FOR SCHOOLS

Reading and Use of English Part 6

In this part, students read a text from which six sentences have been removed and placed in a jumbled order, together with an additional sentence, after the text. Students have to decide which part of the text the sentences have been removed from. This part tests students' understanding of text cohesion and coherence devices and their ability to follow the development of ideas, opinions and events through the text as a whole.

Tips Tell students to pay particular attention to the sentences before and after the gaps. Synonyms or pronouns will often refer forwards or backwards to different ideas. To check their answers, they should be able to identify what these words refer to in the text.

2 Look at sentence A with the class. Elicit ideas of what it could be, for example, a chimpanzee. Students do the same for the other words. Elicit ideas, but don't give the correct answers yet. Tell students that the final words (*such as this*) and the topic (learning words) can also help them decide where the sentence should go. Do not correct students' answers at this stage.

FAST FINISHERS

Ask students to find any other useful clues in the other sentences similar to *such as this* in sentence A. Elicit these when everyone has finished the activity (*B However; D It is the moment; F This happens; G This involves*).

Answers

Students' own answers

3 Look at the example answer with the students. Ask them to work in pairs. One reads the three sentences: the one before the gap, sentence G and the sentence after the gap. The other student listens to make sure it makes sense. Tell students to do the same, although silently, when they complete the activity to check their answers.

4 Tell students to approach this as an exam question, working alone. Set a time limit of ten minutes and encourage students to check their answers when they have finished. Then, nominate three students for each answer. One reads out the sentence before, one reads the missing sentence and one reads the sentence which follows the gap. Each time, ask the class if they think the sentences make sense together and if this is the correct answer. Re-elicit what the underlined words in Exercise 2 referred to (*A dog; B parrots; C crab; D humans; F elephants; G children*) and ask students if their guesses were correct.

MIXED ABILITY

As this is an exam task, students should work alone, but monitor and help where necessary pointing out clues in the text and sentences, for example, for gap 2 ask: 'What kind of creature is this?' (*a crab*); 'Where do crabs live?' (*near the sea, in rocks and on beaches*) and 'What do you think they might use as a tool?' (*a shell*).

Answers

1 G (*This* refers to understanding how a friend feels in the final sentence.)
2 C (*It* refers to the crab in the previous sentence and the rock mentioned in sentence C is an example of a tool.)
3 A (*one* refers to dog/*it* before the gap and the *It* of the next sentence; *things such as this* relates to *ball* before the gap.)
4 B (The paragraph makes the contrast between animals and humans, and the final sentence *Only humans are able to use language with detailed grammar* after the gap links to *can't put individual words together to form complex sentences*.)
5 D (*they* refers to *humans … around 15–18 months old*. The sentence before the gap mentions the mirror stage, which matches *the image they see is actually of themselves*.)
6 F (*they* refers to elephants. The content of the paragraph before the gap refers to elephants in groups, so the mention of *whether or not they are in the same family* fits with this idea.)

» PREPARE FOR THE EXAM TEACHING NOTES AND ANSWER KEY TB PAGE 256

12 The Reading text is recorded for students to listen, read and check their answers.

TALKING POINTS

Ask students to discuss the questions with a partner. Ask one pair to summarise their discussion and then ask the rest of the class if they covered any other points. With weaker classes, you could introduce this activity with a class brainstorm to include topics, such as, other species having more developed senses, human ability to survive in the wild compared with that of animals, the length of time humans take to become adult/independent, use of animals to support humans in their work, exploitation of animals by humans for food and in experiments, etc.

COOLER

Ask students if they have or have ever had a pet. Put the students into groups of four or five with at least one person who has had a pet in each one. Set a time limit of four minutes for groups to discuss examples of intelligence (or a lack of intelligence) that they have noticed. If students haven't had a pet, they can give examples from films or online videos they have seen. Invite each group to share their ideas with the class.

HUMANS: THE SMARTEST SPECIES?

Many animals are said to be intelligent, and some live up to this reputation in surprising and charming ways: whales sing, dolphins enjoy showing off with toys, parrots pick up language and, apparently, an octopus has even learned to take the lid off a jar! This demonstrates a certain amount of drive and determination, but does it mean animals are as intelligent as humans?

There are five commonly recognised signs of intelligence: the ability to make and use tools; problem-solving; the ability to communicate and understand; the capacity for abstract thought (for example, adding numbers up); and the psychological qualities of self-awareness and empathy, among others. The first of these psychological qualities is the ability to realise that you are an individual who is separate from other individuals. Most children start to show basic signs of empathy at an early age. [1] ________ For example, they understand that a friend who has lost his favourite toy must feel upset.

Our ancestors started using stone tools more than 2.5 million years ago. Scientists used to believe that only humans possessed this skill, but we now know that some animals also use tools. Chimpanzees make some unusual ones, from stick brushes for collecting ants to pointed sticks for weapons. Brown bears rub stones against themselves to remove dirt and dead skin from their fur. Even a crab was filmed recently with a tool! [2] ________

Both understanding and producing language are obvious signs of intelligence. Although a dog can't talk, it can understand the names of objects in instructions such as 'Fetch the ball!'. [3] ________ It can also understand verb + noun commands in English, like 'Pick the toy up!', including combinations of verb + noun that it hasn't heard before. This is similar to the understanding of a human child, aged two.

Most animals make sounds to communicate with each other; dolphins make clicking noises, dogs bark and so on. When some parrots hear human language, they can pick it up and repeat it, often to great comic effect. [4] ________ Some chimpanzees 'talk' to humans using sign language, but what they are able to say is fairly limited. Only humans are able to use language with detailed grammar.

There is an interesting test for self-awareness: the mirror test. For humans, the 'mirror stage' occurs around 15–18 months old. [5] ________ To test this with animals, scientists draw a coloured spot on an animal's face. An animal that recognises itself in a mirror always tries to touch or remove the spot. Most animals can't recognise themselves in the reflection in a mirror. Only a small number of animals, including elephants, dolphins and great apes (chimpanzees, gorillas and orangutans) realise they are looking at themselves.

Perhaps the hardest intelligence test of all is for empathy. Empathy is extremely rare in animals, though elephants appear to display it. They are aware of others, care for each other when they are ill, and work together to protect young ones. [6] ________ This kind of behaviour is fascinating, but it is the chimpanzee that is by far the cleverest in the animal kingdom. Some baby chimps have even beaten people in a memory test of numbers! But even though chimpanzees are good at problem-solving and abstract thought, they still can't light fires, cook food or make clothes, which means they are still behind humans when it comes to being the smartest species on Earth.

3 **Read the example answer. Notice how the underlined words can help you to decide which is the correct answer.**

1G: 'This' refers to 'empathy' before the gap. The missing sentence provides a definition of empathy, and an example is provided in the sentence following the gap.

4 **Choose from the sentences A–F the one which fits each gap (2–6). Use the underlined words to help you decide. There is one extra sentence which you do not need to use.**

>> PREPARE FOR THE EXAM PAGE 126

TALKING POINTS

In which ways do you think human beings are not especially smart?

To what extent do humans depend on animals?

Does mankind show animals enough respect? How? / Why not?

GRAMMAR The grammar of phrasal verbs

1 Underline the phrasal verbs in the examples.

1 Some animals live up to this reputation in surprising ways.
2 Dolphins enjoy showing off.
3 They care for each other when they are ill.
4 They have the capacity for abstract thought (for example, adding numbers up).
5 When some parrots hear human language, they can pick it up and repeat it.

2 Match the phrasal verbs in Exercise 1 to the types of phrasal verb in the rules.

There are four types of phrasal verb:

a phrasal verbs without an object
Our car broke down last night.

b separable phrasal verbs with an object
I switched off the TV.
OR *I switched the TV off.*
I switched it off. (NOT ~~*I switched off it.*~~)

c inseparable phrasal verbs with an object
Can you deal with this problem?
Can you deal with it?
(NOT ~~*Can you deal this problem/it with?*~~)

d inseparable three-part phrasal verbs
I'm looking forward to the weekend.

» GRAMMAR REFERENCE AND PRACTICE PAGE 150

3 Read the email. Choose the correct phrasal verbs. In one answer, both options are possible.

I have some bad news about my visit. I'm really sorry, but I need to [1] *put off it / put it off* again. It's my best friend's birthday party the same weekend and I'm helping to organise it. I can't really [2] *get it out of / get out of it*. It's such a pity, as I've been [3] *looking forward to it / looking it forward to*. I'm sorry to [4] *let down you / let you down*. I've even bought my train tickets! I can't get a refund, so I'll have to [5] *throw them away / throw away them*, which is a bit annoying! Are you free on 30th May instead? I think I can get away then. I'd love you to [6] *show around me / show me around* the city. Maybe you could [7] *book us in / book in us* at a restaurant? I will be there, I promise! By the way, please [8] *pass on my thanks / pass my thanks on* to your brother for the book he lent me. It was great!

4 Correct the mistake in each sentence.

1 It's interesting that elephants care each other for when they are sick.
2 I hope this restaurant lives up its reputation!
3 The bus broke it down on the way to the airport.
4 Have you finished with the computer? Don't switch off it – I'll use it now.
5 Please pass my good wishes to your mum!

VOCABULARY Phrasal verbs: learning and thinking

1 Read the sentences and match the phrasal verbs to the meanings (a–f). Which phrasal verb does not need an object?

1 Don't make any sudden decisions about that job offer. Think it through carefully before you decide.
2 My brother wanted to go to the University of Durham, but he didn't get in.
3 Have you backed up your work yet? You wouldn't want to lose it all.
4 You've got to face up to it sometime. The problem won't go away.
5 Mateo always mixes up the words *Tuesday* and *Thursday* in English.
6 Please focus on your work, everyone – no chatting!

a make an extra copy of something held on a computer
b confuse two people or things
c succeed in being chosen for a team or educational institution
d give a lot of attention to
e accept that a difficult situation exists
f carefully consider the possible results of doing something

2 Are the phrasal verbs separable (S) or inseparable (I)? Which sentences have a mistake? Correct the mistakes.

1 I just can't focus anything on today. I've got a headache.
2 I'm going to think my plan through and check I haven't forgotten anything.
3 My cousin is having a party because he got King's College into.
4 You have to face your problems up to. They won't go away on their own.
5 I'm just backing my work up. I'll be with you in a minute.
6 You've mixed our books up. That one's mine.

3 Discuss the questions.

1 Which university is the most difficult to get into in your country?
2 Are you good at focusing on your homework?
3 Which words do you mix up in English?
4 Have you ever come up with a great solution to a problem?

GRAMMAR The grammar of phrasal verbs

WARMER

Tell students that you are going to say some words and they should write the first word that comes into their heads when they hear each one. Give an example. Say *teach* and elicit responses (*students*, *school*, *book*, etc.). Students write the numbers 1–5 on a piece of paper. Ask students to work alone, then read out your words: *1 run out, 2 take off, 3 switch on, 4 pick up, 5 look up*.

Students now compare words in pairs. Ask students what they wrote for each prompt and then ask what all the prompts have in common (*they are phrasal verbs*).

1 Look at the task with students. If necessary, elicit the phrasal verb in sentence 1 from the class and write this on the board (*live up to*). Tell them to only underline the actual phrasal verb, not any objects which might appear between the parts of the verb. Students check in pairs then elicit the answers and ask what each sentence means.

Answers
1 live up to 2 showing off 3 care for 4 adding up 5 pick up

2 When students have done the matching, point out that some phrasal verbs have more than one form depending on the meaning, for example *take off* can be an example of a) *The plane took off* or of b) *I took my shirt off / I took off my shirt*.

Answers
1 d 2 a 3 c 4 b 5 b

» GRAMMAR REFERENCE AND PRACTICE ANSWER KEY TB PAGE 267

3 Look at the first choice with the class and elicit which one is correct (*put it off*) and why the other is incorrect (*when we use an object it can come between or after a separable phrasal verb, but when we use an object pronoun, it has to come between the two parts of the verb*). Students do the rest of the exercise alone and compare answers in pairs. Elicit the answers and the reasons for them (*2 and 3 are inseparable three-part verbs. In 4, 5, 6 and 7, the object pronoun has to come between the two parts of the verb. 8 is a separable phrasal verb and here we use the full object so we can put it between both parts or after the verb*).

With strong classes you could point out that *show around* is always separated, whether we use an object pronoun or a full object.

FAST FINISHERS

Ask fast finishers to think about the meanings of the phrasal verbs used in the text and to write some alternative sentences using the same verbs, for example, *You let me down when you didn't turn up for our meeting yesterday.* Invite students to share these sentences with the class when everyone has finished the activity.

Answers
1 put it off 2 get out of it 3 looking forward to it 4 let you down
5 throw them away 6 show me around 7 book us in
8 both are possible

4 To help weaker students, tell the class that the mistakes could be separating inseparable verbs or there could be a missing word or an unnecessary word in the sentence. When students have finished, elicit the answers and what was wrong with each one. You could also ask students to rephrase the sentences so that they don't use the phrasal verbs, for example, 1 … *elephants look after each other* …; 2 *I hope this restaurant is as good as its reputation suggests.* 3 *The bus stopped working* …; 4 … *Keep the computer on* …; 5 *Give my good wishes to your mum.*

Answers
1 It's interesting that elephants **care for each other** when they are sick. (inseparable)
2 I hope this restaurant **lives up to** its reputation. (three part phrasal verb)
3 The bus **broke down** on the way to the airport. (no object)
4 Have you finished with the computer? Don't **switch it off** – I'll use it now. (object pronoun must come between the two parts)
5 Please **pass on** my good wishes to your mum! (particle missing)

» GRAMMAR WORKSHEET UNIT 3

VOCABULARY Phrasal verbs: learning and thinking

1 Allow the students to work in pairs. Elicit the answers and the types of phrasal verb they are from Grammar Exercise 2 (*1 b; 2 a; 3 b; 4 d; 5 b; 6 c*). Point out that the object in sentence 5 is the whole phrase: *the words Tuesday and Thursday*, so these would all have to go between the two parts of the verb if they separated them.

Answers
1 f 2 c 3 a 4 e 5 b 6 d; *get in* doesn't need an object

2 Students work alone to try to decide which sentences are wrong. When they are ready, they compare ideas with a partner and then rewrite the sentences that are incorrect. Elicit the answers. Ask students to write sentences about other things they have problems focusing on, things they have to think through, problems they have to face up to, how often they back things up on their computer and the last time they mixed something up.

MIXED ABILITY

Tell the students to work alone and read the sentences aloud. Ask them to try to identify the ones which they think sound wrong. Then put weaker students into pairs with stronger students to compare their ideas before they rewrite the sentences correctly.

Answers
1 ✗ focus on anything (I) 2 ✓ (S) 3 ✗ got into (I)
4 ✗ face up to your problems (I) 5 ✓ (S) 6 ✓ (S)

3 Look at the questions with the class and ask students to work alone to write one similar question using one of the other phrasal verbs from Exercise 1. Monitor and help where necessary. Put the students into groups of four. When the students have discussed the four questions from Exercise 3, each group member takes turns to ask the other three students the question they wrote at the beginning of the exercise. Invite groups to tell the class one of the extra questions they discussed and how they answered it.

Answers
Students' own answers

» VOCABULARY WORKSHEET UNIT 3

WRITING An informal letter or email

1 Put the students into groups of three or four. Tell them to first discuss question 1 and then try to come up with a five-point advice sheet to answer the second question. Elicit ideas and ask the class to vote on the three best pieces of advice for learning a new skill.

Answers
Students' own answers

2 Give students five minutes to read the questions and Alex's email. Ask them to underline Alex's questions and any parts in Rob's answer that helped them make their decision.

Answers
No. Rob doesn't directly address the final question.

3 Tell the students to cover the *Prepare to write* box. They find the expressions in the email and then work in small groups to think of other ways they could open and close the email. They then uncover the *Prepare to write* box to see if their ideas were mentioned. Go through the *Prepare to write* box with students. Tell them that it is very useful to memorise at least one of the opening and closing expressions that they can use in lots of different emails and letters. This will save time in the exam, as they won't have to think about what to write.

Answers
a It's great to hear from you b Keep in touch! c Any four of: get into, think through, sign up, get through, pick up, rely on, let down d Any four of: Actually, down at the beach, pretty scary, Anyway, stuff, fine, loads of, guys, Plus, good shape, The thing is; contractions, e.g. can't

4 When students have found the informal alternatives, elicit these and ask how else Rob could have written the same things, for example 4 *Plus you have to be pretty fit.* Allow students to discuss ideas in pairs and elicit ideas.

Answers
1 It's great to hear from you.
2 We're there to help swimmers and surfers who get into difficulties.
3 … this could be pretty scary without any training.
4 Plus you must be in good shape.

5 Look at the question with the class. Elicit that students will have to answer yes or no and then give reasons for their answer. Elicit a few ideas from the class about why it would or wouldn't be a good idea for other teenagers to train to be a lifeguard; this will give weaker students some ideas that they can use. Students then work alone and compare their paragraph with a partner and decide which answer is better. Invite students to read out their paragraph to the class.

Model answer
I think it's a great idea for people to train to be lifeguards, especially if you enjoy swimming. You learn a lot and, one day, who knows, you might need to save someone's life. You can also earn money by working as a lifeguard at an outdoor swimming pool in the summer holidays. It's quite stressful but at least you get to spend time outside in the sunshine – and get paid for it!

PREPARE FOR THE EXAM

B2 FIRST FOR SCHOOLS
Writing Part 2: An informal letter or email
In this part, there are four tasks (questions 2–5) for students to choose from. In questions 2–4, they may be asked to write an article, an email, a letter, a review or a story. For each of these questions, there is a clear context, topic, purpose and target reader. Students should write 140–190 words and make sure they follow the instructions in the task completely. Question 5 is always based on the set reading text. Students should not attempt it unless they have read the set text and prepared for this question beforehand. For more information on the set reading text option, go to the Cambridge Assessment English website: https://www.cambridgeenglish.org/exams-and-tests/first-for-schools/preparation/

Tips Remind students to read the prompt email or letter carefully and make sure they respond to all of the questions. Advise them to cross-check their reply against the original email or letter.

6 Before students start, ask them how many questions they have to answer (*three*). Set a time limit of five minutes for students to think about what they are going to say and to note any useful vocabulary. Tell them not to start writing the email until you tell them to. Weaker students could work together.

7 If you have students preparing for the *B2 First for Schools* exam, set a strict time limit of 40 minutes for this task. Put students into pairs to read each other's emails and ask them to comment on their partner's answer. Has their partner given enough detail and used the right register?

Model answer
Hi Toni,
It's great to hear from you. Learning a language is a great idea! To start with, I don't think it's easy to pick up a new language. It's taken me a long time to learn English. I did a course in America last summer. When you're in the country where a language is spoken, you have more opportunities to practise. My English improved loads over the month I was there – though I still mix words up sometimes.
There are different ways you can learn new words. I like reading magazines. I buy one every month and look up anything I don't know. Then I keep a record of the meanings and use them as soon as I can to help them stick in my memory.
I think it's a brilliant idea for you to learn Italian! Why don't I write to you in Italian? Don't worry – I'll use really easy words and explain them. There are loads of good language-learning websites, too. I don't know any Italian ones because I already speak the language, but I reckon you could find something useful.
Write soon!
Federica

» PREPARE FOR THE EXAM TEACHING NOTES AND ANSWER KEY TB PAGE 258

COOLER
Ask students to swap notebooks, and to write a short reply to their partner's email. They should include two questions which their partner's email doesn't already give the answer to. Look at Rob's email to Alex in Exercise 2. Point out that if students were replying to Rob, they might want to ask how long the lifeguard course took and what exactly he means by being in good shape – how far should you be able to swim? Students swap notebooks and write a response.

WRITING An informal letter or email

1 **Discuss the questions.**

1 What new skills have you learned recently?
2 What is the best way to learn a new skill?

2 **Read the task, then read Rob's email. Has Rob answered all Alex's questions?**

You have received this email from your friend Alex.

> Can you help me with my class project? I have to write about the ways in which people learn a new skill. Please tell me about a skill you have picked up recently. How have you developed this skill? What aspects of it have you found difficult? Would you recommend that other teenagers take up the same skill?
>
> Thanks, Alex

Write your **email**.

Hi Alex

It's great to hear from you. Actually, I got a lifeguard qualification earlier this year, so now I'm spending most Saturdays down at the beach. We're there to help swimmers and surfers who get into difficulties, and this could be pretty scary without any training.

Anyway, to get qualified, I did a course at my local pool. I thought it through carefully before I signed up for it. I'm a strong swimmer and I've always been quite fit, so I got through the physical parts of the course fine, but I found all the stuff on first-aid techniques really challenging. I'm fine with it all now though, and I've picked up loads of practical tips from the more experienced guys I'm working with.

You need to be 15 for lifeguard training. Plus you must be in good shape. The thing is, other people will be relying on your strength and fitness in risky situations and you can't let them down.

Keep in touch!

Rob

3 **Read the *Prepare to write* box, and read Rob's email again. Find:**

a an opening expression
b a closing expression
c four phrasal verbs
d four other examples of informal language

PREPARE TO WRITE Informal letters and emails

In informal letters and emails

- use an informal opening expression.
  How nice to get your news!
  It's great to hear from you.
  Thanks for your email.
- use informal expressions to add ideas.
  To start with, … *Also …* *Plus …*
- use informal language and phrasal verbs.
  I reckon … *Anyway, …* *The thing is …*
  I pick things up quickly.
- use contracted forms.
  don't *can't* *wouldn't*
- use an informal closing expression.
  Take care *Write soon* *Love*
  Keep in touch

4 **Find informal sentences and expressions in the email to match the formal sentences and expressions below.**

1 It was very pleasing to receive your email.
2 Our job is to assist swimmers and surfers who experience difficulties.
3 This could be rather daunting without training.
4 It is also important that you have a good level of fitness.

5 **Rob has not answered the final question in the task. Write a fourth paragraph to Rob's email, answering this question.**

PREPARE FOR THE EXAM

Writing Part 2 (An informal letter or email)

6 **Read the task and plan your answer.**

This is part of an email you received from your English-speaking penfriend, Toni.

> I'd like to learn a language because I can only speak English. Do you think language learning is easy? What's the best way to learn new words? I'd like to learn your language. Can you suggest how I should start learning your language?
>
> Write back soon!
>
> Toni

Write your **email**.

7 **Write your email to Toni.**

- Answer all of Toni's questions.
- Use the tips in the *Prepare to write* box.
- Check your grammar and spelling.
- Write 140–190 words.

4 TAKE IT EASY

ABOUT YOU

Which of these situations typically make you feel stressed?

the amount of homework you have
not having enough money
getting ready for parties
arguing with friends/family

Can you think of other situations?

VOCABULARY Stress

13 **1** **Listen to eight situations and match them to the photos.**

2 **Match the words and phrases to the photos.**

EP

faint | feel dizzy | get in a panic
go over and over something in your mind
have difficulty sleeping | have an upset stomach
lose your temper | lose your appetite

3 **Discuss the questions.**

1. When was the last time you lost your temper?
2. Do you ever get in a panic about exams?
3. Have you ever had difficulty sleeping? When?

READING

1 **Read the headings for an article about stress. Do you agree or disagree? Compare your answers in pairs.**

A Stress is for adults, not people my age.
B A bit of stress helps me to get things done.
C It's not my fault that I get stressed.
D I know how to deal with stress.
E Everyone gets stressed from time to time. It's no big deal.

2 **Read the article quickly. Match the headings in Exercise 1 to parts 1–5 of the article. Use the sentence(s) in bold at the end of each paragraph to help you choose the heading that follows.**

3 **Read the article again. Complete the sentences with one or two words in each gap.**

1. The article suggests that most teenagers have fewer reasons to ________ than adults.
2. The author believes that stress is about more ________ deadlines.
3. Hormones released in stressful situations can both ________ and ________ our energy levels.
4. The article strongly recommends finding time in your day-to-day life ________ and also to relax.
5. Psychologists advise people to try and see the ________ in stressful situations.

4 TAKE IT EASY

Unit Overview

TOPIC	Stressful lives
VOCABULARY	Stress
READING	Under pressure?
GRAMMAR	Modals (1): necessity, obligation, prohibition and advice
VOCABULARY	Phrasal verbs: health
LISTENING	Five opinions about stress
SPEAKING	Offering help
EXAM TASKS	Reading and Use of English Part 4; Listening Part 3

Resources

GRAMMAR REFERENCE AND PRACTICE: SB page 151; TB page 267
PREPARE FOR THE EXAM: SB pages on TB pages 239 and 248; TB pages 255 and 260
WORKBOOK: pages 16–19
PHOTOCOPIABLE WORKSHEETS: Grammar worksheet Unit 4; Vocabulary worksheet Unit 4
TEST GENERATOR: Unit test 4
PRACTICE EXTRA: Unit 4

WARMER

With books closed, tell the students that you are going to give them some situations and they have to write the situation and a number from 1–10 depending on how the situation makes them feel. 1 is completely relaxed and 10 is very stressed. Read the situations out: 'A an important exam; B the night before a holiday; C meeting friends; D speaking a foreign language, and E meeting new people'.

Students then work in small groups of three or four. They tell each other which of the situations make them most stressed and why. Invite each group to tell the class about which situations make them stressed and what number they gave each one.

ABOUT YOU

Read the questions in the *About you* box. If you did the Warmer activity, the students can stay in the same groups to discuss these four situations and think of more stressful situations. Set a time limit of three minutes and then elicit ideas of different situations for the class to discuss how stressful these make them feel.

VOCABULARY Stress

13
1 Ask students to work in pairs to describe what they can see in the photos. Invite students to choose one photo each and describe it for their partner to guess which one it is. Before they listen to the recording, tell students to note down key words they hear and, when you check the answers, elicit any words that helped them to match the speakers to the photos. Students then work in pairs to describe the situation in each photo in their own words, *Speaker 1 (photo D) has just woken up and is late. She looks very worried.* Invite pairs to describe one photo each to the class.

Answers
1 D 2 G 3 H 4 A 5 C 6 B 7 F 8 E

» AUDIOSCRIPT TB PAGE 288

2 Ask the students to try to do as much of the matching as possible without looking up any new words. When they have finished, elicit the answers and the meanings of any new words. (to faint *means to lose consciousness for a short time*; to feel dizzy *is when you feel as if things are moving round and round or you can't stand steadily*; to panic *means to feel a sudden strong feeling of fear which makes it difficult to think clearly*; to lose your temper *means to become angry;* to lose your appetite *means that you are no longer hungry, maybe because you have already eaten or maybe because the food in front of you doesn't look very nice;* an upset stomach *means you feel ill or unwell*; and to go over and over something in your mind *means not to be able to stop thinking about something*)

Answers
A lose your temper B lose your appetite C faint D get in a panic E have an upset stomach F feel dizzy G have difficulty sleeping H go over and over something in your mind

3 Give the class time to think about the three situations alone and then put them in pairs. Set a time limit of three minutes for students to tell each other about the three situations and then invite some pairs to share interesting situations with the class. Students give their own answers.

READING

1 With books closed, write *Stress is for adults, not people my age.* on the board. Elicit responses from the class. First have a class vote on whether they agree or disagree and then invite students to give reasons for their choice. Then give students a few minutes to read the rest of the headings and discuss their ideas with a partner. Students give their own answers.

2 Look at the example with the class. Tell them to read the first paragraph and find any information that would help them to match it with the heading given (*a parent has to … a teenager who has to …; 75% of adults say they feel stressed, 85% of teenagers … say the same thing*). Students may feel that the heading doesn't reflect the paragraph which actually says that stress is for everyone. Elicit the age of the author (*a teenager – it says 'people my age' in the heading*) and point out that the meaning of the heading is that stress should be for adults, not for teenagers, but in fact teenagers also suffer from stress. Students then do the rest of the activity alone and compare answers in pairs. Elicit the answers and how the sentences in bold helped them.

MIXED ABILITY

Allow students to work in pairs. Each person reads two paragraphs and finds the correct headings. They then summarise their two paragraphs and tell each other which headings they think match them.

Answers
2 E 3 B 4 D 5 C

CONTINUED ON PAGE 46

BACKGROUND INFORMATION

A lot of psychologists say that teenagers suffer from more stress than ever before. There are several reasons for this change.

Schools in many countries test their students more often than before. Often this is because the schools themselves are being tested to see if they are keeping up standards. In addition, it is becoming more and more important to get good qualifications in order to get a job, so there is more need to do well in exams and go to university.

Social media has a big effect on stress levels. Students feel the need to look good and have an exciting life, as they constantly compare themselves to their friends. They can be judged by other people and feel the need for their posts to receive positive feedback in terms of comments and likes.

World events can also affect teenagers more than in the past. Serious events used to be reported in newspapers or on television or radio news programmes, which many teenagers could miss. Now, every traumatic event around the world is immediately shared, and it can make people feel as if they are living in a much more dangerous and unfair world than ever before. Teenagers may worry about injustices and natural disasters that they wouldn't have heard about a few years ago. There is constant news about pollution and climate change, which can make teenagers feel powerless.

Friendships and peers is one area where the amount of stress teenagers suffer hasn't changed much when compared to the past. Teens have always considered their social lives to be important. It is important to make and keep friends and bullying has always existed. In addition, the teenage years are the time when young people start having romantic relationships and worry about finding a partner and how to balance their time between the partner and their other friends.

3 Tell students that the words they need may not be written in exactly the same way in the text, so they will have to decide how to make a grammatically correct sentence. Look at the first sentence with the class and remind students that they can only use one or two words. Elicit ideas, for example, *get stressed, become stressed, feel stressed, be stressed, worry*. Tell students that they should read the text carefully and find where each piece of information can be found and then complete the sentences. Allow students to compare answers and elicit ideas.

FAST FINISHERS

Ask fast finishers to find a word in paragraph 1 which means *very surprised* (*astonished*). They then look for other interesting or difficult words in the other four paragraphs. The students write a definition for each word, looking these up in a dictionary if necessary. When everyone has finished the activity, elicit the answers and then invite fast finishers to ask the class to *Find a word in paragraph … which means …* The other students race to find the correct words.

Answers

1 get/feel stressed 2 than (just) 3 increase/boost, decrease/lower 4 for fun 5 positive

14 The Reading text is recorded for students to listen, read and check their answers.

TALKING POINTS

Ask the students the first question as a class. Ask if the stress that teenagers feel is as serious as the stress that adults feel and elicit reasons for their answers. Now put the students into pairs to discuss the second question. Elicit ideas and ask students if they have ever read online articles about how to deal with stress and if they have ever used any of the ideas they have read about.

COOLER

Put students into pairs. Each pair thinks of some of the things which they said make them stressed in the *About you* box at the start of the lesson. They write these down then swap lists with a second pair. They now use their ideas from the *Talking points* activity to write suggestions about how the other pair could deal with their stressful situations. Students then swap advice and read the ideas. Invite students to tell the class about any useful ideas they were given.

UNDER 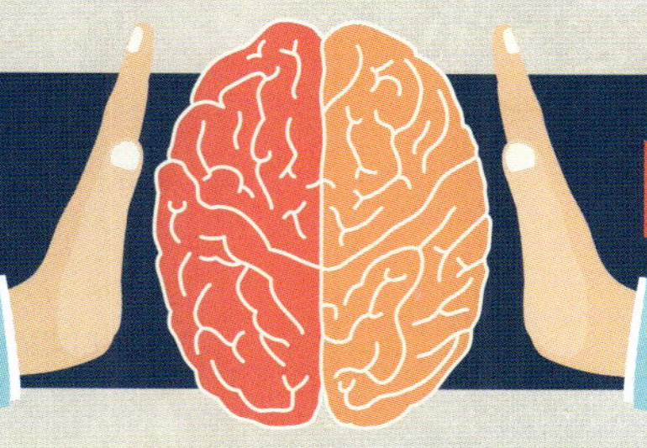 PRESSURE?

14

1 *A Stress is for adults, not people my age.*

Which of these two types of people is more stressed: a parent who has to go to work to earn money to pay bills and bring up a family, or a teenager who has to go to school to study? Surveys report that 75% of adults say they feel stressed on at least three occasions every week. However, an astonishing 85% of teenagers between 14 and 17 say the same thing. What's more, a third of the girls and half of the boys believe the pressure is there every single day. In this age group, the three most frequent causes of stress are schoolwork, parents and problems with friends. **But isn't this just part of life?**

2 ______________________

Very few of us would say we never get stressed. But what does stress mean to you? Is it a piece of work you need to finish for school? Perhaps it's a class you mustn't be late for. If stress was just about deadlines, we would probably be able to keep it under control. However, for most people, it's bigger than this. And it can be a very big deal. But could we get rid of it from our lives? **Do we actually want to?**

3 ______________________

When we are stressed, our body responds to the danger by releasing chemicals called *hormones*. They temporarily increase our heart rate and boost our energy levels. Thousands of years ago, we used this energy to avoid getting attacked by wild animals. So, in small doses, many people find that stress can motivate them. But constant stress can have the opposite effect, leading to feelings of anxiety. At this point, hormones actually lower our energy levels and we risk suffering from a whole range of health problems, such as having difficulty sleeping or losing your appetite. **So how do we avoid this?**

4 ______________________

Most of us know the basics of how to handle stress: we should take regular exercise and eat healthily. Sleep is also important. According to some reports, teenagers ought to get over nine hours of sleep every night. But fighting stress needn't be boring. We must also make some time in our schedule for fun, preferably with friends, and also a little quiet time, when we can relax. We should spend time around positive people, who don't get us down. Helping other people can help us feel less stressed, too, which is why volunteering is a good idea. And if you're getting in a panic, stop what you are doing and take several deep breaths. Pause for a moment and think about all the good things in your life. **Have you tried that? Is everything (or everyone) still stressing you out?**

5 ______________________

A common belief is that our stress comes from all the things we have to do because of *other* people. However, some psychologists believe it's more helpful to think of stress as how we *react* to the things that stress us. The reason is that these things are beyond our control, but we *can* control how we react to them. We've just got to find the right way. One thing we can do is to look for the positive in situations. When your parents say you can't go away with your friends for the weekend because it's too expensive, think of it as an opportunity to do something at home instead. You don't have to choose something boring, like organising your wardrobe: you could spend a day practising that new skateboarding trick or catching up on your favourite TV programmes. Of course, there may be things you *do* have to do before you can go and enjoy yourself. Do you have a tricky essay to write that's due in next week? You'd better do *that*, **but maybe you could see it as a challenge rather than a chore.**

TALKING POINTS

Do you think teenagers get stressed as much as adults?
What do you think is the best way to deal with stress?

GRAMMAR Modals (1): necessity, obligation, prohibition and advice

1 **Read the examples. Then complete the rules with the verbs in the examples.**

1 You don't have to choose something boring.
2 We should take regular exercise.
3 Teenagers ought to get over nine hours of sleep every night.
4 Fighting stress needn't be boring.
5 Is it a piece of work you need to finish for school?
6 Do you have a tricky essay to write that's due in next week? You'd better do that.

We use
a ________, *had better* or *ought to* for advice.
b ________ for necessity.
c ________, (*haven't got to*) or *needn't* for lack of obligation.

GRAMMAR REFERENCE AND PRACTICE PAGE 151

PREPARE FOR THE EXAM

Reading and Use of English Part 4

2 **Complete the second sentence so that it has a similar meaning to the first sentence, using the word given. Do not change the word given. You must use between two and five words, including the word given.**

0 Getting plenty of sleep is necessary when you're very busy. **SHOULD**
You *should get a* lot of sleep when you're very busy.
1 Clare knew that she had to complete all her homework by Friday. **NECESSARY**
Clare knew that ________ her to complete all her homework by Friday.
2 'You need to get to my party on time!' said Daisy. **HAD**
'You ________ late for my party!' said Daisy.
3 There's no need to attend the extra classes. **HAVE**
You ________ to the extra classes.
4 'You needn't wear your uniforms for the school trip,' said the teacher. **DO**
'You ________ wear your uniforms for the school trip,' said the teacher.
5 It would be a good idea if I went to bed early tonight. **OUGHT**
I ________ to bed early tonight.
6 There's no need for me to help my dad. **GOT**
I ________ help my dad now.

PREPARE FOR THE EXAM PAGE 123

3 **Read the examples and complete the rules with the verbs.**

1 We must also make some time in our schedule for fun.
2 Our stress comes from all the things we have to do because of other people.
3 It's a class you mustn't be late for.
4 We've just got to find the right way.

We use
a ________ for prohibition.
b ________, ________ or ________ for obligation.
c *must* or *have got to* when the obligation is our personal opinion.
d ________ when the obligation is not our personal opinion.

4 **Correct the mistake in each sentence.**

1 Simon must to control his temper more.
2 You don't have to use my things without asking first!
3 I really think you can take regular exercise because it's good for you.
4 I'll meet you later because I should go to the doctor's at 3 pm.
5 I haven't done any exercise for ages. I've better do some this week.
6 You haven't eat too much when you're studying or you'll feel sleepy.

5 **Complete the sentences with your own ideas.**

1 I really should …
2 Every day, I have to …
3 At school, we don't have to …
4 Tomorrow, I must …
5 Students mustn't …
6 My parents say I ought to …

VOCABULARY Phrasal verbs: health

1 **Match the phrasal verbs to the meanings.**

EP 1 I threw up after that meal. I think I'm allergic to shellfish!
2 It's taken me weeks to get over this flu.
3 Arguing with my friends really gets me down.
4 I slowly came round after the operation.
5 We all came down with food poisoning in the evening, so we couldn't go out.
6 When I lose my temper, I find it difficult to calm down quickly.

a feel less annoyed or stressed
b make someone feel unhappy
c feel better after an illness or an unhappy event
d be awake again after being unconscious
e become ill
f vomit/be sick (informal)

2 Work in pairs. Turn to page 138.

GRAMMAR Modals (1): necessity, obligation, prohibition and advice

WARMER

Tell students to think about things they should or shouldn't do in order to be less stressed, for example *I should go to bed earlier*. Set a time limit of one or two minutes for students to write ideas alone. Students then get into groups of three or four. They tell each other what they wrote and the other students say whether they also had the same ideas or not. When students have finished, invite groups to tell the class about some of their ideas.

1 Students complete the rules in pairs. When they have finished, elicit an alternative way of saying each sentence, for example, *1 needn't; 2 ought to; 3 should; 4 doesn't have to be; 5 have to; 6 should.*

Answers
a should b need to c don't have to

» GRAMMAR REFERENCE AND PRACTICE ANSWER KEY TB PAGE 267

PREPARE FOR THE EXAM

B2 FIRST FOR SCHOOLS
Reading and Use of English Part 4

This part is a key word transformation task that tests vocabulary, grammar and collocation. It consists of six questions, each with a lead-in sentence, a key word and a gapped sentence. Students must complete the gapped sentence with two to five words, including the given key word. Each question has two marks, one for each part so, for the example, they would get one point for *should get* and one point for *a* (lot of).

Tips Tell students to read the entire sentence for clues about the type of word needed to complete the gap. There might be clues that help them to decide on, for example, which modal verb to use, or which tense is needed to keep the same meaning as the first sentence.

2 Look at the example sentence with the class and the stages they go through to get the correct answer: 1 They know they have to rewrite the sentence using *should*. 2 They have to put the verb in the correct form, so change it from *getting* to *get*. 3 The word *plenty* has changed to *lot of*. They have to remember to add *a* to make the complete phrase *a lot of*. Students complete the activity alone and then compare answers in pairs discussing any mistakes they made.

» PREPARE FOR THE EXAM TEACHING NOTES AND ANSWER KEY TB PAGE 255

Answers
1 it was | necessary for 2 had better | not be 3 do not/don't have to | go / will not/won't have to | go 4 do not | need/have to 5 ought to | go 6 have not/haven't | got to

3 When students have completed the rules, you could point out that, when talking about repeated obligations, we generally use *have to* rather than *have got to*, for example, *I have to take the dog for a walk every day*. *'ve got to* would be used for single events or temporary situations, for example, *My parents are working late today, so I've got to take the dog for a walk this evening*.

Answers
a mustn't b must, have to, have/'ve got to d have to

4 Tell the students that the mistakes may be in the form of the verb following the modal or the wrong modal being used. Look at the first sentence with the class and elicit the problem (must *should be followed by a verb without* to). Students do the rest of the exercise individually and then compare answers in pairs. Elicit what is wrong with each sentence and the correct answers.

Answers
1 Simon **must control** his temper more.
2 You **mustn't use** my things without asking first!
3 I really think you **should / ought to take** regular exercise because it's good for you.
4 I'll meet you later because I **have (got) to go** to the doctor's at 3 pm.
5 I haven't done any exercise for ages. **I'd/had better** do some this week.
6 You **mustn't/shouldn't eat** too much when you're studying or you'll feel sleepy.

5 Elicit that sentence 2 refers to an obligation that is not our personal opinion, but something that someone else has told us to do. Students work alone and then compare ideas in pairs. Monitor and help where necessary. Elicit endings for each sentence and, if students make a mistake with the verb form, try to elicit self-corrections by repeating the incorrect word with questioning intonation, for example, *I really should doing more exercise. Doing?* Students give their own answers.

» GRAMMAR WORKSHEET UNIT 4

VOCABULARY Phrasal verbs: health

1 Put students into pairs and tell them to cover the meanings. Students read through the sentences and try to work out the meanings of the phrasal verbs from context. Students then uncover the meanings and do the matching.

Answers
1 f 2 c 3 b 4 d 5 e 6 a

2 Set a time limit for students to complete the sentences. When the time limit has finished, tell everyone to stop writing, and elicit the correct answers. Students then work in pairs to discuss the questions (0, 2, 4).

Answers
1 came round 2 get over 3 throw up 4 come down with 5 calmed down

3 Look at sentence 2 from Exercise 1 with the class. Write a question using the same phrasal verb on the board, for example *Have you ever had an illness that has taken more than two weeks to get over? What is the best way to get over the flu?* Invite the class to answer the questions and encourage them to give as many details as possible.

Students then look at the questions on page 138 in pairs. If the answer to any of the questions is *no*, students could talk about other people they know. For example, someone they know who has had food poisoning or fainted. Invite students to tell the class about one of their answers. Students give their own answers.

FAST FINISHERS

Tell students to write four sentences about themselves using phrasal verbs. One must be false and three must be true. They should then show their sentences to a partner who must guess which one is false.

» VOCABULARY WORKSHEET UNIT 4

LISTENING

15 **1** Tell students to read through all the sentences before they listen to the recording. Elicit the answer and ask students why some people might have chosen B by mistake. (*The boy mentions exams, exercise classes and his parents, but it is wrong because he talks to his parents about being stressed and mentions the exercise classes as a way of keeping his stress under control.*)

Answer
C

» AUDIOSCRIPT TB PAGE 288

2 Look at the reasons with the students. You may have already mentioned B in the feedback to Exercise 1. Students work in pairs to discuss reasons E–H. Play the recording again if you think it would help the students. Elicit the answers.

Answers
E is not true because although the boy mentions exercise, it is not his main way of fighting stress, but just one of several techniques he uses. F is not true because although he gets in 'a mood', he doesn't say he dislikes his behaviour. G is not true because although the boy mentions different 'tricks', he does not say anyone gave him advice on these. H is not true because the boy does not mention arguing with anyone.

PREPARE FOR THE EXAM

3 **B2 FIRST FOR SCHOOLS Listening Part 3**

16 Briefly review what students need to do in this part of the exam and, if necessary, read out the *B2 First for Schools* information on TB page 30.

Tell students that you will play the recording twice. They should listen carefully on the second listening to make sure they haven't made a mistake. Allow students to compare answers in pairs and then elicit the correct answers and any information students remember from the texts which helped them.

Answers
Speaker 2: D – She is worried about what she needs to do now in order to go to university or get a good job in the future. Speaker 3: G – The *advice* refers to the speaker's teacher and writing a diary is the *technique*. Speaker 4: F – The speaker doesn't like it when she's bad-tempered. Speaker 5: A – The answer is confirmed by a global understanding of the whole text. You do not need letters B, E and H.

» AUDIOSCRIPT TB PAGES 288–289

SPEAKING Offering help

17 **1** When students have listened, elicit the answer and ask for more details, for example: Where is Ben going to get the games from? (*Olivia's house*); Will he see her? (*No, her parents will give Ben the games.*) and Why can't Olivia take the games to Atif? (*She's got band practice and has to finish an essay.*).

Answers
He's going to pick up some of Atif's games from her house and give them to Atif.

17 **2** Students look at the sentences and try to decide which word should go in each gap before they listen again. Elicit some more offers using *Shall I … for you?*

Answers
1 Shall 2 sure 3 like 4 need

» AUDIOSCRIPT TB PAGE 289

18 **3** Tell the students to cover the three questions. They listen to the recording and then discuss what they heard in pairs. Students then uncover the questions and try to answer them together. Elicit the answers.

MIXED ABILITY
Allow weaker students to keep the questions uncovered so they know what they have to listen out for. You could also make copies of the audioscript for them so that, after listening to the dialogue, if they are still unsure of any of the answers, they can refer to the audioscript to help them.

Answers
1 Noah offers to help his mum. 2 He offers to pick his sister up and to do the online shopping. 3 She wants him to make dinner.

18 **4** Look at the different phrases in the *Prepare to speak* box with the class. Elicit the offer made in sentence 1 of Exercise 2 (*Shall I take the games for you?*). Then make the same offer using the other phrases in the box (*Would you like me to take the games for you? Let me take the games for you. I'll take the games for you if you like*). Play the recording and elicit the answers. If you used the *Mixed ability* idea in Exercise 3, ask students to listen without looking at the audioscript and to only refer to the audioscript if they aren't sure of the answers.

Answers
Noah: Would you like me to … ?, Let me …;
Mum: It's OK, I can do it myself. It'd be great if you could. No, don't worry. I can manage that.

» AUDIOSCRIPT TB PAGE 289

5 Give the students one or two examples of things you need to do, for example *I need to write some emails. I need to do some shopping*. Tell the class that no one else can write the emails for you because they are to friends. However, you could ask a friend/family member to go shopping for you. Set a time limit of one minute for students to list their ideas. Students give their own answers.

6 Look at the example with the class. Then ask students to do this in pairs. When they have played both roles, put the students into groups of three. They take turns to play the parts of A and B with the third student listening out for the phrases from the *Prepare to speak* box and noting them down. When all three students have played the role of the listener, ask different students which phrases they heard. Finally, invite one or two pairs to act out their conversation in front of the class. Students give their own answers.

COOLER
Students work alone and write three things they have to do this week on a piece of paper. They can use the same ideas as in Exercises 5 and 6. Students then get into an even number of groups, preferably with five or six students in each. They collect all their pieces of paper together and swap with a second group. The students in each group try to guess who wrote each list and they write the person's name on each piece of paper. They then swap again and see how many the other group guessed correctly.

LISTENING

1 **You will hear a boy talking about stress. Read the sentences carefully. Then listen and decide which of the sentences (A–H) is true for the boy.** 15

A I don't suffer badly from stress.
B Schoolwork and family make me stressed the most.
C I have a range of ways to deal with stress.
D The future is my biggest cause of stress.
E Physical activity is my main way of fighting stress.
F I don't like how I behave when I'm stressed.
G I followed advice on a technique for dealing with stress.
H Arguing with other people makes me stressed.

2 **Read the reasons why A–D in Exercise 1 are true or not true for the boy. Work in pairs and decide why E–H are not true.**

A Not true. He says he does get stressed.
B Not true. Exams stress the boy, but he only mentions talking to his parents.
C True. He says he does a variety of things to keep stress under control.
D Not true. He doesn't mention the future.

PREPARE FOR THE EXAM

Listening Part 3

3 **You will hear four more teenagers talking about stress. For questions 2–5, choose from the list (A–H) what each speaker says about it. Use the letters only once. There are three extra letters which you do not need to use.** 16

Speaker 1 ___*C*___
Speaker 2 ______
Speaker 3 ______
Speaker 4 ______
Speaker 5 ______

SPEAKING Offering help

1 **Listen to the conversation. What is Ben going to do for Olivia?** 17

2 **Listen again and complete the phrases.** 17

like need shall sure

1 ______ I take the games for you?
2 Are you ______? That'd be fantastic, thanks.
3 I'll text you when I leave here if you ______.
4 Thanks, but there's no ______.

3 **Listen to a conversation between Noah and his mother. Answer the questions.** 18

1 Who offers to help who?
2 What offers are made?
3 What does Noah's mother really want him to do?

4 **Read the *Prepare to speak* box. Then listen again. Which phrases do Noah and his mother use?** 18

PREPARE TO SPEAK | Making offers

Making offers
Would you like me to … ?
Shall I … ?
Let me …
I'll … if you like.

Refusing offers
It's OK, I can do it myself.
No, don't worry. I can manage that.
Thanks, but there's no need.

Accepting offers
It'd be great if you could.
Are you sure? That'd be fantastic, thanks.

5 **Write down all the things you need to do this week. Which of them could someone else help with?**

6 **Work in pairs. Then change roles.**

Student A Tell Student B about your list.
Student B Make offers to Student A.
Student A Respond to the offers appropriately.

I've got to finish a project, get some new trainers and buy a birthday present for my dad.

Let me help you with your dad's birthday present.

It'd be great if you could.

LIFE SKILLS LEARNING TO LEARN

TIME MANAGEMENT

LIFE SKILLS

Time management

Life can be very busy! Balancing your school life with your social life and free-time activities can often be tough. Managing your time effectively is a key skill to develop and has many benefits, such as reducing anxiety, performing better at school, and finding it easier to make decisions.

1 **Ask and answer the questions with a partner.**

1 How often do you feel that you don't have enough time to do everything you need to do? Why?
2 How do you feel when you finish work at the last minute or do things late?
3 What kind of things distract or interrupt you when you're trying to concentrate?

2 **Look at the headings and the three photos in the article on the opposite page. Match photos A–C to three of the headings 1–5. Read the article quickly and check your ideas.**

3 **Read the article again and answer the questions.**

1 Is making a list of distractions enough to deal with them? Why? / Why not?
2 What does organisation involve, apart from having everything tidy and in order?
3 What are some of the main reasons for putting something off?
4 Why is it a good idea to start with short periods when you first try using 'timeboxes'?
5 Why shouldn't we do things we like all the time?

4 **Match the highlighted words and phrases in the article to the meanings.**

1 deciding to delay something until a later time
2 a time by which something must be done
3 dealt with something or a situation
4 blocks or pieces of something
5 a very difficult task which requires a big effort

5 **Which of the time management tips from the article do you think are the most useful? Can you think of any other time management tips?**

19 **6** **Look at the chart. How could this be used to help your time management? Listen to a talk on time management for university students and check your ideas.**

URGENCY: HIGH ← → LOW; IMPORTANCE: HIGH ↑ ↓ LOW

	1 Important **and** urgent. You should **do it now.**	**2** Important but **not** urgent. **Do it later.**
	3 Urgent but **not** important. **Ask** someone else **to do it**.	**4** **Not** urgent and **not** important. **Don't waste your time!**

19 **7** **Read the following notes, which a student made in the talk. Listen again and complete them with one or two words in each gap.**

Planning

- is a crucial [1] ________
- creating a study schedule is a [2] ________
- include weekly plan & long-term goals
- helps establish a [3] ________

Study patterns

- pay attention to your own unique study [4] ________
- work out optimum study methods
- have a designated [5] ________
- experiment with study patterns
- alternate between [6] ________ and [7] ________ tasks

Prioritising

- focus on what [8] ________
- balance multiple demands
- use a time matrix to [9] ________ from 1 to 4 by urgency & importance

8 **Complete the sentences with the words in the box.**

behind commitments meet minute stick

USEFUL LANGUAGE

Talking about time management

1 I'm getting ________ with my project.
2 This will help you to ________ deadlines.
3 A study planner will help you to ________ to a schedule.
4 Don't leave things until the last ________!
5 Prioritising tasks will ensure that you meet your ________.

LIFE SKILLS

Learning Objectives

- The students learn about how to manage their time better.
- In the project stage, the students make a poster with time management tips and present it to the class.

Vocabulary

chunks deadline putting things off struggle tackled

BACKGROUND INFORMATION

The history of time management dates back to 1911 when the book *The Principles of Scientific Management* by Frederick Taylor was published. His idea was that there is a best way to do every task and that all employees should be trained to carry out tasks in this way. One of the aims of time management is 'work smarter, not harder'. By cutting wasted time, people should have more time to rest.

In recent times, attention management has started to become an alternative to time management. Because of new technology, our schedule is constantly changing. Emails can arrive at any time and most senders expect an instant response, even if their needs aren't actually very urgent, according to the receiver's schedule. Instead of being able to prioritise, many employees are overwhelmed with work. This can be very stressful but attention management can help. This is the skill of focusing your attention on what you want to do rather than reacting to what other people demand. For this to work, it is necessary for both employer and employee to understand what is best for the business as a whole; the employer so they don't make unreasonable demands and the employee so that they can focus on the things that they are responsible for. This can also be useful for students, especially if they are studying for tests. If several teachers set tests for a similar time, they need to consider what they should give their attention to: exam subjects, homework, relaxation time, chores, etc.

WARMER

Put students into groups of three or four. Ask them to imagine they have just got home from school. They want to use their computer, make a cup of tea, feed the cat, do their homework and check their phone. Ask them to say exactly what order they would do things in, for example *First, I would go upstairs to my room and switch on my computer. Then I would go to the kitchen …* Set a time limit of two minutes then invite the groups to say what order they would do the things in and why. Decide as a class the best way of doing these things in the shortest possible time.

LIFE SKILLS

Time management

Tell students to read the information. Ask them how good or bad they think they are at managing their time. Elicit examples of when they have done something very quickly or wasted a lot of time.

1 Give students a couple of minutes to discuss the questions together. Elicit ideas from different students. Encourage an open-class discussion and help students make connections between their contributions. Then ask them how much they agree with the idea that the more time you have, the longer it takes you to do something.

Answers

Students' own answers

2 Before students do the matching, ask them to work in groups of three. Each student describes one of the photos and what they think it means. The students then work together to do the matching. Set a time limit for them to read the text quickly and elicit the answers and any information students read which helped them to decide.

FAST FINISHERS

Ask fast finishers to think of a photo to illustrate each of the other two headings in the article. When everyone has finished reading, invite students to describe their photos.

Answers

Photo A: 3 Photo B: 5 Photo C: 1

3 Decide whether you want the students to write full sentences for answers or notes, so that everyone does the same thing. When they have finished, elicit the answers and where in the text the information can be found.

MIXED ABILITY

Put students into pairs. Tell them that each question corresponds to one of the five numbered paragraphs. The students look through each paragraph together and, when they have found the answer to the question, they work together to write the answer.

Answers

1 No, because you need to decide what to do about each distraction as well.
2 It's also important to estimate how long things will take to make sure you have enough time to do them.
3 We think it won't be a nice or easy thing to do or that it will be stressful.
4 Because it's realistic and you'll get quick results.
5 Keeping things we like as a reward will mean we enjoy working hard for them.

20 The Reading text is recorded for students to listen, read and check their answers.

CONTINUED ON PAGE 54

4 When students have matched the words to the meanings, elicit the answers and then ask them to work in pairs to think of sentences which are true about themselves using the same words. Give them some examples for yourself, such as: *I always put off marking tests until the last minute. I like working to a deadline because it helps me to focus more.* Monitor and collect examples of good language and errors. After eliciting ideas from different students, share the feedback with the class.

Answers
1 putting things off 2 deadline 3 tackled 4 chunks 5 struggle

5 You could put students into five groups. Each group reads one of the paragraphs 1–5 in the article again. The students then close their books and work together to summarise the tip in one or two sentences. Elicit summaries from each group then the students, still with books closed, decide in their groups which tip they think is the most useful. Elicit ideas from each group with reasons for their choice.

Answers
Students' own answers

19 6 Look at the chart with the students and discuss what it means. Elicit or check meanings for urgent / urgency (*urgent – needs to be dealt with immediately*) and priority / prioritise (*prioritise – to put things in order of importance and urgency so you can decide which to do first*). Students then listen to the recording and discuss what they heard in pairs. Elicit ideas and ask if students make any other similar charts to help them with their work. Tell students that another option is doing things depending on the length of time they take. Some people feel overwhelmed if they have a lot of things to do and so they get rid of the smaller tasks first, even if they are less urgent or important. This helps them psychologically because they then may 'only' have two or three tasks still to do, even if these are time-consuming and urgent. Invite students to say how they prioritise things.

Possible answer
The chart helps students decide what to prioritise, what they can leave for later and what doesn't need doing at all.

19 7 Students read through the notes and write down any words they think they remember, not in the gaps, but next to them. Allow them to listen twice if necessary, and then elicit the answers. Elicit that 'a must' means it is necessary. Follow up by asking students about the advice they heard and whether they think they might use some of the ideas in the future.

Answers
1 skill 2 must 3 routine 4 rhythms 5 study area 6 interesting 7 less interesting 8 (really) matters 9 categorise (things)

» **AUDIOSCRIPT TB PAGE 289**

8 Students work in pairs to complete as much of the exercise as possible. Elicit the answers and the meanings of the different phrases (getting behind *means to be behind schedule*, meet deadlines *means to complete work on time*, stick to a schedule *means to follow it*, the last minute *can mean at any point which is very close to the deadline* (noun)). Elicit or tell students that we can also use this *last-minute* as an adjective, for example, a last-minute flight or holiday is when you book them very close to the time you leave. *Meet commitments* means completing tasks that you have accepted.

Answers
1 behind 2 meet 3 stick 4 minute 5 commitments

PROJECT ***A time management poster***

Look at the introduction to the instructions with the students. Ask them to work alone and note down what they find difficult or easy about time management and examples of when they use it. When they are ready, put them into groups of three or four to discuss the questions, decide who will research what and when and divide up the tasks. Encourage pupils to meet up outside of class to finalise the poster and practise their presentations. Tell them to try to incorporate the *Useful language* into their presentations.

When students have all presented their posters to the class, they work in their groups and discuss the three most useful tips that they heard from the other groups. Elicit ideas from each group and ask for reasons as to why these things are important.

PROJECT EXTENSION

Tell students to think about all the things they have to do in the next week, including schoolwork and personal things such as writing emails or posting blogs. They write them all in a chart similar to that in Exercise 6 on page 28. Tell students to make a schedule for their commitments for the week. Point out that they should update it as they get homework or jobs at home. They then keep a diary in which they say whether or not they succeeded in doing everything they had planned for each day and, if not, what prevented them. When the week is over, invite students to report on how their attempt at scheduling worked and to analyse what worked well and what, if anything, went wrong, for example unrealistic deadlines for certain tasks.

COOLER

Students think about the most distracting thing for them at home – something that prevents them from getting on with their work. Tell all the students to stand up and to mingle and ask each other about what distracts them. They note down how many people have the same problem as them. When students sit down again, put them in groups of three or four to discuss what distracts them and how many other people they talked to with the same problem. They then work together to think of how to avoid such distractions, for example to switch off their phones completely while they are doing homework. Invite groups to share their ideas with the class.

20

TOP FIVE TIME MANAGEMENT TIPS

The majority of adults find managing their time a struggle, and your teenage years can be just as challenging. Trying to split your time between different demands – academic, social, family – can often be a real headache. Learning how to manage your time well will help you to avoid getting behind with your work and to feel calmer and less stressed. Here are our top five tips to get you started.

1 DEAL WITH DISTRACTIONS

Try making a list of all the ways you get distracted. Looking at your phone will be on it, but there will be lots of other things, too. Next, decide how you can control each of the distractions on your list. For example, keeping your phone out of reach or putting it away while you're doing your homework will help you finish a lot faster. You'll be amazed at how much more productive you can be when you've dealt with distractions.

A

B

2 GET ORGANISED

Everything is so much quicker and easier with good organisation. So, before you start studying, make sure that you've got your books, notes and anything else you'll need at hand. Being organised is also about estimating how long tasks or projects will take before you begin them, and making sure that you'll have enough time to dedicate to them. And if you haven't left yourself enough time, always ask for an extension in advance so that your teachers know you need more time to complete something. Never wait until a deadline to announce a delay.

3 DON'T PUT THINGS OFF

Not finishing your work on time, being late, or leaving things until the last minute are all signs of putting things off. Learning to start early enough is a key time management skill. We often avoid starting tasks that we think will be difficult, stressful or unpleasant. But in fact, when we actually start them, we almost always discover that they are not quite as bad as we thought. And often we even end up enjoying doing the thing that we were putting off!

C

4 TIMEBOX

So you've tackled distractions, got yourself organised and stopped putting things off, but are you still finding it difficult to manage your time? Well, it sounds like it's time to try 'timeboxing'. The basic idea here is to set a fixed period of time, or a 'timebox', which you use to do a planned activity. Limiting the number of minutes you work on something will help you break tasks down into manageable chunks and allow you to divide your time between different demands. Start with realistic timeboxes of 5, 10 or 15 minutes and you'll soon see the results.

5 WORK FIRST, PLAY LATER

There's usually something else you'd prefer to be doing instead of studying, like trying to improve your score on the latest game, chatting to friends, or watching a series you're hooked on. Of course, we enjoy these things and they make us feel good. But we also know that we can't do them all the time because then they wouldn't be special any more. So try keeping some things you enjoy doing as a reward for when you finish your work, or complete a number of timeboxes. You'll feel much happier with yourself because you've worked hard for it!

PROJECT

A time management poster

Work in groups of three or four to talk about your own time management. Use these steps to help you.

1. Tell your group about the areas of time management which you find most challenging.
2. Choose time management tips from the article and university tutorial which you would like to try.
3. Don't just think about the present. Which tips and strategies would you like to develop now that could be useful for you in the future?
4. Search online for other time management tips and advice and share what you find with your group.
5. Design a mini-poster with personalised time management tips. Place the poster inside the cover of your notebook or use it as a desktop image.

Present your poster to the class.

REVIEW 1 UNITS 1–4

VOCABULARY

1 Match the words to the meanings.

bestseller	broadcast	cast
the charts	shoot	track

1 show a programme on TV, radio or online
2 all the actors in a film, play or show
3 one song or piece of music on an album
4 an official list of the most popular songs each week
5 use a camera to record a film or take a photo
6 a very popular book that many people have bought

2 Complete the conversations. Use the word pairs in the box in the correct form and the correct order.

bothered / cope	jealous / compare	critical / do
hopeless / decisive	impressed / adventurous	

1 **A:** Would you say you are a ______ person? I mean, do you make your mind up quickly about things?
B: Not really! In fact, I'm completely ______ at deciding what to do.
2 **A:** I think our football manager is quite ______ of us – we never seem to do anything right!
B: I know. We could ______ without his negative comments.
3 **A:** People often ______ me with my 'clever' sister.
B: Do you ever get ______ of her?
4 **A:** Sofia has never had trouble ______ with exam stress.
B: No, but she never gets ______ about anything.
5 **A:** I was really ______ by Alex's art project.
B: Yes, he's been really ______ with colour, hasn't he?

3 Match the phrasal verbs in the box to the meanings.

back up	face up to	focus on
get through	mix up	think through

1 make an extra copy of something held on a computer
2 succeed, e.g. in an exam
3 confuse two people or things
4 give a lot of attention to
5 carefully consider the possible results of something
6 accept that a difficult situation exists

4 Choose the correct verb to complete each phrase.

1 *catch / have / feel* an upset stomach
2 *drop / lose / forget* your temper
3 *take / think / go* over and over things in your mind
4 *lose / feel / be* your appetite
5 *have / get / feel* difficulty sleeping
6 *have / go / get* in a panic

GRAMMAR

1 Choose the correct options.

Tavi Gevinson was just 11 when she [1] *started / had started* her fashion blog, *Style Rookie*. On it, she [2] *posted / was posting* pictures of herself and wrote descriptions of her clothes. At first, people thought the site was fake and that a fashion expert [3] *set / had set* it up. But within a few years, Tavi's site [4] *is attracting / was attracting* thousands of readers. *Rookie*, an online magazine Tavi [5] *has been running / is running* since she was 15, grew from the blog. Tavi [6] *has acted / acted* in several roles in the last few years and has been named one of the most influential teens in the world.

2 Complete the sentences with the present perfect simple or continuous form of the verbs in the box. Use the same verb in each pair of sentences.

do	ring	run	try

1 **a** I can come out now. I ______ my revision.
b I ______ homework for three hours.
2 **a** You look hot. ______ you ______?
b ______ you ever ______ a marathon?
3 **a** Dan ______ to help me with this maths for hours, but I still don't understand it.
b I ______ doing more exercise, but it doesn't seem to help.
4 **a** Clare ______ you several times today.
b Where have you been? I ______ you all morning.

3 Rewrite the underlined part of the sentences with the correct form of the phrasal verbs in the box and a pronoun if necessary.

come across	come down with	hand out
look after	~~make up~~	pass out	throw away

0 No way! I think you invented it! *made it up*
1 Look at this old computer. I found it in the garage.
2 He lost consciousness when he saw the blood.
3 The teacher gave me the papers and asked me to distribute them.
4 I've got a cold. I became ill with it yesterday.
5 My brother's 11. I take care of him sometimes.
6 I don't have any DVDs. I got rid of them recently.

4 Correct the mistake in each sentence.

1 You don't have to get in a panic. It will only make things worse.
2 You needn't be more adventurous with food. Just try things!
3 We have better get going or we'll miss the flight.
4 I'm exhausted. I shouldn't go to bed earlier!
5 I know that your birthday is next week. You mustn't remind me.

REVIEW 1 UNITS 1–4

Overview

VOCABULARY	Arts and media; Personality: adjective + preposition; Verb + preposition; Phrasal verbs: learning and thinking; Stress
GRAMMAR	Simple, continuous or perfect; Present perfect simple and continuous; The grammar of phrasal verbs; Modals (1): necessity, obligation, prohibition and advice
EXAM TASKS	Reading and Use of English Part 1; Reading and Use of English Part 2; Reading and Use of English Part 4

Resources

PHOTOCOPIABLE WORKSHEETS: Grammar worksheets Units 1–4; Vocabulary worksheets Units 1–4; Review Game Units 1–4; Literature worksheet; Speaking worksheet; Writing worksheet

WARMER

Put students into groups of four. Each student in the group looks at a different unit and chooses two vocabulary items that they think the other students may have forgotten. They write down each word and a definition. The students then take it in turns to read out a definition for others in the group to guess the word.

VOCABULARY

1 Before students look at the meanings, ask them to look at the box of words in pairs and see if they can think of their own definitions. Students then uncover the definitions and do the matching. Elicit the answers.

Answers
1 broadcast 2 cast 3 track 4 the charts 5 shoot 6 bestseller

2 Look at 1A with the class and ask what word describes someone who makes their mind up quickly. Elicit the word *decisive* and ask students to check whether the word it is paired with (*hopeless*) fits the next gap (*yes*). Tell students that, if they are sure that one word in a pair is correct, they can be sure that the second word will also be correct. Students work alone and compare in pairs. Elicit answers and the meanings of each word.

Answers
1 A decisive; B hopeless 2 A critical; B do 3 A compare; B jealous
4 A coping; B bothered 5 A impressed; B adventurous

3 Look at the first definition with the class. Elicit the correct answer (*back up*) and ask what sort of things they back up and where they back them up to, for example*, to the cloud, to an external hard drive, to a second computer*, etc. Students then work alone and compare in pairs. Elicit the answers and ask more follow-up questions similar to the first, for example, *What was the last exam you got through?* and *When did you last mix up two people's names?*.

FAST FINISHERS

Ask fast finishers to choose some of the vocabulary from Exercises 1, 2 and 3 and write new sentences which include these words, for example, *I'm hopeless at remembering names.* They should make some of the sentences true for themselves and some false. When everyone has finished the exercise, invite fast finishers to share their sentences with the class. The other students try to guess if the sentence is true for the speaker or not.

Answers
1 back up 2 get through 3 mix up 4 focus on 5 think through
6 face up to

4 When students have chosen the correct verbs and you have checked the answers, tell the class that you are going to say a sentence to illustrate one of the phrases and they have to say which phrase it is. Say, *I'm so nervous about my exams that I'm just not hungry.* Elicit that you have *lost your appetite*. Students now work in pairs and think of similar statements that could illustrate one of the other phrases. Set a time limit of two minutes and then invite pairs to read out one of their statements. The other students say which phrase it matches.

Answers
1 have 2 lose 3 go 4 lose 5 have 6 get

GRAMMAR

1 Give students one minute to read the text quickly and elicit what it is about (*teenage fashion blogger Tavi Gevinson*). Then look at the first sentence with students and elicit the correct verb form and the reason for it. (*We use the past simple to talk about a completed action in the past. We use the past perfect to talk about the earlier of two actions in the past, but there is only one action here.*) Students complete the exercise alone and then compare answers in pairs. If they disagree about any of the answers, ask them to explain which one is correct by thinking about the rules for when we use each tense. Elicit the correct answers.

Answers
1 started 2 posted 3 had set 4 was attracting
5 has been running 6 has acted

CONTINUED ON PAGE 58

2 Look at the first pair of sentences with the class. Elicit that the first person (a) uses the present perfect simple to talk about something specific they have done that is connected to the present moment and the second person (b) uses the continuous form to talk about an unfinished, general activity. Students do the rest of the activity in pairs. Elicit the answers.

MIXED ABILITY

To help weaker students, you could write the verbs to use on the board (2 run; 3 try; 3 ring). Monitor and help where necessary and, if students find it difficult, point out that, even where it is difficult to know which tense to use in one of the gaps, the other gap should be easier to work out, for example, 2b is one specific event in someone's life, 3a is a general activity that is still continuing and 4a talks about several specific events in an unfinished time period. Elicit the correct form for these and then allow students to complete the second sentences in pairs.

Answers

1 a have/'ve done, b have/'ve been doing 2 a Have, been running, b Have, run 3 a has been trying, b have/'ve tried 4 a has rung, b have/'ve been ringing

3 Look at the example with the students and elicit that separable phrasal verbs can be written with the object between the two parts of the verb or after the verb, but when we use an object pronoun, it has to go between the two parts. Students complete the exercise alone then compare answers in pairs. Check the answers as a class.

Answers

1 came across it 2 passed out 3 hand them out
4 came down with it 5 look after him 6 threw them away

4 Ask students to find the modal verb in each sentence. Elicit what these are and tell students that four of the sentences use the wrong modal and one is formed incorrectly. There may be more than one possible answer. Elicit the answers and what was wrong with the original sentence, for example, *1 This means that you can panic if you want to. Problem: A modal to give strong, negative advice is needed.*

Answers

1 You **mustn't** / **shouldn't get** in a panic. It will only make things worse.
2 You **should** / **ought to be** more adventurous with food. Just try things!
3 We **had/'d better get** going or we'll miss the flight.
4 I'm exhausted. I **must** / **should** / **ought to go** to be earlier!
5 I know that your birthday is next week. You **don't have to** / **needn't remind** me.

PREPARE FOR THE EXAM

1 **B2 FIRST FOR SCHOOLS Reading and Use of English Part 1**

Briefly review what students need to do in this part of the exam and if necessary, read out the *B2 First for Schools* box on TB page 26.

As students have looked at this type of task in Unit 2, you could tell them to do this under exam conditions. Allow students ten minutes and then elicit the answers. Where appropriate, elicit the meanings or example sentences of alternative options, for example, *1 A the latest versions of a computer programme, game, etc. 1 B the latest updates to a computer operating system, 1 D the latest episodes of a TV series*. If students made any mistakes, encourage them to write down phrases in their notebooks which include the correct option, for example, *pay attention to something.*

Answers

1 C 2 B 3 A 4 D 5 C 6 A 7 D 8 B

B2 FIRST FOR SCHOOLS
Reading and Use of English Part 2

In this part, students have a text with eight gaps plus an example. They have to decide which word to put in each gap. This tests grammatical items such as auxiliary verbs, relative pronouns, prepositions, articles, phrasal verbs and fixed phrases.

Tips Elicit the sort of words tested in this kind of task. Encourage students to read the sentences with gaps to themselves. Quite often, the missing word will come to mind as they read. Occasionally, although not often, more than one answer is possible. If so, students should only write one of the correct possibilities as, if the other is wrong, they won't get a mark at all. It is also important to spell the words correctly.

2 Look at the example with the students and elicit that this is a present perfect sentence which they can work out from the words after the gap (*ever bought*). Students work alone and compare answers in pairs. Elicit the answers and what they are testing.

Answers

1 out 2 to 3 how 4 been 5 up 6 is 7 have 8 which/that

3 **B2 FIRST FOR SCHOOLS Reading and Use of English Part 4**

Briefly review what students need to do in this part of the exam and if necessary, read out the *B2 First for Schools* box on TB page 49.

Students can do this under exam conditions with a ten-minute time limit. Tell the class that their handwriting must be neat and that they should cross out a word they want to change and write the corrected word beside it if they make a mistake. Elicit the answers and remind the students that there are two points for each part so, for example, in question 1 they would get a point for writing *come down* and a second point for *with*.

Answers

1 come down | with 2 haven't / have not | spoken for
3 come up | with a / the 4 ought to | see 5 apologised for | being
6 do not / don't need | to wear / needn't / need not | wear

COOLER

Have a class survey about which exam task from page 31 the students find the easiest and most difficult and what sort of problems they have when doing them. Then put students into three or six groups. Each group looks at one kind of exam task from page 31. Based on the problems mentioned by the class, the students think of their own tips to help other students prepare for and do well in this kind of task.

PREPARE FOR THE EXAM

Reading and Use of English Part 1

1 For questions **1–8**, read the text below and decide which answer (**A**, **B**, **C** or **D**) best fits each gap.

WANNA BE A FILM CRITIC?

You don't have to have a degree in film studies to **(0)** *review* films. Anyone can be a critic: all you need is to watch the latest **(1)** ________ at the cinema and write about them somewhere online, perhaps through a blog or social media page. However, **(2)** ________ a qualification in the field will make people **(3)** ________ what you have to say more seriously.

What is the day-to-day life of a critic like? Well, he or she may **(4)** ________ several films a day. It may sound like fun, but for every film they see, a critic must **(5)** ________ careful attention to the acting **(6)** ________, the soundtrack, the photography and the costumes. Critics have to make notes at the same time, and may even watch the same film over and over again! They will almost certainly discuss the **(7)** ________ in their critique, and, once it's **(8)** ________, deal with feedback from people who disagree with what they've written. It isn't as easy as it sounds!

	A	B	C	D
0	**(A)** review	**B** remark	**C** reflect	**D** respond
1	**A** versions	**B** updates	**C** releases	**D** episodes
2	**A** winning	**B** obtaining	**C** collecting	**D** establishing
3	**A** take	**B** get	**C** hold	**D** catch
4	**A** glance	**B** regard	**C** observe	**D** view
5	**A** place	**B** bring	**C** pay	**D** note
6	**A** performances	**B** displays	**C** presentations	**D** shows
7	**A** editor	**B** presenter	**C** novelist	**D** director
8	**A** broadcast	**B** published	**C** reported	**D** announced

Reading and Use of English Part 2

2 For questions **1–8**, read the text below and think of the word which best fits each gap. Use only **one** word in each gap.

Fast fashion

If you **(0)** *have* ever bought a trendy T-shirt from a high street shop for £5, then you already know what fast fashion is: cheap clothing that you wear a few times before it wears **(1)** ________. So many of us are addicted **(2)** ________ shopping, and with such bargains to be found, it's no wonder. It's great to be able to show off our purchases to friends and, even better, to tell them **(3)** ________ little we paid for it! And, of course, fast fashion seems a great idea when you're a student and haven't **(4)** ________ earning much while you study.

Unfortunately, we need to face **(5)** ________ to the fact that 'cheap' refers not only to the price, but the wages, too. Fast fashion, as its name suggests, **(6)** ________ produced quickly, and in order to achieve this quick 'turnaround', people **(7)** ________ to sit at machines for long hours, for little pay. We must respond to what's happening in the industry and buy more expensive items **(8)** ________ last for longer.

Reading and Use of English Part 4

3 For questions **1–6**, complete the second sentence so that it has a similar meaning to the first sentence, using the word given. **Do not change the word given.** You must use between **two** and **five** words, including the word given.

0 It's been four years since I started to write this blog. **BEEN**
I *have been writing* this blog for four years.

1 Simon has got flu, so can't play in today's match. **COME**
Simon has ________ flu, so can't play in today's match.

2 It's been a long time since I spoke to Jo. **FOR**
Jo and I ________ a long time.

3 Have you figured out the maths problem yet? **UP**
Have you ________ solution to the maths problem yet?

4 Seeing a doctor is something you should do if you aren't feeling well. **OUGHT**
You ________ a doctor if you aren't feeling well.

5 'I'm sorry I was late,' said James. **APOLOGISED**
James ________ late.

6 Wearing a uniform isn't necessary for students at my school. **NEED**
Students at my school ________ a uniform.

5 PAST TIMES

ABOUT YOU

Which periods of history have you studied at school?
Which periods of history do you find interesting? Why?
What do you know about the history of your local area?

VOCABULARY History

EP **1** Read the quiz. Check the meaning of the words.

21 **2** Do the quiz with your partner. Listen and check. What extra information do you hear?

3 Discuss the questions.

1. In which decade and century were you born? What about your parents?
2. Do women in your country have the vote? When did they get it?
3. Which town/state/region/country are you an inhabitant of?

HISTORY Quiz

1 On which continent did our earliest ancestors live?
a Africa b America c Asia

2 What was New York City called when it was founded in 1624?
a New London b New Paris c New Amsterdam

3 Which tribe of women from an ancient myth gave their name to a South American river?
a the Amazons b the Centaurs c the Titans

4 In which century was the car invented?
a the 18th century b the 19th century c the 20th century

5 In 1900, which country had the most citizens?
a Russia b India c China

6 Which city had the most inhabitants in 1900?
a New York b Tokyo c London

7 In which decade was television first broadcast to the public?
a 1930s b 1950s c 1970s

8 When did all women over 21 get the vote in the UK?
a 1900 b 1918 c 1928

READING

PREPARE FOR THE EXAM

Reading and Use of English Part 2

1 Read the example answer (0) in the first paragraph of the text. What other word could you use instead of *if*?

2 For questions 1–8, read the first paragraph of the text and think of the word which best fits each gap. Use the ideas below to help.

- Look at the words before and after each gap.
- Use only **one** word in each gap.
- There may be more than one correct answer.

» PREPARE FOR THE EXAM PAGE 121

3 Read the questions and discuss possible answers.

1. What alternatives can you think of to an eight-hour sleep?
2. How did sleeping habits change after the invention of artificial lighting?
3. How do the sleep patterns of different cultures and different age groups compare?
4. What is a 'siesta'?
5. What is a 'body clock'?

4 Read the rest of the text and check your answers.

5 Complete the sentences with highlighted words and phrases from the text.

1. How long do you ________ sleep at night?
2. I often have a quick ________ after lunch – eating makes me tired!
3. I never realised, but it ________ that we are at the same school.
4. Did you know that watching TV immediately before bed ________ your sleep?
5. The use of screens in bed is quite ________, but negatively affects sleep.

5 PAST TIMES

Unit Overview

TOPIC	Life in the past
VOCABULARY	History
READING	We used to sleep twice a night ...
GRAMMAR	Present and past habits
VOCABULARY	Expressing frequency
WRITING	An article (1)
EXAM TASKS	Reading and Use of English Part 2; Writing Part 2

Resources

GRAMMAR REFERENCE AND PRACTICE: SB page 152; TB page 267
PREPARE FOR THE EXAM: SB pages on TB pages 237 and 246; TB pages 254 and 258
WORKBOOK: pages 20–23
PHOTOCOPIABLE WORKSHEETS: Grammar worksheet Unit 5; Vocabulary worksheet Unit 5
TEST GENERATOR: Unit test 5
PRACTICE EXTRA: Unit 5

WARMER

Tell students to close their eyes. Say: 'Imagine you have built a time machine which can take you back to any time in the past. You can only use it once. Think about which time you would go back to and why.' Allow 30 seconds of thinking time then tell the students to open their eyes and get into groups of four. The students tell each other their ideas. Invite each group to tell the class which time periods they each chose and their reasons.

ABOUT YOU

If you used the Warmer, keep the students in the same groups to discuss the questions. Read the questions in the *About you* box. Set a time limit of three minutes and then invite groups to share their ideas with the class.

VOCABULARY History

1 Tell students that they are going to do a history quiz. Ask them to focus firstly on the meaning of the words in blue and not the answers to the questions. Ask students to define the words without using a dictionary, if possible. Remind them to look at the whole sentence and to use context clues to help them. Allow students to work in pairs and then check the meanings as a class.

Possible answers

1 ancestors: relatives who lived a long time ago 2 found: start / bring into existence 3 tribe: a group of people who live together, usually in areas far away from cities, and who share the same culture and language; myth: an ancient story about gods and/or brave people, often one that explains an event in history or the natural world 4 century: a period of 100 years 5 citizens: people who have a legal right to live in a particular country 6 inhabitants: people who live in a particular place 7 decade: a period of ten years, especially a period such as 1860 to 1869, or 1990 to 1999 8 get the vote: be officially allowed to vote

21 **2** Ask students to answer the questions in pairs and then ask for a show of hands for each one. Play the recording for students to check their answers. Play the recording again and ask students to take notes. Elicit any facts that students heard, for example, 1 the first humans appeared about 200,000 years ago.

Possible answers

1 a 2 c 3 a 4 b 5 c 6 c 7 a 8 c
1 100,000 years ago, humans started to move out of Africa. 2 The Romans called London 'Londinium'. 3 The Spanish gave the Amazon River its name. 4 Karl Benz made the first car. 5 China had 415 million citizens then. 6 The population of London was around 6.5 million people. 7 The first commercial TVs had black and white pictures. 8 Suffragettes campaigned for women's rights.

» AUDIOSCRIPT TB PAGES 289–290

3 Before students answer the questions, you could point out that, in the 20th century, the decades from 1920 onwards were easy to name (the twenties, thirties, etc.), but the first two decades don't have any commonly accepted name. The most common names for the first two decades of the 21st century are the two thousands (00–09) and the two thousand and tens or twenty-tens (10–19). In the UK, the first decade is sometimes referred to as the noughties – *nought* being another way of saying zero. However, this doesn't work in the USA, as *nought* isn't used in American English. Set a time limit of one minute for students to answer the questions and then elicit answers. Students give their own answers.

READING

PREPARE FOR THE EXAM

1 B2 FIRST FOR SCHOOLS Reading and Use of English Part 2

Briefly review what students need to do in this part of the exam and, if necessary, read out the *B2 First for Schools* box on TB page 58.

Look at the question with the class and elicit the answer. Tell students that sometimes there can be more than one possible answer, for example, where there is a choice between relative pronouns such as *who/that* or *which/that*. In this part of the exam, spelling is important, so students should be careful.

Answer

when

2 Point out that, in the exam, this part has just one, standalone text. The gap fill isn't in one part of a longer text as it is here. Set a time limit of ten minutes and encourage students to check their answers carefully when they have finished.

FAST FINISHERS

Ask fast finishers to identify other words in the text which could have been tested in a task like this. Point out *wake up* and *in the middle of* in the first sentence. When everyone has finished, elicit the answers to the activity and then invite fast finishers to share their ideas with the class.

Answers

1 who/that 2 to 3 are 4 have 5 the 6 no/little 7 too 8 though

» PREPARE FOR THE EXAM TEACHING NOTES AND ANSWER KEY TB PAGE 254

CONTINUED ON PAGE 62

BACKGROUND INFORMATION

Several famous people have had interesting sleeping habits. American President Donald Trump typically sleeps for only three hours to four a night. In 2011, singer Lady Gaga appeared at the Grammy Awards, emerging from a giant egg. Before this, she had suffered from sleep problems and once went three days without sleeping. Reports say that she now sleeps in the giant egg and, as a result, feels more relaxed and no longer has problems sleeping. Musician Florence Welch also suffers from insomnia and even when she does manage to get to sleep, she suffers from terrible nightmares. Einstein, on the other hand, enjoyed ten hours' sleep a night and had naps during the day. Thomas Edison, the inventor, slept for 20 minutes every three hours. People with this habit of regular short sleeps throughout the day are called polyphasic sleepers. Leonardo da Vinci was also a polyphasic sleeper. Shakespeare and Van Gogh both suffered from insomnia, the inability to sleep. Winston Churchill had a two-hour nap every afternoon, even during the Second World War. He then often worked all night. Napoleon had two, two-hour sleeps a day, once at midday and once at five in the morning. Double Nobel prize winner Marie Curie slept with a jar of radium next to her bed as well as carrying the substance around in her lab coat. Her early death was a result of these habits.

3 Look at the first question with the students. Elicit ideas, for example a midday sleep and a shorter sleep at night, and ask students if they ever sleep during the day and, if so, how they feel afterwards. Students then discuss the other questions in pairs. When they have finished, invite students to share their ideas with the class, but do not correct their answers at this stage.

Answers

Students' own answers

4 Before students look at the text, ask them to look at the questions in Exercise 3 and underline key words which will help them find the relevant information in the text, for example, *1 alternatives, eight-hour sleep; 2 habits change, artificial lighting,* etc. Students then read the text carefully and make notes about the answers to the questions in Exercise 3. Allow students to share ideas in pairs and then elicit answers. Finally, in pairs, students discuss how many answers they got right.

MIXED ABILITY

Put weaker students into pairs. Give them some key words to find in the text, for example; *two sleeps, artificial lighting, cultures, age, siesta, body clock.* They work together to find the words and then read the text around these words to answer the questions together.

Answers

1 the two-sleep habit 2 people could stay up later if they wanted to 3 different cultures have different sleep patterns according to their lifestyles; very young and older people tend to get up earlier and go to bed earlier than teenagers 4 a short mid-afternoon sleep/nap 5 the body's function of wanting to be awake or asleep at different times of the day

22 The Reading text is recorded for students to listen, read and check their answers.

5 Ask the students to look at the sentences without looking at the highlighted words. They work in pairs to try to think of words which could go into the gaps, for example, *1 usually, like to.* Elicit ideas and then ask students to uncover the text and do the matching. Finally, elicit the answers and the meanings of the words *(1 usually; 2 a short sleep; 3 a way of saying what happened or what the actual situation was, generally one that was quite surprising; 4 stops something happening properly; 5 popular, often used)*

Answers

1 tend to 2 nap 3 turns out 4 disrupts 5 widespread

TALKING POINTS

Look at the questions with the class and elicit what the last point means, i.e. a society in which things like shops, TV and radio stations, transport and other things carry on all day and night. Put students into groups of three or four and set a time limit for them to discuss their ideas. Invite groups to share their ideas with the class. Follow up by writing the phrases *night owls* and *early birds* on the board. Elicit what the students think these mean and ask them which kind of person they are. (Night owls *are people who work/study best late at night and* early birds *are people who work/study best early in the morning.*)

COOLER

Put students into groups of four or five. Each group looks at the history quiz on page 32. Ask them to write more multiple-choice history questions that they know the answer to. For each question, they should write three alternative answers, one of which is correct. Then invite groups to ask their questions to the class. The other groups race to answer them first. Make a note of which groups answered correctly each time and finish by saying which group won the most points.

WE USED TO SLEEP TWICE A NIGHT …

What happens **(0)** *if* you wake up in the middle of the night? Do you have difficulty falling asleep again? Perhaps you're someone **(1)** ________ becomes frustrated because you can't get back **(2)** ________ sleep straightaway. Then you might begin to get in a panic about being tired the next day, or about problems you **(3)** ________ experiencing, and you go over and over things in your head. Or perhaps you **(4)** ________ woken up after a nightmare and the negative images are still in your mind. Whatever your sleeping habits, in **(5)** ________ 21st century, being awake at night is generally regarded as problematic. This is logical, of course: there's **(6)** ________ point being awake when everyone else is asleep. And if you end up being awake all night, you'll be **(7)** ________ tired to cope well the following day. Even **(8)** ________ in most parts of the world a 'good night's sleep' means more or less eight hours without interruption, it turns out that the concept of an eight-hour sleep is fairly recent.

Naturally, history textbooks tend to only record memorable accounts of wars and empires, of love and death, or bravery and determination. Sleep is something we take for granted, so it rarely comes up. You may have heard that our ancestors used to have two 'sleeps'. This isn't a myth. Historians have noticed references to a 'first sleep' and a 'second sleep' in documents covering several centuries, and in reference to different countries. The first sleep started after sunset and lasted until around midnight. Then people would lie awake for a while and chat or pray. Some neighbours even used to take the opportunity to visit each other between sleeps. After a few hours, they would have their second sleep, which lasted until dawn. In countries with long hours of daylight in summer, people would start work as early as four or five o'clock in the morning.

Artificial lights weren't common a few centuries ago. Only the rich could afford candles and, without electricity, nobody could do anything when it was dark. By the end of the 19th century, lighting had become more widespread as cities installed gas streetlights and domestic gas lamps appeared. All of a sudden, most people had lights and could stay up late if they wanted to. By the time electric lighting was introduced just a century ago, the two-sleep pattern had disappeared.

It's a pity we lost the two-sleep habit because, whether we like the idea or not, being awake for a period at night is both natural and healthy. It follows the body's natural energy and sleep rhythms. It is beneficial psychologically, too: the period between the two sleeps was the perfect time to think about the day ahead and plan for it. The nearest we get to two sleeps these days is the 'siesta', the short mid-afternoon nap still enjoyed in some parts of the world.

The two-sleep habit used to be quite widespread, but it wasn't universal. Sleep patterns have always varied between cultures and still depend on things like light, temperature and health. Hunter-gatherer tribes, for example, only need five or six hours' sleep because they have a much healthier lifestyle than most of the world. Other cultures don't have a fixed time for sleeping, but have much more informal sleep patterns, where individuals sleep for short periods throughout the day or night, whenever they feel tired.

Sleep patterns also vary according to age. While older adults and pre-teens are happy with early mornings in general, teenagers often go to bed later and get up later, too. Either pattern is fine, as long as the person in question gets enough sleep. However, many people are constantly checking their phones, and don't even stop when they go to bed. The blue light emitted by screens disrupts the production of sleep hormones, meaning it is harder to get to sleep and stay asleep. Experts therefore recommend switching screens off two hours before you want to go to sleep. This enables us to listen to our body clock and sleep when our body tells us it's time to do so.

TALKING POINTS

What is 'a good night's sleep' for you?
What difficulties might someone have if they work at night and sleep during the day?
Do you like the idea of living in a 24/7 society?

GRAMMAR Present and past habits

1 **Read the examples. Then complete the rules with the verb forms in the box.**

1 Between sleeps, people **would lie** awake for a while and chat.
2 The two-sleep habit **used to be** quite widespread.
3 Some neighbours even **used to take** the opportunity to visit each other between sleeps.
4 My brother **was always waking** me **up** early when I was younger.
5 Many people **are constantly checking** their phones.
6 Individuals **sleep** whenever they feel tired.
7 I'**m sleeping** a lot because I'm getting over an illness.

past continuous	present continuous (x2)
present simple	*used to* *would*

We use
a ________ for present habits and states.
b ________ (without an adverb) for temporary present habits.
c ________ + *always/constantly* for annoying present habits.
d ________ for past habits and states.
e ________ for past habits (but not past states).
f ________ + *always/constantly* for past habits, especially to criticise or complain.

» GRAMMAR REFERENCE AND PRACTICE PAGE 152

2 **Read the text and choose the correct verb forms.**

BREAKFAST: HERE TODAY, GONE TOMORROW?

Most people [1] *eat / are eating* three meals a day, at least in the USA and northern Europe: breakfast, lunch and dinner. But mealtimes [2] *constantly change / are constantly changing*. In some parts of Asia, Europe and Latin America, people [3] *have / are having* five meals a day, adding a mid-morning snack and a late supper to the list. Our eating habits in the past [4] *would be / used to be* quite different. Let's start with breakfast. Health experts are big fans of breakfast and [5] *are always telling / were always telling* us that it's the most important meal of the day. However, breakfast is in fact a relatively new concept. The ancient Romans, who [6] *are constantly worrying / were constantly worrying* about their health, [7] *were never having / never used to have* breakfast. They [8] *would think / used to think* that one meal a day was sufficient, while three was greedy. It wasn't until the 18th century, when people started working in factories, and did not break for lunch, that they [9] *would have / were having* a big breakfast before going to work. Habits [10] *still change / are still changing*. People may not [11] *feel / feeling* hungry first thing, or they are in a rush, and more and more of us [12] *would miss / are missing* breakfast. Perhaps, after a few hundred years of popularity, breakfast is gradually starting to disappear.

3 **Correct the mistake in each sentence.**

1 I use to play this game with my friends.
2 Nowadays, always we are looking at our phones when we should be asleep.
3 I used to go to bed late while I was on holiday last week.
4 I was always sleeping well when I was a kid, but I don't now.
5 I start school at 8 am, so I used to go to bed early.

4 **Write a sentence for each situation. Use the grammar from Exercise 1.**

0 something that really annoys you
My best friend is always using my phone!
1 something that you do every day
2 a habit from when you were younger
3 something you do that annoys others
4 something you're doing temporarily
5 a fact about you that was true ten years ago, but not any longer

VOCABULARY Expressing frequency

1 **Complete the lists with the words and phrases in the box.**

EP

~~all the time~~ constantly from time to time most days/weeks/months occasionally (every) once in a while rarely regularly seldom

always	*all the time*	________	
often	________	________	
sometimes	________	________	________
almost never	________	________	

2 **Read the rules about expressions of frequency. Then answer the questions using the expressions.**

Single adverbs usually go before the main verb:
*You're **constantly** sleeping.*
Phrases go at the beginning or end of a clause.
*I sleep badly **every once in a while**.*
***From time to time**, I stay up all night.*

How often do you
1 watch documentaries?
2 argue with people?
3 sleep later than 11 am?
4 complain about things?
5 play games on your phone?
6 enter competitions?

3 **Tell your partner six things about yourself, three true and three false. Use an adverb or phrase expressing frequency. Can your partner guess which are false?**

I'm constantly losing my mobile!

Every once in a while, I get up in the middle of the night and watch a film.

GRAMMAR Present and past habits

WARMER
Ask students to think about something they regularly do nowadays that they didn't do five years ago and something they did regularly three to five years ago that they don't do any more. When students have written their ideas, put them into groups of three or four to share what they wrote and give more details about why they stopped the past habit and what made them start the present habit. Invite groups to share the most interesting habits that they discussed.

1 Allow students to work in pairs to do the matching. Elicit the answers and write a simple chart on the board to show when they can use *used to* and *would*:

Single past event: past simple

Past states (e.g. lived, be widespread): past simple, used to

Past habits: past simple (often with an adverb of frequency), used to, would

If they aren't sure, then the past simple is the safest form to use, but it is good to vary this when writing or speaking.

If you did the Warmer, you could then ask the students to talk about their past habits using *used to*, *would* or the past simple.

Answers
a present simple b present continuous c present continuous
d *used to* e *would* f past continuous

» **GRAMMAR REFERENCE AND PRACTICE ANSWER KEY TB PAGE 267**

2 Encourage students to read the whole text before attempting this task, as this will help them with meaning and therefore making the correct choices. Set this as individual work before checking as a whole class. When checking answers, ask for volunteers to explain why each choice is correct, as this will also provide revision of the differences between simple and continuous tenses in the present and past. The answer to 2 isn't an annoying habit, but the use of *constantly* makes the present continuous the best choice.

Answers
1 eat 2 are constantly changing 3 have 4 used to be
5 are always telling 6 were constantly worrying
7 never used to have 8 used to think 9 would have
10 are still changing 11 feel 12 are missing

3 Students work in pairs to find the errors and make the corrections. Elicit the answers and what was wrong with the original. Elicit that *used to* is like any other past simple regular verb. It has an *-ed* ending in positive sentences, but it is written *use to* in questions and negatives.

Answers
1 I **used to** play this game with my friends.
2 Nowadays, **we are always looking** at our phones when we should be asleep.
3 I **went** to bed late while I was on holiday last week.
4 I **always used to sleep** well when I was a kid, but I don't now.
5 I start school at 8 am, so I **usually go** to bed early.

4 Look at the example with the class and elicit alternative habits that could annoy them, for example, *My friends are always arguing.* Students work individually to write their sentences before getting into groups of three or four to discuss their sentences. Invite groups to share their most interesting or surprising sentences with the class.

MIXED ABILITY
Help weaker students by matching each situation in Exercise 4 with the rules from Exercise 1 so they can see which form to use for each sentence. Write these on the board: *0 – c, 1 – a, 2 – d/e, 3 – c, 4 – b, 5 – d.* Monitor and help where necessary to make sure the students' sentences are correct before they get into groups to discuss them.

FAST FINISHERS
Ask students to think of three more similar situations and write a sentence for each, for example, *something you did on holidays in the past but don't do now*. Invite fast finishers to share some of their ideas with the class.

Answers
Students' own answers

» **GRAMMAR WORKSHEET UNIT 5**

VOCABULARY Expressing frequency

1 Give students a few minutes to complete the exercise with a partner. Then check the answers as a class and write the answers on the board. Ask students if they know any other words or expressions to add to each group. Alternatively, with a strong class, ask students to close their books and write *always*, *often*, *sometimes* and *almost never* on the board. Next to *always* write *all the time*, then ask for one more synonym for each word. Books open. Students check the expressions in the box to see if the ones on the board are in the box and then complete the exercise individually.

Answers
always: constantly
often: most days/weeks/months, regularly
sometimes: from time to time, occasionally, (every) once in a while
almost never: rarely, seldom

2 When students have written their answers to Exercise 2, write on the board: *I sometimes go to the cinema.* Ask students to write how often they think this is, for example, once a month, one a week, five times a year, etc. Elicit ideas and point out that, for different people, adverbs of frequency don't always mean the same thing. A parent may say: 'My child is always using his/her phone', but their child may think they don't use it very often, especially compared to their friends. Elicit answers to questions 1–6 and, if necessary, encourage the students to give more details about exactly how often they do something, for example, *I rarely watch documentaries, maybe once or twice a month.*

Answers
Students' own answers

3 Model the exercise by saying two sentences about you (one true and one false), for example, *I rarely used to have a shower when I was a teenager* and *I still sleep in my old bedroom from time to time*. Ask students which one they think is false. Then set the task in the book, reminding them to use an expression of frequency in each sentence. Ask students whether they guessed correctly and elicit some of the true and false sentences they used.

Answers
Students' own answers

» **VOCABULARY WORKSHEET UNIT 5**

WRITING An article (1)

1 If possible, collect some headlines or article titles from newspapers or magazines. Show these to the class or write the titles on the board and ask students what they think each article is about and which title they like best and why. Then put the students into groups of three or four to answer the questions. Invite each group to share the most interesting articles they mentioned.

Answers
Students' own answers

2 Give students a few minutes to complete the exercise individually before checking answers as a whole class. Ask them what they would write about if they were going to write this article.

Answers
1 in an international (English-language) magazine 2 students 3 a hobby or leisure activity I used to do 4 chatty

3 Look at the *Prepare to write* box with the class. Then ask the students to look at the three titles and give an example about what title a's article would be about, for example, *It would be a current hobby and it would give reasons why the author enjoys it.* Students then work in pairs to do the same for titles b and c. Elicit ideas and then ask students to read the article and choose the best title. Elicit the answer and why it is correct (*it talks about the hobby of cycling which the writer now no longer does*).

Answer
b

4 Elicit or tell students what a topic sentence is. (*It is a sentence which sums up the whole paragraph. The rest of the paragraph then gives more details about the information in the topic sentence.*) Look at the first three topic sentences and then ask what further details the rest of the paragraph gives (*A says where he/she got the bike from and how he/she felt; B explains why it gives a sense of freedom and then more details of the cycling the person did; C explains why the person gave up*). Students work alone and write their own sentences. They then compare ideas in pairs. Elicit sentences from different students.

Answers
A I used to ride my bike a lot when I was a kid. B Cycling gives you a great sense of freedom. C When I went to high school, I stopped going to the club. D Possible answer: Now I've got a new hobby.

5 Remind students that good articles tend to address the reader directly and this is what gives them a lively, chatty style. Give students a few minutes to underline some examples of this, then ask them to compare answers with a partner before checking answers as a class.

Answers
In paragraph B they ask the reader a question (*… can't you?*). In paragraph D they make a suggestion (*you should try it!*)
Descriptive language: *I loved having my own way of getting around! It was great fun! I have great memories …; It's just as much fun as cycling, …; which I can't wait to try out.*

PREPARE FOR THE EXAM

B2 FIRST FOR SCHOOLS
Writing Part 2: An article

In this part, students have a choice of task. They may be asked to write an article, an email or letter, a review or a story. As mentioned on TB page 42, there are five tasks in total, but students shouldn't attempt question 5 unless they have read the set reading text. They are given a clear context, topic, purpose and target reader. Students should write 140–190 words. The article is usually for an international magazine or website aimed at teenagers, so the style is quite informal. The writer wants to interest the reader, so there should be some opinion or comment.

Tips Tell students to pay attention to the information given in the input text. This will help them structure their writing and to write in an appropriate register. Topic sentences help the reader understand the article better, as they introduce the idea of each paragraph.

6 If you have students preparing for the *B2 First for Schools* exam, set a strict time limit of 40 minutes for this to mimic exam conditions. If not, you could allow your students more time or set this as homework. Remind them to think of a topic sentence for each paragraph when they are organising their ideas and to try to include two or three direct questions. Ask students to exchange their article with a partner and to comment on the organisation of the article: Does each paragraph have a clear topic? Does the introduction refer to the question? Does the conclusion leave a question or suggestion for the reader? Ask them to underline words they think have been used too often and to suggest replacements. Ask them to circle the language of habits – has the student used a range of structures?

Model answer
My first real hobby
When I was younger, I loved drawing. I spent hours copying cartoons in comics. I think I started when I got a cartoon DVD and the extras included a documentary about the artists at work. For a few years, I used to dream of becoming a cartoonist when I grew up.
I became quite good at drawing for my age. Whenever people came to visit us, my parents would always show them my pictures. Everyone used to say I was really talented, which made me feel really special, as I'm sure you can understand!
When I went to secondary school, I didn't enjoy art classes as much as I'd expected. My biggest problem was that I was self-taught and I found it very difficult to accept other people's advice. I also met new friends and suddenly cartoons seemed a bit childish.
Now, my passion is music. I have been having guitar lessons for three years and I can play quite well. Now my dream is to be in a band. It's funny how we change as we grow older, isn't it?

COOLER

Put students into an even number of groups, each one with three or four students in it. Each group is paired with a second group. The students of each group try to guess what hobbies each member of the other group used to have and what their hobbies are now. If they are friends, they may know the correct hobbies. If not, they can make guesses based on the other students' characters. Elicit how good the guesses were and some of the wrong, or right, guesses that they made.

WRITING An article (1)

1 **Discuss the questions.**

1 What articles have you read recently, in magazines or online?
2 Can you remember any of the titles?
3 What do you think makes an article interesting?

2 **Read the task and answer the questions.**

You see this notice in an international English-language magazine for students.

> **Articles wanted!**
> Write an article about a hobby or leisure activity that you used to enjoy but don't do now. What did you do? Why did you enjoy doing it? What made you give it up? What do you do now?
> Send us your article and see your name in print!

Write your **article**.

1 Where is the article going to appear?
2 Who is going to read it?
3 What is the topic?
4 Do you think the article should be serious or chatty in tone?

3 **Read the *Prepare to write* box. Then read the article and choose the best title.**

a Why I love my hobby
b A hobby I used to have
c Tips for finding a new hobby

PREPARE TO WRITE | Writing articles

In an article

- choose an interesting title.
- organise your ideas into paragraphs.
- include a topic sentence for each paragraph, which tells the reader what the paragraph is about.
- use a lively, chatty style.
- use interesting, descriptive language.
- address the reader directly, for example by asking questions.

4 **Underline the topic sentences in paragraphs A–C. Write a topic sentence for paragraph D.**

5 **Read the article again. How does the writer address the reader directly? What descriptive language is used?**

______

A I used to ride my bike a lot when I was a kid. My older brother gave me his bike when he got a new one, and I loved having my own way of getting around! From then on, I would cycle everywhere I went.

B Cycling gives you a great sense of freedom. You can go where you want and at any time you want, can't you? When I was nine, I joined an after-school cycling club and soon I was regularly taking part in races against my friends. It was great fun!

C When I went to high school, I stopped going to the club. I rarely won races because I wasn't that fast, and I had a lot more homework to do. I have great memories of my time there, though.

D ______ It's skateboarding! I can do it at any time, so it fits in better with school. In fact, I do it most days. It's just as much fun as cycling, but I'm much better at skateboarding. They're building a new skate park in my town, which I can't wait to try out. If you aren't already a skateboarder, you should try it!

PREPARE FOR THE EXAM

Writing Part 2 (An article)

6 **Read the task in Exercise 2 again. Write your article.**

- Use the tips in the *Prepare to write* box.
- Check your grammar and spelling.
- Write 140–190 words.

PAST TIMES 35

6 TOTALLY EMOTIONAL

ABOUT YOU

Which of these emotions have you experienced recently? Why did you feel this way?

anger *fear* *happiness* *satisfaction* *worry*

VOCABULARY Expressing emotions

1 **Match the questions to the photos.**

EP
1 Do you go to school in the morning feeling cheerful about the day ahead?
2 Do you generally feel optimistic or pessimistic about things?
3 Have you ever been scared of anything, like giving a class presentation?
4 Have you ever felt furious with someone, but not said anything?
5 What environmental problems are you most concerned about?

2 **Complete the table with the adjectives with prepositions in Exercise 1.**

Fear	
Anger	
Worry	
Happiness	*cheerful about, …*
Unhappiness	

3 **Ask and answer the questions in Exercise 1.**

23
4 **Listen to Claudia, Ben, Jade and Olly. How are they feeling? Choose the correct options and complete the sentences.**

1 Claudia's fed up with / anxious about …
2 Ben's bad-tempered about / anxious about …
3 Jade's relieved about / over the moon about …
4 Olly's getting depressed about / irritated by …
5 Jade's down about / content with not …
6 Olly's petrified of / fed up with some kind of …

5 **Add the phrases in Exercise 4 to the table in Exercise 2. Use a dictionary to help you.**

6 **Discuss when you last felt …**

- relieved about something
- over the moon about something
- fed up with someone
- irritated by something
- anxious about something

READING

1 **Read the introduction to the article, ignoring the gaps. Which fears are mentioned?**

PREPARE FOR THE EXAM

Reading and Use of English Part 1

2 **Read the introduction again and decide which answer (A, B, C or D) best fits each gap.**

	A	B	C	D
0	A beginning	(B) birth	C start	D origin
1	A predictable	B common	C shared	D usual
2	A phases	B stages	C times	D points
3	A progress	B arrive	C reach	D gain
4	A unexpected	B uncertain	C unlikely	D unsure
5	A emerge	B uncover	C expose	D reveal
6	A take	B fix	C make	D keep
7	A impression	B outcome	C reaction	D impact
8	A up	B over	C into	D on

3 **Look at the names of three phobias. What do you think they mean? Read case studies 1, 2 and 3 and check your answers.**

autophobia nyctophobia scolionophobia

4 **Read the case studies again. Write the correct names.**

1 Who was abandoned in a public place?
2 Whose family almost got into trouble with the law because of a phobia?
3 Whose phobia has made them more sociable?
4 Who recently had a bad experience at a friend's house?
5 Who has been accepted for further education?
6 Whose parents thought his fear was normal?

5 **Match the highlighted words in the article to the meanings.**

1 having your attention taken away from something
2 making you very worried or upset
3 the use of medicine, exercises, etc. to cure a person of an illness or injury
4 silly or stupid
5 likely to cause death

6 TOTALLY EMOTIONAL

Unit Overview

TOPIC	Emotions and fears
VOCABULARY	Expressing emotions
READING	When fear becomes phobia …
GRAMMAR	*be / get used to*
VOCABULARY	Adverbs: type and position
LISTENING	Eight short conversations
SPEAKING	Generalising
EXAM TASKS	Reading and Use of English Part 1; Listening Part 1

Resources

GRAMMAR REFERENCE AND PRACTICE: SB page 153; TB page 267
PREPARE FOR THE EXAM: SB pages on TB pages 236 and 247; TB pages 254 and 259
WORKBOOK: pages 24–27
PHOTOCOPIABLE WORKSHEETS: Grammar worksheet Unit 6; Vocabulary worksheet Unit 6
TEST GENERATOR: Unit test 6
PRACTICE EXTRA: Unit 6

WARMER

Ask the class to close their eyes and listen to you. Tell them that you are going to read out some situations and they should think about how they would feel and what they would do. Read out the following:

1 Their national team wins the football (men's or women's) World Cup.
2 They get into bed and see a large spider on the ceiling above them.
3 They wake up in the morning and the house is empty with no messages saying where the others are.

Students discuss their thoughts in pairs. Invite students to tell the class about their reactions.

ABOUT YOU

Read the questions in the *About you* box and allow the students to think alone for one minute. They then join together in groups of three or four to discuss their experiences. Invite groups to tell the class one or two of the most interesting experiences they talked about.

VOCABULARY Expressing emotions

1 Tell students to cover Exercise 1 and look at the photos A–E. In pairs, they discuss how they think each person is feeling. They then uncover the sentences and do the matching.

Answers
1 C 2 E 3 A 4 B 5 D

2 Ask students which phrase in blue in Exercise 1 shows fear (*scared of*). Students then complete the table alone and compare answers in pairs.

Answers
Fear: scared of
Anger: furious with
Worry: concerned about
Happiness: optimistic about
Unhappiness: pessimistic about

3 Ask the first question to the whole class. If students answer *yes* or *no*, ask them to give reasons why, for example, *No, I don't. I'm usually tired and I know I have to work hard for the next seven hours and will then have to do homework in the evening.* Students ask and answer in pairs. Then, invite one student to ask the first question to any other student in the class. When the second student has answered, they ask a different student the next question and so on.

Answers
Students' own answers

23
4 Play the first recording. Elicit what adjective Claudia uses (*annoying*) and what she is talking about (*her laptop*). Now look at the choice of adjectives in 1 and ask students which one is correct (*fed up with*). Finally, elicit how students could complete the sentence: *Claudia's fed up with her laptop.* Students then listen to the rest of the recording and note down key words for each sentence. When the recording has finished, they choose the correct words and complete the sentences. Elicit the answers.

Answers
1 fed up with her laptop. 2 anxious about being late for the cinema / not getting decent seats at the cinema. 3 over the moon about her present. 4 irritated by the Alex's loud music. 5 down about not getting tickets (on the ticket website). 6 petrified of some kind of spider/insect/animal.

» AUDIOSCRIPT TB PAGE 290

5 Look at the first sentence again with the class and elicit the meaning of the two phrases in blue and which emotions in Exercise 2 they match (*fed up with – unhappiness, anxious about – worry*). Students do the same for the other sentences and complete the table in pairs. Elicit the answers to make sure everyone has completed the table correctly.

Answers
Fear: petrified of
Anger: bad-tempered about, irritated by
Worry: anxious about
Happiness: relieved about, over the moon about, content with
Unhappiness: fed up with, depressed about, down about

6 Put students into groups of three or four to share their ideas. Set a time limit of five minutes. Monitor and listen for interesting stories and invite a few students to share their ideas with the class.

Answers
Students' own answers

READING

1 Tell the class there are nine fears mentioned in total. As soon as someone has found them all, they should put their hand up. When about ten students have finished, stop the activity and elicit the answers. Ask the students if they have any of these fears.

Answers
heights, mice, monsters, the dark, murder, war, looking foolish in front of friends, washing, animals

CONTINUED ON PAGE 70

BACKGROUND INFORMATION

Phobia is a Greek word from *phobos,* which means fear, panic or terror. Many words for phobias come from Greek, although some may have a Latin root or a combination of the two. For example, agrophobia, the fear of open spaces, comes from the Greek word *agro*, which means 'field'. *Claustrophobia*, the fear of enclosed spaces, though, comes from the Latin *claustrum*, meaning 'a place shut in' or 'a confined space'.

Nycto comes from the Greek word for 'night', *nyx* and the Latin word, *nox*. *Auto* is a Greek word meaning 'by oneself, on one's own'. We can see this meaning in the word *autobiography* – writing the story of your own life. Because of words like *automatic* and *automobile*, people often assume it means a machine but, these words actually mean 'to work by itself' or 'to travel by itself'. A driverless car will really be an automobile. *Scolia* comes from the Greek *skhole* and the Latin *schola*. The original meaning was 'free time' because, in Greek time, that was a time when people studied and discussed ideas.

PREPARE FOR THE EXAM

2 B2 FIRST FOR SCHOOLS Reading and Use of English Part 1

Briefly review what students need to do in this part of the exam and, if necessary, read out the *B2 First for Schools* box on TB page 26.

Remind students that, in the exam, this task will be in a standalone text, not part of a longer text. Point out that in some options, students have to choose between words that have a similar meaning, but in other cases, they need to know the meaning and be able to identify the correct word because of the word, for example preposition, verb form, that follows.

Look at the example with the students and elicit why A, C and D are wrong *(they don't make sense here without saying of what; we would need an article e.g.* the + *the word* + of: the beginning of our lives). Students do the activity alone. Set a time limit of ten minutes and elicit the answers and why other choices are wrong.

Answers
1 B 2 C 3 A 4 C 5 A 6 D 7 D 8 C

3 Elicit ideas before students start reading then set a two-minute time limit for students to find the correct answers. Elicit these and share the information from the Background information box if you wish.

Answers
nyctophobia – fear of the dark; autophobia – fear of being alone; scolionophobia – fear of going to school

4 Tell students to read about each person again and make notes on the key information about each one. They then look at the six sentences and see how many they can match. If there are any that they can't match, they have to read the text again to find the answers. Elicit the answers and the information in the texts which helped them.

MIXED ABILITY

Stronger students can work alone and read about all three people. However, you can put weaker students into groups of three and ask them to each read about one person and make notes or underline key information. They then tell each other what they read and, together, they try to match all the questions to the people. If they can't match them all, they read a different text each to try to find the correct match.

Answers
1 Poppy 2 Noah 3 Poppy 4 Mustafa 5 Noah 6 Mustafa

24 The Reading text is recorded for students to listen, read and check their answers.

5 Students look at the words in the text without looking at the meanings. For each word, ask students to find the stem word, i.e. the word they might be given in Reading and Use of English Part 3. Elicit these, what kind of word they are and what they mean (*dead, adj, not alive; fool, n, a stupid person; distress, v/n , a feeling of suffering; distract, v, take someone's attention away from something else; treat, v, to give medical attention to someone*). Students then do the matching.

FAST FINISHERS

Ask fast finishers to make sentences which include the highlighted words, for example*: People sometimes find exams a very distressing experience, especially when they know they have done badly.* When everyone has finished the exercise, invite fast finishers to share their sentences with the class but leaving the highlighted word blank. The other students have to guess which word should be used to complete the sentence.

Answers
1 distracted 2 distressing 3 treatment 4 foolish 5 deadly

TALKING POINTS

Ask students: *Whose phobia in the text do we learn the cause of?* (*Poppy, it started when she was left alone in a shop*). In pairs, students then try to guess why Mustafa and Noah developed a phobia. In the same pairs, students discuss both questions. Elicit ideas and ask if they have ever found that their fear was useful, for example, giving them increased strength and a feeling of calm, forcing them to become more independent, etc.

COOLER

Elicit some common phobias, for example of heights, spiders, injections, flying, etc. Students then work in groups of four or five and say whether anyone in their family or any friends have any phobias. If so, they should tell the group how they react when faced with the thing they are scared of. The other students can ask them questions about their phobia. If no one in the group has a phobia or knows someone with a phobia, the students can make up a story about someone with a phobia. Set a time limit of three or four minutes and invite students to share any interesting stories they discussed.

WHEN ***FEAR*** BECOMES ***PHOBIA*** …

Fear is something we all experience from **(0)** *birth* and for good reason: without it, we would find it difficult to survive. It is thought to be the earliest emotion, evolving millions of years ago.

24

Some fears, such as a fear of heights, are **(1)** ________ to almost all mammals. Other fears, like a fear of mice, are specific to humans and, in this case, possibly result from **(2)** ________ when these rodents carried deadly diseases.

As we **(3)** ________ to adulthood, our fears change. Under the age of seven, fears frequently include imagined monsters or the dark. By ten, children fear events that are real, though extremely **(4)** ________ to happen, like murder or war. When we are teenagers, social fears begin to **(5)** ________, such as looking foolish in front of friends.

The vast majority of us are able to **(6)** ________ our fears under control. However, for others, a fear can get out of control and have a significant **(7)** ________ on their lives. When this happens, a fear has turned **(8)** ________ a phobia. Psychologists recognise over 500 phobias, from ablutophobia (fear of washing) to zoophobia (fear of animals).

CASE STUDY 1
NYCTOPHOBIA

As a child, Mustafa Aksoy used to be terrified of the dark. Until the age of eight, he spent most nights in his parents' room and insisted on leaving a light on. His parents never suspected a problem – after all, such fears are common among young kids. But Mustafa has never got used to sleeping in the dark and he's now 16. He still sleeps with a light on, which is fine, of course. However, Mustafa's nyctophobia can occasionally make everyday life difficult.

'I was at a birthday party last week. Someone turned the lights out while the candles on the cake were being lit,' Mustafa says. 'Even though I knew there was no real danger, I was still petrified of the dark!'

Mustafa can't explain the reasons behind his phobia. However, many phobias result from a distressing experience in childhood.

CASE STUDY 2
AUTOPHOBIA

Seventeen-year-old Poppy Scofield believes that her autophobia – the fear of being alone – comes from an incident when she was ten. She and her mum were shopping in a department store. Suddenly her mum got an urgent phone call from work and became distracted. She left the shop quickly and simply forgot her daughter was with her. Obviously Poppy was in tears until her mum returned, and she's suffered from autophobia ever since.

Although Poppy hasn't entirely got over her fear, she's now used to her autophobia and has several strategies she uses to cope with it. 'Reading or listening to music definitely helps. Plus I deliberately make lots of friends so I'm almost always with someone.'

Both nyctophobia and autophobia are common. But other phobias are quite unusual and, in some cases, possibly difficult to believe.

CASE STUDY 3
SCOLIONOPHOBIA

Scolionophobia has been recognised since the 1960s. Children who suffer from this will feel extreme anxiety about going to school, with symptoms such as headaches and feeling physically sick. For over three years, Noah Jenkins experienced just this. At one point, the school threatened to take Noah's parents to court for keeping their child at home. When his parents proved that Noah was studying at home, the school eventually agreed to help. Now, after a period of psychological treatment, Noah is a typical 18-year-old and is about to leave home for university.

'One of the worst things about that time was the fact that my school didn't believe me,' says Noah. 'They thought I was trying to get out of studying when, in fact, I've always enjoyed learning.'

TALKING POINTS

Why do you think some people suffer from phobias such as scolionophobia?

Do you think fear can be a useful emotion? Why?

TOTALLY EMOTIONAL 37

GRAMMAR be / get used to

1 **Read the examples and the rules. What kinds of words can follow *be/get used to*?**

1 Although Poppy hasn't entirely got over her fear, she's now used to her autophobia.
2 Mustafa has never got used to sleeping in the dark.

a We use *be/get used to* to talk about how familiar something is for someone.
b If you *are used to* something, you are familiar with it. You have experienced it often enough for it to seem normal to you and it is no longer strange.
c If you *get used to* something, you become familiar with it.

» GRAMMAR REFERENCE AND PRACTICE PAGE 153

2 **Choose the correct verbs.**

1 I feel exhausted. I'*m not / don't get* used to staying up so late.
2 We have to speak English in class all the time. At first, we found it hard, but now *we're / we get* used to it.
3 I can't *be / get* used to the school website now they've redesigned it. It's so confusing!
4 It took me several days to *be / get* used to the time change when we went to the USA.
5 Our school starts at 7.30, so I've always *been / got* used to getting up early.
6 I'm *being / getting* used to our new teacher, but I still miss our old one.

3 **Imagine a friend from abroad is coming to live in your country. What will they have to get used to? Write four sentences. Use the ideas in the box and your own ideas.**

daily routine	food	people	weather

You might find it difficult to get used to our sense of humour.

4 **Read the examples. Which one describes a past habit or state?**

1 She's used to being alone now.
2 I used to be terrified of spiders.

5 **Complete the second sentence so that it means the same as the first sentence. Use between two and five words, including *used*.**

1 In the past, I was petrified of dogs.
I ________ petrified of dogs.
2 My new school no longer feels strange to me.
I ________ my new school.
3 Vicki is no longer worried about sleeping in the dark.
Vicki ________ in the dark now.
4 As a child, I was afraid of heights.
I ________ afraid of heights.
5 Did Samuel become accustomed to the cold weather in Norway?
Did Samuel ________ the cold weather in Norway?

6 **Correct the mistake in each sentence.**

1 I've got use to my new school now.
2 Jody can't get use to sharing a room with her sister.
3 You used to your new school timetable?
4 I swam in the lake every weekend as a child, so I was used to deep water quickly.
5 I'm used to my school – I hope that soon it'll feel like I've always been here.
6 I'd prefer to have a smaller car because I got used to them now.

VOCABULARY Adverbs: type and position

1 **Match the examples to the types of adverb.**

1 Fears frequently include imagined monsters or the dark.
2 Our cat spends most nights outside.
3 I was at a birthday party last week.
4 Mustafa can't explain the reasons behind his phobia. However, many phobias …
5 She left the shop quickly.
6 Reading or listening to music definitely help.

a adverbs of time
b frequency adverbs
c adverbs of certainty
d adverbs of manner
e adverbs of place
f connecting adverbs (which link to a previous sentence)

2 **Where in a sentence (beginning, middle or end) are the types of adverb (a–f) in Exercise 1 usually used?**

3 **Write the sentences with the adverbs in the correct positions. More than one answer is sometimes possible.**

1 He can sing. (beautifully)
2 I have been scared of insects. (never)
3 I'll get used to it. (probably)
4 I had an upset stomach. I had difficulty sleeping. (as a result)
5 I get anxious about homework. (usually)
6 I've been getting bad-tempered. (lately)
7 If we leave now, we'll be home. (by nine)
8 She left home. (a few minutes ago, definitely)
9 We have lunch in summer. (outdoors)
10 They were laughing. (loudly)

4 **Ask and answer the questions with a partner.**

1 How are you feeling today?
2 What makes you feel bad-tempered?
3 What's the last thing you felt relieved about?
4 Who makes you feel irritated?
5 Do you ever get anxious about things? What?

38 UNIT 6

GRAMMAR *be / get used to*

WARMER
Ask the class to think of a time when there was a big change in their life, for example, changing school, moving house, etc. Students get into groups of three or four. They tell each other what the change was, how they felt at the time and how they feel now. When students have finished, elicit the most interesting story from each group.

1 When the students have read the information, elicit the answers and the tense of the phrase in purple used to form in each sentence (*1 present simple; 2 present perfect*). Point out that these phrases can be used with different tenses, for example, *I'll never get used to getting up early* or *I'm slowly getting used to being in this class.*

Answers
pronouns or nouns (*her autophobia*) or verbs in the *-ing* form (*sleeping*)

» GRAMMAR REFERENCE AND PRACTICE ANSWER KEY TB PAGE 267

2 Explain that students need to look for clues in the sentences to tell them which tense to use and to decide if *be* or *get* is needed. Elicit the answers and, if necessary, ask for volunteers to explain why each choice is correct. Point out that it is possible to use the present simple (*don't get used to doing something*) when talking about a general fact, not a specific situation, for example, *Elephants don't get used to living in zoos. They don't walk enough and they die younger than expected.*

Answers
1 'm not 2 we're 3 get 4 get 5 been 6 getting

3 You could ask the class whether friends from other countries have visited them, and what they found different. Elicit some ideas from the class about what their friends would have to get used to. Also ask students if they have been to another country and if they found something difficult to get used to. Students can work in small groups, before comparing ideas as a class.

FAST FINISHERS
Ask fast finishers to think of another heading or two and to write a sentence for them too, for example schools, traffic. When everyone has finished, elicit these sentences as well as the sentences for the headings in the book.

Answers
Students' own answers

4 Elicit the answer and the differences between the two structures. In the first, the tense is formed by the verb *to be*. We can use *be used to* to make sentences in different tenses. In the second, *used to* is a past form. In negatives and questions, it changes to *use to*. It is only used to talk about the past. The verb following each structure is also different; the first is followed by the *-ing* form and the second by the infinitive without *to*.

Answer
2

5 Tell students that sometimes, two answers will be possible. Give examples: '*I'm used to getting up early*' and '*I've got used to getting up early*'. Both indicate that getting up early is now normal for the speaker. Students do the exercise alone then compare answers in pairs. Elicit the answers and the possible alternatives for 2 and 3.

MIXED ABILITY
Students can work in mixed-ability pairs to complete the exercise. Check the answers after each of the first two sentences to ensure everyone understands the task, then allow them to finish and elicit the rest of the answers.

Answers
1 used to be 2 am/'m used to / have/'ve got used to
3 has/'s got used to sleeping / is/'s used to sleeping 4 used to be
5 get used to

6 Look at the first sentence with the class and elicit what is wrong (*the spelling of* used). Students work alone and then compare answers in pairs. Check answers as a class.

Answers
1 I've got **used** to the cold weather now.
2 Jody can't get **used** to sharing a room with her sister.
3 **Are you used** to your new school timetable?
4 … so I **got used** to deep water quickly.
5 I'm **getting used** to my school …
6 … I **am / 'm / have got / 've got used** to them now.

» GRAMMAR WORKSHEET UNIT 6

VOCABULARY *Adverbs: type and position*

1 Elicit what an adverb is and what kind of word it can modify (*a verb, an adjective or another adverb*). Students complete the matching in pairs. Elicit the answers then look at type a and elicit what this tells us (*when something happens*). Do the same with the other types.

Answers
1 b 2 e 3 a 4 f 5 d 6 c

2 Elicit where the adverbs are in the example sentences. Point out that some adverbs can often be used in different positions, for example, *sometimes* can come at the start of a sentence, before the verb (or after the verb *to be*) or at the end of the sentence.

Answers
Beginning: adverbs of time (for emphasis), connecting adverbs
Middle: frequency adverbs, adverbs of certainty, adverbs of manner
End: adverbs of time, adverbs of manner, adverbs of place

3 Students work in pairs and decide the most natural position for the adverbs and in which sentences they could be placed in more than one position.

Possible answers
1 He can sing beautifully. 2 I have never been scared of insects.
3 I'll probably get used to it. 4 I had an upset stomach. As a result, I had difficulty sleeping. 5 I usually get anxious about homework.
6 I've been getting bad-tempered lately. / Lately I've been getting bad-tempered. 7 If we leave now, we'll be home by nine. 8 She definitely left home a few minutes ago. 9 We have lunch outdoors in summer. 10 They were laughing loudly.

4 Elicit ways students could answer question 1, for example, *I'm feeling tired today.* Elicit what the adverb is (*today*) and what kind it is (*adverb of time*). Set a time limit of two minutes for students to ask and answer the questions, then invite them to answer the questions in front of the class. Students give their own answers.

» VOCABULARY WORKSHEET UNIT 6

LISTENING

PREPARE FOR THE EXAM

B2 FIRST FOR SCHOOLS
Listening Part 1

In this part, students listen to eight unconnected monologues or dialogues. For each one, there is a three-option multiple choice question. The focus of this part is on genre, identifying speaker feeling, attitude, topic, opinion, purpose, agreement between speakers, gist and detail.

Tips Encourage students to underline key words in the questions and think of synonyms that they may hear in the recording. It is very unlikely that they will hear exactly the same words as in the options.

1 Look at the underlined words in the first question. Ask why the words in the introduction are important (*they tell us who is talking, about what and what information we have to listen for*). Then ask students about the underlined words in the options and to think about what the speaker might say, for example, *A It's a lot more fun than I expected; B It will be very important when I find a job; C Analysing information is really interesting*. Set a time limit of two minutes for students to do the same for the other questions. Students give their own answers.

25 2 Tell students that, in the exam, they hear each extract twice in a row. Here, they will hear all eight once each and then all eight a second time. When they listen for the second time, encourage students to note any synonyms that help them to identify the correct answers. Allow students to compare in pairs, then elicit the answers and reasons for them.

Answers

1 C (The speaker says she knew she would enjoy the course but that it is tougher than she thought it would be, which rules out A as an answer. B is not true as she doesn't have any career ambitions yet.)
2 C (A is not correct as the speaker says his phone is locked and no one will be able to find out anything from it. B is ruled out because he knows he has left it in one of the places he's been to today.)
3 B (The girl knows what the test covers because she mentions how much there is to remember and that she's memorised everything, so A is wrong. C is ruled out because she does not mention any specific facts.)
4 A (The boy says he has quite a bit more to do but doesn't think it will be a problem, which rules out B. C is not true, as there is no indication that he doesn't know what to do – it is maths that he has problems with.)
5 C (Although A and B are plausible reactions to the situation, the father says nothing to indicate that he is annoyed with his daughter, and he offers to go and pick her up.)
6 A (The boy says he's getting used to being on a bike but doesn't express worry about this and mentions that his instructor says things will come in time, which rules out B. C is not correct because he has not learned to ride the bike yet and he doesn't say it was an ambition to do so.)
7 C (The speaker says that experts say we should try to be more optimistic, but this is not the opinion of the speaker, so A is ruled out. B is a plausible option but is not directly referenced.)
8 A (B is ruled out because although the speakers mention its advice, they do not agree about how easy it will be to follow. C is not correct because only one strange phobia is mentioned by the girl, and the boy doesn't comment on it.)

» AUDIOSCRIPT TB PAGES 290–291

» PREPARE FOR THE EXAM TEACHING NOTES AND ANSWER KEY TB PAGE 259

SPEAKING Generalising

26 1 Before students listen, ask them what they think the two people will mention as they talk, for example, the school timetable might be a reason for the worst day of the week. Elicit examples and then play the recording. Elicit which days they talked about and what reasons they gave.

Harry – best, Saturday; reasons – gets up late, phone messages, parents out, loud music, makes breakfast

Elif – worst, Sunday; reasons – tests on Monday, revising, feels tense, can't sleep

Students give their own answers.

26 2 When the students have listened again, elicit answers and then alternative ways of saying each of the expressions, for example, *1 Usually; 2 Almost every Monday / On most Mondays; 3 Usually, I; 4 Usually / Very often; 5 except for*.

Answers

1 H 2 E 3 E 4 H 5 E

» AUDIOSCRIPT TB PAGE 291

27 3 Look at the sentences with the students and elicit words that could complete them, for example, *1 English and Spanish; 2 teachers; 3 Saturdays; 4 spiders*. Students then listen. Ask if anyone guessed any of the words correctly. Ask which ones and then elicit the answers.

Answers

1 science and ICT 2 players on her (football) team
3 Sunday nights 4 public speaking

27 4 Look at the *Prepare to speak* box with the students. Ask which phrase has the same meaning as *ninety percent of the time* (*nine times out of ten*). When students have listened to the recording, elicit the answers and then ask students, 'What happens when you get to school in the morning?' Elicit answers from different students and ask each person to use a different phrase from the box. Give them an example about yourself to start, for example, 'What normally happens is that I get to the staff/teacher's room and make a cup of coffee.'

Answers

Generally speaking (S), Ninety percent of the time (S), For the most part (A), one exception is (A), on the whole (A)

» AUDIOSCRIPT TB PAGE 291

5 Give students time to read the questions and think about their answers before setting this as a pair work discussion. Encourage students to try to give extended answers like the ones given by the speakers in the recordings. Monitor and give help with vocabulary and pronunciation where necessary. Ask pairs to feed any interesting answers back to the class. Students give their own answers.

COOLER

Put students into pairs. Tell the class that one person in each pair has a phobia and the other is interviewing them about it. Give students five minutes to think of what the phobia is and some interesting questions and answers. Monitor and help where necessary. Students then practise their interviews. Invite pairs to carry out their interviews in front of the class.

LISTENING

PREPARE FOR THE EXAM

Listening Part 1

1 **You will hear people talking in eight different situations. Read the questions. Underline the key words that might help you get the correct answers.**

1 You hear a student talking about her degree in psychology. What does she think about it?
  A It's more enjoyable than she thought it would be.
  B It will be very useful for her future career.
  C She finds the research fascinating.

2 You hear a boy telling his friend about losing his phone. How does the boy feel about losing his phone?
  A worried that people can access information on it
  B frustrated that he doesn't know where he left it
  C concerned that he won't be able to use it immediately

3 You hear a girl leaving a voicemail for her friend about a history test. Why is she calling?
  A to find out what it will cover
  B to suggest doing some revision for it together
  C to check some facts before doing it

4 You overhear two friends talking about a school project. What does the boy say about his project?
  A He's feeling optimistic about its progress.
  B He's worried that he won't finish it in time.
  C He's finding it difficult to understand what to do.

5 You hear a father talking to his daughter on the phone. How is he feeling now?
  A annoyed that his daughter hasn't been in touch before now
  B concerned about how his daughter will get home
  C relieved that his daughter is OK

6 You hear a boy telling a friend about learning to ride a motorbike. What is the boy's attitude towards his motorbike lessons?
  A pleased with what he has learned so far
  B worried that he isn't advancing quickly enough
  C satisfied that he has achieved an ambition

7 You hear a psychologist talking about being optimistic and pessimistic. What does she say about this?
  A People should make more effort to be optimistic.
  B It is difficult to balance optimism and pessimism.
  C Pessimism can be useful to people.

8 You hear two friends talking about a programme they have seen about phobias. What do they agree about it?
  A how sympathetic the presenter was
  B how difficult its advice will be to follow
  C how unusual some of the phobias mentioned were

2 25 **Listen. For questions 1–8, choose the best answer (A, B or C). Then listen again and check your answers.**

» PREPARE FOR THE EXAM PAGE 131

SPEAKING Generalising

26 **1** **Listen to Harry and Elif talking about their best and worst days of the week. Which person is more like you?**

26 **2** **Who says these phrases? Listen again and write *H* (Harry) or *E* (Elif).**

1 What normally happens is …
2 Virtually every Monday …
3 As a rule, I …
4 Nine times out of ten, …
5 with the exception of …

27 **3** **Listen to Steffi and Antonio. Complete the sentences.**

1 Two of Steffi's favourite subjects are ________.
2 Steffi gets on really well with the ________.
3 Antonio rarely does his homework on ________.
4 Antonio has a bit of a phobia of ________.

27 **4** **Read the *Prepare to speak* box. Then listen again. Which phrases do Steffi and Antonio use?**

PREPARE TO SPEAK | Generalising

Generalising
Ninety percent of the time …
What normally happens is …
Nine times out of ten, …
Generally speaking, …
On the whole, …
As a rule, …
For the most part, …
Virtually every Monday, …

Exceptions
One exception is …
… with the exception of …

5 **Work in pairs. Interview each other. Use phrases from the *Prepare to speak* box.**

1 Which is your best/worst day of the week? Why? What normally happens on that day?
2 Which is your best/worst time of the year? Why? What generally happens then?
3 What's your favourite lesson at school? Why?
4 Describe a typical weekend for you.

TOTALLY EMOTIONAL 39

CULTURE

COLOURS AROUND THE WORLD

1 **Ask and answer the questions with a partner.**

1. Think about your bedroom, your clothes and your possessions. What colours do you like the most? What colours do you like the least?
2. Do you have a favourite or special colour? What does it mean or represent for you?

2 **What emotions do you associate with the following colours?**

black blue brown green grey
orange purple red white yellow

3 **Read the article on page 41 quickly and compare what it says with your own ideas.**

4 **Read the article again. Discuss these situations with your partner using information from the article.**

1. You want to open a restaurant that serves organic and ecological food. Which colours would you use to decorate it?
2. Your class want to make signs in English to place around your school. Which colours would be effective and eye-catching?
3. You are creating a luxury fashion label. Which colours would you use to advertise your brand?
4. You are making a poster about the importance of a good night's sleep for your health. What colours would you use in the poster?

5 **Match the highlighted words in the article to the meanings.**

1. strong and energetic
2. type or degree of a colour
3. are immediately noticeable
4. the feeling of wanting something that someone else has
5. not clear, bright or shiny

28 **6** **Listen to four people being interviewed about the significance of colours in their cultures. In the table write the country each person is from and the colour or colours they mention.**

Speaker	Country	Colour(s)	Meaning / Use
1			
2			
3			
4			

28 **7** **Listen to the interviews again and complete the last column of the table. Makes notes on the meaning of the colours and how they are used.**

8 **Read the sentences. Look at the underlined phrase in the first sentence. Then choose the correct option in the second.**

USEFUL LANGUAGE

Expressions with colours

1. Sam saw red when I told him. He was really *happy / angry.*
2. He was green with envy when he saw my new phone. It's the *latest / oldest* model.
3. You look like you're feeling a bit blue. *Have you been away? / What's wrong?*
4. The rules are there in black and white. They *could / couldn't* be clearer.
5. Last week, out of the blue, I got a call from Daniel. I was really *miserable / surprised.*
6. He was caught red-handed as he left the museum. It was *obvious / unclear* that he had stolen the painting!

CULTURE

Learning Objectives

- The students learn about the significance of different colours around the world.
- In the project stage, the students research colours in different English-speaking countries and make a poster which they present to the class.

Vocabulary

dull envy jump out shade vibrant

Resources

CULTURE VIDEO AND CULTURE VIDEO WORKSHEET: The meaning of colours

WARMER

Choose something in the classroom which has a particular colour, for example, the walls, a desk, a coat. Tell the class: 'I can see something which is/has the colour … (red).' When students want to guess what it is, they put their hands up. Nominate different students until someone guesses what it is. That student can then choose a different object for the class to guess. Continue the activity until five or six different students have chosen an object and the others have guessed.

1 Put students into groups of three or four to discuss the questions. Set a time limit of three or four minutes and then elicit ideas from different groups. Ask students if there are any colours that they wouldn't wear or colours that they wouldn't put on their bedroom walls.

Answers

Students' own answers

2 Students remain in the same groups as for Exercise 1. Write *blue* on the board and ask what emotions and feelings students think of. Elicit ideas, for example, *calm*, *cold*. Then ask groups to think about the other colours in the box. Elicit ideas from different groups.

Answers

Students' own answers

3 Set a time limit of two minutes for students to quickly look for related adjectives and nouns for each colour. Elicit the answers and ask students if they were surprised by anything they read in the text.

FAST FINISHERS

The text mentions what colours mean in different countries. Ask fast finishers to think about their own country and say what colours are used for what, for example, a bride's wedding dress/outfit, clothes for a funeral and what colours are popular for kitchens, living rooms, etc. When everyone has finished, elicit the answers and invite fast finishers to share their ideas with the class.

Possible answers

Students compare their answers with these ideas from the text.
black – sadness
blue – relaxing, calm, peace, cold, sad, depressed
brown – calming, dull, boring
green – envy
grey – unclear
orange – lively, cheerful
purple – vibrant, bold
red – strong feelings, nervous, embarrassed, excited, angry
white – emptiness
yellow – warmth, happiness, irritating

4 Look at the first situation with the class. Ask what colours might be good for the restaurant. Elicit ideas and then ask students to find reasons for their choices for this and the other three situations in the text. Set a time limit for students to do the task. Monitor and help as necessary. Then, elicit ideas and reasons.

MIXED ABILITY

Ask weaker students to work in pairs and choose two of the situations and concentrate on these. Monitor and help where necessary. When they have finished, they join together with another pair to compare ideas or tell each other about a situation that the other pair didn't look at.

Possible answers

1 Green because it is for plants and nature. Brown because many natural foods are brown.
2 Eye-catching and strong colour choices are purple, red, yellow and orange.
3 White because it is for purity and purple because it is often the colour of royalty, so it is special and luxurious, and black because it indicates elegance.
4 Blue because it is calm, relaxing and is for peace.

29 The Reading text is recorded for students to listen, read and check their answers.

5 Put the students into pairs. One student looks at the meanings and the other looks at the highlighted words. The student looking at the meanings starts by reading out one of the meanings. The other student looks at the highlighted words in the text, reads the sentences containing the words and if necessary the preceding and following sentences in order to decide which word matches the meaning. The student looking at the words then says one of the words and the other student finds the matching meaning. They take turns like this until they have matched all the words.

Answers

1 vibrant 2 shade 3 jump out 4 envy 5 dull

CONTINUED ON PAGE 78

BACKGROUND INFORMATION

The Candoshi tribe of Peru don't have any separate words for colours. When they describe colours, they use words for things that have similar colours, for example, their word for yellow is the name of a yellow bird. Their word for red is the same as the word for ripe fruit and their word for green is the same as for unripe fruit. This may seem strange but the same is true of European languages. Until about the year 1500, there was no word for the colour orange. Instead, it was called yellow-red. The word *orange* is thought to have come from the Arabic word 'naranj' and became used when the fruit became available in markets.

Flowers can be a problem when you go to different countries. We often give flowers when we visit people, but what should we avoid? In parts of France, yellow flowers can symbolise jealousy. In Japan, yellow would be a good choice as it signifies nobility. However, in some parts of central America, yellow flowers are often used to decorate graves. Red flowers, especially roses, are used to say *I love you* in many countries, especially in India where red is the colour most brides choose to wear at their wedding.

28 **6** Look at the instructions with the class. Elicit that they only have to write the countries and the colours, so tell them to put their pens down and just listen carefully for that information. When they have listened, ask them to discuss in pairs what the four countries were and write them down. Ask them which continent each country is on and then, in pairs, they share any other information they remember from the listening before they listen again.

Answers

Speaker 1 China – red Speaker 2 Belgium – pink and blue
Speaker 3 Brazil – purple Speaker 4 Thailand – yellow

28 **7** Before students listen again, tell them to complete any parts of the table they are sure of so that they have less to complete while they are listening. When they have listened, allow students to compare their ideas in pairs and complete anything they missed. Elicit the answers and ask students what information they found most interesting or surprising.

Answers

1 China: red – fire, life and good fortune, used in (happy) festivals, e.g. New Year
2 Belgium: pink and blue – in the past baby boys dressed in pink and girls (light) blue
3 Brazil: purple – sad, death
4 Thailand: yellow – Buddhism, the Earth, the King, Monday

» **AUDIOSCRIPT TB PAGES 291–292**

8 Students work individually and then compare their answers in pairs. Elicit the answers and then ask students to stay in pairs to think of some questions using the phrases, for example, *When was the last time you saw red? What has made you green with envy recently? What do you do when you feel blue? Have you ever proven that you were correct by pointing out rules or other information that are written in black and white? When was the last time you received a message from someone out of the blue? Have you ever been caught red-handed when doing something wrong?* Then, they change pairs and ask and answer their questions. Monitor and listen to the students and invite some of them to share their stories with the class.

Answers

1 angry 2 latest 3 What's wrong? 4 couldn't 5 surprised
6 obvious

PROJECT *Colours in English-speaking countries*

Put the students into groups of four where possible. Read the instructions with the students. Give them one minute to agree on a country for their groups. Ideally, they would research their project together, either using computers at school or together outside school. However, if this isn't possible, tell the students that each member of the group should research one of the bullet points in step 2 and, when it is their turn to give the presentation, they would each present their own point.

Tell the class to listen carefully to all of the presentations and to think of questions to ask their classmates later. Then, invite each group to give their presentation and, when they have finished, allow other groups to ask any of their questions. Students could find out the answers to these at a later time if they can't answer them in the lesson. When the groups have presented their projects, ask them how easy or difficult they found the research as well as how much they worked together and individually on their part of the poster.

PROJECT EXTENSION

Tell the class that they are going to work together to research a non-English speaking country that hasn't been mentioned in the lesson.

Before they start, the whole class brainstorms things which people may need to think about colours, for example giving flowers, wedding clothes, etc. Make sure there is one point for each group. Put the students into groups of four or five and allocate one of the points to each one. They research the importance of colours for their topic and make notes about it. If they can do the research during the lesson, allow five or ten minutes for them to do this. If not, they can do the research at home and present their findings in a future lesson. Invite groups to share their information with the class. Each group presents their information and compares how this is similar or different to their country.

04 **CULTURE VIDEO: The meaning of colours**

When students have completed the lesson, they can watch the video and complete the worksheet.

COOLER

Tell the class that the school has decided to redecorate the classroom and the corridor outside. Students work in groups of three or four to think about what colours to paint the walls, what colour furniture it should have and any other details. They should think of some reasons for their decisions, such as *Yellow walls would cheer up students and make them more likely to work hard.* They could think of practical reasons as well, such as *White walls get dirty more quickly so they are not a good idea.* Set a time limit of three or four minutes and then have a class discussion on what the best colour scheme would be.

What COLOURS really mean

COOL

BLUE is considered to be a relaxing, calm colour, and it's often associated with peace. A pale blue is the typical colour of clear skies and water. It's perhaps for these reasons that blue is the world's most popular colour. On the negative side, blue suggests cold temperatures, as well as low energy. In English, for example, people who are sad or depressed say they 'feel blue'.

GREEN is the colour of plants, so it's often associated with life, nature and growth. In Ireland, people think it brings good fortune, and in Japan, it represents eternal life. However, green also has negative associations in English. It's the colour of envy – 'green with envy' – and people's faces 'turn green' when they feel sick.

PURPLE is a fairly unusual colour in nature. Some minerals are purple and there are plants with purple flowers, but they aren't common. In Europe, purple has been the colour of royalty since ancient times, when purple dye for clothing was rare and very expensive. Purple is often seen as a vibrant and bold colour choice.

WARM

RED is the colour of blood, so it's often associated with life, energy and strong feelings. For example, many people's faces turn red when they are feeling nervous, embarrassed or excited. In English, people also say they 'see red' when they are angry! A splash of red catches our attention, and red objects jump out at us because they appear to be closer than they really are.

YELLOW is the colour of sunlight, so it's often associated with warmth and happiness. It's also the most intense colour, which means a bright shade of yellow can be irritating – imagine a house painted in bright yellow! Yellow things are admired in China, where this colour also represents the Chinese element of earth. In India, yellow is associated with business and financial wealth.

ORANGE is a combination of lively red and cheerful yellow, making it a bright colour that catches our attention. It's also the colour of healthy foods, like oranges, carrots and pumpkins. Because of its high visibility, orange is often used for signs and for emergency equipment, like lifejackets.

NEUTRAL

BLACK is neutral because it absorbs all the colours of light. It's associated with darkness and night, as well as mystery and the unknown. In many countries, black is a serious colour, associated with death and sadness, but also with elegance and authority.

BROWN is the colour of earth, wood and autumn leaves, which makes it a neutral, calming colour. It's also the colour of many foods, such as bread, nuts and chocolate. However, lots of people consider brown dull and boring, especially for clothes.

WHITE is the colour of fresh snow, so it's often associated with cleanliness and purity. In many countries, it's the typical colour of wedding dresses. However, white also suggests emptiness, and in some countries, like Japan, it's linked to death.

GREY is the colour of foggy days, when we can't see clearly. Grey is between black and white, making it the most neutral colour. In English, the phrase 'grey area' is used to describe things that are unclear.

PROJECT

Colours in English-speaking countries

Work in groups of three or four to find out about colours in different cultures and countries. Use these steps to help you.

1. In your group, agree on one of the following countries to research:
   Australia, Canada, Ireland, New Zealand, the UK, the USA
2. Search online for any special colour associations or traditions.
   - Does the country have a national colour or colours?
   - What are the colours of the country's flag? What do they mean?
   - What is the significance of the nine colours mentioned in the article on this page?
   - Are any colours considered to be lucky or unlucky?

Make a poster of your findings and present it to the class.

04 NOW WATCH THE CULTURE VIDEO

7 TELLING STORIES

ABOUT YOU

05 **Watch the video and answer the questions.**

What genres of story do you like?

What makes a good story, do you think?

Do you prefer reading books or watching films?

VOCABULARY Verbs of movement and sounds

1 **Match the sentences to the pictures. Then write the infinitives of the verbs.**

EP

1 Jade leant forward and tapped Megan on the shoulder.
2 Ewan rushed down the street to get his dog, which was trembling with fear.
3 Ollie was kneeling down when his sister slapped him on the back.
4 The door swung open and Butch wandered in.

30 **2** **Listen and decide which verb describes the sounds the people make.**

mumble sigh whisper whistle

3 **Match the sentence halves.**

1 She leant over and whispered
2 He sighed
3 The presenter mumbled his
4 José began to whistle

a introduction to the talk.
b a tune he'd heard on the radio.
c when he realised he'd forgotten his homework.
d her idea in his ear.

READING

1 **Look at the title of the story and the picture. Who do you think the people are? What genre do you think the story is? Read the extract quickly and check your answers.**

PREPARE FOR THE EXAM

Reading and Use of English Part 5

2 **You are going to read an extract from a novel about a detective called Sherlock Holmes and his friend Watson. For questions 1–6, choose the answer (A, B, C or D) which you think fits best according to the text.**

1 What do we learn about Holmes in the first paragraph?
  A He would like more time to spend on his interests.
  B He does not want to share his free time with others.
  C He blames those around him when things go wrong.
  D He feels annoyed when he cannot do what he wants.

Tip: Read paragraph 1. Underline the words which give you the answer.

2 The word 'sneak' in line 24 is used to mean 'move
  A noisily and aggressively'.
  B quietly and secretively'.
  C surprisingly quickly'.
  D extremely slowly'.

Tip: Read the sentences before and after the word carefully to work out the answer.

3 When Watson mentions the thefts in London, Holmes complains because
  A he thinks Watson has got the facts wrong.
  B all of the cases have already been solved.
  C he believes his skills are wasted on such crimes.
  D the weather has caused a big increase in theft.

Tip: Read the conversation between Holmes and Watson about criminals.

4 What does 'it' refer to in line 36?
  A a murder
  B a reason
  C a meeting
  D an appointment

Tip: Underline words A–D in the text. Which one does 'it' refer to?

5 Holmes suggests that his brother Mycroft is someone who
  A uses the railway to get to work.
  B is predictable in his routine.
  C spends most of his time outdoors.
  D is dedicated to his family.

Tip: Read this part of the text carefully to work out the answer.

42 UNIT 7

7 TELLING STORIES

Unit Overview

TOPIC	Story telling
VOCABULARY	Verbs of movement and sounds
READING	The Bruce-Partington Plans
GRAMMAR	Narrative tenses
VOCABULARY	Time phrases
WRITING	A story
EXAM TASKS	Reading and Use of English Part 5; Writing Part 2

Resources

GRAMMAR REFERENCE AND PRACTICE: SB page 154; TB pages 267–268
PREPARE FOR THE EXAM: SB pages on TB pages 240–241 and 246; TB pages 256 and 258
WORKBOOK: pages 28–31
VIDEO AND VIDEO WORKSHEET: Stories
PHOTOCOPIABLE WORKSHEETS: Grammar worksheet Unit 7; Vocabulary worksheet Unit 7
TEST GENERATOR: Unit test 7; Term test 1
PRACTICE EXTRA: Unit 7

WARMER

Write on the board: *It was the third week in November*. Elicit ideas of what the next line of this story could be. Now put the students into pairs to write their own second sentence. Students then pass their story to a different pair, who read what has been written and add a third sentence. Continue like this for three or four more sentences, always making sure the stories go to a different pair. The stories are then returned to their original writers who read what has been written and discuss, without writing, how the story could continue. Invite pairs to give a brief summary of their stories to the class.

ABOUT YOU

05 You can begin the class and introduce the topic of the unit by showing the video and asking students to complete the video worksheet. Read the questions in the *About you* box with the class and check the word *genre* and point out that it is a French word and is pronounced in the French way when used by English speakers /ˈʒɒːnrə/. Students think about the questions alone for a minute and then get into groups of three or four to share their ideas. Have a class vote on the most popular genres of book or film and whether they prefer books or films and elicit why. You could also ask students to discuss these questions: *Who is your favourite author/director? What was the last book you read? What was it about?* Monitor and give positive feedback for interesting ideas.

VOCABULARY Verbs of movement and sounds

1 Before students do this exercise, ask individuals to describe what they can see in each picture. Students work in pairs to do the matching and write the infinitives. Elicit the answers and ask follow-up questions to check their understanding, for example, if a door swings because it moves in two directions, forwards and backwards, what is a swing? (*Something children sit on and go forwards and backwards.*) What part of the body do we use to tap (fingers and feet) and slap (*an open hand*)? What's the difference between to wander and to walk? (*To wander means to go with no specific destination in mind, for example, we wander round the shopping centre when we just want to look at shops in general rather than specific ones.*)

Answers
1 C (lean, tap) 2 B (rush, tremble) 3 D (kneel down, slap) 4 A (swing open, wander)

30 2 Ask the class if they know any of the words before they listen. Play the recording and elicit the answers and what the words mean exactly, i.e., *whisper: to talk very quietly so that other people don't hear what you are saying; mumble: to speak quietly and in a way that is not clear so that words are difficult to understand; sigh: to breath out very deeply and quite loudly in a way which shows sadness or annoyance; whistle: to make a tuneful sound by blowing air through your lips*. Write a short sentence on the board, for example, *It's very hot today.* Nominate different students and ask them to whistle or sigh or to say the sentence on the board in either a whisper or as a mumble.

Answers
1 whisper 2 whistle 3 sigh 4 mumble

» AUDIOSCRIPT TB PAGE 292

3 When students have matched the sentence halves, put them into pairs to check their answers. Tell the students that, when you ask them for the answers, they shouldn't say 1 a, 2 b, etc, they should mime the activity. Invite a pair to mime one of the four sentences, not necessarily the first one. Other students say what sentence they are showing. Choose four different pairs to show the four different sentences.

Answers
1 d 2 c 3 a 4 b

READING

1 Ask students to describe the people they can see in the picture and to guess who they are, where they are and what kind of story it is from. Students may know the stories of Sherlock Holmes, in which case elicit anything they can tell you about the books or film or TV versions of the stories.

Answers
detectives (Sherlock Holmes and Watson), detective story

BACKGROUND INFORMATION

Sir Arthur Conan Doyle was a Scottish doctor, famous for writing crime stories about the detective Sherlock Holmes. The four Sherlock Holmes novels and 58 short stories were published between 1887 and 1927. Holmes solves cases, such as *The Hound of the Baskervilles*, through his logical reasoning and use of forensic science.

CONTINUED ON PAGE 82

PREPARE FOR THE EXAM

B2 FIRST FOR SCHOOLS
Reading and Use of English Part 5

This part is a multiple-choice task. It consists of a text followed by six questions, each with four multiple-choice options. Part 5 tests students' understanding of gist, main idea, tone, purpose, specific detail, attitude, opinion, implication and meaning from context.

Tips Pronoun referents are a common question type in this part, as seen in Exercise 2, question 4. Often the pronoun will refer back to one of the nouns in the sentence immediately before. Tell students to check this as a first option before considering other possibilities.

2 Put the students into pairs. Ask one student to cover the four choices and just look at the first question. Ask the second student to look at the four choices (A–D) for the same question. The first student, who doesn't know what the choices are, underlines in the text all the information about Holmes they think is important and answers the question as if it were an open comprehension question. The second student tries to choose the correct answer by reading the relevant part of the text as in a normal multiple-choice task. When they are ready, the students compare answers; the first reads out their answer, the second reads out the correct option. If the two answers contain the same information the option chosen is probably the correct one. If not, both students look at the choices and decide the correct answer together. Elicit the correct answer and tell the class that these are two ways they can approach this task; by focusing only on the question or by looking at the options and deciding which is correct. Some people prefer the first as there are no distractions from the wrong options, others prefer the second.

Students then complete the reading alone using the technique they prefer. Set a time limit of ten minutes and then allow students to compare answers before asking for feedback.

MIXED ABILITY

Put the students into mixed ability pairs. For each question, they look at two of the options each. When they are ready, they tell each other whether they think neither of their options are correct or if one option is correct.

FAST FINISHERS

Ask fast finishers to think of reasons why each correct answer is the right option. As you elicit the answers, ask the fast finishers to give their explanations. If someone gives the wrong answer, see if other students can explain why it is wrong.

Answers

1 D – He is impatient, and complains when he is forced to be inactive. A is not true as there is no mention of him wanting more time to spend on his hobby; B is ruled out because it is not mentioned; and C is ruled out because although Holmes is complaining, he does not blame his friend for the bad weather.
2 B – This question tests vocabulary above B2 level, where the meaning can be worked out from context (here, with the reference to a *tiger in the jungle*, before making a move).
3 C – Holmes says '*My abilities demand something far more worthy than that*' when referring to the recent thefts. A and B are not suggested in the text and although Watson talks of *a large number of small thefts*, there is nothing to indicate that the weather has caused an increase.
4 A – This question tests backwards reference and Holmes has been talking about an imagined murder.
5 B – Holmes describes Mycroft's behaviour in terms of a train that stays on its rails, which suggests a fixed routine. A is not correct because Holmes does not say that Mycroft uses railways; C is ruled out as Mycroft spends his time in indoor places – his home, his club, his office; and D is not possible as he rarely visits his brother and no other family is mentioned.
6 C – Holmes is bored doing nothing and has a vivid imagination, considering how easy it would be to commit a crime during foggy weather. He is also very excited by the unusual telegram he receives and wants to know what brings his brother to see him. A and D are ruled out because, although he doesn't want to waste his time on minor crimes, he does not suggest he is more intelligent than Watson nor does he doubt his talents. There is nothing to suggest B in the text.

31 The Reading text is recorded for students to listen, read and check their answers.

» PREPARE FOR THE EXAM TEACHING NOTES AND ANSWER KEY TB PAGE 256

TALKING POINTS

Set this as a small group task. For the first question, ask students to list as many stories that they have both read and seen. Then, in groups of three or four, they compare lists and find any that all of them have both read and seen, if possible.

Then ask the second question to the whole class about books and films in general. You could extend the second question by asking students what people might miss or lose from only watching the film. Encourage students to think about the pros and cons of each (for example *there is more time and space in a book for extra detail, and more is left to the reader's imagination; with films you can share the experience with your friends or the rest of the audience*). Students then work in their groups and, for the books and films they chose earlier, they discuss which they liked most and why. Set a time limit of five minutes and then invite groups to share their opinions about one of the books/films with the class.

COOLER

Students work in pairs. Half the pairs, if possible weaker students, write down five verbs from the vocabulary section and think of definitions for them. The other pairs find five words in the reading that aren't verbs and define them. The pairs then join together in groups of four and take turns to define one of their words for the other pair to guess. Elicit some of the words from the text that were chosen and their definitions.

THE BRUCE-PARTINGTON PLANS

SIR ARTHUR CONAN DOYLE

31

It was the third week of November and a thick yellow fog had settled over London. From the Monday to the Thursday, it had rarely been possible from our windows in Baker Street to see even the houses across the street. The first three of these days Holmes had been patiently studying a subject which had been his hobby for some time – the music of the Middle Ages. But when, for the fourth time, we pushed back our chairs from breakfast and saw the heavy brown mist outside the windows, my friend's impatient and active nature could no longer take this dull existence. He wandered restlessly around our sitting room; he bit his nails; he tapped the furniture nervously; and he complained about the inactivity.

'Nothing of interest in the paper, Watson?' he said. I realised that by anything of interest, Holmes was asking about anything of *criminal* interest. There was the news of a revolution, of a possible war and of a likely change of government. However, these were of little interest to my companion. The only criminal reports I could find were very ordinary. Holmes sighed impatiently and continued to wander around the room.

'The London criminal is certainly a dull person,' he said, sounding like a hunter who can find nothing to shoot. 'Look out of this window, Watson. See how people suddenly appear, are briefly seen and then quickly disappear once more into *line 24* the mist. On a day like this, a thief or a murderer could **sneak** round London like a tiger in the jungle. No one would see him until he made his move.'

'There have,' I said, 'been a large number of small thefts.'

Holmes muttered something rude and then turned towards me. 'My abilities demand something far more worthy than that,' he said. 'It is fortunate for this community that I am not a criminal.'

'It certainly is!' I agreed enthusiastically.

'Imagine that I had a good reason to want to kill someone,' continued Holmes. 'How easy it would be on a day like this! I could suggest a meeting, I could make up an appointment *line 36* and **it** would all be over. It is just as well they don't have days of fog in countries where murder is common.'

There was the sound of someone knocking.

'At last!' cried Holmes. 'Here comes something to bring some excitement into our lives.'

He rushed over to open the door. It was the postman with a telegram. Holmes tore it open and before long burst out laughing.

'Well, well! I don't believe it!' he said. 'My brother Mycroft is coming round.'

'And so ...?' I asked.

'And so ...?' said Holmes. 'It is like coming across a train in the middle of the road. Mycroft has his rails, like a train, and he stays on them. His home in Pall Mall, his club, his office in Whitehall – that is where you find him. Once, and only once, has he been here. What disaster can have knocked him off his rails?'

'Doesn't he explain?' I asked.

Holmes handed me his brother's telegram. 'Must see you about Cadogan West. Coming at once. Mycroft.'

'Cadogan West?' I said. I had heard that name.

'It means nothing to me,' said Holmes. 'But it is extraordinary that Mycroft should do something so uncharacteristic. The moon might as well stop going round the Earth.'

from Cambridge Experience Readers, *Holmes: Three Adventures*, adapted by Richard MacAndrew

6 What is implied about Holmes' character in the story extract?

A He believes himself to be more intelligent than Watson.
B He thinks other people are less important than he is.
C He needs to keep his mind occupied.
D He has some doubts about his talents.

Tip: Read the whole text before choosing the answer.

» PREPARE FOR THE EXAM PAGE 124

TALKING POINTS

Which books have you read that have been made into films? What is the difference between stories told in books compared with films?

GRAMMAR Narrative tenses

1 **Look at the underlined verbs in the text on page 43. What tenses are they?**

2 **Complete the rules with the verb forms in the box.**

past continuous	past perfect	past simple

We use narrative verb forms in stories to describe events and actions. We use the

a ________
- to describe the main events of a story, in the order they happened.
- to describe a short action that interrupts an action in the past continuous.

b ________
- to describe an action in progress at a particular time in the past.
- to describe a continuing action interrupted by an action in the past simple.

c ________
- to describe a completed action that happened before a particular point in the past.
- with sequencing expressions (*when*, *after*, *by the time*, *as soon as*) when one event happened before another event.

» GRAMMAR REFERENCE AND PRACTICE PAGE 154

3 **Read six extracts from later in the story about Sherlock Holmes. Choose the correct options.**

1 The man *travelled* / *was travelling* back to Woolwich when he was killed and thrown out of the train.
2 Mycroft Holmes took off his overcoat and *sat down* / *had sat down* heavily in an armchair.
3 At nine o'clock, we *were all sitting* / *had all sat* in the study, waiting patiently for our man.
4 We *just reached* / *had just reached* the dark shadows at the back of the house when we heard footsteps.
5 We were walking past his office when suddenly the man *rushed off* / *was rushing off* into the fog.
6 Lestrade and Mycroft met us outside Gloucester Road Station in the morning. We *left* / *had left* the back door of Oberstein's house open the night before.

4 **Read another extract from later in the story and notice the verb form. Complete the rules.**

Inspector Lestrade suddenly spoke. He had been listening to the conversation with some impatience.

a We use the past perfect continuous instead of the past perfect when we want to talk about a longer action that continued until another past action.
b We form the past perfect continuous with ________ + ________ + *-ing*.

5 **Complete the sentences with the past perfect simple or continuous form of the verbs in the box.**

call	cry	leave	play	rush	shout

1 The man ________ for almost an hour before anyone heard him.
2 By the time the game ended, we ________ for over three hours.
3 I could tell from her eyes that she ________.
4 Josefina was exhausted. She ________ around all morning.
5 The noises outside stopped a few minutes after we ________ the police.
6 I couldn't get into the concert because I ________ my ticket at home.

6 **Choose the correct options.**

1 I *feel* / *felt* relieved when I passed my driving test.
2 Jo *read* / *was reading* her book when she heard a loud noise outside.
3 Aba *went* / *was going* to his friend's house last night and watched TV.
4 I told my brother that I *changed* / *had changed* my mind about going to the party on Saturday.
5 Karl *whistled* / *has whistled* a tune while he waited for the doctor to see him.

VOCABULARY Time phrases

1 **Complete the sentences with the words in the box.**

EP

before (x2)	for (x2)	in	on

1 Holmes tore open the envelope and ________ long, he burst out laughing.
2 I only joined the school in March, but I made lots of new friends ________ no time.
3 He was disappointed not to do better because he'd been studying ________ weeks on end.
4 Callum slapped me on the back happily because we hadn't seen each other ________ some time.
5 I used to catch the bus to school, but the week ________ last, I started cycling instead.
6 We waited there for hours ________ end.

2 **Choose the correct options.**

1 Don't worry, you'll find a holiday job *before long* / *for some time*.
2 I can play computer games *in no time* / *for hours on end*. I never get bored!
3 Thandie practised for her flute exam *for weeks on end* / *before long*.
4 Billy waited *for some time* / *in no time* before a bus finally turned up.
5 Aiden and Finlay went to see the new Spielberg movie *for hours on end* / *the week before last*.
6 The roads were clear and we arrived home *in no time* / *for some time*.

3 » **Work in pairs. Turn to page 138.**

GRAMMAR Narrative tenses

WARMER

Put the students into six or nine groups depending on the class size (three to four students per group). Give each group a number, 1, 2 or 3. Tell group 1 to write down this sentence: 'When I arrived at the cinema, the film started.' Group 2 write: 'When I arrived at the cinema, the film was starting.' Group 3 write: 'When I arrived at the cinema, the film had started.' The groups then discuss exactly what their sentence means in terms of the order of events. Elicit explanations from the different groups. (*1 I got to the cinema and then the film started. 2 I got to the cinema and the opening scene was just coming on. 3 I missed some of the film.*)

1 Look at the text with the class and elicit the names of the three tenses and how we form positive sentences, negative sentences and questions using each one.

Answers
had settled; had … been: past perfect
wandered; bit; tapped: past simple
was asking: past continuous

2 Put students into pairs to match the tenses to the rules and then ask them to think of their own example sentences for each rule, for example, *a I got up, went downstairs and had breakfast. I was drinking coffee when the phone rang.* Monitor to make sure students are using the tenses correctly and elicit examples for each rule.

Answers
a past simple b past continuous c past perfect

» GRAMMAR REFERENCE AND PRACTICE ANSWER KEY TB PAGES 267–268

3 Students work alone and then compare answers in pairs. When everyone has finished, elicit the correct answers and ask students to say what rule each one corresponds to.

MIXED ABILITY

Weaker students also work in pairs but only look at three sentences each. One student starts from number 1 and works down, the other starts from number 6 and works up. Monitor while the students are doing the exercises and help those who are having problems by telling them which rule each sentence corresponds to (1 b, 2 a, 3 b, 4 c, 5 a, 6 c). Once they have completed three sentences each, if there is still time, they tell each other which verb forms they chose and why.

Answers
1 was travelling 2 sat down 3 were all sitting 4 had just reached
5 rushed off 6 had left

4 Ask students to cover the rules box. Read the extract with the class and elicit what tense the phrase in purple is and what it is used for. Students uncover the rules and complete the sentence. Compare the past perfect continuous with the present perfect continuous by comparing two sentences, for example:

'You're wet. What have you been doing?' 'I've been cycling in the rain.'

'You were wet when I saw you yesterday. What had you been doing?' 'I had been cycling in the rain.'

Answers
had been, verb

5 If students aren't sure of which tense to use ask them to imagine that they were doing a present perfect simple or present perfect continuous exercise. With a weaker class, you may want to do this in mixed ability pairs. Monitor and help where necessary and elicit the answers and the fact that 1–4 are describing longer actions whereas the last two are describing single events.

Answers
1 had been shouting 2 had been playing 3 had been crying
4 had been rushing 5 had called 6 had left

6 Look at the first sentence with the class and ask what two tenses the verb is in (*present simple and past simple*). Elicit when we use each one and which we need in this case (*the past because it is talking about a single, completed past action, the verb passed is also in the past simple*). Monitor and help where necessary. Elicit what two tenses the choice is between in each sentence, the correct answer and why it is correct.

FAST FINISHERS

Ask fast finishers to write similar sentences using the incorrect verb form from the sentences, for example, *1 I always feel relieved when I pass tests*. Invite the students to present these sentences and say what rule the sentence illustrates; in this case the present simple for a general truth.

Answers
1 felt 2 was reading 3 went 4 had changed 5 whistled

» GRAMMAR WORKSHEET UNIT 7

VOCABULARY Time phrases

1 Students complete the sentences in pairs. Elicit the answers and what each one means (*1 before long – soon afterwards; 2 in no time – very quickly; 3 for weeks on end – for many weeks in a row; 4 for some time – for quite a long time; 5 the week before last – two weeks ago; 6 for hours on end – for many hours*).

Answers
1 before 2 in 3 for 4 for 5 before 6 on

2 Look at the first sentence with the class. This is a different use of *before long* than in Exercise 1. In Exercise 1, it was a short time after a first event in the past. In this sentence it is used to talk about something happening in the near future. Students complete the activity alone and then compare in mixed ability pairs. Elicit the answers and the meanings of each expression.

Answers
1 before long 2 for hours on end 3 for weeks on end
4 for some time 5 the week before last 6 in no time

3 Look at the first sentence with the students. Elicit what year it is now and what year the year before last was. Elicit that their sentence should be in the past simple. Ask what form the verbs in the other sentences should be in (*2 Present perfect or present perfect continuous; 3 infinitive with* to*; 4 present simple; 5 infinitive with* to). Set a time limit for students to write their sentences. When they compare answers, encourage them to ask for more details, for example: *The year before last I learned how to ski. Really? Where did you go skiing? Did you enjoy it?* etc. Invite students to say one interesting thing they found out about their partner.

Answers
Students' own answers

» VOCABULARY WORKSHEET UNIT 7

WRITING A story

1 Ask students if they have ever looked after someone else's pet or children and whether this was a positive or negative experience. Then ask the class to read the task. Put the students into mixed ability pairs to describe what they think will happen in the story so that stronger students can help weaker students with ideas and language. Ask one or two pairs to tell you their ideas, and ask the rest of the class whether they have a very similar or different story.

Answers
Students' own answers

2 Ask the students to read the story and to compare it to their own version. Of the one or two stories your class heard, which was the most similar to this story?

Answer
Yes

3 Books closed. Ask students what they think a good story should include and write ideas on the board. Take a class vote to decide on the most important order. Books open. Give students a few minutes to read the *Prepare to write* box. Ask whether they think the story in Exercise 2 includes all of these features or not. Then ask them to match paragraphs A to D to the functions in the box. Check answers as a whole class.

Answers
A background information B opening events C developing story D ending

4 Students work alone. Allow students to compare answers in pairs and then invite stronger students to read one sentence of the story aloud each. When a student has a sentence which includes a gap, they use the time expression they think fits. As the students read the sentences aloud, other students check their own answers and correct them if necessary.

Answers
1 Just then 2 Before long 3 After 4 Later

5 Students discuss this in pairs for a few minutes. Ask three different volunteers to each explain the reason for the use of the three verb forms to the whole class.

Answers
had been raining – it started raining before Adam sighed and it was raining continuously until that point (past perfect continuous)
had disappeared – the action of the dog running out of the door started and finished before the action of Adam moving (past perfect)
were shaking – the action of shaking was happening at the time when the boys got on the bus (past continuous)

6 Tell students that in creative writing, it is good to use a wide range of vocabulary. Encourage them not to use the same word too often. Ask students to replace the highlighted words in pairs. They should check they have chosen the correct replacement by re-reading the whole sentence with the replacement in place.

Answers
ran – rushed; shouted – yelled; disappeared – vanished; looked – glanced; see – make out; happily – cheerfully

PREPARE FOR THE EXAM

B2 FIRST FOR SCHOOLS
Writing Part 2: A story

In this part, students have a choice of task. They may be asked to write an article, an email, a letter, a review or a story. As mentioned on TB page 42, there are five tasks in total, but students shouldn't attempt question 5 unless they have read the set reading text. They are given a clear context, topic, purpose and target reader. Students should write 140–190 words. If students choose the story, they should ensure that it links effectively to the first sentence, uses the prompts given and demonstrates both a wide vocabulary and an understanding of narrative tenses.

Tips Tell students to make sure that their story has a clear story line, with coherent linkers and good use of narrative tenses.

7 Give students a couple of minutes to read the task. Then ask them to discuss what they think might happen with a partner. Give them five to ten minutes to organise their ideas and to plan their story further. They could then compare these plans with a different partner.

Answers
Students' own answers

8 Before students start writing, tell them to spend about five minutes noting down useful vocabulary they could use in their stories, especially items from earlier in the unit, such as verbs of movement and sound and time phrases. Also encourage students to use a variety of narrative tenses in their answer. Afterwards, ask them to exchange their story with a partner. Their partner should look at the essay and check that the student has paid attention to each point in the *Prepare to write* box. Using their partner's story, they should underline the different verbs used. How many different tenses has their partner used? Have they used them accurately?

Model answer
Gina hurried over to Ted's house as soon as she heard the news. Her friend had texted to say that Ted had got back from hospital. Two days before, he had broken his arm and injured his right leg playing football, so he needed her help, especially as his parents were away on holiday and his older sister would be out at work all day.
When she got to his house, Gina saw there were three cars parked outside. She wondered whether she should leave – it looked as though Ted already had lots of visitors. She'd expected to see one or two people, but not a big crowd of strangers. Before long, the front door opened and she recognised Ted's football coach, who had come out to get something from his car. He waved at Gina and said, 'Have you come to see Ted? The whole team's inside and we're cooking spaghetti. Why not join us?' Gina said she couldn't stay for lunch, but asked the coach to tell Ted she had called round. She sighed and headed home. She would try again tomorrow.

» PREPARE FOR THE EXAM TEACHING NOTES AND ANSWER KEY TB PAGE 258

COOLER
Students work in groups of three or four. They choose one of their stories to turn into a film. They decide what sort of extra action they could include to make it long enough for a film and then choose well-known actors and actresses to play the parts of the main characters mentioned in the story. Invite each group to present their ideas to the class.

WRITING A story

1 **Read the task and look at the photo below. What do you think might happen in the story?**

You have seen this announcement on your school website.

> **Stories wanted**
>
> We are looking for stories for our website. Your story **must** begin with this sentence:
>
> *Adam wished he hadn't offered to look after Blanca while his cousin was on holiday.*
>
> Your story must include:
>
> - bad weather
> - a search

Write your **story**.

2 **Read the story. Does it contain any of your ideas? Does the story include the ideas mentioned in the task?**

A Adam wished he hadn't offered to look after Blanca while his cousin was on holiday. It had been raining heavily all day, but the dog needed some exercise. Adam sighed and gently stroked the animal's head.

B [1] ________, the front door of the house burst open. Adam's brother ran in and ran straight upstairs. Before Adam could move, Blanca had disappeared out of the open front door. 'Stevie!' Adam shouted. 'Blanca's escaped!' In no time the brothers were chasing after her. She was heading towards the park. Adam whistled loudly, but the dog ignored him. [2] ________, Blanca reached the park and disappeared.

C The brothers searched for the dog for hours on end without success. When they finally got on the bus to go home, they were shaking with cold. [3] ________ ten minutes, Stevie spoke. 'Look. We're going past Suzy's,' he said. Adam looked over at his cousin's house. Through the pouring rain, he could just see a dog on the doorstep. It was Blanca!

D [4] ________ that evening their cousin called and asked about her dog. 'Blanca's been fine,' said Adam happily. 'We took her out for a really long walk today!'

3 **Read the *Prepare to write* box, then read the story again. Match paragraphs A–D to the functions in the box.**

background information | developing the story | ending | opening events

PREPARE TO WRITE | Stories

A good story should

- include all the ideas mentioned in the task.
- be organised into paragraphs.
- have a clear beginning, middle and end.
- use suitable time expressions and different tenses to make it clear when actions happened in relation to other actions.
- use a range of vocabulary to make the story interesting or exciting.

4 **Complete the story with the time expressions.**

After | Before long | Just then | Later

5 **Explain why the writer uses these verb forms in the story.**

had been raining | had disappeared | were shaking

6 **Replace the highlighted words in the story with the words in the box.**

cheerfully | glanced | make out | rushed | vanished | yelled

PREPARE FOR THE EXAM

Writing Part 2 (A story)

7 **Read the task. Discuss what might happen in the story.**

You have seen this advertisement in a magazine.

> **Stories wanted**
>
> We are looking for stories for our magazine. Your story must **begin** with this sentence:
>
> *Gina hurried over to Ted's house as soon as she heard the news.*
>
> Your story must include:
>
> - a meal
> - an accident

Write your **story**.

8 **Write your story.**

- Use the tips in the *Prepare to write* box.
- Check your grammar and spelling.
- Write 140–190 words.

» PREPARE FOR THE EXAM PAGE 130

8 A GREAT PLACE TO LIVE

ABOUT YOU

06 **Watch the video and answer the questions.**

Where do you live and what do you like about it?

What do you think that young people can gain from studying abroad?

VOCABULARY Community

1 **Match the sentence halves. Are the adjectives used for people, places or both?**

EP

WHERE WOULD YOU LIKE TO LIVE?

When I leave home, I'd like to live …

1 somewhere quiet with a **relaxed**
2 somewhere busy and **urban**, with
3 in a place that's **remote** and **rural**, in
4 in a community which
5 somewhere friendly, with a **close** community, where
6 near an **industrial**
7 in a city that's culturally **diverse**, with shops

a the middle of nowhere.
b is **welcoming** and easygoing.
c atmosphere, like a **residential** suburb.
d estate, or in an **inner-city** neighbourhood.
e masses of **affordable** entertainment and leisure facilities.
f and **trendy** restaurants from around the world.
g everyone knows everyone else.

2 **Which kind of place would you like to live in? Discuss the sentences in Exercise 1.**

32 **3** **Listen to David, a British student, asking for advice about a place to study. Answer the questions.**

1 What is he going to do next year? Where?
2 Which adjectives from Exercise 1 describe his home town?
3 Which adjectives describe the city of Bristol?
4 Which adjectives describe the kind of place where he'd like to study?

READING

1 **Read the university recommendations written by five people (A–E). Match two of the recommendations to the photos on page 47.**

2 **Read the question and choose from the five people (A–E). Follow instructions 1–3.**

Which person recommends studying the local language?

1 Look at the underlined key words.
2 Find paragraphs that mention anything related to the underlined words.
3 Read these paragraphs and the question again carefully. Then choose the correct answer.

PREPARE FOR THE EXAM

Reading and Use of English Part 7

3 **Read the recommendations again. For questions 1–10, choose from the five people (A–E). The people may be chosen more than once.**

Which person

1 recommends a particular cold weather activity?
2 understands why one city's inhabitants have a particular approach to life?
3 mentions the quality of education at a recommended place of study?
4 is familiar with a city they do not study in themselves?
5 is impressed by the architecture of the city they recommend?
6 mentions a positive opinion of a programme of study by someone they know?
7 advises keeping an open mind about fellow students?
8 describes one place in a city that they enjoy visiting on a regular basis?
9 says they became relaxed when they went to view the university?
10 mentions one disadvantage for them of the university they attend?

4 **Find words or phrases in the recommendations to match the meanings.**

1 very interesting (A)
2 university buildings and the land that surrounds them (B)
3 in, from or to other countries (C)
4 start living somewhere you are going to live for a long time (D)
5 the size or level of something (E)

8 A GREAT PLACE TO LIVE

Unit Overview

TOPIC	Places where we live
VOCABULARY	Community
READING	University recommendations
GRAMMAR	Future (1): Review
VOCABULARY	*as if / as though*
LISTENING	A talk about a new skate park
SPEAKING	Comparing photographs (1)
EXAM TASKS	Reading and Use of English Part 7; Listening Part 2; Speaking Part 2

Resources

GRAMMAR REFERENCE AND PRACTICE: SB page 155; TB page 268
PREPARE FOR THE EXAM: SB pages on TB pages 244–245, 248 and 250–251; TB pages 257, 259 and 261
WORKBOOK: pages 32–35
VIDEO AND VIDEO WORKSHEET: Where we live
PHOTOCOPIABLE WORKSHEETS: Grammar worksheet Unit 8; Vocabulary worksheet Unit 8
TEST GENERATOR: Unit test 8
PRACTICE EXTRA: Unit 8

WARMER

Ask students to think of the best place they have ever been or somewhere they would like to live in the future. Tell the class that you would like to live in Paris and write the name of the city on the board. Elicit and write adjectives or nouns that relate to Paris, for example *romantic, historic, lively, expensive, tower, arch, good food, cathedral, river* (tell students not to give real names).

Students do the same in their groups. Set a time limit of two minutes. Each group then reads out their words and the other groups try to guess the places.

ABOUT YOU

06 You can begin the class and introduce the topic of the unit by showing the video and asking students to complete the video worksheet. Then, read the questions in the *About you* box. Put students in groups of three or four and elicit one idea for each question, for example, *1 It's quiet and safe. 2 They can learn about a different culture*. Set a time limit of three minutes for students to brainstorm more ideas then invite different groups to share their ideas with the class. Follow up by asking the students if they would think about studying abroad and, if not, why not.

VOCABULARY Community

1 Check students understand the meaning of the adjectives in blue by asking questions, such as *Which word is the opposite of* urban? *(rural); Which word is the opposite of* similar? *(diverse)* and *Which word is a synonym of* friendly? *(welcoming)*. Then ask students to match the two halves of the sentences and decide whether the adjectives are used for people, places or both. Ask students to check their answers with a partner before whole-class feedback. Elicit different ways of rephrasing each sentence, for example, *1 in a quiet, peaceful area of homes away from the city centre; 2 in a built up area with cheap entertainment; 3 in the countryside a long way from anywhere; 4 in a friendly, relaxed place; 5 a place where the residents chat to each other and get to know each other; 6 near factories or a manufacturing area or close to the city centre; 7 in a place where there are different cultures living together and there are fashionable restaurants*. If the students are from the same area, elicit which sentences describe it best. If not, ask them to describe the area that the school is in.

Answers
1 c 2 e 3 a 4 b 5 g 6 d 7 f

2 Look at the first sentence with the whole class and elicit some advantages and disadvantages of living there (*safe, friendly, boring*). Students do the same for the other places and then choose the best place for them, discussing their reasons in pairs. Invite students to share their opinions with the class.

Answers
Students' own answers

32 3 Ask students to read the questions. Ask if anyone knows where Bristol is. (*It is in the west of England near the Welsh border*.) Play the recording twice for students to take notes. Allow them to check their answers with a partner before whole-class feedback. Ask students to consider the answer to question 4 and suggest where John could study in their own country.

Answers
1 He is going to study abroad. He doesn't know where yet.
2 quiet, close, rural, remote, residential
3 industrial, relaxed
4 urban, trendy, diverse, welcoming

» AUDIOSCRIPT TB PAGE 292

READING

1 Ask the students to look at the two photos and say what they can see, where they think the places are and what they think each place is like. They then read the texts and find any words which help them to match the places described to the photos. When they have finished, elicit the five places mentioned in the texts and ask the students what they know about the different cities. You could give them some information about each university or city from the Background information box on page 90.

Answers
Recommendation A – Barcelona – photo bottom left (Sagrada Familia cathedral); recommendation E – Mexico City photo top right (Aztec pyramids, Teotihuacán)

2 Look at the instructions with the students. Elicit different ways of saying the underlined words, for example, *learning to speak … (for example Spanish)*. Elicit who made this recommendation and what words they used.

Answers
Ayaz (lines 4–7 of text B) says *It would make a difference if you learned some Turkish before coming.*

CONTINUED ON PAGE 90

BACKGROUND INFORMATION

The University of Barcelona has about 63,000 students and is generally recognised as being one of the best universities in Spain. It was King Alphonse V who created the Estudi General of Barcelona by unifying university education in 1450. The building mentioned in the text, The Forum, is a triangular building which was built for the Universal Forum of Cultures exhibition in 2004.

Koç University was established in 1993 and is now generally recognised as the best university in Turkey. There are about 7,000 students and over 95% of the courses are taught in English. The campus overlooks the Black Sea and Bosporus Strait.

Macquarie University is situated 15 km north-west of Sydney city centre. The university has its own railway station and there are several trains an hour to the centre of the city. When it opened in 1964, it became Sydney's third university.

Milan has seven universities including the University of Milan, Bocconi University (a business-focussed university) and the Politecnico di Milano, which is considered to be the best university in Italy. The total student population in the city is about 185,000.

Tecnológico de Monterrey was established in 1943 in the city of Monterrey in the north-east of Mexico. It is 200 km from the border with the USA. Since then it has expanded and now has 31 campuses in 25 different cities in Mexico.

PREPARE FOR THE EXAM

3 B2 FIRST FOR SCHOOLS Reading and Use of English Part 7

Briefly review what students need to do in this part of the exam and, if necessary, read out the *B2 First for Schools* box on TB page 17.

Encourage students to read each text before looking at the questions, noting key information in each one. This means that, when they look at the questions they have to match, they should be able to decide which texts they correspond to more quickly. Set a ten-minute time limit and elicit the answers as well as the information in the text which helped them to do the matching.

MIXED ABILITY

Put weaker students into pairs to compare the key information they noted when reading the different texts before they start doing the matching. This will enable them to add any information that they missed but their partner found.

FAST FINISHERS

Ask fast finishers to note the use of any synonyms and rephrasing in the text which gives the same information as the questions. When you elicit the answers to the activity, elicit this information as well, for example, *1 a cold weather activity – make use of the ski slopes.*

Answers

1 E (you should definitely make use of the ski slopes of Popocatépetl volcano)
2 C (Sydney really is an impressive city – no wonder everyone living here is so optimistic.)
3 B (It has an excellent reputation for its teaching)
4 D (I know Milan quite well because we visit relatives there every New Year. … I've already decided I'm going to settle there when I'm older.)
5 A (There are Gaudí's crazy, nature-inspired houses and his extraordinary Sagrada Familia cathedral, as well as incredible contemporary buildings like The Forum on the outskirts.)
6 E (A friend on the architecture course highly recommends it.)
7 D (You may find yourself sitting next to some very stylish classmates, but don't be put off)
8 A (my favourite spot is Parc de la Ciutadella, near the Old Town. … I spend a great deal of time there and it's somewhere I return to frequently.)
9 B (When I visited, the campus seemed quite a close community, which made me feel at home)
10 C (for me, the only drawback is the location)

33 The Reading text is recorded for students to listen, read and check their answers.

4 You could do this in groups of five. Each student looks for one of the words. When they have found their word, they help any other students who are finding it difficult to find their word. When they have all five words, tell students to close their books or cover the text and Exercise 4. Read out the meanings in a different order and elicit the words for each of them. You could follow up by asking the students to work in small groups to make sentences using the words. Invite groups to share their ideas and check that they have used the words correctly.

Answers

1 fascinating 2 campus 3 overseas 4 settle 5 scale

COOLER

Write these words on the board: *urban*, *dull*, *industrial*, *inner-city*, *welcoming*, *diverse*. Ask students to work in pairs and to note down the opposites of these words (*rural*, *interesting*, *residential*, *remote*, *unfriendly*, *similar*). In feedback, add the opposites to the board. Then erase the original words, and see if students can remember them from the opposites remaining.

UNIVERSITY RECOMMENDATIONS

Five young people recommend their favourite cities to study in

33

A MARTA

It sounds as if you'd love Barcelona. The main university dates from the 1450s, and there's a huge student population in the city, making it very culturally diverse. The inner-city neighbourhoods are full of fascinating streets, and there are squares with trendy cafés. The city isn't all old, though. There are Gaudí's crazy, nature-inspired houses and his extraordinary Sagrada Familia cathedral, as well as incredible contemporary buildings like The Forum on the outskirts. La Rambla is always busy with people walking up and down looking at the stalls, but my favourite spot is Parc de la Ciutadella, near the Old Town. There's always a performance or something going on. I spend a great deal of time there and it's somewhere I return to frequently. It's beautiful in every season. I'll probably go after lectures tomorrow.

B AYAZ

How about Turkey? I'm about to start at Koç University, 30 km from Istanbul city centre. It has an excellent reputation for its teaching, and international students are welcome. It would make a difference if you learned some Turkish before coming, but don't worry about the classes – all of the university's undergraduate degrees are taught in English. When I visited, the campus seemed quite a close community, which made me feel at home, and it's set in woodland, so it feels as if you're in the middle of nowhere, even though the city isn't far away. Istanbul itself is exciting because it's where the East meets the West and the old part of the city is a United Nations World Heritage Site.

C THOMAS

It would make sense to go to an Australian university – they cater for overseas students of all nationalities and languages. I'm at Macquarie University in Sydney and I love it. The campus is surrounded by parkland, so it actually feels as if it's quite rural. There's a friendly atmosphere and for me, the only drawback is the location. I live quite a distance away and there's only one bus an hour. There isn't much to do near the university, so most students meet up in a place called Surry Hills. There's always something going on there – I don't go very often myself, but there's an event there tomorrow I'm going to. The city has a fantastic outdoors lifestyle, and at the weekends you can check out the city's world-famous beaches – when the weather's warm enough, that is! Sydney really is an impressive city – no wonder everyone living here is so optimistic.

D VALERIO

You should consider Milan. Lots of places offer undergraduate degrees in architecture, often in English. I know Milan quite well because we visit relatives there every New Year. It's a lively university city, so you'll have a great social life. It's a major cultural centre too, with everything from theatre and opera to festivals and pop concerts. After you've spent a few weeks there, you'll never want to leave. I've already decided I'm going to settle there when I'm older. Milan is the centre of the Italian fashion industry, so it's great for window-shopping. You may find yourself sitting next to some very stylish classmates, but don't be put off – underneath, people are welcoming and down-to-earth.

E ABRIL

I study geography at the Tecnológico de Monterrey university, where all the classes are in English rather than Spanish. A friend on the architecture course highly recommends it. Mexico City is a massive urban centre with millions of things to do – you'll certainly never be bored. There are restaurants from every continent and lots of surprises – you should definitely make use of the ski slopes of Popocatépetl volcano at the weekends. And you can easily make your way out to the Aztec pyramids in the ancient city of Teotihuacán. If you're into archaeology, you'll definitely be impressed by the scale of the ruins. I'm a real fan and I'm going again next weekend.

TALKING POINTS

Which of the universities recommended would you like to study at? Why?

Do you think every young person should go to university? Why? / Why not?

A GREAT PLACE TO LIVE 47

GRAMMAR Future (1): review

1 Read the examples. Then complete the rules with the verb forms.

1 I'**m about to** start at Koç University …
2 It's a lively city, so you'**ll have** a great social life.
3 I've already decided I'**m going to settle** there when I'm older.
4 You **may** find yourself sitting next to some very stylish classmates.
5 It's beautiful in every season. I'**ll** probably **go** after lectures tomorrow.
6 There's always something going on there – there'**s** an event there tomorrow.
7 I'm a real fan and I'**m going** again next weekend.

be about to	*be going to*	*may*
~~present continuous~~	present simple	*will* (x2)

We use
a *present continuous* for plans and arrangements.
b ________ for regular, timetabled events.
c ________ for decisions you've just made.
d ________ for plans and intentions.
e *be going to* and ________ to make predictions.
f ________ / *might* / *could* for things that are possible in the future.
g ________ for events that are going to happen very soon.

» GRAMMAR REFERENCE AND PRACTICE PAGE 155

2 Read the examples and complete the rules. Do you use the same verb forms in your language?

1 After you'**ve spent** a few weeks there, you'll never want to leave.
2 I'm going to settle there when I'**m** older.

After time conjunctions (e.g. *when, after*), we use ________ simple or ________ perfect to talk about the future.

3 Read the text and choose the correct options.

We've been talking about what we [1] *do* / *'re going to do* after we [2] *will leave* / *leave* school. I [3] *won't start* / *'m not starting* university immediately because I've decided to have a year out, but I [4] *'ll definitely do* / *'m definitely going to do* a course the year after. I haven't chosen a subject yet. I'm fascinated by human behaviour, so I [5] *'m studying* / *might study* anthropology or social sciences, but I [6] *'ll make* / *am making* a decision later. I [7] *'m talking* / *'m about to talk* to a careers adviser. After I [8] *will speak* / *have spoken* to her, I'll have a clearer idea.

48 UNIT 8

4 Correct the mistake in each sentence.

1 Have you decided what you going to do at uni?
2 I think I call my friend Anna to see how she is.
3 We could to visit the market in town.
4 The train will leaves at exactly 8 am every morning.
5 I go to the shop and get some more chocolate.

5 Complete the sentences about you. Then compare your answers.

1 When I'm older, …
2 I … university.
3 After I've done my homework, I …
4 This weekend, I …
5 I'm about to …

VOCABULARY *as if / as though*

1 Choose the correct meaning for each example.

EP
1 *It feels* ***as if*** */* ***as though*** *it's going to rain.*
a It's definitely going to rain.
b I think it's going to rain.

2 *It sounds* ***as if*** */* ***as though*** *we won't have enough money.*
a I don't think we will have enough money.
b We may have enough money.

3 *He was behaving* ***as if*** */* ***as though*** *he'd received some bad news.*
a He may have received some bad news.
b He might receive some bad news.

4 *It looks* ***as if*** */* ***as though*** *the train's going to be late.*
a The train might not be late.
b The train will probably be late.

2 Read the examples again and complete the rules.

1 We use *as if* and *as though* to talk about situations that *seem to be true* / *are definitely true*.
2 *As if* and *as though* have *the same meaning* / *different meanings*.

3 Make sentences about the people in the picture. Use *look + as if / as though*.

buy a paper	cross the road
get some crisps	like keeping fit
need a new umbrella	~~see something annoying~~
shout to a friend	walk into the lamppost

1 *She looks as though she's seen something annoying.*

GRAMMAR Future (1): Review

WARMER

Put the students into five groups. Give each group a task to discuss:

1 Plans you have for the next few days
2 Arrangements you have made with other people for the next few days
3 Events that are timetabled that you regularly go to
4 Something that could possibly happen in the next few days
5 A prediction about your future life

Set a time limit of three minutes for groups to discuss ideas and then invite each group to share their ideas with the class. For each group, write one of their ideas on the board in note form, without using the correct grammatical form, for example 1 – go shopping / Saturday, 2 – have a party / Friday. When the students have done Exercise 1, you could elicit the correct grammatical forms for the notes on the board from the class.

1 Look at the first sentence with the class and ask: *Has the speaker started university?* (*No*) and *Will they start soon?* (*Yes*). Students look at the other sentences in pairs and decide what they mean and then complete the activity. Elicit the answers and alternative sentences using the language in purple, for example, *We're about to look at some grammar rules* and *You'll have a great time if you come to our party,* etc.

Answers
b present simple c will d be going to e will f may g be about to

» GRAMMAR REFERENCE AND PRACTICE ANSWER KEY TB PAGE 268

2 Look at the first sentence and rephrase it to show why we use the present perfect, for example, *I've spent a few weeks here now and I don't want to leave!* For the second sentence, tell students that there are several time expressions, which are followed by the present simple even though they refer to the future, for example, *if, when* and *as soon as.*

Answers
present, present

3 Students should read the text all the way through first before making their decisions so they get a feel for the overall meaning and time frame. Then ask them to work in pairs to choose the correct verb forms. Remind them to look at the rules in Exercise 1 to help them. Check answers as a class.

FAST FINISHERS

Ask fast finishers to look at the first sentence of the text and then think about what they would say if they were in this situation. When everyone has finished the exercise, invite fast finishers to tell the class about what they might do after they leave school.

Answers
1 're going to do 2 leave 3 'm not starting 4 'm definitely going to do / 'll definitely do 5 might study 6 'll make 7 'm about to talk 8 have spoken

4 Tell students to work alone and write the correct sentences on a piece of paper. They then swap papers with a partner. Elicit the answers and tell students to correct their partner's sentences where necessary. Students then swap back their answer sheets to see how many they got correct.

Answers
1 Have you decided what you **'re/are** going to do at uni?
2 I think I **'ll/will** call my friend Anna to see how she is.
3 We could ~~to~~ visit the market in town.
4 The train ~~will~~ leaves at exactly 8 am every morning.
5 I **'ll/will** go to the shop and get some more chocolate.

5 Elicit how the students could continue the first sentence, for example; *I think I'll …, I'm going to …; I might …* or *I'd like to … .* You could give an answer about yourself first, such as *When I'm older, I'm going to retire and travel around the world.* Monitor and help if necessary. When students have compared in pairs, invite students to share some of their ideas with the class.

Answers
Students' own answers

» GRAMMAR WORKSHEET UNIT 8

VOCABULARY *as if / as though*

1 Explain that in this exercise *as if* and *as though* are synonyms (not words they have to choose between). Read the sentences 1–4 aloud and ask for a show of hands for the two options each time. If there is disagreement, ask one person who voted for *a* and one who voted for *b* to explain their choice. In stronger classes, you could tell students that English speakers sometimes use *look/sound/feel* with *like* instead of *as if/as though*. This is grammatically incorrect. In correct English, *like* is followed by a noun (*He looks like a teacher*) whereas *as if / as though* are followed by a verb phrase.

Answers
1 b 2 a 3 a 4 b

2 Look at this with the whole class and elicit the answers. Then, ask students for more examples of the structure, such as *It looks as if some of the students are going to fall asleep!* You could put students in pairs to think of some more sentences and then invite them to share these with the class.

Answers
1 seem to be true 2 the same meaning

3 Look at the example sentence with the class. You could ask students to cover the ideas and try to make their own sentences about the people in the picture first, then look at the box and use the ideas given to make sentences. When you have elicited sentences, invite students to share their own sentences with the class if they are different, and see if other students can guess who they refer to.

MIXED ABILITY

Put weaker students into pairs and encourage them to write sentences for three of the people and then talk about them so that they have more time to think about the correct forms to use. Monitor and help where necessary. Once they have written three sentences, tell them to try to talk about the other people in the picture without writing about them.

Possible answers
2 It looks as if he's buying a paper. 3 It looks as though the cyclist is about to cross the road. 4 It looks as if he's getting some crisps. 5 It looks as though she likes keeping fit. 6 It looks as if he's shouting to a friend. 7 It looks as though he's about to walk into a lamppost. 8 It looks as if she needs a new umbrella.

» VOCABULARY WORKSHEET UNIT 8

LISTENING

1 Look at the first gap with the students. Tell them not to think of a specific word, for example *teacher* but the kind of word it could be, for example, a job, a kind of person (man, woman). Students work in pairs to think about the kind of information they need for each gap. Elicit ideas from different pairs.

Possible answers

1 a job title 2 a loan or other form of money 3 an event 4 an amount of money 5 a verb with the *-ing* form 6 information / photos or something similar you can see on a website 7 an event aimed at making a decision 8 a material 9 something printed you can look at 10 a kind of building

PREPARE FOR THE EXAM

B2 FIRST FOR SCHOOLS
Listening Part 2

In this part, students listen to a monologue and have to complete ten sentences. The focus is on listening for detail and identifying specific information and stated opinion; often the sentences are in the form of statements of opinion, e.g. *Anna was impressed by …* . Students shouldn't rephrase the words in the recording and won't need more than three words in each gap. Most gaps require only one or two words. Numbers can be written in numerical form.

Tips Tell students to read the sentences with the missing words carefully before listening, and think about the type of information that might be needed to complete each one. Minor spelling mistakes won't be penalised unless it makes the answer unclear.

34 2 Tell students to use abbreviations while writing so that they don't spend too long writing and miss the next piece of information. As long as they can understand their notes, they will have time to write the answers in full when the recording has finished. Do not check the answers.

34 3 When students compare answers, tell them not to change their answers yet or fill in any gaps that they missed. Ask them to notice the correct information when they listen again and write the answers then. Elicit the answers and ask how many of their guesses in Exercise 1 were correct.

Answers

1 restaurant owner 2 (government) grant 3 concert 4 200,000 5 planning 6 video clips 7 vote 8 steel 9 drawings 10 factory

» AUDIOSCRIPT TB PAGES 292–293

» PREPARE FOR THE EXAM TEACHING NOTES AND ANSWER KEY TB PAGE 259

SPEAKING Comparing photographs (1)

1 Look at the instructions with the students and tell them not to write a full script of what to say but just brief notes. Write this list vertically on the board: *similarities – small, rural …; differences –; advantages –; disadvantages –; my home town –*

Students work in pairs. Set a time limit of two minutes then elicit ideas and add them to the board. Students give their own answers.

35 2 When students have listened, they compare notes in pairs. Elicit what the speakers said and ask students whether they think the answers were good or not and why.

Answers

1 similarities: small, rural, peaceful, not many facilities, not culturally diverse; differences: size and design of the houses, weather, standards of living, wealth
2 six (size, facilities, crime, community style, weather and lifestyle)
3 Students' own answers

» AUDIOSCRIPT TB PAGE 293

36 3 Go through the *Prepare to speak* box with the class. When they have listened to Track 35 a second time, elicit the full sentences used for each phrase that the speakers used. Play Track 36 to confirm answers.

» AUDIOSCRIPT TB PAGE 293

PREPARE FOR THE EXAM

B2 FIRST FOR SCHOOLS
Speaking Part 2

In this part, students have an individual one-minute 'long turn' each with a brief 30-second response from the second student afterwards. In turn, students are given two photographs to talk about. The second student shouldn't say anything until asked to by the examiner.

Tips The question that students should address is written above the photos so they don't have to remember it, but they should listen carefully to the instructions and make sure they answer the question asked, for example, Thalía has to talk about what people might enjoy about life in the two villages. It can feel quite unnatural to speak about a picture for one minute as it's not something most people do in normal life. Give students a range of pictures to practise speaking about to make the task seem more natural.

4 Put the students in pairs and nominate who will be student A in each pair. Give the students about 20 seconds to read the instructions and think about what they are going to say. Remind them that in the exam they won't read the instructions, they will have to listen carefully to the examiner. When they are ready, tell them when to start and tell them again when one minute has passed. Do the same for the 30 seconds B has to speak for. Students give their own answers.

5 Students turn to page 138 and read the instructions. Repeat the procedure for Exercise 4, telling students when the time has passed. Now invite three students to act out the exam in front of the class. One plays the role of the examiner and chooses the task in either Exercise 4 or 5. The other two play the roles of students A and B. The examiner reads out the instructions and times the activity. Students give their own answers.

» PREPARE FOR THE EXAM TEACHING NOTES AND ANSWER KEY TB PAGE 261

COOLER

Tell students to look at the two photos on pages 138–139 again. They work alone to think of a different question they could ask Student A and B in an exam using these two photos, for example, *What time of year would you like to visit them?*, *Which looks most similar to where you live?*, etc. Monitor and help with ideas where necessary. Then put students into groups of three. The students take turns in playing the role of examiner, asking the other two students their questions. When they have finished, ask students if the other two students listened to the task carefully and answered the questions they were asked.

LISTENING

1 **You will hear a teenager called Anna Asher talking about a new skate park. Read the sentences and predict what you might hear.**

Anna says that the leader of the action group is a **(1)** __________ who works locally.

Anna was pleased that the group leader was able to help them apply for a **(2)** __________.

Anna and her friends raised money by arranging a **(3)** __________ and doing different jobs.

After six months, the group had almost reached their target of **(4)** £ __________.

A local resident became involved in **(5)** __________ the project.

Anna was impressed by the **(6)** __________ on one company's website.

A **(7)** __________ was held at a community meeting to agree who would design the skate park.

Anna says that **(8)** __________ is the main material used in a jump for BMX riders called the 'whale tail'.

Anna liked the **(9)** __________ which the main designer gave the group to look at.

The skate park was built on land where a **(10)** __________ once stood.

PREPARE FOR THE EXAM

Listening Part 2

2 **Listen. For questions 1–10, complete the sentences with a word or short phrase.** (Audio 34)

3 **Compare your answers with your partner's. Then listen again and check.** (Audio 34)

» PREPARE FOR THE EXAM PAGE 132

SPEAKING Comparing photographs (1)

1 **You are going to compare two photographs. Look at the photographs below. They show two different kinds of village. Then read points 1–3 and make notes. Think about:**

1. similarities and differences between the two photographs
2. advantages and disadvantages of living in each village
3. how your home town differs from these villages

2 (Audio 35) **Listen to Thalía and Oleg comparing the photographs in an exam. Answer the questions.**

1. What similarities and differences between the photographs does Thalía mention?
2. How many comparisons does Oleg make between St Petersburg and the villages in the photographs?
3. How many of your ideas do they mention?

3 (Audio 36) **Read the *Prepare to speak* box. Then listen to Thalía and Oleg using the phrases.**

PREPARE TO SPEAK Comparing and contrasting

The main difference is …
Both of these places are …
Neither place looks as though …
It looks …, whereas the other village is …
While the village in the first photograph has …, the village in the second photograph has …
On the other hand, I assume that …

PREPARE FOR THE EXAM

Speaking Part 2

4 **Work in pairs.**

Student A: Compare the two photographs. Say what advantages and disadvantages the people living in these villages may have. Use phrases from the *Prepare to speak* box.

Student B: Which of these two villages would you prefer to live in? Why?

5 » **Turn to page 138 and complete the task.**

» PREPARE FOR THE EXAM PAGE 134

LIFE SKILLS CREATIVITY AND INNOVATION

CREATIVE WRITING

1 **Ask and answer the questions with a partner.**

1 How easy do you find it to express your thoughts and feelings? Can you give an example?
2 When was the last time you wrote a piece of creative writing using just your imagination? What was it? How did you feel?

2 **In pairs, think of some tips and ideas for writing creatively. Then read the text on the opposite page quickly and see if any of your ideas are mentioned.**

3 **Read the text again and complete the sentences with one or two words in each gap.**

1 Poetry, storytelling and sharing experiences are a form of ________ for many people.
2 Start by writing about ________ and ________ that you know personally.
3 Besides writing as much as you can, you should also be doing lots of ________.
4 As far as possible, aim to ________ things clearly and in detail.
5 Looking forward to people reading your writing can give you a feeling of ________.

4 **Match the highlighted words in the text to the meanings.**

1 something that is silly or stupid
2 attract and keep someone's attention
3 showing your personality, emotions or ideas, especially through art, music or acting
4 to a great degree
5 at the beginning of something

LIFE SKILLS

Creative writing

Creativity means using our imagination to create something new or unusual. Creative writing is an excellent way to explore our own creativity. Learning creative writing skills can help us to express our thoughts and feelings more clearly. It can also build confidence and help us become better readers and writers.

5 (37) **Listen to a radio interview with Zack, a creative writing expert. What do the creative writing exercises all have in common?**

6 (37) **Listen again and match the creative writing exercises (1–4) to the writing area that each one develops (a–e). There is one extra writing area that you don't need.**

Creative writing exercises	Writing areas
1 Round Robin	a point of view
2 Who on Earth is it?	b creative descriptions
3 What's in a list?	c plot development
4 Guess the celebrity!	d elements of a story
	e character development

7 **Complete the sentences with the words in the box.**

background	collaborate	imagination
interests	provoke	

USEFUL LANGUAGE

Talking about creative writing

1 We need to use our ________.
2 It's a good idea to write a description of the character's ________.
3 The opening lines should ________ a reaction in the readers.
4 We can express our personal ________ in our creative writing.
5 Try to connect and ________ with other writers.

LIFE SKILLS

Learning Objectives

- The students learn how to use their imagination to be more creative in their writing.
- In the project stage, the students use tips on creative writing that they heard in the recording to help them create a piece of written work. They then share their work with the class.

Vocabulary

hook hugely nonsense opening self-expression

BACKGROUND INFORMATION

Before humans could read and write, stories were passed on from generation to generation by people telling them. The oldest surviving printed story is Gilgamesh from about 2100 BC. This epic poem tells the story of Gilgamesh, the king of Uruk and Enkido, a wild man created by the gods.

In the 4th century BC, Aesop's fables were first written down. His stories are still popular today and each one contains a message about life. Many popular sayings that we use today come from Aesop's stories, for example, A bird in the hand is worth two in the bush; Look before you leap and Slow and steady wins the race. This last one comes from perhaps his most famous story, *The Hare and the Tortoise*.

Creative writing courses can be taken at universities, online or at evening classes. As well as training the students to write, they also introduce students to a wide range of writing styles.

WARMER

Write a sentence on the board: *A man walked down a street.* Put students into small groups of three or four. Tell the groups that this is the beginning of a story. They should work together to write the first paragraph by making the first sentence more interesting and then adding more information by answering questions readers might want to know (what, where, when, how, why). Set a time limit and then ask each group to read out their introduction.

LIFE SKILLS

Creative writing

Tell students to read the information. Ask students what kinds of creative writing they can think of, for example, novels, short stories, poems, scripts, essays. Ask which creative, imaginative authors or writers the students like and why.

1 Before students look at the questions, elicit if they create anything by asking, 'Do you write stories, poems, blogs or scripts?'; 'Do you make your own video games?' and 'Do you draw pictures, design video games or make comics?'. Put students into groups of four to discuss what they do and invite groups to share their information with the class. Students then work in pairs to discuss the questions in the book together. Elicit ideas from different students then ask them if they ever write for an audience, for example, by posting something online or if they ever write just for themselves.

Answers

Students' own answers

2 Elicit or give the students an example to start, for example, '*use real events that have happened to you or people you know so that you don't have to think about what happened and can concentrate on being creative with descriptions and imagining why it happened and how people felt*'. Set a time limit of two minutes for pairs to think of more tips before they look at the text. Elicit what ideas were mentioned and any other tips they thought of which weren't mentioned.

Answers

Students' own answers

3 Set a time limit of ten minutes. Tell students that sometimes the correct words will be exactly the same as in the text but on other occasions they will have to change the word, for example, from a noun to a verb. When students have finished, they can compare in pairs before giving the answers.

FAST FINISHERS

Ask fast finishers to think of a great line from a story, poem or song lyric that they think is a good example of creative writing. If possible, allow them to use their phones to look up the line to check that they can remember it perfectly. When everyone has finished the reading, elicit the answers and then invite fast finishers to share their examples with the class, explaining why they like them so much.

Answers

1 self-expression 2 places, characters 3 reading 4 describe 5 excitement

38 The Reading text is recorded for students to listen, read and check their answers.

4 Tell students to cover the meanings and to look at the highlighted words and the sentences they appear in. Ask them to work in pairs to try to decide what they mean and then look at the meanings to see how close their guesses were.

Answers

1 nonsense 2 hook 3 self-expression 4 hugely 5 opening

CONTINUED ON PAGE 98

37 **5** Before students listen, put them into groups of four to discuss what they do before they start writing a story or something else creative, for example, *research information, talk to other people, think about how the story begins and ends,* etc. Set a time limit of two minutes for them to share ideas. Invite each group to share their ideas with the class. Stronger students or classes could also try to guess what the creative writing exercises they are going to hear about might have in common. When the students have listened, elicit the answer to the question and ask the students if any of the activities were similar to their own ideas.

Answer

All of them are for creative writing in groups.

37 **6** Students look at the creative writing exercises (1–4) and what they teach (writing areas, a–e) and discuss any that they can remember. When they have listened again, elicit the answers. Then put the students into four or more groups. Give each group an activity to listen out for. Play the recording again and the students in each group make notes about their activity. They then work together to share the information they heard and discuss how to explain the activity to the class. Give them two or three minutes and then invite groups to explain their activity. Encourage the other students to make notes as they will need to carry out one of the activities in the project.

Answers

1 c 2 e 3 d 4 a

>> **AUDIOSCRIPT TB PAGES 293–294**

7 Tell the students to look at the words in the box and see how many they know or can guess the meanings of. They then complete as many of the sentences as they can and try to guess any they don't know. Elicit the answers and what the words mean. Ask follow-up questions, for example, *When did you last use your imagination?; What are your personal interests?* or *When do you collaborate with other people?.* Also give them other tasks, for example, put the students in pairs and ask them to describe the background of a character from a book or a film. Invite students to tell the class without mentioning the character's name. The other students guess who the character is. Finally, read a famous opening line and ask the class what it means and how they react to it, for example *'If music be the food of love, play on.'* (from *Twelfth Night* by Shakespeare).

MIXED ABILITY

With weaker classes, put students into groups of five. Each student looks at one of the words in the box, using a dictionary if necessary to find out what it means. They each then explain their word to their group and tell them which sentence they think it completes. Elicit the answers and the definitions students found. Stronger students could write their own sentences using some of the words in the box and read these out when everyone has finished.

Answers

1 imagination 2 background 3 provoke 4 interests
5 collaborate

PROJECT *Creative writing in groups*

Look at the instructions with the students. If you did the extra activity in Exercise 6, the students will know exactly what each writing exercise entails. If not, you could play track 37 again and elicit details of each. Have at least one group for each task. Allow the students time to do the activity in the classroom, preferably about 20 minutes to half an hour. If they choose to do *Who on Earth is it?* they can use a photo of someone who isn't famous from the Student's Book.

When students present their writing to the class, they can also give feedback to the class about how they felt during the activity and whether they would recommend it, both as a way to help their writing and as an enjoyable activity to do together. When all the students have finished their presentations, invite students to say which activity/activities apart from their own they thought was the most interesting or useful and why.

PROJECT EXTENSION

After the students have all completed and presented their writing activities, ask them to think alone about anything they learned from the activities that they might use again, for example, when they are asked to write a story at home or in an exam, and how they could adapt them so that they could still be helpful even without anyone else to work with. Students then discuss their ideas in pairs or small groups and work together to make a poster with their ideas about what they can do to improve their writing when working alone. Display these around the classroom so that all the students can look at them.

COOLER

Have some quotes about writing on pieces of paper and display them around the room. Tell the students to walk round the class in pairs looking at the quotes and discussing what exactly they mean and which ones they find the most interesting or inspirational. They should note these down on a piece of paper. When students have read them all, invite students to discuss their favourite quotes and why they like them. You could follow up by asking students to look up other quotes in their pairs and then invite each pair to present their quote to the class.

https://www.inc.com/glenn-leibowitz/50-quotes-from-famous-authors-that-will-inspire-yo.html

Examples:

'If there's a book that you want to read, but it hasn't been written yet, then you must write it.' – Toni Morrison

'Read, read, read. Read everything – trash, classics, good and bad, and see how they do it. Just like a carpenter who works as an apprentice and studies the master. Read! You'll absorb it. Then write. If it's good, you'll find out. If it's not, throw it out of the window.' – William Faulkner

'Here is a lesson in creative writing. First rule: Do not use semi-colons … All they do is show you've been to college.' – Kurt Vonnegut Jr.

'I kept always two books in my pocket, one to read, one to write in.' – Robert Louis Stevenson

'You can make anything by writing.' – C.S. Lewis

CREATIVE WRITING 101

Why 101, I hear you ask? Well, 101 is the number often used to describe an introductory course in something, one where students don't need any previous knowledge of the subject. So if you have no, or very little, experience of creative writing, then you're reading the right article!

Creative writing is an art – the art of painting with words. It's not academic or technical, but something freer – a form of self-expression. Creative writing entertains an audience through storytelling or poetry and sharing common human experiences like fear, love, hope or joy. It can also be found in many different places, such as on stage, on the big screen, or in a speech delivered to a room full of people. And of course, in a novel or short story.

When you begin your creative writing journey, write about places and characters that you are familiar with and use language that you already know. Your personal background and experience are a great place to start! Later, be brave and use your imagination to write about things that you're not familiar with: places, periods in history or even a whole new world! There are those who think that creative writing is nonsense because it's not about real people and situations. In fact, that's exactly the beauty of it.

It's important that you write what you really want to write first, focusing completely on telling the story you want to tell. Then, when you re-read your writing, you can make changes so that it sounds as if you are *speaking* to your audience. In addition to writing as often as you can, you also need to be reading, and reading a lot! Surround yourself with literary works and become absorbed in each unique world.

Aim to hook your readers from the very first moment. The opening sentences should provoke a reaction in your reader, like making them laugh, or curious to know what happens next. Make your reader feel some kind of emotion. Try to use detailed descriptions – using sensations such as smells, sounds and feelings – in your writing whenever possible, ones that will create clear images in the reader's mind. Finally, allow your characters to tell the story through what they themselves do and say.

Last, but definitely not least, make sure that you enjoy the writing process. And when it comes around, finishing your first story will be a hugely satisfying moment. The excitement of looking forward to it being published and read by others will really make you feel like a writer!

PROJECT *Creative writing in groups*

Work in groups of three or four to practise your creative writing. Use these steps to help you.

1 Choose one of the group creative writing exercises from the radio interview.
2 Complete the exercise together and take turns to share your writing with the class.
3 Discuss your reaction to each group's writing and agree on some feedback to help them improve their story.

REVIEW 2 UNITS 5–8

VOCABULARY

1 Match the words to the meanings.

ancestor century citizen decade myth tribe

1 a group of people who have a traditional way of life
2 a period of ten years
3 someone who lives in a particular town or city
4 an ancient story that may explain an event in history
5 a period of 100 years, especially used in giving dates
6 a relative who lived a long time ago

2 Complete the sentences by adding an adverb from the box in the best place.

constantly occasionally regularly

1 He goes to the swimming pool, most often on a Saturday.
2 She's so careless! She's breaking things.
3 He apologises to people, but very rarely.

alternatively definitely outside

4 She's been ill for weeks now, so she needs to see a doctor.
5 It's lovely and sunny. Why don't we have lunch?
6 You may use the computers in the library. You can use the laptops in room 23.

3 Match the sentence halves.

1	I don't get anxious	a	of heights.
2	I'm so fed up	b	with this awful weather!
3	I'm petrified	c	about exam results.
4	He's furious	d	with second best.
5	I was a bit irritated	e	about what you said.
6	I'm never content	f	by all their questions.

4 Complete the conversation with suitable adjectives.

Adrian: Has your family always lived in Moscow?
Olga: No. In fact, my grandparents grew up in a really [0] *remote* area called Altai.
Adrian: That's in the middle of nowhere!
Olga: Yes, but they loved it. The [1] r________ way of life at that time was much more [2] r________ than the motorways and [3] i________ estates of modern [4] u________ life. It's a beautiful area, and their village was a [5] c________ community where everyone knew everyone else. The people were much more friendly and [6] w________ than in a city.

GRAMMAR

1 Complete the sentences with the correct forms for present and past habits.

1 When I was younger, I ________ into trouble. (constantly / get)
2 We ________ in the sea every day as children. (swim)
3 You ________ reasons not to visit these days! (always / find)
4 I'm lucky because I ________ my friends most weekends. (see)
5 He ________ of headaches. He should see a doctor. (constantly / complain)
6 My cousin and I ________ games for hours when we were children. (play)

2 Complete the sentences with the correct future form of the verbs in brackets.

1 When you ________ (finish) your exams, you'll be able to relax.
2 'Have you chosen a university course yet?' 'Yes, I ________ (study) Italian.'
3 The bus ________ (leave) in 20 minutes.
4 I think I ________ (buy) some new headphones with the money my grandma's given me.
5 Jed's still here, but he ________ (about to / leave), so you'll have to be quick if you want to talk to him.
6 I'm stuck in traffic, so I ________ (arrive) a bit late. I'm not sure what time yet.
7 The food all looks lovely. I think I ________ (have) a piece of that cake.
8 I ________ (meet) Jen on Saturday morning. Why don't you come too?

3 Complete the sentences with the correct form of *be/get used to*.

1 I had never driven a car before, but I ________ it quite quickly once I started.
2 I ________ washing up; I do it all the time.
3 The course was hard at first because I ________ still ________ studying for eight hours a day.
4 When we were living in Madrid, I ________ watching films in Spanish.

4 Correct the mistake in each sentence. There may be more than one way to correct the mistake.

1 Every night, we were going to the cinema and it was fantastic.
2 My mother told me that the old lady who was telling us stories died.
3 I've been disappointed many times in my life, so I have used it.
4 He saw a woman he never met before.
5 Try drinking more water and you are going to see a difference in how awake you feel!

REVIEW 2 UNITS 5–8

Overview

VOCABULARY	History; Expressing frequency; Expressing emotions; Adverbs: type and position; Community
GRAMMAR	Present and past habits; *be / get used to*; Narrative tenses; Future (1): review
EXAM TASKS	Reading and Use of English Part 1; Reading and Use of English Part 2; Reading and Use of English Part 3

Resources

PHOTOCOPIABLE WORKSHEETS: Grammar worksheets Units 5–8; Vocabulary worksheets Units 5–8; Review Game Units 5–8; Literature worksheet; Speaking worksheet; Writing worksheet

WARMER

Put students into groups of three or four. Give each group a grammar point from the previous four units, but do this quietly so that other groups can't hear. The groups think of an example sentence for their grammar point. Invite each group to read out their sentence and ask the other groups to say what the grammar point is.

VOCABULARY

1 Tell the students to cover the meanings and look at the box of words. They choose one that they are sure they know the meaning of. Students then mingle and tell each other which word they chose and what it means. Allow students to talk to as many people as possible in about two minutes, then they sit down again and complete the matching. Ask students how close other people's meanings were to the ones given in the book.

Answers

1 tribe 2 decade 3 citizen 4 myth 5 century 6 ancestor

2 Students work alone and then compare answers in pairs. Elicit the answers and then invite students to make the first three sentences true for themselves. Model the first sentence about yourself, for example, *I rarely go to the swimming pool, about once or twice a year*.

MIXED ABILITY

As there are two parts to this activity, you could tell the weaker students which adverbs match the first three sentences and then just ask them to rewrite the sentences with the adverbs in the correct place. For the second group of sentences, ask the students to match the adverbs to the correct sentences and only think about where they should go when they have matched all three. If they don't have time, they can wait until you get feedback from other students.

Answers

1 He regularly goes …
2 She's constantly breaking …
3 He occasionally apologises …
4 … she definitely needs to see …
5 … Why don't we have lunch outside?
6 … Alternatively, you can use the laptops in room 23.

3 Tell students to cover the endings. Elicit the meaning of each adjective and then ask students to work in pairs make notes of how they could complete each beginning so that they are true for them. They then uncover the endings to do the matching and see if they used the correct prepositions in their examples. Elicit the answers and some of the students' own endings that they thought of before doing the exercise.

FAST FINISHERS

Ask fast finishers to think of questions to ask using the same adjective + prepositions that are used in the exercise. These can be open (*What do you get anxious about?*) or closed (*Do you get anxious about exam results?*). When everyone has finished and you have elicited the answers, invite fast finishers to ask their questions to the class and elicit answers from different students.

Answers

1 c 2 b 3 a 4 e 5 f 6 d

4 Tell students to read the dialogue very quickly without worrying about the gaps yet. Elicit where Olga lives now (*Moscow*) and where her grandparents grew up (*Altai*). Ask if Olga is generally positive or negative about Altai (*positive*). Students then work in pairs to think about what the missing words could be. Elicit the answers and what each word means.

Possible answers

1 rural 2 relaxed 3 inner-city 4 urban 5 close 6 welcoming

GRAMMAR

1 Elicit when we use *used to* (*past habits and states*), the past or present continuous for habits (*when they are seen to be annoying*) and *would* (*past habits but not states*). Tell students that sometimes more than one answer may be possible. Students work in pairs. Monitor and help where necessary. Elicit the answers and any alternatives that students may have written.

Answers

1 was constantly getting 2 used to / would swim 3 're/are always finding 4 see 5 's/is constantly complaining / constantly complains 6 used to / would play

2 Tell students to work alone and then compare answers in pairs. If they have different answers, they should look at the rules on Student's Book page 48 to try to decide the best answer. Elicit the answers and which rule each one corresponds to.

Answers

1 finish 2 'm/am going to study 3 leaves 4 'll/will buy 5 's/is about to leave 6 'm/am going to arrive 7 'll/will have 8 'm/am meeting

CONTINUED ON PAGE 102

3 Elicit when we use *to be used to* (*when a situation seems normal*) and when we use *get used to* (*with different tenses to show what stage of getting used to something we are at*). Elicit that *(have) got used to* has the same meaning as *am used to* because both show that the stage of getting used to something has now finished. Students work in pairs. Elicit the answers and the situation now for each sentence (*1 the speaker is used to driving and they got used to it in the past; 2 it's normal for the speaker; 3 probably the speaker is now used to studying because they are talking about the past; 4 The speaker may have got out of the habit again now as they don't live in Spain any more.*).

Answers

1 got used to 2 'm/am used to 3 was, getting used to
4 got used to / was used to

4 Look at the instructions with the class and tell them that there are three ways of correcting the first sentence. Elicit what these three ways are (*past simple, used to, would*) and why all three are possible (*because this is a habitual action in the past*). Students work alone and then compare answers in pairs. Elicit the answers and any alternatives that students have written to make sure they are correct.

Answers

1 Every night, we **went** / **used to go** / **would go** to the cinema and it was fantastic.
2 My mother told me that the old lady **who told** / **would tell** / **used to tell** us stories died.
3 I've been disappointed many times in my life, so I **have got used to** / **I'm used to** it.
4 He saw a woman he **had never met** before.
5 Try drinking more water and **you'll see** a difference in how awake you feel!

PREPARE FOR THE EXAM

1 **B2 FIRST FOR SCHOOLS Reading and Use of English Part 1**

Briefly review what students need to do in this part of the exam and if necessary, read out the *B2 First for Schools* box on TB page 26.

Remind students that it is often possible for them to reject one or two choices so that, even if they aren't sure of the correct answer, they have a better chance of guessing correctly. Tell them to always read all four options. Set a time limit of ten minutes and ask students to work alone under exam conditions. Elicit the answers and ask students what each one tests, for example, *1 tests adjectives + prepositions*. Ask the students if there are any words in the options that they weren't sure the meaning of while they were doing the exercise. If students mention any, write them on the board. Invite students to define one of the words on the board and the other students guess which word it is.

Answers

1 B 2 D 3 A 4 C 5 D 6 A 7 C 8 D

2 **B2 FIRST FOR SCHOOLS Reading and Use of English Part 2**

Briefly review what students need to do in this part of the exam and if necessary, read out the *B2 First for Schools* box on TB page 58.

Elicit the kinds of words that are tested in this part of the exam, for example pronouns, articles, phrasal verbs, linking words, fixed expressions, auxiliary verbs. Look at the example with the students and ask what this is testing (*a fixed expression*). Set a time limit of ten minutes and then elicit the answers and what each gap is testing. (*1 zero conditional form; 2 get used to something; 3 as if / as though; 4 present continuous; 5 time expression; 6 would for past habits; 7 as a result – causative linking expression; 8 present perfect*)

Answers

1 when/if/whenever 2 got 3 though/if 4 are 5 to 6 would
7 as 8 has

B2 FIRST FOR SCHOOLS
Reading and Use of English Part 3

In this part, students have a text with eight gaps plus an example. They also have eight stem words in capitals at the end of each line with a gap in it (not immediately after the gap as here). They have to decide the correct form of the stem word to fit each gap. This tests the student's knowledge of prefixes and suffixes and their overall understanding of the text.

Tips Tell students to read through the whole text first to get an understanding of what it is about. For each gap they should decide what kind of word is needed, for example, noun, adverb and then whether it is singular or plural (noun), positive or negative (adjective) etc.

3 Set a time limit for students to read the text quickly and elicit what it is about (*How Scandinavians are often found to be the happiest with their lives.*). Remind students to think carefully about whether nouns are plural or singular and whether adjectives are positive or negative. They should read the text around the gaps carefully to make sure they don't lose marks unnecessarily by failing to notice that a plural noun or negative form of an adjective is needed. Set a time limit of eight minutes as they have already read the text and then elicit the answers. Elicit how students know the last gap is a negative noun (*we need an idea which is positive because it contrasts with the idea of paying higher taxes. However, the text says that they express less of this noun so it makes sense that they express less of a negative emotion if they are positive*).

Answers

1 apparently 2 enjoyment 3 belief 4 optimistic 5 residential
6 trendy 7 living 8 dissatisfaction

COOLER

Put students into groups of three or four. Tell the groups to look at the three exam tasks they have just completed. They discuss together the difficulties in doing each type of task and to rank them in order of difficulty. Invite the groups to share their ideas with the class and have a whole class vote on which task they find the easiest and most difficult.

PREPARE FOR THE EXAM

Reading and Use of English Part 1

1 **For questions 1–8, read the text below and decide which answer (A, B, C or D) best fits each gap.**

The new novelist

Amanda Wright, aged 17, has surprised everyone she knows by writing for weeks **(0)** *on* end to produce a full-length science-fiction novel. She frequently worked right through the night to complete the 375-page story, *Parallel Decades*.

Amanda's teachers and family began to get **(1)** ________ about her when she stopped being her usual cheerful self. She **(2)** ________ her appetite, fell asleep during classes and would wander around **(3)** ________ quietly to herself about imaginary characters and faraway civilisations.

No one had a clue what was going on, until a teacher asked her to talk about the most important thing she'd **(4)** ________ in her life. 'I've written a novel,' she said. The class fell silent with astonishment. Back at home, her parents learned what Amanda had been doing and were immensely proud of her. When it turned **(5)** ________ that this was the reason for her moods, they **(6)** ________ with relief. Finally, Amanda's odd behaviour made sense.

Does Amanda plan to write a **(7)** ________ of books? She is quite decisive about it. 'No, I won't! I just don't have the **(8)** ________. I'm exhausted!' she laughs.

	A	B	C	D
0	in	to	(C) on	at
1	pessimistic	concerned	furious	irritated
2	overlooked	forgot	missed	lost
3	muttering	whistling	yelling	cheering
4	earned	realised	achieved	reached
5	round	up	over	out
6	sighed	whispered	said	mumbled
7	version	chain	series	course
8	power	push	force	drive

Reading and Use of English Part 2

2 **For questions 1–8, read the text below and think of the word which best fits each gap. Use only one word in each gap. There is an example at the beginning (0).**

Funny PHOBIA?

Every **(0)** *once* in a while, my old phobia reappears. It happens **(1)** ________ I see eggs on someone's plate. I never liked them as a child, and I've never **(2)** ________ used to their unpleasant texture and horrible taste. It's an irrational fear – it isn't as **(3)** ________ I think that the eggs **(4)** ________ actually going to do me any harm – but it isn't quite as unusual, or as funny, as you might think. The phobia even has a name: ovaphobia.

From time **(5)** ________ time, when my sister and I were really young, and Mum told us it was eggs on toast for lunch, I **(6)** ________ start to feel anxious about it. My sister laughed and held up bits of egg on her fork in front of my face. It was a joke to her, but **(7)** ________ a result, I became even more worried about having to eat them. Eventually, my mum realised how serious my phobia was, and she **(8)** ________ never cooked them since!

Reading and Use of English Part 3

3 **For questions 1–8, read the text below. Use the word given in capitals to form a word that fits in the gap. There is an example at the beginning (0).**

THE HAPPIEST PLACE ON EARTH

Norwegians are officially the most **(0)** *cheerful* (CHEER) people on Earth, according to a recent survey. The survey asked around 1,000 people a simple question: 'Where, on a ladder of ten steps, do you stand: at the bottom or at the top?' According to the findings, the people of Norway **(1)** ________ (APPEAR) stand above the rest of us, with a score of 7.54 out of ten!

Scandinavian countries often come out ahead of other places when it comes to **(2)** ________ (ENJOY) of life, and they certainly seem to hold the **(3)** ________ (BELIEVE) that their lives are pretty good. So what makes Scandinavians so **(4)** ________ (OPTIMIST)? Is it living in a pleasant **(5)** ________ (RESIDENT) neighbourhood? Is it having access to nice shops and **(6)** ________ (TREND) restaurants? Is it living in rural rather than more industrial locations?

While Scandinavians do have a better standard of **(7)** ________ (LIFE) than other countries and express less **(8)** ________ (SATISFY) with their lives, they pay higher taxes, too. The difference in happiness levels may be due to the fact that these taxes pay for better facilities in the community.

9 A BRIGHT FUTURE

ABOUT YOU

Do you feel positive or negative about the future? Are you generally an optimistic or pessimistic person?

VOCABULARY Collocations

1 Complete the quiz with the verbs in the box.

EP

achieve	go	have (x2)	looks	
make (x2)	making	put	see	take

OPTIMISTIC? PESSIMISTIC? REALISTIC?

Are you an optimist, a pessimist or a realist? Read the statements and decide on your scores from 1 (= strongly disagree) to 5 (= strongly agree).

1. I'm good at _______ **the best of** a bad situation.
2. I think the future of mankind _______ **bright**. For instance, one day, science will _______ **an end to** major diseases.
3. I'm always willing to _______ **a go** at something new. I always _______ **opportunities** that come my way and I _______ **the most of** them.
4. I rarely think it's my fault when things _______ **wrong**.
5. I _______ more **strengths** than **weaknesses**.
6. I really think I'll be able to _______ **a difference** to the world one day.
7. I hope I will _______ all my **goals** in life.
8. I often _______ **the best** in people, rather than **the worst**.

2 Match the phrases in Exercise 1 to the meanings.

- **a** make something stop happening *put an end to*
- **b** attempt to do something
- **c** try to be positive about a bad situation
- **d** improve a situation
- **e** notice the most positive/negative qualities
- **f** seems likely to be good or successful
- **g** succeed in your aims
- **h** use occasions to do or say something
- **i** have good/bad qualities
- **j** develop problems
- **k** take full advantage of something because it may not last long

39

3 Listen to the conversation. Write Joseph's scores for each quiz question.

4 Read the quiz again and decide on your scores. Work in pairs and give reasons for your answers.

5 Add up your scores for each question, then turn to page 138.

1. What does the quiz say about Joseph?
2. What does it say about you / your partner? Do you agree?

READING

1 Read the article quickly and answer the questions.

1. What is the text about?
2. Is each expert optimistic or pessimistic about future technologies?
3. Can you think of any themes that link the inventions?

2 Read the article again. Correct these sentences.

1. By the middle of this century, travelling to Mars will be a common event for us all.
2. Driverless cars will probably be similar in appearance to today's cars.
3. The main application for exoskeleton suits will be in manufacturing.
4. New forms of clothing will help athletes improve their physical abilities.
5. People in the future will use smartphones to communicate and go online.
6. Students will use VR technology in combination with printed textbooks.

3 Match the highlighted words in the article to the meanings.

1. happening often, so not considered special or unusual
2. areas of work or study
3. see something happen
4. taxis (informal)
5. giving the ability to

9 A BRIGHT FUTURE

Unit Overview

TOPIC	Our future lives
VOCABULARY	Collocations
READING	2050: A glimpse into the future
GRAMMAR	Future (2): continuous and perfect
VOCABULARY	Adjective and noun suffixes
WRITING	An essay (2)
EXAM TASKS	Reading and Use of English Part 3; Writing Part 1

Resources

GRAMMAR REFERENCE AND PRACTICE: SB page 156; TB page 268
PREPARE FOR THE EXAM: SB pages on TB pages 238 and 246;
TB pages 255 and 258
WORKBOOK: pages 36–39
PHOTOCOPIABLE WORKSHEETS: Grammar worksheet Unit 9;
Vocabulary worksheet Unit 9
PRACTICE EXTRA: Unit 9

WARMER

Tell the students to close their eyes and imagine it is 25 years in the future and they now have secondary school-aged children of their own. They should imagine what their child's classroom looks like and what happens in a normal lesson. Tell them to keep their eyes closed for one minute, then put them into groups of three or four to share their ideas. Invite students from different groups to share some of their ideas with the class.

ABOUT YOU

Read the *About you* box with the class and ask them to think about something that they are going to do in the near future, for example, planning a party or preparing for an exam, and also about the longer-term future and things like their life after school, career, etc. Students then discuss their ideas in pairs. Elicit who is optimistic and nominate one or two to give examples, then do the same for pessimistic students.

VOCABULARY Collocations

1 Ask students to look at the quiz heading and say what they think *realistic* means (*accept things as they are. A realistic person is not optimistic or pessimistic and makes practical decisions about what they can do*). Set the exercise for students to complete individually. Tell students not to do the quiz yet, but just to complete the sentences. Check answers as a whole class.

Answers
1 making 2 looks, put 3 have, take, make 4 go 5 have 6 make 7 achieve 8 see

2 Ask students whether they already know the meaning of any of the phrases in blue, but don't ask for the answers yet. They should do the matching exercise individually and then compare answers with a partner. Check answers. Ask students to identify antonyms and synonyms (for example *strengths/weaknesses, the best of / the most of*).

Answers
b have a go c make the best of d make a difference e see the best/worst f looks bright g achieve (all your) goals h take opportunities i have strengths/weaknesses j go wrong k make the most of

39
3 When students have listened to the recording, elicit the scores and then ask the students to listen again, but this time paying attention to how Joseph answers. They should note down any phrases he uses to talk about the future. Allow students to compare answers in pairs then elicit phrases from the class, for example, *that might happen, are going to keep improving, I won't be … but I'm definitely going to try to …, Maybe I'll …* Ask how many times he answered with the single word *Yes* or *No* (*none*). Tell students to try to give longer answers similar to Joseph's when they discuss the questions.

Answers
1 two 2 three 3 one 4 one 5 four 6 four 7 three 8 five

» AUDIOSCRIPT TB PAGE 294

4 Set a time limit of about five minutes for the activity. Monitor and encourage students to give explanations or examples for their answers if they aren't saying much.

Answers
Students' own answers

5 Before students look at page 138 ask them what they think the quiz says about them and Joseph. When students have checked at the back of the book, ask if they think the quiz gave an accurate picture of what they are like. Follow this up by going through each question in the quiz and inviting different students to tell the class how they answered each one and what reasons they gave.

Answers
1 Joseph scores 23 and is described as realistic.
2 Students' own answers

READING

1 Ask students to look at the two pictures on page 55 and elicit what they can see and whether they think these things will happen in the near future. Set a time limit of three minutes for students to read the text quickly. They then get into groups of three or four to discuss the questions and share any information they found. Invite groups to answer one of the questions.

Answers
1 the future of technology 2 They are optimistic.
3 transportation and superhuman technology

CONTINUED ON PAGE 106

BACKGROUND INFORMATION

It is very difficult to predict the future. Here are some wrong predictions:

1895 – A British physicist said that it was impossible to make a flying machine that was heavier than the air.

1916 – Charlie Chaplin didn't think the cinema's popularity would last, because audiences would want live performances on stage.

1903 – A bank president advised a customer not to invest in the Ford Motor Company because cars were just a temporary fashion, whereas horses would always be here.

1913 – Inventor Lee De Forest was accused of selling fake shares in his company because his idea was to transmit the human voice across the Atlantic and a US District Attorney thought the idea was ridiculous.

1926 – Lee De Forest himself said that it would never be possible to send a spaceship to the moon.

1946 – Movie producer Darryl Zanuck claimed that people would soon get bored of watching television.

1955 – The president of a vacuum cleaner company predicted that we would use nuclear-powered vacuum cleaners within ten years.

1968 – *Business Week* magazine thought it would be difficult for Japanese car makers to sell many cars in the USA.

1995 – The founder of the company 3Com (a digital electronics manufacturer) thought the internet would collapse in 1996.

2005 – Steve Chen, the co-founder of YouTube, was worried about his company's future as he said that 'There's just not that many videos I want to watch'.

2 Give the students ten minutes to read the text again. As they are reading they should note where the information for each sentence in Exercise 2 can be found in the text but not answer it yet. When they have read the whole text carefully, they can go back to each of the six points and find out the correct information. Students compare their correct sentences to make sure they have the same information. Elicit the answers then ask the students to think about the predictions made and discuss in groups which ones they agree with and which ones they disagree with. Invite groups to share their ideas with the class.

MIXED ABILITY

Put weaker students into groups of three. Each student reads one or two of the paragraphs and makes notes of the key information they contain. The students then share the information they read and look at the six sentences together. The student who read about each sentence tries to say what is wrong with it. If they aren't sure, the other students also look at the paragraph and try to find the correct information.

Answers

1 Only professional astronauts will travel to Mars.
2 Driverless cars will probably look more like steel boxes than today's cars.
3 Exoskeleton suits will mostly be used outside the workplace, for example to help people with back and leg injuries walk again.
4 New forms of clothing could help the police and firefighters in emergency situations.
5 People in the future will use jewellery with a virtual screen instead of using a smartphone.
6 Students will use VR technology instead of textbooks.

40 The Reading text is recorded for students to listen, read and check their answers.

3 Put students into groups of three or four to discuss which words they think match which meanings. Elicit the answers and give more details about the words and phrases, i.e. a *field* of study or employment can either be very specific, for example *I'm a biologist who specialises in the field of human cell growth* or, as in the text, a general term: *I work in the field of education, but I'm not a teacher, I'm a school inspector*. In the context of the text, *commonplace* has the same meaning as *common*, meaning *regular* or *usual*. Sometimes, though, *common* has a different meaning. We use the word *cabs* in both the UK and the USA. Taxi drivers are often referred to as *cabbies*. *Enabling* comes from the word *able to*. If you *enable* someone to do something, you make them able to do it. *Witness* can be a verb or a noun and is often used when talking about crimes or news events.

FAST FINISHERS

Ask fast finishers to look for other words in the text which they think some people won't know. They look up the words they find and write down the dictionary definition. When everyone has finished the exercise, elicit the answers and then invite fast finishers to read out their definitions and say which paragraph the word appears in. The other students then try to find the word.

Answers

1 commonplace 2 fields 3 witness 4 cabs 5 enabling

TALKING POINTS

Look at the questions with the class. Tell them that if they think it isn't important for technology to keep developing, they can argue why not. Also, tell them to use their imaginations for the second question as it is almost impossible to predict future technology so far in advance. You could share the Background information with them to illustrate this. Put students into groups of three or four and set a time limit of three minutes. At the end of that time, invite each group to share one of their predictions with the class.

COOLER

Ask students to work with four to six other students they know quite well. Each person should take a piece of paper and write their name at the top. They should then pass this to their left and the next person should write a sentence about something this person will do in the future (for example *Max will move to Paris. Anna will study architecture.*). Students then fold the piece of paper so that only the name can be seen and not the prediction. They then pass this on to their left again and repeat until the piece of paper gets back to the named person. Students then open their paper and see if they agree with their friends' predictions. Ask some volunteers to share some funny or interesting predictions as a class.

2050: A glimpse into the future

Have you ever wondered what we'll be doing in 2050? By the middle of this century, new technology will have changed the way we live our lives beyond recognition. Experts from the fields of transport, health and education share some interesting predictions about what lies ahead.

40

Missions to Mars

The idea of astronauts travelling to Mars may seem like something out of a science fiction movie, but humans may set foot on the red planet sooner than you think. According to experts, by 2050, we will already have been travelling to Mars for some years, with the first trips by astronauts expected as early as 2025. Some companies are even planning to establish a permanent settlement on our neighbouring planet, where trained crews will be able to live and work to further our understanding of the solar system. While missions to Mars will still likely only be for professional astronauts in 2050, it's expected that space tourism around the Earth and Moon will be relatively commonplace.

The death of the smartphone

You probably can't image life without your smartphone, but, according to technology experts, it's likely that these devices will have disappeared by 2050. But don't worry, you'll still be able to keep in touch with your friends or surf the web when you're out and about, thanks to advances in 'augmented reality', or AR, a technology which lays computer-generated images onto a user's view of the real world. Rather than walking around chatting on smartphones, people will instead be wearing small items of jewellery, such as bracelets, that can create a virtual screen that they can use to access and control all the apps they need.

Driverless taxis

If space travel isn't your thing, what about self-driving vehicles? Next year, a US company will be starting a trial of a driverless taxi service in Arizona, and experts think that in as little as ten years' time, we'll all be ordering driverless vehicles instead of traditional cabs to carry us from A to B. These driverless vehicles are likely to look more like a steel box rather than a recognisable car shape, but whatever form they take, there are so many companies in competition to bring us this new form of transport that the next generation won't even need to learn to drive!

Bionic bodies

Fancy being a real-life superhero? The car manufacturer Hyundai has developed an exoskeleton suit, which is a kind of mobile machine that can be worn in factories to make it easier to do jobs such as lifting heavy objects. But in the future, the main applications of this technology are expected to be outside the workplace. Exoskeleton suits have the potential to be hugely beneficial for people with back and leg injuries who currently have to use a wheelchair, enabling them to walk again. Other kinds of bionic clothing may give us superhuman properties, such as 'Spider-Man' suits. These are a softer version of the exoskeleton suit without all the machinery, that give the wearer extra strength or make them run faster. These could be useful for the police and firefighters to help protect them in dangerous situations and allow them to reach people more rapidly in an emergency.

Virtual reality classrooms

Virtual reality (VR) technology is already pretty advanced, and experts believe it could become commonplace in classrooms in the next 10 to 20 years. So, perhaps instead of opening your books at the beginning of a lesson, you'll put on a VR headset! Instead of studying from printed textbooks, apps will allow students to 'travel' via VR to places like the Great Barrier Reef in Australia, where they can observe underwater life and witness the environmental effects of tourism and climate change. This will be a valuable way for students to learn about the world from the comfort of their own classrooms.

TALKING POINTS

Why do you think it's important for technology to keep developing?

What technologies do you think there will be in 50 years' time?

A BRIGHT FUTURE 55

GRAMMAR Future (2): continuous and perfect

1 **Read the examples. How do we form the future continuous, future perfect and future perfect continuous?**

1 Next year, a US company **will be starting** a trial of a driverless taxi service in Arizona.
2 **Will** driverless cars **be driving** us around in as little as ten years' time?
3 It's likely that smartphones **will have disappeared** by 2050.
4 By 2050, we **will** already **have been travelling** to Mars for some years.

2 **Complete the rules with *continuous*, *perfect* or *perfect continuous*.**

We use the
a future ________ for an action that will be in progress in the future or an action that is planned for the future.
b future ________ for an action that will be complete at a future time.
c future ________ to say how long an action has been in progress at a future time.

» GRAMMAR REFERENCE AND PRACTICE PAGE 156

3 **Complete the predictions about life in 50 years' time using the future continuous or future perfect. Which predictions do you agree with?**

1 Technology ________ (put) an end to our energy problems and people ________ (generate) most of their electricity from the sun.
2 We still ________ (not find) life on other planets by then, but some of us ________ (live) on them.
3 I definitely ________ (not work) because I ________ (earn) enough money to retire!
4 Many people will live until they are 150, as scientists ________ (discover) a cure for all diseases.

4 **Choose the correct verb forms.**

1 This time next week, we *'ll sit* / *'ll be sitting* on the beach in Spain!
2 I *'m waiting* / *'ll be waiting* for you at ten outside the space museum.
3 People's homes *will change* / *will be changing* a lot in the near future.
4 Will you *be visiting* / *have visited* anywhere interesting when you go to Africa?

5 **Make sentences about your future in three years' time. Use the future continuous, future perfect or future perfect continuous. Compare your sentences with your partner's.**

1 study at university – Yes/No?
2 travel abroad without your parents – Yes/No?
3 learn English – How long?
4 live with your parents – Yes/No?
5 learn to drive – Yes/No?
6 do an interesting job – Yes/No?

VOCABULARY Adjective and noun suffixes

1 **Look at the adjectives from the article on page 55. What are the noun forms of the words? What suffix has been added in each case?**

1 Missions to Mars will still likely only be for **professional** astronauts in 2050.
2 These could be **useful** for the police and firefighters …
3 … to help protect them in **dangerous** situations.

2 EP **We use suffixes to change word classes, for example from a verb to a noun or adjective. Find the correct forms of the words in the article on page 55.**

1 *settle* (verb) → ________ (noun)
2 *driver* (noun) → ________ (adjective)
3 *recognise* (verb) → ________ (adjective)
4 *compete* (verb) → ________ (noun)
5 *value* (noun) → ________ (adjective)

PREPARE FOR THE EXAM

Reading and Use of English Part 3

3 **Read the text and decide which kinds of word are needed in each gap. How do you know?**

HAPPINESS AND HEALTH
Dutch teenagers have it all!

Scientists have often linked **(0)** *emotional* **(EMOTION)** problems, such as depression, to illness, but, until recently, there has been little research into how happiness can be **(1)** ________ **(BENEFIT)** to your health. However, a new study has indicated a close **(2)** ________ **(RELATION)** between them. Conversely, a lack of **(3)** ________ **(ENJOY)** of daily activities and a pessimistic **(4)** ________ **(PERSONAL)** are closely associated with illness. The link between happiness and health is good news for teenagers, as a second report has found that 16- to 17-year-olds express higher levels of **(5)** ________ **(SATISFY)** with their lives than any other age group.

Furthermore, the **(6)** ________ **(MAJOR)** of teenagers also say they are optimistic about the future. And one study has shown that the happiest and healthiest teenagers of all are Dutch. So, what's different about Dutch teenagers? We're often told that having an **(7)** ________ **(ACT)** lifestyle makes us feel better. Dutch teenagers report spending more time than average watching TV and doing little exercise, yet a **(8)** ________ **(REMARK)** 95% of them still say they are content with their lives! Perhaps it is doing what you enjoy that matters most!

4 **Complete the text in Exercise 3. Use the word given in capitals to form a word that fits in the gap.**

» PREPARE FOR THE EXAM PAGE 122

5 » Work in pairs. Turn to page 139.

GRAMMAR Future (2): continuous and perfect

WARMER

Tell students to think of three times in the future but on the same day as the lesson. You can model this by saying, '4 pm, 9 pm, 1 am'. Ask students what they think they will be doing at one time and what they think they will have done before another time. Give model sentences for your times, for example, 'At 4 pm, I'll be marking homework. By 9 pm, I'll have finished my dinner. At 1 am, I'll be sleeping.' Students do the same in pairs.

1 Students work in pairs to think of how the tenses are formed. Use a simple sentence to show the differences in meaning between different tenses, for example:

Tomorrow at 8 pm I will fly to the USA. (This tells us when I will leave.)

Tomorrow at 8 pm I will be flying to the USA. (This tells us we will be in the middle of flying, but we don't know for how long.)

By 8 pm tomorrow, I will have flown to the USA. (This tells us that the flight will have finished, but we don't know exactly when.)

By 8 pm tomorrow, I will have been flying for three hours. (This tells us that the flight will still be continuing and tells us when it started.)

Answers

Future continuous: *will + be + -ing;* future perfect: *will + have +* past participle; future perfect continuous: *will + have been + -ing*

2 Go through the rules with the students and elicit which sentence in Exercise 1 matches each rule (*1 a – planned; 2 a – in progress; 3 b; 4 c*).

Answers

a continuous b perfect c perfect continuous

» GRAMMAR REFERENCE AND PRACTICE ANSWER KEY TB PAGE 268

3 Look at the first sentence with the students. Elicit the best tenses to use and then ask students to do the rest of the exercise in pairs. Elicit the answers.

Answers

1 will have put, will be generating 2 won't have found, will be living 3 won't be working, will have earned 4 will have discovered

4 Students work alone and refer to the rules if they aren't sure. They then compare answers in pairs. Elicit the answers and why the alternative is wrong.

Answers

1 'll be sitting 2 'll be waiting 3 will change 4 be visiting

5 Look at the first prompt with the class. Ask, 'Will you have studied at university in three years?' (*No* – this would mean that you had finished your studies.) 'Will you be studying at university in three years?' (This depends on the age of the students. If they have two more years left at school, this is possible.) 'How long will you have been studying at university?' (If the answer to the last question is *yes*, the students could answer this, for example, *In three years, I'll have been studying at university for three months*.) Students then write their own sentences. Monitor and help where necessary. When students have compared with their partner, invite them to share some of their sentences with the class.

Possible answers

1 I'll / will / won't / will not be studying at university. 2 I 'll / will / won't / will not have travelled abroad without my parents. 3 I'll/ will have been learning English for … years. 4 I'll / will / won't / will not be living with my parents. 5 I'll / will / won't / will not have learned (how) to drive. 6 I'll / will / won't / will not be doing an interesting job.

» GRAMMAR WORKSHEET UNIT 9

VOCABULARY Adjective and noun suffixes

1 Look at the sentences with the class and elicit the suffixes. Point out that, the suffix was added without any other necessary changes but this isn't always the case, e.g., when *-al* is added to a word ending in *-e*, the *-e* is dropped (practice – practical); when *-ful* is added to a word ending in *-y*, the *-y* changes to *-i* (beauty – beautiful) and when *-ous* is added to words ending in *-e*, the *-e* is dropped (fame – famous).

Answers

1 profession(-al) 2 use(-ful) 3 danger(-ous)

2 Elicit the answers and what the words mean. Again, elicit that, although the final *-e* is dropped before *-able* and *-ion*, it isn't dropped before *-ment*.

Answers

1 settlement 2 driverless 3 recognisable 4 competition 5 valuable

PREPARE FOR THE EXAM

3 **B2 FIRST FOR SCHOOLS Reading and Use of English Part 3**

Briefly review what students need to do in this part of the exam and if necessary, read out the *B2 First for Schools* box on TB page 102.

Students should read the text quickly to get an overall understanding and to think about what kind of word is needed in each gap. Elicit that the word needed in the example is an adjective which describes the problems. Students work in pairs to think of what kinds of words are needed in the other gaps, but don't try to complete the gaps yet.

Answers

1 adjective 2 noun 3 noun 4 noun 5 noun 6 noun 7 adjective 8 adjective

4 Tell students all the words are testing suffixes but, in the exam, there will be more variety and it is usual to have at least one prefix. Elicit the answers and focus on the spelling of *beneficial* as it may cause problems.

Answers

1 beneficial 2 relationship 3 enjoyment 4 personality 5 satisfaction 6 majority 7 active 8 remarkable

» PREPARE FOR THE EXAM TEACHING NOTES AND ANSWER KEY TB PAGE 255

5 When students have completed the sentences, elicit the words to make sure they all have the correct words before they start asking and answering. Set a time limit of three minutes for students to ask and answer the questions then invite students to share their ideas with the class.

Answers

1 driverless 2 recognisable 3 remarkable 4 personality 5 enjoyment

» VOCABULARY WORKSHEET UNIT 9

WRITING An essay (2)

1 Remind students about Speaking Part 2 in the *B2 First for Schools* exam in which they have to compare two photos. Tell them to try to speak for one minute each about the photos then elicit ideas from the class.

Answers
Students' own answers

2 Write the two points from the task on the board: *keeping in touch* and *hobbies*. Elicit one way of how keeping in touch is easier nowadays and write this on the board, for example *social media*. Elicit one idea for hobbies too and write this on the board, for example *sports*. Students then work alone to add more ideas. Elicit these and add them to the board and elicit the students' own ideas for the third part and write these on the board too.

MIXED ABILITY
If weaker students have problems thinking of their own ideas, put them in groups to discuss each point. Monitor and help the groups with ideas and tell them that in the exam they will have plenty of time to think of an idea as well as useful vocabulary for the two points given to them in the task, so they shouldn't panic.

Answers
Students' own answers

3 If possible, you could photocopy the essay and cut it into four separate paragraphs. Students close their books and work in pairs or small groups to try to put the essay in the correct order. They should ignore the highlighting for now. Elicit the correct order and ask students how they know. They then open their books to check and answer the questions. Check answers together and then ask students whether they agree with the opinions in the essay, giving reasons for their opinion.

Answers
1 Students' own answers 2 technology and safety

4 Look at the functions with the class and elicit simple words or phrases that can be used for these things, for example *1 and; 2 I think; 3 so; 4 Overall*. Students then complete the gaps with the highlighted words from the text. Elicit why the words in the essay are better than the simple ones that you elicited at the start of the exercise (*they show that the writer has a good range of vocabulary*).

FAST FINISHERS
Ask fast finishers to try to add more words to each function. When everyone has finished, elicit the answers and invite fast finishers to share their extra vocabulary items with the class, for example *1 In addition; 2 As far as I'm concerned, I believe; 3 Therefore; 4 To sum up*.

Answers
1 Moreover, Furthermore 2 In my view 3 As a result
4 On balance

5 Give students time to read the *Prepare to write* box and make sure the meanings are clear. Then ask them to complete this task individually. Elicit the answers and point out that all these phrases can be used to start a sentence or can go in the middle of the sentence, for example *I'm an optimist, unlike my brother*.

Follow up by writing on the board:

Unlike my …

In comparison with my …

My … wants to … , whereas I want to …

Compared to … I …

In ten years, I'll … , which will be great, but on the other hand …

Students work in pairs to complete the sentences in a way which is different to the sentences in the exercise, for example, *Unlike my parents, I use social media a lot*. Monitor and help where necessary and invite students to share some of their sentences with the class.

Answers
1 Unlike 2 In comparison with 3 whereas 4 Compared to
5 on the other hand

PREPARE FOR THE EXAM

6 **B2 FIRST FOR SCHOOLS Writing Part 1: An essay**

Briefly review what students need to do in this part of the exam and if necessary, read out the *B2 First for Schools* box on TB page 22.

Give the students five minutes to think about their ideas and what vocabulary they can use. Tell them not to start writing the actual essay yet. Remind them about topic sentences and how these are used to introduce the ideas in each paragraph. Then, look at the topic sentences in the essay in Exercise 3. For each paragraph, ask a question based on the topic sentence, for example: 'What sort of things do adults say about when they were young? What sort of opportunities do teenagers have? How was life more straightforward in the past?' Students give their own answers.

7 Give students a time limit of 40 minutes to write their essay. When they have finished, they swap essays with a partner and give each other feedback on their ideas and how they compared and contrasted ideas.

Model answer
There is no way of predicting the future with accuracy, but in my view, young people's lives will be very different in 25 years' time. With the many new technologies that will be invented, our lives will both change *and* improve.
The internet has made learning more accessible than it was for previous generations. In future, there could be brain implant technology to assist our studies: research is already being carried out in this area.
Smart technology in the field of entertainment will allow us to access exciting applications. On the one hand, we may see fewer traditional forms of entertainment, such as cinema, but on the other hand, there may be new leisure places where we spend time in alternative worlds.
One of the greatest changes will be in terms of how we interact with our environment. The negative effects of climate change have meant that we've already become much 'greener'. The technologies of the future will help us do an even better job of protecting the world we live in.
On balance, I believe that the next generation will have quite a different life to ours.

COOLER
Write three topics on the board, for example, *music, fashion* and *films*. Ask students to work in pairs to write sentences comparing each area today with what it was like 50 years ago. Then tell them to write sentences about each area using the future forms from this unit. Ask students to get into groups of four with a different pair to compare ideas then discuss some of the ideas as a class.

WRITING An essay (2)

1 **Look at the two photos. Discuss the questions.**

1 When do you think these photos were taken?
2 How are the lives of the people in each photo different?

2 **Read the task. Add more information and your own idea to the notes.**

> **'Life is better for young people now than it was 50 years ago.' Do you agree?**
>
> Notes
>
> Write about:
>
> 1 keeping in touch with friends and family
> 2 hobbies
> 3 ________ (your own idea)

3 **Read the essay and answer the questions.**

1 Did the writer mention any of your ideas from Exercise 2?
2 What subjects other than hobbies or keeping in touch with friends and family did the writer mention?

It is common to hear adults talk about how things were different when they were young. Some believe life has improved dramatically for young people, whereas others feel life was simpler when they were young.

On the one hand, in comparison with 50 years ago, teenagers' lives are full of opportunities. Technology has made it easy for us to learn about anything and make friends with people who share similar interests. Moreover, we can easily stay in touch with friends and family, wherever they are in the world.

On the other hand, life was more straightforward half a century ago. While young people today are obsessed with their computers and phones, these things didn't exist when our grandparents were young. Furthermore, unlike now, parents weren't constantly anxious about their children's safety. As a result, young people would spend more time playing sport outside, or being sociable with their friends.

In my view, compared to now, life was definitely less complicated for young people 50 years ago. On balance, however, I believe life today is more interesting and enjoyable, as long as we make the most of our lives and the opportunities we receive.

4 **The highlighted words and phrases in the essay are used to organise ideas. Write the words next to the functions.**

1 Adding a new point: ________, ________
2 Introducing a personal opinion: ________
3 Showing a logical consequence: ________
4 Summing up: ________

5 **Read the *Prepare to write* box and find the expressions in the essay. Then choose the correct options below.**

> **PREPARE TO WRITE** Comparing and contrasting
>
> These expressions are used to compare and contrast ideas:
>
> *in comparison with/to*
> *compared to/with*
> *unlike*
> *while/whereas*
> *on the one hand / on the other hand*

1 *While / Unlike* my brother, I'm an optimist.
2 *In comparison with / Compared* my friends, I get to go out a lot.
3 My best friend wants to get a job after he leaves school, *whereas / compared to* I want to do a degree.
4 *Compared to / On the one hand* many young people, I have an easy life.
5 In ten years, I'll have my own place, which will be great, but *whereas / on the other hand* I'll be paying for everything myself!

PREPARE FOR THE EXAM

Writing Part 1

6 **Read the task. Add more information and your own idea to the notes.**

> **'In 25 years, young people's lives will be very different to how they are now.' Do you agree?**
>
> Notes
>
> Write about:
>
> 1 studies
> 2 entertainment
> 3 ________ (your own idea)

7 **Write your essay. Use all the notes and give reasons for your point of view.**

- Organise your essay into paragraphs.
- Use phrases from the *Prepare to write* box to compare and contrast the present and the future.
- Use expressions from Exercise 4 to organise your ideas.
- Check your grammar and spelling.
- Write 140–190 words.

10 SURPRISE!

ABOUT YOU

07 **Watch the video and answer the questions.**

What's the biggest surprise you've ever had?

Do you like surprises? Why? / Why not?

VOCABULARY Phrases with *in, out of, at, by*

41 **1** **Listen and match the speakers (1–5) to the topics (a–f). There is one extra topic.**

a an unexpected extra
b a surprise invitation
c an unexpected visit
d a surprise party
e a surprise wedding
f a shock result

41 **2** **Complete the sentences with the words in the box. Listen again and check.**

EP

at fault	at risk	by accident	~~by chance~~
in advance	in all	in detail	in secret
out of character	out of nowhere		

0 It was only *by chance* that I glanced through the door.
1 The whole concert lasted over two hours ______.
2 Unfortunately, he found out about it ______.
3 I'd left an email open ______.
4 He burst into my room ______.
5 It's not exactly ______ for my brother to turn up like that.
6 United are now ______ of finishing the season without any trophies.
7 United's goalkeeper was partly ______ for the goal.
8 She refused to speak ______ about the ceremony, but said that it had taken place ______ a couple of weeks ago.

3 **Match the phrases in Exercise 2 to the meanings.**

a before a particular time
b including all the information about something
c altogether
d without telling other people
e unusual in terms of someone's personality
f suddenly and unexpectedly
g without intending to do something, not on purpose
h when something happens because of luck
i responsible for something bad that has happened
j in a situation where something bad is likely to happen

4 **Discuss the questions with your partner.**

1 Has anyone you know acted in a way that was out of character? What did they do?
2 Would you ever have an argument with someone even if you knew you were at fault?
3 Do you tend to plan your free time in advance?
4 Have you ever broken anything by accident?
5 Do you think it's mean to talk about friends in secret?

READING

1 **Read the article quickly and choose the best alternative title (A–C).**

A Why we should ban flash mobs
B The world's best flash mobs
C The evolution of flash mobs

PREPARE FOR THE EXAM

Reading and Use of English Part 6

2 **Six sentences have been removed from the article. Read sentences A–G and notice the underlined words.**

A As a result of such unwelcome incidents, some cities have banned flash mobs.
B They began organising flash mobs all over the world, often through social media and text messaging.
C Despite this, they kept a close eye on the participants.
D Over the next three months, he organised seven successful flash mobs in shops, hotels, parks and stations all around New York.
E They have realised the potential of promoting their products by creating unexpected events in public.
F Recently, over a million people took part in one, at different times on the same day, in over 25 cities around the world.
G One afternoon, he emailed 60 friends, inviting them to meet at a small local shop at exactly 7.24 pm.

3 **Choose from the sentences A–G the one which fits each gap (1–6). Use the underlined words to help you decide. There is one extra sentence which you do not need to use.**

4 **Replace the bold phrases with the correct form of the highlighted phrasal verbs in the article.**

1 I've got used to Sam **arriving** late.
2 They're **doing** tests to see if the building is safe.
3 Jem has **thought of** an idea for the end-of-term party.
4 When we got back, Nate had already **tidied up** after the party.
5 I didn't enjoy that book, but don't let that **discourage** you.

10 SURPRISE!

Unit Overview

TOPIC	Unexpected moments
VOCABULARY	Phrases with *in, out of, at, by*
READING	Flash mob fun
GRAMMAR	Modals (2): modals in the past
VOCABULARY	Extended meanings of words
LISTENING	A radio interview about a surprise
SPEAKING	Expressing surprise
EXAM TASKS	Reading and Use of English Part 6; Reading and Use of English Part 4; Listening Part 4

Resources

GRAMMAR REFERENCE AND PRACTICE: SB page 157; TB page 268
PREPARE FOR THE EXAM: SB pages on TB pages 242–243, 239 and 249; TB pages 255–256 and 260
WORKBOOK: pages 40–43
VIDEO AND VIDEO WORKSHEET: Surprises!
PHOTOCOPIABLE WORKSHEETS: Grammar worksheet Unit 10; Vocabulary worksheet Unit 10
TEST GENERATOR: Unit test 10
PRACTICE EXTRA: Unit 10

WARMER

Talk to students about fortune tellers and what they do. Tell them to imagine they go to a fortune teller who tells them the following:

(Write these on the board or dictate them and ask students to write them down.)

In 20 years' time, you will be living in a different country. You will have three children. You will be famous. You will have climbed to the top of Mount Everest. You will have sailed across the Atlantic.

Students now get into groups of three or four and discuss which of these would be the most surprising and which they wouldn't be surprised by.

Set a time limit of three minutes and then elicit ideas from different groups.

ABOUT YOU

07 You can begin the class and introduce the topic of the unit by showing the video and asking students to complete the video worksheet. Then put the students into pairs to discuss the questions in the *About you* box. Invite students to share any interesting surprises with the class.

VOCABULARY Phrases with *in, out of, at, by*

41 **1** Students look through the topics. Elicit what they think the first one could be referring to, for example *some extra food with a meal*. When students have listened, elicit the answers and what each topic was about (*a extra songs at a concert; d a party the speaker had organised for someone; c brother visiting from university; f United drew 2–2 with City; e a famous singer's wedding*)

Answers
1 a 2 d 3 c 4 f 5 e
Extra topic: b a surprise invitation

41 **2** Look at the example with the students and ask what the sentence means, for example, *I wasn't expecting to see anything and there was no real reason for me to look through the door.* Tell students to complete the sentences and then to compare their answers with a partner. Play the recording for students to check their answers, pausing after each speaker if necessary.

Answers
1 in all 2 in advance 3 by accident 4 out of nowhere
5 out of character 6 at risk 7 at fault 8 in detail, in secret

» AUDIOSCRIPT TB PAGE 294

3 Students look at the sentences in Exercise 2 without looking at the meanings in Exercise 3 and try to guess what each phrase means. They then look at the meanings to check their ideas. Elicit the answers and then ask stronger students to either reword the sentences in Exercise 2 using the meanings in Exercise 3 and to make any other changes necessary, for example *It was only because of luck that I glanced through the door*, or explain them in their own words, for example *8 She didn't say much about the ceremony, but said that it had taken place a couple of weeks ago and they had decided not to tell anyone about it at the time.*

Answers
a in advance b in detail c in all d in secret e out of character
f out of nowhere g by accident h by chance i at fault j at risk

4 Look at the first question with the class and invite students to give examples. If they can't, you could tell them about someone you know (or make up a story about someone acting out of character). Monitor and help students while they are discussing the other questions and then invite pairs to share interesting stories or ideas with the class.

Answers
Students' own answers

READING

1 Ask students what a flash mob is and invite them to describe flash mobs they have seen online, in person or even been a part of. Ask the class how they would feel if one started in front of them at the local shopping centre. Then set a time limit for students to read the text quickly and choose the best alternative title. Elicit ideas and reasons for their answers.

Answer
C

CONTINUED ON PAGE 114

BACKGROUND INFORMATION

Bill Wasik's first successful flash mob took place on 17th June 2003. The participants split into four groups and only got together just before the event began. The flash mob happened on the ninth floor of Macy's Department Store, in the rug department. The word was added to the Oxford English Dictionary the following year.

Some other famous flash mobs include:

A flash mob which was made up of about 1,000 musicians, including 50 members of the German Symphony Orchestra, happened at a shopping centre in Berlin when they suddenly started playing classical music for the shoppers.

At the party for the 24th season of *The Oprah Winfrey Show* the audience suddenly started a coordinated dance routine while the Black Eyed Peas were singing their song 'I Gotta Feeling'. 800 professional dancers had learned the dance moves in advance and, before the show started, they taught them to the audience members around them.

One of the biggest flash mobs was in Mexico City in 2009 when almost 14,000 people danced to the song 'Thriller' together. This record entered into the *Guinness World Records*.

A flash mob at a shopping centre in Florida was stopped by two policemen who, to the audience's delight and surprise, then joined in with the dance routine. But was it planned?

PREPARE FOR THE EXAM

2 B2 FIRST FOR SCHOOLS Reading and Use of English Part 6

Briefly review what students need to do in this part of the exam and if necessary, read out the *B2 First for Schools* box on TB page 38.

Remind students that there are always clues in both the sentences which have been removed and the sentences before and after the gaps in the text, which help students decide where the sentences should go.

Look at the first sentence with the class. Ask, 'Why is *As a result* useful?' (*Because it refers to an incident that has happened before the gap.*). Ask why the word *banned* could be important (*There could be more details of such bans after the gap.*).

Students look at the other sentences in pairs and discuss how the underlined words can help them to complete the activity.

FAST FINISHERS

Ask fast finishers to look for other words in the sentences which may be useful when trying to match the sentences to the correct gaps, for example, *B They* (*Who are they?*); *C the participants* (*in what?*); *E They* (*Who are they?*).

3 Set a time limit of ten minutes for students to do the activity. If they finish early, encourage them to look at all the underlined words and see if they can explain what or who they refer to. Elicit the answers and how the underlined words helped them.

MIXED ABILITY

Allow weaker students to get together to share ideas from Exercise 2 before they start the reading. They can then work in pairs or groups of three to complete Exercise 3. Monitor and help where necessary.

Answers

1 G (*he* refers back to Bill Wasik, and his *60 friends* are referred to in the sentence after the gap as *They*.)
2 D (the missing sentence mentions seven more events and these are referred to in the phrase *Each time* immediately after the gap.)
3 B (the underlined phrases in sentence B are matched in the text by *everywhere* before the gap and *modern urban culture* afterwards.)
4 F (the paragraph is describing the annual *international* pillow fight and the missing sentence talks about this event occurring in *25 cities around the world*. The city of San Francisco is then mentioned after the gap.)
5 A (the missing sentence refers to *incidents* caused by flash mobs, and immediately before the gap, one such incident is described, where thousands of rail passengers were seriously inconvenienced.)
6 E (the missing sentence talks about product promotion, which is matched in the text by *commercial opportunities*.)
Extra sentence: C

42 The Reading text is recorded for students to listen, read and check their answers.

4 Students cover the sentences in Exercise 4 and look at the highlighted words in yellow. They work in pairs to try to define the words together, using the context of the sentences to help them. Monitor and note down good language use and mistakes for feedback. Elicit ideas and then students rewrite the sentences in Exercise 4. Tell them to be careful to use the correct tense so that the meaning stays the same. Elicit the answers and invite students to use the phrasal verbs in different sentences, for example, *twenty people turned up to the school drama club auditions.*

Answers

1 turning up 2 carrying out 3 come up with 4 cleared up
5 put you off

TALKING POINTS

Look at the questions with the class and ask them for an example from the text of a flash mob which was annoying (*the silent disco which delayed trains in London*) and one which wasn't just entertainment (*the Heathrow Airport flash mob which was for an advert*). Students then discuss the questions in small groups. Invite groups to share their ideas with the class. You could mention some flash mobs which have raised awareness and money for different charities if students don't think of this themselves, for example an End Hunger flash mob in St Paul, USA, which raised $84,000.

COOLER

Put students into groups of four or five. Ask students to plan a flash mob. Where and when will it be? What will participants do? How will they advertise it? Will it be for fun or will it have a serious purpose? Set a time limit of three or four minutes and then invite groups to share their ideas with the class. If students want to actually choreograph a routine for a future lesson, encourage them to do so.

FLASH MOB FUN

Imagine it's Saturday at a busy shopping centre. People are doing all the things you'd normally expect – chatting on phones, looking in shop windows and so on. Then suddenly, the people in front of you stop moving. They're completely still, frozen in the middle of whatever they were doing. You look around. There are more of these people – perhaps a hundred or so. Other shoppers look just as confused as you are. Several minutes go by and the frozen people remain in exactly the same positions. Then, as suddenly as they stopped, they begin moving again, as if nothing had happened. You've just experienced a flash mob!

The definition of a flash mob is 'a group of people who meet suddenly in a public place, perform an unusual act for a brief time, then quickly leave'. A US man, Bill Wasik, came up with the idea. [1] ________ They shouldn't say anything to the assistants or each other, he told them. They didn't need to buy anything. They just had to browse for precisely seven minutes and then leave. It would have been the world's first flash mob. However, someone had warned the police, and when Bill and his friends arrived, the police were waiting, and the flash mob couldn't go ahead.

Bill wasn't put off by this failure, however, and started planning the next event. [2] ________ Each time, Bill's friends received their invitations by email. They met at an exact time, carried out their instructions, such as forming a queue or just clapping, and then they left.

Before long, stories and videos of these funny and often bizarre events appeared online. Wasik's idea instantly captured the attention of creative people everywhere. [3] ________ These methods of communication helped spread the message far and wide. Flash mobs quickly became part of modern urban culture and the phrase was even added to the Oxford English Dictionary.

One of the most popular events has been the annual international flash mob pillow fight. [4] ________ However, the event in San Francisco left a park covered in thousands of feathers! It was estimated that it would cost thousands of dollars to clear up the mess. The organisers posted a message online. 'We shouldn't have left such a mess,' they wrote. 'We're sorry.'

Flash mobs are not only potentially costly, though. There is also a danger that they can get out of control. When a 'silent disco' was advertised at a London station, the instructions to anyone who saw it were to bring music, wear headphones and dance. The organiser needn't have worried whether anyone would come: 12,000 people turned up! After 45 minutes, the station was closed, trains were delayed and thousands of passengers were furious. [5] ________

Since the early days of flash mobs, the events have developed into commercial opportunities for companies. [6] ________ In one mobile phone advertisement, for example, a crowd of 500 singers and dancers flooded into Heathrow Airport's arrivals hall to greet people who had just got off flights. The performers had rehearsed in secret for months before the day, and the company was terrified it would go wrong. However, the resulting advert more than lived up to everyone's expectations and has been seen by millions.

TALKING POINTS

Do you think people find flash mobs fun or annoying? Why?

Are flash mobs just entertainment, or can they have a more serious purpose?

SURPRISE! 59

GRAMMAR Modals (2): modals in the past

1 **Read the examples. What type of word follows *would have*, *should(n't) have* and *needn't have*?**

1 It would have been the world's first flash mob.
2 We shouldn't have left such a mess.
3 I should have sent the invitation to more people.
4 The organiser needn't have worried.
5 They didn't need to buy anything.

2 **Complete the rules with some of the modal verbs from Exercise 1.**

We use
a *would have* + past participle to imagine something in the past that didn't happen.
b ________ or *shouldn't have* + past participle to criticise or express a regret about the past.
c ________ + past participle to talk about something which happened but wasn't necessary.
d ________ + infinitive to talk about something which didn't happen because it wasn't necessary.

» GRAMMAR REFERENCE AND PRACTICE PAGE 157

3 **Choose the correct modal verbs.**

1 He *wouldn't / shouldn't* have driven when he was so tired. He put all our lives at risk.
2 You *needn't / wouldn't* have bought me a present.
3 We left at eight because we *didn't need to be / needn't have been* there until nine.
4 I'm glad I didn't see that spider. I *should / would* have been petrified!
5 I *needn't / shouldn't* have watched that film. I'm going to have difficulty sleeping tonight.
6 You *should / would* have told us you were going to be late. We were really concerned.

PREPARE FOR THE EXAM

Reading and Use of English Part 4

4 **Complete the second sentence so that it has a similar meaning to the first sentence, using the word given. Do not change the word given. You must use between two and five words.**

1 It was wrong of you to use my phone without my permission. **SHOULD**
You ________ before you used my phone.
2 It wasn't necessary for you to panic. **HAVE**
You ________ in a panic.
3 It was unfortunate that he went without checking the train times in advance. **SHOULD**
Before going out, ________ the train times.
4 It was a bad idea for me to walk home on my own. **NOT**
I ________ home on my own.
5 Why didn't you tell me you were going out? **SHOULD**
You ________ me know you were going out.
6 We had no homework last night. **NEED**
We ________ do any homework last night.

5 **Correct the mistake in each sentence.**

1 We needn't have gone shopping so we stayed at home and watched TV.
2 You would have seen the doctor about your cough. It sounded awful.
3 I should have gone skating with you yesterday. Why didn't you ask me?
4 You didn't have cooked, but I'm glad you did!
5 My brother wouldn't have told Mum and Dad about the surprise I'd planned for them. It was annoying!

6 **Complete the sentences about you. Then compare them with your partner. Ask more questions to find out details.**

1 Yesterday, I would have … , but …
2 Last weekend, I shouldn't have …
3 This morning, I didn't need to …
4 Last week, I needn't have …
5 Last year, I should have …

VOCABULARY Extended meanings of words

1 **Read the examples. What do *frozen* and *flooded* mean here? What is their literal meaning?**

1 They're completely still, frozen in the middle of whatever they were doing.
2 A crowd of 500 singers and dancers flooded into Heathrow Airport's arrivals hall.

2 EP **Complete the sentences with the correct form of the words in the box.**

boil	bright	flood	freeze	hit	weigh

1 You're an excellent student with a ________ future.
2 The students have been ________ by the news that their favourite teacher is leaving.
3 Mind if I leave the door open? It's ________ in here.
4 Having ________ up the pros and cons, he's decided to go to university.
5 She ________ when she saw the spider.
6 I opened the curtains and light ________ into the room.

3 EP **What do you think the words mean in these sentences?**

1 Simon is hardly an angel.
2 My memory is foggy.
3 The police grilled the suspect.
4 The good news lifted everyone's mood.
5 Josie sailed through her exams.
6 Molly and her sister have a stormy relationship.

4 » **Work in pairs.** **Turn to page 139.**

GRAMMAR Modals (2): modals in the past

WARMER

Ask students to think of: something they have done which they are sorry about because it was a mistake or it ended badly, and something they had a chance of doing but didn't do which would have been a good thing to do. Students discuss their ideas in groups of three or four.

1 Ask four different students to read the first four sentences aloud. Then ask the class what the form of the word is that follows each modal. Elicit *have* and that this is the same form as the present perfect but it is better to think of it in terms of *have* + past participle so that they don't write *has* instead of *have* by mistake.

Answer
past participle

2 When students have completed the rules, elicit the answers and ask which of the things mentioned in Exercise 1 happened. Ask questions for each sentence: 1 'Did the flash mob happen?' (*No*); 2 'Did they leave a mess?' (*Yes*); etc.

Answers
b should have c needn't have d didn't need to

» GRAMMAR REFERENCE AND PRACTICE ANSWER KEY TB PAGE 268

3 Before students choose the correct words, elicit whether the actions that are mentioned took place or not. Students then work alone, using the rules and the sentences in Exercise 1 to help them. Elicit the answers and corresponding rules.

Answers
1 shouldn't 2 needn't 3 didn't need to be 4 would 5 shouldn't 6 should

PREPARE FOR THE EXAM

4 B2 FIRST FOR SCHOOLS Reading and Use of English Part 4

Briefly review what students need to do in this part of the exam and if necessary, read out the *B2 First for Schools* box on TB page 49.

Point out that students must use between two and five words and that each question is worth two marks, with one mark for each part of the answer that is correct. Tell the class that, in the exam, this task will test different structures and vocabulary items, not just past modals. Remind students that most of the past modals will need the past participle of a verb, some of which they have to think of from the context. Students work alone then compare answers in pairs. Check the answers as a whole class.

Answers
1 should have | asked (me) / should have | asked / got | my permission 2 needn't | have got 3 he should | have checked 4 should not | have walked 5 should | have let 6 didn't/did not | need to

5 Look at the first sentence with the class. Ask them If they went shopping (*No, they stayed at home.*). Ask, 'Which verb form do we use to talk about something that didn't happen because it wasn't necessary?' (*didn't need to + infinitive*) and then elicit the correct sentence (*We didn't need to go shopping …*). Students then do the rest of the exercise alone. Elicit the correct answers and which rule each sentence corresponds to.

Answers
1 We **didn't need to go** shopping …
2 You **should have seen** the doctor about your cough.
3 I **would have gone** skating with you yesterday.
4 You **needn't have cooked**, but I'm glad you did!
5 My brother **shouldn't have told** Mum and Dad …

6 Look at the sentences and elicit what each one refers to, for example *1 something you didn't do; 2 something you did that you regret or want to criticise* etc. When students have finished, set a time limit of three minutes for them to discuss their sentences and invite students to share some of their ideas with the class. Students give their own answers.

FAST FINISHERS

Fast finishers can think of an extra sentence for each time period using a different modal verb, for example, *Yesterday, I should have …* They share these sentences with the class when students have finished their discussions.

» GRAMMAR WORKSHEET UNIT 10

VOCABULARY Extended meanings of words

1 Look at the sentences with the class and elicit the two meanings of each word. Ask the students if they can use the words in the same way in their own language. You could give more examples of both meanings of the words, for example: 'Do you ever buy frozen food from the supermarket? Have you ever seen an animal frozen in the lights of the car, too scared to run away?'

Answers
frozen – not moving; the literal meaning is 'turned into ice'
flooded – quickly entered in large numbers / in a large quantity; the literal meaning is 'caused something to be filled with water'

2 Look at the words in the box and elicit the literal meanings of each. Students work alone to complete the sentences then compare answers in pairs. Again, ask students if the same words have similar meanings in their language.

MIXED ABILITY

Allow weaker students to use dictionaries or their phones to look up alternative meanings of words they aren't sure of.

Answers
1 bright 2 hit 3 boiling 4 weighed 5 froze 6 flooded

3 Elicit the literal meanings of the words in blue. Students then work in pairs to think what the sentences mean. Elicit the answers and ask which ones were the easiest and which were the most difficult to guess.

Possible answers
1 someone who is very good and kind 2 unclear 3 asked a lot of questions for a long time 4 improved / made happier 5 easily passed 6 involving a lot of arguments and shouting

4 Set a time limit of three minutes for students to discuss the questions. Then elicit answers from different pairs. Students give their own answers.

» VOCABULARY WORKSHEET UNIT 10

LISTENING

1 Put the students into groups of three or four to discuss the questions. Invite students to share their ideas with the class. Students give their own answers.

PREPARE FOR THE EXAM

B2 FIRST FOR SCHOOLS
Listening Part 4

In this part, students listen to an interview or an exchange between two speakers and answer seven multiple-choice questions. The focus is on identifying opinion, attitude, detail, gist, main idea and specific information.

Tips Encourage students to look at each question and identify whether they need to listen for an opinion, the speaker's attitude, a main idea or specific information. When they listen, all three choices will be mentioned in some way but only one will give the correct information, so they need to listen carefully to see why two are incorrect.

43 2 Tell students to cover up Exercise 3. They look at the questions in Exercise 2 before listening. When they have listened, allow them to compare answers in pairs and then elicit the answers and any details that they remember.

Answers
1 No, it wasn't. 2 It was her best friend Jenny's idea.
3 Her actual birthday isn't until tomorrow.

43 3 Students look at the question and three choices in pairs and discuss which answer they think is correct. They then listen again and say why C is correct and why the other two answers are incorrect.

Answers
C

» AUDIOSCRIPT TB PAGES 294–295

44 4 Tell the students they will hear the recording twice, so they can mark the answer they think is correct the first time they listen and then check again on the second listening. Allow students to compare answers in pairs, then elicit the correct answers and the information in the conversation that helped them to decide.

Answers
2 A (B is not correct because the uncle only invented the story about the friend to prevent Amanda from finding out about the surprise; C isn't true because he did sit with them.)
3 B (A is incorrect because the restaurant had an eating area upstairs; C is not supported by what Amanda says, but is plausible as the upstairs area was getting busy.)
4 A (B is suggested by the fact that the sister was filming the event, but there is no suggestion that Amanda was uncomfortable with this; C is incorrect as Amanda says she was *almost* in tears.)
5 B (A is ruled out because the adults, including her parents, only stayed for an hour; C is wrong as Amanda doesn't say her mum was worried about saying a few words.)
6 A (B is not correct because when she mentions effort, she refers to friends making the effort for her and that she is likely to help them in the future. C is not correct because she says that being the centre of attention is not for her.)
7 C (A is not correct because the parents weren't worried about paying for the party; B is ruled out because Amanda says that her parents knew she'd appreciate it.)

» AUDIOSCRIPT TB PAGE 295

» PREPARE FOR THE EXAM TEACHING NOTES AND ANSWER KEY TB PAGE 260

SPEAKING Expressing surprise

45 1 Play the recording and elicit what Zoe is talking about (*a writing competition*) and what the surprising fact was (*a girl they know, Lisa, won it*).

Answer
He's surprised that Lisa Winters won a writing competition.

45 2 When students have listened, elicit the answers.

Answers
1 amazing 2 guessed

» AUDIOSCRIPT TB PAGE 295

46 3 Before students listen, elicit what Zoe was about to say and ask students to guess what the news was, for example, *someone stole Michael's bike*. Ask students to guess what Michael will be most surprised about, then play the recording and elicit the answer.

Answer
That someone took the bike back to the shop where it had been taken from.

46 4 Look at the *Prepare to speak* box with the students. Play the recording again, elicit the phrases used and then ask the students to work in pairs to say the expressions in the box showing they are very surprised. Choose one or two students to say the phrases with the correct intonation.

Answers
Jared: Was he?, Really?, You're kidding!, No way!
Michael: It was the last thing I expected.

» AUDIOSCRIPT TB PAGE 295

5 Choose one of the ideas in the box and elicit one or two possible pieces of surprising news from the class. Set a time limit of three or four minutes for students to write their pieces of news in their notebooks.

Answers
Students' own answers

6 Look at the example with the students and ask how the first speaker could continue the conversation, for example, *I know. It was the last thing I expected!* Allow students to practise their conversations and then invite a few pairs to act out a conversation in front of the class.

Answers
Students' own answers

COOLER
Write three topics on the board: school, friends, home. Ask students to write three things that would surprise them, one for each topic, for example, school – *The teacher allows us to go home early*. When they have finished, put the students into groups of three or four to share their ideas. The groups then try to agree on the most surprising thing for each topic. Invite students to share their ideas with the class.

LISTENING

1 Has anyone ever thrown you a surprise party? Have you ever been to a surprise party for someone else? What happened?

PREPARE FOR THE EXAM

Listening Part 4

2 (43) **Listen to part of a radio interview and answer these questions.**

1 Was it normal for Amanda and her friend to go to this café?
2 Whose idea was it to go to the cinema?
3 What does Amanda say about her actual birthday?

3 (43) **Listen again and choose the best answer to question 1.**

1 Why didn't Amanda suspect her friends were organising something on Saturday?
A They often went to a café before seeing a film.
B She had invited her friends to go to the cinema.
C Saturday wasn't actually her birthday.

4 (44) **You will now hear the complete radio interview. For questions 2–7, choose the best answer (A, B or C).**

2 When Amanda's uncle arrived at the restaurant, Amanda thought he
A seemed uncomfortable.
B was in a hurry.
C would prefer to be alone.

3 What did Amanda think about Jenny's suggestion to go downstairs?
A It was strange because they weren't going to eat.
B It wasn't worth moving because they had to leave soon.
C It was a good idea because it might be quieter there.

4 When Amanda first saw the party, she
A was surprised to see certain people there.
B felt unhappy about being filmed.
C became emotional and cried.

5 What does Amanda say about her parents?
A They stayed longer than she would have liked them to.
B Her dad gave a special performance for her.
C Her mum seemed concerned about making a speech.

6 What has happened as a result of Amanda's party?
A She has recognised how positive her relationships with friends are.
B She has made more effort to spend time with people she likes.
C She has become more confident about receiving attention.

7 What did Amanda's parents think about the idea of a surprise party?
A They were concerned about the cost.
B They didn't think Amanda would enjoy it.
C They were worried it would be too much work.

» PREPARE FOR THE EXAM PAGE 133

SPEAKING Expressing surprise

(45) 1 **Listen to the conversation. What is Jared surprised about?**

(45) 2 **Listen again and complete the extracts**

1 Did she? That's ________ !
2 I'd never have ________ Lisa was a good writer.

(46) 3 **Listen to another conversation. What are both Michael and Jared surprised about?**

(46) 4 **Read the *Prepare to speak* box. Then listen to Michael and Jared again. Which expressions do you hear?**

PREPARE TO SPEAK | Expressing surprise

I'd never have guessed.
It was the last thing I expected.
You're kidding!
That's amazing!
No way!
Really?
Was he?, Did she? (echo questions)

5 **Write three pieces of surprising news about yourself. Use the ideas in the box or your own ideas.**

an accident | a birthday present | moving house | someone you met | something you bought | something you read online

6 **Work in groups.**

- Tell each other your news and react.
- Use phrases from the *Prepare to speak* box.

I got a scooter for my birthday!

Did you? You're so lucky!

CULTURE

PERCEPTIONS OF TIME

1 **Ask and answer the questions with a partner.**

1 Do you think more about your past or your future? Why?
2 Do you ever feel that sometimes time goes more slowly or quickly than usual? In what situations?

2 **Read the title and the first paragraph of the article on page 63. How do you think that the language a person speaks can affect the way they perceive time? Read the article quickly and check if any of your ideas are mentioned.**

3 **Read the article again and answer the questions.**

1 How do English and German speakers talk about future events differently?
2 What effect might this difference have on the way that English and German speakers manage their money?
3 How do English and Spanish speakers talk about periods of time differently?
4 Who might think about their future being 'below' them. Why?

4 **Match the highlighted words and phrases in the article to the meanings.**

1 notice or understand the difference between two things
2 feeling that you must do something quickly
3 is in the future
4 form a picture of someone or something in your mind
5 passes very quickly

47 **5** **Listen to three people talking about time and culture. Match the summaries (A–C) to the speakers (1–3).**

A The way in which people think about time individually can be classified into two different groups, each with different perspectives or habits related to time.
B Generally, there are two different ways that cultures view time. The first way is as a sequence or line. The second is to see time as a cycle and something that doesn't start or end.
C The academic study of time uses two different groups to help us understand how time relates to culture and non-verbal communication.

47 **6** **Listen again. Are the sentences true (*T*) or false (*F*)?**

1 People in future-orientated cultures have a relaxed view of time.
2 Western cultures usually see time as a sequence of events or a line.
3 Meeting deadlines is very important in cyclical time cultures.
4 The main priority for people who like multi-tasking is reaching goals and getting results.
5 Time is very valuable in places like Japan.
6 In polychronic cultures, people pay more attention to other people's needs rather than deadlines.

7 **Read the sentences 1–6. Match the phrases in bold to the meanings a–f.**

a certain to happen, but you do not know when
b at the last minute and before it was too late
c not having more time available
d for the moment / temporarily
e the result will be known or seen in the future
f find and dedicate time to doing something

USEFUL LANGUAGE

Expressions with *time*

1 Just stay there **for the time being** and I'll call you in a while.
2 You got here **just in time**. I was about to leave!
3 It's really important to **make time** for yourself and your family.
4 I'm not sure if I made the right decision, but **time will tell**.
5 Well, that's it for today. I'm afraid we're **out of time**.
6 Your parents will find out! It's only **a matter of time**.

CULTURE

Learning Objectives

- The students learn about how language affects our view of time.
- In the project stage, the students investigate different attitudes to time by creating a questionnaire to ask different people and then they present the results of the questionnaire to the class.

Vocabulary

distinguish flies lies ahead rushed visualise

Resources

CULTURE VIDEO AND CULTURE VIDEO WORKSHEET: Sensing language

BACKGROUND INFORMATION

Language can show how different cultures have different views about our relationship with time. For example, does time move or do we move? In English, we can say both that the time is coming nearer (for example *summer is coming*) or that we are moving towards a future event (for example *we're getting closer and closer to our exams*).

In English, we say the past is behind us and the future is ahead of us. In Aymara, a language spoken in some parts of Bolivia and Peru, they see these concepts differently. For them, the past is in front of us because we can see in front of us, just as we can know what happened in the past but we can't see behind us or see what the future will bring.

The Kuuk Thaayorre tribe of aborigines in Australia see time as being from east to west so, when they are facing south, the past is to the left and the future to the right, as in many Western societies. However, when they sit facing north, they see time from right to left and when they face east, time comes towards them. For them, time is related to the world around them.

Another tribe, the Amondawa people of South America, have no words for time or time periods such as years or months. They don't refer to their ages, but have different names for the different stages they go through in their lives. However, although they don't have these concepts in their own language, tribe members understand and use them correctly when they learn Portuguese.

WARMER

Put the students into groups of four or five. Elicit a topic, for example, animals. Tell the students they have to say the name of an animal in turn and if they can't think of one, they are out. Stop the activity after one minute and ask the students how they felt. Elicit a different topic, for example, fruit, and do the same again, but this time, tell the students they only have three seconds to think. The other students count down and, if they run out of time, the student is out. Again, allow one minute and afterwards ask students if they felt any differently because of the time limit.

1 Set a time limit of one minute for students to discuss the questions in pairs then invite students to share their ideas as a class. Ask them if they think their answer for the first question will change as they grow older and, if so, why.

Answers
Students' own answers

2 Tell students not to read more than the first paragraph yet. When they have finished, they discuss their ideas as a class. Give them three minutes to then read quickly through the text and elicit any ideas that were mentioned.

Answers
Students' own answers

3 Set a time limit of ten minutes for students to read the text and find the information. They then cover the text and work in pairs to answer the questions in their own words. Elicit the answers and ask the students what they think about the ideas in the text.

FAST FINISHERS

Tell fast finishers to get into pairs and, ask them to discuss what other facts they found out and how similar or different they think their language is compared to those in the text. When everyone has finished, elicit the answers and then invite fast finishers to share their information and ideas with the class.

Answers
1 English speakers have special tenses/structures for talking about the future. German speakers use a present simple structure.
2 Because they use a future tense, English speakers see the future as more distant and so don't feel the same need to save for it. For German speakers, the future seems closer and more real, and therefore they think they need to save for it.
3 English speakers talk about time in terms of distance, or length. Spanish speakers tend to use words of size and volume to talk about time passing.
4 A Mandarin speaker, because they write their words vertically, from top to bottom, and so they visualise time that way too.

48 The Reading text is recorded for students to listen, read and check their answers.

4 When students have done the matching task, ask if their language has an equivalent phrase to *time flies*. You could also tell them that there is another phrase, *time stands still*, which means that time seems to stop or go very slowly.

Answers
1 distinguish 2 rushed 3 lies ahead 4 visualise 5 flies

CONTINUED ON PAGE 122

47 **5** Read the three summaries with the class. For A, elicit that this is about individuals and how they see time. Students then work in pairs and look for the key words or phrases in each (*A think, individually, two groups, different perspectives or habits; B cultures, line / cycle – doesn't start or end; C academic, study, groups, culture, non-verbal communication*). When students have listened, they discuss in pairs which summary matches each person and what key words they heard in the recording to help them. (Speaker *1 – B: cultures, entire nations, United States, Western cultures, linear, sequential, cyclical, big wheel; Speaker 2 – A: personal attitude, profile one, you prefer, you like, profile two, etc.; Speaker 3 – C: study, non-verbal communication, first group, timetables, second group, needs.*)

Answers

Speaker 1 B Speaker 2 A Speaker 3 C

47 **6** Tell the students to read through the sentences and underline key words so they know exactly what they are listening for. When they have listened, allow students to compare answers in pairs. You could then play the recording again and ask students to note key words which helped them to identify the answers. Elicit the answers and what the speakers said.

Answers

1 F People in future-orientated cultures are usually very time-conscious, which can be stressful.
2 T
3 F Deadlines are less important than flexibility in cyclical time cultures.
4 F Reaching goals and getting results is important, but the most important things are sharing experiences with people and forming strong relationships.
5 T
6 T

» **AUDIOSCRIPT TB PAGES 295–296**

7 Ask students to cover the meanings in Exercise 7. Then, look at the phrases with the class and elicit what the sentences mean. Students then do the matching. Elicit the answers and check students understand the difference in meaning between *in time* and *on time*. (*On time* means at an agreed time. *In time* means at a time before something happens. Sometimes, they are similar, but, for example, you could be late for a train, so not on time, but, if the train is also late and you catch it, you would be in time for it.) Put students into groups of three or four to brainstorm any other phrases which include the word *time* they know in English, for example *from time to time, a long time*. Students then think of how these could be translated into their own language and see which have a literal translation and which use different ideas; some might not have an equivalent at all. Invite groups to share their ideas with the class.

MIXED ABILITY

To make the activity easier for weaker students, write a choice of two answers for each expression on the board, for example: 1 a, d; 2 b, c; 3 e, f; 4 d, e; 5 c, f; 6 a, b.

Answers

1d 2b 3f 4e 5c 6a

PROJECT ***Investigating attitudes to time***

Put the students into groups of four where possible. Look at the instructions with the class and elicit a possible question for each of the four headings, for example: *Is it important for people to be on time for meetings? Should people save regularly? Is it OK to ask for an extension to a deadline? Is it important to prioritise tasks when you have more than one thing to do at a time?* Tell students that Yes/No answers like these are better on a questionnaire as it is easier to find some clear results. Instead of Yes/No answers, they can have a number between 0 (not at all) to 5 (yes, vital). Allow students time in the lesson to create their questionnaires and make sure they all write the same questions so that they can compare the answers they are given by friends and family.

Set a realistic time limit for students to ask their questions outside the classroom. Encourage them to ask as many people of different ages as possible, with a minimum of five people overall. They then get together to compare answers and create a summary of the results, noting any obvious differences between answers given by different generations.

When the groups have presented their projects, if there were any differences noted between generations, ask the class why they think these differences exist.

PROJECT EXTENSION

Tell the class to imagine that someone is coming to visit their country. Students work in the same groups as for the project. Half the groups should make a list of advice for the visitor about attitudes to time, for example *if you are invited to someone's home at 7 pm, you should arrive no earlier than 7.15!* The other half should make a list of information about when things happen (timetables, holidays, etc.), for example, *Shops usually open at 8 am and close at 6 pm, but on Sundays most shops are shut*. They think of at least five pieces of advice or information. When they are ready, invite groups to share their ideas with the class and have a class discussion of what the students like or dislike about attitudes to time in their country.

08 **CULTURE VIDEO: Sensing language**

When students have completed the lesson, they can watch the video and complete the worksheet.

COOLER

Ask the students if they have ever read a story or seen a film which involves time travel. Give them an example, for example *A sound of thunder* by Ray Bradbury. Say: 'A company takes people back in time to hunt dinosaurs, but there are rules about which ones you can kill *(dinosaurs which will die anyway almost at that exact point in time)*. There is also a floating walkway so the hunters don't damage any living thing. One hunter panics and falls off the path and runs through the forest. When they get back home, there are small but obvious changes in the world. The hunter looks at his shoe and sees he has stepped on a butterfly and this has changed how things have evolved.' Ask the students what changes may have happened and why they think the death of a butterfly could have caused these changes. (*In the book, there were changes in spelling of some words and a different outcome in a recent election. The changes were caused by very small changes in evolution as a result of the butterfly dying early.*) Students then discuss a film or story they know in groups of three or four. When they are ready, they explain the plot to the class.

CAN THE LANGUAGE YOU SPEAK CHANGE HOW YOU VIEW TIME?

48

Time always moves forward at exactly the same rate, but our experience of it can change dramatically. Think about how slowly time seems to pass when you're bored, waiting for something or doing something you don't want to do … But time flies when you're having fun or feeling rushed! Well, new research suggests that the language we speak can affect how we perceive time, and even how we manage our money!

A group of Australian economists has suggested that the way a language 'talks' about the future can affect the way its speakers save their money. Many languages have clearly defined tenses or structures that they use to talk about the future. For example, when making plans, an English speaker might say 'I'll buy a new car next year' or 'I'm going to buy a new car next year'. They wouldn't say 'I buy a car next year'. It has been suggested that speakers of such languages are less likely to save for the future because they see future events as being more distant and less connected to the present. So what about speakers of languages that don't distinguish the future from the present grammatically? They view the future as closer and more real, and so are more likely to save money for it. Speakers of German and Mandarin Chinese, for example, typically talk about the future using a present simple construction: *I buy a car next year*. However, critics of this theory claim that these are just generalisations and many other, more important factors determine people's spending and saving habits.

A different study suggests that the language we use to talk about the duration of an event affects how we think about time. For example, speakers of languages that use mostly 'distance' words to describe time perceive time differently from speakers of languages that use mostly 'volume' words. English and Swedish are examples of languages that generally use distance words to describe time, for example, asking how *long* a film lasts, talking about the *length* of a holiday, or taking a *short* break. Languages like Spanish and Greek, on the other hand, mainly use words of size and volume, for example, asking how *much* time a lesson will last, or taking a *small* break. The study suggests that these differences can affect the speakers' ability to accurately estimate periods of time in different situations.

But it's not just the way we *talk* about language that affects the way we perceive time. Linguists say that the way we read and write our native language also affects the way we visualise time. For example, most languages, including English, are written horizontally from left to right. Speakers of these languages imagine time as a horizontal line with the past behind them, while their future lies ahead of them. However, Mandarin is traditionally written vertically, and therefore its speakers visualise time vertically, from top to bottom. They see the past as being above them and the future below them.

It's fascinating when you start to consider how language affects not only our sense of time, but also the way we think in general and our perception of the world. Take some time to think about it!

PROJECT *Investigating attitudes to time*

Work in groups of three or four to investigate the attitudes towards time amongst people you know. Use these steps to help you.

1. Create a questionnaire about people's views on the following areas:
   - punctuality
   - saving money
   - meeting deadlines
   - prioritising tasks
2. Ask people you know, such as friends and family members, to fill in the questionnaire.

Present the results of your questionnaire to the class.

08 NOW WATCH THE CULTURE VIDEO

11 WE ARE FAMILY

ABOUT YOU

09 **Watch the video and answer the questions.**

Who do you get on with best in your family? Why?

Do you think it's important to know about your family history?

What do you think makes a happy family?

VOCABULARY Phrasal verbs: relationships

1 Match the pairs of sentences.

EP

1 Sarah really looks up to her father.
2 My eldest sister looks down on me.
3 Luke takes after his father.
4 My family always stick together.
5 I don't want to fall out with you.
6 My brother's gone off his girlfriend.
7 Lisa has just finished with her boyfriend.
8 I didn't hit it off with Jake.
9 I can always count on my parents.
10 Anna won't let you down.

a He's 1.92 m tall, the same as his dad.
b She makes me feel completely unimportant.
c I found him very difficult to talk to.
d I think they're going to split up.
e We never fall out and we're very close.
f I hate getting into arguments.
g They'll always help me if I need them to.
h He's a very good role model for her.
i She's single again now.
j If she says she'll help, she will help.

49 **2 Listen to the conversations and answer the questions you are asked.**

3 Ask and answer the questions about your family or friends with a partner.

1 Have you ever met someone and hit it off with them immediately?
2 Have you ever let anyone down? How?
3 Who can you really count on?
4 Who do you look up to? Why?
5 Who do you take after?
6 Have you ever felt that someone looks down on you? Who?
7 Does your family stick together?
8 Have you ever gone off someone? Why?
9 Have you ever finished with a girlfriend or boyfriend?
10 How often do you fall out with friends?

READING

PREPARE FOR THE EXAM

Reading and Use of English Part 2

1 Read the example answer (0) in the first paragraph of the text. What type of word is given in the gap?

2 For questions 1–8, read the first two paragraphs of the text and think of the word which best fits each gap. Use only one word in each gap.

3 Read the rest of the text. Match the sections (A–C) to the headings (1–5). There are two extra headings.

1 Long-distance love
2 Opposites attract
3 Family nightmares
4 Wrong number
5 Staying local

4 Answer the questions.

1 What 'mistake' did Attis make?
2 Why did the Palestino fans take pity on Nobu?
3 Why didn't Rachana like Amir at first?

11 WE ARE FAMILY

Unit Overview

TOPIC	Family and relationships
VOCABULARY	Phrasal verbs: relationships
READING	How we met …
GRAMMAR	Relative clauses
VOCABULARY	Compound adjectives
WRITING	An article (2)
EXAM TASKS	Reading and Use of English Part 2; Writing Part 2

Resources

GRAMMAR REFERENCE AND PRACTICE: SB page 158; TB page 268
PREPARE FOR THE EXAM: SB pages on TB pages 237 and 246; TB pages 254 and 258
WORKBOOK: pages 44–47
VIDEO AND VIDEO WORKSHEET: Families
PHOTOCOPIABLE WORKSHEETS: Grammar worksheet Unit 11; Vocabulary worksheet Unit 11
TEST GENERATOR: Unit test 11
PRACTICE EXTRA: Unit 11

WARMER

Tell students to write five sentences with *would have … but / shouldn't have / didn't need to / needn't have / should have* about members of their family. Three of the sentences should be true and two should be false, for example, *My sister should have bought some new shoes last week.*

Students read their sentences aloud to a partner who should guess which ones are true. Tell pairs to ask each other a question about the three true sentences. Ask two or three pairs to report back to the class.

ABOUT YOU

09 You can begin the class and introduce the topic of the unit by showing the video and asking students to complete the video worksheet. Put students into groups of three or four to discuss the questions in the *About you* box. Set a time limit of three or four minutes, then invite students to share their ideas with the class. Ask students if any of them know anything about the generations before their grandparents.

VOCABULARY Phrasal verbs: relationships

1 Students can do the matching alone and then compare answers in pairs. Monitor and help where necessary. Elicit the answers and the meanings of the verbs in blue.

Answers
1 h 2 b 3 a 4 e 5 f 6 d 7 i 8 c 9 g 10 j

49 2 Play the first question and elicit what this means (*someone Olivia trusts to be on time because they are always punctual*). Play the recording and elicit the answer. Now play the rest of the recording. Allow students time to compare their answers. When the students have listened, play the recording again, pausing after each question to elicit what it means and then playing the extract to elicit the answer.

Answers
1 her dad 2 her grandma 3 Not very well – they didn't have anything in common. 4 his parents 5 Mateo's brother looks down on him. 6 Nicholas has fallen out with his cousin.

» AUDIOSCRIPT TB PAGE 296

3 Look at the first question with the class and invite students to tell the class about someone they hit it off with straightway. Encourage other students to ask more questions to find out more details. Re-elicit the meanings of the different phrasal verbs if necessary and put students in pairs to discuss the questions. Monitor and encourage students to give as much detail as possible. Monitor and note down interesting answers and good use of the phrasal verbs to give as feedback. Then invite some students to share their stories with the class.

Answers
Students' own answers

READING

PREPARE FOR THE EXAM

1 **B2 FIRST FOR SCHOOLS Reading and Use of English Part 2**
Briefly review what students need to do in this part of the exam and, if necessary, read out the *B2 First for Schools* box on TB page 58.

Point out that in this part, the students are not given options to choose from, so it is important that they use their language knowledge to predict the type of word needed and to also think about issues such as collocation.

Ask students if their families have always lived in the same area, and tell them that they are going to read three interesting family stories from round the world. Write a verb (*have*), conjunction (*however*), adverb (*as*), determiner (*another*), preposition (*of*) and article (*the*) on the board, and ask students to identify the parts of speech. Then tell students to look at the question and the example gap and ask them to put their hands up if they think they would have written the correct word. Elicit that this is the *-ing* form of a verb. Ask how the students could be sure that *to be* is the wrong answer (*we can only write one word in each gap in this task*).

Answer
a verb form

2 If you have students preparing for the *B2 First for Schools* exam, set a time limit of ten minutes for this task. Tell students that to complete the gaps, they need to think about what type of word is missing. Remind them that, in the exam, the gapped text is a standalone text, not part of a longer one. After students have completed this individually, they should check their answers before comparing them with a partner. Remind them that sometimes more than one answer is possible. Check answers as a whole class.

Answers
1 This/That 2 is 3 after 4 such 5 what 6 all 7 it 8 each/every

CONTINUED ON PAGE 126

BACKGROUND INFORMATION

Talcahuano is an important port in south-central Chile. It is named after the local tribal chief who lived in the area when the Spanish arrived. It translates as 'Thundering Sky'. The local football club, Club Deportivo Huachipato, was formed in 1947 and plays in the Chilean Premier Division. Club Deportivo Palestino was founded in 1920 by Palestinian immigrants.

The first large scale movement of Japanese immigrants to Chile were 126 miners who arrived in 1903, although, according to a census taken in 1875, there were two Japanese citizens living in the country at that time. Now, there are estimated to be about 2,600 Japanese people living in the country.

Marrakesh is a city in the mid-south-west of Morocco, the fourth largest in the country. It is a major tourist destination and most famous for its main square, the Jemaa el-Fnaa, one of the best-known squares in Africa, where you can find food stalls and many different forms of entertainment. Marrakesh grew as a trading post and rest stop on the Saharan trade routes as there is a large oasis to the north of the city which supplied water to the city and made farming possible.

Mumbai used to be called Bombay. It is on India's west coast and is the biggest city in India, with a population of about 12 million in the city proper and around 21 million in the metropolitan area. It is also the wealthiest city in the country and home to the Indian film industry: Bollywood. It is the financial capital of India and home to both the central bank and the country's stock exchange.

3 Look at the headings with the students. Ask them to think of what they could refer to, for example, *1 Two people living in two different countries. Perhaps one got a job abroad or their family emigrated. 2 Two people with different personalities fall in love. 3 Two people fall in love, but their families don't accept their partners and make life difficult for them. 4 Someone made a phone call to the wrong person and it led to a long-term relationship. 5 An extended family who all still live in the same town or village and where so many of the people are related*. Students discuss their own ideas in pairs. Monitor and help as necessary. Elicit ideas about what they could be about then tell the students to read the texts and do the matching. Elicit the answers and how close the students' guesses were to the real stories.

You could follow up by putting the students into small groups and asking them to write a short text for one of the two unused headings. Invite the groups to read their stories to the class.

Answers

A 4 B 1 C 2

4 Tell students to read the texts again without writing anything. They then cover the texts and discuss what they found out in pairs. Together they write the answers to the three questions in their own words. Monitor and help if necessary. Check answers as a whole class. Then elicit which of the three texts they found most interesting and why.

MIXED ABILITY

Weaker students can work in groups of three, with each student reading a different section of the text and finding the answer to their question. They then tell each other the answers. Stronger students could try to answer the questions in pairs without reading the texts again and then read the texts to see if there were any details they didn't remember.

FAST FINISHERS

Ask fast finishers to think of another question they could ask for each of the three people, for example, *Why did Attis decide to ring the woman again?* (*There had been something in her voice which had really appealed to him*). When everyone has finished, elicit the answers to the questions in the book and invite the fast finishers to ask their questions for other students to answer.

Answers

1 He dialled the wrong number.
2 Because he was on his own.
3 She thought he was rude and arrogant because he didn't talk much and stared at her.

50 The Reading text is recorded for students to listen, read and check their answers.

TALKING POINTS

In pairs, students discuss these questions together. Set a time limit of three minutes and then elicit ideas from different students. Ask the students which family member or friend they think they can count on most and who lets them down the most often. You could give the class one or two quotes about a family and ask them what they think of them, for example:

'Happiness is having a large, loving, caring, close-knit family … in another city.' George Burns, comedian

'As much as they make you mad, interrupt you, annoy you, curse at you, try to control you, these are the people who know you the best and who love you.' Jenna Morasca, actress

COOLER

Ask students to draw their own family tree including grandparents and parents' brothers and sisters (and their families). Then ask them to describe their family to a partner. They should ask about each other's family to try to find out any interesting stories or facts. Invite students to talk about someone special in their family.

HOW WE MET ...

No one says that **(0)** *being* part of a family is easy, but families do generally provide us with the love, comfort and security we need. **(1)** ______ is partly because of a shared history, which is often recorded in photos. What many families enjoy doing **(2)** ______ looking back at the people and events in their lives through these photos. And it's always fun to see which of our ancestors we take **(3)** ______.

Family members also like to share things they remember, **(4)** ______ as fond memories of their relatives, or amusing stories of **(5)** ______ grown-ups did when they were small. Perhaps most of **(6)** ______, we enjoy hearing about how our parents and grandparents first got to know each other. The more unusual or romantic the story, the more we enjoy hearing **(7)** ______. The same stories are often told over and over again without losing their impact, and bring families closer together **(8)** ______ time they hear them.

Here are some family stories of how people met.

50

A MARKOS FAFOUTAKIS
Athens, Greece ______

It was love at first sight for Markos's grandparents, despite the fact that they had fallen out before they met face to face. It all started when his grandfather, Attis Fafoutakis, called a friend. Marie Wouters, who had just moved to Greece from Belgium, answered the phone. When she explained that she didn't know the friend Attis was looking for, Attis got a little annoyed. But when Marie repeated her number slowly, Attis realised his mistake. He was in a hurry, so he simply hung up. Later, Attis couldn't stop thinking about the woman he had spoken to. There had been something in her voice which had really appealed to him and so he decided to start all over again. Attis redialled the number that he had called by accident and used all his charms to apologise to Marie. She forgave him and they ended up chatting for ages. In fact, they got on so well that they arranged to meet, and the rest is history.

B PANCHO YAMAMOTO
Talcahuano, Chile ______

Pancho Yamamoto's parents didn't exactly hit it off the first time they met. The Yamamotos moved from Japan to Chile to work in the mines around 1915. Pancho's father, Nobu, was a big fan of Huachipato, a football team from his home town of Talcahuano. Nobu took pride in going to every Huachipato match and one winter, he travelled 500 km to Santiago de Chile, where Huachipato was going to play against Palestino. At the match, he was surprised to find that he was the only Huachipato fan in the stadium. The Palestino fans laughed and whistled at lonely Nobu throughout the game. Then, when the game ended, some of them took pity on him, invited him for dinner and they soon forgot all about their teams' rivalry. One Palestino fan, Carolina Fernández, had been laughing at Nobu all along, like the others. But she knew it was wrong, so she made an effort to get to know him during dinner. Despite living at different ends of the country, they started writing letters to each other – in all about 200 passed between them before they got married.

C LUCINDA SHAH
Marrakesh, Morocco ______

Lucinda Shah tells us about how her parents almost didn't get together …

Lucinda's mother, Rachana, who is Indian, grew up in Mumbai and ended up working as an actress in London. Lucinda's father, Amir, a film producer whose work is mainly in the UK, was born in India to an Afghan father and a Scottish mother. Amir Shah met Rachana in 1999 through a mutual friend, Carrie. 'She thought we'd get on well, and invited us both to a dinner party,' says Rachana. Unfortunately, it wasn't love at first sight. 'I thought he was rude and arrogant!' she continues. 'I'm very confident and chatty, whereas he hardly spoke and just kept staring at me.' When Amir had left the party, Rachana shared her doubts with her friend. 'Carrie told me that Amir was shy and that the more he liked someone, the quieter he was. She said it was a good sign!' Rachana decided to give Amir another chance, and the pair met up for coffee. 'This time,' says Rachana, 'I asked Amir lots of questions about his work, and we chatted for the rest of the afternoon and we really hit it off!'

TALKING POINTS

How do family relationships differ from friendships?

Do you think friends can be more important than family in certain situations?

GRAMMAR Relative clauses

1 Read the examples and underline the relative clauses. Are they defining (D) or non-defining (ND)?

1 Marie Wouters, who had just moved to Greece from Belgium, answered the phone.
2 Attis couldn't stop thinking about the woman he had spoken **to**.
3 Attis redialled the number that he had called by accident.
4 There had been something in her voice which had really appealed to him.
5 Lucinda's father, whose work is mainly in the UK, was born in India.
6 Nobu travelled to Santiago de Chile, where Huachipato was going to play against Palestino.

2 Read the rules and check your answers.

a A defining relative clause gives essential information about a noun. We:
- can leave out the relative pronoun if it is the object of the clause.
- cannot leave out the relative pronoun if it is the subject of the clause.

b A non-defining relative clause adds extra information about a noun. We:
- cannot leave out the relative pronoun.
- do not use *that* for people or things.
- always use commas before and after the relative clause.

» GRAMMAR REFERENCE AND PRACTICE PAGE 158

3 Read the examples in Exercise 1 again. Where is the bold preposition in example 2?

4 Read the text. Add a relative pronoun before each relative clause. Put the relative pronoun in brackets if you can leave it out. Add commas where necessary.

We went to the island of Rhodes, which is where my ancestors used to live.

I'll never forget our family holiday in Greece. We went to the island of Rhodes is where my ancestors used to live. It's an area has a fascinating history, and my parents wanted to find the village they used to live in. We couldn't find any records could help us, but eventually we found a village just like the one in the old photos we had been given. We asked in a café and we were introduced to an old man great-grandparents had lived next to our old family home. The house had been knocked down, but it was nice to make a connection with someone knew a bit about our family history.

5 Rewrite the sentences using relative clauses.

0 I have a cousin the same age as me. She is really good fun.
I have a cousin the same age as me, who is really good fun.
1 That's Shelly. She wants to buy my bike.
2 Our apartment has views across the whole city. It was built five years ago.
3 My uncle is now a teacher at our school. He always played with us as children.
4 Here's the money. I owe you it for the concert ticket.
5 This is a photo of my grandparents. They got married in 1967.

6 Correct the mistake in each sentence.

1 I went with my wife and son is two years old.
2 The area, wich has lots of farms, is great for walking.
3 At the café, we met a girl which my friend Saif knows.
4 The beach, who is really long and wide, is perfect for playing ball games.
5 There are 30 students will attend the class.

VOCABULARY Compound adjectives

1 Complete the compound adjectives. Use the past participle form of the words in the box.

EP

age	balance	behave
~~build~~	organise	pay

0 Sam is tall and weighs 86 kg. He's fairly well-*built*.
1 The holiday was well-______, thanks to my mum.
2 My dad's 45, so I guess he's middle-______.
3 I try to eat a well-______ diet.
4 My aunt has a very well-______ job.
5 I can't stand badly ______ pets! My dog's so good!

2 Complete the sentences. Combine one word from each box to form compound adjectives.

EP

grown high last ~~long~~ self short

confident ~~distance~~ minute tech term up

0 We make a lot of *long*-*distance* phone calls.
1 Mark is really ______-______. He doesn't mind performing in front of huge audiences.
2 My uncle's living with us at the moment, but it's only a ______-______ arrangement. He's moving out to his own place soon.
3 I've got two ______-______ cousins who are a lot older than me. They have their own homes and families now.
4 There's always a lot of ______-______ equipment in our house because my mum's a software developer.
5 We didn't book the football tickets until the day before the match. It was a ______-______ decision, so we were lucky to get seats.

3 » **Work in pairs. Turn to page 139.**

GRAMMAR Relative clauses

WARMER

Tell students to complete the following sentence: *The person sitting next to me is wearing …* Write an example on the board: *The person sitting next to me is wearing a cool T-shirt.* Now write the start of another two sentences about the same person on the board: *1 He/She …* and *2 His/Her …* . Elicit how students could complete the sentences: *He has got brown hair. His dad is a doctor.* Students do the same about the person they wrote about originally. Tell them NOT to write the person's name.

Now elicit how you can combine your sentences so that they contain relative clauses: *The person sitting next to me, who has got brown hair, is wearing a cool T-shirt. The person sitting next to me, whose dad is a doctor, is wearing a cool T-shirt.*

Students do the same with their sentences. Collect these in and read some out. Students guess who the sentences refer to.

1 Ask the students to do this in pairs without any explanations. Don't check the answers yet.

2 Read through the rules box with the class. Then look at each sentence in Exercise 1. Read out the sentences without the relative clauses and ask the students if they make sense, for example, *1 Yes, the relative clause just gives extra information. 2 No, we don't know which woman.* Also point out that sentence has omitted the relative pronoun and elicit what it could be (*who/that*).

Answers

1 Marie Wouters, <u>who had just moved to Greece</u>, answered the phone. (ND) 2 Attis couldn't stop thinking about the woman <u>he had spoken to</u>. (D) 3 Attis re-dialled the number <u>that he had called by accident</u>. (D) 4 There had been something in her voice <u>which had really appealed to him</u>. (D) 5 Lucinda's father, <u>whose work is mainly in the UK</u>, was born in India. (ND) 6 Nobu travelled to Santiago de Chile, <u>where Huachipato was going to play against Palestino</u>. (ND)

» **GRAMMAR REFERENCE AND PRACTICE ANSWER KEY TB PAGE 268**

3 Point out that we can place the preposition before the relative pronoun, for example *to which, from whose.* However, when we do this with *who*, we have to use a different word, *whom*: *to whom*, *from whom*, etc. This is more formal than placing the preposition at the end of the sentence.

Answer

at the end of the relative clause

4 Look at the example with the students. Elicit the sentence without the relative clause (*We went to the island of Rhodes.*). Elicit that the relative clause adds extra information, so this is non-defining. That means we cannot omit the relative pronoun and we can't use *that* in place of *which*. Students do the exercise alone then compare answers in pairs. Elicit the answers and what kind of relative clause each one is.

Answers

I'll never forget our family holiday in Greece. We went to the island of Rhodes, **which** is where my ancestors used to live. It's an area **that/which** has a fascinating history, and my parents wanted to find the village (**that/which**) they used to live in. We couldn't find any records **that/which** could help us, but eventually we found a village just like the one in the old photos (**that/which**) we had been given. We asked in a café and we were introduced to an old man **whose** great-grandparents had lived next to our old family home. The house had been knocked down, but it was nice to make a connection with someone **who/that** knew a bit about our family history.

5 Look at the example with the class and elicit that it is a non-defining relative clause, so the pronoun must be used; we can't use *that* in place of *who* and we need to separate the clause with a comma. Also elicit that the pronoun *she* has been replaced with the relative pronoun. Tell students that there is more than one correct answer for some sentences. Students work in pairs. Elicit the answers and information about each sentence.

Answers

1 That's Shelly, who wants to buy my bike.
2 Our apartment, which has views across the whole city, was built five years ago. / Our apartment, which was built five years ago, has views across the whole city.
3 My uncle, who is now a teacher at our school, always played with us as children. / My uncle, who always played with us as children, is now a teacher at our school.
4 Here's the money that/which I owe you for the concert ticket.
5 This is a photo of my grandparents, who got married in 1967.

6 Elicit what the relative clause is in the first sentence (*is two years old*), ask if it is non-defining (*yes, it gives extra information about the son*) and what is missing (*a comma and the relative pronoun* who). Students do the rest alone. Elicit the answers and students' explanations.

Answers

1 I went with my wife and son, **who** is two years old.
2 The area, **which** has lots of farms, is great for walking.
3 At the café we met a girl ~~which~~ **who/that** my friend Saif knows.
4 The beach, ~~who~~ **which** is really long and wide, is perfect for playing ball games.
5 There are 30 students **who/that** will attend the class.

» **GRAMMAR WORKSHEET UNIT 11**

VOCABULARY Compound adjectives

1 Elicit what a compound adjective is (*an adjective formed of two words: an adverb or adjective and a second adjective*). Students do the exercise alone. Elicit the answers and what the words mean.

Answers

1 organised 2 aged 3 balanced 4 paid 5 behaved

2 Tell students to look at the sentences without looking at the word pools. For each one, they should think of what the missing words mean, for example, *1 not shy, outgoing; 2 not for a long time*, etc. Students then look at the words and complete the sentences. Elicit the answers and the meanings of the words.

Answers

1 self-confident 2 short-term 3 grown-up 4 high-tech
5 last-minute

3 Students to turn to page 139 and read the instructions. Encourage the students to give extended answers with reasons for their answers. Monitor and listen for interesting responses and invite these students to share their answers with the class.

Answers

Students' own answers

» **VOCABULARY WORKSHEET UNIT 11**

WRITING An article (2)

1 Tell students they are going to read an article entitled 'Someone I admire'. Ask them to write down the name of someone they admire and to then tell their partner why they admire this person. Ask students to read the text and answer the question. Check the answer with the whole class.

Answer
His brother taught him to be more thoughtful.

2 Draw students' attention to the notice and tell them to read it quickly. Then ask students to read Sebastian's article again and answer the questions with a partner. Elicit ideas from one or two pairs.

FAST FINISHERS
Ask fast finishers to think of three questions they would like to ask Sebastian about his older brother. When everyone has finished the exercise, elicit the answers then invite fast finishers to share their questions with the class. Ask other students to use their imagination to answer the questions.

Answers
1 Students' own answers (for example *My brilliant brother!*) 2 yes 3 'Do you have a friend or family member that you look up to?' is answered in paragraph 1. 'What makes this person special?' is answered in paragraph 2. 'What have you learned from him or her?' is the subject of paragraph 3. 4 He asks the reader questions, for example *Can you think of someone who you really look up to?*, which encourage them to compare Sebastian's experiences with their own.

3 Give students a few minutes to do the matching exercise. Check answers as a whole class. You could then look back at the Reading and Use of English task on pages 64–65 as that tested an *-ing* form as a subject (example) and an expression for emphasis (gap 2).

Answers
Questions: *Can you think of someone who you really look up to? Who has been a big influence in your life?*
-ing forms as subjects: *Talking to my parents didn't help*
Structures which add emphasis: *The thing I admired most about him was …, What I've learned more than anything is …*

4 Tell students to use between one and four words in each sentence. Look at the first sentence with the class and elicit that they need to use the *-ing* form of the verb *to meet*. Give students a few minutes to complete the rest of the exercise and to compare their answers with a partner. Check answers as a whole class.

MIXED ABILITY
Tell weaker students to use the highlighted sentences from the article as a model for these sentences but warn students that they may have to change the tense, for example 2 and 3 are in the present simple, so the second sentences must also be in the same tense. Students work in pairs.

Answers
1 Meeting 2 (that) admire most 3 I love most 4 Spending time 5 What I find 6 I like most is / I really like is

PREPARE FOR THE EXAM

5 **B2 FIRST FOR SCHOOLS Writing Part 2: An article**

Briefly review what students need to do in this part of the exam and if necessary, read out the *B2 First for Schools* box on TB page 66.

Ask students to think about the target audience before they start writing, and to consider the types of things that would interest their reader. This will help them to write in a suitable style and register.

Look at the instructions with the class. Elicit the topic sentences in the article in Exercise 1 and then give students five minutes to work alone to plan their article. Weaker students could use the first two sentences of the article in Exercise 1 in their own writing if they are unsure about how to start.

Answers
Students' own answers

6 If you have students preparing for the *B2 First for Schools* exam, set a strict time limit of 30 minutes as they have already had time to plan their ideas. Once students have finished, ask them to swap articles with a partner and to highlight examples of the target structures their partner has used. Ask them to underline any opinions and comments they think are interesting, and discuss one or two examples as a class.

Model answer
My fantastic grandmother!
Do I have someone I really look up to? Yes – my grandmother. She's great! Growing up on a small farm in the middle of nowhere, her parents (my great-grandparents) had very little money. My grandmother was the youngest of seven children and they had a hard life – sometimes they didn't even have enough food to eat. But despite how hard my grandmother's life was as a child, she still managed to study hard and now she even runs her own company. She also had three children of her own, including my dad.
My grandmother is special because she has achieved so much on her own, and she believes that anyone can do anything if they try hard enough. She always gives me and my cousins great advice and encouragement, especially when things aren't going so well, like at school.
I've learned a lot from my grandmother. No matter what problems life gives her, she deals with them with a smile on her face – and she never gives up! I'm quite a determined person, too, and I'm sure this comes from my grandmother!

COOLER
Write on the board: … *is a place which I love*; … *is a person who I admire* and … *is something which I can't live without.*
Students complete the sentences so they are true for them. They then get into groups of three or four and have to try to guess what the other people in the group wrote. When they have finished, elicit some of the things that students wrote and some of the wrong guesses they made.

WRITING An article (2)

1 **Read the article. In what way has Sebastian's brother influenced him?**

Someone I admire

by Sebastian Duchamps

Can you think of someone who you really look up to? Is there anyone who you can rely on, no matter what? For me that person is my older brother, Louis.

When I was 13, he had a big impact on my life. I was having problems with a gang at school who used to bully me all the time. Talking to my parents didn't help because they don't understand teenage stuff, but I did talk to my brother about it. Discussing the issues with him made a huge difference to me. The thing I admired most about him was his patience. I must have talked about the same problem 100 times, yet he always listened as if it was the first time. I think that makes him a pretty grown-up person.

Louis has been a really important influence on me ever since. What I've learned more than anything is the importance of being thoughtful. Instead of sounding sympathetic and then forgetting all about friends' problems, I listen properly now.

What about you? Who has been a big influence in your life?

2 **Read the task, then read Sebastian's article again. Answer the questions.**

You see this notice in an English-language magazine for teenagers.

> **Articles needed!**
> Do you have a friend or family member that you look up to?
> What makes this person special?
> What have you learned from him or her?
> The best articles will be published in our magazine.

Write your **article**.

1. Can you think of a more interesting title for Sebastian's article?
2. Does Sebastian answer the three questions in the task?
3. How does he organise his answers?
4. How does Sebastian get the reader's attention?

3 **Read the *Prepare to write* box. Match the sentence structures in the *Prepare to write* box to the highlighted parts of the article.**

PREPARE TO WRITE | Varying sentence structure

You can make your writing more interesting by varying your sentence structure. Try using

- questions.
- *-ing* forms as subjects.
- structures which add emphasis.

4 **Complete the second sentence so that it means the same as the first. Use ideas from the *Prepare to write* box to help you.**

1. I met Adam and that changed my life.
   .... Adam changed my life.
2. I admire her kindness the most.
   What I .... is her kindness.
3. I love my uncle, especially his sense of humour.
   The thing .... about my uncle is his sense of humour.
4. I spent time with my aunt, and that helped me become more confident.
   .... with my aunt helped me become more confident.
5. I find his determination really amazing.
   .... amazing is his determination.
6. I really like his positive attitude to life.
   The thing .... his positive attitude to life.

PREPARE FOR THE EXAM

Writing Part 2 (An article)

5 **Read the task in Exercise 2 again and plan your own article.**

- Think of a family member or friend.
- Make notes. Think of examples which will help you to answer the questions and develop your ideas.
- Put your ideas in order.
- Think of a topic sentence to begin each paragraph.
- Think of an interesting title.

6 **Write your article.**

- Try to vary your sentence structure.
- Remember to address your reader to get their attention.
- Check your grammar and spelling.
- Write 140–190 words.

12 MAKING A DIFFERENCE

ABOUT YOU

Which of the photos below do you like best? Why? Do you think seeing these things can make a difference to how people feel?

VOCABULARY Verbs of communication

1 How many of the photos can you match with each sentence?

EP

1. This was done to **cheer** people **up**.
2. This is probably intended to **amuse** people.
3. This is intended to **highlight** a cause or problem.
4. This is to **congratulate** someone.
5. I think this is there to **stimulate** people to think.
6. Whoever did this wanted to **speak out** about an issue.
7. Things like this **reassure** people that things will work out well.
8. I think it is there to **spread** happiness.
9. This one's obviously there to **promote** a business.

51 **2** Listen to James and Rosie discussing photos A–D. Which **verb(s)** do they associate with each photo?

3 Discuss three things that …

- cheer you up.
- you'd like to speak out about.
- amuse you.

READING

1 Read the text quickly. What is a random act of kindness? Give two examples.

PREPARE FOR THE EXAM

Reading and Use of English Part 5

2 Read the text again. For questions 1–6, choose the answer (A, B, C or D) which you think fits best according to the text.

1 When Sarah was at the supermarket, she says that she felt
- **A** content about having spent time with her friends.
- **B** pleased by the success of her earlier shopping trip.
- **C** worried about being able to fulfill her father's request.
- **D** concerned about the motives of someone who approached her.

2 What reason does Alison give for helping others?
- **A** She is keen to give something back to people who have helped her.
- **B** She enjoys seeing people's delight at receiving an offer of help.
- **C** She likes the way doing things for other people makes her feel.
- **D** She finds it interesting to try out helpful new activities.

3 What is suggested about Alison in the fourth paragraph?
- **A** She was impressed by how rapidly random acts of kindness became popular.
- **B** She was enthusiastic about the idea of improving her mood through physical contact.
- **C** She was motivated to think of some random acts of kindness to carry out herself.
- **D** She was encouraged to do something in return for the person who helped her.

4 What does 'merely' mean in line 49?
- **A** easily **B** barely **C** simply **D** slightly

5 What was Sarah's attitude when she first heard about *caffè sospeso*?
- **A** She thought it was unfair to customers who had to pay for their coffee.
- **B** She realised that it was something she'd like to do.
- **C** She believed it could be confusing for customers.
- **D** She found it a highly unusual concept.

6 In the final paragraph, we understand that Sarah feels
- **A** disappointed so few people want to help others.
- **B** hopeful for a future where people are nicer to one another.
- **C** optimistic that she would benefit from others' kindness one day.
- **D** keen to appear as generous as the people she had recently come across.

12 MAKING A DIFFERENCE

Unit Overview

TOPIC	Helping others
VOCABULARY	Verbs of communication
READING	Random acts of kindness
GRAMMAR	The passive (1): review; Causative *have/get*
VOCABULARY	*both, either, neither*
LISTENING	A talk about a busker
SPEAKING	Discussing options
EXAM TASKS	Reading and Use of English Part 5; Listening Part 2; Speaking Part 3 and Part 4

Resources

GRAMMAR REFERENCE AND PRACTICE: SB page 159; TB page 268
PREPARE FOR THE EXAM: SB pages on TB pages 240–241, 248 and 252–253; TB pages 256, 259 and 262
WORKBOOK: pages 48–51
PHOTOCOPIABLE WORKSHEETS: Grammar worksheet Unit 12; Vocabulary worksheet Unit 12
TEST GENERATOR: Unit test 12
PRACTICE EXTRA: Unit 12

WARMER

Ask students to think about people, events, dates and places that have been important in their life. Tell them to write down a sentence for each one using a relative clause, for example, *I really liked my first primary school teacher, who taught me to read.*

Tell students to discuss their sentences with a partner who should ask more questions about each one. Monitor and give positive feedback. Ask one or two pairs to feed back on their discussion.

ABOUT YOU

Look at the photos with the class and elicit descriptions of what they can see in each one. Ask students if they have ever seen anything similar. Then, put them into pairs and read the *About you* box with the class. Set a time limit of two minutes for students to discuss the questions in pairs and then invite students to share their ideas with the class. Ask the class if there are any ideas in the photos that they don't like and, if so, why.

VOCABULARY Verbs of communication

1 Elicit the meaning of each sentence with the class. Students then work in groups of three to discuss which sentences could match each photo. Tell students there may be more than one correct answer. Monitor and help with ideas where necessary. Invite groups to share their ideas for one sentence, giving reasons why they matched that sentence to the photos they chose.

Answers
Students' own answers

51 2 Play the first part of the recording and elicit the two verbs used to describe photo A. Ask the class if they agree with James and Rosie. Tell students that not all the verbs used are from Exercise 1 and play the rest of the recording. When students have listened, they compare answers in pairs. Elicit the verbs used for each photo. You could follow up by asking students to work in pairs and have a similar conversation about photo E, either using verbs from Exercise 1 or other verbs that the students think are appropriate.

Answers
A amuse, cheer up B congratulate
C highlight, speak out, stimulate D promote, advertise, persuade

» AUDIOSCRIPT TB PAGES 296–297

3 Look at the three points with the class and write one idea that is true for you for each on the board, for example: *cheers me up – the sun shining in the morning; something I'd like to speak out about – people throwing rubbish on the ground; amuses me – animal videos on the internet.* Give students one or two minutes to think of ideas alone, then put them into groups of three or four to share their ideas. Monitor and prompt quieter students to join in the discussion. Invite groups to share things that they all feel the same way about, i.e. things that cheer them all up, amuse all of them or which they would all like to speak out about.

Answers
Students' own answers

READING

1 Set a time limit of two minutes for students to find the answer to the question and two examples. They then discuss what they found out in pairs. Elicit the answers and ask the students if they have ever done something kind for someone they don't know or have had a stranger do something kind for them. If anyone answers *yes*, elicit more details.

Answers
Doing a favour for someone you have never met before, and for no special reason. Two examples from: helping to carry the shopping, picking up litter from someone's garden, swapping places with the person behind you in a queue.

CONTINUED ON PAGE 134

BACKGROUND INFORMATION

Sick Puppies are an Australian band which formed in 1997. They play grunge / alternative metal music. There are two stories about how they got their name. The first is that when they were trying to think of a band name, one of the band members came home and found his father reading the book *Sick Puppy* by Carl Hiaasen. The other story is that they were rehearsing in a garage and a puppy came in and was sick. Then one of their fans said, 'That's one sick puppy' and the name stuck.

The Free Hugs Movement was set up in Sydney in 2004, two years before the Sick Puppies video. The video had been viewed over 78 million times by September 2019 and made the campaign and the band famous. The person who started the movement said that he had arrived back in Australia after living in the UK and that he had watched people coming off the plane being greeted by friends and relatives and wished there was someone there to greet him. So, he made a sign saying Free Hugs and stood on a busy pavement and waited for people to come and give him a hug. The first person came up to him after about 15 minutes and the campaign had started.

PREPARE FOR THE EXAM

2 B2 FIRST FOR SCHOOLS Reading and Use of English Part 5

Briefly review what students need to do in this part of the exam and, if necessary, read out the *B2 First for Schools* box on TB page 82.

Remind students that all four of the options will probably be mentioned in some way, but only one of them will be the correct answer. They can check their answers, if they have time, by trying to show why the other three options are incorrect. This is especially important where the correct answer may not be very obvious, for example, question 3. Set a time limit of ten minutes and elicit the answers with information from the text which shows that these are the correct options.

MIXED ABILITY

Allow weaker students to work in pairs. Monitor and help where necessary. As some students finish the exercise, they could join a pair of weaker students and help them to find the information for any questions that they haven't yet answered so that they don't need to spend so much time looking through the whole text.

Answers

1 D (*when this happened to me, I was a little suspicious. Why would someone want to help me carry my bags all the way home?*)
2 C (*'It makes me happy that I've done something to benefit others,' explained Alison.*)
3 A (*A few days later, Alison came across the video for* All the Same *by the band Sick Puppies, which shows the first Free Hugs group hugging shoppers in Sydney. 'The video went viral and incredibly got millions of views!' … As a result of this, the idea spread quickly and there are now Free Hugs campaigns in most countries.*)
4 C (This could also be translated as *just/only*.)
5 D (*I could hardly believe my ears …*)
6 B (*I felt glad to witness such generosity of the human spirit. Wondering whether charity and kindness could become the philosophy of the modern age …*)

52 The Reading text is recorded for students to listen, read and check their answers.

3 Look at the title of the text again and re-elicit what it means. You could ask further questions, such as: 'Are the acts planned in advance or not?' (*No, they are sudden reactions to a situation.*). Elicit from this the meaning of *random*. Ask students what a random number is (*one which is chosen without any thought or planning, for example, when drawing numbers for the lottery*). Students then do the rest of the exercise together, using the context of each sentence to help them. Elicit the answers and ask follow-up questions to check the students' understanding, for example: 'Are you a regular at any shop or café?' 'What video do you know that has gone viral?' 'Have you ever seen anyone doing anything suspicious?' 'Which parts of your town are worst for litter?'.

FAST FINISHERS

Ask fast finishers to find more words in the text which they don't know or think that other students might not know. They write a definition for the words, using a dictionary if necessary. When everyone has finished the exercise, elicit definitions from fast finishers and ask the other students to find the words they define.

Answers

1 regulars 2 random 3 suspicious 4 went viral 5 litter

TALKING POINTS

Put students into small groups and ask them to discuss the first question. Elicit ideas and ask which acts they liked the least and why. Then look at the second question with the class and ask them to imagine different scenarios, for example different people offering help – a middle-aged woman, a person their own age, a young child, someone in a foreign country who they can't understand, etc. – to see if their reactions would be different. Set a time limit of two or three minutes for students to discuss their ideas then invite students to share their ideas with the class.

COOLER

Students work in groups of three or four and try to think of other kind acts they could do for strangers. Give them three minutes to think of an idea then invite each group to share their ideas with the class. Ask the class to try to agree on one act of kindness that they could try to offer in the future and ask them to report back to the class in a future lesson if they do this.

RANDOM ACTS OF KINDNESS

52

By Sarah Longman

Have you experienced a 'random act of kindness'? Imagine the scene: you've been out shopping all day with friends. You're loaded with bags and heading home. Then your dad calls and asks if you can pick up a few things at the supermarket on the way back. You do the shopping, then, standing outside the supermarket, wonder how you're going to get everything home. Another customer approaches you. 'Need a hand?' she asks. What should you say?

As a matter of fact, when this happened to me, I was a little **suspicious**. Why would someone want to help me carry my bags all the way home? 'It's just a **random** act of kindness!' the woman said. She reassured me it was no problem, and I accepted her offer with relief.

As we were walking along, the woman introduced herself as Alison and told me that many people had been kind to her in the past. Now she wanted to do something for someone else. She explained that random acts of kindness are doing favours for someone you have never met before, and for no special reason. The whole idea is simply to cheer strangers up. I was amused by the idea myself, and asked whether she did this all the time. 'I like to do a few random acts every once in a while. It makes me happy that I've done something to benefit others,' explained Alison. 'It could be any number of things, from picking up **litter** in a stranger's garden to swapping places with the person behind you in a queue. As far as I'm concerned, by far the best part is watching people's reactions. Some people are comfortable with it immediately, others are doubtful initially, and a few don't want to be helped at all.'

Alison's interest in helping others began when she was hugged by a complete stranger at a bus stop on a trip to the United States. An old lady was standing there with a sign that said *Free Hugs*. When Alison asked her what it meant, the woman just hugged her. 'It made a difference to my day,' she said. While Alison was waiting, the woman hugged several other people – young and old, men and women. A few days later, Alison came across the video for *All the Same* by the band Sick Puppies, which shows the first Free Hugs group hugging shoppers in Sydney. 'The video **went viral** and incredibly got millions of views!' she said. As a result of this, the idea spread quickly and there are now Free Hugs campaigns in most countries. Millions of people have been inspired by the idea, which has gone beyond **merely** giving hugs to include other random acts of kindness like the one I experienced from Alison.

A few weeks later, I went into a café to get a takeaway coffee. While I was being served, a man walked in behind me and asked, 'Are there any free coffees?' I could hardly believe my ears, especially when the barista said, 'Yes.' The customer got the barista to give him a coffee – for nothing. Then the barista crossed off a mark on the blackboard. When the man had left, I asked the barista what was going on. '*Caffè sospeso,*' he explained. 'It's an old tradition from Naples, in Italy. It means 'suspended coffee' in Italian, and it's when someone who's had good luck or who is feeling generous orders two coffees, one to drink and one a *sospeso*, for a future customer who needs a coffee but can't afford one. We take the payment and add a mark here on the board. Then people can come in and ask if we have any *sospesos* – any free coffees. We don't promote it, but our **regulars** know we do it.'

In a world where we are often let down by people's behaviour, I felt glad to witness such generosity of the human spirit. Wondering whether charity and kindness could become the philosophy of the modern age, I ordered a cappuccino 'to go' – and one *caffè sospeso*.

3 Match the **highlighted** words and phrases in the text to the meanings.

1. people who often go to a particular shop, restaurant, etc.
2. done or chosen without any plan or system
3. not trusting someone
4. became very popular very quickly on social media
5. small pieces of rubbish that are left in public places

TALKING POINTS

Which of the random acts of kindness in the text appeals to you the most? Why?

How do you think you would react if someone offered you a random act of kindness? Why?

GRAMMAR The passive (1): review

1 **Read the passive examples. What tenses are they?**

1 She **was hugged** by a complete stranger.
2 While I **was being served**, a man walked in behind me and asked …

2 **Read the rules. Why is the passive used in each sentence in Exercise 1?**

We use the passive
a when who or what does something is unknown, unimportant or obvious.
b to emphasise the person who receives an action, rather than the person who does the action.
We use *by* if it is important to add who or what does something.

» GRAMMAR REFERENCE AND PRACTICE PAGE 159

3 **Complete the text with the passive form of the verbs in brackets.**

Free hugs STOP the city

Members of the Free Hugs Campaign [0] *have been asked* (ask) to go home early after their annual meeting caused chaos this evening. Although thousands of members [1] ________ (invite), organisers only expected a few hundred to turn up. They were wrong, and huge numbers of people arrived. Roads around the city centre [2] ________ (block) by the enormous crowds for three hours earlier today, and even now drivers [3] ________ (advise) to avoid the area until midnight. Police are warning that public transport [4] ________ (might / affect) until later tonight as well. 'Throughout the day, we [5] ________ (impress) by the organisers,' said a police spokesperson. And 'I [6] ________ (never / hug) by so many people in one day!' he added.

4 **Correct the mistake in each sentence.**

1 The food was really tasty. It makes by my dad.
2 This game can be play online.
3 The pool was closed because it has been repaired.
4 This is the most powerful book that was written in the last decade.

Causative *have/get*

5 **Read the examples and answer the questions.**

1 I needed to **have** my bags **carried**.
Who did the writer think should carry her bags?
2 I was pleased to **get** my shopping **delivered**.
Who was delivering the writer's shopping?
3 The customer **got** the barista **to give** him a coffee – for nothing.
Who gave the customer a coffee? Did the customer pay?

» GRAMMAR REFERENCE AND PRACTICE PAGE 159

6 **Write sentences using the verbs in the box and the causative.**

cut	redeliver	repair	~~replace~~	wash

0 Your dad's watch stops.
He could have/get the batteries replaced.
1 Your sister's hair is too long.
2 Your mum's car was dirty.
3 The screen on your phone has cracked.
4 They tried to deliver a parcel while I was out.

VOCABULARY *both, either, neither*

1 **Read the examples. Then match the words to the meanings.**

You've **both** got heavy shopping bags to carry.
Both (**of** my) bags are full of shopping.
Is **either of** you tired?
I'll carry **either** this bag **or** that one.
Neither of you has any energy left.
Neither you **nor** your friend has any energy left.

1 both	a one or the other
2 either (… or)	b one and the other
3 neither (… nor)	c not one or the other

2 **Choose the correct options.**

1 Both of them *is* / *are* mine.
2 Either George or Sam *is* / *are* lying.
3 Neither Sam nor Jo *was* / *were* willing to help.

3 **Write one or two words in each gap.**

1 You can go along ________ Park Street or Market Street – ________ ways are fairly quick.
2 A police officer and a taxi driver were offered hugs, but ________ them accepted.
3 Two students asked me if I'd like a free hug, so I had hugs from ________ them!

4 » **Work in pairs. Turn to page 139.**

GRAMMAR The passive (1): review

WARMER

Ask the class: 'What happened to you yesterday?'. Tell them to work in pairs and tell their partner everything they can remember, for example *I missed the bus; I got a B+ in Spanish*, etc. Give them two minutes to discuss their ideas and then invite students to tell the class. As the students speak, write any passive verb forms they use on the board. If no one uses a passive, write one or two of their ideas on the board, e.g. *I got a B+* and, at the end of the activity, elicit how students could say this using the starter: *I was … (given a B+)*.

1 Remind students how to form the passive on the board (the correct form of *be* + past participle) and add one or two sentences as examples. Ask students to read the examples in the exercise and identify the tenses used.

Answers
1 past simple passive 2 past continuous passive

2 Look at the question with the class and ask them not to look at the rules box yet. They look at both sentences and say why the passive is better than the active (*1 We are talking about the woman, so she is more important than the person who hugged her. The active form would be fine as well. 2 It is obvious that a barista is doing the serving and it would sound strange to start the sentence with 'While a barista was serving me …'*). Students then do the matching.

Answers
1 b. The person receiving the action is the one the speaker wants to emphasise. 2 a. It isn't important who was serving the speaker.

» GRAMMAR REFERENCE AND PRACTICE ANSWER KEY TB PAGE 268

3 Students should work in pairs and use clues in the text to decide which tense is best and then write the correct passive form. Elicit the answers and why each verb form is used.

FAST FINISHERS

Fast finishers try to rewrite the text so that it uses active forms, for example *Someone has asked members of the Free Hugs Campaign to go home early …* Point out that students may need to add subjects not mentioned in the original text or those mentioned in later sentences, for example *3 The police are advising / have advised drivers …* When students have finished, they work in pairs to decide which sentences sound OK in the active and which sound strange (*Most are apart from the last sentence*).

Answers
1 had been invited 2 were blocked 3 are being advised / have been advised 4 might be affected 5 've/have been impressed 6 've/have never been hugged

4 Students work alone. Elicit the mistakes and ask students how they know each one is wrong (*1* it makes *is an incorrect active form because the food doesn't make anything and the phrase 'by my dad' also indicates that the passive is needed; 2 we need the past participle form of the main verb;* 3 it has been repaired *implies that it is fine now;* 4 the last decade *means in the decade up to now so it is unfinished*).

Answers
1 The food was really tasty. It **was made** by my dad.
2 This game can be **played** online.
3 The pool was closed because it **was being** repaired.
4 This is the most powerful book that **has been** written in the last decade.

Causative *have/get*

5 Look at the exercise with the class and elicit the answers. Remind the students that, with this structure, it is the verb *to have* / *to get* which changes form depending on the tense. Write: *I always have my bags carried.* on the board and elicit the tense (*present simple*). Elicit different tenses, for example the present continuous: *I'm having my bags carried.*

Answers
1 someone else 2 someone else
3 the barista; No, the customer didn't pay.

» GRAMMAR REFERENCE AND PRACTICE ANSWER KEY TB PAGE 268

6 Look at the example sentence with the class. Elicit what other tenses they could use which would make sense, for example: *He's going to get the batteries replaced; He should have the batteries replaced; He needs to get the batteries replaced,* etc. Students complete the exercise alone and compare answers in pairs. If they have used different tenses, they decide together if they are both correct.

Possible answers
1 She should/could have/get it cut.
2 She had/got it washed. / She could have had/got it washed.
3 You could/should have/get it repaired.
4 You should/could/will have to have/get it redelivered.

» GRAMMAR WORKSHEET UNIT 12

VOCABULARY *both, either, neither*

1 Give students a few minutes to read the sentences and then complete the matching exercise with a partner.

Answers
1 b 2 a 3 c

2 Tell the students to cover Exercise 1. Read these sentences aloud and ask students for a show of hands for each option. They then look at Exercise 1 and find the correct answers.

Answers
1 are 2 is 3 was

3 Students work alone then compare their answers in pairs. Elicit the answers and what each sentence means (for example, *1 You have a choice of Park Street or Market Street – there is no difference. 2 The police officer and the taxi driver refused to be hugged. 3 I had hugs from the first and second student.*).

Answers
1 either, both 2 neither of 3 both of

4 Look at the first dialogue with the class and elicit how to complete the final part (*We're both hungry!*). Students then do the same for the other dialogues. Invite different pairs to act out one dialogue and then ask students to work in pairs to find something they both like or do and something that neither of them like or do. Elicit ideas from different pairs.

Possible answers
1 We're both hungry!
2 Neither of us has got any money left.
3 We can visit either one or the other.
4 either/both of you excited about our holiday?
5 Neither Leroy nor Heather is playing football today.

» VOCABULARY WORKSHEET UNIT 12

LISTENING

53 **1** With books closed, read the rubric and play the recording. Elicit what Amy heard and ask students about any buskers / street musicians they have heard and what they thought of them.

Answer
a violinist playing in an underground station

PREPARE FOR THE EXAM

2 B2 FIRST FOR SCHOOLS **Listening Part 2**

53 Briefly review what students need to do in this part of the exam and, if necessary, read out the *B2 First for Schools* box on TB page 94.

Tell students to read through the gapped text and to think about the kind of word which should go in each gap. Elicit the answers, but tell students that, even if they remember the exact answer, they should only tell you the kind of word missing, for example *1 a job; 2 a place,* etc. Students then listen and complete the words and phrases. Allow students to compare in pairs. Elicit the answers.

Answers
1 journalist (job: the main distractor is *freelance editor*, which is the job she did previously. Shop assistants and waiters are jobs that the other people she sees do)
2 ticket hall (place: the distractors are the *underground passages* and the *platform*, but these are not where she first heard the music)
3 exceptional (adjective: the distractor is *wonderful,* but this describes the music)
4 casual clothes (clothes: *smart evening dress* and *work clothes* are the distractors, but the musician is not wearing these)
5 cap (object to hold money: the distractor is *violin case* – this is closed, so is not how she is collecting money)
6 looked up (action: the distractors are *smiled* and *greeted*, but this is only what Amy expected her to do, not what she did)
7 radio programme (noun: the distractors are *TV series* and *well-known advert,* but Amy dismisses these when she remembers the radio programme)
8 impressed (feeling: *surprised* is the distractor. This is not how Amy felt about the performance. It was the musician who was *embarrassed*, not Amy)
9 wedding (place/event: the distractor is *concert*, but this is not where Amy saw the violinist play)
10 public places (place: the distractors are *theatres* and *music venues* but these are not what the musician finds interesting)

» AUDIOSCRIPT TB PAGE 297

SPEAKING Discussing options

54 **1** Elicit how the choices in the box might help disabled children. Play the recording and check answers.

Answers
1 access to school, computer gaming, going shopping, going out at the weekend, tidying up
2 going out at the weekend

» AUDIOSCRIPT TB PAGES 297–298

55 **2** Tell students they will hear all of the expressions apart from two. Play the recording for them to identify which ones and elicit the answers from a volunteer.

Answers
All except *Are you referring to … ?* and *What else?*

» AUDIOSCRIPT TB PAGE 298

PREPARE FOR THE EXAM

B2 FIRST FOR SCHOOLS
Speaking Part 3 and Part 4

In Part 3, students have a two-way conversation together. They are given spoken instructions with written stimuli. The focus is on sustaining interaction, exchanging ideas, expressing and justifying opinions, agreeing/disagreeing, suggesting, speculating, evaluating and reaching a decision through negotiation. In Part 4, the students each answer questions on a related topic to that of Part 3.

Tip Highlight to students the importance of the concept of interaction. Students should actively listen to and respond to their partner and not just simply think of, and state, their own opinion.

56 **3** Play the instructions and elicit what the students have to do. Encourage them to look at each point in turn, discussing how it may affect the answer to the question, for example, the first point might be an argument against students helping because they have so much schoolwork to do. On the other hand, students may also think they have plenty of free time and could organise their time to do both. Monitor and note interesting answers to give as feedback. When they have finished, invite one pair to carry out the task in front of the class. Students give their own answers.

MIXED ABILITY

Weaker students can write three of the expressions from the *Prepare to speak* box each; one asking for clarification and two from the Keeping talking section. The student who starts the conversation begins by saying: *Let's start with …* . As they have their conversation, they cross out the phrases they wrote down when they use them so that they can be sure they used three each. Stronger students could aim to use all of the phrases and tick them off as they say them.

» AUDIOSCRIPT TB PAGE 298

4 You could do this in groups of three. Each student takes a turn to play the part of the examiner and asks the other two students two of the questions. While they are listening, they note down any of the phrases from the *Prepare to speak* box that they hear the students using. When everyone has finished, discuss the questions as a class. Students give their own answers.

» PREPARE FOR THE EXAM TEACHING NOTES AND ANSWER KEY TB PAGE 262

COOLER

Each student writes four sentences on a piece of paper: two starting with *I like …* and the other two starting with *I don't like …* They mingle and say their sentences to other students. When they find a partner with whom they agree about at least one of their four sentences, they sit down together. After two minutes, if some students still haven't sat down, tell them to try to find one thing that isn't on their pieces of paper that they both agree about. Stop the activity after another minute and tell the students to sit down with whoever they are with at that time, even if they don't agree with anything the other person wrote. Ask the students who found a partner to make sentences using *both of us* or *neither of us* about the sentences they agree on.

LISTENING

53 **1** You will hear a woman called Amy Linton talking about something she heard recently. What was it?

PREPARE FOR THE EXAM

Listening Part 2

2 53 **Read the sentences below carefully. Try to work out what kinds of answer are needed. Then listen again and, for questions 1–10, complete the sentences with a word or short phrase.**

MUSIC IN THE CITY

Amy works as a **(1)** __________ in London.
Amy first heard violin music when she was in the **(2)** __________ at the station.
Amy uses the word '**(3)** __________' to describe how well the woman was playing the violin.
Amy was amused to see that, unlike her, the violinist was wearing **(4)** __________.
The violinist had put a **(5)** __________ on the ground for people to put money in.
When a little boy stopped to listen, the violinist **(6)** __________ briefly.
Amy realised that she knew the piece of music from a **(7)** __________ she'd listened to.
When the music stopped, Amy felt **(8)** __________ by what she had heard.
Amy realised that she'd seen the violinist once before at a **(9)** __________.
The violinist said she liked to play in **(10)** __________ because the sound was always interesting.

SPEAKING Discussing options

54 **1** Listen to Alexandra and Johann talking as part of a speaking exam. They are talking about giving help to disabled children in the local community.

1 Tick (✓) the five things that they talk about.
2 What do they both agree they would help with?

access to school computer gaming going out at the weekend going shopping homework reading and writing sports tidying up

55 **2** Read the *Prepare to speak* box. Then listen to part of the conversation again. Which expressions do you hear?

PREPARE TO SPEAK | Keeping talking

Starting to talk
Let's start with …

Asking for clarification
What exactly do you mean?
Are you referring to … ?

Keeping talking
Again, as with … , we could …
What else? / Anything else?
I was just going to say that …
Do you want to add anything?

PREPARE FOR THE EXAM

Speaking Part 3 and Part 4

3 56 **Work in pairs. Listen to the instruction and look at the task for one minute. Then complete the task. Use phrases from the *Prepare to speak* box.**

having time for schoolwork
spending free time with friends
learning from older people
Is it a good idea for students to spend time helping elderly people in their local community?
getting practical skills
understanding other people's lives

4 **Ask and answer the questions with a partner.**

1 What are the most common ways in which people help others?
2 How important is it to help other people?
3 Do you think it can be difficult for people to ask for help? Why?
4 Why do you think some people do not want to be helped?
5 If you don't offer help, you won't receive it. Do you think this is true?
6 'People only help others when they want something in return.' Do you agree?

» PREPARE FOR THE EXAM PAGES 136–7

LIFE SKILLS COLLABORATION

VOLUNTEERING

1 **Ask and answer the questions with a partner.**

1 Have you ever volunteered? What for?
2 Do you know anyone who volunteers? What do they do?

2 **In pairs, make a list of things you could do as a volunteer and organisations you could help. Then read the text on the opposite page quickly and see if any of your ideas are mentioned.**

3 **Read the text again and answer the questions.**

1 What can you learn about if you volunteer locally?
2 Why will volunteering look good on future university or job applications?
3 What key question should you ask yourself to find the right volunteer role for you?
4 Who could you contact if you're interested in the arts?
5 Why is it better to begin by dedicating less time and then increase your involvement slowly?

4 **Match the highlighted words and phrases in the text to the meanings.**

1 a safe place to live and be protected
2 happening without most people knowing about it
3 collecting money for a cause or charity
4 responsibilities which are part of your role
5 the set of characteristics that make a good leader

LIFE SKILLS

Volunteering

There are many ways that you can volunteer. You may want to support a cause that is important to you, or volunteer for an activity which allows you to explore your interests. Volunteering is a great way to gain new skills and new experiences, and to show how responsible you can be.

57 **5** **Listen to a talk about summer volunteer programmes abroad. Put the topics mentioned in the correct order.**

A Financial considerations and suggestions ____
B Benefits of participating in a volunteer programme ____
C Types of volunteer programmes abroad 1
D Planning a summer volunteering experience ____
E Final preparations ____

57 **6** **Listen again and complete the sentences with between one and three words in each gap.**

1 If you enjoy spending time with children, you might want to try teaching ______________.
2 Volunteering can help increase ______________ and improve your ability to adapt.
3 Asking organisers ______________ can help you feel fully informed about volunteering.
4 Travel and accommodation are examples of the ______________ you will probably need to pay.
5 You'll need to organise your travel ______________ and write a ______________ list.

7 **Complete the sentences with the words in the box.**

budget	build	host	intercultural
reviews	sustainable		

USEFUL LANGUAGE

Choosing and planning a summer volunteer opportunity

1 Volunteering will help you to ________ relationships.
2 You'll develop your ________ understanding.
3 Is the project ________?
4 Find ________ online from previous participants.
5 Working out your ________ will be key.
6 Research the ________ country carefully.

LIFE SKILLS

Learning Objectives

- The students learn about different kinds of voluntary work and advantages of being a volunteer.
- In the project stage, the students research different kinds of summer volunteer programmes and present them to the class.

Vocabulary

behind the scenes duties fundraising leadership shelter

BACKGROUND INFORMATION

A survey in the UK has shown that 15 years ago, young adults aged 16–24 did less voluntary work than any other age group, but now, they do more than any other age group. However, the total amount of voluntary work done has fallen. It is believed that young people are doing more to boost their chances of finding a good career, but those already in work have less free time in which to do voluntary work.

WARMER

Put the students into groups of three or four. Ask them to think about times a teacher or headteacher has asked students if they can help. Give one or two examples, for example: *Could someone help me carry these boxes? Could a few students stay after class and get the hall ready for a meeting?* Make it clear that you don't want examples where students are told to do something. Students think of as many ideas as possible in two minutes. Invite groups to share their ideas with the class.

LIFE SKILLS

Volunteering

Tell students to read the information. Ask them if they can think of a definition for *to volunteer*, for example, *to offer do work with no expectation of reward or payment,* or *to do something for someone else that you don't have to do*. Elicit ideas from the class.

1 Ask students to discuss the questions in pairs. Tell them that, even if they haven't done voluntary work similar to that mentioned in the *Life skills* box, they may have volunteered to do the sort of things mentioned in the Warmer above. When students have finished, invite those who have done voluntary work to tell the class what they did. Encourage other students to ask them questions to find out more details.

Answers

Students' own answers

2 Elicit one or two ideas before the students look at the text, for example, *helping at a local hospital, picking up litter for an environmental group*. Set a time limit of two minutes for students to make their lists. Monitor and note any interesting ideas. Then give the students two minutes to look at the text. Elicit what was in the text and any other ideas they had.

Answers

Students' own answers
Mentioned in text: local music festival, local animal shelter, local sports league, local fundraising event, helping people with special needs, neighbourhood food bank, local museums, environmental organisations

3 Set a time limit of ten minutes. Ask the students to read the questions and write the answers in their notebooks. When they have finished, they compare answers in pairs. Elicit the answers and where in the text the information can be found.

MIXED ABILITY

Put students into pairs. Tell them to work together to find the answer to the first question. They then look for two of the other answers each, 2 and 4 or 3 and 5. They then tell each other the answers and where they found the information in the text.

Answers

1 You can learn about social issues which are facing your community.
2 Because you'll develop a range of transferable skills.
3 What are you (am I) interested in?
4 You could contact local museums.
5 So that volunteering doesn't interfere with your study time.

58 The Reading text is recorded for students to listen, read and check their answers.

4 Students cover Exercise 4. Look at the highlighted words with the class. Ask students if they recognise any of them and elicit definitions for any they think they know. They then look at the sentences containing any words they don't know or aren't sure of and try to work out the meanings from context. Students then uncover the exercise and do the matching.

FAST FINISHERS

Ask fast finishers to read the text quickly to find examples of words formed from a root word. They try to identify the kind of word it is and the root word from which it comes, for example, *satisfaction – noun, from satisfy – verb*. While students are doing the exercise, write a table on the board with three columns marked *adjective, noun, verb*. When everyone has finished, invite students to share their words with the class and write them in the appropriate columns in the table on the board. Encourage all students to copy the table into their notebooks.

Answers

1 shelter 2 behind the scenes 3 fundraising 4 duties
5 leadership

CONTINUED ON PAGE 142

57 **5** Tell students that they are going to listen to someone talking to young people about doing voluntary work abroad. With books closed, students think about things they usually do before going on a school trip or a foreign holiday, for example looking at maps to see where they are going, and discuss their ideas in small groups. With books open, look at the first topic and elicit what the person might say, for example, *You don't get paid for doing voluntary work so, if you need money, it might be better to look for a paid job instead*. Students then work in the same groups to think of what the person may say about the other topics. Elicit ideas, then play the recording. Elicit the order in which the topics were mentioned and anything else the students remember about each topic.

Answers

A4 B2 C1 D3 E5

57 **6** Tell students to read through the sentences and think about what the missing words could be. When they have listened again, they complete the gaps and check that their answers make grammatically correct sentences. Allow students to compare answers in pairs and then elicit the answers. If a student answers, for example, *questions* for sentence 3, ask the class if anyone has any more information for this gap.

Answers

1 languages or sports 2 your confidence 3 specific questions 4 costs 5 documents, packing

>> AUDIOSCRIPT TB PAGE 298

7 Tell stronger students to cover the words in the box and to look at the gapped sentences in the *Useful language* box. Elicit what word could go in the first gap, for example, *improve* or *strengthen*. Students work in pairs to think of possible words for the other gaps. Allow weaker students to keep the box uncovered and think about which word goes in which gap. Elicit ideas from the stronger students and then ask them to uncover the word box to complete the sentences. Weaker students listen to their ideas and use these to help them make the correct choice. Elicit the answers and what the words mean.

Answers

1 build 2 intercultural 3 sustainable 4 reviews 5 budget 6 host

PROJECT *Choosing a volunteer programme*

Look at the instructions with the class. If possible, allow students to use computers or their mobile phones to look for volunteer programmes in the class. Set a time limit of five minutes for this and then put them into groups of three or four. They tell each other about the volunteer programmes that they found and have three minutes to do this and to agree on which one to choose. They can now do steps 2 and 3 at home or in class. Groups should also assign different aspects of research that each person can later present, for example one person can present information about the duties, one person the costs and other practical information and one person can look at reviews.

During the presentation, each student presents their part of the project and, at the end, they all give their opinions about why they would like to go on it.

After each group has presented their project, encourage other students to ask questions about the volunteer programme. When everyone has finished, invite students to say which of the other projects they found the most interesting and why.

PROJECT EXTENSION

Tell each group to imagine that they did voluntary work for their chosen programme. Write the following headings on the board: *What we did, How we felt, Who we met, Good and bad points of the programme*. Set a time limit of five minutes for students to discuss ideas for each heading. Now ask groups to think of questions they would ask other groups about their experience, for example *How many hours did you have to work each day? What did you do in your free time? What responsibilities did you have?* They should write at least one question for each of the other groups. Set a time limit of three or four minutes for this. Now invite one group to come to the front of the class. They explain what the programme they went on was and give details based on the headings written on the board. The other groups now ask them one of their questions about their experience. Repeat with the other groups so that they are asked different questions each time.

COOLER

Write in the centre of the board the words *Volunteering at school*. Draw six lines leading from this to different parts of the board. At the end of one of the lines write *Keeping the school grounds tidy*. Ask students what volunteers would have to do and when, for example, *They may pick litter up themselves every day when school finishes or they may organise a different class to pick litter up during a break*. Elicit more ideas about this kind of voluntary work, what equipment would be needed, how long it would take and the kind of person who would be interested in this type of volunteering. Students now work in groups and try to do the same for five other possible activities, thinking of what the activity is, when and where it would take place and who it would suit. Monitor and help with ideas where necessary and note good ideas. Set a time limit of about six minutes, then elicit ideas from different groups and complete the diagram on the board. When it is complete, ask the students which idea would be most useful and whether they might volunteer for it. It may be possible to actually implement some of the ideas to show the students that their ideas can be valuable to the school.

CAN YOU SPARE SOME TIME?

So you're thinking of volunteering and wondering how to find out more about it? Whatever the reasons for wanting to volunteer, there are many benefits. Firstly, through helping others locally, you'll become more aware of the social issues which are facing your community. Obviously, you'll also end up meeting new people and that will help you to develop a sense of empathy and better understand the needs of others.

Apart from the satisfaction you'll feel from knowing that you're making a difference to your community, volunteer work will also look great on future applications for university or a job! That's because, while you're volunteering, you'll develop a range of transferable skills such as time management, organisation, leadership and conflict resolution. These skills, and many more, will be very useful to you both now and in the future!

Volunteering is basically like having a job (but an unpaid one!) and you'll need to take it seriously. Finding the right area to work in is very important when looking for a volunteering opportunity, and the best way to do this is to sit down and think about it carefully first. Do you feel passionate about any particular social or environmental issues? Would you prefer to be working with members of the public or working behind the scenes? Realistically, how much time will you have to offer? But probably the most important question of all is: what are you interested in?

If you're interested in music, could you help out at a local music festival? Or if you're keen on becoming a vet or a zoologist, why not approach a local animal shelter and ask if they need help caring for the animals? Maybe you're into sports? Well, talk to a local sports league or the organisers of a local fundraising event, like a run, and ask how you could play a part.

Perhaps you'd just like to be with others and help people. How about supporting people with special needs, or lending a hand at your neighbourhood food bank? Or maybe the arts are more your thing? Local museums are always looking for volunteers to lead visitor tours of their galleries and exhibits. If you're not a big fan of museums and prefer the outdoors, try contacting an environmental organisation and see what initiatives they're involved in locally.

Your duties as a volunteer will depend on the exact role you choose. However, there are a few things to consider which are relevant to all volunteering opportunities. Firstly, think carefully about how much time you can dedicate. It's much better to start off with a smaller time commitment and gradually increase your participation as you become more involved. You don't want your volunteering to interfere with your study time. You'll also need to think about how to get to the place where you'll be volunteering. Are there buses or trains, or will someone give you a lift? And lastly, remember that you might need to do some basic training before you can begin, and there could be a minimum age requirement for the volunteer role that you're interested in.

Ready to expand your horizons? Get out there and start looking – there's a volunteer opportunity waiting just for you!

PROJECT

Choosing a volunteer programme

Work in groups of three or four to choose and research a summer volunteer programme. Use these steps to help you.

1. Search for summer volunteer programmes online and decide on one which everyone would like to do.
2. Research your chosen programme or project. Find information about what it involves and how to apply for it.
3. Search for images and videos of people participating in the programme. Find some reviews from previous participants.
4. Create a short presentation about your chosen programme and take turns to share your individual reasons for wanting to do it.

Present your work to the class.

REVIEW 3 UNITS 9–12

VOCABULARY

1 **Match the two parts of the phrases.**

1	make the	**a**	goals
2	put an	**b**	best of something
3	have a	**c**	go at something
4	achieve your	**d**	best in people
5	see the	**e**	end to something

2 **Complete the meanings with the words in the box and a preposition.**

accident advance character fault secret

1 When you do something before it's needed, you do it ________.
2 When you do something you wouldn't normally do, you act out ________.
3 When you do something and hide it from others, you do it ________.
4 When you're responsible for something that's going wrong, you're ________.
5 When you do something you didn't mean to do, you do it ________.

3 **Complete the conversations with a compound adjective that means the opposite of the underlined words. Use the words in the box.**

badly last self short well

1 **A:** Is Martin the tall slim boy?
B: No, he's the ________-built one.
2 **A:** Did you plan your holiday well in advance?
B: No, it was a ________-minute decision.
3 **A:** Were the students good?
B: There were a few ________ behaved boys, but nothing serious.
4 **A:** Is your brother's job abroad permanent?
B: No, it's only a ________-term contract.
5 **A:** Is Louise still as shy as she used to be?
B: No, she's much more ________-confident now.

4 **Rewrite the underlined phrases using the phrasal verbs in the box. Make any other changes necessary.**

fall out go off let down look down on stick together take after

1 I feel terrible about disappointing Tom, but I'm just too tired to go out tonight.
2 We always support each other in my family.
3 My brother is a lot like our dad.
4 I've stopped enjoying chocolate.
5 My sister and I are constantly having arguments, but we always make up again.
6 It always feels as if Susanna is thinking that I'm less important than her.

GRAMMAR

1 **Choose the correct options.**

1 By the end of the year, we'll *be finishing* / *have finished* this book.
2 Maybe we could borrow my dad's car. He won't *be using* / *have used* it today.
3 I might be tired on Saturday evening, as I'll *have revised* / *have been revising* all day.
4 I will have been learning Spanish *by the time we go to Madrid.* / *for a year soon*.
5 I can give Mike the key. I'll *be seeing* / *have seen* him later.
6 Emily's going to university next year. She'll *have finished* / *have been finishing* school then.

2 **Choose the correct options.**

1 I *shouldn't* / *wouldn't* have done the shopping if I'd known we were going out.
2 Sally made all the arrangements in advance, so we *didn't need to do* / *shouldn't have done* anything.
3 You *shouldn't* / *wouldn't* have let John down yesterday. He needed your help.
4 I'm glad I didn't wear my jacket. I *shouldn't* / *wouldn't* have been comfortable.
5 I *should* / *would* have persuaded Josie to come and see that film. She'd have loved it.
6 It was an easy history test. I spent ages learning dates, but I *needn't* / *wouldn't* have.

3 **Complete the sentences with *who*, *that*, *which*, *whose*, *where*, *when* or *why*. Write the word in brackets if you can leave it out.**

1 This is the hospital ________ Sam's dad works.
2 We waited for Marcus, ________ eventually turned up 30 minutes late.
3 Sam's the girl ________ mum you met.
4 Can I borrow the book ________ you were reading?
5 Do you know the date ________ we have to hand in our essay?
6 I don't know the reason ________ he left.

4 **Correct the mistake in each sentence.**

1 You mentioned that you have to leave by 4.50 pm. That's not a problem, we will have been finished by then.
2 The time that the show should start was 19.30, but it started 45 minutes later.
3 Your group has been booked into the Palace Hotel, which address you will find in the leaflet.
4 That time we spent together was great, because I made some good new friends, which are some of my closest.
5 I inspired to read the book after I had watched the film.

REVIEW 3 UNITS 9–12

Overview

VOCABULARY	Collocations; Phrases with *in, out of, at, by*; Phrasal verbs: relationships; Compound adjectives
GRAMMAR	Future (2): continuous and perfect; Modals (2): modals in the past; Relative clauses; The passive (1): review
EXAM TASKS	Reading and Use of English Part 2; Reading and Use of English Part 3; Reading and Use of English Part 4

Resources

PHOTOCOPIABLE WORKSHEETS: Grammar worksheets Units 9–12; Vocabulary worksheets Units 9–12; Review Game Units 9–12; Literature worksheet; Speaking worksheet; Writing worksheet

WARMER

With books closed, write the following gapped words on the board:

_ _ _ _ _ _ _ _ _ _ _ _ _ _ _ _ *and* _ _ _ _ _ _ _ (*Future continuous and perfect*)

_ _ _ _ _ _ *in the* _ _ _ _ (*Modals in the past*)

_ _ _ _ _ _ _ _ _ _ _ _ _ _ _ (*Relative clauses*)

The _ _ _ _ _ _ _ (*The passive*)

Put students into two groups. Tell them to guess one letter at a time and they will get a point for every time that letter appears. When they think they know all the words, they can guess them, but if they are wrong, the other team wins the points for the words they get wrong. They can't say individual words, they must know them all. The winning group is the one with the most points. Elicit what the groups know about each grammar point.

VOCABULARY

1 Put the students into pairs to do the matching. Elicit the answers then say, 'I always wanted to be a writer and now my first book has been published.' Elicit which phrase this illustrates (*achieve your goals*). Students work in pairs to choose one of the other phrases and think of a sentence to illustrate it. Invite some pairs to say their sentences and ask the other students to guess the phrase.

Answers

1 b 2 e 3 c 4 a 5 d

2 Students work in pairs to complete the sentences. Elicit the answers and what each phrase means. Divide the class into two halves. Ask the students in one half of the class to write one of the prepositions from the exercise on a piece of paper: *in, out of, in, at, by*. Tell the students in the other half to write one of the words from the word pool on a piece of paper. The students now mingle. As soon as they find someone who they can complete a phrase with, they sit together. When it is obvious that the students who are left standing can't find a partner, they find a seated pair who their word matches. Elicit the phrases from each pair and what their phrase means.

Answers

1 in advance 2 of character 3 in secret 4 at fault 5 by accident

3 Look at the first dialogue with the class. Elicit what *slim* means and what compound word could have an opposite meaning. Students then do the rest of the exercise in pairs. Elicit the answers and the meanings of the phrases in A's utterance and in B's reply.

Answers

1 well 2 last 3 badly 4 short 5 self

4 Look at the first sentence with the class and elicit what changes students might have to make when using a phrasal verb, for example, they would have to use the *-ing* form, as that is the form used in the original sentence and they would have to decide whether the phrasal verb is separable or not in order to decide where to write the name *Tom*. Students work alone and then check in pairs. Elicit the answers and what kind of phrasal verb each is (*1 separable; 2 no object – if we wrote* we stick each other together, *it would mean with glue; 3 inseparable; 4 inseparable; 5 inseparable; 6 three part, inseparable*).

MIXED ABILITY

Allow mixed ability students to work together in pairs. Monitor and help where necessary. Allow them to use a dictionary to look up the meaning of the phrasal verbs in the box so that they have more time to concentrate on the form of the sentences.

Answers

1 letting Tom down / letting down Tom 2 stick together
3 takes after 4 gone off 5 falling out 6 looking down on me

CONTINUED ON PAGE 146

GRAMMAR

1 Look at the exercise with the students and elicit that it tests the difference between the future continuous, future perfect and future perfect continuous. Elicit what we use each one for (*continuous – something that will be in progress at a future point, perfect – something that will have been completed at a future point, perfect continuous – to say how long an activity has been in progress at a future time*). Students work alone, then compare answers in pairs. Elicit the answers and why each choice is the correct one.

Answers
1 have finished 2 be using 3 have been revising
4 for a year soon 5 be seeing 6 have finished

2 Students work alone to complete the exercise. Elicit the answers and what each sentence means, for example *1 I didn't know we were going out so I did the shopping. 2 We didn't do anything because Sally did it all. 3 It was wrong of you to let John down*, etc.

Answers
1 wouldn't 2 didn't need to do 3 shouldn't 4 wouldn't 5 should
6 needn't

3 Ask students when we use each relative pronoun and when we can't use *that* (*for non-defining relative clauses for people or things*). Students do the exercise alone then compare answers in pairs. Elicit why we can leave out the relative pronouns in the final three sentences (*they are defining relative clauses where the relative pronoun refers to the object of the sentence*).

Answers
1 where 2 who 3 whose 4 (that/which) 5 (when) 6 (why)

4 Students work in pairs. Elicit the answers and why the original sentences were wrong. Look at sentence 3 and remind students that we can use *whose* for people and objects, for example *We live in the house whose roof you can see from here*.

Answers
1 … That's not a problem, we will **have finished** by then.
2 The time that the show **should have started** was 19.30, but it started 45 minutes later.
3 Your group has been booked into the Palace Hotel, **whose** address you will find in the leaflet.
4 … I made some good new friends, **who** are some of my closest.
5 I **was inspired** to read the book after I had watched the film.

PREPARE FOR THE EXAM

1 **B2 FIRST FOR SCHOOLS Reading and Use of English Part 2**
Briefly review what students need to do in this part of the exam and if necessary, read out the *B2 First for Schools* box on TB page 58.

Look at the example with the students and elicit that this is a past modal. Set a time limit of ten minutes for students to complete the exercise alone and then allow them to compare answers in pairs. Tell students that, occasionally, more than one answer will be possible. Elicit the answers and what each gap is testing, for example, *1 passives, 2 relative pronouns,* etc.

Answers
1 was 2 who 3 or 4 be 5 Although/Though/While
6 by/on/with/using/through 7 whose 8 would

2 **B2 FIRST FOR SCHOOLS Reading and Use of English Part 3**
Briefly review what students need to do in this part of the exam and if necessary, read out the *B2 First for Schools* information on TB page 102.

Look at the example with the students and elicit that *friendship* is a noun and we know it is singular because it is preceded by the article 'a'. Tell students to read the text quickly before they start completing the gaps. Set a time limit of ten minutes and tell students to be careful and check that they have used negatives where necessary. Elicit the answers and how they know the last word is negative (*the article* an *shows us that a vowel is needed and the fact that the writer couldn't reach the goal shows that it wasn't realistic.*).

FAST FINISHERS

Tell students to look at the Reading and Use of English Part 2 text and find more examples of words which could be tested in a Part 3 task. When everyone has finished the activity, elicit the answers and then invite students to share the words they found (possible answers: *scientist – from science, activity – from active, unexpected – from expect, pleasures – from please, expectation – from expect, pleasurable – from please*).

Answers
1 difference 2 practical 3 strength 4 encouragement 5 effective
6 valuable 7 beneficial 8 unrealistic

3 **B2 FIRST FOR SCHOOLS Reading and Use of English Part 4**
Briefly review what students need to do in this part of the exam and if necessary, read out the *B2 First for Schools* box on TB page 49.

Look at the example sentence with the class. Remind them of the word limit and that they can't change the form of the word in capitals. Students work alone. Elicit the answers and ask the students if *was given a certificate as a reward for* could also be correct (*no, it uses too many words*).

Answers
1 was given | a certificate for 2 (of) my suitcases | are
3 'll/will have | swum 4 being persuaded | by
5 should have/should've | invited 6 I was being | told

COOLER

Write on the board: ______ *you experienced a random act of ______ (KIND).* Elicit that the first missing word is *Have* because this is a present perfect simple question, and the correct form of *kind* needed is *kindness.* Tell students this was from one of the reading texts in Units 9–12. In groups they should look for another sentence which they can do the same thing with: have one gapped word and one word formation gap. When they are ready, they take turns to write their sentence on the board for other students to complete.

PREPARE FOR THE EXAM

Reading and Use of English Part 2

1 **For questions 1–8, read the text below and think of the word which best fits each gap. Use only one word in each gap.**

WHY PEOPLE LIKE SURPRISES

I hate surprises, and I wouldn't **(0)** *have* believed anyone who said they really liked them. That is until I read about a fascinating experiment that **(1)** ________ carried out by neuroscientists in America, **(2)** ________ wanted to find out why some people appear to like surprises and others don't. During the experiment, the scientists poured either water **(3)** ________ juice into the mouths of those who had agreed to be involved. Sometimes the subjects knew which one they were going to **(4)** ________ given, and sometimes they didn't.

(5) ________ some of the subjects had previously stated that they didn't like surprises, their brains told a different story. As the water or juice was put into their mouths, the subjects' brain activity was recorded **(6)** ________ machines. Images showed that their brains responded more strongly to the unexpected pleasures than the subjects might have thought. This surprised the scientists, **(7)** ________ expectation was that the brain **(8)** ________ respond to any pleasurable substance.

Reading and Use of English Part 3

2 **For questions 1–8, read the text below. Use the word given in capitals to form a word that fits in the gap.**

90 ACTS OF KINDNESS

'I had a great **(0)** *friendship* (**FRIEND**) with my grandfather,' says 17-year-old Josie Taylor. 'He was kind, and made a big **(1)** ________ (**DIFFERENT**) to those around him, simply by being friendly. When he passed away at the age of 90, I decided to do 90 acts of kindness in his memory. I'm a **(2)** ________ (**PRACTICE**) person, so I thought I'd use my main **(3)** ________ (**STRONG**) – cooking – to make others happier.

With **(4)** ________ (**ENCOURAGE**) from my grandmother, I baked a cake for a neighbour. He was thrilled! That was when I realised how **(5)** ________ (**EFFECT**) one small act can be.

I learned a **(6)** ________ (**VALUE**) lesson from my acts: I noticed that even a kind word or smile can be **(7)** ________ (**BENEFIT**) in terms of well-being – for both the person who receives it and the one who gives it. With all my schoolwork, finding time to do 90 acts of kindness was an **(8)** ________ (**REAL**) goal and I couldn't reach it. But I did make time to say hello to neighbours and help people when they needed it!'

Reading and Use of English Part 4

3 **For questions 1–6, complete the second sentence so that it has a similar meaning to the first sentence, using the word given. Do not change the word given. You must use between two and five words, including the word given.**

0 Oh, no – you don't have any chocolate left and I don't have any either! **US**
Oh, no – *neither of us* has any chocolate left!

1 Because we did well, the teacher gave everyone in the class a certificate. **WAS**
Everyone in the class ________ doing well.

2 This suitcase of mine is heavy and so is that one! **MY**
Both ________ heavy.

3 Next December, I'm going to swim across the lake. **HAVE**
By the end of December, I ________ across the lake.

4 Is Simon persuading you not to go to the cinema? **PERSUADED**
Are you ________ Simon not to go to the cinema?

5 It would have been a good idea to invite Alex to my party, but I didn't. **SHOULD**
I ________ Alex to my party, but I didn't.

6 I could see my classmates laughing while the teacher was telling me off. **BEING**
While ________ off by the teacher, I could see my classmates laughing.

13 LEADING THE WAY

ABOUT YOU

What do you think are the qualities of a good leader?
Which of these qualities do you think you have?

VOCABULARY Leadership and achievement

EP **1** Read the quiz. Check the meaning of the words and phrases.

Team player? Team leader?

1 I rarely doubt my ability, as I'm confident and have high self-esteem. ☐
2 I include everyone in activities and treat people fairly. ☐
3 I'm conscientious and always take a lot of care with my work. ☐
4 I'm motivated and can get a lot done when I put my mind to it. ☐
5 People think of me as a sympathetic person who is always ready to listen. ☐
6 I react negatively to bossy people and don't enjoy being told what to do. ☐
7 I set myself targets and I have a lot of drive. ☐
8 I'm willing to be different and stand out from the crowd. ☐

2 Read the quiz again and decide on your scores from 1–3 (1 = not true for me, 2 = sometimes true for me, 3 = always true for me).

3 Add up your scores for the quiz, then turn to page 140. What does the quiz say about you? Do you agree?

59 **4** Listen to four people. Which of them do you think would make a good leader? Why?

59 **5** Listen again. Complete the sentences with the correct names: *Phoebe*, *Mo*, *Nathan* or *Ruby*.

1 ________ doubts that he/she will ever be a leader.
2 ________ has improved his/her self-esteem through doing an activity.
3 ________ isn't very sympathetic towards people who lack drive and try to get out of doing things.
4 ________ admits to being quite a bossy person.

READING

60 **1** Listen to someone talking about the *Three Dot Dash* challenge. What do all the teenagers' ideas have in common?

2 Read the profiles of four teenagers taking part in *Three Dot Dash*. In pairs, decide which basic need each teenager is addressing.

education food health shelter

PREPARE FOR THE EXAM

Reading and Use of English Part 7

3 Read the profiles again. For questions 1–10, choose from the teenagers (A–D). The teenagers may be chosen more than once.

Which teenager
1 has been recognised for their project in their own country?
2 has improved the lives of people in several countries through their idea?
3 is working locally on their project, but wishes to expand it to other locations?
4 has worked with the kinds of people their project helps for a long time?
5 has involved their relatives closely in their project?
6 was motivated when they suffered from a personal experience?
7 is initially aiming their project at primary school children?
8 did some research to find out the extent of a problem?
9 has helped individuals to get back in contact with each other?
10 combined different interests to create something students would enjoy?

13 LEADING THE WAY

Unit Overview

TOPIC	Leaders and leadership skills
VOCABULARY	Leadership and achievement
READING	*Three Dot Dash* Challenge
GRAMMAR	The passive (2): other structures
VOCABULARY	Phrasal verbs with *up*
WRITING	A formal letter or email
EXAM TASKS	Reading and Use of English Part 7; Writing Part 2

Resources

GRAMMAR REFERENCE AND PRACTICE: SB page 160; TB page 268
PREPARE FOR THE EXAM: SB pages on TB pages 244–246; TB pages 257–258
WORKBOOK: pages 52–55
PHOTOCOPIABLE WORKSHEETS: Grammar worksheet Unit 13; Vocabulary worksheet Unit 13
TEST GENERATOR: Unit test 13
PRACTICE EXTRA: Unit 13

WARMER

Ask students to think about a person who is a good leader and some reasons for this. The person can lead anything, for example a sports team, a business, a political party. Students should then work in groups of four and tell each other who their person is and the reasons for their choice. Invite groups to tell the class about one or two of the leaders they chose and why they chose them.

ABOUT YOU

Look at the questions with the class. Put the students into groups of three to discuss the first question together. Students then discuss each other's leadership qualities. Ask each group which member they think has the best leadership qualities and what they are.

VOCABULARY Leadership and achievement

1 Students stay in groups of three to discuss the meaning of the words in blue. Tell them not to do the quiz yet, but make sure they understand the sentences. Set a time limit of two or three minutes and then elicit or tell the class what each sentence means.

Answers
1 doubt: feel uncertain; self-esteem: belief in your qualities and abilities 2 fairly: equally 3 conscientious: always doing your work with a lot of care 4 motivated: enthusiastic or determined because you really want to do something; put one's mind to it: give your full attention to something 5 sympathetic: understanding and caring 6 bossy: always telling people what to do 7 targets: things to achieve; drive: energy and determination to achieve things 8 stand out: be very noticeable

2 Look at the instructions with the class and make sure they understand what to do. When they have finished, elicit their totals and ask them what they think a higher or lower score means.

Answers
Students' own answers

3 Students work in groups of three again, the same groups as they were in for the *About you* box. They tell each other what they found out about themselves and see how similar this is to what they said about themselves before. Invite groups to share their ideas with the class.

Answers
Students' own answers

59 4 Tell students to make notes about what the four people say. When they have listened to the recording, students compare their notes in pairs or groups of three and decide together whether or not each person would make a good leader and why. Invite groups to share their ideas with the class and see if the class can come to an agreement on who would be good leaders.

Possible answer
Nathan and Ruby would make the best leaders. Mo just wants to be one of the crowd, and Phoebe doesn't work well as part of a team. Nathan has leadership experience (football team captain) and Ruby enjoys being in charge.

59 5 Students read the sentences and discuss who they think each sentence is about. When they have listened again, elicit the answers and the words used by each person. (*Mo – I think I'll always be this way … I don't need to be the one in charge; Nathan – he made me captain … I'm more confident in myself and what I can achieve now; Phoebe – I can't stand people who make excuses … I haven't got time for people who don't want to do anything; Ruby – I'm always telling them what a bad idea everything is – how someone should have done something*)

Answers
1 Mo 2 Nathan 3 Phoebe 4 Ruby

» AUDIOSCRIPT TB PAGE 298

READING

60 1 Ask students if any of them lead a local club or organisation. Tell them that they are going to listen to someone talking about a challenge set for teenagers by a charitable organisation. Check they understand the meaning of *in common* (*in the same way as someone else*). Play the recording and elicit the answer. Then, discuss with the class what basic human needs are.

Answer
They all want to solve problems related to basic human needs.

» AUDIOSCRIPT TB PAGE 299

CONTINUED ON PAGE 150

BACKGROUND INFORMATION

The Three Dot Dash Global Teen Leaders Challenge is organised by the We Are Family Foundation. The Foundation gets its name from one of Nile Rodgers' most famous songs, which he wrote for the disco band Sister Sledge in 1979. The band was made up of four sisters, with the surname Sledge. It was the first song he composed for a group other than his own band, Chic. As a writer, producer and musician, Nile Rodgers has been involved in records which have sold over half a billion copies in total, including records by David Bowie, Madonna, Lady Gaga and Christina Aguilera.

2 Check meaning of *addressing* (*dealing with a problem*). Ask students to scan the texts to find what need each teenager is addressing. Give them a time limit of two or three minutes to do this. Tell them to compare their ideas with a partner before checking answers as a whole class. Ask students to give any details they can remember about how and why they are addressing these needs, for example: *Hector knows that students appreciate being involved in their learning, so he uses fun activities to teach them. Yash broke his glasses and realised how important they are and how many people can't afford them, so he found a way of distributing unwanted glasses to children in developing countries. Natasha's sister brought home some food from work which was going to be thrown away, so Natasha she started collecting bread to give to poor people. Anoop helps homeless people get back in contact with family and friends.*

MIXED ABILITY

For stronger students, re-elicit the basic needs discussed in Exercise 1. If you didn't elicit the needs then, you can brainstorm them now and write them on the board. Tell students to cover up the word pool in Exercise 2 before doing the task.

Answers

A education B health C food D shelter

PREPARE FOR THE EXAM

3 B2 FIRST FOR SCHOOLS Reading and Use of English Part 7

Briefly review what students need to do in this part of the exam and, if necessary, read out the *B2 First for Schools* box on TB page 17.

Remind students that the words used in the text won't be the same as those in the questions. Also point out that, if they go through the questions one by one, they will have to keep re-reading the texts to find which ones they match. That's why it is important to read all the texts quickly first and to underline or note down key information in each, so that it is easier and quicker to do the matching. Set a time limit of ten minutes and elicit the answers and the information in the text which helped them to do the matching.

FAST FINISHERS

Ask fast finishers to find distractors in the text, i.e. words or phrases that are similar to the words in the questions but don't give the same answer. When everyone has finished, elicit the answers and then invite fast finishers to share any distractors they found, for example, in question 5 Anoop's mother is mentioned, but not as someone involved in the project.

Answers

1 D (Anoop was included in the '20 under 20' list, which celebrates the top 20 young people under the age of 20 in Canada who are brilliant innovators and who stand out from the crowd.)
2 B (The first clinic to be started was in Mexico and has already given thousands of young children the glasses they need. This initial success has led to further clinics overseas)
3 C (Natasha set up FoodSync in New York, but she's setting herself high targets and really wants her idea to be adopted all over the country.)
4 D (Anoop started volunteering at homeless shelters at a young age. … Project HELLO … was founded when Anoop was 16.)
5 C (With the help of friends and family, … Natasha began collecting food from two bakeries in her home town of Scarsdale, New York, and delivering it to homeless shelters and retirement homes.)
6 B (Yash Gupta's project was inspired by breaking his glasses! While he was waiting for a new pair, Yash had to go to school for a week without them. Unable to see clearly, Yash soon found keeping up in class difficult.)
7 A (The website is aimed at 7 to 11-year-olds to begin with.)
8 B (Yash went online to do a bit of research into poor sight and discovered that around 130 million people worldwide depend on their glasses every day. Furthermore, he learned that an astonishing 300 million need glasses but can't afford them.)
9 D ([Project HELLO] aims to put homeless residents in Vancouver, Canada, in touch with lost family and friends.)
10 A (he took two of his favourite passions – computer programming and the environment – and did something with them. Hector knew that, in general, young children and teenagers appreciate being involved in their learning)

61 The Reading text is recorded for students to listen, read and check their answers.

TALKING POINTS

In pairs, students discuss the two questions. For the second question, ask students to list at least five qualities. Elicit the qualities needed from the class and write them on the board. Then ask each pair to choose just three qualities and to rank them in order of importance. Ask two or three pairs to tell the class their order and explain their reasons.

COOLER

Tell students they are going to work in groups to think of a different idea for a project like those in the reading texts. Put them into groups of four or five and tell them that one person in each group should not take part in the discussion but make notes about the ideas to present to the class later. When students have decided who will do this, take those students away from the groups and quietly tell them, so that the groups can't hear them, that their job is not to note down the group's decisions but to note down which students acted as leaders in their group and how they acted, for example, did they listen to others or impose their ideas on the group? Set a time limit of five minutes then ask the note takers to tell the class what they noticed.

Three Dot Dash Challenge

61

A HECTOR FERRONATO

Hector Ferronato has never had any doubt that he wants to make a difference in the world. So for his project, he took two of his favourite passions – computer programming and the environment – and did something with them. Hector knew that, in general, young children and teenagers appreciate being involved in their learning and would put their minds to work when they were involved. So he and two friends created 'The World of Piatã', a website about the adventures of a young Brazilian girl. Visitors are taught about environmental issues through fun and motivating games. The website is aimed at 7 to 11-year-olds to begin with, but Hector wants to expand it to older children and start a revolution in environmental education.

B YASH GUPTA

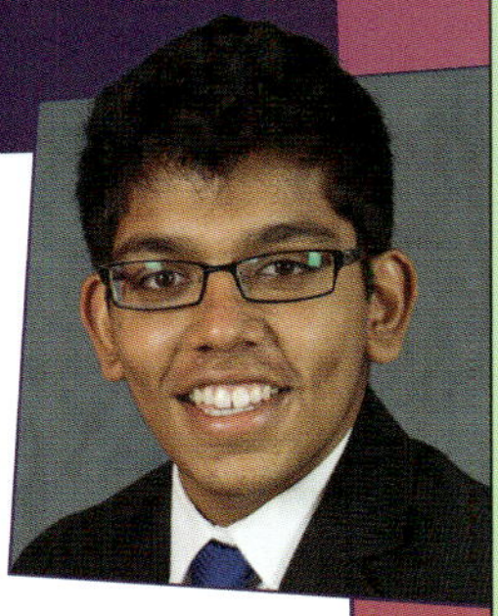

Yash Gupta's project was inspired by breaking his glasses! While he was waiting for a new pair, Yash had to go to school for a week without them. Unable to see clearly, Yash soon found keeping up in class difficult. Yash went online to do a bit of research into poor sight and discovered that around 130 million people worldwide depend on their glasses every day. Furthermore, he learned that an astonishing 300 million need glasses but can't afford them. In developing countries, around 10% of children at primary school, between 6 and 11, have poor vision and often struggle in class as a result. So sympathetic Yash set up *Sight Learning*, which distributes unwanted glasses to eye clinics to give children their vision back. The first clinic to be started was in Mexico and has already given thousands of young children the glasses they need. This initial success has led to further clinics overseas, and Yash has insisted on being involved in each of them.

C NATASHA SURI

For Natasha Suri, it all began when her older sister got a part-time job at a bakery. One evening, Natasha's sister turned up at home with a huge bag of bread and cakes that the bakery had been planning to throw away. Natasha was shocked at the amount of wasted food in the USA, where one in six people don't get enough to eat every day. She started thinking about how this food could be distributed to people who needed it. With the help of friends and family, and her own drive, Natasha began collecting food from two bakeries in her home town of Scarsdale, New York, and delivering it to homeless shelters and retirement homes. This led to the website *FoodSync*. Natasha had this built for her to give live reports on the availability of leftover food and those in need of it. In just a few months, she had delivered 500 kg of food that would have gone in rubbish bins. Natasha set up *FoodSync* in New York, but she's setting herself high targets and really wants her idea to be adopted all over the country.

D ANOOP VIRK

Anoop Virk, from Canada, has always been passionate about helping people and started volunteering at homeless shelters at a young age. Having been brought up by a single mother, Anoop is aware of the importance of both family and friends in our lives. She knew that there were many organisations providing essentials to the homeless, but wanted to do something different. Project HELLO (Helping Everyone Locate Loved Ones) was founded when Anoop was 16. It aims to put homeless residents in Vancouver, Canada, in touch with lost family and friends. In three years, Project HELLO has reconnected 300 people with their friends and family through letters, phone calls and even face-to-face meetings, increasing their happiness and self-esteem. In addition to her invitation to Three Dot Dash, Anoop was included in the '20 under 20' list, which celebrates the top 20 young people under the age of 20 in Canada who are brilliant innovators and who stand out from the crowd.

TALKING POINTS

Why do you think some people are motivated to try and help others?

What qualities do you think young people need to take on the Three Dot Dash challenge?

LEADING THE WAY 77

GRAMMAR The passive (2): other structures

1 **Read the examples and complete the rules with *be*, *to be* or *being*.**

1. Natasha **wants** her idea **to be adopted** all over the country.
2. **The first clinic to be started** was in Mexico.
3. Yash has insisted **on being involved** in each of them.
4. She started thinking about how this food **could be distributed** to people who needed it.
5. Hector knew that, in general, young children and teenagers **appreciate being involved** in their learning.

There are some special structures for the passive.
We use

a ________ + past participle after some verbs (*appreciate*, *enjoy*, *feel like*, etc.).
b ________ + past participle after some verbs (*want*, *hope*, etc.).
c ________ + past participle after prepositions.
d ________ + past participle after *the first*/*second*/*last* + noun.
e ________ + past participle after modal verbs.

» GRAMMAR REFERENCE AND PRACTICE PAGE 160

2 **Complete the second sentence so that it means the same as the first sentence. Use a passive form.**

0. They invited her first.
   She was the first person *to be invited*.
1. He hates it when people criticise him.
   He hates ________.
2. They blame me all the time and I am fed up with it.
   I am fed up with ________.
3. Maybe we can sell the tickets online.
   The tickets could ________.
4. We must treat everyone fairly.
   Everyone must ________.
5. I hope they make me team captain soon.
   I hope ________.
6. They told me last.
   I was the last ________.

3 **Write the sentences in the passive form.**

0. I hate / tell / what to do.
   I hate being told what to do.
1. Everyone expects / criticise / from time to time.
2. He insisted on / put / in charge.
3. The first student / award / a prize was from my class.
4. The singer appreciates / take / seriously as an actor.
5. You will / give / the results of your exam this week.

4 **Choose the correct sentence in each pair.**

1. **a** The shop was closed because it was be repaired.
   b The shop was closed because it was being repaired.
2. **a** She wants to be recognised as one of the best rock climbers in the country.
   b She wants being recognised as one of the best rock climbers in the country.
3. **a** We saw the guy being carried out to sea.
   b We saw the guy be carried out to sea.
4. **a** Would you enjoy to be woken by the sound of waves?
   b Would you enjoy being woken by the sound of waves?

5 **Work in pairs. Take turns to complete the sentences with a passive verb and your own ideas.**

1. I can't stand being …
2. I dream of being …
3. I prefer being … to being …
4. In a few years, I hope to be …

VOCABULARY Phrasal verbs with *up*

1 **Complete the sentences with the correct form of the phrasal verbs in the box. Check your answers in the profiles on page 77.**

keep up	set up	turn up

1. One evening, Natasha's sister ________ at home with a huge bag of bread and cakes.
2. Natasha ________ *FoodSync* in New York.
3. Unable to see clearly, Yash soon found ________ in class difficult.

2 **Match the phrasal verbs in Exercise 1 to the meanings.**

a start a company or organisation
b arrive or appear
c be able to understand what is happening

3 **Match the phrasal verbs to the meanings.**

1. If you want to be heard, you'll need to **speak up**.
2. I **made up** an excuse about being busy because I couldn't be bothered to go.
3. I was waiting outside the station when a young man **came up to** me.
4. The film didn't quite **live up to** my expectations.

a approach someone
b talk louder
c be as good as hoped
d invent something that isn't true

4 **Ask and answer the questions.**

1. Which of your friends always turns up last when you meet?
2. Do you find it easy to keep up with schoolwork?
3. Have you ever been to an event that didn't live up to your expectations?
4. Are you good at making up stories?
5. Have you ever set up a club or something similar?

GRAMMAR The passive (2): other structures

WARMER

With books closed, elicit how we form the passive (*the verb* to be + *past participle*) and forms of the passive that the students covered in Unit 12, for example, the present simple, past simple, etc. On the board, write: *Last week, we ______ (tell) how to use the passive* and elicit that the missing words are *were told*.

Then write:

'I didn't need ______ how to use the passive.'

'I can't stand ______ how to use different structures.'

'I think it's good ______ how to use different structures.'

Students work in pairs to try to complete the sentences with the verb tell in the correct passive form (*to be told, being told, to be told*). Elicit ideas and tell students they are going to look at similar forms.

1 Students complete the exercise in pairs. Elicit the answers and the fact that, if we use *to* + infinitive of a verb in the active, we use *to be* + past participle in the passive. If we use the *-ing* form in the active, we use *being* + past participle in the passive, and if we use just the verb in the active we just use *be* + past participle in the passive. Ask students to make a passive sentence using *look forward*, for example, *I look forward to being chosen as your student representative.*

Answers
a being b to be c being d to be e be

» GRAMMAR REFERENCE AND PRACTICE ANSWER KEY TB PAGE 268

2 Look at the example sentence with the students and elicit which rule it matches (*d*). Tell students to look at the verbs used in the active sentences and think about what form of verb follows them to work out what form of *to be* is used in the passive. Students work alone then compare answers in pairs.

MIXED ABILITY

Put weaker students into pairs and go through the sentences with them, asking them for alternative sentences using the active form in the first two sentences, for example, *I hate going to bed early* and *I'm fed up with waiting for my friends.* Elicit that both these forms are followed by the *-ing* form, so they will take *being* in the passive form.

Answers
1 being criticised 2 being blamed all the time 3 be sold online
4 be treated fairly 5 to be made team captain soon 6 to be told

3 Look at the example with the class and ask why we use *being* here (*because* hate *is followed by the* -ing *form of the verb*). Students complete the exercise alone and compare in pairs before you elicit the answers.

FAST FINISHERS

Elicit an active form for the example sentence, such as *I hate people telling me what to do*. Ask fast finishers to try to make some of the other sentences active. When everyone has finished, invite fast finishers to share their sentences with the class (*1 Everyone expects people to criticise them …; 2 He insisted that we/they put him …; 3 The first student they awarded a prize to was …; 4 The singer appreciates it when people take her …; 5 I / Your teacher will give you …*).

Answers
1 Everyone expects to be criticised from time to time.
2 He insisted on being put in charge. 3 The first student to be awarded a prize was from my class. 4 The singer appreciates being taken seriously as an actor. 5 You will be given the results of your exam this week.

4 Look at the first pair of sentences and elicit which one makes sense and why (*1b because the repairing was in progress.*). Students do the same with a partner with the other three pairs of sentences. Elicit the answers and reasons for the correct answers.

Answers
1 b 2 a 3 a 4 b

5 Look at the instructions with the class and elicit why it is not possible for the students to say, *I can't stand being late* for the first sentence. (*It is a grammatically correct sentence, but doesn't use a passive verb.*) Monitor and listen for interesting sentences and invite students to share their sentences with the class.

Answers
Students' own answers

» GRAMMAR WORKSHEET UNIT 13

VOCABULARY Phrasal verbs with *up*

1 If students aren't sure of which sentence to put each phrasal verb in they can look at the profiles on page 77 before they complete the gaps. Don't elicit the answers yet.

Answers
1 turned up 2 set up 3 keeping up

2 When students have matched the meanings to the phrasal verbs, elicit the answers to Exercise 1 using a phrasal verb and a non-phrasal verb, for example, *1 Natasha's sister turned up at home / Natasha's sister arrived home; 2 Natasha set up the organisation* FoodSync */ Natasha started the organisation FoodSync; 3 Yash found keeping up in class difficult. / Yash found understanding what was happening in class difficult.* Make sure students don't use the preposition *at* after *arrived* in sentence 1.

Answers
a set up b turn up c keep up

3 Students work in pairs to match the sentences to the meanings. Tell stronger students to cover the meanings and to try to work out the definitions of the phrasal verbs from the context. They then uncover the meanings and do the matching. Elicit the answers and ask students to write different sentences using the phrasal verbs.

Answers
1 b 2d 3 a 4 c

4 Students work in groups of three or four to discuss the questions. Set a time limit of five minutes. Monitor and note interesting answers and invite students to share their ideas with the class.

Answers
Students' own answers

» VOCABULARY WORKSHEET UNIT 13

WRITING A formal letter or email

1 Look at the exercise with the whole class. Elicit who you might write a letter of complaint to and for what reason, for example, *to a shop if something you bought wasn't as good as they claimed*. Elicit the answers and then ask students if they have ever written a formal email or letter and, if so, who to and why.

> **Answers**
> to make a complaint; to apply for a part-time job; to request information about a college course

2 Before students discuss the questions, ask 'What is a children's holiday club?' and 'What sort of activities do children do there?' (*It is a place where children can go during the school holidays while their parents are at work. They play and do different interesting activities such as drawing, singing, sports and other things.*) Ask students if they have ever been to one and what they thought of it. Also ask what the leader would do (for example, *thinking of activities for other staff to do, helping when there are problems, etc.*). Students read the task alone then discuss the questions in pairs. Elicit answers from different pairs.

> **Answers**
> 1 creative and confident, good with children 2 Some examples of why you are suitable for the role; reasons why you enjoy working with children, whether you are available to work at weekends
> 3 Students' own answers

3 Look at the rubric with the class and re-elicit how many questions there are in the task and what they are. Students read the letter and answer the questions alone then compare answers in pairs. Elicit the answers and ask the students what useful topic vocabulary Bethany has used in the letter (for example *advertisement, apply, position, suitable, experience, volunteered, in charge, responsible, application*).

> **Answers**
> No, she doesn't (she does not mention whether she is available at weekends). Yes, she would be suitable for the role because she enjoys spending time with children and has experience of working with them.

4 If you elicited topic vocabulary in the previous exercise tell the students that, as well as words which are suited to the topic of the letter, there are other words and phrases that can be used in formal letters regardless of the topic. Go through the *Prepare to write* box with the class. Ask students to find the phrases alone then elicit the answers.

> **Answers**
> a Dear Sir/Madam b Any five of: I have seen, I would like, I would be, I am, they are, I would be, you would consider c I believe that, I would be grateful if, I look forward to hearing from you d Yours faithfully

5 Students discuss their ideas in pairs. Ask students to put their hands up for either a or b and then ask the students who chose b why it is better. (*It is more formal, it uses better vocabulary such as* available *and* commitments *and it starts with the word* Unfortunately *to show that Bethany is sorry.*)

> **Answer**
> b

PREPARE FOR THE EXAM

6 **B2 FIRST FOR SCHOOLS Writing Part 2: A formal letter or email**

Briefly review what students need to do in this part of the exam and if necessary, read out the *B2 First for Schools* box on TB page 42.

When writing the formal letter or email, students should ensure that they answer all the questions and use a suitable writing style for the task. For a formal letter or email, they should avoid contractions and informal phrases. Tell students to organise their email clearly with an introduction saying why they are writing and the other information in two or three separate paragraphs and ensure they start and finish the email appropriately.

Allow students to work in pairs to plan their emails. They identify the three pieces of information needed and think about which phrases from the *Prepare to write* box they can use. They could also brainstorm other useful vocabulary for the letter, for example, *I would like to study physics at university.*

Set a time limit of five minutes. Monitor and help where necessary.

7 Set a time limit of about half an hour for the writing, as students have already planned their work. When they have finished, ask students to work in pairs and to swap their emails with a second pair so that no pair has their own emails. The students read the two emails as if they were organising the quiz show and should decide which person to choose for the quiz team. They then get together with the other pair and tell each other who they chose and why.

> **Model answer**
> Dear Ms Ryan,
> I have seen the advertisement on the school notice board and I would like to apply to be a team member on the TV science quiz show.
> I would like to take part in the show because I enjoy quizzes. I often do quizzes at the after-school club I go to, and I always get good results. I also think it would be very interesting to visit a TV studio and find out how programmes like this are made.
> I have always loved science and I believe that I have a good knowledge of the subject. I am interested in all kinds of science – biology, chemistry and physics – and I hope to work as a scientist one day. I also enjoy working with other people to achieve goals and I believe that would make me a good team member.
> I would be grateful if you would contact me if you think I would be a useful addition to the team.
> Yours sincerely,

COOLER

Put the students into groups of four or five. Ask them to write some questions for a science quiz. Set a time limit of three or four minutes then tell each group they are going to organise a quiz for the other students. They can organise it how they like, for example asking each group a question in turn, asking questions and seeing who answers first, asking individuals from each team, etc. Then, invite each team in turn to ask their questions to the other groups.

WRITING A formal letter or email

1 **Tick (✓) the situations which require a formal letter or email.**

to make a complaint ☐
to enquire how a relative is ☐
to apply for a part-time job ☐
to request information about a college course ☐
to tell your news to a friend ☐

2 **Read the task and answer the questions.**

You have seen this advertisement for a holiday job in your town.

> **Children's holiday club leader wanted!**
> We're looking for a creative and confident leader for our children's holiday club.
> Why would you be suitable for the role? What do you enjoy about working with children? Are you available at weekends?
> If you're capable of inventing and running fun activities for 4 to 11-year-olds, we'd love to hear from you.

Write your **letter**.

1 What kind of person are they looking for?
2 What information do you need to include in your application?
3 Would *you* be suitable for this role? Why? / Why not?

3 **Read Bethany's application. Has she answered all the questions in the advert? Do you think she would be suitable for the role? Why?**

> Dear Sir/Madam,
>
> I have seen the advertisement for children's holiday club leader on your website and I would like to apply for the position.
>
> I believe that I would be suitable for the role because I already have some experience of working with children. Last summer, I volunteered at a local sports club, where I taught young children how to play tennis. I also have two younger brothers, and my parents often leave me in charge when they go shopping, for example. I often invent interesting games for them to play and I am responsible for their safety.
>
> I enjoy working with children because they are interested in everything and they're good fun, too. I like how they think about the world and how much energy they have. They enjoy life!
>
> I would be grateful if you would consider my application and I look forward to hearing from you.
>
> Yours faithfully,
>
> *Bethany Ward*

4 **Read the *Prepare to write* box, then read Bethany's application again. Find:**

a an opening expression
b five formal full forms
c three other formal phrases
d a closing expression

PREPARE TO WRITE | Formal letters and emails

In formal letters and emails:

- use formal titles.
  Dear Mr Thompson / Ms García
  Dear Sir/Madam
- use a formal opening expression.
  I have seen your advertisement …
  I would like to apply for …
  I am writing to enquire/complain about …
- use full rather than contracted forms.
  do not *cannot* *would not*
- use formal language.
  I believe that … *I would be grateful if …*
  I would like to know … / Could you tell me …
- use a formal closing expression.
  emails: *Best regards* *Best wishes* *Yours*
  letters: *Yours sincerely* *Yours faithfully*

5 **Bethany hasn't answered the final question in the task. Choose the best sentence (a or b) to answer the question.**

a I won't be able to work at weekends because that's when I spend time with my friends, but I can do plenty of hours during the week.
b Unfortunately, I am not available at the weekends due to other commitments, but I am fully available during the week.

PREPARE FOR THE EXAM

Writing Part 2 (A formal letter or email)

6 **Read the task and plan your answer.**

You have seen this advertisement on the school notice board.

> **Take part in a science quiz show on TV!**
> We're looking for team members from around the country to take part in a science quiz show on TV.
> Write and tell us why you would like to take part. Tell us about your interest in science and why this would make you a good participant on the show.

Write your **email**.

7 **Write your email to apply for the science quiz show.**

- Answer all of the points in the advert.
- Use the tips in the *Prepare to write* box.
- Check your grammar and spelling.
- Write 140–190 words.

14 GETTING THERE

ABOUT YOU

10 **Watch the video and answer the questions.**

Describe the longest journey you've ever been on.
What's the best journey you've ever been on?
Which types of holiday do you think are best suited to young people?

VOCABULARY Phrasal verbs: transport

1 **Read the sentences and match them to the photos (A–L).**

EP

1 I was **held up** because there was an accident further down the road.
2 I **broke down** in the middle of nowhere.
3 Come on, **speed up** a bit – we're going to be late!
4 I put my foot on the brake, and the car **slowed down**.
5 The train **pulled into** the station exactly on time.
6 As I got to the platform, the train was **pulling out** of the station.
7 The taxi **pulled up** outside our house.
8 The police officer told the driver to **pull over** to the side of the road.
9 I found it really hard to **keep up with** her.
10 I **ran over** some glass and got a puncture.
11 The bus **drove off** without waiting.
12 I **ran into** the back of the car in front when it stopped suddenly.

62 **2** **Listen to eight situations and decide what is happening or has happened. Use the phrasal verbs in Exercise 1.**

1 Sophie's dad has driven off without her.

READING

1 **Look at the pictures opposite. What do you think they show? Read the first paragraph of the article and check your answers.**

2 **Read the article about the Hyperloop quickly. Choose the best alternative title (A–C).**

A International public transport
B Public transport of tomorrow
C Futuristic airplanes

3 **Read the article again and answer the questions.**

1 What will the Hyperloop system look like?
2 Which two systems gave Musk the idea for the Hyperloop?
3 Aside from passengers, what else will the Hyperloop be able to carry?
4 Why wasn't Musk impressed with California's high-speed rail project?
5 For what reasons will Hyperloop be better than other forms of transport?
6 What is Elon Musk's attitude to the plans he created?
7 How are plans progressing to make the Hyperloop a reality?

4 **Match the highlighted words and phrases in the article to the meanings.**

1 make the effort
2 using something to help you
3 for no particular reason
4 goods carried by trains, trucks, ships or aircraft
5 moving somewhere very quickly

14 GETTING THERE

Unit Overview

TOPIC	Travel and transport
VOCABULARY	Phrasal verbs: transport
READING	The high-speed Hyperloop
GRAMMAR	Reported speech
VOCABULARY	Reporting verbs
LISTENING	Five people talking about bad travel experiences
SPEAKING	Linking ideas
EXAM TASKS	Reading and Use of English Part 4; Listening Part 3; Speaking Part 1

Resources

GRAMMAR REFERENCE AND PRACTICE: SB page 161; TB page 268
PREPARE FOR THE EXAM: SB pages on TB pages 239, 248 and 250; TB pages 255 and 260–261
WORKBOOK: pages 56–59
VIDEO AND VIDEO WORKSHEET: Travelling
PHOTOCOPIABLE WORKSHEETS: Grammar worksheet Unit 14; Vocabulary worksheet Unit 14
TEST GENERATOR: Unit test 14; Term test 2
PRACTICE EXTRA: Unit 14

WARMER

Put students into groups of three or four. Allocate each group a form of transport, for example, *car, train, plane,* etc. They write ten related words for their form of transport, for example, *drive*, *petrol*, *car park*, etc. These can be verbs or nouns. When they have written their ten words, they join up with a group with a different form of transport. The groups take turns to tell each other their form of transport and then the other group have one minute to say any words related to that form of transport and see how many of the other group's words they can say in that time. Elicit how many words each group guessed, any words that weren't guessed and any new words suggested by the groups.

ABOUT YOU

10 You can begin the class and introduce the topic of the unit by showing the video and asking students to complete the video worksheet. Students then get into groups of three to discuss the questions in the *About You* box. They each describe journeys they have been on. Invite students to share stories of their journeys with the class and then discuss the final question as a class.

VOCABULARY Phrasal verbs: transport

1 Before students read the sentences, ask them to work in pairs and to describe what they can see in each photo. Elicit ideas and write any interesting vocabulary that isn't included in the exercise on the board, for example *traffic jam*, *passengers*. Students then do the matching in pairs. Elicit the answers and the meanings of the words in blue. (*held up – delayed; broke down – the car stopped working; speed up – go faster; slowed down – went slower; pulled into – arrived at; pulling out – leaving; pulled up – stopped; pull over – stop in a place you can park; keep up with – go at the same speed as; ran over – drove/cycled over/on top of; drove off – left; ran into – bumped/crashed into*)

Answers

1 A 2 G 3 L 4 H 5 C 6 B 7 J 8 D 9 K 10 F 11 E 12 I

62 2 Play the recording once for students to choose a phrasal verb for each situation. Then play the whole recording a second time. Encourage students to take short notes about the situations. Students then work in pairs to decide the situation each time. When they have finished, play the recording again, stopping after each situation and invite students to say what is happening in each one. You could follow this up by asking the students to choose one of the phrasal verbs not used in the situations in the recording and write a short dialogue to illustrate it. Invite pairs to act out these dialogues and see if the other students can guess which phrasal verb it shows.

Possible answers

2 They've been held up. 3 They've broken down. 4 He's having trouble keeping up with his friend. / He can't keep up with his friend. 5 They've pulled over to the side of the road. 6 They've run over a box. 7 They're about to pull into the station / They're pulling into the station. 8 They're speeding up. / They are pulling out to overtake a lorry.

» AUDIOSCRIPT TB PAGE 299

READING

1 Students discuss the pictures in pairs for one minute. Elicit what they can see and what they think the pictures show. Then give the students one minute to read the first paragraph of the text. Ask them for their answers and what information the text gives about the transport, for example, *maximum speeds, the date they should be ready*.

Answers

The pictures show a future form of transport called the Hyperloop.

2 Set a time limit of two minutes for students to skim-read the article. Elicit the answer and why the other two answers are wrong (*A because it talks about cities which are fairly close together. The journeys could be international in, for example, Europe, but the example given is between Los Angeles and San Francisco; C they aren't airplanes. It is a form of transport which uses magnets and runs in a tube*).

Answer

B

CONTINUED ON PAGE 158

BACKGROUND INFORMATION

Elon Musk was born in South Africa. Even as a young boy, he was so obsessed with inventions that he would often get lost in his daydreams and his parents actually took him to the doctor to check his hearing because of this. He moved to Canada at the age of 17 to study at Queen's University and three years later, he went to the USA to study business and physics at the University of Pennsylvania. He then went to Stanford University in California to do a PhD in energy physics, but dropped out after two days to take advantage of the opportunities presented by the growth of the internet.

His first internet company was Zip 2, which he sold in 1999 for $307 million. He then set up X.com, which became PayPal. He sold that to eBay for $1.5 billion. His other companies include Space X, which became the first private company to send supplies to the International Space Station. He invested in Tesla Motors, which produces electric cars, in 2004 and became its chairman. In 2017, he also started the Boring Company, which aims to build tunnels to reduce the amount of traffic on city streets (*to bore* means to make deep, round holes in a hard surface).

The fastest train in the world in 2019 was the Shanghai Maglev, which could reach speeds of up to 430 kph. Maglev is short for 'magnetic levitation'. The train doesn't have wheels but floats on a magnetic field between the train and the tracks. It travels the 30 km between Shanghai Airport and the city centre in 7 minutes 20 seconds.

There are Space Mountain rides at five of the six Disney parks in the world, but the original opened in Florida in 1975. Because you travel in the dark and there are some sudden drops, it feels faster than it actually is. The top speed of the ride is 45 kph. The original ride was rebuilt for the 50th anniversary of Disneyland, and Neil Armstrong, who was the first man on the moon, officially opened the new ride.

3 Before students read the text, ask them to underline the key words in each question, for example *1 Hyperloop system / look like*. Elicit these and then set a time limit for students to read the text and note where the information needed to answer each question can be found. They then cover the text and work in pairs to discuss the answers to each question. Finally, they uncover the text again and write the answers.

FAST FINISHERS

Ask fast finishers to think of one or two more questions they could ask about the text. When everyone has finished the exercise, elicit the answers and then invite fast finishers to ask their questions to see if the other students can answer them.

MIXED ABILITY

Students work in pairs or groups of three. They divide the questions between themselves and find the answers to their questions. They then tell each other what they found out and show each other where in the text the information was written.

Answers

1 a raised tube on columns with capsules travelling inside it
2 the office mail system and the California high-speed rail project
3 cars and freight 4 It was likely to be slow and expensive.
5 It will be faster, safer and more convenient, weather-proof, sustainable and efficient 6 He wants other people to improve on them 7 A capsule has already been created and there are plans to start building a track.

63 The Reading text is recorded for students to listen, read and check their answers.

4 Students cover the meanings of the words. Read the sentences with the highlighted words with the class. Then, elicit what the highlighted words could mean. Students then uncover the meanings and complete the exercise. You could follow this up by putting students into groups of four. Two students search for two more useful words or phrases in the first column of the text and the other two look in the second column. They write definitions for their words, using paper or online dictionaries. Each pair then tells the other two students their two definitions and each of the pairs tries to find the other pair's two words. Invite students to share some of their words and definitions with the class.

Answers

1 bother 2 with the aid of 3 for the sake of it 4 freight
5 whizzing

TALKING POINTS

Look at the first question with the class and ask how people usually travel between major cities in their country: by plane, train, car, bus. Elicit any problems with each, for example, pollution, traffic jams, accidents, etc. Also ask students if there is any high-speed rail travel in their country and, if so, ask those who have used it to say what it was like. Students then work in groups of three to discuss the two questions. Set a time limit of two minutes and then elicit ideas.

COOLER

Elicit two countries in the world from the students and write them on the board. You could draw a very basic map to show where they are or allow students to look them up on computers or mobile phones. Put students into groups of three or four and tell them that they are scared of flying so they have to decide how to travel between the two countries. There is no time or cost limit. Students work together to plan their route. Set a time limit of three minutes then invite students to share their ideas with the class.

THE HIGH-SPEED HYPERLOOP

Can you imagine whizzing through a tube from city to city at speeds of 1,200 kilometres an hour? Well, this could soon be a reality with the 'Hyperloop', a futuristic form of transport in which passengers will speed between cities in capsules travelling faster than the speed of sound. By as early as 2030, some of us could be zooming around in what will be not only the world's fastest form of transport, but the safest and most efficient, too.

So, where did the idea come from? Billionaire technology entrepreneur Elon Musk came up with the idea after being inspired by the tubes which are used to transport mail between offices in some buildings. In Hyperloop, with the aid of strong magnets, long capsules will float through airless tubes that are raised above the ground on columns. This will virtually eliminate friction, allowing the capsules to reach speeds higher than any other form of land transport. Musk compares the experience to that of an amusement park ride, saying it will be 'like getting a ride on Space Mountain at Disneyland'. He hopes that the Hyperloop capsules will transport passengers, as well as cars and freight. This will speed up people's journeys, avoid them being held up in traffic jams, and reduce the number of polluting vehicles on the roads.

Musk decided to work on a new and innovative form of transport after reading about California's high-speed rail project. While Musk agreed that it would be good if there were an alternative to having to drive or fly, he didn't think high-speed rail was the answer. Since it would be slower and more expensive than it would be to fly, this would mean few passengers would actually bother with the system.

Musk wasn't just being critical for the sake of it, but was considering ways in which a public-transport system could be made better. This, according to Musk, means making a system that is not only faster but safer, more convenient, weather-proof, sustainable and efficient – all the things that he believes the Hyperloop can do. 'You want the future to be better than the past,' he says.

Hyperloop is intended for cities which are less than 1,500 kilometres apart and which have high volumes of traffic travelling between them. The system would allow passengers to travel between, for example, Los Angeles and San Francisco, a distance of over 600 kilometres, in under 30 minutes. That's five hours less than it currently takes to drive in a car. What's more, Musk thinks there could be as many as 70 capsules operating at any one time, pulling into and out of 'stations' every 30 seconds!

Although Musk doesn't intend to be involved in building a full Hyperloop network himself, he published a design and invited feedback to see if people could find ways to improve it.

The idea is that other companies use the design to develop and test their own Hyperloop systems. And it may not be too far into the future that Musk's ideas come into being. 'I know there are various companies that are trying to create the Hyperloop,' he said. The first full-scale capsule has already been constructed and revealed at a special ceremony, and rival companies HyperloopTT and Hyperloop One are working hard to get projects off the ground in various places. HyperloopTT, for instance, already has plans to start building a Hyperloop track to replace Abu Dhabi's rail network.

However, with such high speeds and long distances involved, the process won't be straightforward, and some leading engineers have raised concerns about the safety of the technology. After a successful test by Hyperloop One at speeds of 110 km/h over a short distance in the Nevada Desert, Philippa Oldham, a senior engineer at the Institution of Mechanical Engineers, said that Hyperloop could only ever be used by the public if the right safety systems were put in place. She added, 'Whilst this was a successful first trial, the speeds were still relatively low, so it will be interesting to watch the development of this programme.'

So, who knows, with some amazing minds behind the Hyperloop, we may soon be travelling hundreds of kilometres in a matter of minutes.

TALKING POINTS

Would a Hyperloop transport system benefit your country? How?

Do you think there are any advantages to travelling more slowly?

GRAMMAR Reported speech

1 **Read the direct and reported speech. Why do the tenses sometimes not change? Read the rules and check.**

1 You want the future to be better than the past.

Musk says that you want the future to be better than the past.

2 It will be like getting a ride on Space Mountain at Disneyland.

Musk says it will be like getting a ride on Space Mountain at Disneyland.

3 Whilst this was a successful first trial, the speeds were still relatively low.

Oldham said that whilst this had been a successful first trial, the speeds had still been relatively low.

a When we report sentences we usually change the tense, e.g. present simple → past simple.
b We <u>don't</u> usually change the tense when we are talking about
- general truths and opinions.
- an event which is not in the past.

In these cases, we often use a reporting verb in the present simple or present perfect, e.g. *says*, *agrees*, *has said*, etc.

» GRAMMAR REFERENCE AND PRACTICE PAGE 161

2 **Choose the correct verb forms.**

1 'It's quicker to pull up at the back door than stop outside the main door.'
Tom says it *'s / was* quicker to pull up at the back door than stop outside the main door.
2 'You should learn to drive.'
He said I *should learn / should have learned* to drive.
3 'You must carry your passport with you at all times.'
The law says you *had to / must* carry your passport with you at all times.
4 'The holiday will be my first without my parents.'
Sarah points out that the holiday *will / would* be her first without her parents.
5 'We're going there tomorrow.'
Dad told me last week that they *were / 're* going there the next day.

3 **Tick (✓) the sentences which are right, and correct the mistakes in the other sentences.**

1 My parents told us that we will spend our holidays in the Netherlands that summer.
2 My dad said it was worth the long journey to see something so incredible.
3 I asked where my case was, and someone told me it was in the lost property office.
4 She wanted to know why I am slowing down.
5 Johanna told me that the bus has driven off without her.

4 **Complete the reported-speech sentences.**

1 'The hotel won't take guests under 18.'
The travel agent says ________
2 'I want to take a year off before university.'
My sister told my parents ________
3 'My mum's a better driver than my brother.'
Amy reckons ________
4 'I've been travelling through Europe in the holidays.'
Dylan said ________
5 'We've been waiting for over an hour!'
Amy claims ________

VOCABULARY Reporting verbs

1 **Read the sentences. <u>Underline</u> the reporting verbs and check their meaning.**

EP

a My sister agreed to slow down.
b My grandparents insisted that I went home early.
c Tom persuaded his friend to overtake the car in front.
d My parents forbade me from travelling home alone.
e The woman enquired whether the trains were on time.
f The police officer pointed out that his driver's licence wasn't valid.
g She recommended travelling after the rush hour.
h He confessed to driving above the speed limit.

64 **2** **Listen and match the speakers to the sentences in Exercise 1.**

PREPARE FOR THE EXAM

Reading and Use of English Part 4

3 **Complete the second sentence so that it has a similar meaning to the first sentence, using the word given. Do not change the word given. You must use between two and five words, including the word given.**

1 'It's best to leave your passports in the hotel safe,' the receptionist told them. **RECOMMENDED**
The ________ passports in the hotel safe.
2 'It was me who lost the tickets,' Jo said. **CONFESSED**
Jo ________ the tickets.
3 'I definitely locked the door before I left,' Sam said. **INSISTED**
Sam ________ the door before he left.
4 'Do you think I should pull over here?' Karen asked. **ENQUIRED**
Karen ________ pull over there.
5 'Going camping would be a brilliant idea. Let's go!' Mum said to me. **PERSUADED**
Mum ________ camping.
6 'Getting a family room will be cheaper,' the travel agent said. **POINTED**
The travel agent ________ a family room would be cheaper.

4 » **Work in pairs. Turn to page 140.**

GRAMMAR Reported speech

WARMER

Write on the board: *I want you to go to London tomorrow.*

Tell the class that your mother said this to you a few weeks ago. Put students into groups of three and ask them to report the sentence starting: *My mother said …* Set a one-minute time limit and then elicit the correct form (*My mother said that she wanted me to go to London the next/following day.*) and the parts of the sentence that they needed to make changes to (*pronouns, tense, time reference words*).

1 Students work in pairs to discuss the sentences and corrolate them with the rules. Elicit the answers (*1 b (opinion); 2 b (an event which is not in the past); 3 a)*) and tell students that, in exams when reported speech is tested, for example in a Reading and Use of English Part 4, it will be obvious whether or not the tense change needs to be made.

» **GRAMMAR REFERENCE AND PRACTICE ANSWER KEY TB PAGE 268**

2 Ask students to do this task individually, and encourage them to think about the reason for the correct answer in each case. They should look at the tense of the reporting verb to give them a clue. Check answers and reasons.

Answers
1 's 2 should learn 3 must 4 will 5 were

3 Ask students what tense the reporting verb is in the first sentence (*past*) and tell them to look at the time expression (*that summer*). Ask if we need to change the tense of the sentence (*yes*) and elicit that *will* should change to *would*. Students work in pairs. Check answers as a whole class.

Answers
1 My parents told us that we **would** spend our holidays in the Netherlands that summer. 2 ✓ 3 ✓ 4 She wanted to know why I **was** slowing down. 5 Johanna told me that the bus **drove off** without her.

4 Look at the sentences with the class and elicit the tense of the reporting verbs in each case. Ask how this will affect how the students finish the sentences (*they won't change the tense where the reporting verb is in the present*). Students complete the sentences alone and then compare answers in pairs. Then, check answers as a class.

Answers
1 (that) the hotel won't take guests under 18. 2 (that) she wanted to take a year off before university. 3 (that) her mum's a better driver than her brother. 4 (that) he 'd/had been travelling through Europe in the holidays. 5 (that) they 've/have been waiting for over an hour.

» **GRAMMAR WORKSHEET UNIT 13**

VOCABULARY Reporting verbs

1 Look at the first grammar exercise and elicit what reporting verb was used (*said/says*). Now look at Exercise 2 and elicit other reporting verbs used (*points out / told*). Elicit how the sentence after *told* differs from the sentence after *said* (*We need an object after* told. *We don't use an object after* said). Students then look at the verbs in Vocabulary Exercise 1. Elicit the answers and look at the sentence structure in each case. (*agree to, insist that + object, persuade + object + to, forbid + object + from + -ing form, enquire whether, point out that, recommend + -ing form, confess + to + -ing form*).

Answers
Underlined words: a agreed (said yes) b insisted (said I had to) c persuaded (encouraged/convinced) d forbade (said I couldn't) e enquired (asked) f pointed out (explained) g recommended (said it was a good idea to) h confessed (admitted to)

64 **2** Put students into eight groups and allocate them one sentence from Exercise 1 each. They have to think of a very short dialogue which matches their sentence but without using any of the words in the sentence.

Set a time limit and then invite each group to read out their dialogue while the others guess the sentence it matches. Play the first conversation and elicit the reporting verb used. If they suggest *agreed*, tell them that it is true that Speaker 2 agrees with Speaker 1, but try to elicit a verb for what Speaker 1 says. Say, 'You really MUST go home now', with emphasis on the word *must* and elicit that the person is insisting. Play the rest of the recording. Students compare ideas in pairs. Play the recording again, stopping after each conversation to elicit the answers.

Answers
1 b 2 f 3 a 4 c 5 g 6 e 7 h 8 d

» **AUDIOSCRIPT TB PAGE 299**

PREPARE FOR THE EXAM

3 **B2 FIRST FOR SCHOOLS Reading and Use of English Part 4**

Briefly review what students need to do in this part of the exam and, if necessary, read out the *B2 First for Schools* box on TB page 49.

Tell students that all the verbs in this exercise appear in Exercise 1, so if they aren't sure of what form to write the verb in or whether it needs an object, they should check the sentences there. When students have finished, allow them to compare in pairs before eliciting answers.

MIXED ABILITY

Tell students to work in pairs and to use Exercise 1 to help them write the correct form. Focus their attention on the structure in Exercise 1 and prompt the students to use the same structure for the information in Exercise 3, for example for sentence 1 say, 'We need the person speaking (*the receptionist*), the reporting verb (*recommended*) the verb in the correct form – look at Exercise 1 sentence g – (*leaving*) and the correct pronoun (*their*)'.

Answers
1 receptionist recommended | leaving their 2 confessed to | losing / confessed that she | had lost 3 insisted that | he 'd/had locked 4 enquired if/whether | she should 5 persuaded me | to go 6 pointed out | that (getting)

4 Look at the example with the class. You could ask the students to read the five sentences and elicit which verb matches each one before they start. Tell students to try to do it without looking at page 82. Elicit the sentences and see if students can correct each other if they make mistakes.

Answers
1 My dad forbade me from going on my brother's motorbike.
2 My mum insisted that I eat/ate something.
3 Beth pointed out that Charlie / to Charlie that he couldn't stop there.
4 The attendant recommended parking / that I/we/he, etc. park by the station.
5 The woman enquired where the nearest bus stop was.

» **VOCABULARY WORKSHEET UNIT 14**

LISTENING

1 Books closed. Ask students to work in pairs to make a list of problems they might have whilst travelling. Elicit some examples from different pairs. Books open. Ask students to look at the photos and to work with a partner to explain what they think each travel problem is. Find out if anyone in the class has experienced any of the problems shown or brainstormed earlier. If so, invite students to share their experiences or ask students to tell the class about travel problems they have heard about on the news.

Possible answers

A The car has broken down and they are waiting for a mechanic.
B The road is closed, so they have to find an alternative route.
C Passengers at an airport are rushing to their gate because they are late for their plane.
D The boy fell off his bike and broke his arm.

65
2 Before students listen, put them into groups of three or four and ask them to think of one key word that each person might say. Elicit these and write each group's suggestions on the board under the letters A–D to match the photos. When students have listened and done the matching, ask each group if their words were mentioned.

Answers

Speaker 1 C Speaker 2 D Speaker 3 no photo Speaker 4 A
Speaker 5 B

PREPARE FOR THE EXAM

3 **B2 FIRST FOR SCHOOLS Listening Part 3**

65
Briefly review what students need to do in this part of the exam and, if necessary, read out the *B2 First for Schools* box on TB page 30.

Tell students to read through the sentences. They may remember some of the answers from the first listening, but they shouldn't write anything until they listen again. When they have listened again, allow them to compare their answers in pairs and discuss anything they remember about the five situations. Elicit the answers and the information from the recordings which helped them. (*1 totally his fault; 2 I tripped … broke my wrist; 3 came down with some virus; 4 the car suddenly broke down; 5 We should've realised*)

Answers

Speaker 1 G Speaker 2 E Speaker 3 D Speaker 4 F
Speaker 5 C

» AUDIOSCRIPT TB PAGES 299–300

SPEAKING Linking ideas

66
1 Read the questions with the students and elicit what the people might say about each, for example, *a It's slow / expensive / very good in the capital.* Elicit the order and ask if the speakers mentioned any of the students' ideas in their answers.

Answers

1 e 2 a 3 h 4 g 5 c 6 f 7 d; b is not answered

66
2 Read the *Prepare to speak* box with the class before playing the recording. After listening to the recording, elicit the answers. Put students into pairs and tell them to think of their own sentences using the different linking expressions. Monitor and help where necessary and then elicit some of the sentences from different pairs.

Answers

Anita: besides that, as well as, but sometimes, as I was saying
Marco: like, anyway, such as, however

» AUDIOSCRIPT TB PAGE 300

3 Look at question e in Exercise 1 with the class and elicit what Anita talked about during her answer. You could play this part of the recording again if necessary. Elicit that she mentions that *she is learning to drive, how she felt during her first lesson, what she is looking forward to about passing, the cost of travelling by car compared to public transport.* Encourage students to give similarly extended answers to question b. Monitor and note interesting answers and invite students to share their answers with the class. Students give their own answers.

4 Give students a time limit to think about the questions. Tell them not to try to script their answers but just make very brief notes; for example, *bus – school / every day.*

FAST FINISHERS

Ask stronger students to think of one or two questions they could ask as a follow up to some of the questions in Exercise 1, for example, *a What do you think needs improving most? Do you think it is better than in other countries?* When they do Exercise 5 they can ask these questions if their partner has problems thinking of something to say.

PREPARE FOR THE EXAM

5 **B2 FIRST FOR SCHOOLS Speaking Part 1**

Briefly review what students need to do in this part of the exam and, if necessary, read out the *B2 First for Schools* box on TB page 30.

Remind students that they should try to give extended answers, but not deviate from the question. So, for question a, they could mention different forms of transport and say whether they are getting better or worse. They shouldn't talk too much about a journey they have been on, but could compare transport in their country with that in a different country using a personal anecdote. Try to put stronger students with weaker ones so that stronger students can help them to give more extended answers by asking follow-up questions. The students could talk for 30 seconds about each question, so eight minutes altogether for the activity or, to reduce the time, you could tell each student to ask and answer four of the questions. Allow weaker students to keep their books open to refer to the *Prepare to speak* box so they can use as many of the phrases as possible during their answers. Monitor and note interesting answers and invite students to share some of their answers with the class. Students give their own answers.

COOLER

Put students into different pairs to those they were in for the last exercise. Each student reports what their partner said during the previous activity, using present reporting verbs for things which are still true, for example *He says that he uses the bus every day*, or past reporting verbs for other information, for example *She said that the best journey she had been on was when she went to Spain …* Monitor and correct where necessary. Then, invite students to share sentences with the class.

LISTENING

1 Look at photos A–D. Can you explain the travel problem in each photo? Have you experienced any of these problems yourself?

65 **2** You will hear five people talking about bad travel experiences. Match the people to the photos. Which person's story doesn't match a photo?

PREPARE FOR THE EXAM

Listening Part 3

3 65 Listen again. For questions 1–5, choose from the list (A–H) what each speaker says. Use the letters only once. There are three extra letters which you do not need to use.

A I was too young to understand why something went wrong.
B A joke I played ended in difficulty.
C The problem we had was our own fault.
D Illness prevented me from enjoying myself.
E An accident temporarily interrupted the trip.
F An unexpected event delayed our arrival.
G I blame someone else for what happened.
H Nobody could have predicted such a situation.

Speaker 1 ......
Speaker 2 ......
Speaker 3 ......
Speaker 4 ......
Speaker 5 ......

SPEAKING Linking ideas

66 **1** Listen to Anita and Marco answering questions about travel and transport. Number the questions in the order they answer them. There is one extra question.

a What's public transport like in your country?
b How often do you use public transport? (Which form of transport do you use most?)
c How do you spend your time when you're travelling on public transport or by car?
d Tell us about an interesting journey you've made recently.
e Do you like travelling by car? (What do you like about it?)
f What's the longest journey you've ever made? (Did you enjoy it?)
g Do you ever travel by bike? (What's good about doing that?)
h Have you ever been on holiday by plane? (Did you enjoy travelling by plane? Why? / Why not?)

66 **2** Read the *Prepare to speak* box. Then listen again. Who uses each linking word or phrase? Write A (Anita) or M (Marco).

PREPARE TO SPEAK | Linking ideas

Giving examples
like ... such as ...

Adding information
as well as ... besides that ...

Returning to an earlier point
as I was saying ... anyway ...

Showing contrast
but sometimes ... however ...

3 In pairs, answer question b in Exercise 1.

4 Make notes on your answers to the other questions in Exercise 1. Think about how you can link your ideas together.

PREPARE FOR THE EXAM

Speaking Part 1

5 Ask and answer the questions with a partner.

- Ask the questions from Exercise 1.
- Answer using words or phrases from the *Prepare to speak* box.

CULTURE

GAP YEARS

1 **What do you think a 'gap year' is? What kind of things do you think people do on one? Read the article quickly and check your ideas.**

2 **Read the descriptions of four people and choose the best gap year experience from the article for each one. Compare your ideas with your partner's.**

1 You like to feel useful and that you are helping others. You'd also like to go abroad and use your communicative skills.
2 You know exactly what you want to study at university, but it's a very difficult course to get a place on. Therefore, you want to use a gap year to make your CV more attractive.
3 You like getting to know new people and finding out about how they live. You are also looking for an experience that will help boost your confidence so you can do more things by yourself.
4 You love the idea of going backpacking, but you want to get some money in your wallet at the same time!

3 **Match the highlighted words and phrases in the article to the meanings.**

1 doesn't interest you
2 officially register for and be accepted on a course
3 showing good judgement
4 when someone learns a job and skills from an expert
5 travelling with all your possessions and clothes in one big bag

67 **4** **In pairs, make a list of pros and cons for taking a gap year. Then listen to a talk by a school careers advisor. Does he mention any of your ideas?**

67 **5** **Listen again and choose the correct answer for each of the questions.**

1 What warning does the speaker make at the beginning of his talk?
A Thinking about the advantages and disadvantages of a gap year can take a long time.
B Your parents might want to decide whether or not you can go on a gap year.
C Taking a gap year isn't the right thing to do for all young people.

2 Why is it good to take a gap year between finishing school and starting university, rather than doing it later in life?
A Young people feel refreshed and ready for new challenges at this age.
B Young people have few commitments in life to deal with at this age.
C Young people's parents can pay for their gap year.

3 When doing a gap year job, being young and inexperienced
A can be a disadvantage.
B can be an advantage.
C has neither a positive nor negative impact.

4 For what type of people is a gap year **not** suitable?
A People who are motivated and responsible.
B People who are goal-orientated.
C People who like to have deadlines.

5 What recommendation does the speaker give at the end of the talk?
A Young people should be prepared to explain to other people why they want to do a gap year.
B Young people should always follow their parents' advice.
C Young people should talk to other people for advice about whether to do a gap year or not.

6 **Complete the sentences with the words in the box.**

candidate	consideration	distraction
financial	motivate	practice

USEFUL LANGUAGE

Talking about plans for life after school

1 You may need to take several things into ________.
2 This is exactly what makes you the perfect ________ for the job.
3 University is a major ________ investment.
4 You have to be able to ________ yourself.
5 You'll learn lots of things that you can put into ________ at university.
6 A year out could become a ________.

84 CULTURE

CULTURE

Learning Objectives

- The students learn about what a gap year is and the sorts of things that young people do during the year.
- In the project stage, the students prepare a presentation about an ideal gap year and present it to the class.

Vocabulary

apprenticeship backpacking enrol isn't your thing wisely

Resources

CULTURE VIDEO AND CULTURE VIDEO WORKSHEET: Gap years

WARMER

With books closed, ask the class to think about the next ten years of their lives. For each year, they should write the main events that they will probably experience. Write an idea on the board, for example *1. Year 12 of school: start learning to drive; 2. Year 13 of school, final exams, 18th birthday, driving test, go to university / get a job*.

Students write their own lists then compare answers in pairs or small groups. Ask the students if anyone decided to have a year out between finishing school and going to university or starting work.

BACKGROUND INFORMATION

Gap years started to become popular in the 1960s. The original aim was for students from different countries to exchange cultural ideas and prevent future wars from happening. From the 1960s, a number of companies were created in the UK to make it easier to find voluntary work or adventure. For example, in 1967, an organisation called Project Trust sent three volunteers from the UK to Ethiopia. Later, in 1973, a man named Graham Turner bought a bus and started offering overland bus trips from the UK to Kathmandu in Nepal. Then, in 1978, Prince Charles and Colonel John Blashford-Snell offered an expedition voyage following the route around the world taken by Sir Francis Drake in the 16th century.

Other countries also have gap years. In Belgium, every employee is allowed one year off (one year's time credit which can be taken over a number of years) from their job so they can enjoy other experiences. In Denmark, gap years became so popular during the 1990s that only about 25% of students went straight from school to university. In 2009, the country introduced a law which gives students a bonus if they don't take a gap year.

1 If you did the Warmer activity, students may be able to guess what a gap year is. Elicit ideas from the class then allow them two minutes to skim read the text to find some ideas about what people do on gap years. Elicit the answers and ask students if they know anyone who has taken a year out or would like to have one.

Answers
Students' own answers

2 Set a time limit of ten minutes for students to read the text carefully and do the matching. Elicit the answers and ask students what information in the texts helped them to decide which experience matched which person (*1 – feel useful – feel you're doing something constructive, abroad – abroad / somewhere new in the world, communicative skills – teach languages; 2 you know exactly what you want to study – the specific degree they want to study, very difficult to get a place on – competition for places is usually very high (if students say this, point out that it refers to work experience), make your CV more attractive – not mentioned; 3 getting to know new people – meet lots of people, finding out about how they live – discover new cultures, boost your confidence – become much more independent; 4 go backpacking – travelling / hostel for backpackers, want to get some money – get paid for your time / paid employment.*)

MIXED ABILITY

Tell weaker students to work in pairs. Each student looks at two descriptions and underlines key words which show them what they have to look for, for example *1 feel useful, helping others, abroad, communicative skills*. When they have done this, point out that they can do the matching just by looking at the four headings in the text. Check that they have done this correctly and then ask them to find information in the texts which match the words in the descriptions, for example, *feel useful – feel you're doing something constructive*.

Answers
1 volunteering 2 work experience 3 travel 4 paid work

68 The Reading text is recorded for students to listen, read and check their answers.

3 Tell the class to cover the text. Look at the meanings and, for each one, try to elicit what the words may be, for example, *1 could be bored, not your first choice*, etc. Don't tell the students if they are right or wrong. When they have thought of ideas for each meaning, they uncover the text and do the matching. Elicit the answers.

Answers
1 isn't your thing 2 enrol 3 wisely 4 apprenticeship
5 backpacking

CONTINUED ON PAGE 166

67 **4** Elicit one or two ideas for and against the idea from the class and write these on the board. Set a time limit of two minutes for students to make their lists; then, put pairs together in groups of four to share their ideas and add the other pair's ideas to their own lists. Invite groups to share their ideas with the class and write these on the board.

Before students listen, ask them if they have a careers advisor at school and, if so, what they think he/she would say if they said they were thinking of taking a gap year. They could also discuss in pairs what they think other people would say about the idea of taking a gap year, for example, a best friend, a family member or another teacher from school.

Students then listen to see which ideas the careers advisor mentions. Elicit the answers and ask if they agree with the advisor or not, giving reasons for their answers.

Answers
Students' own answers

67 **5** Tell students to look at the questions without looking at the choices, so that they know what they are listening out for. Tell them to try to make very short notes in answer to each question as they listen, still without looking at the choices if they can avoid it. When they have listened, they compare notes in pairs and then look at the three choices to see which one corresponds most closely to what they noted down. Elicit the ideas and ask students what they noted down for each question.

Answers
1 C 2 B 3 B 4 C 5 A

» **AUDIOSCRIPT TB PAGE 300**

6 Ask the class to cover the *Useful language* box, then, read out the words in the word pool. Put students into six groups and walk to each group, writing one of the words on a piece of paper so that the other groups don't know which word they have. The students look up their word in a dictionary or online and write a definition for it. Ask each group to read out their definition and the other groups write down the word they think it defines. When all six groups have read out their definitions, elicit the answers and ask each group how many they got right. Students then uncover the *Useful language* box and complete the sentences.

FAST FINISHERS

Ask fast finishers to look at the sentences in the *Useful language* box and to think of further details they could add to give examples or further explanations of the words, for example *1 You need to take several things into consideration, for example, what you hope to achieve during the year, how much it will cost you and whether it will help you in your studies or not*. When everyone has finished, invite fast finishers to share their ideas with the class.

Answers
1 consideration 2 candidate 3 financial 4 motivate 5 practice
6 distraction

PROJECT ***Choosing and planning a gap year***

Look at the instructions with the students. As a class, they brainstorm ideas of gap years they could do. Make a note of some of the ideas on the board to help weaker students later on. Students then work alone, either at home or in the classroom on computers to find out what sort of opportunities are available. They may be able to find an organisation which offers placements, in which case they can get details from the organisation's website about costs, etc.

Students then decide alone how they would like to present the information. Encourage them to use a multimedia presentation if they can. Set a fairly short time limit for the presentations, as each student will be doing this alone, which will mean there are a lot for the students to listen to.

When students have presented their projects, ask them which idea, apart from their own, they found the most interesting.

PROJECT EXTENSION

Tell the students to imagine that they have been on a gap year and are now at university. Their old school has invited them to return to talk to current students about the gap year. They could talk about things such as what they did, things they learned about themselves and whether they think it was a good idea or not. They can also give the audience tips on how to find gap year activities. Students work in groups of three or four to prepare their speeches. They can do this in the classroom or at home. When they are ready, invite each group to choose a speaker. Each speaker in turn addresses the class as if they were addressing a hall full of younger students. When everyone has finished, ask the class if they think it would be useful for their school to invite ex-students to talk to them about gap years, university life, finding a job or other topics.

11 **CULTURE VIDEO: Gap years**
When students have completed the lesson, they can watch the video and complete the worksheet.

COOLER

Put the students into pairs. Tell each pair that one of them has decided to take a gap year before going to university. The other student is a worried friend or parent who doesn't know anything about gap years and thinks it is a terrible idea. They work together to create a dialogue between the two people, with the worried person asking questions and the student reassuring them. Set a time limit of about five minutes then allow the pairs to practise their dialogues before inviting them to act out their dialogue in front of the class.

ARE YOU READY FOR A GAP YEAR ADVENTURE?

So, the end of life as you know it is in sight! What's next? Straight to university? Maybe the world of work is calling you? Or perhaps the next thing for you is an apprenticeship in a company? Whatever your next step may be, don't forget that there is another option: a gap year! Essentially, this is taking a year-long break between school and university to … well, this is the unbelievable bit: to do whatever you like!

GAP YEAR FACT

*Approximately **10%** of students in the UK, Australia and New Zealand take a gap year before they enrol at university.*

Now, I don't mean sitting around and watching TV series all day or spending a year at the beach! I'm talking about something that will energise you after all those years of sitting down in a classroom. An experience to reward yourself for all your hard work and open new doors to the future. Interested? I thought you would be! I'm talking about taking a gap year. While they remain uncommon in many countries, gap years have long been popular in countries like the UK, Australia and New Zealand. Let's take a look at just a few of the amazing things you could get up to on yours.

68

TRAVEL

Pack your bags and go and explore the world! Yes, travel is always one of the most popular gap year choices. You'll discover new cultures, meet lots of people and become much more independent. How about backpacking across Asia, taking a train through Europe, or flying to Australia? The possibilities are endless. The world's a big place and the only limit is your wallet!

VOLUNTEERING

Does travelling appeal to you, but you're the type of person that needs to feel you're doing something constructive? In that case, taking part in a volunteer programme abroad may be the best gap year option for you. You can help other people while supporting a good cause and gaining valuable life skills. You could sign up to teach languages to children, participate in wildlife conservation, or help to build infrastructure in remote villages. And best of all, you'll be satisfying your desire to see somewhere new in the world at the same time.

PAID WORK

You may like the idea of spending a year travelling and keeping yourself busy, but you'd prefer to get paid for your time. Well, paid employment is definitely a gap year option, too. There are plenty of jobs around the world in agriculture or working in the tourism industry, like working in a hostel for backpackers. Of course, finding paid work near where you live is also an option if travelling isn't your thing.

WORK EXPERIENCE

Getting paid in a job that's easy to find might sound good. However, some people's priority is to get work experience that is relevant to the specific degree they want to study for in the future. This could take the form of a work placement or internship, and be over a period of several weeks to a year. However, if this is your gap-year choice, make sure you apply early. This type of work experience is popular, and competition for places is usually very high. Besides, many of these positions are unpaid, so if you need to make some money for university, this probably isn't an option for you.

In the past, I've heard people referring to gap years as a year *off*, but the reality is far from that. The most important thing is to spend the time wisely. Whichever of the ideas above sounds most interesting to you, it'll be a year full of new, exciting experiences and valuable life lessons!

PROJECT *Choosing and planning a gap year*

Prepare a presentation about your ideal gap year. Use these steps to help you.

1. Which of the gap year choices from the article would you most like to do?
2. Choose a specific destination, job, programme, etc. for your ideal gap year.
3. Find out more about your choice, including images and videos if possible.
4. Prepare a presentation to talk about your ideal gap year.

Present your research to the class.

11 NOW WATCH THE CULTURE VIDEO

15 THE BIGGER PICTURE

ABOUT YOU

12 **Watch the video and answer the questions.**

What national or global issues do you feel concerned about? Explain why you are concerned.

Do you think that young people should have a role in government? Why? / Why not?

VOCABULARY Global issues: nouns and verbs

1 **Match the sentence halves. Check the meaning of the verbs.**

EP

1 Aid agencies are cooperating
2 We've collected
3 Cars should be banned
4 The local council has been criticised
5 You seem to think I don't support
6 It's great that Ann's been elected

a for not dealing with litter in the city.
b your views on animal rights.
c £100 for an anti-poverty charity.
d with the state government.
e as leader of the school council.
f from busy city streets.

69 **2** **Listen to six people using these nouns and verbs and check your answers to Exercise 1.**

69 **3** **Complete the sentences with the noun form of the verbs in Exercise 1. Listen again and check.**

EP

ban collection cooperation criticism election supporter

1 Unfortunately, ________ between the two organisations hasn't worked out.
2 Sometimes we organise a food ________ for a local homeless hostel.
3 A ________ on private cars would make a huge difference in the city centre.
4 There has been further ________ of the local council for closing down leisure facilities in the area.
5 I'm a great ________ of animal rights.
6 I'm so proud of her for winning the ________!

READING

1 **Read the title of the text. What do you think *MYP* and *UKYP* could mean? Read the first two paragraphs of the text to find out.**

PREPARE FOR THE EXAM

Reading and Use of English Part 1

2 **Read the first two paragraphs of the text again and decide which answer (A, B, C or D) best fits each gap.**

	A	B	C	D
0	A containing	(B) consisting	C involving	D forming
1	A act	B run	C set	D lay
2	A ensure	B reassure	C assure	D secure
3	A sense	B influence	C aspect	D theme
4	A demonstrate	B represent	C produce	D regard
5	A recently	B shortly	C freshly	D newly
6	A stay	B keep	C live	D hold
7	A presented	B provided	C supplied	D given
8	A consequence	B impression	C reaction	D impact

3 **Read the whole interview. Choose the best summary of it (A–C).**

A Charity talks about her personal experiences of being an MYP and gives a few examples of specific projects she has worked on.
B Charity mentions some of the things she achieved as an MYP and gives advice to readers who may wish to be elected as MYPs.
C Charity describes the range of people you are likely to meet as an MYP and how to handle them.

4 **Complete the sentences with highlighted words and phrases from the text.**

1 We need to strike a ________ between good service and price.
2 What ________ does Jon play in the organisation?
3 I'll help you tidy up ________ for help with this assignment.
4 Honesty is ________ when you want people's cooperation.
5 Suzy spends a ________ of her time supporting worthy causes.

15 THE BIGGER PICTURE

Unit Overview

TOPIC	Global issues
VOCABULARY	Global issues: nouns and verbs
READING	MYPs @ UKYP
GRAMMAR	Modals (3): deduction
VOCABULARY	Phrases with *in*
WRITING	An essay (3)
EXAM TASKS	Reading and Use of English Part 1; Writing Part 1

Resources

GRAMMAR REFERENCE AND PRACTICE: SB page 162; TB page 268
PREPARE FOR THE EXAM: SB pages on TB pages 236 and 246; TB pages 254 and 258
WORKBOOK: pages 60–63
VIDEO AND VIDEO WORKSHEET: The big picture
PHOTOCOPIABLE WORKSHEETS: Grammar worksheet Unit 15; Vocabulary worksheet Unit 15
TEST GENERATOR: Unit test 15
PRACTICE EXTRA: Unit 15

WARMER

Put the students into groups of four. Ask them to think of a country other than their own where they would be happy to live. Ask them to list reasons why it would be a good place, for example, *employment, good climate*, etc. When students are ready, invite each group to share their ideas with the class. Note the reasons for their choices on the board. Elicit which factors are human-made and which are natural. Then ask students to think of problems in the world, both natural and those caused by humans and write their ideas on the board.

ABOUT YOU

12 You can begin the class and introduce the topic of the unit by showing the video and asking students to complete the video worksheet. Then look at the *About you* box with the class and put the students into groups of three or four to answer the questions. Elicit their ideas and ask them to rank the five most important global issues facing the world today. When students have done this, invite one group to share their ideas with the class. Then ask other groups if they have any different issues in their top five and, if so, invite them to share these with the class.

VOCABULARY Global issues: nouns and verbs

1 Students work in pairs. Ask them to discuss the meanings of the words in blue and only look them up if they don't know them or are unsure. Don't elicit the answers yet.

69 **2** Play the first part of the recording and elicit that the person used phrase 1d. Ask the students what the problem was that the person was talking about (*a tornado in Oklahoma*). Ask them to do the same for the other five speakers, check their answers to Exercise 1 and make notes about the problem or situation in each one (*2 long-term unemployment / low wages / homelessness; 3 traffic congestion and parking; 4 litter and rubbish; 5 animal rights; 6 school council elections*). Allow students to compare ideas in pairs and elicit the answers, then check the meanings of the words in blue in Exercise 1.

Answers
1 d; cooperate – work together 2 c; collect – get money by asking people to give it 3 f; ban – forbid 4 a; criticise – express disapproval of sb/sth 5 b; support – agree with 6 e; elect – choose by voting

69 **3** Read the words in the box with the students. Ask them which one refers to a person (*supporter*). When students have completed the sentences, play the recording and then elicit the answers. Ask the students to work in pairs to rephrase the sentences in the exercise so that they don't use the words in the box, for example, *1 The two organisations aren't able to work together well*. Ask students to do the same for the other sentences and elicit ideas (*2 We ask people to give us food for the homeless hostel. 3 A law against cars driving in the city centre would make a huge difference. 4 People have made negative comments about the local council's decision to close down leisure facilities in the area. 5 I believe in animal rights. 6 I'm proud that she won more votes than the other candidates.*).

Answers
1 cooperation 2 collection 3 ban 4 criticism 5 supporter 6 election

» AUDIOSCRIPT TB PAGES 300–301

READING

1 Look at the title with the class. Ask them to put their hands up if they can guess the meanings of the letters. If all the students don't put their hands up, write UK on the board and elicit what that stands for (*United Kingdom*). Then, write MP and ask if anyone knows what this means (*Member of Parliament*). Elicit ideas from different students and write these on the board without saying if they are right or wrong, then set a time limit of one minute for students to read the first part of the text and find the answers.

Answers
Member of Youth Parliament; United Kingdom Youth Parliament

CONTINUED ON PAGE 170

BACKGROUND INFORMATION

UK voters elect 650 Members of Parliament (MPs) to represent their interests in the House of Commons. MPs assess and propose new laws, and examine government policies.

The UK Parliament is the supreme legislative body in the United Kingdom. Its head is the Sovereign of the United Kingdom (currently Queen Elizabeth II) and its home is the Palace of Westminster in London.

The House of Commons is the lower house of the UK Parliament, and is where MPs meet. The House of Lords is the second house. Together, these are called the 'Houses of Parliament.'

The UKYP consists of 369 elected members all aged between 11 and 18. Anyone of this age can vote for a local representative or stand for election. Elections are held each year. The members meet at an annual conference as well as an annual debate in the House of Commons. They also run campaigns and meet local politicians to discuss young people's concerns. The MYPs are not affiliated to any political party. They stand as independents and campaign on individual issues.

The West Midlands is a region of England, and home to the second most populous city, Birmingham.

PREPARE FOR THE EXAM

2 **B2 FIRST FOR SCHOOLS Reading and Use of English Part 1**

Briefly review what students need to do in this part of the exam and if necessary, read out the *B2 First for Schools* box on TB page 26.

Remind students that in the exam this task will be a standalone text, not a part of a longer text. Look at the four options in the example and note that they all have the same form, the gerund, as this task tests the meaning of the words, not which is grammatically correct. Elicit how they would be able to tell that *consisting* is the correct word (involving *and* containing *aren't followed by* of *and, to have a similar meaning with* form, *we would need the past participle,* formed of). Tell the students that even if they have no idea of an answer, they should guess as there is a chance they will be correct and they don't lose marks for wrong answers. Set a time limit of ten minutes for students to complete the task then allow them to compare in pairs. Elicit the answers and ask students how easy or difficult they find this task-type.

MIXED ABILITY

Allow weaker students to work in pairs and use a dictionary to look up any words they aren't sure of. This will also help them with any collocations or set phrases that the task is testing, for example, *have an impact on*.

Answers
1 B 2 A 3 C 4 B 5 A 6 C 7 D 8 D

3 Read the three summaries with the class and elicit the key words in each, for example, *1 personal experiences, examples of specific projects; 2 things she achieved, advice, wish to be elected; 3 range of people, how to handle them.* When students have read the text, they discuss which summary they think is best in pairs. Elicit ideas and ask students to give examples of what Charity has achieved and the advice she gives to people hoping to become MYPs. (*Achievements: She appeared on national TV and radio, she has grown in confidence and learned the art of socialising and negotiating. Advice: be brave, do the best you can, don't be afraid to ask questions*)

Answer
B

70 The Reading text is recorded for students to listen, read and check their answers.

4 Tell students to cover the text. They look at the sentences and think of one or two words which could go into each gap, for example, *1 balance*. Elicit ideas and then ask students to uncover the text and do the matching. Elicit the answers and the meanings of the words.

FAST FINISHERS

Ask fast finishers to think of their own sentences using the highlighted words and phrases, for example, *I spend a great deal of money on clothes.* When everyone has finished, elicit the answers and then invite fast finishers to share their sentences with the class.

Answers
1 balance 2 role 3 in return 4 key 5 great deal

TALKING POINTS

Look at the first question with the whole class. Ask, 'Which issues affect young people aged between 18 and 24 today?' If students have trouble thinking of issues, encourage them to brainstorm as a class some general areas first, such as education, housing, employment, entertainment. Elicit any laws which have helped young people in recent years and any which have been bad for young people. Ask why politicians care/don't care about young people (e.g. *under 18s/16s can't vote, fewer younger people vote than older people*). For the second question, students work in groups of three or four. Elicit one or two ideas from the class and write these on the board, for example *doing voluntary work*, and then set a time limit of three minutes for students to think of their own ideas. Invite groups to share their ideas with the class and find out if any students do things to help improve their society.

COOLER

Tell students that they are applying to be members of a youth parliament. Ask them to consider the key things they would like to work on whilst in power, and to prepare a brief speech. Before students start writing their speeches, ask them to think about ways of starting and closing a presentation. Then, brainstorm some useful language as a class and write it on the board. Put students into groups of five or six. Students should deliver their speeches in their groups and each group should elect its MYP. In feedback, ask each group who they chose and why. Then invite those students to give their speeches to the class.

70

MYPs @ UKYP

The UK Youth Parliament is a youth organisation in the United Kingdom, **(0)** *consisting* of elected members aged between 11 and 18. There are currently hundreds of MYPs who meet with MPs and local politicians, organise events, **(1)** .... campaigns, make speeches, hold debates and **(2)** .... the views of young people are listened to by decision-makers. A key **(3)** .... of any MYP's job is making certain they **(4)** .... the views of the young people in their area. We talked to Charity Mhende about the position she has **(5)** .... taken up as an MYP.

Charity, your year as a Member of the Youth Parliament must have been a really interesting experience. Did it (6) .... up to your expectations?
It was absolutely amazing! I have grown so much and have been **(7)** .... so many incredible opportunities. I really believe now that you have to make the most of every opportunity that comes along, as it could be something that has a long-lasting **(8)** .... on your life.

'YOU HAVE TO MAKE THE MOST OF EVERY OPPORTUNITY THAT COMES ALONG.'

It can't have been easy, though, doing this on top of your schoolwork and everything else that a normal 15-year-old likes to do! Did anything suffer?
For some people, being involved in the UKYP means they end up giving up their social lives, but it shouldn't be like that. It's all about getting a good work–life balance. At the same time, you always have to remember that you only get what you give. If you put in the work, you will get loads back in return.

And what did you focus on as an MYP?
I was elected as one of the Media Representatives for the West Midlands, where I live, so I was heavily involved in media work. And my year was when history was made – we were the first non-Members of Parliament to be allowed to debate in the House of Commons like real politicians. It was my role to make sure the press knew about it and that our work got recognised. My biggest achievement was being on the national TV news and on the radio.

You must be very proud of that. It sounds like the experience might have changed your approach to life. Has it?
Yes! I have definitely grown in confidence and I have learned the art of socialising and negotiating, because communication is key if you want to get something done. In this role, you can make links with decision-makers and people that could help you a great deal in the future. You just need to take the opportunities that come your way.

'DON'T BE AFRAID TO ASK QUESTIONS!'

Some situations must have been quite scary, in that they were completely new for you. What advice would you give other teenagers in that position?
Well, it's true that you might be put into unexpected situations, but you just need to be brave and do the best you can. And don't be afraid to ask questions! Youth workers, staff and other MYPs will all be happy to help you. You will meet so many people and have loads of new challenges, but it will all be worth it in the end.

TALKING POINTS

Do you think politicians represent the views of young people?
In what ways can young people help to improve their society?

GRAMMAR Modals (3): deduction

1 **Read the examples. Is each sentence about the past, the present or the future?**

1 You **must be** very proud of that.
2 You can make links with people that **could help** you a great deal in the future.
3 The experience **might have changed** your approach to life.
4 Some situations **must have been** quite scary.
5 It **can't have been** easy.

2 **Complete the rules with the modal verbs in the box.**

can't	could	couldn't	may
may not	might	might not	must

We use modal verb + infinitive to make guesses about the present and future.
We use modal verb + *have* + past participle to make guesses about the past.
We use

a ______ for things we are certain are true.
b ______ or ______ for things we are certain are not true.
c ______, ______ or ______ for things that are possible.
d ______ or ______ for things that are unlikely.

» GRAMMAR REFERENCE AND PRACTICE PAGE 162

3 **Choose the correct options.**

1 Carla *couldn't have stuck* / *must have stuck* that poster here. She's trying to advertise her charity event.
2 There's someone at the door. It *must be* / *can't be* Dan; he's not around today.
3 Jacob often does collections for this group, so he *must be* / *couldn't be* a supporter of our ideas.
4 We're waiting for an important document. There was a postal strike last week, so that *must delay* / *might have delayed* it.
5 Kids from that school *couldn't damage* / *couldn't have damaged* the car. They are banned from entering the car park, and it's always locked.
6 Their friends are away, so they *mustn't have* / *might not have* anyone to talk to.
7 My brother usually keeps in touch, but we haven't heard from him for ages. I'm not sure, but there *can't be* / *may be* some sort of problem.
8 Tina has sent a few text messages of support, so she *could lose* / *can't have lost* her phone.

4 **Correct the mistake in each sentence by replacing the bold words with one or two words.**

1 You **could** not believe this, but it's true – Andy's passed his guitar exam at last!
2 Within a few years, many people in the country **can** be living in poverty.
3 Our holiday was OK. It could **be** much worse than it was.
4 It **could** have been Mandy who left the window open – there's no one else it could have been.
5 You **must** left the book at home if it isn't in your bag.

5 **Look at the photos. In pairs, make guesses about the situations.**

VOCABULARY Phrases with *in*

1 **Charity Mhende used the phrase *in return*, meaning 'in exchange'. Match the phrases to the meanings.**

EP

1 in the light of
2 in general
3 in progress
4 in favour of
5 in actual fact
6 in turn

a happening or being done now
b one after another
c considering the whole of something
d to emphasise what is true or give information
e because of, considering
f approving of a plan or idea

2 **Complete the sentences with the phrases in Exercise 1.**

1 People thought the politician had suggested a ban on advertising, but ______ he'd said something quite different.
2 Josh and Liam are ______ splitting up the band. They aren't getting on any more.
3 ______ the bad weather, the match has been postponed until next weekend.
4 Let's speak to everyone ______ and then report any criticism or positive comments back to the class.
5 Building work is ______, so the library will remain closed until Friday.
6 Apart from your studies, how are things going for you ______?

3 » **Work in pairs.** **Turn to page 140.**

GRAMMAR Modals (3): deduction

WARMER

Invite a student to come to the front of the class. Give the student a piece of paper with this text: *You are waiting for someone to come to the classroom. They are late.* Ask the student to mime the situation, for example, they should keep looking at the door and their watch and look anxious. Ask the class to guess the situation. Note down any ideas using modal verbs. Now invite a second student to the front. Their piece of paper could say: *You lost your new, expensive mobile phone this morning on the way to school.* The student mimes feeling sad and others guess what's wrong. Again, note any uses of modal verbs. Write any modals they used on the board. If no one used any modals, ask the class, 'How might … feel now?' and 'What can he/she do?'

1 Students discuss the sentences in pairs. Elicit the answers and tell students to look at sentences 1 and 4. Ask them what this tells them about the modal *must* (*it can be used for the present and past*). Now look at the second sentence and elicit how *could* can also be used in the past and present (*could have helped, can help*).

Answers
1 present 2 future 3 past 4 past 5 past

2 Students complete the rules in pairs. Remind them that for things we are certain aren't true (for present deductions) we use *can't*, not *couldn't*, e.g. *It can't be ten o'clock already*. Also, we very rarely use contracted forms of *might not* or *may not* so students should avoid using these. Ask students to work in pairs and to make three sentences with present deductions. Monitor and help where necessary making sure that the students use the correct form. Invite students to share their sentences with the class.

Answers
a must b can't, couldn't c could, may, might
d may not, might not

» GRAMMAR REFERENCE AND PRACTICE ANSWER KEY TB PAGE 268

3 Look at the first sentence with the students. Elicit that the two choices either say that we are certain she didn't put up the poster or we are certain that she did. Elicit the correct choice and why it is correct (*she is advertising a charity event*). Students do the rest of the exercise alone then compare their choices in pairs. Help weaker students by eliciting whether 4, 5 and 8 are talking about the present or past so they can choose the correct option more easily (*they all refer to the past*). Elicit the answers.

FAST FINISHERS

Tell the students to look at sentences 1 and 2. Tell them to try to think of how to complete both sentences using the unused option, for example *1 Carla couldn't have stuck that poster here. It's about the school trip and she isn't going on it. 2 There's someone at the door. It must be Dan. He said he would come at about 5 o'clock.* When everyone has finished the activity, elicit the answers and invite the fast finishers to share their ideas with the class.

Answers
1 must have stuck 2 can't be 3 must be 4 might have delayed
5 couldn't have damaged 6 might not have 7 may be
8 can't have lost

4 Students complete the activity alone then compare answers in pairs. Elicit the answers and why the students used the words they did to replace the ones in the originals (*1 it is possible, not definitely untrue; 2 we don't use* can *be for things that are possible; 3 we are talking about a past holiday; 4 we are sure that it was Mandy; 5 the person has used the correct modal and tense but has left out a word*).

Answers
1 might/may 2 could/may/might 3 have been 4 must
5 must have

5 Ask students to try to guess both what is happening and what has happened. Elicit ideas for each photo from different pairs. Focus on the students' use of modals of deduction and encourage them to use a range of modals. It may be useful to teach or elicit the phrase *There must/might/can't have been …* . You could follow this up by putting students into mixed ability pairs. They work together to draw their own pictures showing something that has just happened. Display the pictures and allow students to wander round the room looking at them and trying to guess what has happened. When they have looked at all of the pictures, collect them and show them to the class, one at a time, and elicit ideas of what they show.

Answers
Students' own answers

» GRAMMAR WORKSHEET UNIT 15

VOCABULARY Phrases with *in*

1 Books closed. Write: *We took it in turn to speak to the author.* on the board and underline *in turn*. Ask students to explain what it means (*one after another*). Tell students to complete the task individually and then check answers together.

Answers
1 e 2 c 3 a 4 f 5 d 6 b

2 Look at the first sentence with the class and elicit which phrase should complete it. Students then work in pairs to do the exercise. They then compare answers in different pairs. Elicit the answers and re-elicit what each sentence means, for example, *1 but what is actually true is that …; 2 approve of splitting up; 3 Because of the bad weather …; 4 Let's speak to everyone, one after the other; 5 Building work is happening at the moment …; 6 … how are things going for you generally?.*

Answers
1 in actual fact 2 in favour of 3 In light of 4 in turn 5 in progress
6 in general

3 Tell students to think alone for one minute about how to complete the sentences. They then tell each other their ideas. Invite pairs to share one or two of their sentences with the class. Encourage students to ask follow-up questions for some of the sentences, for example, *Why are you in favour of banning …?*

MIXED ABILITY

Allow weaker students to complete the sentences together rather than taking turns. They can then join together with a second pair to take turns to complete them.

Answers
Students' own answers

» VOCABULARY WORKSHEET UNIT 15

WRITING An essay (3)

1 Look at the diagram for employment with the class and elicit what the other words mean. Elicit that all the headings refer to finding a job. Now write on the board: *At work* and elicit words which could go on a diagram for this topic, for example, *salary, hours, colleagues, boss*. For each word, elicit possible collocations, for example, *high/low salary, long/short hours, friendly/helpful colleagues, demanding/ sympathetic boss*. Students then work in pairs to make two more diagrams. Allocate two topics to each pair so that all four topics are used in class. Invite four students to write their diagrams on the board, each student covering one of the four topics. Then elicit other words that could go in each topic from the rest of the class. Encourage all students to copy the environment diagram in their notebooks as this will help them in the writing task.

Answers
Students' own answers

2 Before students look at the essay, ask them to note down all the words connected to employment and/or education that they find. Elicit the answer and the words they found, for example, *job opportunities, get work, unemployment, employers, experience, unpaid jobs, world of work, learn, study, subjects, university*.

Answer
both

3 Tell students to read the three questions and then read the essay again. They then discuss in pairs which question the essay matches and how they know this. (*a It does say that it is easier to get into university and harder to find work than in the past but it also talks about travel which isn't related to a at all. b It talks about work, university and travel and mentions grandparents, although only in relation to studying. It doesn't really talk about life skills, though.*)

Answer
c

4 Look at the *Prepare to write* box with the class. Elicit other linking words that they know, for example *so, because, as well as*, etc. Students then look through the essay in pairs to find the words in the box and to try to find more examples. Elicit any they find, for example, *and, but, just to, on the other hand, whereas*.

Answers
All the linking words are in the essay.

5 Ask students to work in pairs to complete the sentences using the words from the box. Check answers as a whole class. Write *even though* and *provided* (*that*) on the board and elicit one more example sentence for each from the class, then write these on the board. This will provide extra help for weaker students when they come to write their essay in exercise 7. You could follow this up by writing *Issues facing my generation* on the board. Ask students to write sentences on this topic using the linking words from the box, for example *My generation should have a good standard of living, provided that we deal with the environmental issues our society is facing.* Tell students to discuss their ideas with a partner, before whole-class feedback.

Answers
1 or 2 once 3 now 4 provided 5 even though

PREPARE FOR THE EXAM

6 **B2 FIRST FOR SCHOOLS Writing Part 1: An essay**

Briefly review what students need to do in this part of the exam and if necessary, read out the *B2 First for Schools* box on TB page 22.

Remind students of the environment diagram that they created in Exercise 1. Point out that the topic for their own idea shouldn't overlap with the other two prompts given. Students choose a problem of their own either from the environment diagram or a new idea. Invite the class to share their ideas so that weaker students can use one of these if they prefer it to their own idea.

7 Give students some advice on writing an effective introduction. For example, the first sentence should get the reader's interest. The introduction should start with general points and move to more specific information. You could allow students to work in pairs to think of an eye-catching first sentence for the essay. Invite some students to share these with the class to help other students with their own opening sentences.

Give students time to do the task. Set a strict time limit of 30 minutes if students are preparing for the *B2 First for Schools* exam. This takes into account the time they have spent planning and thinking of an opening sentence. When they have finished, students check their work then swap their essays with a partner. When reading their partner's essay, they should underline any linking expressions from this lesson and note any useful topic vocabulary that they didn't include in their own essay. Invite students to share any vocabulary that their partner used which they liked. Then ask them to work together to suggest solutions to the problems they wrote about. In feedback, ask two or three pairs to present their solutions to the class.

Model answer
Our world has many environmental problems, which have been mainly caused by humans. However, most governments are now working to solve these issues, or so they tell us, and scientists are also doing their best to find solutions.
The world's population is rising rapidly and this could lead to food shortages unless the situation is carefully managed. Farmers may have to use different methods to increase the amount of food they produce, which could present new problems for the countryside.
Pollution remains a big problem, even though there have been attempts to reduce the quantity of emissions from homes, factories, transport and power stations. However, in the future, cars and planes will need to be even cleaner, perhaps powered by alternative forms of energy instead of petrol.
Another problem is the amount of plastic rubbish we create and many countries are unable to recycle the plastic that people throw away. Fish and other creatures are dying because they swallow plastic objects that they can't digest.
To sum up, these problems are likely to continue unless we find solutions. Once we take action, we may be able to save our planet for future generations.

COOLER
Ask students to work in small groups to discuss questions a and b from Exercise 3. Tell them to brainstorm their ideas and produce a mind map to plan their essay. If you would like to give your students more practice, ask them to write the essay for homework.

WRITING An essay (3)

1 **Look at the diagram about employment. Choose two more topics and create a diagram for each.**

1 education
2 health
3 travel
4 the environment

2 **Read the essay. Is it about employment, education or both?**

This is a complex question, and conditions vary greatly around the world. In my own country, there are no job opportunities, or very few. Once teenagers leave school aged 16–18, they often find it very hard to get work. Youth unemployment is 50% higher than it was ten years ago. Employers these days are happy to take on young people, provided they already have some experience, but it can be difficult for young people to get experience in the first place. That's why many young people accept unpaid jobs, just to learn more about the world of work.

On the other hand, the opportunities to learn are much greater than they used to be. It is possible to study a wider range of subjects today and it is much easier to get into university. My grandfather never had the chance to attend university, whereas a large percentage of today's generation will do so.

Young people today have a lot more opportunity to travel now that there are lots of low-cost airlines and you can plan trips online. They say that travel broadens the mind, and it has never been easier to gain experience of other cultures.

In conclusion, even though the job market is difficult at the moment, today's young people still have more opportunities than their parents and grandparents did.

3 **Choose the question that matches the essay in Exercise 2.**

a How has access to education and work changed over the past two generations?
b What life skills can young people acquire today that their grandparents couldn't?
c Does society offer more or fewer opportunities for young people today?

4 **Read the *Prepare to write* box and find the linking words in the essay.**

PREPARE TO WRITE | Linking words (1)

We use linking words to join short sentences together to make complex sentences:
I've got a car. I can visit you more often.
→ *I can visit you more often* ***now*** *that I've got a car.*
You can use these linking words to join sentences:
even though, now (that), once, or, provided (that).

5 **Complete the sentences with the linking words and phrases in the box.**

even though   now   once   or   provided

1 The situation at school has been improving, ... that's what we've been told.
2 Are you sure you want to leave? Remember that you can't criticise the group .... you've left.
3 She's enjoying the position .... that she's got more responsibility.
4 I'll lend you my camera, ... you look after it properly.
5 She did really well, ... she had had relatively little experience.

PREPARE FOR THE EXAM

Writing Part 1

6 **Read the task. Add more information and your own idea to the notes.**

'Existing environmental problems will continue to cause harm if we don't act to solve them.'
Do you agree?

Notes
Write about:
1 population growth
2 pollution
3 .... (your own idea)

7 **Write your essay.**

- Write about all the ideas in the notes.
- Use linking words to make complex sentences.
- Check your grammar and spelling.
- Write 140–190 words.

16 NEW AND IMPROVED!

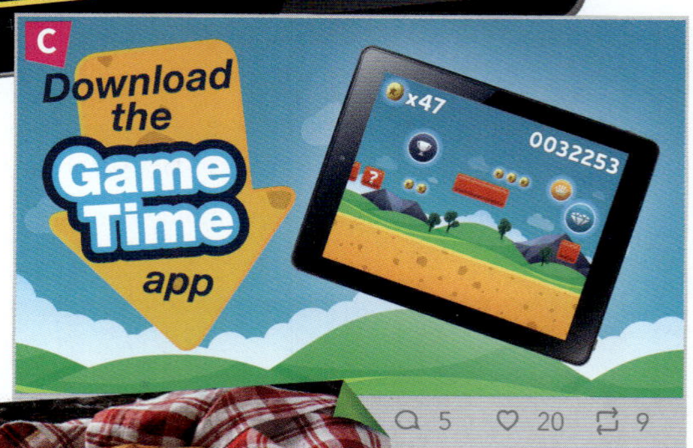

ABOUT YOU

Which current TV adverts do you love or hate? Why?
What do you think makes a good advert?

VOCABULARY Advertising: nouns and verbs

71 **1 Look at the adverts. Listen to Daniel and Jade talking and answer the questions.**

1. Which ad don't they talk about?
2. Which ads does Daniel actually like? Why?
3. Who do you think the products are aimed at? Why?
4. How does Daniel's attitude to advertising change during the conversation?

71 **2 Complete the sentences. Listen again and check.**

EP

ad breaks | aimed at | appeal to | consumer | launching | product placement | sample | sponsored

1. Jade enjoys the ________ on TV.
2. Jade said that the gaming app advert would ________ Daniel, but isn't ________ non-gamers like her.
3. Jade sometimes gets a free ________ of an advertised product in a magazine.
4. The car manufacturer they hear is ________ a new model.
5. Jade says Daniel is a ________ like everyone else.
6. Jade says Daniel is influenced by ________ in programmes.
7. The football team they're supporting is ________ by a bank.

3 Discuss the questions.

1. What do you think of the ad breaks on TV?
2. Who sponsors the biggest football clubs in your country?
3. Are you ever offered free samples of products?
4. Do you ever notice product placement in TV shows? Does it have an effect on you?

READING

1 Read the text quickly. What is the main idea?

A Most advertisers have started to use guerrilla marketing.
B Guerrilla marketing involves new and clever methods.
C Viral marketing is the latest trend in online advertising.
D Guerrilla marketing will take over from traditional advertising.

PREPARE FOR THE EXAM

Reading and Use of English Part 2

2 For questions 1–8, read the first two paragraphs of the text and think of the word which best fits each gap. Use only one word in each gap.

3 Answer the questions.

1. Why is body advertising an uncommon sight?
2. Why is viral marketing relatively cheap?
3. Why isn't viral marketing guaranteed to succeed?
4. Why do actors doing undercover marketing have to be unknown?
5. What is the risk associated with undercover marketing?
6. Why isn't reverse graffiti against the law?

16 NEW AND IMPROVED!

Unit Overview

TOPIC	Advertising and marketing
VOCABULARY	Advertising: nouns and verbs
READING	Guerrilla marketing
GRAMMAR	Conditionals (1): review
VOCABULARY	Adverb + adjective collocations
LISTENING	A talk about an unusual advertising campaign
SPEAKING	Expressing opinions
EXAM TASKS	Reading and Use of English Part 2; Listening Part 2; Speaking Part 3 and Part 4

Resources

GRAMMAR REFERENCE AND PRACTICE: SB page 163; TB pages 268–269
PREPARE FOR THE EXAM: SB pages on TB pages 237, 248 and 252–253; TB pages 254, 259 and 262
WORKBOOK: pages 64–67
PHOTOCOPIABLE WORKSHEETS: Grammar worksheet Unit 16; Vocabulary worksheet Unit 16
TEST GENERATOR: Unit test 16
PRACTICE EXTRA: Unit 16

WARMER

Bring in five adverts from magazines, but remove the product and company name. Ask students to work with a partner to make sentences about what the adverts could be for, using *could*, *might*, *can't* and *must*, for example, *It must be for a mobile phone*. Discuss some ideas as a class.

ABOUT YOU

Elicit one advert that all or most of the students know. Pretend that you have never seen it and ask the class to describe it and the aims of it, and elicit their opinions of the advert. Read through the questions with the class. Students then work in groups of three or four to discuss the two questions. Invite each group to share their ideas with the class.

VOCABULARY Advertising: nouns and verbs

71 **1** Look at the adverts with the class. Invite four different students to describe one advert each and say what it is advertising and what the message in each one is, for example, *this car gives you freedom and excitement*. Students then listen to the recording and discuss their answers in pairs. Elicit the answers and then ask the class to look at the pizza advert. Tell them to imagine they are sitting at home when this flyer is delivered to their door. One person should be enthusiastic about it and suggest trying the pizzas, the other should be sceptical. Allow them to prepare a short dialogue about the flyer and the pizzas; give them time to practise it. Monitor and help with ideas where necessary and note any interesting dialogues or good use of language. Invite one or two pairs to act out their conversations in front of the class.

Answers

1 the pizza ad (D)
2 The gaming app (C) because he's gamer and it's free, and the car ad (A), as he finds out the company are launching a new model.
3 Students' own answers
4 He realises that he is also a consumer, and is also influenced by ads.

71 **2** Tell students to work in pairs and to read through the sentences. They should discuss which words they think fit the gaps but only complete the sentences they are sure about. Play the recording for students to listen, check and complete their answers. Elicit the answers and ask the pairs to think of a definition for each word or phrase. Invite students to share their ideas, for example, *an ad break is a time in the middle of a TV programme or between TV programmes when adverts are shown.*

Answers

1 ad breaks 2 appeal to, aimed at 3 sample 4 launching 5 consumer 6 product placement 7 sponsored

» AUDIOSCRIPT TB PAGE 301

3 Put students into groups of three to discuss the questions. Monitor and note interesting ideas. When students have discussed the questions in their groups, discuss them as a class. Ask more questions, for example, 'Do you avoid watching films on TV because of ad breaks? Do you think that football clubs should reject sponsorship from certain industries, for example, gambling or alcohol? When you see people in the supermarket giving away free samples of chocolates or other snacks, do you ever go back more than once?' You could also ask them whether they use ad blocking software online. After the discussion, give feedback on some of the good ideas and mistakes you heard.

Answers

Students' own answers

READING

1 Write the title of the reading text on the board and ask whether any of the students understand what it means (*a marketing strategy that uses cheap and unconventional methods*) or if they can give any examples of it. Look at the four options with the class and set a time limit of three minutes for students to skim read the text and find the answer. Elicit the main idea and how students know. (*All the sub-titles are examples of the new and clever methods of advertising or marketing.*)

Answer

B

CONTINUED ON PAGE 178

BACKGROUND INFORMATION

Before the internet and social media, an early form of guerrilla advertising that reached a large audience was aerial advertising. In 1922, a pilot flew over Times Square in New York and wrote a phone number by 'skywriting'. This requires a special kind of smoke which is expelled as the pilot writes letters in the sky by manoeuvring the plane. It was for a hotel and, according to newspaper reports, over 47,000 people tried to phone the number in the next three hours. Very soon, companies were using skywriting as advertising. In 1940, Pepsi used a total of 2,225 skywriting messages in northern, central and southern USA. The practice only started dying out when TV became more and more popular and allowed companies to reach a large audience with adverts.

The term Guerrilla Marketing was invented by the writer Jay Conrad Levinson and was based on guerrilla warfare, a type of fighting based on the element of surprise, which is usually carried out by small groups of armed civilians against a professional army. Guerrilla marketing uses low cost and unconventional methods of advertising which are memorable because they are not usually expected.

PREPARE FOR THE EXAM

2 **B2 FIRST FOR SCHOOLS Reading and Use of English Part 2**

Briefly review what students need to do in this part of the exam and if necessary, read out the *B2 First for Schools* box on TB page 58.

Remind students that, in the exam, there will be just one standalone gapped text. It won't be a part of a longer text. Elicit what kinds of words are tested, for example, *pronouns, auxiliary verbs, set phrases, prepositions*, and look at the example with the class. Ask how they could know that the correct answer is *will*. (*The sentence is a first conditional sentence which is formed with an* if *clause:* If + *present simple, and a* will *clause:* will + *infinitive.*) Set a time limit of ten minutes for students to complete the exercise. Elicit the answers and what each one tests (*1* as well as *+ gerund; 2, 4, 5, 6, 7 are all set phrases; 3 relative pronoun; 8 present continuous or verb in present simple*).

FAST FINISHERS

Ask the fast finishers to look at one of the other paragraphs in the text and to find a sentence which includes a word which could be tested in this type of activity. When everyone has finished, elicit the answers to the exercise and invite fast finishers to come to the front of the class to write their sentences on the board, with the word they are testing gapped. Other students close their books or cover the text and try to guess what the missing word is, for example: *You need to promote the game cheaply if you have _____ money for publicity. (little).*

Answers

1 being 2 to 3 which 4 of 5 No 6 with 7 as
8 is/involves/means/entails

3 Tell the students to read the text carefully and to note key words, not full sentences, in order to answer the questions, for example, *1 Make film / YouTube*. When they have finished, they cover the text and work in pairs. They look at the notes they made for each question and use these to write complete answers, for example, *1 It's cheap because you don't have to pay to put the advert on TV, you can upload it to YouTube for nothing.* Monitor and help where necessary and elicit the answers. Elicit one or two for each question because there will be more than one way to phrase each answer.

MIXED ABILITY

Put students into groups of four. Two of the students work together to answer questions 1–3 and two work together to answer 4–6. When they have finished, the pairs tell each other what the answers to their questions are and show them the information in the text.

Possible answers

1 Because it can look very strange, possibly offensive, so not many people are willing to wear it.
2 Because you don't have to pay for broadcasting.
3 Because it relies on individual viewers to share it.
4 Because if people recognised the actors, they would know the conversation wasn't real and the marketing campaign would fail.
5 If people realise that the conversation isn't genuine, they might start to strongly dislike the company.
6 Because it cleans things rather than damages them, and there are no laws against cleaning.

72 The Reading text is recorded for students to listen, read and check their answers.

TALKING POINTS

Re-elicit the four types of guerrilla marketing mentioned in the text and ask the students if they have seen any of these in real life or any other kinds of alternative marketing. Students then discuss the questions in pairs. Encourage them to add examples and justify their opinions. Elicit some ideas after a few minutes. Give positive feedback for interesting ideas and comments during class feedback.

COOLER

Elicit four things that individuals or companies could advertise, for example, *a new café, a new film, a free concert in their town, a chocolate bar*. Write these on the board and then put the students into groups of three or four. They have to decide the best way to advertise each and give reasons for their choice. Set a time limit of three minutes and then elicit ideas and reasons from the class and try to come to an agreement. Write their ideas on the board, for example: *café – body advertising, a new film – viral marketing, a free concert – reverse graffiti, a chocolate bar – undercover marketing.*

The groups then choose one of these and discuss in more detail, for example, the café: *We could have groups of teenagers with body art advertising the café walking in the town centre. They could also hand out flyers.*

Give the groups three or four minutes to discuss the ideas and then invite them to share their ideas with the class.

GUERRILLA MARKETING

Wherever you are in the world, if you switch on the TV or open a magazine, you **(0)** *will* probably see an advert. Love it or hate it, publicity is a fact of modern life. For the keen consumer, ads can provide entertainment as well as **(1)** ________ informative. Attractive logos, witty slogans and beautifully designed ads are seen by some as a welcome addition **(2)** ________ their TV viewing. Others, however, who watch TV to relax, feel they live in a busy world in **(3)** ________ adverts are simply an annoying interruption. For them, adverts are a waste **(4)** ________ resources and their appearance is visual pollution. **(5)** ________ matter what your feelings are, ads are becoming more sophisticated every day. They have developed hand in hand **(6)** ________ technological advances. In the early days, they appeared **(7)** ________ simple printed messages, before being heard on the radio and seen on TV, and later popping up on computer or phone screens. Today, 'guerrilla' marketing **(8)** ________ using ever more innovative techniques – usually imaginative and sometimes irritating – to get ads seen.

BODY ADVERTISING

How would you like an advert painted on your body? It would have to be somewhere visible such as your forehead or even your eyelids! Body advertising looks striking, some might say offensive, but the ads can usually be washed off after a couple of days. Still, it's no wonder you don't see it very often. It is either used to advertise to a specific, local audience, who see the advert in person, or photos of the body advertising are intended to go viral.

VIRAL MARKETING

Imagine that you're a computer games developer and you're trying to launch a new BMX racing game on a limited budget. You need to promote the game cheaply if you have little money for publicity, so you commission a short film with talented but unknown BMX riders. The film is dramatic and fast-moving, following a crazy ride around an inner-city neighbourhood to a soundtrack of heavy rock music. The clip shows the riders arriving home exhausted, lying on the sofa and playing your game. It ends with your logo and a link to your website. A BMX magazine uploads the video to YouTube and you're very lucky: viewers love it. If the clip is shared and 'liked' enough, you could end up with millions of views. If the same clip had appeared as a TV ad, it would have cost millions to broadcast it. How many viral videos like this have you watched and shared and how many products have you helped to promote for free?

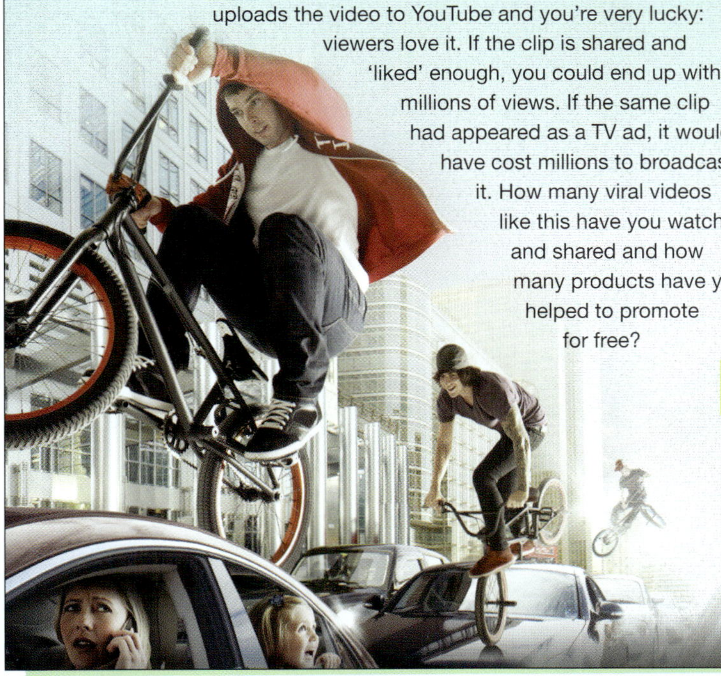

UNDERCOVER MARKETING

Actors are sometimes paid to raise awareness of products secretly. For example, a phone company might place an actor with their latest mobile in a city centre location. The actor approaches passing strangers, the type of person the phone is aimed at, and asks, 'Would you mind taking a photo of me on my phone?' While their photo is being taken, the actor chats with the potential customer about what an amazing phone it is. It's no good using well-known actors: undercover marketing only works if the actors' identities and motives remain secret. It would damage a company's reputation if consumers realised it was marketing. Undercover marketing is expensive, but effective, because an interaction with a real person is much more believable and memorable than any other kind of advertising.

REVERSE GRAFFITI

If you sprayed an image onto a wall, you'd probably get arrested – graffiti is illegal in many places. But reverse graffiti is clever, as there's no need to break the law. To create reverse graffiti, you cut words and shapes into a sheet of plastic. Then lay the plastic against a flat surface and spray water and cleaning products into each gap. The result is a clean, bright image surrounded by a dirty bit of wall or pavement. It is cheap and there are no laws against cleaning, which means it is popular with street artists who want to create beautiful images in unloved urban locations. Photos of the best reverse graffiti ads can be seen by millions globally if they go viral.

TALKING POINTS

Which guerrilla marketing techniques do you think are most likely to be effective? Why?

Do you think that guerrilla marketing will ever replace advertising on TV or online? Why? / Why not?

GRAMMAR Conditionals (1): review

1 **Read the examples and answer the questions.**

1. If you switch on the TV or open a magazine, you will probably see an advert.
   Is it certain or possible you will see an ad?
2. If the same clip had appeared as a TV ad, it would have cost millions.
   Did the ad appear on TV? Did it cost millions?
3. You need to promote the game cheaply if you have little money for publicity.
   Is this a possibility or a true statement?
4. It would damage a company's reputation if consumers realised it was marketing.
   Was the company's reputation damaged?

2 **Read the examples again and complete the rules with the words in the box.**

future	general	past	likely

We use the
- **a** zero conditional to talk about ________ truths.
- **b** first conditional for ________ events in the future.
- **c** second conditional for impossible or unlikely situations in the ________.
- **d** third conditional for imaginary results of ________ situations that never happened.

» GRAMMAR REFERENCE AND PRACTICE PAGE 163

3 **Match the sentence halves.**

1. If you take LongLife vitamins,
2. You wouldn't have been late
3. If I wasn't using my laptop,
4. If it's raining later,
5. This door makes a loud noise

- **a** she'll probably get the bus.
- **b** of course I'd lend it to you.
- **c** you'll be healthy forever.
- **d** unless you open it carefully.
- **e** if you'd left home on time.

4 **Correct the mistake in each sentence.**

1. If the doorbell would ring, the dog barks loudly.
2. If that ad comes on again, I'd turn the TV off!
3. If I would see those guys again, I'd be able to identify them.
4. You would have had fun if you came to the party.
5. If I were you, I will get some snacks during the ads.

5 **Complete the conditional questions. Then ask and answer with a partner.**

1. If you ________ your phone, what would you do? (lose)
2. What ________ yesterday if your classes had been cancelled? (you / do)
3. What ________ when it's hot? (you / wear)
4. If you ________ your exams, will you go to university? (pass)
5. Where ________ if you had £1 million? (you / go)

VOCABULARY Adverb + adjective collocations

1 **Complete the sentences with the adverbs in the box.**

EP

ecologically	environmentally	financially
globally	incredibly	regularly
scientifically	well	

1 It's fast, it's cheap, it's ________ friendly. Travel by Metro!

2 Take VitX every day – ________ proven to give you extra energy. Remember – always take vitamins as part of a ________-balanced diet.

3 Get all the latest sports news using our ________ updated app.

4 This ________ recognised brand is a bestseller on every continent.

5 Don't you want to be ________ independent? Work part-time from home and earn extra cash now!

6 WEPRINT
Our printers use ________ safe inks and they're ________ economical to run.

2 **Complete the second sentence using the correct form of the bold words.**

0. This work is so **easy** it's **ridiculous**!
   This work is *ridiculously easy*!
1. Your brother always **dresses** in **nice** clothes.
   Your brother is always ________.
2. It's **amazing** how **tasty** this dish is.
   This dish is ________.
3. I am **involved** in their project quite **actively**.
   I am ________ in their project.
4. The railway is **located** at a **convenient** distance from the college.
   There's a ________ railway station near the college.
5. My dad has a **natural talent** for telling jokes.
   My dad is a ________ comedian.
6. The recipe says you have to **chop** the onions **finely**.
   The recipe requires ________ onions.

3 » **Work in pairs. Turn to page 140.**

GRAMMAR Conditionals (1): review

WARMER

Write the word *If* on the board. Ask students to work alone and write a sentence about advertising starting with this word. Students then get into groups of three or four to share their sentences. Ask them if the tenses in their sentences are the same and elicit examples from different groups.

1 Students do the exercise in pairs. Elicit the answers and ask how they know, for example, *1 The word* probably *tells us it is likely but not certain. 2 This is looking at a hypothetical past situation, one that didn't happen. 3 This is always true. 4 This is looking at a hypothetical present or future situation, not a specific situation.*

Answers
1 possible 2 No, No 3 a true statement 4 No

2 Before students look at the rules, elicit the types of conditional sentence in Exercise 1 (*1 first; 2 third; 3 zero; 4 second*). Students then complete the rules. Elicit the answers and ask students to make their own sentences using each of the four conditionals.

Answers
a general b likely c future d past

» **GRAMMAR REFERENCE AND PRACTICE ANSWER KEY TB PAGES 268–269**

3 Tell students to cover the endings of the sentences and just look at the beginnings. Elicit how they could end. Elicit that 1 could be the start of a zero or first conditional sentence, but 4 couldn't be because it is talking about later, not a general truth. Students do the matching then elicit the answers. Ask students how to complete sentence 5 using *if* (*if you don't open it carefully*).

Answers
1 c 2 e 3 b 4 a 5 d

4 Students correct the sentences alone then compare answers in pairs. Point out that, often the wrong sentences are made up of a beginning using one type of conditional and an ending using a different one; therefore, they may be able to correct the sentence in more than one way. Students compare answers in pairs. Elicit the answers and what was wrong with the original sentences.

FAST FINISHERS

Tell the students to look at sentence 5 and elicit or tell the students that we often use this sentence beginning to give advice. Fast finishers think of *If I were you* sentences that they can share with their friends in the class. When everyone has finished correcting the sentences, elicit the answers to the exercise and allow fast finishers to share their sentences with the students they have written the advice for.

Possible answers
1 If the doorbell **rings**, the dog barks loudly.
2 If that ad comes on again, I **will/'ll turn** the TV off!
3 If **I saw** those guys again, I'd be able to identify them.
4 You would have had fun if you **had come** to the party.
5 If I were you, I **would get** some snacks during the ads.

5 Read the first question with the class and ask what kind of conditional it is (*second*) and how they know (*the second half of the sentence uses* would + *infinitive*). When students have completed the verb forms, elicit the answers to make sure they are correct and then students ask and answer the questions in pairs. Ask the students the five questions and invite a few students to share their answers with the class.

Answers
1 lost 2 would you have/'ve done 3 do you wear 4 pass
5 would you go

» **GRAMMAR WORKSHEET UNIT 16**

VOCABULARY Adverb + adjective collocations

1 Remind students that collocations are two or more words that often go together. Tell students that these adverbs modify, i.e. give extra information about, the adjectives that follow, and point out that, apart from *well*, they end in *-ly*. Ask them to complete the exercise individually and then check answers. Elicit the meanings of some of the phrases, for example, *environmentally friendly = good for the environment*.

Answers
1 environmentally 2 scientifically, well 3 regularly 4 globally
5 financially 6 ecologically, incredibly

2 Tell students that these sentences will take the same form as in Exercise 1 so the first word in each case will be an adverb and the second will be an adjective. Look at the in example sentence with the class. Ask why it isn't *easily ridiculous* (*because we know the work is easy and want to say how easy it is*). Monitor and help where necessary and then elicit the answers.

MIXED ABILITY

Go through all the sentences with weaker classes to elicit or show them what adjective we want to modify in each case (*1 how the brother is dressed; 2 how tasty it is; 3 how involved I am; 4 how close the railway station is located; 5 how talented the father is; 6 how the onions should be chopped*). They then work in pairs to form adverbs from the words in bold. Stronger students could write their own sentences using some of the collocations. When everyone has finished, invite these students to share their sentences with the class.

Answers
1 nicely dressed 2 amazingly tasty 3 actively involved
4 conveniently located 5 naturally talented 6 finely chopped

3 Read the questions on page 140 with the class and elicit what they mean, for example, *1 You eat healthily and have the vitamins and nutrients you need. 2 When you stop relying on anyone else for money*. Monitor and note interesting answers and invite students to share their answers with the class. You could follow this up by asking pairs to choose two other collocations from Exercise 1 on page 92 and writing a similar question for each. Pairs then join together in groups of four to ask and answer their questions. Invite students to share one or two of their questions and answers with the class.

Answers
Students' own answers

» **VOCABULARY WORKSHEET UNIT 16**

LISTENING

1 Look at the first line in the text with the students and elicit what students think the key words are, for example, *recently, role*. These words tell us when it happened, what she took up and where. Students do the same for the other sentences. Elicit ideas and ask students what they have to listen out for in each one (*1 a kind of role; 2 a person/company; 3 a noun; 4 an age range; 5 a kind of advertising; 6 an adjective; 7 a place; 8 a person or company; 9 a kind of advertising; 10 people*).

Possible answers

1 recently, role 2 originally thought, parcel, from 3 favourite item, personalised 4 The Emissary, aims, appeal, age
5 Advertisers, believe, best, advertising, age group
6 uses, describe, strategy 7 tickets, local 8 contacted, talk, new campaign 9 asked, promote, clothing, strategy, advertising
10 excited, meet, well-known, launch event
Predictions: Students' own answers

PREPARE FOR THE EXAM

2 **B2 FIRST FOR SCHOOLS Listening Part 2**

73 Briefly review what students need to do in this part of the exam and if necessary, read out the *B2 First for Schools* box on TB page 94.

When the students have listened twice, allow them to compare answers in pairs. Elicit the answers and make sure that students have written the plural form for 10. Tell students that minor spelling mistakes are allowed if they don't impede understanding so, for example, writing recommendation with two *c*s or one *m* would be fine.

Answers

1 head girl 2 bookshop 3 diary 4 15–19 5 recommendation
6 smart 7 stadium 8 publicity agency 9 undercover
10 journalists

» AUDIOSCRIPT TB PAGES 301–302

3 Ask the class to cover the text in Exercise 2 and elicit what the text is about from the class. Students then work in groups of three to discuss the questions. Monitor and note interesting ideas and then invite groups to share their ideas with the class. Students give their own answers.

SPEAKING Expressing opinions

1 Remind the students of the different kinds of advertising they read about earlier on in the unit and draw a diagram on the board. Write: *How to advertise?* in the centre with lines leading from it. At the end of one line write: *target customers*. Ask students how the type of advertising may change if a company is selling to young people, rich people, etc. Students then work in groups of three to think of more factors that could influence the decision. Elicit ideas and reasons and add the ideas to the diagram on the board. They then discuss the question as a class. Students give their own answers.

74 2 Read the instructions with the class. Elicit what they think the answer will be. Students then listen. Elicit the answer and any other interesting ideas that Sun and Johann have, for example, *pop-ups are a nuisance.*

Answer

Viral ads

» AUDIOSCRIPT TB PAGE 302

75 3 Elicit any phrases the students remember and then play the recording for students to make a note of the answers. Ask them to write S or J next to the phrases used depending on who uses them. When you have elicited the answers, ask the students what viral advertising is (*like viral videos, it means marketing content which becomes a huge success by being spread by social media users very quickly*). Give the students an example, for example, the fidget spinner which became a huge success thanks to social media. Students then discuss any other viral adverts that they know about as a class.

Answers

Johann: I imagine that, If you think about it, the good thing about … is, I reckon
Sun: It seems to me that, as I see it, From the point of view of, I get the impression that,

» AUDIOSCRIPT TB PAGE 302

PREPARE FOR THE EXAM

4 **B2 FIRST FOR SCHOOLS Speaking Part 3 and Part 4**

Briefly review what students need to do in this part of the exam and if necessary, read out the *B2 First for Schools* box on TB page 138.

Look at the task and remind the students about how Sun and Johann approached the task, i.e. they discussed each idea in turn giving their opinions. Tell the students that, even if one option seems better than any of the others, the idea is not to agree immediately but to use the time allowed to show that they can express opinions, justify opinions and agree and disagree politely.

Tell students that they have two minutes for this task in the exam and should keep talking until the examiner tells them to stop. They should do the same now, all starting when you tell them to and they should keep talking until you tell them to stop. Students give their own answers.

5 Tell the students to take turns asking the questions so that one student asks questions 1, 3 and 5 and the other asks 2, 4 and 6. Monitor and note interesting answers. When everyone has finished, discuss all six questions with the class, eliciting their ideas and reasons. Write any useful feedback on the board. Students give their own answers.

COOLER

Put the students into groups of four. Tell them to imagine they work for an advertising agency and they are going to give a talk to companies about successful advertising. They have to think of some conditional sentences to convince the companies about the benefits of advertising. Write two examples on the board:

If companies don't advertise, they don't sell.

If you use a Hollywood actor in your adverts, you will make more money from extra sales than it will cost to pay the actor.

Elicit what conditionals these are (*zero and first*). Set a time limit of three minutes for students to write their own sentences. Monitor and help where necessary. Invite each group to share their sentences with the class.

LISTENING

1 You will hear a girl called Sophia Spencer talking about an unusual advertising campaign. **Underline** key words in sentences 1–10 below and predict what you might hear.

PREPARE FOR THE EXAM

Listening Part 2

2 Listen and, for questions 1–10, complete the sentences with a word or short phrase. Listen again and check. (73)

AN UNUSUAL ADVERTISING CAMPAIGN

Sophia recently took up the role of **(1)** ________ in her school.

Sophia originally thought that the parcel she received must be from a **(2)** ________.

Sophia's favourite item in the box was a personalised **(3)** ________.

The band called The Emissary aims to appeal to girls in the **(4)** ________ age group.

Advertisers believe that a **(5)** ________ is the best form of advertising for Sophia's age group.

Sophia uses the word '**(6)** ________' to describe what she thought of the advertiser's strategy.

Sophia was given tickets for a performance held in a local **(7)** ________.

Sophia was contacted by a **(8)** ________ who wanted to talk to her about a new campaign.

Sophia was asked to promote clothing through a strategy known as '**(9)** ________ advertising'.

Sophia was excited to meet some well-known **(10)** ________ at a launch event in London.

3 Discuss the questions.

1. What do you think of undercover advertising?
2. What would you do if you were Sophia?
3. How would you feel if an ad agency wanted to work with you?

SPEAKING Expressing opinions

1 How do you think companies make decisions on what kind of advertising to use?

2 (74) Look at the task below, then listen to the conversation. What form of advertising do Sun and Johann agree is the best value for companies?

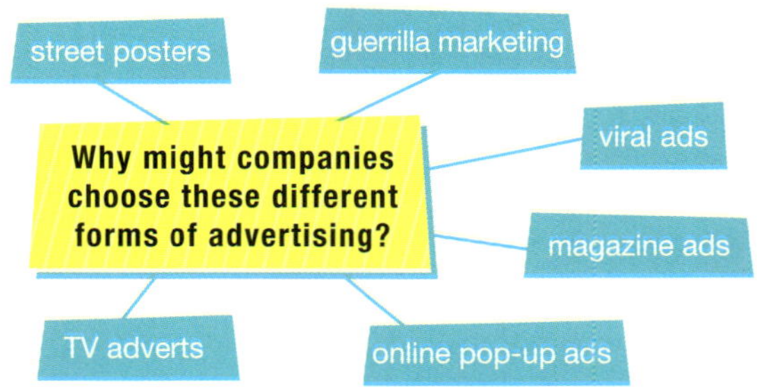

3 (75) Read the *Prepare to speak* box. Then listen to Sun and Johann using the phrases. Which expressions do you hear?

PREPARE TO SPEAK Expressing opinions

Expressing opinions
I assume/imagine/reckon (that) …
I get the feeling/impression that …
The good/bad thing about … is …
As I see it, …

Justifying opinions
It seems to me that …
On the one hand, … on the other hand, …
From the point of view of …
If you think about it, …

PREPARE FOR THE EXAM

Speaking Part 3 and Part 4

4 Work in pairs. Complete the task in Exercise 2. Use phrases from the *Prepare to speak* box.

5 Ask and answer the questions with a partner. Use phrases from the *Prepare to speak* box.

1. Do you think companies would sell less if they didn't advertise their products?
2. Do you think it's true that watching adverts always makes people want to buy things? (Why? / Why not?)
3. Some people think advertising can be harmful because it encourages people to buy things they can't afford. Do you agree? (Why? / Why not?)
4. Some people say it is wrong to show adverts for toys during children's shows. Do you agree? (Why? / Why not?)
5. Do you think it would be better if there were no adverts on TV? (Why? / Why not?)
6. Some people think that adverts can be more entertaining than the actual shows. What do you think?

LIFE SKILLS CRITICAL THINKING

ASSESSING ADVERTISING

LIFE SKILLS

Assessing advertising

Advertisers use many techniques and tricks to try to influence the way we think and feel, often on a subconscious level, in order to get us to buy or use their products and services. It's therefore important to be aware of advertising and have the necessary skills and tools to be able to assess ads properly and make well-informed decisions when it comes to spending our money.

1 Ask and answer the questions with a partner.

1. How many adverts do you think you see in a typical day?
   a 40 **b** 400 **c** 4,000
2. Do you have a favourite advert at the moment? Why do you like it?
3. How do you think adverts try to make us buy or consume things?

2 Read the first three paragraphs of the article on page 95 quickly. Which of these sentences is the best summary?

A We only look at the adverts we're really interested in, and their influence on us is limited.
B Adverts come in a surprising variety of forms and it's easy to see how they influence us.
C Most adverts today are found online and they aim to increase our desire for something.

3 Read the whole article and answer the questions.

1. Why might the number of 4,000 ads not be precise?
2. What do ads try to do after they have been successful in getting you to look?
3. Why do adverts include people who are similar to you?
4. Is it hard to identify examples of product placement? Why? / Why not?
5. How can assessing advertising critically make you feel more confident about your choices?

76 **4** Listen to a media studies teacher giving a talk to a group of students about common advertising techniques. Number the techniques in the order she mentions them.

________ the bandwagon effect
________ association
________ fear and embarrassment
________ celebrity endorsements

76 **5** Listen again and choose the best answer (A, B or C).

1. In her introduction, the teacher says that adverts are
   A simply images of and information about products.
   B designed to be eye-catching.
   C designed to influence us without us realising.
2. The association technique is when advertisers
   A try to make people feel happy and attractive.
   B use positive images in their ads.
   C try to sell their products to people in different countries.
3. The second technique mentioned might be used in an ad for
   A deodorant.
   B a smartphone.
   C washing-up liquid.
4. What does the teacher point out about celebrity endorsements?
   A Products promoted by celebrities tend to be more expensive.
   B Celebrities often don't really use the products they advertise.
   C Brands create products imitating the style of clothes that celebrities wear.
5. The bandwagon effect is when advertisers try to make us feel that
   A we're the first to try a product.
   B we're the only ones not using a product.
   C we don't have much time left to enjoy a product.

LIFE SKILLS

Learning Objectives

- The students learn about advertising and how it persuades people to buy things.
- In the project stage, the students critically assess an advert and present their assessment to the class.

BACKGROUND INFORMATION

The first TV advert was shown in 1941 on New York TV channel WNBT and was for a watchmaker called Bulova. The advert was shown before a baseball game and the company is believed to have paid less than $10 to show it.

The first online advert was on Wired magazine's website, HotWired. The company whose advert it was paid $30,000 for three months and about 44% of visitors to the website clicked on the advert. Nowadays, only about 0.06% of website users click on adverts.

The first example of celebrity endorsement for a product was probably when the British company Wedgewood made a tea set for the King's wife in 1765. The company then got the official title 'Potter to her Majesty'.

In 2015, an American named Ron Marshall decided to count all the adverts he was exposed to in one day to see if the 4,000 number was accurate. Including radio and TV ads, logos on gadgets and clothing that he used and the packaging of the food in his kitchen, he reached 487 adverts before he had finished his breakfast and gave up counting.

WARMER

Put students into groups of three or four. Ask them to think of something they have in their bags and decide how they would try to convince the other members of their group to buy it. To start, give an example of an object you have, such as a school book, and use adjectives (for example *useful, easy, reasonably priced, essential*) as well as a more general description (*This attractive and light-weight book is perfect for any student of English.*). When students have advertised their objects in groups, invite each group to present one object to the class.

LIFE SKILLS

Assessing advertising

Tell students to read the information. Ask students if they have ever bought something just because they saw it advertised. Elicit what, how it was advertised and whether it was a good purchase or not.

1 Allow students to discuss the questions together. Elicit ideas from different students then ask them if an entertaining advert is more likely to make them buy something or whether they just look at it as entertainment rather than an advert.

Answers

1 c 2–3 Students' own answers

2 Before students read the article, ask them to read the summaries and guess which one is the correct answer and why they don't think the other two will summarise the article, for example, *I don't think 1 is true. I think they have a lot of influence over some people.* Ask students to read the three paragraphs and elicit the correct answer. Elicit from the class which pieces of information in the text helped them to decide. (*… print, on TV, … popping up … watching our favourite series, playing games or streaming music … internet or using apps … ads on the way to and from school or when we're out shopping … Ads … affect us emotionally and encourage us to buy something.*)

FAST FINISHERS

Ask fast finishers to think of which types of adverts mentioned in the text they see while walking to and from school or while out shopping, for example, billboards, signs on buses, etc. When all the students have finished reading, ask the fast finishers to share their ideas with the class.

Answer

B

3 Decide whether you want the students to write full sentences for answers or notes, so that everyone does the same thing. Ask students to find the information as they are reading and then to cover the text and try to answer the questions in their own words.

MIXED ABILITY

Put weaker students into pairs. One student, the stronger of the two, reads the first column of the text and answers questions 1–3. The other, weaker student, reads the second column and answers questions 4–5. When they have finished, they discuss the answers to the questions and show each other where the relevant information can be found. They then decide together on the wording of their answers. Monitor and help where necessary.

Answers

1 It depends on our definition of an ad. / It's difficult to prove.
2 They try to affect us emotionally and then encourage us to buy something.
3 Because it creates the idea that the brand or item will make you more like them so you feel 'better' than you are.
4 It can be really difficult to spot these because the products are 'hidden'. However, you notice them subconsciously.
5 Because you will feel much more in control.

77 The Reading text is recorded for students to listen, read and check their answers.

CONTINUED ON PAGE 186

76 **4** Read the four techniques and ask students how they think they could work Students may not be able to guess the first two but should have some ideas about the last two. Do not correct their answers as they will learn more about them in the next exercise. Ask students to make notes about each technique as they listen. Elicit the order they are mentioned and what the four techniques involve.

Answers

1 association 2 fear and embarrassment
3 celebrity endorsements 4 the bandwagon effect

76 **5** Give students one or two minutes to read through the questions and to think about any answers they remember. When they have listened again, allow them to compare answers in pairs and share any information they can remember from the recording. Elicit the answers and the information that helped them to decide. (*1 on a subconscious level, without us noticing it; 2 use positive images in their ad; 3 common in beauty and hygiene products; 4 he or she probably doesn't actually use the products being promoted in real life; 5 everyone is already using their product … we're the only ones who aren't*)

You could follow this up by asking the students to try to think of adverts they know which use the four techniques or use their imagination to think of other products which could be advertised using these techniques. For example, *the bandwagon effect – an advert for a new mobile phone which shows a group of happy people using the phone and one person, on their own, looking at the screen of a very old phone. Association – a car driving on a beautiful, empty road with an elegantly-dressed driver. Fear and embarrassment – looking at clothes washed in a cheap washing powder and seeing that they aren't as clean as other people's. Celebrity endorsements – a famous writer being used to advertise a laptop for writing on or a singer endorsing a throat medicine which helps them to sing better when they have a cold.* Students work in groups of three or four and then present their ideas to the class.

Answers

1 C 2 B 3 A 4 B 5 B

» **AUDIOSCRIPT TB PAGES 302–303**

6 Tell students to look at the gapped sentences without looking at the words in the box. They work in pairs to try to think of words which could go into each gap and, then, they uncover the word pool to complete the sentences. Elicit the answers. Ask students follow-up questions using some of the vocabulary, for example: *What do you associate with summer / school / Sundays? Which adverts do you know target people's health worries? Which products can you name that have celebrity endorsements? Is there anything that advertisers have made you feel as if you are missing out on?*

Answers

1 subconscious 2 associate 3 targets 4 endorsements
5 missing out

PROJECT ***A critical assessment of an advert***

Look at the instructions with the students. Put them into groups of four. If possible, bring in some magazines or newspapers for students to choose a print advert or ask them to bring in a magazine each that they can cut up. You could also record some radio or TV adverts or watch some online adverts during the lesson. If it isn't possible do this in class, ask them to choose the advert(s) they want to present at home and then, in the following lesson, allow a few minutes for the groups to get together and discuss which adverts they thought about and to agree on the best ones. You could ask each group to present two: a print advert and a digital one.

Students then discuss aspects of the advert that they can present, for example, one student can give a simple description of the advert, another can talk about which technique the advert uses, a third can say whether or not they think the advert is effective (with reasons) and the fourth could suggest ways in which the advert could be improved.

When all the groups have presented their adverts, the class discuss which they think was the best/worst print and digital advert and why.

PROJECT EXTENSION

When the students have presented their adverts tell the groups to swap adverts with each other. The groups now look at the advert(s) they have been given and imagine they are an advertising agency which has been given the contract to create adverts for this company (these companies). They work together to decide on a better way of advertising the product(s). They don't have to produce an advert but they do have to present their ideas to the class, for example, they could describe the picture to be used in a print ad, the words/slogan to be used, and they could describe the digital ad and whether or not they would use a celebrity to help to sell the product. When students are ready, each group presents their ideas to the class and explains why they think their ideas will make the advert(s) better.

COOLER

Students think of two questions to ask other students in the class about adverts that weren't asked during the lesson, for example, *1 When you go to the cinema, how do you feel when there are adverts before the film starts? 2 Which celebrity would be most likely to persuade you to buy something?* Students then mingle and ask and answer each other's questions. When students have finished, invite some of them to tell the class what they found out.

Do you REALLY want to buy it?

Some studies estimate that we're exposed to up to 4,000 adverts every day! That seems like a huge amount, so let's have a think about how that could add up. First of all, it depends on our definition of an ad. Many people believe that this includes seeing a logo or a product's packaging, as well as more obvious adverts in print, on TV and those popping up while we're watching our favourite series, playing games or streaming music online.

In fact, when we're on the internet or using apps, we're constantly being bombarded by ads. We're also exposed to a huge number of ads on the way to and from school or when we're out shopping. While the exact figure of 4,000 might be difficult to prove, what's very clear is that we see a massive number of adverts in our daily lives.

A large amount of the advertising we see is designed to make us want something. Now, you might think that you don't let adverts influence your opinion about things. But in reality, that's very difficult to demonstrate. Why is it that we really want one thing, but don't want another because we 'know' that it's not fashionable? More often than not, it depends to a large extent on the adverts we've seen. Ads usually aim to grab our attention, affect us emotionally and encourage us to buy something.

Persuasive advertising doesn't always send positive messages. Many adverts exploit our worries and make us feel less self-confident, more unattractive, or like we're not part of a group because we don't have the 'right' things. This is often done by using peer influence on social media, where people of a similar age to you are pictured with the product being advertised. From a psychological point of view, this works because it creates the idea that the brand or item will somehow 'make' you become 'better' than you are. We need to take a step back and look at adverts from an independent and critical perspective. Feeling confident and informed enables us to assess and control the influence adverts can have on us.

And it's not just the obvious adverts which we need to assess critically. Product placement – when companies use media like TV shows, films or games to promote their brands and new products – has become the norm in the world of advertising. Perhaps your favourite character is wearing a certain brand of clothing or enjoying a new drink. Or a singer you like has the latest mobile in her new music video. Product placement can come in many forms, but it's usually very difficult to spot the product because it is 'hidden'. However, you can be sure that your brain has 'seen' it on a subconscious level. Try spotting product placements and you'll be amazed at how widespread it is!

There are some key lessons to learn here. When you want to buy a specific product or brand, ask yourself a few questions before you make a decision: What does it 'mean' to you to have this thing? Is the product attractive because of how it looks, feels or sounds? Or do you perhaps find it attractive because it's associated with the celebrity, model or setting used to advertise it? Assessing advertising in this way will make you feel a lot more in control of your choices and spending decisions.

6 Complete the sentences with the words and phrases in the box.

associate endorsements missing out subconscious targets

USEFUL LANGUAGE

Assessing an advert critically

1 Advertisers try to influence us on a ________ level.
2 Companies try to ________ positive images with their products.
3 This ad ________ people's fear of having bad skin.
4 Many brands use celebrity ________ to sell their products.
5 The aim of this advert is to make us feel like we're ________.

PROJECT

A critical assessment of an advert

Work in groups of three or four to critically assess an advert. Use these steps to help you.

1 Search for and choose a selection of adverts from print and digital sources.
2 Decide together on one advert that you'd like to work on.
3 Use the ideas from the article and the techniques from the talk to perform a critical analysis of the advert.
4 Create a presentation to share your assessment.

Present your work to the class.

ASSESSING ADVERTISING 95

REVIEW 4 UNITS 13–16

VOCABULARY

1 Complete the sentences with the words in the box.

conscientious doubt self-esteem sympathetic targets

1 Mike seems nice, but he isn't very ________ to other people's problems.
2 Arran's a very ________ boy and always hands his work in on time.
3 Suzanne's got pretty high ________. She has a lot of confidence in herself.
4 I'm always full of ________ about being able to do new things.
5 It's important to set realistic ________ so you can achieve them.

2 Complete the sentences with the correct form of the phrasal verbs. Use a word from A and a word from B.

A break keep live pull speak

B down out up up to up with

1 My scooter ________ all the time. It's really unreliable.
2 Can you ________ a bit? I can't hear you very well.
3 I got to the platform as the train was ________, so I missed it.
4 Did the party ________ your expectations?
5 It's hard to ________ Steph because she walks so fast.

3 Choose the correct options.

1 The world's leading phone brand has just *launched* / *aimed* a budget model for the first time.
2 It is aimed at *samples* / *consumers* who can't afford the £500+ products that have made the brand so successful.
3 The phone will *appeal* / *sponsor* to people who want a good-quality phone for a lower price.
4 The new product is being shown during TV *product placement* / *ad breaks* and is likely to be very successful.
5 A local store has agreed to *sponsor* / *launch* our football team, which means we don't have to close the club down!

4 Match the sentence halves.

1 It's an environmentally
2 I eat a fairly well-
3 I am financially
4 There are no scientifically
5 It's a globally

a friendly car.
b independent.
c proven benefits.
d recognised brand.
e balanced diet.

GRAMMAR

1 Choose the correct options.

1 Joe *must* / *can't* be on holiday because I saw him this morning.
2 The thief *might have* / *can't have* stolen your bag. It's locked in the car, remember!
3 Be careful! You *might* / *can* fall off the ladder.
4 Tina *might not have* / *can't have* wanted to go to the party. I thought she looked a bit tired.
5 That man *could not have* / *can't have* paid his bill. Look – the waiter's running after him!
6 You *must* / *can't* have been really pleased when you got a new phone for your birthday.

2 Complete the sentences with the passive form of the verbs in brackets.

1 I love ________ for dinner. (take out)
2 You won't be the last person ________ this question. (ask)
3 Were you pleased ________ a prize for your essay? (award)
4 Who else should ________ to the party next week? (invite)
5 Why does he always insist on ________ first? (serve)
6 No one likes ________ at. (laugh)

3 Complete the conditional sentences using the <u>underlined</u> words.

1 It's a pity you missed the barbecue last week. <u>you / love / it / if / you / go.</u>
2 Alex will be here in a few minutes. We've met him before, so I'm sure <u>we / recognise / him / when / he / arrive.</u>
3 Exercise is so important to me. <u>if / I / not / do / it / regularly, / I / feel / unhealthy.</u>
4 Imagine winning a £1,000 holiday! <u>if / you / win / one / who / you / take?</u>
5 I know you didn't go to university, but <u>what / you / study / if / you / go?</u>
6 You know about science, don't you? <u>if / you / heat / iron / what temperature / it / melt / at?</u>

4 Correct the mistake in each sentence.

1 How much do you expect to be pay in your holiday job?
2 These programmes must not watched by really young children.
3 David told by the security guard that photos were forbidden in the palace.
4 John said me he had some good news.
5 Now I can email on my tablet, I needn't to get annoyed about how slow my laptop is.
6 I died if the men that were fishing had not called the police.
7 I will offer you a 10% discount if you booked for 18 months.

REVIEW 4 UNITS 13–16

Overview

VOCABULARY	Leadership and achievement; Phrasal verbs with *up*; Phrasal verbs: transport; Advertising: nouns and verbs; Adverb + adjective collocations
GRAMMAR	The Passive (2): other structures; Reported speech; Modals (3): deduction; Conditionals (1): review
EXAM TASKS	Reading and Use of English Part 1; Reading and Use of English Part 2; Reading and Use of English Part 4

Resources

PHOTOCOPIABLE WORKSHEETS: Grammar worksheets Units 13–16; Vocabulary worksheets Units 13–16; Review Game Units 13–16; Literature worksheet; Speaking worksheet; Writing worksheet

WARMER

Ask students to work in groups of four. They look at the vocabulary sections of the previous four units and choose one word. They then each write one correct definition for the word and three incorrect definitions; these should not be obviously wrong. Each group in turn then presents their word and the four group members read out one definition each. The other groups have to guess which is the correct definition. They write the name of the person who they think gave the correct definition on a piece of paper and hold these up. Each correct group wins a point.

VOCABULARY

1 Put the students into pairs to complete the sentences. When students have finished, elicit the answers and ask them to rephrase the sentences to show they understand the meanings of the words, for example, *1 Mike seems nice, but he isn't understanding of people with problems.*

Answers
1 sympathetic 2 conscientious 3 self-esteem 4 doubt 5 targets

2 Look at the first sentence with the whole class. Ask them to first read the sentence and ask what is wrong with the scooter. (*It is very unreliable.*) Elicit the phrasal verb required and then ask what tense it needs to be in and how the students know (*present simple for regular habits*). Elicit the correct form and students do the rest of the exercise alone. Elicit the answers, the meanings of the phrasal verbs and what tense each phrasal verb should be in.

Answers
1 breaks down 2 speak up 3 pulling out 4 live up to
5 keep up with

3 Look at the first sentence with the class. Ask them what the sentence means (*that the company has started selling a cheap phone for the first time*). Elicit that this is talking about putting a new product on the market and that the correct word is *to launch*. Elicit what other context we use the word *launch* with (*to launch a rocket*). Students do the rest of the activity alone then compare answers in pairs. Elicit the answers and what the sentences mean.

MIXED ABILITY

For weaker classes, elicit the meaning of the choices of the words before asking students to do the activity in pairs.

Answers
1 launched 2 consumers 3 appeal 4 ad breaks 5 sponsor

4 Put students into pairs. Tell half the pairs in the class to cover the beginnings of the sentences and the other half to cover the endings. They have to try to make a full sentence using the half they can see. The pairs then get together in groups of four and tell each other how they began or ended each sentence. Finally, they all uncover the sentences and do the matching as a group of four. Elicit the answers and what the sentences mean.

Answers
1 a 2 e 3 b 4 c 5 d

GRAMMAR

1 Look at the first sentence with the class. Elicit the meanings of the two modal verbs: *I'm sure Joe is away on holiday / I'm sure Joe isn't away on holiday*. Students then look at the ending of the sentence and say which makes more sense. Students work alone then compare answers in pairs. Elicit the answers and why each choice is the correct one. (*2 It's not possible because it is safely locked away. 3 We don't use* can *to talk about possible true situations in the present. 4 We aren't sure enough to say* can't have. *5 We don't use* could not *to talk about negative deductions. 6 A new phone is a good present to have so we can be certain that the person was pleased. There is also a clue in the words used. With the negative form* can't *we would say:* You can't have been very pleased *meaning* not really pleased.)

Answers
1 can't 2 can't have 3 might 4 might not have 5 can't have
6 must

CONTINUED ON PAGE 190

2 Look at the first sentence and ask the students to make an active sentence using the verb in brackets, for example, *I love taking my friends out for dinner*. Elicit that *love* is followed by the *-ing* form and elicit how they would form the passive form of the verb (*being taken out*). Students then do the rest of the exercise in pairs. Elicit the answers.

Answers
1 being taken out 2 to be asked 3 to be awarded 4 be invited 5 being served 6 being laughed

3 Look at the first sentence with the class. Ask if it is about the past, present or future (*past*). Ask if the person being spoken to went to the party (*no*). Elicit that this is talking about a hypothetical past and elicit the conditional needed (*third*) and the form (If + *past perfect* + would + have + *past participle*). Students complete the exercise in pairs. Elicit the answers and the kinds of conditionals in each sentence.

FAST FINISHERS

Tell fast finishers to look at questions 4 and 5 and elicit that the questions are in the second and third conditionals. Ask students to think of questions they could ask using both kinds of conditional. When everyone has finished, elicit the answers and invite fast finishers to ask their questions to other students in the class.

Answers
1 You would/'d have loved it if you had/'d gone. 2 we will/'ll recognise him when he arrives. 3 If I do not/don't do it regularly, I feel unhealthy. 4 If you won one, who would you take? 5 what would you have studied if you had/'d gone? 6 If you heat iron, what temperature does it melt at?

4 Look at the first sentence and elicit what the problem is and what this is testing. (*The verb* pay *should be in the past participle form; passives*) Students complete the activity alone and compare in pairs. Elicit the answers and what each sentence is testing (*2, 3 passives; 4 reported speech; 5 modals; 6, 7 conditionals*).

Answers
1 How much do you expect to be **paid** in your holiday job? 2 These programmes must not **be** watched by really young children. 3 David **was** told by the security guard that photos were forbidden in the palace. 4 John **told me/said** he had some good news. 5 Now I can email on my tablet, I needn't ~~to~~ get annoyed about how slow my laptop is. 6 I **would have died** if the men that were fishing had not called the police. 7 I will offer you a 10% discount if you **book for** 18 months.

PREPARE FOR THE EXAM

1 **B2 FIRST FOR SCHOOLS Reading and Use of English Part 1**

Briefly review what students need to do in this part of the exam and if necessary, read out the *B2 First for Schools* box on TB page 26.

Look at the example with the class and elicit the meaning of supports (*helps in some way*). Remind students that, if they aren't sure of the answer they can usually reduce the choice by rejecting one or two words because of meaning or sentence structure. Allow ten minutes for the activity and then elicit the answers.

Answers
1 A 2 A 3 A 4 C 5 D 6 C 7 C 8 B

2 **B2 FIRST FOR SCHOOLS Reading and Use of English Part 2**

Briefly review what students need to do in this part of the exam and if necessary, read out the *B2 First for Schools* box on TB page 58.

Look at the example with the students and elicit that *constantly* is an adverb which describes how often something happens and that the missing word, *being,* is part of a present continuous passive form. Students read the text quickly to see what it is about and then work alone. Set a time limit of ten minutes and remind students to be careful to spell the words correctly or they will lose marks. Elicit the answers and what kind of structure each word is a part of, for example, *1 verb + infinitive with to; 2 first conditional,* etc.

Answers
1 to 2 If/When 3 then/can 4 have/need 5 be 6 where 7 by 8 been

3 **B2 FIRST FOR SCHOOLS Reading and Use of English Part 4**

Briefly review what students need to do in this part of the exam and if necessary, read out the *B2 First for Schools* box on TB page 49.

Look at the example sentence with the class. Elicit that *that she should* is not possible here as it is grammatically incorrect to use *should* with *to* (get a new phone). Students complete the activity alone and compare sentences in pairs. Elicit the answers and what each sentence is testing. Point out that this type of exercise commonly tests passives and reporting verbs.

Answers
1 admitted (that) | it was she/her 2 wouldn't mind | being / If I was 3 must have | been 4 if it | had been 5 had | recommended the café to 6 criticised me | for making

COOLER

Write on the board: *A bad day.*

The police stopped me while I was cycling home.

Ask students to write a sentence saying why they had a bad day. It doesn't have to be true and doesn't have to involve the police. When they are ready, write:

If you … the police wouldn't have stopped you.

Elicit different ways of completing the sentence, for example, *If you hadn't been cycling on the pavement … If your lights had been on … If you had been wearing a helmet …*

Students now work in groups of four. They tell each other about their bad day and the other students make third conditional sentences saying how the bad situation could have been avoided.

Monitor and note interesting ideas and invite groups to share some of their sentences with the class.

PREPARE FOR THE EXAM

Reading and Use of English Part 1

1 **For questions 1–8, read the text below and decide which answer (A, B, C or D) best fits each gap.**

The Teamwork Challenge Award for Scouts

The Scouts is an organisation for 6- to 25-year-olds around the world, which **(0)** *supports* young people in developing important life skills, such as teamwork and leadership. Through a range of interesting and varied activities, which include everything from kayaking to looking after animals, Scouts **(1)** ________ skills and character. This enables them to become **(2)** ________ and not rely on others for support.

The Teamwork Challenge Award is incredibly useful, teaching team members to **(3)** ________ with the group to set **(4)** ________ and reach goals. To gain the award, Scouts must prove what role they have fulfilled within teams, take part in team-building exercises, and **(5)** ________ up in Scout forums. While Scout meetings are in **(6)** ________, members are encouraged to express their opinions about items on the agenda.

Participating in such activities helps young people form strong relationships and **(7)** ________ out from the crowd when it comes to finding employment. Many former Scouts go on to **(8)** ________ up businesses, or become teachers and leaders, Olympic athletes and even astronauts!

	A	B	C	D
0	**A** influences	(**B**) supports	**C** persuades	**D** promotes
1	**A** build	**B** create	**C** produce	**D** raise
2	**A** independent	**B** individual	**C** available	**D** free
3	**A** cooperate	**B** help	**C** aid	**D** assist
4	**A** achievements	**B** ambitions	**C** targets	**D** plans
5	**A** chat	**B** talk	**C** discuss	**D** speak
6	**A** performance	**B** completion	**C** progress	**D** action
7	**A** step	**B** look	**C** stand	**D** hold
8	**A** do	**B** set	**C** make	**D** put

Reading and Use of English Part 2

2 **For questions 1–8, read the text below and think of the word which best fits each gap. Use only one word in each gap.**

NEW PUBLIC TRANSPORT

Interesting ways of keeping citizens moving are constantly **(0)** *being* employed around the world. In many cities, large numbers of people have already been persuaded **(1)** ________ cycle or use electric scooters because they're quick and cheap. **(2)** ________ you cycle, you'll often arrive before a car, bus or train. Some people use public hire systems. With their credit card or phone, they **(3)** ________ release a bike or scooter from wherever it has been left in the street and ride it for as long as they like. Sometimes the first hour is free, and they then **(4)** ________ to pay a small fee for subsequent periods.

The first large-scale cycle system to **(5)** ________ introduced was the Vélib in Paris, **(6)** ________ tens of thousands of bicycles are now ridden every day **(7)** ________ people of all ages. Without the Vélib's enormous success, several hundred other cities around the world, including London, New York, Barcelona and Mexico City, might not have **(8)** ________ able to fund their own bicycle-hire systems.

Reading and Use of English Part 4

3 **For questions 1–6, complete the second sentence so that it has a similar meaning to the first sentence, using the word given. Do not change the word given. You must use between two and five words, including the word given.**

0 'You should get a new phone,' Stevie said to Maria. **THAT**
Stevie told Maria *that she ought* to get a new phone.

1 Sara said, 'It was me who broke Dan's headphones.' **ADMITTED**
Sara ________ who had broken Dan's headphones.

2 It would be good to get an invitation to Cheryl's wedding, but I'm not too bothered about it! **MIND**
I ________ invited to Cheryl's wedding, but I'm not too bothered about it!

3 I'm sure João was at work yesterday because his car was in the car park. **BEEN**
João ________ at work yesterday because his car was in the car park.

4 The advert was going to cost $1 million, but the film company never made it. **IF**
The ad would have cost $1 million ________ made.

5 'I've had a recommendation from someone about this café,' Jan said. **RECOMMENDED**
Jan said that someone ________ him.

6 Jules said to me, 'You always make such a mess!' **CRITICISED**
Jules ________ such a mess.

17 MAKING HEADLINES

ABOUT YOU

13 Watch the video and answer the questions.

Where do you hear or read the news?

Who or what is in the news at the moment that you're particularly interested in? Why?

VOCABULARY The media

1 Read the quiz. Match the phrases in the quiz to the meanings below.

EP

What's the purpose *of the media?*

The media is there to …

1. help me keep up to date with the sports results ☐
2. celebrate achievements such as discoveries and firsts ☐
3. gossip about celebrities ☐
4. tell me what's making headlines around the world ☐
5. make fun of public figures ☐
6. comment on current events ☐
7. keep people amused ☐
8. cover interesting stories ☐

- **a** give positive information about successes
- **b** help someone feel interested and happy
- **c** give opinions about the news
- **d** deal with news items which people may want to know about
- **e** talk about people's private lives
- **f** be an important news story in the media
- **g** make unkind jokes about someone
- **h** have the latest information about the news, sport, etc.

78 **2** Listen to eight short recordings. What is happening in each one? Use the phrases in Exercise 1 in your answers.

3 Read the quiz again and tick the statements you agree with. Compare your answers with your partner.

4 Think about recent news stories. Which statements in Exercise 1 do they match?

READING

1 Look at the photos and read the article quickly. What does it give advice about?

- **A** how to write a realistic news story
- **B** how to deal with a particular kind of journalism
- **C** how to ignore news which may be harmful

PREPARE FOR THE EXAM

Reading and Use of English Part 3

2 Look at the example answer (0) in the first paragraph of the article. What type of word is it?

3 For questions 1–8, read the first three paragraphs of the article. Use the word given in capitals to form a word that fits in the gap.

4 Read the whole article and answer the questions.

1. Why can fake news be a problem?
2. How do fake news stories appear to be real?
3. What advice is given about checking whether a story is genuine or not?
4. Why are people tempted to read fake news stories?
5. What does the text say about quotes in news stories?
6. What is the advice given in the article's conclusion?

5 Match the highlighted words and phrases in the article to the meanings.

1. where something comes from
2. can be trusted
3. arranged
4. words someone else has said or written
5. make us notice something

17 MAKING HEADLINES

Unit Overview

TOPIC	The news
VOCABULARY	The media
READING	Fake news: what is it and how can you spot it?
GRAMMAR	Conditionals (2): mixed
VOCABULARY	Phrasal verbs: the media
WRITING	A review
EXAM TASKS	Reading and Use of English Part 3; Writing Part 2

Resources

GRAMMAR REFERENCE AND PRACTICE: SB page 164; TB page 269
PREPARE FOR THE EXAM: SB pages on TB pages 238 and 246; TB pages 255 and 258
WORKBOOK: pages 68–71
VIDEO AND VIDEO WORKSHEET: The news
PHOTOCOPIABLE WORKSHEETS: Grammar worksheet Unit 17; Vocabulary worksheet Unit 17
TEST GENERATOR: Unit test 17
PRACTICE EXTRA: Unit 17

WARMER

Tell students to work in groups of three or four. Ask them to think about newspapers, the internet and TV and ask the groups to think of how these could be an advantage or a disadvantage to famous people. You could give them one example from the previous unit and write on the board: *Advantage: Famous people can earn money from advertising.* Set a time limit and then invite students to share their ideas as a class. Follow up by asking students if they like reading about celebrities in the media and if so why or why not.

ABOUT YOU

13 You can begin the class and introduce the topic of the unit by showing the video and asking students to complete the video worksheet. Then, read the questions in the *About you* box with the students and allow them to discuss their ideas as a class. Try to find one or two interesting stories before the lesson in case students can't think of any ideas. Elicit some places where you can hear or read the news, for example, *radio, newspaper, online*. Now write three headings on the board: *local, national, international* and elicit one recent news story for each heading. Students now work in groups of three or four to discuss the questions together. Monitor and note any interesting answers and invite students to share these with the class.

VOCABULARY The media

1 Tell the students to cover the meanings and to look at the sentences in pairs. Elicit what the first sentence means, for example, *to help me know the latest results*. Together students do the same with the other sentences. Elicit ideas about what each sentence means and then ask students to uncover the meanings in the book. Elicit the answers but don't elicit any opinions about the statements yet.

Answers
1 h 2 a 3 e 4 f 5 g 6 c 7 b 8 d

78 2 Before students listen, put them into eight groups and give each group one of the statements in Exercise 1 to look at. Ask them to think of three key words that they might hear in a short dialogue about their statement, for example, *1 team, win, result; 2 invention, first, science,* etc. Elicit these ideas and write them on the board. As students listen, they match the recordings to the statements and see how many of the key words they hear. Elicit the answers and any words the students heard.

Answers
1 gossiping about (celebrities) 2 keeping (people) amused 3 keeping people up to date (with sports results) 4 making fun of (a public figure) 5 covering (interesting) stories 6 commenting on current events 7 celebrating achievements (such as discoveries) 8 making headlines

» AUDIOSCRIPT TB PAGE 303

3 Look at the instructions with the class and write a table on the board with three headings: *Does the media do this? Should the media do this?* and *Do I use the media for this?* Students copy this and, for each sentence in the quiz, they write a tick or cross under each heading of the table. Set a time limit of two minutes for students to think alone and then two minutes to compare their ideas with a partner. Monitor and note interesting ideas from the students and invite them to share their ideas with the class.

Answers
Student's own ideas

4 Re-elicit the news stories students mentioned in the *About you* task and discuss with the class which statements they match. Students then work in groups of three or four to think of other stories and match them to the statements. Elicit ideas and, for each story suggested by groups, ask if anyone knows anything about it and whether they found it interesting or not.

Answers
Students' own answers

READING

1 Give students two minutes to quickly read the text and look at the photos. Elicit the answer and ask students if they have ever heard the term *fake news* before and whether they can give any examples. You could give them some examples from the background information box.

Answer
B

CONTINUED ON PAGE 194

BACKGROUND INFORMATION

Although fake news stories have existed for many years, the term became famous in 2016 when the editor of Buzzfeed noticed a lot of completely untrue stories about the US presidential elections all coming from the same town in Eastern Europe. The motivation seemed to be earning money by gaining hits on social media and from advertising, rather than trying to change people's voting intentions.

PREPARE FOR THE EXAM

2 B2 FIRST FOR SCHOOLS Reading and Use of English Part 3

Briefly review what students need to do in this part of the exam and, if necessary, read out the *B2 First for Schools* box on TB page 102.

Remind students that, in the exam, this will be a standalone text and not the first part of a longer text. In addition, the words in brackets appear at the end of the line the corresponding gap is in rather than immediately after the gap. When you have elicited that the word in the example is an adverb, ask the students what it is describing (*it's an adverb of certainty saying how likely the action is to have happened*).

Answer

adverb

3 Ask the students to read the paragraphs quickly without writing anything. Then give the students nine minutes to do the task alone. Students compare answers in pairs. Elicit the answers and how students knew which type of word was needed in each case, especially for 2, 4 and 6 (*2 is negative because it is misleading, not true; 4 is not harmful because it causes no problems; 6 is a plural noun because there is no indefinite article, which would be needed if it were singular*).

MIXED ABILITY

Put weaker students into pairs or groups of three. Look at the first three gaps with them and elicit the kinds of words needed in each, for example, *1–2 an adjective to describe a fake news story; 3 an adverb describing how sure the writer is that fake news isn't a new phenomenon*. Elicit the correct form of the three words and then allow students to work together on the rest of the exercise.

Answers

1 misleading 2 untrue 3 definitely 4 harmless 5 damaging 6 politicians 7 advertising 8 factual

4 Students read the text and answer the questions individually and then compare their answers in groups of three or four. Invite groups to give the answer to one of the questions and, after each one, ask the other groups if they agree or if they have answered the question in a slightly different way.

Answers

1 It can damage people's reputations, people are made fun of, and readers are led to believe that 'facts' are true when they aren't.
2 They are laid out in a similar way to genuine news items, with a headline, photos, and the name of the news provider.
3 Do a search for the news provider and check it is known; look the story up on a well-known news site; look for missing details such as logos or names of journalists.
4 They are convincing and contain information we want to read, such as gossip.
5 They can be made up, and do not necessarily mean a story is genuine.
6 Be critical of what you read online.

79 The Reading text is recorded for students to listen, read and check their answers.

5 Students do the matching alone then compare answers in pairs. Elicit the answers and ask follow-up questions to check the students' understanding, for example: 'Which sources did you use for your last history project?' (*names of books or websites*); 'Who is this quote from: "I have a dream"?' (*Martin Luther King*); 'Can you think of an advert which grabs your attention?'; 'Can you think of someone famous who you think is trustworthy (or untrustworthy)?' and 'How is a newspaper front page usually laid out?' (*a big headline, with the journalist's name under it, then the story with smaller sub-headings and photos*).

FAST FINISHERS

Ask fast finishers to create their own sentences using three of the highlighted words. Elicit these example sentences after checking answers to Exercise 5.

Answers

1 source 2 trustworthy 3 laid out 4 quote 5 grab our attention

TALKING POINTS

Before students read the questions, elicit that fake news is news which has been made up and isn't true. Give students other examples of news and ask if they think this also counts as being fake, for example: *true stories but only giving one side of an argument and deliberately not mentioning the other side's point of view; news stories which have been paid for by companies or countries but which are written as if they were news items; and tweets or posts by celebrities which advertise a product but don't tell their followers that they have been paid to mention the product.*

Students then work in small groups to answer the questions. Set a time limit of three minutes and then discuss the questions as a class.

COOLER

Re-elicit some of the news stories the students have mentioned during the lesson. Discuss how headlines are important for grabbing the readers' attention. Choose one story and elicit ideas for a good eye-catching headline. Write these on the board. Students now work in groups of three or four to think of headlines for some of the other stories they have mentioned. Set a time limit of three minutes then elicit ideas from different groups.

FAKE NEWS:

WHAT IS IT AND HOW CAN YOU SPOT IT?

79

If you're on social media and like to keep up to date with the news, you'll almost **(0)** *certainly* (CERTAIN) have read at least one fake news story, if not dozens. So, what *is* fake news? Well, it's a story which is deliberately **(1)** ______ (MISLEAD). In other words, it's partially or entirely **(2)** ______ (TRUE).

While making up news is **(3)** ______ (DEFINITE) not a new phenomenon, social media is helping it to reach bigger audiences than ever.

Many stories are relatively **(4)** ______ (HARM) and cause no problems. Some, however, can actually be **(5)** ______ (DAMAGE) to people's reputations, especially for people in power, like **(6)** ______ (POLITICS).

There are several reasons why news is made up. One is to get people clicking onto a website which promotes companies' **(7)** ______ (ADVERT) campaigns and earns the site more money. Other reasons include attempting to influence readers' opinions or making fun of public figures. Some readers are unaware that these stories may not be **(8)** ______ (FACT).

How can we distinguish between what is fake news and what is a genuine news article? Many fake stories have the appearance of a real news item, and as a result of this, they're shared, reaching many millions of people worldwide. They are laid out like actual news stories, with a headline, photos of the people mentioned in the article, and often indicate who the news provider is. This makes it very difficult for readers to determine whether a story is real or fake.

One of the ways in which it is possible to find out whether a story is genuine is to do a search for the news provider. We are all familiar with the big news providers in our own countries, and we know that they're trustworthy. If the provider isn't one you've ever heard of, or something makes you suspect it isn't a recognised source, then it probably isn't. If you have any doubts about the story, you can verify it by looking on a well-known news site, such as the BBC. If it appears there, then you can safely assume it's real, since genuine providers check facts and make sure their stories are true. In addition to checking the provider and verifying the story, you can also look out for things like missing logos or the names of journalists being left out, which credible news stories always include.

The problem is that fake news headlines can be very convincing and cover what seem to be interesting events. This makes us want to read them and catch up on what's happening, especially if they appear to be gossiping about stars: 'Top Hollywood couple split up!' Or if they make absurd claims: 'Scientists say you can survive on chocolate!' Headlines like this are guaranteed to grab our attention and draw us in. And if you think that the presence of a quote makes a story more likely to be true, think again. These can also be made up, and this is where someone's reputation may be affected.

Here's your checklist for spotting fake news:

- Is the source reliable? Do you recognise the news provider and is their logo visible?
- Is the journalist's full name on the piece? You can look them up, too!
- Did someone you know and trust share the story with you?
- Can you find the same story on a reputable news site?
- Does the story *seem* fake? If so, it probably is!
- And finally, remember to be critical about what you read online – especially if you plan on including facts or quotes in school assignments.

MAYOR SAYS HE **HATES** OUR CITY

Miracle fruit makes you TALLER!

TALKING POINTS

What are the consequences for people of believing fake news?

Do you think social media sites should ban advertising? Why? / Why not?

MAKING HEADLINES 99

GRAMMAR Conditionals (2): mixed

1 **Read the examples and answer the questions.**

1 If you hadn't read this article, you wouldn't know how to spot fake news.
Did you read this article?
Do you know how to spot fake news?

2 If I weren't aware of fake news, I might have believed that fake story.
Are you aware of fake news?
Did you believe the fake story?

2 **Match the examples in Exercise 1 to the rules.**

Mixed conditionals combine elements of the second and third conditional. We use them:

a to talk about an imaginary situation in the present that is affected by a past action:
if + past perfect, *would/might/could* + infinitive.

b to talk about an imaginary situation in the past that is affected by a present situation or permanent conditions:
if + past simple, *would/might/could* + *have* + past participle.

» GRAMMAR REFERENCE AND PRACTICE PAGE 164

3 **Complete the mixed-conditional sentences.**

0 We haven't got wi-fi because our router stopped working last night.
We *would have* wi-fi if our router *hadn't stopped working last night*.

1 We speak English, so we understood the report.
We ________ the report if we ________ English.

2 This is a safe area, so I didn't lock the back door.
If this ________ a safe area, I ________ the back door.

3 You're wet because you didn't bring an umbrella.
If you ________ an umbrella, you ________ wet.

4 You're a hard worker, so you passed your exams.
You ________ your exams if you ________ a hard worker.

5 David missed the bus. That's why he isn't at home now.
David ________ at home now if he ________ the bus.

4 **Decide which two sentences are correct. Correct the mistakes in the three incorrect sentences.**

1 If I weren't such a fast runner, I wouldn't have missed the bus this morning.
2 If it weren't so wet, we could have gone to the park today.
3 If I didn't have my calculator today, I wouldn't have taken much longer with this homework.
4 You would be in trouble now if you haven't done your homework.
5 If you had taken a headache tablet as I suggested, you would be out cycling now.

5 **Write questions using mixed conditionals.**

0 Today's a weekday, but what (you / do / this morning / if / Saturday)
would you have done this morning if it were a Saturday?

1 The internet was launched in the 1980s, but (if / they / not invent / it / how / life / be / different)

2 You aren't a millionaire, but (where / you / go / on holiday / last summer / if / be / millionaire)

3 You haven't left school yet, but (if / you / already / leave / where / live)

4 Mobile phones became popular in the 1990s, but (how / you / communicate / with your friends / if / they / not become popular)

6 **Ask and answer the questions in Exercise 5.**

VOCABULARY Phrasal verbs: the media

1 **Match the sentence halves.**

EP
1 I managed to get the point across
2 He followed up his TV interview
3 The news item brought up an
4 I got out my tablet and caught up on
5 These points were left out
6 His family backed him up
7 The programme looked into
8 We need to clear up

a with a Twitter conversation for fans.
b to the audience.
c of the article about guerrilla marketing.
d the issue of fees for higher education.
e interesting point about equality.
f after he confessed he was lying.
g a few problems before we can move on.
h all the latest gossip on social media.

2 **Replace the underlined words and phrases in the email with a phrasal verb from Exercise 1 with a similar meaning.**

Dear Jonas,

While I'm [1] learning the latest information about how everyone's getting on, I just want to confirm your responsibilities as the newsletter editor. Your main role is checking the content of the blogs. I [2] mentioned the issue of sources when I spoke to some of the writers a while back, so do make sure you [3] emphasise to them the importance of using accurate sources. They mustn't [4] forget to include their references either. It's the webmaster's job to learn about and [5] solve problems, such as photos that don't upload, so don't worry about those. Let me know if you want me to [6] check the accuracy of any sources and references. I'm here to [7] support you, as you know. If you want, we can [8] take further action connected to this email with a meeting to talk about things in more detail.

See you soon,
Clare

3 **In pairs, make sentences with the phrasal verbs from Exercise 1.**

GRAMMAR Conditionals (2): mixed

WARMER

Re-elicit how we form third conditional sentences (If + past perfect + *would* + *have* + *past participle*). Write this sentence on the board: *If I hadn't stayed up so late last night, I wouldn't have woken up late.*

Elicit that the person went to bed late and woke up late. Ask students to imagine how that affected the person, for example, *they were late for school, they missed a train,* etc. Ask how you think the person feels now, for example, *tired*.

Write this sentence on the board: *If I hadn't stayed up so late last night, I ______ tired now.*

Elicit the missing words (*wouldn't be/feel*) and that the sentence is now a mix of the third and second conditional.

1 Students look at the first sentence. Elicit which part talks about the past (*the first part*) and which talks about the present (*the second part*). Do the same for the second sentence. Students then answer the questions in pairs.

Answers
1 Yes, Yes 2 Yes, No

2 Read the rules box with the class and elicit which sentence matches which idea. Explain to students that the first sentence is more common as we often think about how an imaginary past event could affect the present.

Answers
1 a 2 b

» GRAMMAR REFERENCE AND PRACTICE ANSWER KEY TB PAGE 269

3 Look at the example sentence with the students. Ask what the present situation is (*there is no wi-fi*) and what the past event was (*the router stopped working*). Tell students to do the same with the other sentences if they aren't sure which part to put into the second conditional and which in the third. Students work in pairs. Elicit the answers and which rule each one corresponds to.

MIXED ABILITY

Put weaker students into pairs or groups of three. You could tell them which rule each sentence corresponds to before they start (*1, 2, 4 – b; 3, 5 – a*). They then follow the patterns in the rules box to complete each sentence.

Answers
1 would not/wouldn't have understood, did not/didn't speak
2 was not/wasn't/were not/weren't, would/'d have locked
3 had/'d brought, would not/wouldn't be 4 would not/wouldn't have passed, were not/weren't 5 would/'d be, had not/hadn't missed

4 Students look at the sentences alone and try to work out which are correct. They then compare ideas in pairs and rewrite the incorrect sentences. Elicit the answers and ask what was wrong with the original sentences.

Answers
1 If I **weren't** such a fast runner, I **would** have missed the bus this morning.
2 correct
3 If I didn't have my calculator today, I **would have taken** much longer with this homework.
4 You would be in trouble now if you **hadn't** done your homework.
5 correct

5 Elicit how to form questions using the second and third conditional and show how they can be written in two different ways:

Would you have missed the bus if you could run faster? If you could run faster, would you have missed the bus?

What would your life be like if mobiles hadn't been invented? If mobiles hadn't been invented, what would your life be like?

Look at the example and show that it uses the first part of a third conditional question and the second part of a second conditional question. Students then work in pairs to write the other questions. Monitor and help where necessary and then elicit the answers.

Answers
1 if they had not/hadn't invented it, how would life be different?
2 where would you have gone on holiday last summer if you were a millionaire?
3 if you had/'d already left, where would you live?
4 how would you communicate with your friends if they had not/hadn't become popular?

6 Ask the example question to the class and encourage students to use a full conditional form to answer, for example, *If it were a Saturday today, I would have … this morning.* Students then ask and answer the other questions in pairs. When they have finished, elicit questions and answers from different pairs.

As a follow up, you could put the students into small groups and ask them to write two mixed conditional questions of their own to ask to the class. When they are ready, invite the groups to ask their questions to the class and elicit answers. Students give their own answers.

» GRAMMAR WORKSHEET UNIT 17

VOCABULARY Phrasal verbs: the media

1 Match the first sentence as an example and then ask students to complete the exercise individually. Check answers. Extend the task by asking students to define the phrasal verbs with a partner (see Answers). Elicit a definition for each one and check whether all students agree with each definition.

Answers
1 b (make someone understand something)
2 a (take further action) 3 e (raise) 4 h (get up to date on)
5 c (not include) 6 f (support) 7 d (examine) 8 g (solve)

2 If you have already looked at the definitions of the phrasal verbs, this exercise should be straightforward. Do the first one together as an example and then set the rest as an individual task. Check answers. If students haven't defined the phrasal verbs, take the opportunity to define any that they struggle with.

Answers
1 catching up on 2 brought up 3 get across 4 leave out
5 clear up 6 look into 7 back you up 8 follow up

3 Give each pair a letter, A or B. Pair A make sentences using the first four phrasal verbs and Pair B using the other four phrasal verbs. When they are ready, they join together in groups of four. Ask students to read their sentences aloud to the other pair, but without saying the phrasal verb. The other pair should guess what the missing phrasal verb is. Invite groups to share any challenging ones with the class. Students give their own answers.

» VOCABULARY WORKSHEET UNIT 17

WRITING A review

1 Before students look at the exercise, elicit some news sites that the students read and invite them to say whether they think the sites are reliable and interesting or not. Ask students to quickly read the review and say what it is reviewing (*a magazine for teenagers*) and what the reviewer likes about it (*interesting articles, original stories, amazing photos*). Students then answer the questions.

Answers
1 teenagers who are into writing, art and photography
2 The style is lively. *Are you into, tired of, check out, full of, interesting, amazing*

2 Students read both texts and discuss the answers in pairs. Elicit their answers and ask the class if the review would persuade them to buy the magazine and why.

FAST FINISHERS

Ask fast finishers to note down useful adjective-noun or adverb-adjective phrases from review B, for example *trivial gossip, refreshingly different*. When everyone has finished the exercise, elicit the phrases and what they mean.

Answers
1 B 2 B This style is more appealing because of its lively and informal language and because it addresses the reader directly and writes as one teenager to another.

3 Look at the *Prepare to write* box with the class and elicit examples of phrases from the start of the review in Exercise 1 (informal phrases: *be into, boring old, it's full of*; direct questions: *Are you into …*? Phrasal verbs: *check out;* a friendly tone: *Are you …*). Students then do the same for review B. Allow them to work in pairs and elicit examples from the class.

Answers
a stuffed full of, for a start, makes a nice change, love its style, And the best thing is, look out for it
b Do publishers really think we only want to read trivial gossip? Who wants to read poems aimed at children?
c brings up, backed up, get across, lets down, stand outs, look out for
d As we know, I know you'll, use of 'we' and 'us'

PREPARE FOR THE EXAM

B2 FIRST FOR SCHOOLS
Writing Part 2: A review

In this part, students have to answer one question out of a choice of four writing tasks. As mentioned on TB page 42, there are five tasks in total, but students shouldn't attempt question 5 unless they have read the set reading text. They are given a clear context, topic, purpose and target reader and should write 140–190 words. The review should describe something which the writer has experienced personally, for example, a film, holiday, product, etc. and give the reader a clear impression of what it is like. The review should contain a clear description, opinion with explanations and will usually finish with a recommendation to the reader.

Tips Tell students that the review is usually written for an English-language magazine, newspaper or website. Make sure students are aware that who they are writing for is important in terms of register, and that this will affect their choice of grammar and vocabulary. If it is aimed at teenagers, they should make their writing fun, informal and friendly.

4 Give students time to read the task and then ask them to cover it or close their books. Ask what the review is of (*a news website*), who it is for (*an international student's forum*) and what questions they have to answer (*why you use it, what information you have found and why it is interesting, who you would recommend it for and why*). Allow five minutes for students to plan their reviews, noting down useful expressions, phrasal verbs and other ideas. You could allow weaker students to plan together. Monitor and help where necessary.

5 If you have students preparing for the *B2 First for Schools* exam, set a strict time limit of 40 minutes minus the time they have spent planning. When they have finished and checked their own work, ask students to look at their partner's review and to check it against the instructions in the Student's Book. They should check it for informal phrases, friendly tone, direct questions and phrasal verbs, as well as for all the listed bullet points.

Model answer
The greatest news website for young people
I often catch up on the news online via teenkidsnews.com. I visit the site because it's full of fascinating news stories. Are you interested in the world like I am? Then you'll love it, too. It has eye-catching photos with attention-grabbing headlines which make you want to read the stories. It definitely stands out from other websites of its kind.
There's some cool stuff on the site. Today, for example, I've not only read an article which cleared up the reasons why it's so difficult to predict the weather, but there was a feature about how pianists' brains are different from other people's, and it was followed up with an interview with a famous pianist. Not only can you read about what's happening in the news, but in the entertainment world, too. There's also information about careers, health, and a ton of other topics.
I would recommend this website to other people my age. The articles are informative, current and entertaining. I think it's essential for young people to know what's happening in the world: it keeps us informed, develops our opinions and helps us to engage in interesting conversations with other people.

COOLER

Students work in groups of four. They discuss the websites they chose for the review and tell each other why they like the website and what sort of information it contains. When they are ready, the groups choose one of the websites they discussed and present it to the class. Other students can give their opinions about the website or, if they don't know it, ask for more information. When they have all presented their websites have a class survey of each one with four choices: *I like it, I don't like it, I know it* and *I don't know it* to find out which site is the most well-known and which is the most popular.

WRITING A review

1 **Read the first paragraph of a magazine review.**

1 Who do you think the review is aimed at?
2 Do you think the style is lively or serious? Which words and phrases tell you this?

THINK INK: NEWS AND VIEWS FOR TEENAGERS

Are you into writing and art, but tired of the same boring old magazines? Then you should check out 'Think Ink'. It's a new magazine especially for teenagers who are into writing, art and photography. It's full of interesting articles and original stories. The photos are amazing, too.

2 **Read two options, A and B, for the rest of the review and answer the questions.**

1 Which has a similar style to the first paragraph?
2 Which option do you think is more appropriate for a review? Why?

A

It seems to be the case that magazines for teenagers tend to concentrate on celebrities and fashion. Arguably, publishers fail to understand their market if they see celebrity culture as a teenager's chief concern and don't look into other issues which concern young people. However, 'Think Ink' is not in this category because its readers are treated like adults. What's more, the content is entirely created by its readers, which makes it unique and genuinely attractive to a teenage audience.

Nevertheless, it has to be said that the poetry section is rather disappointing. If the poems hadn't seemed so childish, they would be a little more appealing. On the other hand, the articles feature many original topics, and the fiction is generally excellent. While 'Think Ink' isn't perfect, it is a thoroughly good read and highly recommended.

B

As we know, most magazines for teenagers are stuffed full of articles about celebrities and fashion. Do publishers really think we only want to read trivial gossip? Teenage magazines get very boring after a while, but 'Think Ink' is refreshingly different. For a start, it treats its readers like adults, and brings up fascinating points which are backed up with detailed arguments. That makes a nice change, and I know you'll really love its style! And the best thing is that we, the readers, write everything that's in it, giving us the opportunity to get across ideas that a teenage audience will relate to.

I feel that the poetry section lets the magazine down a bit. Who wants to read poems aimed at children? But then again, the creative fiction really stands out, and the articles are excellent as well. 'Think Ink' is definitely worth a read, so look out for it!

3 **Read the *Prepare to write* box, and read review B again. Underline examples of:**

a informal phrases
b direct questions
c phrasal verbs
d a friendly tone

PREPARE TO WRITE Language for reviews

Reviews written for teenagers will generally

- have a friendly tone rather than a formal one.
- contain informal phrases, such as *really cool* and *stuff like that*.
- use direct questions, which address the reader personally.
- include phrasal verbs, such as *get across* and *stand out*.

PREPARE FOR THE EXAM

Writing Part 2 (A review)

4 **Read the task and plan your answer.**

You see a notice on an international students' forum asking for reviews of news websites.

Submit a review!

We are looking for reviews of news websites. Write us a review of a website you know well, telling us:

- why you use this website
- what information you have found on the website and why it is interesting
- who you would recommend the website to and why.

Write your **review**.

5 **Write your review.**

- Use the tips in the *Prepare to write* box.
- Give your review a title and organise it into paragraphs.
- Express your opinion and make a recommendation.
- Check your grammar and spelling.
- Write 140–190 words.

MAKING HEADLINES 101

18 CREATIVE CAREERS

ABOUT YOU

14 Watch the video and answer the questions.

Have you ever worked during the school holidays? What did you do?

Have you ever done any work experience? What was it like?

How do you think that schools and parents can help young people prepare for their futures?

VOCABULARY The world of work

1 **Read the list of aspects a job might have. Then look at photos A–F and decide which aspects apply to these jobs.**

EP

- **a** having to work long hours
- **b** using a hobby to make a living
- **c** being able to take lots of time off
- **d** doing something that is rewarding
- **e** having to meet deadlines
- **f** being well paid
- **g** being badly paid
- **h** having to work shifts

2 **Can you think of another job for each of the aspects in Exercise 1?**

80 **3** **Listen to Sofia, Martin and Tara. Which of the jobs in the pictures A–F would be most appropriate for each person?**

80 **4** **Listen again. Why is each job appropriate for each person? Use the aspects of work in your answers.**

Sofia: artist. She wouldn't need to meet deadlines or work shifts …

5 **Discuss the questions.**

1. Which person is most like you? Why?
2. Which aspects from Exercise 1 will be important to you in your future job?

READING

1 **Read the blog post quickly. Which career does Emily seem to be most attracted to?**

PREPARE FOR THE EXAM

Reading and Use of English Part 5

2 **Read the blog post again. For questions 1–6, choose the answer (A, B, C or D) which you think fits best according to the text.**

1 From the first paragraph, we understand that Emily
- **A** believes she still has a chance of becoming famous.
- **B** is worried about how much she'll earn in the future.
- **C** is undecided about her future plans.
- **D** thinks most teenagers want to become famous.

2 In line 23, 'making it' means
- **A** becoming successful in a chosen field.
- **B** being discovered at a very young age.
- **C** deciding to follow up on a hidden talent.
- **D** having the chance to earn some money.

3 What does Emily think about having a career in finance?
- **A** The work might be too difficult for her.
- **B** The hours would be too physically demanding for her.
- **C** The job wouldn't be appropriate for her.
- **D** The career is morally unacceptable to her.

4 What do Emily's parents agree is important to her career choice?
- **A** that she gains further qualifications
- **B** that she tries out a number of different jobs
- **C** that she avoids the mistakes they both made
- **D** that she finds something she is enthusiastic about

5 Emily feels that law and medicine
- **A** are careers she can't take seriously.
- **B** require too much studying.
- **C** are professions she wouldn't be able to do.
- **D** have a predictable career path.

6 What steps has Emily taken towards finding work?
- **A** She's arranged some work experience.
- **B** She's shown her blog to some local newspapers.
- **C** She's researched the kinds of work she'd like to do.
- **D** She's applied for a degree in journalism.

18 CREATIVE CAREERS

Unit Overview

TOPIC	Work
VOCABULARY	The world of work
READING	The Big Decision
GRAMMAR	Uses of verb + *-ing*
VOCABULARY	Word pairs
LISTENING	An interview about a T-shirt business
SPEAKING	Agreeing and disagreeing
EXAM TASKS	Reading and Use of English Part 5; Listening Part 4

Resources

GRAMMAR REFERENCE AND PRACTICE: SB page 165; TB page 269
PREPARE FOR THE EXAM: SB pages on TB pages 240–241 and 249; TB pages 256 and 260
WORKBOOK: pages 72–75
VIDEO AND VIDEO WORKSHEET: Jobs
PHOTOCOPIABLE WORKSHEETS: Grammar worksheet Unit 18; Vocabulary worksheet Unit 18
TEST GENERATOR: Unit test 18
PRACTICE EXTRA: Unit 18

WARMER

Put the students into groups of four. The students start by working alone and writing down two jobs that they might like to do in the future and two they wouldn't want to do. They should write these in a random order. They then get into groups of three or four and take turns reading out their four jobs. The other students guess which are the two they would like to do and which the ones they wouldn't like to do. They then discuss all the jobs and say what is good or bad about each one. Invite groups to tell the class about some of the jobs they discussed.

ABOUT YOU

14 You can begin the class and introduce the topic of the unit by showing the video and asking students to complete the video worksheet. Then, read the questions in the *About you* box and students exchange ideas and answer the questions in groups of three or four. Monitor and note any interesting replies and invite students who answered *yes* to the first and third questions to share their experiences with the class.

VOCABULARY The world of work

1 Look at the photos with the class. Elicit what kind of job each one shows, what skills the people doing the jobs would need and ask students how they think the people feel, and how they themselves would feel if they were to do these jobs. Students then work in pairs to match the aspects to the photos. Elicit ideas and the meanings of the highlighted words.

Possible answers

A being well paid, doing something that is rewarding
B having to work shifts, being well/badly paid, working long hours
C using a hobby to make a living, being able to take lots of time off, doing something that is rewarding, being badly paid
D doing something that is rewarding, working shifts, being well paid, working long hours
E doing something that is rewarding, meeting deadlines, being well paid
F work long hours, being well/badly paid, doing something that is rewarding

2 Look at the first aspect in blue with the class and elicit other jobs in which people have to work long hours, for example, *lorry driver*. Set a time limit of two minutes and elicit ideas from different pairs. Students give their own answers.

80 3 Tell students not to write anything while they are listening but just try to get an impression of each person. When they have listened to all three people they compare ideas in pairs. Elicit ideas and ask about any information that the students remember from the recording which helped them to choose.

Possible answers

Sofia: artist (photo C)
Martin: builder (photo F)
Tara: doctor (photo D) or barrister (photo A)

80 4 Tell students to write the names of the three people in their notebooks. As they listen, they note down the things they want from their job and the things they don't want (for example *work in an office, something creative, working with my hands, repetitive, paperwork, feel stressed, challenges me, demanding, professional, dealing with people, travel on business*). Allow students to compare answers then elicit the answers and the meanings of any new vocabulary.

Answers

Sofia: She doesn't want to work shifts or work in an office. She wants to do something that is creative and rewarding.
Martin: He doesn't want to meet deadlines. He wants to be able to take lots of time off, and he wants to make a decent living.
Tara: She doesn't mind working long hours. She wants a well-paid job, like a doctor or lawyer.

≫ AUDIOSCRIPT TB PAGE 303

5 Students work in groups of three and four. Allow them to think about the questions for one minute then, ask each person in turn to give their answer. Monitor and note interesting ideas and invite students to share these with the class. Students give their own answers.

READING

1 Set a time limit of four minutes for students to read the text. When they have finished, put them in pairs to compare answers and discuss what they learned about Emily.

Answer

journalism

CONTINUED ON PAGE 202

BACKGROUND INFORMATION

There are different ways of searching for a suitable career. One idea is looking at job families. You choose an area that you think would be of interest, for example, journalism and publishing, and then find out related jobs, for example, copywriter for a marketing company, proofreader, web editor, media researcher, etc. Each one might require different skills and qualifications so you can choose the one best for you.

Generally, the factors that lead to higher satisfaction at work are

- doing work that is engaging and interesting with freedom to work as you wish and a variety of tasks
- helping others and seeing the results of your help
- doing something you're good at
- working with people you like and who support you
- work that allows you to enjoy your personal life
- work that doesn't have any major negative aspects to it such as a long journey to work and back, very low wages, an unfair boss and long hours.

PREPARE FOR THE EXAM

2 B2 FIRST FOR SCHOOLS Reading and Use of English Part 5

Briefly review what students need to do in this part of the exam and if necessary, read out the *B2 First for Schools* box on TB page 82.

Remind students that the information in the wrong options is usually mentioned in the text but in a way that shows that these options are incorrect. In that way, each question is like four True/False questions in which we know only one sentence is true. If students find that they are distracted by the four options, they can try to answer the questions in their own words without looking at the options. When they have found the answer, they should find that the choice of correct option is easy to identify.

Set a time limit of ten minutes for students to do the activity and then allow them to compare answers in pairs. Elicit the answers and the reasons for their choices.

FAST FINISHERS

Ask fast finishers to underline any new vocabulary in the text and to look it up in a dictionary. After checking answers to Exercise 2, ask fast finishers to read the definitions out loud to the class, but tell them not to name the word. The rest of the class should try to find the words in the text. Then, students can choose two words and write one sentence for each word.

MIXED ABILITY

Allow students to work in pairs. For each question, each student looks at two of the options and decides whether they are correct or not. If between them they find one correct option, they are probably correct. If they find more than one or none, they have to work together to see which option is the right one.

Answers

1 C (Emily says *The only thing that's clear to me …*, which supports C and rules out A. There are words to suggest options B and D but these are not correct.)
2 A (The phrase *make it* means *become successful*. The sentences before and after the phrase help to clarify the context. The previous sentence explains that very few baseball players end up working for a professional team, and the following sentence says that it will be difficult for musicians to earn money if they are not discovered early.)
3 C (Although Emily recognises that finance careers offer high salaries, it would not satisfy her need for a job which would allow her time off and she would not find it rewarding. A is wrong as we know she is good at economics and maths; B is not supported by the text in terms of being *physically* demanding; and D is not mentioned.)
4 D (Emily's father *talks about being passionate about whatever you do* and her mother *holds the same view*. Although qualifications are mentioned, A is wrong as they are not stated in relation to Emily; B is not mentioned; and C is ruled out because her father has no regrets about his career choices.)
5 D (The answer is supported by the last two sentences of the fifth paragraph. A is tempting because Emily writes *Until recently, I might have laughed at them* but it is wrong because Emily states she is now *jealous* of her friends' plans; B is not correct because Emily says she doesn't mind hard work; and C is wrong because although she questions whether she'd be capable, she is not conclusive about this.)
6 B (The answer is supported where Emily states *I've already written to several local newspapers … referencing my blog and asking them to take a look at it*. A is wrong because she has not been offered any work experience yet; C and D are wrong because she *has been looking into relevant courses* but not the kinds of work she'd like to do and she hasn't applied for a course.)

81 The Reading text is recorded for students to listen, read and check their answers.

TALKING POINTS

Ask the first question to the class and, if anyone says *yes*, elicit what career they are interested in and what planning they have done. Students then work in groups of three or four and think of advantages and disadvantages of following their parents' advice. Set a time limit of two minutes and then elicit ideas from the class.

COOLER

Students work in pairs. One plays the role of a career adviser and the other plays themself. The career adviser thinks of some questions to ask using the aspects from Vocabulary Exercise 1, for example, *Would you mind working long hours?* When they are ready, they ask their partner their questions and note the answers. They then swap roles. When they have both asked and answered their questions, they think about some careers advice for their partner and tell each other what jobs would or wouldn't suit them.

81

THE BIG DECISION

BY EMILY PARKER Posted 8th April

With just over a year of school to go, sooner or later I'll be making some decisions about my future. This has left me wondering whether I want to spend another few years studying or whether I'm actually ready to start making a living. The only thing that's clear to me right now is that my vague teenage dreams of making films, singing in a band, competing in the Olympics or generally earning a fortune while socialising with celebrities are becoming more and more unlikely. It's probably nothing unusual, but I've just come to the realisation that, although I'm good at lots of things, I'm not *brilliant* at anything.

I'm not upset by this. Research about teenagers' career ambitions reveals that those prioritising fame and fortune above other ambitions are likely to earn 20% less in adult life than teenagers who have realised that their futures may be less glamorous. And even if I did have a genuine talent, the statistics aren't encouraging. In baseball, for example, by far the largest sport in the US, only the top 250 amateur players out of every 300,000 will be selected for the professional leagues. For musicians, there's even less chance
line 23 of **making it**. Unless you are discovered before your twenties, which is incredibly unlikely, you'll probably struggle to make a living from your talent.

At school recently, we did an online questionnaire about our academic strengths, interests and career priorities. The aim was to give us all some ideas for the future. OK, so economics and maths are my best subjects. But while having a career in finance might be well paid and earn me far more than most people get, is it really rewarding and would I be able to take plenty of time off?; two things I consider important in a job. And besides, don't people like bankers have to get up really early in the morning? I can do that, but really, *every* morning?

My parents, trying desperately not to influence my decisions, have so far offered limited guidance. My dad, who went into construction straight from school and doesn't regret a thing, talks about being passionate about whatever you do. My mum, a teacher, holds the same view. However, on balance, she feels that qualifications gave her more options when she was ready to decide. But, now and then, I get the feeling she'd rather have done something different.

Most of my friends are in the same position as me. One or two have decided on degrees in medicine or law. Until recently, I might have laughed at them – it takes a long time to qualify in those subjects. I don't mind hard work, but only for something I definitely want to do. And saving someone's life in an operating theatre or giving speeches in a court seems so grown up. Now I'm actually jealous of their plans. Forgetting about the hard work for the moment, or even whether I'd be capable of doing those jobs, their futures are more or less decided: a degree, training and then work. In ten years, they'll all have enjoyable careers.

One thing I do feel positive about is the response I've had to this blog. People seem to enjoy reading it, so I've been wondering whether journalism might be my 'thing' and whether I could make a living with my writing. I've already written to several local newspapers to arrange some work experience and, in my applications, I've been able to prove my interest in journalism by referencing my blog and asking them to take a look at it. I haven't had any replies yet, but I remain hopeful. I've also been looking into relevant courses at local colleges and at some universities, but the length of time required to do a full degree is putting me off. Naturally, I'll keep you updated, so come back soon and I might have some exciting news about my future!

TALKING POINTS

Have you started planning for your future yet?

Do you think it's important for young people to follow their parents' advice when planning their futures?

GRAMMAR Uses of verb + *-ing*

1 **Match the examples to the rules.**

1 People seem to enjoy reading my blog.
2 This has left me wondering whether I want to spend another few years studying.
3 Giving speeches in a court seems so grown up.
4 My dreams of making films are unlikely.
5 I've been looking into relevant courses.
6 My parents, trying desperately not to influence my decisions, have so far offered limited guidance.

We use verb + *-ing*
a as part of continuous verb forms.
b after prepositions.
c after certain verbs, e.g. *like, admit, keep.*
d as the subject, or part of the subject, of a verb.
e after certain phrases, e.g. *spend time.*
f in participle clauses, to give more information about a noun.

» GRAMMAR REFERENCE AND PRACTICE PAGE 165

2 **Complete the story with the *-ing* form of the verbs in the box.**

be	beat	~~invent~~	live	realise
study	think	turn	win	

Hannah Herbst discovered that she liked [0] *inventing* things when she was just 13, after [1] ________ a robot-making competition. At 15, Hannah found out from her penfriend in Africa that many people [2] ________ there didn't have electricity. She started [3] ________ about how she could help and came up with BEACON (Bringing Electricity Access to Countries through Ocean Energy), an invention which captures energy from waves.

Hannah, [4] ________ that many millions of people without electricity live close to the sea, created a simple device that would change their lives. It consists of a plastic tube with a propeller at one end and a hydroelectric generator at the other. The flow of the water creates power by [5] ________ the propeller, which is connected to the generator. [6] ________ light, portable and cheap makes the device particularly practical. [7] ________ hundreds of other young inventors, Hannah was named 'America's Top Young Scientist' for BEACON. Now in her late teens, Hannah is [8] ________ computer science at university. Her future looks bright!

3 **Correct the mistakes in the sentences. There may be more than one mistake.**

1 Your idea about find a job before start college is great.
2 We had loads of fun design a new toy for children.
3 Offer greater bonuses has contributed to raise the motivation of our young sales team.
4 Mason likes use his brain and enjoys do puzzles.
5 Teresa, believe she would help me do my work more quickly, actually slowed me down.

4 **Work with a partner and complete the sentences about you. Use the *-ing* form of a verb.**

1 I can't stand …
2 I spend a lot of time …
3 I don't think it's worth …
4 I'm thinking of … one day.

VOCABULARY Word pairs

1 **Read about word pairs. Then read the examples and match the word pairs to the meanings.**

EP

Word pairs are two words that are joined by a conjunction (usually *and* or *or*). They often have a similar meaning or opposite meanings.

1 Sooner or later, I'll be making some decisions.
2 We walked up and down the corridor, but couldn't find the careers office.
3 My dreams are becoming more and more unlikely.
4 Now and then, I get the feeling she'd rather have done something different.
5 The teacher told us over and over again how important it is to get qualifications.
6 One or two have decided on medicine or law.
7 Their futures are more or less decided.
8 Ideas go round and round in my head, but I still haven't decided on a career.

a almost or approximately
b sometimes, but not very often
c a few
d eventually
e increasingly; as time passes
f in one direction and then in the opposite direction
g moving in a circle without stopping
h happening or done many times

2 **Complete the sentences with the words in the box.**

down	later	less	more (x3)
now	one	over (x2)	round (x2)
sooner	then	two	up

1 We speak online ________ and ________, but in general, we're not in touch any more.
2 We walked ________ and ________ the park for over an hour, but couldn't find you.
3 You should think about it now. ________ or ________, you'll need to make a decision.
4 James has ________ or ________ decided. He's almost definitely going to university.
5 When she heard the news, she started jumping ________ and ________ with excitement.
6 It's becoming ________ and ________ expensive to do a degree.
7 I've got ________ or ________ ideas about my future. But I'm far from certain.
8 I rang the number ________ and ________ again, but got no answer.

3 » **Work in pairs. Turn to page 140.**

GRAMMAR Uses of verb + *ing*

WARMER

With books closed, ask the students to write any sentence they like which includes an *-ing* form of a verb. When they have finished, write a table on the board with the following four headings: *Continuous tense; verb + -ing form, -ing form as subject, preposition + -ing form*.

For each heading ask students to put their hands up if their sentence is or includes an example of this form and elicit one or two examples from the students. Write these on the board in the table. You don't have to write the whole sentence, just the relevant verb form, for example *I'm trying to… I love swimming… Teaching is …, Thanks for coming…* If no one puts their hands up for one or more of the headings, elicit or give students an example of this kind of sentence.

1 Students do the matching in pairs. Elicit the answers and, if you didn't do the Warmer activity, elicit more examples of each kind of sentence. Elicit or tell students that sentence 6 is like a reduced relative clause (*My parents, who are trying desperately …*).

Answers

1c 2e 3d 4b 5a 6f

» GRAMMAR REFERENCE AND PRACTICE ANSWER KEY TB PAGE 269

2 Look at the instruction with the class. Elicit that, as they know that all the verbs need the *-ing* form, all they have to think about is the meaning of the verbs and where they should go in the text. Students work alone and compare answers in pairs. Before they start comparing, ask students to spell each word to make it more challenging. Remind them that verbs ending in *e* usually drop the *e* when *-ing* is added. Elicit the answers and which rule each use of the *-ing* form corresponds to.

MIXED ABILITY

Put students into pairs and give some clues to students, for example 1, 7 – should these be *beating* or *winning*? 3, 5 – should these be *realising* or *thinking*? Monitor and help students where necessary. You could make all the gaps a choice of two if necessary (2, 8 *living* / *studying*, 5, 6 *being* / *turning*).

Answers

1 winning (b) 2 living (f) 3 thinking (c) 4 realising (f)
5 turning (b) 6 Being (d) 7 Beating (f) 8 studying (a)

3 Tell the students that, as well as finding the mistakes and deciding which verbs should be written with the *-ing* form, they should also decide which rule each one corresponds to. Students work alone and compare answers in pairs. Elicit the answers and rules. Point out that although state verbs, such as *believe* and *understand*, are not usually used in continuous forms, they can have an *-ing* form when used as the subject of the sentence, in participle clauses (as in sentence 5), after a preposition and after certain verbs and phrases.

Answers

1 Your idea about **finding** a job before **starting** college is great. (b)
2 We had loads of fun **designing** a new toy for children. (e)
3 **Offering** greater bonuses has contributed to **raising** the motivation of our young sales team. (d), (b) 4 Mason likes **using** his brain and enjoys **doing** puzzles. (c), (c) 5 Teresa, **believing** she would help me do my work more quickly, actually slowed me down. (f)

4 Tell students to write their own sentences and also to try to guess what their partner has written. When they have both finished, they start by saying what they think their partner has written and then tell each other their own sentences. Partners should ask follow-up questions. Encourage them in particular to ask *Why* questions and to ask other partners to justify their opinions, where appropriate. Invite students to share some of their sentences with the class. Students give their own answers.

» GRAMMAR WORKSHEET UNIT 18

VOCABULARY Word pairs

1 With books closed, read the explanation aloud and write on the board:

… and …

… or …

Give students some clues for word pairs and try to elicit them by saying 'a popular form of music that Elvis Presley sang' (*rock and roll*); 'the colour of films before they were made in colour' (*black and white*); 'what people often use to eat meals with' (*knife and fork*), 'a kind of reading comprehension task' (*true or false*) and 'two possible reactions to an idea' (*for or against*).

Students then open their books and complete the exercise. You can extend this activity by asking students to write three sentences about themselves using the word pairs. Tell them to share their sentences with their partner and ask questions to find out more information about each one.

Answers

1d 2f 3e 4b 5h 6c 7a 8g

2 Tell students to think of the meaning which is needed and then to complete the sentence. Students work alone and compare in pairs. Elicit the answers and the meanings of the sentences.

FAST FINISHERS

Ask fast finishers to think of a question they could ask other students in the class about the information in the sentences, for example, *Is there anyone you speak to online now and then? Have you ever walked round and round somewhere looking for someone?* etc. When everyone has finished the activity, elicit the answers and then invite the fast finishers to ask their questions to the class.

Answers

1 now, then 2 round, round 3 Sooner, later 4 more, less
5 up, down 6 more, more 7 one, two 8 over, over

3 Look at the questions with the students and give some example answers for yourself, for example, *When I have worries going round and round in my head, I go for a walk and try to concentrate on the things I can see around me. Then I feel better, and, sometimes work out how to solve my worries.* Before the students ask and answer the questions, ask them to think of a similar question using a different phrase from Exercise 1. When the students have asked and answered the questions in the exercise, they can change partners and ask their final question to their new partner. Invite students to share some of their own questions with the class. Students give their own answers.

» VOCABULARY WORKSHEET UNIT 18

LISTENING

PREPARE FOR THE EXAM

1 B2 FIRST FOR SCHOOLS Listening Part 4

Briefly review what students need to do in this part of the exam and if necessary, read out the *B2 First for Schools* box on TB page 118.

Look at the first question with the students and elicit that *Aiden*, *idea* and *business* are all key words as that is what they need to listen out for. In the options, useful words could be *parents suggested, neighbours, supply, clothes, profitable*. Students do the same in pairs for the other questions. Monitor and help with ideas where necessary. Elicit ideas and remind students that all of the options will be mentioned in some way but only one will be correct.

Possible answers

1 Aiden, idea, business, parents suggested, neighbours, supply, clothes, selling used items, profitable
2 problem, ran out of space, weren't enough good T-shirts, too long to repair
3 business, now, brother, creates, buys, other countries, sells, original designs
4 paperwork, grateful, help, lack of skill, isn't much
5 hardest, school, work, doesn't, do his best, business more interesting, school, isn't, flexible
6 friends, useful suggestions, fed up, not interested
7 summer jobs, working hard, success, deal with people, making a living

82 **2** Tell students that they will hear the recording twice. They should use the second listening to check their ideas so that they can be sure they haven't made a mistake. Elicit the answers and the information in the recording which helped them to decide.

Answers

1 C (A is wrong because although he chatted to his dad about selling T-shirts, it was Aiden who had the idea; B is ruled out as he says there *was no shortage of stuff*.)
2 B (A is wrong because although he admits that *at one point, our garage … was pretty full*, there is no suggestion that he ran out of space; C is wrong because the mention is of T-shirts being *impossible to fix*.)
3 C (A is incorrect because his brother only pointed out designs on the web; B is wrong because although Aiden used to import T-shirts, he no longer does this.)
4 A (B is not correct because although he finds it challenging, he does not express surprise, and C is wrong because his parents *do a fair amount of it*.)
5 A (B is not mentioned and C is wrong because the online school he attends is very flexible.)
6 C (A is wrong because it is his family who give him useful suggestions and B is ruled out because it is only sometimes that Aiden can't see his friends, when he is busy.)
7 B (A is not correct because although he worked for little money, he doesn't mention anything about it being the key to success; C is ruled out because the jobs he did were for *not much money*.)

» AUDIOSCRIPT TB PAGES 303–304

SPEAKING Agreeing and disagreeing

1 Before students look at the questions ask them to choose one photo and describe it to their partner. The partner listens and says which photo it is. Students then discuss the questions together. Set a time limit of three minutes. When students have finished, invite different pairs to describe one of the jobs without saying what the job is using the aspects of a job vocabulary from page 102. The other students guess the job.

Answers

Students' own answers

83 **2** Read the instructions with the class. Elicit the answers and the questions asked. Ask students to listen again to note any phrases used to ask for each other's opinions.

Answers

1 All of them except the cleaner (B). 2 Yes, they do. 3 Yes, Conor does. He asks 'What do you think?' and 'What do you reckon?'.

83 **3** Look at the *Prepare to speak* box with the class. When they have listened once more and given the answers, point out that *Fair enough* is used slightly differently to the other phrases. In the recording Leila was quite negative about being a waiter but Conor pointed out an advantage of the job. That's when Leila used *Fair enough*. She used it to agree with Conor even though he was disagreeing with her argument. Give the students another example, for example: '*Let's go shopping.*' '*No, it'll be busy. And it's a nice day. We should do something outside.*' '*Fair enough. How about going cycling?*'.

Answers

Conor: I can't really see the point of; That's a good point; I agree up to a point, but
Leila: I'm not sure about that; I'm with you on that; I'm not convinced; Absolutely; Fair enough; I'd rather I didn't

» AUDIOSCRIPT TB PAGE 304

4 Tell the students to discuss the first two questions as if they were doing an exam task. First, they have two minutes to discuss the first question. When they have finished, ask students how many of the phrases from the *Prepare to speak* box they used. They now do the same thing for the second question and try to use phrases they didn't use before. Finally, discuss the third question with the class and encourage students to ask each other's opinions and agree and disagree using the phrases in the box.

Answers

Students' own answers

COOLER

Put students into groups of three or four. Each person chooses a different job from the photos on page 105. They then imagine they have been doing this job for several weeks and that they have now met up and are discussing their jobs. Students ask each other what they are doing, and what they like and dislike about their jobs. Set a time limit of four minutes and then invite students to tell the class what they said about their jobs.

LISTENING

PREPARE FOR THE EXAM

Listening Part 4

1 **You will hear an interview with a boy called Aiden Cass, who started up his own T-shirt business. Read the questions and <u>underline</u> the words that might help you when you listen.**

1 What gave Aiden the idea for his business?
A One of his parents suggested it.
B His neighbours couldn't supply him with enough clothes.
C He realised selling used items could be very profitable.

2 The most **significant** problem that Aiden encountered was that
A he ran out of space to keep the T-shirts in.
B there weren't enough good T-shirts to sell.
C the T-shirts took too long to repair.

3 How does Aiden's business work now?
A His brother creates the T-shirts that it sells.
B He buys T-shirts from other countries.
C He sells T-shirts with original designs.

4 How does Aiden feel about paperwork?
A grateful to receive help with it
B surprised by his lack of skill with it
C pleased that there isn't very much to do

5 The hardest thing for Aiden about combining school and work is that
A he doesn't always do his best at school.
B he often finds his business more interesting.
C his school isn't very flexible.

6 In general, how do Aiden's friends feel about his business?
A They're eager to make useful suggestions.
B They're fed up because they can't spend time with him now.
C They're not as interested in it as he expected.

7 Summer jobs taught Aiden
A how working hard is the key to success.
B how to deal with people well.
C the importance of making a living.

2 82 **Listen to the interview. For questions 1–7, choose the best answer (A, B or C). Then listen again and check.**

SPEAKING Agreeing and disagreeing

1 **Work in pairs. Look at the photos of summer jobs. Answer the questions.**

1 What are the good and bad things about each job?
2 Would you like to do this as a job? Why? / Why not?

83 **2** **Listen to Conor and Leila discussing five of the jobs in the photos. Answer the questions.**

1 Which jobs do they talk about?
2 Do they take turns to talk?
3 Do they ask each other's opinions?

83 **3** **Read the *Prepare to speak* box. Then listen again. Who uses each phrase? Write C (Conor) or L (Leila).**

PREPARE TO SPEAK Agreeing and disagreeing

Agreeing

I'm with you on that.	Absolutely!
That's a good point.	Fair enough.

Disagreeing

I'm not sure about that.
I can't really see the point of …
I'm not convinced.
I agree up to a point, but …
I'd rather I didn't …

4 **Discuss the questions. Use phrases from the *Prepare to speak* box to agree or disagree with each other.**

1 What kind of things might you learn from the summer jobs in Exercise 1?
2 Which would you most or least like to do?
3 Do you think it's a good idea for teenagers to do summer jobs? Why? / Why not?

CULTURE

FAN CULTURE

1 **Ask and answer the questions with a partner.**

1 Are you a big fan of anything?
2 What do you think 'fan culture' means?

2 **Read the article on page 107 quickly. Which of the following are mentioned?**

1 the origins of the word *fandom*
2 examples of fandoms
3 things that participants in fandoms do
4 searching for the right fandom for you
5 how to start a fandom
6 advantages and disadvantages of fandoms

3 **Read the article again and answer the questions.**

1 Which group of fans are not normally considered to be members of a 'fandom'?
2 How does 'fan fiction' differ from normal fiction?
3 How can feeling a connection with a character, celebrity or show help people?
4 How do members of fandoms help each other?
5 What are the signs of an obsessive fan?

4 **Match the highlighted words and phrases in the article to the meanings.**

1 a series of films that have the same or similar titles and are about the same characters
2 sharing the same opinions, ideas or interests
3 very likely
4 feeling that you are in the right place or group
5 when too much of something pleasant becomes unpleasant

84 **5** **Listen to an interview about spoilers. Number the topics in the order you hear them.**

A a brief history of spoilers in entertainment
B reasons why some people like to see spoilers
C what a spoiler is
D trying to keep the details of a film secret

84 **6** **Listen to the interview again and decide whether the statements are true (*T*), false (*F*) or not mentioned (*NM*).**

1 The presenter doesn't know what her guest is going to talk about.
2 People tell spoilers about books, films, TV shows, etc. because it makes them feel powerful.
3 Spoilers have only existed since the arrival of social media.
4 Filmmakers always avoid putting spoilers in trailers.
5 The social media campaign against spoilers by fans of *Fantastic Beasts* was a success.
6 In the study mentioned by the lecturer, spoilers made the story less enjoyable to readers.

7 **Complete the sentences with the words in the box.**

admiration	characters	connection
lose	obsessive	participants

USEFUL LANGUAGE

Talking about fans and fandoms

1 They are active ________ in the *Whovian* fandom.
2 The subject of their ________ is Taylor Swift.
3 She felt a strong ________ with her favourite character.
4 *Shipping* is when fans want people or ________ to form relationships.
5 Sometimes fans ________ themselves in a character's experience.
6 ________ fans are often referred to as 'stans'.

106 CULTURE

CULTURE

Learning Objectives

- The students learn about fans and fandoms.
- In the project stage, the students research a fandom and present their findings to the class.

Vocabulary

belonging franchise like-minded too much of a good thing undoubtedly

Resources

CULTURE VIDEO AND CULTURE VIDEO WORKSHEET: Fantastic fans

BACKGROUND INFORMATION

In 1893, Sir Arthur Conan Doyle decided to kill off Sherlock Holmes in *The Adventure of the Final Problem*. When the story came out, many fans in London wore black armbands to mourn his death. It was the first sign of organised fandom. In 1934, an official Sherlock Holmes fan club, The Baker Street Irregulars, was set up and, in 2010, the first female only Sherlock Holmes fan club, The Baker Street Babes, was formed.

Doctor Who is a British TV series made by the BBC. It first started in 1963. The series is about 'the Doctor', an alien time lord who can travel in time and space in his spaceship which looks like a police telephone box but which is 'bigger on the inside'. There aren't many of these in existence now but, when the series started, they were a common sight in Britain. When the Doctor dies, he regenerates into a new body so the character can continue with a new actor. In 2017, the Doctor regenerated into a female for the first time. The name 'Whovians' was first used by the American fan club but it is now used more widely. There is even an Australian quiz show called *Whovians* in which celebrity fans answer questions and discuss the show.

Fan fiction is nothing new. *Old Friends and New Fancies*, a sequel to the novels of Jane Austen, was published in 1913. There are over 200 books of fan fiction based on Jane Austen novels. The Baker Street Journal, a magazine devoted to Sherlock Holmes, included fans' own stories including 'self-insert fiction' where the writer meets the characters and becomes a part of the story.

WARMER

Read out some categories, for example 1 TV series; 2 film series; 3 band or singer; 4 team; 5 vlogger, and ask the class to write down their favourite for each.

When students have finished, ask them to share their ideas in pairs and say how much they like each one, for example: *My favourite TV series is* Stranger Things. *I've watched every episode four or five times!* Invite students to share some of their ideas with the class and ask if anyone follows any celebrities on social media or if they have managed to get a selfie with anyone famous.

1 Elicit the difference between a fan of something and someone who just likes something, for example, *a fan may spend more time reading about the thing they like or collecting items associated with it*. Students then discuss the questions and share their ideas as a class. If the students aren't sure, tell them that *fan culture involves taking part in collective activities such as going to conventions or creating something*, for example blogs or videos.

Answers

Students' own answers

2 Set a time limit of three minutes for students to skim read the text quickly. When they have finished, they discuss in pairs which of the things in Exercise 2 they found information about and any details they can remember. Ask students to close their books. Ask about each of the six things in the exercise and elicit any details students found out about each one. (*For 2, examples of fandom include Potterheads, Whovians, Swifties and Sherlock Holmes fandom. For 3, activities include attending Comic Cons, creating and sharing fan fiction and fan art. For 6, advantages include helping each other out with advice and support, getting involved in social activism, forming relationships, increasing their sense of belonging; disadvantages include finding it hard to feel empathy for people who don't share their interest, feeling frustrated, disliking non-fans.*)

Answers

2, 3 and 6 are mentioned.

3 Students work alone to find the information needed to answer each question. They then cover the text and discuss the answers in pairs. With the text still covered, elicit the answers and see how much detail students can give. Ask what they learned from the text, for example *I didn't know that Harry Potter fans were called Potterheads!*

FAST FINISHERS

Look at the different words and phrases made from the word *fan*, for example *fanatic, fandom, fan fiction*. Ask fast finishers to find other examples of word building or phrases using other words; for example, *benefit – beneficial, comic – comic cons* (comic conventions). When everyone has finished, invite fast finishers to share the words they found with the class. (Useful words include: *obsessive, participants, subculture, admiration, imaginary, relationship, connection, momentarily, activism, universal, interpersonal, enthusiastic, like-minded, empathise, psychological.*)

Answers

1 sport(s) fans
2 Fans write their own stories, using characters from their favourite film, TV series, etc.
3 They feel a part of something bigger, and 'lose' themselves in a character's experiences, which can help them forget about their own worries and problems for a short time.
4 They give each other advice and support.
5 Finding it hard to feel empathy for people in other groups, disliking non-fans.

CONTINUED ON PAGE 210

85 The Reading text is recorded for students to listen, read and check their answers.

4 Tell students to cover the meanings and look at the highlighted words. Ask the students for an example of a movie franchise (for example, *Marvel superheroes films*). They look at the second word and ask if the writer is certain or uncertain about the reason (*certain*). For the third word, ask what people can belong to (*a club, an organisation,* etc.) and how they might feel if they have a sense of belonging (*feel a part of a club or group*). For the next word, ask, 'What is your mind?' (*the part of the body which allows you to think and feel*) and ask what you might have in common with like-minded people (*interests, opinions,* etc). Finally, ask what good things it is possible to have too much of and why, for example *fast food – unhealthy, free time – get bored*). Students then do the matching activity alone.

Answers
1 franchise 2 like-minded 3 undoubtedly 4 belonging
5 too much of a good thing

84 **5** Look at the questions and elicit what a spoiler is (*details of a film or programme that reveals important information about what is going to happen*). Ask the students if they have ever read or been told a spoiler before they saw a film or TV series and how they felt. You could also elicit any steps the students take to avoid spoilers. Encourage students to make brief notes about each of the points mentioned. Elicit the order and any other details students remember from the recording.

Answers
1 C 2 A 3 D 4 B

84 **6** Tell students to read through the sentences and discuss in pairs anything they think they can remember from the first listening task. Students then listen and discuss the sentences again. Elicit the answers and the information in the text which helped them to decide. Follow up by having a class survey to see who hates spoilers and who doesn't mind knowing the ending or important details before they see a film or TV series. Invite students to say why.

MIXED ABILITY

Put weaker students into pairs and tell one student to listen out for 1, 3 and 5 and the other to listen for 2, 4, 6. They then share the information they heard and what they think the answers should be.

Answers
1 F (She doesn't say what the show is going to be about because she doesn't want to spoil the surprise for listeners.)
2 T
3 F (Spoilers have existed throughout history.)
4 F (Filmmakers sometimes intentionally put spoilers in trailers as a marketing technique.)
5 NM (The lecturer doesn't say whether the campaign was a success or not.)
6 F (In the study, readers who read the story with spoilers enjoyed it more than those who read the story without spoilers.)

» **AUDIOSCRIPT TB PAGES 304–305**

7 Students may have looked at some of these words in the Fast finishers activity for Exercise 3. Look at the words in the box and elicit which two refer to people (*characters, participants*). Ask what verbs *admiration* and *connection* are formed from (*to admire, to connect*) and what noun can be formed from *obsessive* (*obsession*). Students then complete the sentences in pairs. Elicit the answers and ask students to try to rephrase the sentences, for example, *1 They take an active part in the Whovian fandom. 2 They admire Taylor Swift.*

Answers
1 participants 2 admiration 3 connection 4 characters 5 lose
6 Obsessive

PROJECT ***Researching a fandom***

Remind students or re-elicit the areas in which fandom is important, for example *comic books, films, TV series, musicians (bands and singers), vloggers*. Write these on the board. Put the students into groups of four where possible. Look at the first point with the class and try to ensure that all the groups are going to research a different fandom. Allow them five minutes in the lesson to decide on what they are going to research and how they are going to divide up the work involved. Once the presentations are ready, students should also work together in their groups to think of questions they would like to know the answers to about the other fandoms. If they don't hear the answers to their questions during the presentations, they can ask their questions after the presenatations to find out the information.

When the groups have presented their projects, ask them what the most interesting or the strangest thing they found out about the fans they were researching.

PROJECT EXTENSION

Allocate each group an area to think of: TV series, film, comic book or musician. They must think of one example in that area that they all like or know well but which no one did a presentation on. They then work together to create their own fandom group. They decide on a name for their group and what sort of activities their group will do and what things they create to show their fandom. They can be imaginative and create logos or images to represent their fandom.

When they are ready, each group presents their ideas to the class and the class work together to decide which fandom group they liked best.

15 **CULTURE VIDEO: Fantastic fans**

When students have completed the lesson, they can watch the video and complete the worksheet.

COOLER

Ask students to complete the question 'Are you a fan of …?'. Students then mingle and ask other students in the class. When they answer each other's questions, they should give details about why they are or aren't fans. Set a time limit of three or four minutes and then invite students to share some of the interesting answers they were given.

FAN OR FANATIC?

Did you know the word 'fan' is short for 'fanatic'? This is because in the past, many people held negative views about fans, confusing their passion with obsessive behaviour. But things have changed, and psychologists now talk about fans as 'active participants in a culture or community'. This change in attitude has drawn our attention to 'fandoms', which is a subculture made up of people who are fans of the same thing, who share a common interest and who connect with other fans. The subject of their admiration could be a TV series, a band, a series of books, a movie franchise, a celebrity or any other form of culture or interest. Although supporters of a sports team or sportsperson can be said to be members of fandoms, the term isn't usually used for sports fans. Popular fandoms include *Potterheads* (yes, you guessed it – for Harry Potter fans), *Whovians* (Doctor Who fans) and *Swifties* (Taylor Swift fans).

Members of fandoms often take part in activities like attending Comic Cons, which are conventions for fans of comic genres, or creating and sharing new 'fan fiction'. This is when fans themselves write their own short stories using the characters from their favourite TV, book or film series, or even their favourite singers or actors. The term *shipping* is often used in fandoms and it comes from the word 'relation**ship**'. This is when fans would like to see real-life people or fictional characters form a romantic relationship. Fans create fan fiction or art of the imaginary relationship and often publish it on the internet.

Fandoms are not a new idea – in the late 19th Century, fans of Sherlock Holmes created what's considered to be the first fandom.

FANTASTIC FANDOMS

85

People become fans for many different reasons. But, undoubtedly, a big reason is to feel a strong connection with a favourite character, celebrity or show. Their story or struggle can feel like our own, and fans experience being a part of something much bigger than themselves. Some fans also find that they can let go of their own identity and 'lose' themselves in a character's experiences. They can step into Harry Potter's shoes and empathise with his fears and triumphs. This can be beneficial, as it allows them to momentarily forget about the worries and problems in their own lives. In addition, studies have found that many fans contribute to the real world in positive ways. They participate in social activism and form networks with other fans where they can help each other with advice and support.

Human beings have an almost universal need to form and maintain some kind of interpersonal relationship with others. Fandom participants can increase their sense of belonging by building large communities – spaces where fans can be enthusiastic about their passions – with like-minded people from all over the world. And many fans also get together in real life at conventions.

TAKING FANDOM TOO FAR?

Fandoms are not without their negative side, though, and too much of a good thing can also lead to unwanted consequences. Obsessive fans, often referred to as 'stans', can find it really hard to feel empathy for people in other groups, or towards anyone who doesn't share their interest. Feeling frustrated and disliking or even hating non-fans is a sure sign that someone is experiencing the negative side of fandom.

While having interests and being part of a community are good for our psychological well-being, fans shouldn't let their fandom become their whole world. It's important to have a range of different interests and hobbies.

PROJECT
Researching a fandom

Work in groups of three or four to research a fandom. Use these steps to help you.

1. Search for and then agree on a fandom you all want to know more about.
2. Research information about the fandom.
   - What does it call itself?
   - Does it have conventions or fan meetings?
   - What do the fans wear?
3. Find some images or videos of the fans.
4. Create a presentation.

Present your research to the class.

15 NOW WATCH THE CULTURE VIDEO

19 POINTS OF VIEW

ABOUT YOU

Do you have strong opinions and beliefs?
What issues in the news concern you the most at the moment?

VOCABULARY Opinions and beliefs

1 **Look at photos A–D. What issue do you think each photo represents?**

86 **2** **Listen and match the conversations to photos A–D. What issue is being discussed in each conversation?**

3 **Match the sentence halves.**

EP
1 You have to bear in mind
2 I've never been
3 They could,
4 You should keep an open mind
5 I'm totally against students
6 I'd go along with

a convinced by that argument.
b about allowing mobile phones in schools.
c that their careers are short.
d using their phones at school.
e that view.
f to my mind, easily get another job after playing.

7 What are your views on
8 It's hard to deny that it
9 As far as I'm concerned,
10 I suspect this is true,
11 There's no doubt
12 I firmly believe in

g that you're more independent when you're older.
h enjoying yourself while you've got the chance.
i people just need to eat less meat.
j vegetarianism?
k must be better for you.
l to be honest.

86 **4** **Listen again and check.**

5 **Work in pairs. Look at photos A–D again. What is your opinion on these issues? Discuss your opinions. Use phrases from Exercise 3.**

READING

1 **Read the article about the teenage brain quickly, ignoring the gaps. According to the article, which statement is true?**

A Teenagers need to spend less time thinking about their emotions.
B Teenage brains have some advantages and disadvantages over adult brains.
C The differences between adult and teenage brains are now becoming understood by scientists.
D Adults need to make more of an effort to understand the way teenagers think.

PREPARE FOR THE EXAM

Reading and Use of English Part 6

2 **Six sentences have been removed from the article. Choose from the sentences A–G the one which fits each gap (1–6). There is one extra sentence which you do not need to use.**

A This is the area we use for thinking carefully about something in order to make a decision.
B Dramatic conclusions like this might have made good headlines at the time, but we now know that evidence for any truth in them is weak.
C If teenagers spend more time with adults, there is more opportunity for them to learn how to make thoughtful decisions.
D It is able to absorb huge amounts of information, and the opportunity is there to make the most of this by putting energy into learning, experimenting and seeking out new experiences.
E All participants were asked to identify the feelings their expressions represented.
F During the discussions, the young people reacted more emotionally than the adults, and researchers concluded that emotions develop faster than the parts of the brain that help people to manage them.
G However, a number of studies using brain scanning equipment have since led to an understanding that it is the teenage brain itself that is not the same as an adult one.

19 POINTS OF VIEW

Unit Overview

TOPIC	Our thoughts and brains
VOCABULARY	Opinions and beliefs
READING	Explaining your brain
GRAMMAR	Subject–verb agreement
VOCABULARY	Plural nouns
WRITING	An essay (4)
EXAM TASKS	Reading and Use of English Part 6; Writing Part 1

Resources

GRAMMAR REFERENCE AND PRACTICE: SB page 166; TB page 269
PREPARE FOR THE EXAM: SB pages on TB pages 242–243 and 246; TB pages 256 and 258
WORKBOOK: pages 76–79
PHOTOCOPIABLE WORKSHEETS: Grammar worksheet Unit 19; Vocabulary worksheet Unit 19
TEST GENERATOR: Unit test 19
PRACTICE EXTRA: Unit 19

WARMER

Put the students into groups of three or four. Ask them to think of any statements that their friends or family have made over the last few days that they have either strongly agreed or disagreed with, for example, *My sister said that it's a waste of money to drink in cafés, but I disagree. It's a nice place to meet friends and you can make one drink last a long time.* Set a time limit of three minutes then invite students to share some of their ideas with the class.

ABOUT YOU

Read the questions in the *About you* box with the students. Give students a minute to think alone about their answers to the two questions then put them in groups of three or four to discuss their ideas. Invite students with strong opinions to tell the class what they are.

VOCABULARY Opinions and beliefs

1 Elicit descriptions of what the students can see in the photos. Next, look at photo A with the class and give students one or two ideas about what it could represent, for example, *it could be someone who is eating a vegetarian or vegan burger and who is strongly against eating meat.* Students then work in pairs to think of more ideas for each of the photos.

Answers
Students' own answers

86 **2** When you have played the recording, elicit the order and the issues in each. Tell students to work in pairs. One student writes down the first speaker's opinion and the second writes down alternative ideas said by the other speaker. Play the recording again and elicit what the two speaker's opinions on each issue were (see teaching notes in Exercise 5 for opinions). Don't ask for the students' opinions yet.

Answers
1 B how much professional sportspeople are paid
2 C should students be able to have their phones in school
3 A healthy eating and vegetarianism
4 D is it better to be a teenager or an adult

3 Students work alone and match either the first six sentence halves or the halves in the second group. They then get together in pairs and tell each other what they think and correct each other if they think their partner is wrong. Do not correct their answers yet.

86 **4** Play the recording and pause it after each dialogue. Elicit which sentences were used in that conversation and then do the same for the other three conversations (*Conversation 1: 1–3; Conversation 2: 4–6; Conversation 3: 7–9; Conversation 4: 10–12*). When you have elicited all the sentences, elicit which phrases are used for giving an opinion, agreeing and disagreeing.

Answers
1 c 2 a 3 f 4 b 5 d 6 e 7 j 8 k 9 i 10 l 11 g 12 h

» AUDIOSCRIPT TB PAGE 305

5 Re-elicit the opinions given by the two speakers in each dialogue and any reasons they give for them (*1 sportspeople are paid too much, short career, earn as much in six months as most people in a lifetime, could get a different job after playing; 2 students shouldn't bring phones into school, check them often, distracting, maybe not a ban; 3 vegetarianism is better for you, some meat is very fatty and unhealthy, should eat less meat; 4 being an adult is better than being a teenager, adults have more freedom, more independent, more responsibilities too, enjoy yourself while you can*). Students then have similar dialogues about each issue; making sure to give their opinions. Monitor and help where necessary and encourage students to use the phrases in blue. When the students have finished, discuss the issues as a class.

Answers
Students' own answers

READING

1 Set a time limit of three minutes for students to read the text quickly and allow them to discuss their ideas in pairs. Elicit which statement is true and how the students know. (*scientists now believe there is no doubt that teenagers' brains work quite differently to adults' brains. … As far as scientists are concerned, it is clear that the teenage stage is significant for the brain …*)

Answer
C

CONTINUED ON PAGE 214

BACKGROUND INFORMATION

Scientists have identified five different kinds of decision making: rational, dependent, intuitive, avoidant and spontaneous. The rational style means logically thinking about the pros and cons of a decision. Intuitive people rely on their feelings and experience. Dependent people tend to ask for advice from other people. The avoidance style means that people try to put off decision making for as long as possible. The spontaneous style means making decisions quickly without much or any thought. Research hasn't found any clear differences between decision-making styles at different ages.

However, as teenagers' brains work differently to adults' brains, there are things they are more and less likely to do. Things they are more likely to do are:

- act on impulse without thinking of the consequences
- misunderstand social cues
- get into fights
- take risks and have accidents.

Things they are less likely to do are:

- think before they act
- change the way they behave.

Injuries causing death in teens aged 15–19 is about six times higher than for 10–14-year-olds. This can be partly explained by greater opportunity for risk, for example, being able to drive or stay out late, but it also shows that teenagers do take more risks and can act more wildly than younger children and adults. This is reflected in car insurance rates which start falling as people go past the age of 20. However, insurers still believe there is a greater risk right up to the age of 25.

PREPARE FOR THE EXAM

2 B2 FIRST FOR SCHOOLS Reading and Use of English Part 6

Briefly review what students need to do in this part of the exam and if necessary, read out the *B2 First for Schools* box on TB page 38.

Remind students that, in this activity, they have to use clues in the text and the sentences to decide where they should go. These can be based on the content of the text or pronouns or other words in the sentences which link to people or things in the preceding or following sentences.

Look at sentence A with the class and elicit that 'This is the area' obviously links back to something just mentioned in the text. If we put the sentence in the correct gap, we should know what the area is. Tell students to spend the first minute looking at the sentences and underlining words which could link in some way with ideas in the text. They then compare their ideas in pairs. Set a time limit of ten minutes for the reading and then elicit the answers and the words and phrases in the sentences and text which helped them to decide.

FAST FINISHERS

Tell any fast finishers to look back at the text and underline any sentences they find interesting or surprising, for example, *teenagers' brains work quite differently to adults' brains*. Elicit some examples after checking the answers to Exercise 2.

MIXED ABILITY

You could help weaker students by telling them which sentence isn't needed. Also, while they are looking at the sentences before they do the reading, monitor and help them identify which words are important and what they might expect to see in the text around the sentences.

Answers

1 G (this sentence refers to what has happened since the time people believed hormones were responsible for differences in behaviour and thought. It also links to the following sentence in the text about the fact that teenage and adult brains are different from each other.)
2 E (the missing sentence outlines the experiment, and the sentence after the gap gives the results of the study.)
3 A (the word *area* in the missing sentence refers back to the part of the brain known as the frontal cortex.)
4 F (the missing sentence refers to how the teenagers reacted during the experiments and what the researchers concluded, which links to the sentence following the gap: *This explains …*)
5 B (the missing sentence links to the example of a *dramatic conclusion*, that playing video games or watching too much TV is *biologically unhealthy*.)
6 D (the word *It* in the missing sentence refers back to *The brain* in the previous sentence.)
Extra sentence: C

87 The Reading text is recorded for students to listen, read and check their answers.

3 Look at the first highlighted word with the students. Ask, 'Which stage does everyone go through?' (*being a teenager*) and 'What might the highlighted word mean?' (*going from starting teenage life to finishing it*). Students then look at the other words in pairs, discussing what they might mean before doing the matching. Elicit the meanings of the words and elicit alternative situations in which each could be used, for example, ask: 'What controversial topics do your parents not like talking about?' and 'What difficult situations do people have to go through in their lives?'.

Answers

1 controversial 2 patterns 3 adulthood 4 go through 5 stress

TALKING POINTS

Put students into groups of three or four and read the questions together as a class. Ask them to think of the examples given in the text first and then to try to think of their own examples. Set a time limit of three minutes and elicit ideas.

COOLER

Look at this sentence from the final paragraph of the text: *This may be by studying, by gaining new skills such as creating music or art, or by exploring the world.*

Put students into groups of three or four and ask them to discuss new skills they have learned since becoming a teenager and skills they would like to learn before they reach the age of 20.

Set a time limit of three minutes and then invite groups to share their ideas with the class.

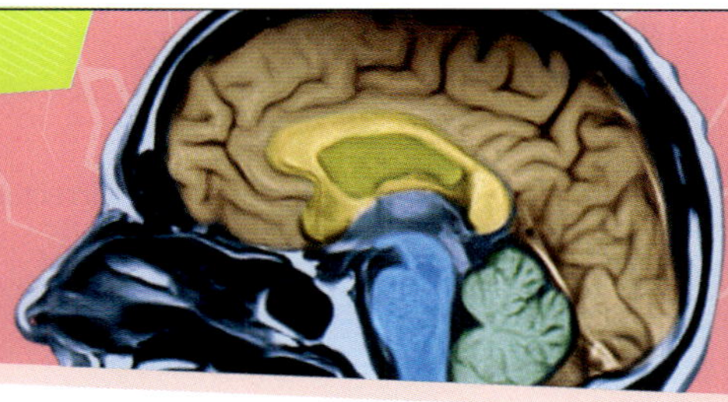

EXPLAINING YOUR BRAIN

87

Being a teenager is not unique to humans, although this stage in life lasts longer than the similar phase does for, say, primates or whales. But why do animals, and in particular humans, go through this stage? Scientists have offered different views on this: some believe long human lifespans have simply made room for this growth phase. Others think these years are needed to learn about the complex ways in which humans behave socially. The truth is that no one is even close to knowing about the brain, but scientists are getting nearer to understanding its complexities.

By the age of 12, the human brain is fully grown in size, and scientists once firmly believed that it was also fully developed. While they recognised that teenage behaviours and thoughts often differ from those of adults, including things like sleeping patterns and ideas about the world, scientists blamed these on hormones, the chemicals that control the way the human body grows and develops. [1] ________ In short, scientists now believe there is no doubt that teenagers' brains work quite differently to adults' brains.

In one study, teenagers and adults were shown photos of people's faces. [2] ________ The results surprised researchers. One of the pictures was of someone with an apparently obvious look of fear on their face. All the adults in the test were able to recognise this, but the teenagers believed the face was either surprised or angry. What accounted for this difference in interpretation?

Using scanning equipment, scientists observed which parts of the brain were active during the experiment. The adults used the part of their brain called the frontal cortex. [3] ________ In contrast, the teenagers' brain activity was in the amygdala, the region that handles instant reactions, which are often emotional. What's more, the older the teenagers in the group were, the more they used the frontal cortex for mental processing, just as adults do.

Another study asked groups of teenagers and their parents to talk about potentially controversial subjects, such as the amount of freedom teenagers should be given. The researchers found that young people with a larger amygdala are likely to have stronger opinions on such subjects than those who don't and, as a result, parents and teenagers are more likely to end up in conflict with each other. [4] ________ This explains why teenagers genuinely feel angry or upset by events that adults may think are insignificant.

Initially, some people used the research to support the argument that it could be biologically unhealthy for teenagers to play video games or watch a lot of TV. [5] ________ Fortunately, such ideas have since been abandoned. However, most scientists stress that while considerable progress has been made in our understanding of the teenage brain, our overall knowledge of the brain is still very limited. They encourage us to bear in mind that drawing too many conclusions from research is irresponsible.

As far as scientists are concerned, it is clear that the teenage stage is significant for the brain because of its flexibility. [6] ________ This may be by studying, by gaining new skills such as creating music or art, or by exploring the world. The important news is that the teenage years are a time of great change for the brain and a time when young people start to develop to their full potential as they move towards adulthood.

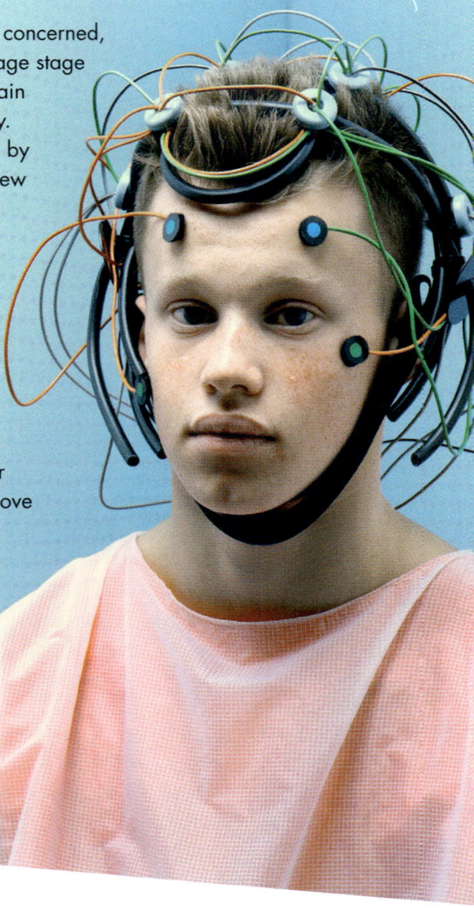

3 **Match the highlighted words and phrases in the article to the meanings.**

1. causing disagreement
2. the particular ways that something is often done
3. the time when someone is an adult
4. experience a difficult or unpleasant situation or event
5. emphasise something in order to show that it is important

TALKING POINTS

In what ways do teenagers and adults think differently?
What can scientists learn by studying people's brains?

GRAMMAR Subject–verb agreement

1 **Read the examples and choose the correct options.**

1. However, a number of studies *has* / *have* since led to an understanding that …
2. The truth is that no one *is* / *are* even close to knowing about the brain.
3. One of the pictures *was* / *were* of someone …
4. Drawing too many conclusions from research *is* / *are* irresponsible.
5. The important news *is* / *are* that the teenage years are a time of great change for the brain …

2 **Match the examples in Exercise 1 to the rules.**

We use a singular verb
- **a** when the subject of the verb is an *-ing* form.
- **b** with uncountable nouns, including those that end in *-s*, e.g. *physics*.
- **c** after words such as *everyone*, *someone*, *anyone*, etc.
- **d** after the expression *one of*.

We use a plural verb
- **e** after the expressions *both of*, *a couple*, *a number of*.

With collective nouns, we can use a singular or plural verb, e.g. *My family live/lives in Spain*.
But the noun *police* always takes a plural noun, e.g. *The police are looking for two men*.

» GRAMMAR REFERENCE AND PRACTICE PAGE 166

3 **Choose the correct verb form.**

1. One of my friends always *go* / *goes* to school by car.
2. The information you gave me *was* / *were* useful.
3. If anyone *have* / *has* any questions, ask them now.
4. Living abroad for the last few years *has* / *have* made it impossible to keep up with everyone.
5. I've tried to keep an open mind, but I can't help thinking that maths *is* / *are* just pointless!

4 **Complete the first part of the article with the present simple singular or plural form of the verbs in brackets.**

You've changed my mind!

You've just been to the cinema and all of your friends [1] ________ (agree) that the film was brilliant. But one of you [2] ________ (feel) differently: you! Do you express your real views, or do you go along with the crowd? Plenty of us [3] ________ (do) the latter and it's hard to deny that everyone [4] ________ (tell) a little white lie from time to time to fit in. However, news [5] ________ (come) from an experiment in the United States that agreeing with people like this actually [6] ________ (have) a strong effect on your mind and can even change it permanently!

5 **Read the second part of the article and correct six mistakes with subject–verb agreement.**

If, to our mind, someone are attractive, a region of our brain called the orbitofrontal cortex becomes active. In an experiment, a number of people was shown photos of faces and gave scores based on how attractive they thought the faces were. Next, everyone were told they had given much lower scores than a nationwide survey of the same faces. The process of scoring the faces were repeated, and the scientists observed the activity in the orbitofrontal cortex. The scores on this occasion were higher than the first time and the activity in the orbitofrontal cortex was also higher. Therefore, one of the researchers' conclusions were that following the opinion of a larger group lead to people changing their own opinion.

6 **Work in groups. Find something that …**

1. all of you are convinced by.
2. a number of you firmly believe in.
3. one of you is totally against.
4. no one believes in.
5. some of you suspect is true.

VOCABULARY Plural nouns

1 **The nouns in the example are always plural. Can you think of any other nouns that are always plural?**

He spent his savings on lots of new clothes.

2 **Read the sentences. Which nouns should be plural? Change the nouns, then match them to the meanings.**

0. Please help yourselves to ~~refreshment~~, everyone. *refreshments*
1. This term in English, we've been looking at the lyric of some famous songs.
2. Look in the content at the beginning and find the unit about money.
3. Leaving my belonging all over the house is guaranteed to drive my parents mad.
4. We live on the outskirt of London, near the river.
5. I'd love to study in such beautiful surrounding.

- **a** a list in a book that tells you what the book contains
- **b** the place where someone or something is and the things that are in it
- **c** the areas of a town or city furthest away from the centre
- **d** food and drinks available at an event, meeting, etc.
- **e** the words of a song
- **f** the things that someone owns

3 » **Work in pairs. Student A, turn to page 139. Student B, turn to page 141.**

GRAMMAR Subject–verb agreement

WARMER

Put the students into groups of three or four. Ask students to find something that they all like and an activity that none of them does. Write on the board: *We all …; Everyone in the group …; No one in the group …* and *None of us …* When students are ready, ask them to use the cues on the board to make sentences about their group. Monitor and correct the verb forms they use if necessary (*We all like / Everyone likes, No one in the group plays / None of us play …*).

1 Set this as an individual task and then check answers as a whole class. In feedback, ask students to explain their answers. They can then confirm or refine their understanding in Exercise 2.

Answers

1 have 2 is 3 was 4 is 5 is

2 Ask students to match the rules to the sentences in Exercise 1 in pairs before checking answers as a whole class. Look at the notes about collective nouns and ask students why someone might say: 'My favourite team is Liverpool. The team are playing well today.' (*In the first sentence, we look at the team as a single thing. In the second, we are really talking about all the players in the team.*)

Answers

1 e 2 c 3 d 4 a 5 b

» GRAMMAR REFERENCE AND PRACTICE ANSWER KEY TB PAGE 269

3 Before students start the exercise, ask them to read through the sentences and decide how many take the plural verb form. When they have found the answer, they should put their hand up. When someone puts their hand up, elicit the answer (*0*) and then ask students to choose the correct options.

FAST FINISHERS

Ask fast finishers to write alternative sentences for 1 and 5. The first one should start with: *One of my friends …* and the second one should be similar to the end of the fifth sentence but about a different subject, for example, *English is …* When everyone has finished the exercise, invite fast finishers to share their sentences with the class.

Answers

1 goes 2 was 3 has 4 has 5 is

4 Look at the first gap with the class and elicit the correct verb form (*agree*) and why it is correct (all of *is followed by the plural verb form*). Students complete the exercise alone and then compare in pairs. Elicit the answers and which rules each gap corresponds to.

Answers

1 agree 2 feels 3 do 4 tells 5 comes 6 has

5 Put students into pairs. Each one reads out a sentence from the text in turn and their partner listens to see if it sounds correct or not. When they have read the whole text, if they haven't found all six mistakes, they read the text together and find the wrong verb forms. Elicit the answers.

MIXED ABILITY

You could help weaker students by telling them to read through the text quickly and find phrases mentioned in Exercises 1 and 2. Elicit these (*someone, a number of, everyone, one of the*). Students then work together to change the verb forms after these phrases. If they have time, they can then try to find the final two errors which both follow a subject which includes an *-ing* form.

Answers

1 someone **is** attractive 2 a number of people **were** shown
3 Next, everyone **was** told 4 the process of scoring the faces **was** repeated 5 one of the researcher's conclusions **was** that
6 following the opinion of a larger group **leads**

6 Put the students into groups of three or four and set a time limit of three minutes to find the five things. Change the groups so that students are now with students from different groups. They tell each other what ideas their groups came up with. Monitor and collect examples of mistakes and good use of language for feedback. Invite each group to share one of two of their findings with the class.

Answers

Students' own answers

» GRAMMAR WORKSHEET UNIT 19

VOCABULARY Plural nouns

1 Put the students into groups of three or four and set a time limit for them to list as many words as they can which are always plural. When the time limit is up, ask the groups how many words they have got and elicit ideas from the group with the most. Then invite other groups to add any words that the first group didn't think of.

Possible answers

glasses, jeans, scissors, sunglasses, trousers, shorts

2 Tell the stronger students to cover the meanings of the words (a–f). Elicit the plural nouns and ask the stronger students for their own definitions. They then uncover the meanings and do the matching. Weaker students will find the matching easier after having heard the ideas from stronger students. Check the answers as a class. You could follow up by asking students to write three sentences about themselves using the words from Exercises 1 and 2. Two sentences should be true and one should be false. Tell students to read their sentences aloud to a partner who should guess which one is false. Ask students to share any funny examples in feedback.

Answers

0 d 1 e lyrics 2 a contents 3 f belongings 4 c outskirts
5 b surroundings

3 When students look at the activities tell them not to show each other their one so they have to listen carefully to each other's sentences. When they have finished, they can look at both exercises together and correct the wrong words. Elicit the answers from the class.

Answers

1 not correct – *news* 2 not correct – *surroundings* 3 correct
4 not correct – *contents* 5 correct 6 not correct – *outskirts*

» VOCABULARY WORKSHEET UNIT 19

WRITING An essay (4)

1 Ask students to discuss this question in pairs. They should think of at least two reasons for their answer. Elicit ideas and reasons from the class and write these on the board under two headings *Yes, it should* and *No, it shouldn't*.

Answers
Students' own answers

2 Look at the task with the class and elicit a reason why health, learning and transport may influence whether students should start school later, for example, *health: teenagers need more sleep; learning: because students get up early every day, they are often exhausted by the end of the week and can't concentrate; transport: school starts at the same time as most people's work so it is a very busy time on the roads*. Also elicit one other possible idea for point 3 (e.g. *breakfast*). Students work in groups of three or four to think of more ideas for questions 1 and 2. Monitor and note down good language use for feedback. Then students share their ideas as a class.

Answers
Students' own answers

3 Set a time limit of two minutes for students to read the essay; then, allow them to compare answers in pairs. Elicit which of their ideas were mentioned in the essay and any other new ideas they found. Then ask students if they agree or disagree with the writer and why.

Answers
Ideas in the text:
Health: need more sleep
Learning: not time for breakfast – don't pay full attention
Transport: may not get lifts from parents
Other: longer working day for teachers

4 Ask students to make a list of the different kinds of linking words from the *Prepare to write* box that are used in the essay, and check answers as a whole class. When students have chosen the correct words in the exercise, elicit the answers and what kind of linking words were needed for each sentence. You could ask students to rewrite the sentences with an alternative linking word with a similar meaning to check their knowledge of how each word affects sentence structure. For example, 1 *in order to* (*He left early in order to catch the last bus.* 2 *despite* (*Despite leaving early, she missed the bus.*).

Answers
Linking words from the text: however, in order to, as a result, whereas, while, consequently, therefore, on the other hand, as, despite
1 so 2 Even though 3 consequently 4 as 5 despite 6 whereas 7 as 8 Since

PREPARE FOR THE EXAM

5 **B2 FIRST FOR SCHOOLS Writing Part 1: An essay**
Briefly review what students need to do in this part of the exam and, if necessary, read out the *B2 First for Schools* box on TB page 22.

Point out that the essay should be between 140 and 190 words and it should address two points given in the task and one more point of the student's choosing. Also highlight that students need to give reasons for their opinion and not just simply state their opinion. Then, set a time limit of five minutes for students to think of ideas and make their notes. Encourage them to think of words related to homework, for example, *doing exercises, revision, studying* and synonyms for *discourage*, for example, *put off*. Allow weaker students to work in pairs or small groups and monitor and help them with ideas where necessary.

Answers
Students' own answers

6 Tell students to write their essay. If you have students preparing for the *B2 First for Schools* exam, set a strict time limit of 30 minutes for this task and provide less support. The time limit corresponds to the time they will have in the exam minus the time they have already spent planning their essay. If not, you can be more flexible with the timing and give more help. In pairs, students exchange their essays and provide feedback on the task. They should highlight any linking words and suggest other ones that could have been used.

Model answer
Not many students at my school would claim that they enjoy doing homework, but, despite this, there are ways in which homework could be less unpopular.
Firstly, it shouldn't take too long to do. Two hours of homework in the evening is a reasonable amount and, in order to ensure that there isn't more, there could be a homework timetable so that different teachers don't all set homework at the same time and for the same day.
Students also need to be aware of why we are given homework. Homework allows us to reflect on what was done in class. It also trains us to be independent learners, which will help when preparing for exams.
In addition, homework could be made more enjoyable. While repetitive written exercises can be boring, making presentations or watching educational videos to discuss in future lessons would be more interesting and motivating.
In my opinion, too much boring homework can discourage students from wanting to learn. Therefore, it is important to ensure that there is less homework and, provided that the homework set is interesting and varied, students won't be discouraged from learning.

COOLER
In groups of four, ask students to make a list of other changes they would make to their school, for example, more after-school activities, more PE, an extra foreign language, etc. Encourage students to think of the reasons for these changes and what the result might be. Invite each group to present one of their ideas to the class and then hold a class vote to find out the most popular suggestion.

WRITING An essay (4)

1 What time does your school start and finish each day? Should it start or finish earlier or later?

2 Read the task and answer the questions.

> **'Students who are 15 and older should start and finish school an hour later.'**
> **Do you agree?**
> Notes
> Write about:
> 1 health
> 2 learning
> 3 *transport* (your own idea)

1 The student has added their own idea. What other ideas could you add?
2 What advantages and disadvantages can you think of to do with health, learning and transport?

3 Read the essay. Which of your ideas are mentioned? What other ideas are mentioned?

Changing the timing of the school day is a complex issue. However, such a policy might benefit teenagers, who are often so busy with after-school activities and homework that they are rarely in bed before 11 pm.

In my country, students need to get up by 7 am in order to arrive at school for 8 am. As a result, teenagers get fewer than eight hours' sleep, whereas the recommended minimum is 9.5 hours per night. This may well start to affect their health. In addition, while some young people manage to eat breakfast before they leave home, others arrive at school hungry and, consequently, do not always pay full attention in lessons. Some even pretend to be ill to gain more time in bed, therefore missing important work in class. Starting later would help in this respect.

On the other hand, other problems might occur. Teenagers who rely on their parents for transport could experience difficulties, as the parents might have already left for work. Furthermore, even though teachers might support the change, their working hours would be longer.

On balance, despite the drawbacks, it seems worth experimenting in selected schools. A decision could then be made based on the results.

4 Read the *Prepare to write* box and find examples of the different kinds of linking words in the essay. Then choose the correct options below.

PREPARE TO WRITE Organising essays

We use linking words to link clauses and make sentences longer. Linking words can express

- contrast: *although, even though, whereas, despite*
- purpose: *so, so that, in order that*
- reason: *because, as, since, for this reason*
- result: *consequently, therefore*

1 He left early *so / despite* he could catch the last bus.
2 *So that / Even though* she left early, she missed the bus.
3 I got home very late and *because / consequently* I felt exhausted the next day.
4 I was late for school, *as / although* I overslept.
5 I got a bad mark in the exam, *despite / since* all the work I did.
6 Some people work well in the mornings, *therefore / whereas* others work better later in the day.
7 I couldn't get a lift to school, *as / in order that* my parents had already left for work.
8 *In order to / Since* the exam has to be fair, everyone must do it at exactly the same time.

PREPARE FOR THE EXAM

Writing Part 1

5 Read the task. Add more information and your own idea to the notes.

> **'Having a lot of homework discourages students from wanting to learn.'**
> **Do you agree?**
> Notes
> Write about:
> 1 the time spent on doing homework
> 2 how useful homework is
> 3 .... (your own idea)

6 Write your essay. Use all the notes and give reasons for your point of view.

- Organise your essay into paragraphs (see page 13).
- Use language to compare and contrast (see page 57).
- Use linking words to link clauses and make your sentences longer (see page 89).
- Check your grammar and spelling.
- Write 140–190 words.

20 SPEAK UP

ABOUT YOU

What idioms do you know in your own language?
What idioms do you know in English?

VOCABULARY Idioms

1 **Look at the list of idioms. Which meanings do you think are the most likely? Why?**

EP

1 break the ice
- **a** make people feel more relaxed in a social situation
- **b** explain why people feel a certain way

2 break someone's heart
- **a** make someone feel nervous
- **b** make someone feel extremely sad

3 take your breath away
- **a** make you feel anxious and impatient
- **b** make you feel surprise and admiration

4 be a piece of cake
- **a** be sweet and tasty
- **b** be very easy

5 cross your mind
- **a** come into your thoughts for a short time
- **b** make you change your mind

6 have an eye for something
- **a** want something very much
- **b** be good at noticing certain things

7 be a pain
- **a** be very sore
- **b** be annoying

8 lose track of time
- **a** not be aware of what time it is
- **b** not be able to find time for something

88 **2** **Listen and choose the correct meanings in Exercise 1.**

3 **Discuss the questions.**

1. What is the best way to break the ice when you meet new people?
2. Have you ever seen something that took your breath away? What?
3. Is there anything that your friends find difficult that you think is a piece of cake?
4. When was the last time you were late because you'd lost track of time?

READING

1 **Read the title of the article on page 113. What might the article be about? Then read the article quickly and check your ideas.**

PREPARE FOR THE EXAM

Reading and Use of English Part 3

2 **For questions 1–8, read the first three paragraphs of the article. Use the word given in capitals to form a word that fits in the gap.**

3 **Read the article again and answer the questions.**

1. Why do teenagers have an influence on language change?
2. What examples does the text give of how English has changed lately?
3. What are the standard question tags for these questions? What question tag do some young people use instead?
   - **a** *You texted me, ________?*
   - **b** *You like this game, ________?*
4. How does the language of texting differ from standard English?
5. How does texting affect texters?
6. How does the saying, 'Everything rolls on, nothing stays still' relate to languages?

4 **Match the highlighted words in the article to the meanings.**

1. planned or controlled by a particular person or thing
2. the ability to read and write
3. hurting or damaging
4. informal language that is only used by people who belong to a particular group
5. although

5 **Discuss the questions.**

1. Do you use slang when you are speaking to your friends? Give some examples.
2. Are you sometimes criticised for using the 'wrong' language? In what situations?
3. Think of examples of words in English and in your own language that
   - **a** are borrowed from other languages.
   - **b** are often shortened.
   - **c** come from technological developments.

20 SPEAK UP

Unit Overview

TOPIC	Different languages
VOCABULARY	Idioms
READING	'Teen speak' We love it!
GRAMMAR	Determiners
VOCABULARY	Commonly confused words
LISTENING	Eight short conversations
SPEAKING	Comparing photographs (2)
EXAM TASKS	Reading and Use of English Part 3; Listening Part 1; Speaking Part 2

Resources

GRAMMAR REFERENCE AND PRACTICE: SB page 167; TB page 269
PREPARE FOR THE EXAM: SB pages on TB pages 238, 247 and 250–251; TB pages 255, 259 and 261
WORKBOOK: pages 80–83
PHOTOCOPIABLE WORKSHEETS: Grammar worksheet Unit 20; Vocabulary worksheet Unit 20
TEST GENERATOR: Unit test 20; Term test 3; End of Year test
PRACTICE EXTRA: Unit 20

WARMER

Put students into groups of three or four and ask them to think of some of the problems a learner of their language would have. Give examples for English: spelling, pronunciation, lots of tenses, phrasal verbs which have more than one meaning, etc. Set a time limit of two minutes and elicit ideas.

ABOUT YOU

Read the *About you* box with the students. Elicit a definition of an idiom (*a phrase which has a different meaning to the literal translation of the words used*). Give the students an example of an idiom which is different in different languages, for example *It's raining cats and dogs* has many equivalents:

It's raining shoemakers' apprentices. (Danish)

It's raining pilot whales. (Faroese)

It's raining old women with clubs. (Afrikaans)

It's raining old women. (Dutch)

Students work in groups of three or four to think of idioms they know in English. Set a time limit of two or three minutes and invite groups to share their ideas with the class.

VOCABULARY Idioms

1 Read the idioms with the class and ask if they have any idioms using the same, or similar, expressions in their own language. In pairs, students go through the idioms and guess the likely meanings. Elicit ideas but do not tell the students what the correct answers are at this stage.

Answers
Students' own answers

88 2 When students have listened, elicit the answers. Then, play the recording a second time and ask students to make notes about each dialogue, including the situation, the place or anything that happened. Students compare notes in pairs then elicit the situations in each case and what the speakers were talking about. (*1 The man was at a rehearsal. He told a joke to break the ice. 2 They are watching TV. Seeing an ad for a TV programme which showed cows in small sheds broke the girl's heart. 3 Walking up in the Alps. The view from the hotel of the Alps took the woman's breath away. 4 The girl's history homework was a piece of cake. 5 The girl had been out late and hadn't contacted her mum. It never crossed the girl's mind that her mum might be worried about her until she saw tears in her eyes. 6 The girl has a great eye for detail and she used her memory to draw a picture of the city centre. 7 Getting to and from the friend's 15th floor flat is a real pain. 8 The man can lose track of time when he is on holiday at the beach.*)

Answers
1 a 2 b 3 b 4 b 5 a 6 b 7 b 8 a

» AUDIOSCRIPT TB PAGE 305

3 Look at the first question with the class. Re-elicit what the man did in the first dialogue in Exercise 2 to relax everyone (*tell a joke*). Ask the class for other ideas, and encourage them to talk about situations where they broke the ice or someone else did while they were there. Students then discuss the other questions in groups of three. Monitor and note interesting ideas and invite students to share their ideas with the class.

Answers
Students' own answers

READING

1 Allow students to discuss their ideas about the title in pairs for one minute without reading the text and then ask the class for ideas. Ask them to give examples of words or phrases that they use in their own language, or English expressions, which they rarely or never hear adults using. Ask them if there were any words or expressions they used to use a lot which have now become unfashionable. After students have predicted what the text will be about, give them three minutes to read the text quickly to check, as well as finding any examples of teen speak mentioned in the text. Elicit these and ask students if these words are used by young people in their own country (for example *wicked* for wonderful, *bad* for good and *sick* for very cool).

Answers
Students' own answers

CONTINUED ON PAGE 222

BACKGROUND INFORMATION

Each year hundreds of new words are added to official English language dictionaries depending on how often they are used in everyday language. These often include words used by teenagers or people using technology. Before this happens, researchers look to see how often the words appear in print or on the internet. The word should have been in existence for five years to ensure that it isn't a very temporary thing. A database collects about 150 million words used each month. The public can also make suggestions, but these have to be checked by an editorial team before they are approved. Words are never removed from the dictionary even if they go out of fashion. Some of the latest words added include:

bae: boyfriend or girlfriend (This is a word which originated in American English. New words can originate from the UK, other English-speaking countries or any other languages.)

e-bike: an electric bike

gym bunny: someone who uses the gym a lot

noob: a person new to a computer game, forum or similar

Words which have previously appeared can also be given extra definitions, for example in March 2019, *favourite* had a new definition added as a verb meaning to store a link to a web page as a bookmark.

PREPARE FOR THE EXAM

2 B2 FIRST FOR SCHOOLS Reading and Use of English Part 3

Briefly review what students need to do in this part of the exam and if necessary, read out the *B2 First for Schools* box on TB page 102.

Elicit that the differences between the task here and in the exam is that here the gap fill is part of a longer text, whereas in the exam it is a standalone text. Also, the words in brackets appear after the gap here, whereas in the exam they will be at the end of the line. Tell students to read the first three paragraphs again quickly and elicit what each one is about. (*The first is asking about the readers' use of different kinds of words with different people, the second explains that teen speak is nothing new and the third compares teen speak with jargon used by people in different professions.*)

Now look at the example with the students and elicit that this is a plural noun. We know it must be plural because it says *some words or …* Students do the rest of the task alone and compare in pairs. Elicit the answers and what kind of word each one is.

Answers

1 comparison 2 criticism 3 specific 4 remarkable 5 objections 6 specialist/specialised/specialized 7 medical 8 Naturally

3 Put students into pairs and ask them to read the questions and discuss any of the answers they think they can remember. Then give students time to read the text carefully and, when they have finished, ask them to cover the text and discuss the answers again and write them in their own words in their notebook. Monitor and help where necessary. Elicit the answers.

MIXED ABILITY

Pair weaker students with stronger ones. As they read through the text, the stronger student can show their partner where the relevant information is and help them to formulate the answers in a different way to the phrases in the text.

Answers

1 They change standard grammar and vocabulary to mark the difference between them and older generations.
2 Changes of lexical meaning (e.g. *wicked*) and grammatical use (e.g. *innit* as a question tag).
3 a didn't you, innit b don't you, innit
4 It uses acronyms and emojis.
5 Texting helps people's reading and writing.
6 The phrase means that language changes constantly, as does everything else in life.

89 The Reading text is recorded for students to listen, read and check their answers.

4 Students look at the highlighted words in the text and, without reading anything else, they tell each other, in pairs, if they know what any of them mean. For the words that neither student knows, they read the sentences they appear in and try to work out the meaning from context. They then do the matching. Elicit the answers and other examples of words followed by *-led*, for example, *student-led lessons*.

FAST FINISHERS

Ask fast finishers to look for more words in the text that other students might not know. They look up the meanings of the words and, when everyone has finished and you have elicited the answers, ask the fast finishers to read out their meanings for the other students to try to find the words.

Answers

1 -led 2 literacy 3 harming 4 slang 5 albeit

5 Put students into groups of three or four to discuss the first two questions. Set a time limit of four minutes and then elicit ideas from different groups. Then, with students in the same groups, set a quiz about the origin of some English words. Tell them that you will read ten words aloud and they should write down the language they think the word comes from. You can use any words, but here are some suggestions: kangaroo (Aboriginal), aubergine (Arabic), ketchup (Chinese), angst (German), biology (Greek), bangle (Hindi), karaoke (Japanese), mammoth (Russian), macho (Spanish), dad (Welsh). You could help students by giving them multiple-choice options. Elicit their ideas and then discuss the third question in the exercise with the whole class. Students give their own answers.

TALKING POINTS

Look at the question with the class and give them an example. Tell students that we now use a lot more abbreviations instead of words to save time while texting. Write some examples on the board and elicit what they mean, for example, *c u l8r* (*see you later*), *afaik* (*as far as I know*), *b4* (*before*), *gr8* (*great*), *atm* (*at the moment*), *lol* (*laugh out loud*), *thx* (*thanks*). Tell students not to think of abbreviations, but other types of imagery which people use to save time, such as emojis, memes, GIFs, videos, photos, voice notes. Students work in groups of four. Set a time limit of two minutes and elicit ideas, discussing each one as a class.

COOLER

Talk to students about emojis and how they can be used in messages. Put students into pairs and ask them to write a sentence using as many emojis as possible in place of words. They then swap sentences with a different pair to work out what their partner's sentence means. Pairs then get together to see if they were correct.

'TEEN SPEAK' We love it!

89

Do you use some words or **(0)** *expressions* **(EXPRESS)** with your friends and other ones with your family? Maybe you use very different language in **(1)** ______ **(COMPARE)** with older generations, or perhaps you receive **(2)** ______ **(CRITICISE)** from teachers for using the 'wrong' language at school.

Slang that is **(3)** ______ **(SPECIFY)** to teenagers is common in most languages, as are complaints about it from older people. However, in spite of the claims made by some adults that teenagers are 'ruining' their language, in fact changes to standard grammar and vocabulary are nothing new, and aren't, therefore, particularly **(4)** ______ **(REMARK)**. Since the time of the Ancient Greeks, there have always been plenty of **(5)** ______ **(OBJECT)** to young people's language use.

Groups with similar interests adapt language to suit their purposes: think of the **(6)** ______ **(SPECIALISE)** language used in the legal and **(7)** ______ **(MEDICINE)** worlds. Known as 'jargon', these words mark out those who use them as belonging to a specific group. **(8)** ______ **(NATURE)**, teenagers also want to make it clear which social group they belong to, and changing the language you use is a great way to do this.

One way in which teenagers change their language is to introduce new vocabulary or change the meaning of existing words. Some recent examples of 'teen speak' show how big these changes in meaning can be. For young people, *wicked* doesn't mean *very bad* as it does for older generations, but *wonderful; bad* can mean *good*, and *sick* has taken on the meaning of *very cool*. These uses don't always last for long. Indeed, words come in and out of use very quickly, and it can be hard to keep up.

Young people also make changes to grammar. One example of a teen-led change to English grammar is the use among some young people of *innit* (a shortened form of *isn't it*) as a substitute for all question tags, e.g. *You texted me, innit?* or *You like this game, innit?* It has been suggested that this 'simplification' is a by-product of texting and instant messaging. Although some people are concerned that this trend towards 'text speak' is harming the language, well-known linguist Professor David Crystal doesn't agree. According to Crystal and many other linguists, the fact that teenagers use text speak, acronyms (LOL) and emojis 🙂 doesn't mean the end of the language. Says Crystal, 'Texting is just a new type of English that has evolved as a result of internet technology. It hasn't had any impact on the rest of the language. The big myth is that texting is somehow harming the language. There is no evidence of that. All the recent research shows the best texters are actually the best spellers. The more they text, the better their literacy is, as it gives them the practice in reading and writing they wouldn't otherwise have.'

Although teenagers are often criticised for ignoring linguistic rules and destroying the language by those keen on imposing standard grammar rules, we should bear in mind that languages aren't fixed. All languages change over time, albeit at different rates and for a lot of different reasons. Vocabulary evolves as speakers need new words to describe new concepts or consumer goods, for example. Where would we be without all those new words such as *app* and *e-reader* that have come into the language as a result of modern technologies? Grammar also changes over time, which explains why many present-day native English-speakers find Shakespeare's 16th-century plays difficult to read. Our use of language changes naturally as we go through life, too; we continually pick up new words and phrases and integrate them into our speech.

Some adults may not always like the way teenagers speak to each other, but realising that language change is inevitable and that teenagers are integral to this process might help older generations feel better about it. People have always complained that standards are declining among the younger generation, but as the Greek philosopher Heraclitus observed more than 2,500 years ago, 'Everything rolls on, nothing stays still.'

WICKED

sick

LOL

innit

TALKING POINTS

How have modern ways of communicating changed the way we use language?

SPEAK UP 113

GRAMMAR Determiners

1 **Read the examples and choose the correct options. Check your answers in the rules.**

1 Perhaps you receive ***the*** / **–** criticism from teachers for using ***the*** / ***a*** 'wrong' language at **–** / ***the*** school.
2 There have always been ***much*** / ***plenty of*** objections to young people's language use.
3 All languages change over time … for ***a bit of*** / ***a lot of*** different reasons.
4 This explains why ***much*** / ***many*** present-day speakers find Shakespeare's 16th-century plays difficult to read.
5 Changing the language you use is **–** / ***a*** great way to do this.

We use
a *a* or *an* before a singular countable noun, for referring to one of many things, or one that is not specific.
b *the* before any noun, for referring to something in particular or something already mentioned.
c – before any noun, for referring to things generally.
d *some*, *any*, *plenty of*, *a lot of*, *lots of* before uncountable and plural countable nouns.
e *much*, *(a) little*, *a bit of*, *a small/large amount of* before uncountable nouns.
f *many*, *(a) few*, *several*, *a small/large number of* before plural countable nouns.

GRAMMAR REFERENCE AND PRACTICE PAGE 167

2 **Read the sentences and explain the difference in meaning between them.**

0 a She has **a little** money to spend.
b She has **little** money to spend.
a She has some money to spend. ('A little' means a small amount but it is enough.)
b She doesn't have very much to spend. ('Little' means a very small amount and it is not enough.)

1 a They gave me **little** help.
b They gave me **a little** help.

2 a **Few** people here can speak Chinese.
b **A few** people here can speak Chinese.

3 a We get **a little** rain in summer.
b We get **little** rain in summer.

4 a Latin is offered by **few** schools these days.
b Latin is offered by **a few** schools these days.

5 a I speak **little** French.
b I speak **a little** French.

3 **Correct the mistake in each sentence.**

1 We apologise for sending a wrong phone to you.
2 Hi, Ciaran! I have a good news for you!
3 Yesterday I went to shops and bought some new clothes.
4 There are few biscuits left if you'd like some with your coffee?
5 I don't think you'll have many fun on the language-exchange programme.

4 **Complete the text with the correct determiners. There may be more than one correct answer.**

FOREIGN-ACCENT SYNDROME

Olga Grigorieva, a Russian schoolgirl from Novgorod, passed out one day while she was in [1] ________ art class. When she came round, a nurse told her to drink [2] ________ of water and to get [3] ________ rest. When Olga thanked [4] ________ nurse and stood up, she noticed that [5] ________ of her classmates were giggling. Olga asked them what was wrong and then she noticed her own voice. She was speaking Russian with [6] ________ English accent!

Olga was suffering from 'foreign-accent syndrome', where people suddenly, sometimes after an operation or accident, start speaking with [7] ________ foreign accent. Like a large [8] ________ of other people with the syndrome, Olga was, naturally, upset. A person's speech forms part of their personality, after all.

Olga's case was even more unusual because she didn't speak [9] ________ English at all before her fall. It was her accent, not the language, that was different. Slowly her old Russian accent returned, but she has learned to say a [10] ________ things in English as well.

VOCABULARY Commonly confused words

1 **Choose the correct options.**

1 Which is your favourite *way* / *means* of transport?
2 What is the best *means* / *way* to practise English?
3 I'll visit you if the *journey* / *way* isn't too long.
4 What is the best *way* / *journey* to the beach?
5 You'll have plenty of *possibilities* / *opportunities* to meet people at university.
6 There's *a possibility* / *an opportunity* my sister will be at the party.
7 Why won't you let me play my music? I'm only trying to have *funny* / *fun*.
8 I've never thought Logan was very *fun* / *funny*, but everyone else laughs at his jokes.

2 **Complete the sentences with words from Exercise 1.**

1 Did you have a good ________ or was the traffic bad?
2 I haven't had the ________ to read your blog yet.
3 He told us a very ________ joke!
4 I know the ________ to school from here.
5 There's a ________ I'll be late, I'm not sure yet.
6 I really enjoyed my holiday. It was great ________.

3 **Complete the sentences with the verbs in the box.**

damage guess harm injure know observe

1 How did you ________ your leg?
2 The rain won't ________ you or your equipment.
3 Please don't ________ the furniture.
4 Can you ________ how old I am?
5 The headteacher is going to ________ this class.
6 I have read the essay title, but I don't ________ what it means.

GRAMMAR Determiners

WARMER

With books closed tell students that determiners are words placed in front of a noun to make it clear what the noun refers to. Write a word on the board, for example *chair(s)*. Put the students into pairs and ask them to think of as many words as possible, that are not adjectives, that could come before the word *chair* or *chairs*. Give an example to start: *a chair*. Set a time limit of one minute and elicit any words the students think of.

1 Students choose the correct words in pairs and do the matching (*1c, b, c; 2f; 3d; 4f; 5a*). Elicit the answers then ask students to try to think of example sentences for the two unused words and phrases; *much* and *a bit of* (which both match rule e). Elicit examples from different pairs. Make sure that both examples are used with uncountable words.

Answers

1 –, the, – 2 plenty of 3 a lot of 4 many 5 a

» GRAMMAR REFERENCE AND PRACTICE ANSWER KEY TB PAGE 269

2 Look at the example with the class. Students then read the other sentences in pairs and discuss the differences between them. Elicit the answers and then ask why sentences 1 and 3 use *little* and 2, 4 use *few* (*1, 3 are uncountable nouns and 2, 4 are countable nouns.*).

Answers

1 a Not much help was given.
  b Some help was given.
2 a Not many people here can speak Chinese.
  b Some people here can speak Chinese.
3 a There is some rain in summer.
  b There isn't much rain in summer.
4 a Not many schools offer Latin these days.
  b Some schools offer Latin these days.
5 a I can hardly speak any French.
  b I can speak some French.

3 Tell students to work alone. When they have corrected all the sentences they work in pairs and take it in turns to explain the mistakes as if the other student had made them in a piece of written work and they were the student's teacher. They shouldn't just say what is wrong but why it is wrong. Do the first one with the class, for example *1 This is talking about a specific, known phone so we need the definite article.* Then elicit explanations from different students for the other sentences.

Answers

1 We apologise for sending ~~a~~ **the** wrong phone to you.
2 Hi Ciaran, I have ~~a~~ **some**/– good news for you!
3 Yesterday I went to **some/the** shops and bought some new clothes.
4 There are **a** few biscuits left if you'd like some with your coffee.
5 I don't think you'll have ~~many~~ **much** fun on the language exchange programme.

4 Look at the first gap with the class. Elicit the correct answer. If someone suggests *her*, tell them that it is correct but it isn't one of the words focused on in Exercise 1. Students complete the text alone and then compare in pairs. Elicit the answers and which rule they correspond to.

Answers

1 an 2 plenty/lots/a lot 3 some 4 the 5 some/lots/a lot/a few 6 an 7 a 8 number 9 any 10 few

» GRAMMAR WORKSHEET UNIT 20

VOCABULARY Commonly confused words

1 Ask students to complete the exercise individually and then check answers as a whole class. Other words that are commonly confused are false friends, i.e. words that look similar to words in the students' own language, but which have a different meaning. For example, *sensible* in French means *sensitive*, but it means *using good judgement* in English. Other words are commonly confused because an English-sounding word is used in the mother tongue, for example, *handy* in German means *mobile phone* but it means *useful* in English. If you know of any similar problems students have because of their own language, use these to extend the exercise.

FAST FINISHERS

Ask fast finishers to look at sentence 2 and to write some sentences describing the best way to practise English. When everyone has finished the activity, elicit the answers and invite fast finishers to share their ideas with the class.

Answers

1 means 2 way 3 journey 4 way 5 opportunities 6 a possibility 7 fun 8 funny

2 Ask students to complete the sentences individually and then check the answers as a class. If they are confused about the uses of *opportunity* and *possibility*, tell them that we use *opportunity* to talk about a situation in which we can do something that we want to do; for example, *I had the opportunity to go to university when I was younger but I didn't. Now I wish I had gone.* We use *possibility* to talk about something that may happen or be true. An example is, *The possibility that there is life on other planets has always inspired scientists.* We don't say have **the** possibility but we do say have **the** opportunity, for example *I would love to have the opportunity to meet the prime minister* NOT ~~… have the possibility to meet …~~.

Answers

1 journey 2 opportunity 3 funny 4 way 5 possibility 6 fun

3 Ask students to work with a partner to explain the meaning of the words in the box. Ask, 'Which words do you think are commonly confused with one another?' (e.g. *damage, harm* and *injure*). Feed back as a class and then tell students to complete the exercise. Check the answers and when we use each word. (*We use* injure *to talk about hurting a part of the body. We use* damage *to talk about breaking, tearing, etc. an object. It is also used with things like the brain, eyesight and hearing. We use* harm *as a more general word meaning to hurt a person or cause something like electronic equipment to stop working.* for example *Be careful. This could harm you (general). How? Will it injure me or damage my eyesight?*)

Answers

1 injure 2 harm 3 damage 4 guess 5 observe 6 know

» VOCABULARY WORKSHEET UNIT 20

LISTENING

PREPARE FOR THE EXAM

1 B2 FIRST FOR SCHOOLS Listening Part 1

90 Briefly review what students need to do in this part of the exam and if necessary, read out the *B2 First for Schools* box on TB page 74.

Give the students one minute to read through the questions before playing the recording. Remind them that, they will hear each recording twice in a row in the exam, not once all the way through and then a second time all the way through. Elicit that the text will contain synonyms of the key words in the questions so it is important for students to think about what they might hear. Look at the first question with the class and elicit synonyms for the key words in each option (for example, *A sections – parts, variety – different kinds; B borrow – take out, longer periods – more time, a greater length of time; C Staff – the people working there, librarians, employees; unhelpful – disinterested, locating – finding*). Divide the class into seven groups and give each group one question to look at. They find the key words and think of synonyms that might be heard. Elicit their ideas before playing the recording. When students have listened twice, allow them to compare answers in pairs and elicit the answers and any information students heard which helped them choose the correct answer or reject the other options. Elicit any of their synonyms that were used.

Answers

1 B 2 B 3 B 4 C 5 B 6 A 7 C 8 A

» AUDIOSCRIPT TB PAGE 306

SPEAKING Comparing photographs (2)

1 Put students into pairs and give each student a letter: A or B. Student A should cover photo B and Student B should cover photo A. They then describe their photos to each other and say what they can see and what the people are doing. They then decide together which choice connects them.

Answer

3 Communicating with others

91 **2** Ask the students to note down any good items of topic vocabulary that they hear, i.e. words describing what the person can see, not their opinion. Elicit which photo Andrea was describing and then the words he used that students noted down (for example: *a group of, sitting together, communicating with each other, guy, screen, boss, informal, paying attention, a meeting of some kind*).

Answer

B

» AUDIOSCRIPT TB PAGE 306

92 **3** Before you look at the *Prepare to speak* box, elicit topic vocabulary that Andrea might use when describing the other photo. Write the ideas on the board. Then look at the *Prepare to speak* box with the class elicit any phrases that the students remember hearing which showed how sure or unsure Andrea was about the situation. Play Track 91 again and elicit the phrases used (*I'm not sure, I get the impression, it looks like, It must be*). Now play Track 92. Elicit the phrases used and then play the recording again for students to see which of the words and phrases they predicted Andrea mentioned, and see if there were any they didn't think of (*in a room, learning, practising, classroom, language class, teacher, sign language, people of different ages*).

Answers

They seem, it doesn't look as though, Maybe it's, I get the impression that, I think, they might be

» AUDIOSCRIPT TB PAGES 306–307

4 Elicit one or two sentences from the class, for example for Photo A: *They might be deaf.* Then set a time limit of two minutes for students to think of more possible sentences using the phrases in the box. Elicit ideas from different pairs and, if there are some phrases that no one has used, elicit ideas for these from the class.

MIXED ABILITY

In weaker classes, tell half the pairs to make sentences using the first four phrases in the box and half the pairs to use the other four phrases. When they have done this, put them into groups of four to share their sentences with each other. Monitor and help them with ideas. Students in stronger classes can try to use as many of the phrases as possible.

Answers

Students' own answers

PREPARE FOR THE EXAM

5 B2 FIRST FOR SCHOOLS Speaking Part 2

Briefly review what students need to do in this part of the exam and, if necessary, read out the *B2 First for Schools* box on TB page 94.

Tell the students to work in pairs. One student in each pair should keep their book open at page 115. While their partner is talking, they should note any phrases from the *Prepare to speak* box that they use. When they have compared the photos and Student B has answered the follow-up question, allow students to change roles so that Student B does the first part of the task and Student A the second part. Monitor and note any good phrases used as well as mistakes. Give feedback to students to the class, firstly pointing out the positive things about their talk and then making suggestions about how to improve it, if appropriate. Invite one or two pairs to do the activity in front of the class.

Answers

Students' own answers

COOLER

Students work in groups of three. Individually, they look through the book to find examples of two photos with a similar theme. When they have found their photos, they write an exam task question similar to the one they have just looked at. They then each take turns in playing the role of examiner. They ask the other two students to turn to the relevant page and then tell them the questions they have to answer. Monitor and help with the choice of questions and make sure they have a follow-up question for the second student.

LISTENING

PREPARE FOR THE EXAM

Listening Part 1

1 (90) **You will hear people talking in eight different situations. For questions 1–8, choose the best answer (A, B or C).**

1 You hear two friends talking about their college library. What does the boy think of it?
A Some sections don't have a variety of books.
B You should be able to borrow books for longer periods.
C Staff can be unhelpful in locating books.

2 You hear a linguist talking about endangered languages. What does she say about languages?
A Languages represent one of man's most important skills.
B Language loss could result in loss of historical knowledge.
C There will be fewer regional cultures if languages die out.

3 You hear two friends talking about a novel they have read. They agree that
A it was well-written.
B the writing was very descriptive.
C its main character was realistic.

4 You hear a teacher talking to her students about the school holidays. During the holidays, she wants them to
A make an effort to keep in touch with one another.
B catch up on any schoolwork they have missed.
C keep a brief record of experiences they have.

5 You hear two friends talking about speaking two languages. The boy says that people who speak two or more languages
A can interact better with people in other cultures.
B are able to do certain things better than other people.
C should be able to learn further languages without difficulty.

6 You hear a student adviser talking about young people starting university. The man advises new students to
A prepare themselves for a different approach to studying.
B find out as much as possible about the town or city they are going to.
C meet as many people as possible.

7 You hear two friends talking about a long-distance running race. What is the girl worried about?
A whether she will finish the race or not
B how big a problem her clothing will be
C who will see her take part in the race

8 You hear a boy telling a friend about a blog he writes. What does he regard as a priority?
A controlling the length of what he produces online
B increasing the number of followers that he has
C finding new topics to interest his readers

SPEAKING Comparing photographs (2)

1 **You are going to compare two photographs. Look at the photographs. What is the connection between them?**

1 Social conversation
2 Learning a foreign language
3 Communicating with others

2 (91) **Listen to Andrea talking about one of the photos. Which photo is he talking about?**

3 (92) **Read the *Prepare to speak* box and listen to Andrea talking about the other photo. Which phrases does he use?**

PREPARE TO SPEAK | Speculating

It looks as if/though they're … / It looks like …
He/She/They might/could be (learning …)
I think they're about to …
Perhaps/Maybe it's …
I get the impression that …
They seem/look …
They/It must be …
Clearly they're …

4 **Work in pairs. Speculate about the two photos. Use phrases from the *Prepare to speak* box.**

PREPARE FOR THE EXAM

Speaking Part 2

5 **Turn to page 141 and complete the task.**

SPEAK UP 115

LIFE SKILLS STUDY SKILLS

PREPARING FOR EXAMS

LIFE SKILLS

Preparing for exams

Preparing for and taking exams can be both scary and stressful. Exams form a big part of university life too, and they are also a reality for many different professions. Learning how to prepare for them effectively is key to your future in many ways.

1 **Ask and answer the questions with a partner.**

1 How do you feel when you have to take exams?
2 What routines or techniques do you use to prepare for exams?
3 How do you cope with exam-related stress?

2 **Read the article on the opposite page. Match the headings (A–E) to paragraphs 1, 2, 5, 8 and 9.**

A Get up and do something!
B Create a revision timetable
C Study when you're wide awake!
D Make flash cards
E Get some Zzzzzs

3 **What is the difference between an *early bird* and a *night owl*? Which one are you? Can you give some examples to explain why?**

4 **Read the article again and complete the sentences with two or three words in each gap.**

1 When you've calculated how long to spend on each subject, begin your revision as ________.
2 The recommended rest time for each 60 minutes you spend revising is ________.
3 If you study while listening to music, remember that ________ can make it difficult to concentrate.
4 You should try to eat a lot of ________ and snack regularly around exam time.
5 If you don't ________, you might forget what you studied the day before!

5 **Match the highlighted words and phrases in the article to the meanings.**

1 improvement or increase
2 try to learn a lot very quickly before an exam
3 short sleep, especially during the day
4 a plan that gives events or activities and the times that they will happen or be done
5 a combination of the correct types and amounts of food

93 **6** **Listen to a study-skills tutor having a conversation with two students. Put the topics mentioned in the correct order.**

A Moving and stretching ___
B Focusing on progress ___
C Not panicking, planning instead ___
D Making a note of your worries before going into an exam ___
E Thinking positively ___

93 **7** **Listen again and complete the sentences with between two and six words.**

1 When she plans her revision schedule, Lucia feels …
2 If you're worried before an exam, the tutor suggests …
3 When you have exams, it's important to believe in yourself so that you don't focus …
4 Thinking about a memory that makes you happy will motivate you to …
5 Try not to be hard on yourself and celebrate …
6 Stretching and moving around will help you …

8 **Complete the sentences with the words in the box.**

achieving	cope	mindset
plan	well-being	

USEFUL LANGUAGE

Coping with exam stress

1 I want to find ways to help me ________ with exam stress.
2 Writing a study ________ will save time in the long run.
3 I'm trying to keep a positive ________ before my exams.
4 Thinking about a happy memory can give us a sense of ________.
5 Focus on making progress and not on ________ perfection.

116 LIFE SKILLS

LIFE SKILLS

Learning Objectives

- The students learn about how to study and prepare for exams effectively.
- In the project stage, the students prepare a campaign to improve exam preparation and present it to the class.

Vocabulary

balanced diet boost cram power nap schedule

BACKGROUND INFORMATION

The origin of the phrases *night owl* and *early bird*, which appear in the Reading text, are based on the habits of the owl, which hunt at night and sleep during the day and small birds which rise early to look for worms (*the early bird catches the worm* – appeared in a book of proverbs in 1605). Research has found that early birds are more productive than night owls. However, studies suggest that night owls can be more creative. Benjamin Franklin once said, 'early to bed and early to rise makes a man healthy, wealthy, and wise' but there is no evidence that this is true. The big problem for night owls is that school and most work suits early birds better.

WARMER

With books closed, dictate ten words from the text on page 117 for students to note down, for example: 'chart, alert, concentrate, distraction, visuals, summaries, hydrated, oxygen, energy, stressful'. Tell the students that this isn't a spelling test, so they shouldn't worry too much if they are not sure of how to spell any of the words. Tell them that they now have one minute to memorise the words. After one minute, tell them to put their notes away and, in pairs, try to remember all ten words.

When the students have done this, elicit any techniques they used in the one minute to try to memorise the words. You can also write the words on the board for students to check their spelling if necessary.

LIFE SKILLS

Preparing for exams

Tell students to read the information. Ask students if they have ever been taught how to prepare for exams and, if so, who by and what ideas they were given. Ask students which tips they have found the most useful.

1 Set a time limit of three minutes for students to discuss the questions together. Students then get together in groups of four to share their ideas. Invite students to tell the class any good techniques they learned from the other people in their groups.

Answers

Students' own answers

2 Look at the five headings with the class. On the board, write: *1 Get up and do something!* Under this write: *activities, sports, exercise, outside, rest*. Tell the students that these are words that you think could appear in the relevant paragraph. They do the same for the other four headings in pairs. While they are discussing ideas, write the other four headings on the board. Then elicit ideas and write them under the corresponding heading. When students have done the matching, elicit which of their words they found in the text.

Answers

A 8 B 1 C 2 D 5 E 9

3 These expressions are used at the start of paragraph 2. Elicit what an owl is and then ask the class what they think these two phrases mean (see Background information for origin of these phrases). Ask students to mingle to find out if students are night owls or early birds. When they find someone who is the opposite to them, they sit down together. When the people still standing can't find a partner, they join a pair already seated to make a group of three and discuss why they think they are a night owl or an early bird.

Answers

An *early bird* is a person who likes to get up and do things very early in the morning. A *night owl* is a person who is more awake and works best in the late evening or at night.

4 Tell students that the words needed for the gaps may be exactly the same as in the text or they may have to change them slightly. Students work alone and then compare answers in pairs. Elicit the answers and then look at each piece of advice with the class and ask them if they do the things suggested in 1, 2, 4 and 5. Ask, 'Do you ever listen to music while studying?' and if they do check whether or not they ever become distracted by the lyrics of the music.

FAST FINISHERS

Ask fast finishers to look at other pieces of advice in the text and rephrase the sentences from the text, for example: *If you don't drink enough water, you may suffer from ______ (headaches and/or tiredness)*. When everyone has finished, elicit the answers to the exercise and invite fast finishers to read out their sentences, leaving out the key information from the text. The other students have to guess what the words are.

Possible answers

1 early/soon as possible 2 15 minutes 3 the (song) lyrics 4 brain foods 5 sleep enough

94 The Reading text is recorded for students to listen, read and check their answers.

CONTINUED ON PAGE 230

5 Students work in pairs to discuss the meanings of the highlighted words from context and match them to the definitions. Check answers as a whole class. Ask students follow-up questions, for example: 'Do you cram at the last minute or start revising a long time in advance? What do you eat for an energy boost? Do you have a daily schedule that you try to keep to? Do you think your diet is balanced? How often do you have a power nap?'

Answers
1 boost 2 cram 3 power nap 4 schedule 5 a balanced diet

93 6 Look at the topics with the class and write: *A Moving and stretching* on the board. Ask the students to think about studying and exam stress and imagine what the speaker might say about this. Elicit ideas and write these on the board, for example, *It's good to move and stretch after sitting and studying for a long time.* Students then work in pairs to think about what the speaker might say about the other headings. Elicit ideas. When the students have listened, ask them to say which of their ideas were mentioned. *(A get up when you feel tension in shoulders or neck, or your back or legs start to ache … will release tension and help you relax; B don't worry about achieving perfection, just on getting better than before, celebrate successes; C planning saves time and makes you calmer because targets are more realistic; D it makes you more relaxed; E believe that you can be successful, stop and think of a happy memory that makes you smile)*

Answers
1 C 2 D 3 E 4 B 5 A

93 7 Students work in pairs to discuss anything they remember from the recording. When they have listened a second time, elicit the answers and ask students if they are the same or different to Lucy and ask for reasons why, for example, *I feel different when I plan a revision schedule: I get even more stressed when I see all the work I have to do!*

Possible answers
1 more relaxed. 2 writing down the things you're worried about.
3 on failure. 4 spend (a bit) more time studying.
5 your/any successes. 6 release tension (in your body) and relax.

» **AUDIOSCRIPT TB PAGE 307**

8 Students look at the sentences without looking at the words in the box and try to think of a word which could go in each gap. When they have looked at them all, they uncover the word pool and complete the sentences. Elicit the answers and encourage students to note down the new words, in phrases where necessary, for example, *cope with, a sense of well-being*.

MIXED ABILITY
Put the students into pairs and tell them to look up the meanings of the words in the box in a dictionary or online. They then share the definitions they found and do the sentence completion together. Strong students can write alternative sentences with the words in the box.

Answers
1 cope 2 plan 3 mindset 4 well-being 5 achieving

PROJECT *A campaign about exam preparation*
Look at the instructions with the students and, for the first point, re-elicit any areas that students could give advice for, such as exercise, food, socialising, treats, timetables, etc. and elicit any of their own ideas. Put them into groups of three or four and set a time limit for them to brainstorm different ideas and choose the best three. If students can't think of any new ideas, tell them to use their favourites from the text or they can use the ideas elicited at the beginning of the task. Set a realistic time limit for students to create their projects if doing them at home, preferably at least a week. Tell the class that each student should present a different part, as well as all of them giving a personal anecdote about their own exam preparation techniques.

When students have all presented their campaigns to the class, they work in their groups and discuss the three best pieces of advice that they heard from the other groups. Elicit ideas from each group and ask for reasons as to why they were impressed by these ideas.

PROJECT EXTENSION
Students stay in their original groups and discuss how they have prepared for exams in the past and what they could have been doing better. They then think about how they might use the best pieces of advice they heard from other groups in the future. They could also note any of the tips and techniques from the presentations that they have used in the past.

COOLER
Students write down one thing which they wish they could change at exam time, for example, *I get very stressed, I can't sleep. It's difficult to concentrate on my notes, etc.* When they are ready, they mingle and tell each other their problems. Everyone they talk to has to think of some advice to give them to help them; for example, *When you feel stressed, you should go for a walk and look around you. Try to concentrate on things you see around you and forget the exams for a while.* Set a time limit of four minutes. Students then sit in groups of four and tell each other their problem and the best advice they were given. Invite groups to share their ideas with the class.

TOP TIPS FOR EXAM SUCCESS!

There are lots of things you can do to prepare for exams. Try out these great tips and you'll see the difference when it comes to results time!

94

1 ______________________

Exams are often close together, so you'll probably be revising for various subjects at the same time. Work out how much time you can dedicate to each subject and make a chart of what you need to do when. Then start revising as early as possible, especially if you tend to cram at the last minute!

2 ______________________

Are you an early bird? Or perhaps you're a night owl? Planning your revision timetable around when your mind is most alert will make revising much easier! But no matter what time of day you study best, you ought to take a 15-minute break for every hour of study in order to give your brain some much needed rest.

3 STUDY TECHNIQUES MATTER

Some people use model exam answers to review what they've studied. You might find that studying with music really helps you concentrate, although be careful, because the lyrics can also be a big distraction! Get together with friends from class to talk through what you've learned and explain difficult things to each other. But if it quickly turns into social chat, group study might not be for you.

4 KEEP YOUR NOTES TIDY

Organising your notes into different sections will make your life a lot easier. Make sure that you ask a classmate or teacher for notes on any classes that you've missed. Good notes should include plenty of visuals like mind maps. And always use different coloured pens to highlight important points.

5 ______________________

Reduce your notes to summaries, and then write the most important facts from the summaries. Some students like to use a Q&A format, with a question on one side and an answer on the other. Take these everywhere you go – you never know when you'll get a few minutes to test yourself. Use them regularly and you'll be amazed how much you remember!

6 DRINK PLENTY OF WATER

Your brain needs to stay hydrated to work well. It's easy to forget to drink when you're studying a lot, and you can get headaches and feel tired as a result. Avoid drinks with caffeine or excessive amounts of sugar, and drink lots of water or herbal teas instead.

7 EAT PROPERLY AND SNACK HEALTHILY!

Just like sugary drinks, sweets and chocolate give you a quick energy boost. However, at exam time, it's preferable to eat foods which give you a slow release of energy. Make sure you have a balanced diet which includes plenty of 'brain foods' like cereals, pasta, oily fish, chicken, vegetables and salads. And snack regularly on things like nuts or fruit.

8 ______________________

Your brain needs lots of oxygen to work well, and exercise moves oxygen around your body. Going for a walk, a swim or playing a team sport should form a part of your daily schedule. And don't forget to exercise your eyes by blinking and looking away from your books or screen regularly. Tired eyes aren't good for reading!

9 ______________________

As well as hydration, good food and oxygen, your brain needs plenty of rest. Sleep is key, especially the night before an exam, and without it, it's easy to forget what you've studied! You should aim for a good eight hours of quality sleep. A power nap of 15–30 minutes can also give you some energy before you start a revision session.

10 AVOID STRESS

Do your best to avoid any situations that you know you find stressful. And remember that the day before an exam, you're not studying to learn new things, but to review what you've already studied.

PROJECT

A campaign about exam preparation

Work in groups of three or four to prepare a campaign to improve exam preparation. Use these steps to help you.

1. Brainstorm advice and techniques for preparing for exams and coping with exam-related stress.
2. Decide together on the three best ideas to include in your campaign.
3. Come up with a main message and slogan for your campaign.
4. Decide how you will promote the campaign to students in your school. Choose from different media such as posters, a web page, presentations, etc.
5. Include some personal stories about your own exam preparation experiences.

Present your work to the class.

REVIEW 5 UNITS 17–20

VOCABULARY

1 Complete the sentences with the words in the box.

comment	injured	keep
keeping	mind	suspect

1 How do you ________ up to date with what's happening in the world?
2 To my ________, it's important to be aware of news so you can ________ on current events intelligently.
3 I ________ you may have ________ your ankle when you jumped off that wall. Let's take a look at it and find out.
4 I like chilling out with a good book. A great adventure series is ________ me amused at the moment!

2 Complete the sentences with the jumbled verbs in the box.

ahctc	evela	igrnb	kbac	teg

1 I hate to ________ this up, but you owe me £10.
2 My holiday gave me time to ________ up on sleep.
3 Please help me make a list for the party. I might ________ out something important.
4 I tried to ________ my point across at the meeting, but I'm not convinced people understood.
5 When I tell Mum about the stain, will you ________ me up that it wasn't my fault?

3 Match the two parts of the phrases.

1 make
2 meet
3 be
4 take lots
5 work
6 do

a deadlines
b shifts
c a living
d something rewarding
e of time off
f well paid

4 Complete the sentences with the idioms. Make changes to the idioms as necessary.

be a pain	be a piece of cake	break my heart
lose track of time	take my breath away	

1 I finished the test 15 minutes early. It ________.
2 Is it two o'clock yet? I've ________.
3 My phone's battery rarely lasts the whole day. Having to recharge it during the day ________.
4 It ________ when the last series of that programme ended. I used to love it so much.
5 The view from our hotel room ________. We could see right across the whole city.

GRAMMAR

1 Complete the mixed conditionals with the correct form of the verbs in brackets.

1 I wouldn't be here now if Abby ________ (not mention) the game.
2 If we had sorted out the problems earlier, we ________ (not be) in this mess today.
3 I ________ (take) the summer job if it were a bit better paid. But I had to turn it down.
4 Tom could apply for medicine if he ________ (study) biology, but he did maths, physics and chemistry.
5 If my brother ________ (not be) such a pain, I might have invited him to the festival. He's too young.

2 Complete the sentences with the correct form of the verbs in brackets. Use the *-ing* form, the infinitive with *to*, or the infinitive without *to*.

1 I hate ________ told what ________. (be, do)
2 ________ in mind how long it will take ________ there, I think we should leave now. (bear, get)
3 Despite Ollie ________ the best cook, we took turns ________ the meals on holiday. (be, make)
4 He denies ________ Joe, but admits he's been ________ about it. (tell, think)
5 ________ in a shop made me ________ how much I would hate that kind of job. (work, realise)

3 Choose the correct verb forms.

1 I like most of my classmates, but a couple *is / are* a pain.
2 The news about his accident *has / have* really upset me.
3 I think starting your own business *sound / sounds* like hard work.
4 One of my friends *work / works* in that café.
5 *Is / Are* anything in those film reviews positive?

4 Choose the correct options. Sometimes there is more than one possible answer.

I've got [1] *a / the / some* summer work in a local pizza restaurant. [2] *A / The / –* job itself is OK, and at least I'm earning [3] *some / a bit / a few* money. I spend [4] *a lot of / several / much* time taking orders over the phone, but I also make [5] *much / a large number / a bit* of pizzas, too. There are always [6] *a few / a bit of / a little* pizzas left at the end of [7] *an / the / –* evening, but I've gone off them now!

5 Correct the mistake in each sentence.

1 I would have been happier right now if you had done your homework.
2 I don't enjoy to shop all the time.
3 I really want to spend time to go sightseeing.
4 Life nowadays is so full of things to be done, that people forget that their health are important.
5 Whilst spending a few time in Barcelona, I have been looking for different kinds of activities which you could do in a single week.

REVIEW 5 UNITS 17–20

Overview

VOCABULARY	The media; Phrasal verbs: the media; The world of work; Idioms
GRAMMAR	Conditionals (2): mixed; Uses of verb + *ing*; Subject–verb agreement; Determiners
EXAM TASKS	Reading and Use of English Part 1; Reading and Use of English Part 3; Reading and Use of English Part 4

Resources

PHOTOCOPIABLE WORKSHEETS: Grammar worksheets Units 17–20; Vocabulary worksheets Units 17–20; Review Game Units 17–20; Literature worksheet; Speaking worksheet; Writing worksheet

WARMER

Put the class into two groups. Choose one student from each group to sit at the front of the classroom facing the other students. Tell the students that the two students at the front can't look at the board. The students facing the board have to define the word or phrase you write and the two at the front have to guess it. The students facing the board can't spell, translate or say the word(s). Whoever guesses the word or phrase first wins a point for their team. Swap both students after each correct guess. Examples to use: *make fun of, more or less, lyrics, outskirts, gossip about, bear in mind, break the ice*.

VOCABULARY

1 Tell students to cover the word pool. In pairs, they try to think of words which could go in the gaps. Write any ideas on the board without commenting on whether they are correct or not, for example *1 get, keep, stay*. Elicit ideas and then allow students to open their books and complete the activity. Elicit the answers and what the phrases mean and cross out any wrong words on the board that you elicited earlier. (Some other answers may be possible.)

Answers

1 keep 2 mind, comment 3 suspect, injured 4 keeping

2 Tell students to close their books. Write the jumbled words one at a time on the board and tell the students to put their hands up as soon as they know what the words are. When they have worked out all five words, they open their books and complete the sentences. Alternatively, you could write the verbs on the board for weaker students and ask stronger students to cover the jumbled letters and try to guess the missing verbs. Elicit the answers and the meanings of the phrases.

Answers

1 bring 2 catch 3 leave 4 get 5 back

3 When the students have done the matching elicit the first phrase, *make a living* and a sentence which could show what it means, for example, *I like my job but it is difficult to make a living as an artist*. Students then make sentences for the other phrases in pairs. Monitor and help where necessary. Then, elicit sentences to make sure they have used the phrases properly.

Answers

1 c 2 a 3 f 4 e 5 b 6 d

4 Read the idioms in the box and elicit the meanings of each and an example of something that can be a pain, be a piece of cake, break someone's heart, take someone's breath away or which can make you lose track of time. Students then complete the sentences. Elicit the answers and then, in pairs, ask students to rephrase them as if the person they are talking to doesn't understand the idioms, for example, *1 'It was a piece of cake.' 'Sorry?' 'I mean, it was very easy.'*

Answers

1 was a piece of cake 2 lost track of time 3 is a pain
4 broke my heart 5 took our/my breath away

GRAMMAR

1 Re-elicit which two conditionals are mixed (*second and third*) and their uses (*to talk an imaginary situation in the present that is affected by a past action; to talk about an imaginary situation in the past that is affected by a present situation or permanent conditions*). Look at the first sentence with the class and ask what the first part of the sentence shows (*an imaginary present situation*) and what is needed (*an imaginary past event*). Students complete the sentences alone and compare in pairs.

MIXED ABILITY

Put weaker students into pairs and tell them that sentences 1, 2, 4 follow the same pattern (*if* + past perfect + *would / could* + infinitive) and 3, 5 follow the opposite pattern (*if* + past simple + *would / might* + have + past participle). Tell them to watch out for sentences that are written the other way round or those that need negative forms. Students work together to complete the sentences.

Answers

1 hadn't/had not mentioned 2 wouldn't/would not be
3 'd/would have taken 4 'd/had studied
5 wasn't/was not/weren't/were not

2 Students complete the sentences in pairs. Before eliciting the answers, ask: 'How many of the sentences with the first word gapped take the *-ing* form?' Elicit answers and then tell the students that the correct answer is all of them. Then ask how many of the sentences with a second gap take the *to* + infinitive form. Tell the students the correct answer is three of them. Then, elicit that one sentence has two *-ing* forms and in another one, the second gap is the infinitive without *to*. Check the answers as a class.

Answers

1 being, to do 2 Bearing, to get 3 being, to make/making
4 telling, thinking 5 Working, realise

CONTINUED ON PAGE 234

3 Students work alone and compare answers in pairs. Elicit the answers and why each verb form is chosen (*1 a couple of them = two people are; 2* the news *always takes a singular verb form; 3 starting your own business is a single action = it sounds like; 4 one of my friends = one person = he/she works; 5 indefinite pronouns* anyone, something, nobody, *etc. are followed by a singular verb form*). You could extend the activity by asking students to think of ideas of their own for some of the phrases; for example, A couple of my classmates …, The news about…., One of my friends …., Is anything ….? Elicit ideas and make sure students have used the correct verb form for the first three.

Answers
1 are 2 has 3 sounds 4 works 5 Is

4 Tell students to look at the instructions and ask, 'Which quantifiers would it be possible to use in the same gap?' (for example, *some / a few / a number of*). Students then do the activity in pairs. Elicit the answers.

Answers
1 some 2 The 3 some 4 a lot of 5 a large number 6 a few 7 the

5 Students work in pairs to decide why each sentence is incorrect. They then play the role of teacher and student and take turns to explain what the problem is in each case and what the correct form should be. Elicit the problems and correct answers. For example, *1 The tense indicates a past problem but we are talking about a present situation. 2 We don't follow* enjoy *with* to.

Answers
1 I would ~~have been~~ **be** happier right now if you had done your homework.
2 I don't enjoy ~~to shop~~ **shopping** all the time.
3 I really want to spend some time ~~to go~~ **going** sightseeing.
4 Life nowadays is so full of things to be done, that people forget that their health ~~are~~ **is** important.
5 Whilst spending ~~a few~~ **some** / **a little** time in Barcelona, I have been looking for different kinds of activities which you could do in a single week.

PREPARE FOR THE EXAM

1 **B2 FIRST FOR SCHOOLS Reading and Use of English Part 1**
Briefly review what students need to do in this part of the exam and if necessary, read out the *B2 First for Schools* box on TB page 26.

Remind the class that this part of the exam tests vocabulary. Look at the example with the class and elicit what the other words generally refer to, for example, *compose a piece of music, publish a newspaper or book, broadcast a TV or radio show*. Remind students that, if they aren't sure, they can usually dismiss one or two of the choices so there is more chance of choosing the correct answer. Set a time limit of ten minutes and then elicit the answers and what the words mean.

FAST FINISHERS

Ask students to imagine they were Seb at the interview. In the text it says that Seb's enthusiasm made him the ideal candidate. Students work in pairs and think of some interview questions and answers. When everyone has finished, elicit the answers to the exercise and then invite fast finishers to act out their interviews for the class.

Answers
1 D 2 C 3 A 4 B 5 C 6 A 7 B 8 D

2 **B2 FIRST FOR SCHOOLS Reading and Use of English Part 3**
Briefly review what students need to do in this part of the exam and if necessary, read out the *B2 First for Schools* box on TB page 102.

Give students one minute to read the text and elicit what it is about. (*Why some English native speakers don't bother to learn a foreign language and why this is a shame.*) Set a time limit of nine minutes to reflect the fact that they have read through the text already and elicit the answers. Ask how many people knew that gap 3 is negative and how they knew. (*The text suggests a negative emotion as it has already said they don't see the point of learning a language.*)

Answers
1 concerned 2 totally 3 impatient 4 means 5 achievement 6 improved 7 rewarding 8 satisfaction

3 **B2 FIRST FOR SCHOOLS Reading and Use of English Part 4**
Briefly review what students need to do in this part of the exam and if necessary, read out the *B2 First for Schools* box on TB page 49.

Look at the example with the class and elicit that this is an example of a mixed conditional. The speaker is talking about the hypothetical past result (finishing their homework) of a present situation (someone who is constantly talking). Allow ten minutes for students to complete the exercise and allow them to compare answers in pairs. Elicit the answers and what each one is testing.

Answers
1 had not/hadn't | brought up 2 a lot of | time 3 a number | of 4 of us | will be 5 only | a little / only | a bit of 6 or later | you are

COOLER

Put students into groups of three or four. Write the four parts of the exam (*Reading and Use of English, Listening, Writing, Speaking*) on the board. Ask the students to work together to try to agree on the order of difficulty for the four papers, giving reasons for their answers. Monitor and note interesting ideas then invite different groups to share their ideas with the class.

PREPARE FOR THE EXAM

Reading and Use of English Part 1

1 For questions **1–8**, read the text below and decide which answer (**A**, **B**, **C** or **D**) best fits each gap.

The world's best summer job?

When an international holiday company **(0)** *advertised* a job for someone to test their water slides, they didn't expect so many people to apply. Incredibly, over 2,000 people did, but lucky Seb Smith, a British student, **(1)** ________ from them all.

Potential candidates needed to be 'mad about water parks', '**(2)** ________ to travel' and 'happy to get wet at work.' Seb **(3)** ________ his application with a funny video of himself testing a slide in his local park.

He will now spend three months travelling the world and judging new water slides which have been **(4)** ________ at the company's 20 water parks. **(5)** ________ in mind that all Seb's accommodation and travel expenses are free, it's hard to **(6)** ________ that the job is pretty well paid, too: Seb will earn an amazing £20,000!

'I'm absolutely over the **(7)** ________,' said Seb, 'and I can't wait to get started.' A spokesman for the company said Seb's enthusiasm made him the ideal person for the **(8)** ________ of water-slide tester.

	A	B	C	D
0	**A** composed	**B** published	(**C**) advertised	**D** broadcast
1	**A** put out	**B** came out	**C** brought out	**D** stood out
2	**A** agreeing	**B** obliging	**C** willing	**D** encouraging
3	**A** backed up	**B** cleared up	**C** faced up	**D** picked up
4	**A** begun	**B** launched	**C** served	**D** started
5	**A** Taking	**B** Crossing	**C** Bearing	**D** Thinking
6	**A** deny	**B** refuse	**C** decline	**D** reject
7	**A** sun	**B** moon	**C** Earth	**D** world
8	**A** part	**B** function	**C** purpose	**D** role

Reading and Use of English Part 3

2 For questions **1–8**, read the text below. Use the word given in capitals to form a word that fits in the gap.

WHAT'S THE POINT OF LEARNING A LANGUAGE?

Many native English speakers are of the firm **(0)** *belief* (**BELIEVE**) that they needn't bother learning another language. As far as they are **(1)** ________ (**CONCERN**), the people they come into contact with through business or travel already speak English. It isn't that they are **(2)** ________ (**TOTAL**) against the idea of learning languages, but simply that they don't see the point. They often get **(3)** ________ (**PATIENCE**), too, when it's suggested that they should make more of an effort.

What they're missing out on is a **(4)** ________ (**MEAN**) of understanding other cultures, and a whole range of skills which would almost certainly benefit them. Language learners not only gain a sense of **(5)** ________ (**ACHIEVE**) from being able to communicate with others across the globe, but also have **(6)** ________ (**IMPROVE**) memory, enhanced listening skills and better job opportunities.

Learning another language can be highly **(7)** ________ (**REWARD**), and it isn't necessary to reach fluency, either. Managing a conversation in another language, however basic, often leads to a great deal of **(8)** ________ (**SATISFY**) and pride.

Reading and Use of English Part 4

3 For questions 1–6, complete the second sentence so that it has a similar meaning to the first sentence, using the word given. **Do not change the word given.** You must use between **two** and **five** words, including the word given.

0 You keep talking and that's why I still have homework to do. **WOULD**
If it wasn't for you talking, I *would have done* my homework by now.

1 The media raised the issue of fake news, otherwise no one would know about it. **BROUGHT**
You wouldn't know about fake news if the media ________ the issue.

2 Jake takes ages getting ready to go out! **LOT**
Jake spends ________ getting ready to go out!

3 Several families have lived in this house over the years. **NUMBER**
Over the years, ________ families have lived in this house.

4 We're both going to go to the event at the town hall tomorrow night. **WILL**
Both ________ going to the event at the town hall tomorrow night.

5 The family doesn't have much money to spend on holidays. **ONLY**
The family has ________ money to spend on holidays.

6 Eventually, you will have to make a decision about what job you'd like to do. **ARE**
Sooner ________ going to have to make a decision about what job you'd like to do.

PREPARE FOR THE EXAM
B2 FIRST FOR SCHOOLS

READING AND USE OF ENGLISH

Reading and Use of English Part 1 Multiple-choice cloze (Unit 2, Unit 6, Unit 15, Review 1, Review 2, Review 4, Review 5)

EXAM INFORMATION

Reading and Use of English Part 1

- You will read a short text with eight gaps, each representing a missing word or phrase.
- There are eight four-option multiple-choice items, one for each gap.
- You should choose the correct answer to fill each gap.
- There is one example, to show you what to do.

1 Read the article quickly for general meaning. What alternative title could you give the article?

2 Look at the example (0). All four options are verbs. Why is A the correct answer?

3 Now read the exam instructions and complete the task.

For questions **1–8**, read the text opposite and decide which answer (**A, B, C** or **D**) best fits each gap. There is an example at the beginning (**0**).

EXAM TIPS

Look at the words around the gap to see if the missing word is part of a phrase or collocation. When you have finished, read the text again and check your answers.

0	**(A)** rise	**B** widen	**C** move	**D** progress
1	**A** aim	**B** hunt	**C** search	**D** track
2	**A** occupied	**B** urban	**C** engaged	**D** crowded
3	**A** inhabitants	**B** populations	**C** members	**D** public
4	**A** well-paid	**B** affordable	**C** modest	**D** low-priced
5	**A** take	**B** get	**C** make	**D** keep
6	**A** occasions	**B** chances	**C** capabilities	**D** opportunities
7	**A** diverse	**B** separate	**C** assorted	**D** variable
8	**A** profit	**B** gain	**C** promote	**D** benefit

CITY LIVING

Today, over half of the world's population live in cities, and this percentage is likely to **(0)** *rise* significantly in the future. More and more people are moving to cities in **(1)** ________ of employment and a better life. Their lives are becoming more **(2)** ________ and less rural, with 'mega cities', which have over 10 million **(3)** ________, emerging around the globe.

Some cities are more **(4)** ________ to live in than others, but residents with earning power can **(5)** ________ the most of city living, as cities provide many attractions, such as excellent shopping **(6)** ________, trendy restaurants and numerous other leisure facilities. What's more, anyone who lives in a city can take advantage of how culturally **(7)** ________ it is, how convenient it is, and how many interesting people there are to meet. There are certainly negative aspects of living in a city, such as overcrowding and pollution, but the general picture is that cities greatly **(8)** ________ those who live there.

Reading and Use of English Part 2 Open cloze
(Unit 5, Unit 11, Unit 16, Review 1, Review 2, Review 3, Review 4)

EXAM INFORMATION

Reading and Use of English Part 2

- You will read a short text with eight gaps.
- You should decide which word fits in each gap.
- You should write only one word for each gap.
- There is one example, to show you what to do.

1 **Read the text quickly for general meaning. Then look at the example. What kind of word is it (noun, preposition, determiner, article, etc.)?**

2 **Now look at the gaps in the text. Which gap (or gaps) require ...**

- a conjunction
- a verb form
- part of a comparative structure
- part of a phrase
- a determiner
- part of an infinitive
- a preposition

3 **Now read the exam instructions and complete the task.**

For questions 1–8, read the text below and think of the word which best fits each gap. Use only one word in each gap. There is an example at the beginning (0).

EXAM TIPS

Check your spelling before writing your answers. The words must be spelled correctly. When you have finished, read the whole text again and make sure the word you've chosen makes sense.

CROCODILES

Not **(0)** *all* crocodiles in Australia are threatening to humans. Freshwater crocodiles, known **(1)** ________ 'freshies', do not attack people, and being shy by nature, they prefer **(2)** ________ stay away from them altogether. Their habitat includes rivers and natural pools in northern regions of the country, and fish are therefore the creatures' main source **(3)** ________ food. Freshies do, however, consume a variety of small animals and insects as well.

Saltwater crocodiles (or 'salties'), on the **(4)** ________ hand, are dangerous creatures. They are also **(5)** ________ of the largest living creatures on our planet. Unlike freshwater crocodiles, which usually grow to around two metres in length, male adult salties **(6)** ________ been known to reach an incredible seven metres, **(7)** ________ this is rare. Like freshies, salties also eat fish and birds, but they are more **(8)** ________ happy to hunt larger animals, too, including horses and cattle. The 'saltwater' name is actually misleading, because these giant reptiles are just as content living in rivers and swamps inland.

PREPARE FOR THE EXAM
B2 FIRST FOR SCHOOLS

Reading and Use of English Part 3 Word formation
(Unit 9, Unit 17, Unit 20, Review 2, Review 3, Review 5)

EXAM INFORMATION

Reading and Use of English Part 3

- You will read a short text with eight gaps.
- There are eight words which you should change to fit the gap.
- You should only use the word which is on the same line as the gap.
- You must use all the words.
- There is one example, to show you what to do.

1 **Look at the example and gaps 1–4 in the text and read the explanations below. Notice that the answers require a suffix, a prefix or both.**

Example: The gap is followed by a noun, which suggests that the missing word is an adjective.
Question 1: The plural verb and *their* shows that the answer must be people (*psychologists*).
Question 2: The gap is after the main verb and an adverb is needed (*exactly*).
Question 3: A noun is needed after *There is* (*agreement*).
Question 4: Here, you must understand the meaning of the whole sentence to know that an adjective with a negative prefix is needed (*unlikely*).

2 **Look at question 5. What part of speech is needed in the gap: an adverb or an adjective? Choose *cheerfully* or *cheerful*.**

3 **Now read the exam instructions and complete the task.**

For questions 1–8, read the text below. Use the word given in capitals at the end of some of the lines to form a word that fits in the gap in the same line. There is an example at the beginning (0).

EXAM TIPS

Decide which part of speech is needed for each gap. Remember that you may need to make a word negative, and can use a prefix or suffix to do so. When you have finished, check your answers make sense and are spelled correctly.

Identity and the *Individual*

The whole concept of **(0)** *personal* identity is fascinating. A lot of meaningful research has been carried out in this area, and **(1)** ________ continue to spend their working lives exploring its deep questions. Do our personalities stay **(2)** ________ the same over time? Given that our childhood experiences are so different to what we encounter as adults, there is **(3)** ________ among experts working in the field that this is **(4)** ________ to be the case.

PERSON
PSYCHOLOGY
EXACT
AGREE
LIKE

Do we even have just one 'self' or various 'selves' according to who we are with? A teenage boy may engage in **(5)** ________ conversation with his elderly grandmother about hobbies and homework, whereas his **(6)** ________ could be somewhat different when he is with other teens. The **(7)** ________ of us will act differently according to who we are with at any given time. Our desire to gain **(8)** ________ of a group often influences what we do and say in different situations, whether this is for better or worse.

CHEER
BEHAVE
MAJOR
MEMBER

Reading and Use of English Part 4 Key word transformation
(Unit 4, Unit 10, Unit 14, Review 1, Review 3, Review 4, Review 5)

EXAM INFORMATION
Reading and Use of English Part 4

- You will read six separate questions, each with a pair of sentences, one complete and one incomplete.
- You should complete the second sentence using between two and five words, including the key word given in bold.
- The second sentence should have the same meaning as the first sentence.
- You must not change the key word.
- There is one example, to show you what to do.

1 **Look at the example below. What changes have taken place in the second sentence?**

0 Medical research recommends reducing the amount of salt you consume. **DOWN**
According to medical research, you *should cut down on* the amount of salt you consume.

2 **Look at questions 1 and 2 in Exercise 3. Which one tests a dependent preposition?**

3 **Now read the exam instructions and complete the task.**

For questions 1–6, complete the second sentence so that it has a similar meaning to the first sentence, using the word given. Do not change the word given. You must use between two and five words, including the word given.

EXAM TIPS
Make sure the second sentence means the same as the first. Then check your spelling and grammar carefully.

1 A majority of students selected Jackie as the best singer in the school's talent competition. **VOTED**
More students ________ any other singer in the school's talent competition.

2 I'll only phone next week if it is absolutely necessary. **REALLY**
Next week, I won't phone ________ to.

3 I didn't like the new fashion at first, but I don't mind it now. **USED**
It has taken me a while ________ the new fashion.

4 Doing homework needn't be a chore if you work with your friends. **HAVE**
It ________ be a chore doing homework if you work with your friends.

5 There wasn't much food left over after the party. **SMALL**
Only ________ food was left over after the party.

6 To my mind, travel is a waste of time. **FAR**
As ________, travel is a waste of time.

PREPARE FOR THE EXAM
B2 FIRST FOR SCHOOLS

Reading and Use of English Part 5 Multiple choice (Unit 7, Unit 12, Unit 18)

EXAM INFORMATION

- You will read a fiction or non-fiction text.
- There are six four-option multiple-choice questions.
- The questions are in the same order as the information in the text.
- You should read the text carefully and choose only one option per question.

1 **Read the article on page 125 quickly. What is *Southfields*?**

A a documentary about old skateboarding movies
B a documentary about the award-winning skateboarder Stuart Laker
C a documentary about skaters in an area of London

2 **Read question 1 below. Then look at the highlighted part of the first paragraph, which confirms the answer. Why are A, B and D wrong?**

3 **Now read the exam instructions and complete the task.**

You are going to read an article about a film-maker called Stewart Laker and a skateboarding film he has made. For questions 1–6, choose the answer (A, B, C or D), which you think fits best according to the text.

1 What made the writer want to watch the film *Southfields*?
A the fact that it was made for younger audiences
B the reputation of the person who directed it
C the location where the film is set
D the publicity she had read about it

EXAM TIPS

Read the relevant paragraph and underline where you think the answer is. Check that the other three options are wrong.

2 Stewart Laker tells the writer that *Southfields*
A explores certain aspects of growing up.
B draws attention to an unfamiliar side of urban life.
C highlights the value of having a particular passion.
D shows how people benefit from overcoming physical challenges.

3 In the third paragraph, the writer expresses admiration for the way *Southfields* shows how
A extreme the lifestyle of skateboarders can be.
B different skateboarders are from each other.
C separate skateboarders are from the rest of society.
D skateboarders use language imaginatively.

4 The writer suggests the action scenes in *Southfields*
A may well have benefitted from more careful planning.
B must have required many repeated attempts to get them right.
C would have been better if more advanced film equipment had been used.
D could only have been made by someone with in-depth knowledge of skateboarding.

5 What does 'have a knack for' in line 52 mean?
A have a talent for
B have an interest in
C have problems with
D have time for

6 How does Laker feel about skateboarding being included in the Olympic Games?
A concerned about how it will affect people already involved in the sport
B unsure whether it will attract more people to the sport
C confident that it will result in better facilities for the sport
D hopeful that it will lead to improved safety in the sport

SOUTHFIELDS

Jennie Burgess meets Stewart Laker, the director of a new skateboarding movie.

People have always filmed skateboarding. As a skateboarder myself, I've watched hundreds of videos of young skateboarders displaying their skills and many skateboarding movies – dramas, usually based in some urban landscape in the USA, in which the main characters are teenage skateboarders. These movies often aren't very good, and when I first read about *Southfields* – directed by a well-known, award-winning maker of adverts for skateboarding equipment – I suspected more of the same. It wasn't until someone told me it was about young people in my home town, London, that I thought I'd give it a try. I'm glad I did.

When I meet Stewart Laker, he has his skateboard with him. He skates every day and says it makes him feel good. 'You concentrate on bumps in the street, how steep a ramp is, how to jump over a concrete block, and not getting hurt. This takes your mind off other things. You see that in *Southfields*. By losing themselves in what they're doing, the skaters are often dealing with other issues – the changes they're experiencing as they move towards adulthood, complicated feelings about family and friends, the desire for independence. Those things are what the film's really about – skateboarding's the context.'

Most of Laker's cast are skateboarders from an area of the city the film is named after, and parts of the storyline are based on their real-life experiences. There's a tendency to view skateboarders as all weird, wild, long-haired teenage boys who wear torn clothes, communicate with strange words, and can't fit in with the way most people live. While two of Laker's skaters are like that, we also meet 14-year-old Sam, a promising pianist; Maria, who's studying medicine; and 22-year-old Fatima, who's a qualified accountant. Their fascinating individual stories are followed in convincing detail; what brings them together is their love for the sport.

How interesting non-skateboarders will find the skateboarding action scenes in *Southfields,* I can't be certain. They were clearly filmed by someone with a great deal of personal experience of the sport – they capture what it's really like. Many scenes are filmed from the ground looking upwards. The shots are often shaky, as if taken with a small, hand-held camera rather than the large, modern, sophisticated devices that Laker assures me he actually filmed with. We see the skateboarders practising the same trick again and again – usually failing, very occasionally succeeding. That's skateboarding, though – thrills, dangers, frustrations and rare satisfactions.

As in all skateboarding films, music plays a key part. Skaters' musical tastes vary, so it's no surprise that the soundtrack includes Scandinavian heavy metal, Colombian *reggaeton*, African jazz, UK hip-hop and Korean pop. There are also tunes that Laker has included in an attempt to recall the soundtracks of skateboarding films made 20, even 50 years ago; but, rather than achieving this aim, these songs make the film seem a little dated. Laker does **have a knack for** arranging the songs to support the story – we see Maria, who is confident and dynamic, skating to fast, electronic dance music, while shy, sensitive Sam gets a quieter, thoughtful piece. These choices skilfully reflect the skaters' individual personalities and further highlight how diverse the skating community is.

One young skateboarder in the film talks about representing her country at the Olympic Games. How does Laker feel about skateboarding becoming an Olympic sport? Does it mean that more skateparks will be built? 'How many more courts have been built since tennis became an Olympic sport?' he replies. With media coverage of the Olympics, the general public will know what skateboarding is like and realise how impressive the top skaters are. However, it's not clear if this will translate into people actually taking up the sport. Will more regulations be introduced to make the sport safer? 'Some probably will,' Laker says. 'It's an extreme sport – accidents obviously happen. But if it becomes very regulated, we'll lose something special about it, although there isn't much danger of that happening.'

PREPARE FOR THE EXAM 125

PREPARE FOR THE EXAM
B2 FIRST FOR SCHOOLS

Reading and Use of English Part 6 Gapped text
(Unit 3, Unit 10, Unit 19)

EXAM INFORMATION
Reading and Use of English Part 6

- You will read a text from which six sentences have been removed.
- There are seven sentences to choose from.
- You should read the text carefully and choose only one sentence to fill each gap.
- There is one sentence which you do not need to use.

1 **Read the text quickly. Choose the best alternative title for the text.**

A How companies benefit from advertising
B How adverts encourage you to buy
C How to create a successful advert

2 **Choose the option which fits in the first gap. Why is this the correct option?**

3 **Now read the exam instructions and complete the task.**

You are going to read an article about advertising. Six sentences have been removed from the article. Choose from the sentences A–G the one which fits each gap (1–6). There is one extra sentence which you do not need to use.

EXAM TIPS
Look for meaning and language in the sentences which link to the text around the gap. Then read each paragraph with your answer in place to check it makes sense.

A Another proven advertising technique involves featuring a celebrity who gives a personal recommendation for their chosen brand.

B Advertisements like this are, predictably, broadcast more frequently at certain times of year.

C A sunny image of smiling teenagers enjoying their favourite soft drink by the pool may well persuade you to follow their example.

D By releasing such an impressive set of facts about this special feature, the advertiser expects you to commit to the product without a second thought.

E So, the orange juice that provides 75% of your daily requirement of vitamins will be bought in preference to other soft drinks where no such claim is made.

F In other words, they can create a need that you didn't even know you had.

G This personalisation of products helped them reconnect with the public, and convince those who had not tried the product before to give it a go.

The art of advertising

ADVERTISEMENTS work in different ways according to how they have been developed. Of course, the objective is the same – to persuade you, the consumer, to purchase a product – but the techniques employed to do this vary a great deal.

Some adverts are designed to appeal directly to your emotions, both positive and negative. **1** ______ The suggestion is that if you do so, you will end up feeling as satisfied as they are.

Witnessing pain and suffering can play on your feelings just as effectively. Seeing someone in an advert with a heavy cold who gains instant relief from the product being advertised should register in your memory that this is the remedy to seek out the next time you are sneezing helplessly. **2** ______ In this particular case, the advert would be shown during the peak period of winter coughs and colds.

A different approach that is adopted for other kinds of advert relies on convincing the consumer to buy a product based on real scientific evidence or statistics. **3** ______ This appeal to reason appears to be highly effective where personal health and fitness is concerned.

4 ______ Involving such people in this way gives a product status, and makes potential customers want to associate themselves with those promoting the product. Whatever image the person endorsing the brand has will supposedly be passed onto the consumer when they purchase the brand themselves.

One recent kind of advertising campaign involves the consumers themselves. For example, one big name brand, Coca-Cola, produced products with common first names on the label. **5** ______ Another popular brand, the chocolate nut spread Nutella, made it possible for customers to request an individual label with their own name printed on it.

There are many other strategies employed by brands to make you, the consumer, want to go out and purchase their products right away. **6** ______ In addition to promising happiness and status, advertisers also take advantage of consumers' FOMO (fear of missing out). So, if all your friends have the latest smartphone, the chances are, you'll want it too. Companies will even resort to scare tactics (if you don't buy this product, a particular problem will get worse) to make you buy a product.

PREPARE FOR THE EXAM
B2 FIRST FOR SCHOOLS

Reading and Use of English Part 7 Multiple matching
(Unit 1, Unit 8, Unit 13)

EXAM INFORMATION

Reading and Use of English Part 7

- You will read either a single text which is divided into sections, or several short texts about the same subject.
- There are ten questions which you should match to each section.
- You can use each section more than once.

1 Look at questions 1 and 2. Which asks about an opinion? Does it ask about a positive or negative opinion?

2 In this part of the exam, information which appears to be relevant may be found in another section of the text, but it will not answer the question correctly. Look at question 2. Then read texts A and B. Underline the information which appears to match the question. Then decide whether A or B is the right answer.

3 Now read the exam instructions and complete the task.

You are going to read an article about four teenage tennis players and their fitness. For questions **1–10**, choose from the teenagers (**A–D**). The teenagers may be chosen more than once.

EXAM TIPS

Read the questions first and underline important words. Then read the texts quickly to find the information you need.

Which teenager

disapproves of an aspect of her fellow players' behaviour?	1
arranges additional matches as part of her fitness plan?	2
acknowledges that she could make more effort to be healthy?	3
admits that a chosen form of physical exercise could be risky?	4
is following a plan which has been created especially for her?	5
praises the advice and support she has been given on diet?	6
makes a particular effort to prepare well before a match?	7
would like to start working on a certain technique with her coach?	8
is confident that she can overcome a weakness in her performance?	9
believes some people think that the sport requires little effort?	10

TEENAGE TENNIS PLAYERS AND THEIR FITNESS

A ALEXANDRA

Being part of the top college tennis team means I have to stay in great shape. So, however hard I'm studying, not a day goes by without some form of exercise, although I might only actually do tennis practice three times a week. Swimming and long-distance running suit me better than organising extra games, allowing me to build up my strength. These activities also provide useful thinking time for essays, so my brain gets a proper workout. Our fitness trainer keeps an eye on general food intake and comes up with really helpful suggestions about what to eat and when. Not everyone listens to him, though, which I think shows little respect for what he's contributing to the team effort. Then again, I tend to ignore advice on sleep patterns, while the others are pretty good at observing the early nights rule, so I maybe shouldn't criticise them!

B KATE

Our team practice sessions are scheduled after school finishes and focus on movement around the tennis court and general technique. I also set up further sessions on court with friends, so there's no shortage of tennis! Some players do other sports to keep fit, but that's not my thing. I do lift weights, but my body's still growing, so I need to be careful how I do it, even though it's evidently good preparation for long matches. Up to a point, taking in high-energy products on court helps with any lack of stamina, but I can't deny that as time goes on through the match, it's tough to keep going. I'm doing extra workouts right now to tackle this and I expect to see some benefit from that soon. Maybe I should seek advice on eating a balanced diet, too. We don't get much official support on that, which could actually make all the difference in big matches.

C TAMARA

I always make sure I get myself ready properly for any match, whether I'm playing against someone experienced or someone without as much experience as me. I reckon that's great practice for when I turn professional – if I ever do! This means getting a good night's sleep and then eating the right stuff – some protein, fruit or energy bars. I've done my own research into what I should do and when, and I'm sure that's helped me improve my game. At the moment, I'm increasing my fitness levels with my coach, who's developed a training programme to suit my own personal needs. I do a series of jumps and sprinting, which reflect the movements you do on court. The professionals make the sport look easy, and friends seem surprised when I tell them how demanding it is. Tennis matches can go on for hours, so you can lose by not being fit enough.

D MICHELA

Every time I have a spare hour or two, you'll see me heading down to the courts by my house, looking out for someone to have a game with. I'm self-taught, which means I've picked up a few bad habits which I'm now trying to undo. I've just found a trainer at the local club who's agreed to do some sessions with me, and I'm making progress. I still need to develop a stronger serve, so that's what I want to look at next with him. So far, we've spent time building up my stamina so I can keep going for longer. I haven't taken any of it too seriously until now, but I'm quite keen to become a better player, though I know I'll probably never play professionally. I never really considered that what I ate had an impact on my playing ability, and I know I ought to eat fewer burgers and more lean protein, like fish.

PREPARE FOR THE EXAM
B2 FIRST FOR SCHOOLS

WRITING

Writing Part 1 Writing an essay (Unit 1, Unit 9, Unit 15, Unit 19)

EXAM INFORMATION
Writing Part 1

- You will be given a question or statement and asked whether you agree with it.
- You are also given two ideas which you must include in your essay.
- Your essay must also contain a third idea of your own which does not overlap with the first two ideas. This 'own idea' is **not** the conclusion.

1 Read the task. Which two ideas below (A–C) would be relevant as a third idea?

A developing talent **B** time in the day
C social skills

In your English class you have been talking about sport. Now your English teacher has asked you to write an essay for homework. Write your essay using **all** the notes and giving reasons for your point of view.

> **'Sport should be a compulsory subject for teenage schoolchildren.'**
> **Do you agree?**
> **Notes**
> Write about:
> 1 keeping fit
> 2 teamwork
> 3 ________ (your own idea)

2 Complete the advice with the words in the box.

conclusion	grammar	introduction	
language	paragraphs	plan	spelling

1 Make a ________ before you begin writing.
2 Start your essay with an ________, where you explain what it will cover.
3 Organise your essay in ________.
4 Include a ________ at the end.
5 Don't use ________ which is too informal.
6 Check your essay for ________ and ________.

3 Now read the exam instructions and complete the task.

You **must** answer this question. Write your answer in **140–190** words in an appropriate style.

EXAM TIPS

Remember to include a relevant third idea. Time how long it takes you to write your essay – you should spend no longer than 40 minutes on it.

Writing Part 2 A choice of writing task (Unit 3, Unit 5, Unit 7, Unit 11, Unit 13, Unit 17)

EXAM INFORMATION
Writing Part 2

- You are given a choice of four questions. These may include an article, a letter or email, an essay, a review or a story.
- You should choose **one** question only.
- Question 5 is about a set text. You shouldn't choose this question if you haven't studied the set text in class.
- You should write 140–190 words.

1 Read the task, then answer the questions to help you think of ideas for your story.

1 What do you think has happened in the room to cause Sofie to leave?
2 Where do you think Sofie will go next?
3 Has someone been unable to keep a secret?
4 How might a phone be involved in the story?

You have seen this announcement in an English-language magazine.

> **Write a story!**
> We are looking for stories about strong emotions to publish in the next issue of our magazine. Your story must **begin** with this sentence:
> *Sofie was so angry that she stood up and ran out of the room, shutting the door loudly behind her.*
> Your story must include:
> - a secret
> - a phone

2 Which of these tips could you use for writing a story? Tick all that apply.

- have a clear storyline ☐
- use descriptive vocabulary ☐
- use a range of grammatical structures ☐
- add lots of detail ☐
- use direct speech ☐
- use humour ☐
- use narrative tenses ☐
- write an unexpected or dramatic ending ☐

3 Now read the exam instructions and complete the task.

Write your story. Write your answer in **140–190** words in an appropriate style.

EXAM TIPS

Decide how you will continue from the first sentence before you start writing. Remember to include the two things listed.

LISTENING

Listening Part 1 (Unit 6, Unit 20) Multiple choice

EXAM INFORMATION

Listening Part 1

- You will listen to eight unrelated extracts of about 30 seconds each.
- You will hear one or two speakers each time.
- There is one three-option multiple-choice question to answer for each extract.

1 **Read question 1. What is it important to listen out for?**

95 **2** **Listen to the extract for question 1. Choose the best answer (A, B or C). Why are the other options incorrect?**

1 You hear two friends discussing a novel.
What do they agree is impressive about it?
A how believable the characters are
B how clearly the plot develops
C how well the places are described

2 You hear a boy talking on the phone about some homework.
He is worried because he
A doesn't have the right materials.
B can't complete everything in time.
C hasn't got enough ideas to include.

3 You hear two friends talking about social media.
What do they both say about it?
A It's a good way to connect with new people.
B It helps them to remember past events.
C It occupies time which would otherwise be boring.

4 You hear a girl telling her friend about moving house.
How does she feel about it?
A sad about having left her old home
B upset not to have more space
C disappointed with the location

5 You hear a teacher talking to his class about being a good citizen.
What does he want them to do after the lesson?
A talk about what it means
B carry out some online research
C put some ideas into action

6 You hear an announcement at a railway station.
The purpose of the announcement is to inform customers that
A there are likely to be some delays.
B there is a replacement service available.
C some work is being carried out on the tracks.

7 You hear a boy talking to his sister about climbing.
What is he doing?
A advising her to do something
B reminding her to do something
C offering to help her do something

8 You hear two friends talking about the girl's temporary job.
The girl thinks that her work should be
A better organised.
B more highly paid.
C done at a different time.

96 **3** **Now read the exam instructions and complete the task.**

You will hear people talking in eight different situations. For questions 1–8, choose the best answer (A, B or C).

EXAM TIPS

Choose the answer you think is correct at the first listening. Check your answer when the recording is repeated.

PREPARE FOR THE EXAM
B2 FIRST FOR SCHOOLS

Listening Part 2 Sentence completion (Unit 8, Unit 12, Unit 16)

EXAM INFORMATION
Listening Part 2

- You will listen to one person speaking for between three and four minutes.
- There are ten questions in the form of incomplete sentences.
- As you listen, you should complete each sentence with a word or short phrase.
- The questions are in the same order as the information you hear.

1 Look at the title. What do you think the recording will be about? What do you think Jamal does?

2 Read the sentences. What kind of information would complete each sentence?

97 **3** Now read the exam instructions and complete the task.

You will hear a girl called Cristina talking about a musician called Jamal Edwards. For questions **1–10**, complete the sentences with a word or short phrase.

EXAM TIPS
Read the sentences before listening to predict what kind of information is missing. Check your answers when you listen to the recording the second time.

JAMAL EDWARDS and his music website SBTV

The first video Jamal uploaded to the internet showed **(1)** ________ in London.

Jamal was interested in music which combined garage and **(2)** ________.

Some of Jamal's early music videos were filmed in **(3)** ________, which people found very original.

Jamal started saving money for equipment when he was working in a **(4)** ________.

Jamal set up his website when his videos had been viewed more than **(5)** ________ times.

Cristina likes looking at the **(6)** ________ which are posted on the SBTV website.

Jamal acknowledges that he wasn't good at **(7)** ________ when his business started to become serious.

Jamal used to **(8)** ________ staff because he was shy.

Cristina likes the fact that Jamal encourages people to build their **(9)** ________ in order to become successful.

Jamal was not keen on becoming **(10)** ________ after what happened to his mother.

Listening Part 3 Multiple matching (Unit 2, Unit 4, Unit 14)

EXAM INFORMATION
Listening Part 3

- You will hear five individual speakers, talking about a common theme.
- You should choose the option which matches what each speaker says.
- There are eight options (A–H) to choose from.
- There are three options which are not used.

98 **1** Read options A–H below. Which subject (A–C) do you think they all relate to? Listen to the first speaker and check your ideas.

A studying science
B wildlife holidays
C volunteering

2 Read the exam instructions in Exercise 3. Underline the key words in the options which you need to listen out for.

99 **3** Now complete the task.

You will hear five short extracts in which university students are talking about doing voluntary work on conservation projects in different parts of the world. For questions **1–5**, choose from the list (**A–H**) what each speaker says they enjoyed most about the experience. Use the letters only once. There are three extra letters which you do not need to use.

EXAM TIPS
Be careful – sometimes an option seems possible, but it isn't a match. Check your answers when you listen to the recording the second time.

A saving the life of individual animals
B getting to see a wide variety of environments
C having the chance to do challenging tasks
D getting close to a very rare animal
E being responsible for collecting important data
F using relevant previously learned information
G learning more about various local traditions
H being able to view the beautiful surroundings

Speaker 1	1
Speaker 2	2
Speaker 3	3
Speaker 4	4
Speaker 5	5

Listening Part 4 Multiple choice (Unit 10, Unit 18)

EXAM INFORMATION

- You will hear an interview or conversation lasting between three and four minutes.
- There are seven multiple-choice questions with three options (A, B and C).
- You should choose the option which answers each question.

100 **1** **Listen to an interviewer introduce a guest called Maria Smith on a radio programme. What has Maria done recently?**

2 **Look at the questions. Which ones ask about people's emotions and opinions?**

101 **3** **Now read the exam instructions and complete the task.**

You will hear an interview with a teenager called Maria Smith, who's talking about carrying out a survey into her generation's views on the future. For questions 1–7, choose the best answer (A, B or C).

1 Maria says that she became interested in the topic of her survey after
A hearing her friends discussing their plans.
B feeling worried about her progress at college.
C being encouraged to think about her future.

2 Maria's biggest challenge while working on her survey was
A preparing suitably worded content.
B analysing all the results thoroughly.
C persuading enough students to complete it.

3 What did Maria identify as being of concern to many students?
A being accepted at the right university
B getting a job that is suitable for them
C having an adequate standard of living

4 On the subject of technology, Maria says that many students seem to be
A convinced that it will continue to develop.
B dissatisfied with the range of products available.
C uneasy about needing it for everything they do.

5 When Maria read responses to a question about success, she felt
A surprised by what people considered important.
B disappointed that people gave little detail.
C pleased that people were so ambitious.

6 What does Maria plan to do with the data she has collected?
A publish it online
B write a report explaining her findings
C encourage other people to read about what she did

7 How does Maria feel after having carried out the survey?
A more confused than she was previously
B confident that she will make good decisions
C regretful that she has wasted valuable time

EXAM TIPS

Underline the key words in the questions before you listen. Check your answers when you listen to the recording the second time.

PREPARE FOR THE EXAM
B2 FIRST FOR SCHOOLS

SPEAKING

Speaking Part 1 Interview
(Unit 2, Unit 14)

EXAM INFORMATION

Speaking Part 1

- The examiner will ask you some questions.
- The questions will be about you, your interests and your life.
- You should answer the questions, expressing your opinion about various topics.

1 **Look at the questions. Which three topics are they about?**

- How often do you use social media?
- What do you like finding out about on the internet?
- How do you usually travel to school or work?
- Do you use public transport to travel around?
- What do you enjoy doing with your family and friends in your free time?
- Is there a new hobby you would like to do in the future?

102 **2** **Listen to Sara answering some of the questions. Which ones is she asked?**

3 **Read the questions below. Ask and answer them with a partner.**

1

What kind of books do you like?

I like fantasy books best.

What do you like about them?

They're really imaginative and take you into a different world.

2 What was the last special occasion you celebrated? What did you do to celebrate?
3 Do you have any interesting hobbies? Tell me what you like about it/them.
4 Who do you enjoy spending time with? What kind of things do you do when you spend time with him/her?
5 Tell me about a TV programme you've seen recently. Would you recommend it to other people? Why? / Why not?

EXAM TIPS

Give longer answers, not just *Yes* or *No* answers. Don't worry if you get stuck. The examiner will ask you another question. You will not lose marks for this.

Speaking Part 2 Long turn
(Unit 8, Unit 20)

EXAM INFORMATION

Speaking Part 2

- The examiner will give you two photographs.
- You should compare the photographs for about one minute and answer the question given.
- You will also be asked to comment (for about 30 seconds) on your partner's photos.

1 **You are going to compare two photographs. Look at photographs 1 and 2 on page 135. They show teenagers doing different things in their free time. Think of ideas for the question above them.**

103 **2** **Listen to Álvaro comparing photographs 1 and 2. How many of your ideas does he include?**

3 **Work in pairs.**

Candidate A: Look at photographs 3 and 4 on page 135. They show teenagers doing different outdoor activities. Compare photographs 3 and 4 and say what you think the teenagers are enjoying about these activities.

Candidate B: Which of these activities would you prefer to do? Why?

4 **Work in pairs.**

Candidate B: Look at photographs 5 and 6 on page 135. They show teenagers studying in different ways. Compare photographs 5 and 6 and say what you think the advantages are of studying in these different ways.

Candidate A: Do you prefer studying alone or in a group? Why?

EXAM TIPS

Compare the two photographs, making sure you answer the question you are asked about them. Be careful to make comparisons rather than simply describing the photos separately. Don't interrupt the other candidate when they are talking about their photos. The examiner will make it clear when it is your turn to speak.

What do people like about doing these activities?

1

2

What do you think the teenagers are enjoying about these activities?

3

4

What are the advantages of studying in these different ways?

5

6

PREPARE FOR THE EXAM
B2 FIRST FOR SCHOOLS

Speaking Part 3 Collaborative task
(Unit 12, Unit 16)

EXAM INFORMATION
Speaking Part 3

- You will have a conversation with another candidate lasting about three minutes.
- The examiner will give you a question to discuss, with five ideas to help you discuss the question.
- You will talk together for about two minutes, then the examiner will stop you.
- The examiner will then ask you to talk together for another minute before making a decision based on the task.

104 **1 Read the task, then listen to Sara and Álvaro. Do they think all of the ideas might be interesting to young people?**

Some young people would like to find out more about the history of the area where they live. Here are some ways they could find out about the history of their area and a question for you to discuss.

Talk to each other about how interesting young people would find these ways of finding out about history.

105 **2 Listen to the examiner. What do the candidates have to do next?**

106 **3 Listen to Sara and Álvaro make their decision. Which way of finding out about history do they choose?**

107 **4 Work in pairs. Listen to the examiner, then complete the task in Exercise 1.**

EXAM TIPS
Make sure you take turns in the conversation, and give your partner chances to speak. Don't be afraid to ask the examiner to repeat the questions if you need to hear them again.

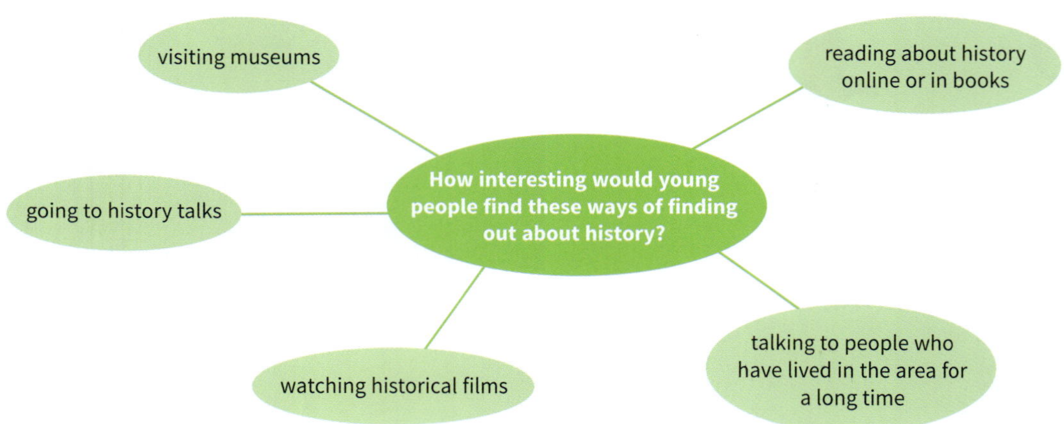

Speaking Part 4 Discussion
(Unit 12, Unit 16)

EXAM INFORMATION

- You will continue the discussion on the topic you talked about in Speaking Part 3.
- The examiner will ask questions for you both to answer.

108 **1 Read the questions, then listen to Sara and Álvaro. Which questions do they answer?**

- How can talking to the older generation help young people learn about the past?
- Do you think people should look to the future rather than the past? (Why?)
- Why are people so interested in their own family's history?
- Why do you think history museums should be interactive, with activities for visitors to do?
- How can history lessons be made interesting at school?
- Do you think certain periods of history are more important for young people to find out about than others? (Why? / Which ones?)

108 **2 Listen again. What do they say about each question they are asked?**

3 Ask and answer the questions in Exercise 1 with a partner.

How can talking to the older generation help young people learn about the past?

Life was often harder in the past. I think older people can help young people feel hopeful about the future and teach them what they've learned in life.

EXAM TIPS

Remember to talk to your partner during the discussion. Give reasons for your answers.

READING AND USE OF ENGLISH

Reading and Use of English Part 1

Multiple-choice cloze (Unit 2, Unit 6, Unit 15, Review 1, Review 2, Review 4, Review 5)

Remind students of the format of Reading and Use of English Part 1 and refer them to the exam information and tips boxes. This part is also practised in the Student's Book on pages 14, 31, 36, 53, 86, 97 and 119 and in the Workbook on pages 8, 24 and 60.

1 Give students two minutes to quickly read the text, ignoring the gaps. Elicit a few possible titles from the class.

> **Possible answers**
> Living in a city / City life

2 Ask students to identify the part of speech they would need in gap 0 (*a verb, as it follows the word* to). Then ask them to look at the options in Exercise 3. Ask a volunteer to explain why A is correct.

> **Answer**
> Because the verb *rise* collocates with the noun *percentage*.

3 Ask students to complete this exercise individually. Then tell them to compare their answers with a partner before checking as a whole class. Remind students of the importance of learning collocations as set phrases, for example *make the most of something*, as it is important in Part 1, Part 2 and Part 4 of the Reading and Use of English paper.

> **Answers**
> 1 C 2 B 3 A 4 B 5 C 6 D 7 A 8 D

» **TEST AND TRAIN: Exam Practice: Reading and Use of English Part 1**

Reading and Use of English Part 2

Open cloze (Unit 5, Unit 11, Unit 16, Review 1, Review 2, Review 3, Review 4)

Remind students of the format of Reading and Use of English Part 2 and refer them to the exam information and tips boxes. This part is also practised in the Student's Book on pages 31, 32, 53, 64, 75, 90 and 97 and in the Workbook on pages 20, 44 and 64.

1 Give the students 30 seconds to skim read the text. Ask them to tell you two interesting facts about crocodiles that they found out and then elicit what kind of word *all* is.

> **Answer**
> determiner

2 Before doing the exercise, elicit an example of each word type from students and write them on the board. Then ask the class to work in pairs to decide what type of word is needed in each gap. Check answers as a whole class.

> **Answers**
> 1 part of a phrase 2 part of an infinitive 3 part of a phrase
> 4, 5 determiner 6 verb form 7 conjunction
> 8 part of a comparative structure

3 Ask students to complete the gaps individually and then check answers as a whole class.

> **Answers**
> 1 as 2 to 3 of 4 other 5 one 6 have 7 (al)though/but 8 than

» **TEST AND TRAIN: Exam Practice: Reading and Use of English Part 2**

Reading and Use of English Part 3

Word formation (Unit 9, Unit 17, Unit 20, Review 2, Review 3, Review 5)

Remind students of the format of Reading and Use of English Part 3 and refer them to the exam information and tips boxes. This part is also practised in the Student's Book on pages 53, 56, 75, 98, 112 and 119 and in the Workbook on pages 38, 68 and 80.

1 Tell the students to look the first four gaps without reading the instructions to Exercise 1 and ask them to identify what is needed in each word. They then check their answers against the explanation.

2 Refer students to question 5 and ask them to decide on the answer in pairs. Before you elicit the answer, ask what word the gap describes (*conversation*) and what kind of word this is (*noun*). Elicit that we need an adjective (*cheerful*) because adjectives describe nouns, whereas adverbs describe verbs and adjectives.

Answer

adjective – cheerful

3 Ask students to discuss with a partner the type of word they think they will need in each of the final three gaps. Then ask them to try to do the exercise together. Remind students that it's useful to make a note of different forms of a word when recording vocabulary.

Answers

1 psychologists 2 exactly 3 agreement 4 unlikely 5 cheerful
6 behaviour 7 majority 8 membership

» **TEST AND TRAIN: Exam Practice: Reading and Use of English Part 3**

Reading and Use of English Part 4

Key word transformation (Unit 4, Unit 10, Unit 14, Review 1, Review 3, Review 4, Review 5)

Remind students of the format of Reading and Use of English Part 4 and refer them to the exam information and tips boxes. This part is also practised in the Student's Book on pages 26, 31, 60, 75, 82, 97 and 119 and in the Workbook on pages 18, 42 and 59.

1 Ask students to read the instructions to Exercise 1 and ask how the second sentence differs from the first. Remind students that there are two points for each question and ask how they think the points might be awarded here. (*It could be one point for writing* should *or* ought to *and one point for identifying the phrasal verb correctly.*)

Answer

recommends is replaced with the modal verb *should*, and *reducing* has been replaced with the phrasal verb *cut down* which is followed by *on* before a noun.

2 Tell the students not to complete the second sentences yet, but just think about the words needed. Have a hands up vote on whether 1 or 2 contains a dependent preposition and elicit what it is.

Answer

Question 1 tests a collocation (*vote for* someone).

3 Tell students to do the activity alone and then compare answers in pairs. If they have different answers, ask them to each close their eyes in turn and listen to their partner to see which sentence sounds incorrect. Elicit the answers and what each question tests (*1 collocation and phrasal verbs; 2 modals; 3 get/become used to something; 4 needn't and doesn't have to; 5 quantifiers; 6 a set phrase for giving opinions*).

Answers

1 voted for Jackie | than (for) 2 unless | I really have/need
3 to get/become | used to 4 does not/doesn't | have to
5 a small | amount of 6 far as | I am/'m concerned

» **TEST AND TRAIN: Exam Practice: Reading and Use of English Part 4**

Reading and Use of English Part 5

Multiple choice (Unit 7, Unit 12, Unit 18)

Remind students of the format of Reading and Use of English Part 5 and refer them to the exam information and tips boxes. This part is also practised in the Student's Book on pages 42, 68 and 102 and in the Workbook on pages 28, 48 and 72.

1 Make sure students understand the difference between fiction (*about imaginary characters and events*) and non-fiction (*about real facts and events*). Then give them one minute to read the text to answer the questions.

Answer

C

2 Ask students to highlight the key words in each of the options in question 1. Then give them one or two minutes to think of synonyms or similar expressions. Tell them to compare the options with the highlighted part of the text.

Answer

The writer says: *It wasn't until someone told me it was about young people in my home town, London, that I thought I'd give it a try.* So, the fact that it was located in London is what convinced her to watch it. A is incorrect because the fact that most of the characters are teenagers doesn't necessarily make it a film for younger audiences. B and D are incorrect because neither what she read about the film nor the fact that director is well-known as a maker of adverts for skateboarding equipment made her want to watch it.

3 Ask students to work with a partner to answer the questions. Check answers as a class and ask students to justify their answers by referring to the text.

Answers

1 C 2 A 3 B 4 D 5 A 6 B

» **TEST AND TRAIN: Exam Practice: Reading and Use of English Part 5**

Reading and Use of English Part 6

Gapped text (Unit 3, Unit 10, Unit 19)

Remind students of the format of Reading and Use of English Part 6 and refer them to the exam information and tips boxes. This is also practised in the Student's Book on pages 20, 58 and 108 and in the Workbook on pages 12, 40 and 76.

1 Give the students two minutes to read the text quickly and decide on the best title. Allow students to compare ideas in pairs and then elicit the answer and reasons for their choice.

Answer

B (The text is about how companies use advertising to persuade people to buy their products.)

2 Ask students to read the whole paragraph that the first gap appears in. Elicit what the sentence before and after the gap are about (*before the gap it talks about adverts appealing to emotions; the sentence after the gap refers to something that will make customers satisfied*). Elicit that the right choice will tell us what the action is that will make us satisfied and who they are. Students discuss the correct answer in pairs. Elicit this and ask, 'What will make us satisfied?' (*drinking the soft drink*) and 'Who are they?' (*smiling teenagers*).

Answer

1 C (It gives an example of an advert appealing to positive emotions. It refers to the fact that the consumer will feel as good as the people in the advert if they buy the product.)

3 Students work alone and, when they think they have matched a sentence to a gap, they check that they know what pronouns and other words and phrases, in both the text and the sentence, refer to. Elicit all the answers and the information which helped them.

Answers

1 C 2 B 3 E 4 A 5 G 6 F

» **TEST AND TRAIN: Exam Practice: Reading and Use of English Part 6**

Reading and Use of English Part 7

Multiple Matching (Unit 1, Unit 8, Unit 13)

Remind students of the format of Reading and Use of English Part 7 and refer them to the exam information and tips boxes. This part is also practised in the Student's Book on pages 10, 46 and 76 and in the Workbook on pages 4, 32 and 52.

1 Ask students to read the questions and elicit which one asks for an opinion and how they know (disapproves *shows an opinion;* arranges *is an activity*).

> **Answer**
> Question 1 asks for an opinion. The word *disapproves* shows that you need to look for a negative opinion.

2 Set a time limit for students to find the information. Elicit the two sentences so that all the students know what to look at, even if they didn't find them themselves. Students then decide which matches the question and why.

> **Answers**
> The words *organising* and *games* appear in Text A, although this is not actually the answer to question 2 as she says swimming and long-distance running are better than extra games. The answer is in B: *I also set up further sessions on court with friends, so there's no shortage of tennis!*

3 Students work alone and, when they think they have matched a question to a text, they mark the information in the text which helps them to decide. When they have finished, they compare answers in pairs and, if they have different answers, try to find the correct answer together. Elicit all the answers and the information which helped them.

> **Answers**
> 1 A 2 B 3 D 4 B 5 C 6 A 7 C 8 D 9 B 10 C

» **TEST AND TRAIN: Exam Practice: Reading and Use of English Part 7**

» **TEST AND TRAIN: Practice Test: Reading and Use of English**

WRITING

Writing Part 1

Writing an essay (Unit 1, Unit 9, Unit 15, Unit 19)

Remind students of the format of Writing Part 1 and refer them to the exam information and tips boxes. This part is also practised in the Student's Book on pages 13, 57, 89 and 111 and in the Workbook on pages 7, 39, 63 and 79.

1 Ask students to read through the instructions and then work in pairs to answer the question. Elicit why the other idea isn't a good one. (*It would be useful if writing about considerations when timetabling sports lessons, but not when deciding whether or not sport should be compulsory.*)

Answers
A and C

2 Tell students to complete the list of advice individually. Then ask them to compare their answers with a partner before whole-class feedback. Students, in pairs, then write one more tip for example, *link your arguments with words, such as* in addition, on the other hand, etc. Invite students to share these with the class.

Answers
1 plan 2 introduction 3 paragraphs 4 conclusion 5 language 6 grammar, spelling

3 Ask students to spend a few minutes brainstorming and organising their ideas. Monitor and check and then ask students to compare their plans with a partner. Weaker students could brainstorm together. Give students 40 minutes to write their essay. They then swap essays with a partner to check them against the list of advice from Exercise 2.

Model answer
In general, I agree with the statement, because health and fitness are crucial to people of all ages, and it is good to start sport at a young age so that it becomes part of your daily routine.
Combined with a good diet, regular physical activity ensures that people stay fit and healthy, protecting them against disease and improving well-being.
By being encouraged to do sports and exercise, young people also have the opportunity to learn important life skills, such as working in a team. This will help them not only at school but also when they start work.
What is equally important to my mind is that playing sports can help to develop talent in teenagers. If sport was not offered free at school, it might mean some teenagers miss out on opportunities to improve and get noticed.
In all, every effort should be made to ensure that sport is included in the school timetable. The benefits of exercise are just as important as academic achievement.

» **TEST AND TRAIN: Exam Practice: Writing Part 1**

Writing Part 2

A choice of writing task (Unit 3, Unit 5, Unit 7, Unit 11, Unit 13, Unit 17)

Remind students of the format of Writing Part 2 and refer them to the exam information and tips boxes. This part is also practised in the Student's Book on pages 23 (informal letter/email), 35 (article), 45 (story), 67 (article), 79 (formal letter/email) and 101 (review) and in the Workbook on pages 15, 23, 31, 47, 55 and 71.

1 Ask students to look at the instructions and set a time limit of one minute for them to think of ideas alone. They then get into groups of four to share their ideas.

Answers
Students' own answers

2 Tell the class to read the list. Ask them to put their hands up when you read out each of the tips if they think it could be used for writing a story. When you have finished, elicit that the correct answers is that they can all be used.

Answer
All of them

3 Set the writing task for students to do. Then ask them to work in groups of four and to read their stories to each other. Each group must choose the story they think is the best and say why. Ask each group to read their best story out loud and to explain the reasons for their choice.

Model answer
Sofie was so angry that she stood up and ran out of the room, shutting the door loudly behind her. How could her best friend Lulu have done this? She had always trusted Lulu to keep a secret, and yet this time, she had let her down badly.
Sofie headed towards the park, and began to calm down a little. Just then her phone rang. It was Lulu. She told Sophie to look at her phone messages. Sophie checked and saw that she had accidentally shared the message to Lulu with a whole group of friends. That's how they knew. Not because of anything that Lulu had told them. Sofie was embarrassed, but relieved as well that she could still trust her best friend after all.
The two girls arranged to meet up in the park immediately. Sofie gave Lulu a big hug and apologised for being so mad at her when it was all her own fault. They ended up laughing about it and got back to doing what best friends do – sharing secrets with each other.

» **TEST AND TRAIN: Exam Practice: Writing Part 2**

» **TEST AND TRAIN: Practice Test: Writing**

LISTENING

Listening Part 1

Multiple choice (Unit 6, Unit 20)

Remind students of the format of Listening Part 1 and refer them to the exam information and tips boxes. This part is also practised in the Student's Book on pages 39 and 115 and in the Workbook on pages 27 and 83.

1 Tell students to read through the question and underline key words in both the question and the options. Elicit ideas from the students (*novel, agree, impressive, believable, characters, clearly, plot, well, places, described*).

Answer

What impressive thing the friends agree about.

95 2 Allow the students to listen twice; once to try to identify the correct answer and the second time to note information which helped them to decide. Elicit the correct answer and then invite students to say why the other two were wrong.

Answer

A (They don't agree that the plot was clear. The girl says, 'I found the story a bit hard to follow at times', whereas the boy says, 'That wasn't an issue for me.' They don't agree about the descriptions of the cities either. The boy says, 'I was less keen on the descriptions of Liverpool and Manchester.' whereas the girl says, 'That didn't bother me.' They agree that Jake's character and his friends' behaviour were true to life - the boy says, 'He was really true to life somehow, and I thought that was brilliant,' and the girl says, 'Good point … his friends behaved just like we do at times, didn't they?')

» AUDIOSCRIPT TB PAGE 307

96 3 Give students time to read through the questions to make sure they know what they are listening for. Then play the recording twice for students to answer the questions. When students are checking their answers, ask them why the other options didn't quite match.

Answers

1 A 2 C 3 B 4 A 5 C 6 B 7 C 8 A

» AUDIOSCRIPT TB PAGES 307–308

» TEST AND TRAIN: Exam Practice: Listening Part 1

Listening Part 2

Sentence completion (Unit 8, Unit 12, Unit 16)

Remind students of the format of Listening Part 2 and refer them to the exam information and tips boxes. This part is also practised in the Student's Book on pages 49, 71 and 93 and in the Workbook on pages 35, 51 and 67.

1 Give the students 30 seconds to read the title and discuss their predictions in pairs. Elicit some ideas from the students.

Possible answer

A person called Jamal Edwards and a music website that he set up, called SBTV. He may be a musician or other person involved in music somehow.

2 Look at the first gap with students. Elicit that this is something you can see in London. It could be a singular noun or a plural or uncountable noun. Students then look at the other gaps in pairs. Elicit ideas from the class.

Answers

1 a noun – something you can see in London 2 a type of music 3 a place 4 a place where people work 5 a number 6 a plural noun – something you can see on a website 7 a noun or verb, something you can be good at – possibly a school subject 8 a verb 9 a noun 10 an adjective or noun

97 3 When students have listened once, allow them to compare ideas in pairs but tell them not to change their own answers yet. They then listen again and check and correct their answers if necessary. Elicit the answers.

Answers

1 foxes 2 hip-hop 3 cars 4 (clothes) shop 5 39 million 6 news stories 7 finance(s) 8 email 9 confidence 10 famous

» AUDIOSCRIPT TB PAGES 308–309

» TEST AND TRAIN: Exam Practice: Listening 2

Listening Part 3

Multiple matching (Unit 2, Unit 4, Unit 14)

Remind students of the format of Listening Part 3 and refer them to the exam information and tips boxes. This part is also practised in the Student's Book on pages 17, 27 and 83 and in the Workbook on pages 11, 19 and 59.

98 **1** Ask students to look at the three subjects and discuss in pairs what they might hear in a talk about each one. Elicit ideas and then play the recording. Elicit the answer and what the speaker said which helped them decide.

Answer

C

» **AUDIOSCRIPT TB PAGE 309**

2 Look at A with the class and elicit that keywords (*saving, life, individual animals*). 'individual' is important as someone may talk about looking after animals or saving entire species, neither of which would match this sentence. Students work in pairs. Elicit ideas and why the key words could be important.

Possible answers

A saving the life of individual animals
B getting to see a wide variety of environments
C having the chance to do challenging tasks
D getting close to a very rare animal
E being responsible for collecting important data
F using relevant previously learned information
G learning more about various local traditions
H being able to view the beautiful surroundings

99 **3** Allow students to listen twice and then compare answers in pairs. If they have different answers, they try to justify their answer by referring to what they heard in the text. Elicit the answers and the information that helped them.

Answers

1 A 2 F 3 H 4 D 5 E

» **AUDIOSCRIPT TB PAGE 309**

» **TEST AND TRAIN:** Exam Practice: Listening Part 3

Listening Part 4

Multiple-choice (Unit 10, Unit 18)

Remind students of the format of Listening Part 4 and refer them to the exam information and tips boxes. This part is also practised in the Student's Book on pages 61 and 105 and in the Workbook on pages 43 and 75.

100 **1** Ask students to read the information on Part 4. When students have listened to the introduction elicit what Maria has done and what sort of questions the interviewer might ask her.

Answer

She has created and completed a survey online about what students of her own age think about the future.

» **AUDIOSCRIPT TB PAGE 309**

2 Look at the first question with the students. Ask if this is about emotions and opinions. (*No, it isn't. Although it talks about when she became interested in the topic, it's more about facts, asking exactly when she became interested.*) Students discuss the other questions in pairs. Elicit the answers and how students know (*words such as* seem to be, felt *and* feel *show that these are not facts*).

Answers

4, 5 and 7

101 **3** Remind students that all three options may be mentioned in some way but two will be in such a way that it is clear they are the wrong answer. Students listen twice to check their answers and see if they can identify why the other two options are wrong. Elicit the answers and any information students can remember from the recording which helped them.

Answers

1 C 2 A 3 B 4 C 5 A 6 C 7 B

» **AUDIOSCRIPT TB PAGES 309–310**

» **TEST AND TRAIN:** Exam Practice: Listening Part 4

» **TEST AND TRAIN:** Practice Test: Listening

SPEAKING

Speaking Part 1
Interview (Unit 2, Unit 14)

Remind students of the format of Speaking Part 1 and refer them to the exam information and tips boxes. This part is also practised in the Student's Book on pages 17 and 83.

1 Ask students to read the questions to identify the topics. Then put students into groups of three. Each student chooses one of the topics and the others ask them the questions on that topic.

Answers
the internet, transport, free time

102 2 Play the recording twice. On the first listening ask students to identify the questions asked. On the second listening, ask them to pay attention to Sara's replies and say whether they were the same as or different to the ones they gave in Exercise 1. Elicit her answers.

Answers
1 How do you usually travel to school or work?
2 What do you enjoy doing with your family and friends in your free time?
3 How often do you use social media?
4 Do you use public transport to travel around?

» AUDIOSCRIPT TB PAGE 310

3 Look at the example questions and answers with the class and encourage them to try to give both responses to the first question to make it a longer answer. They could make the answer even longer by talking about their favourite fantasy book. Tell students to try not to look at the questions their partner is asking and to see if they can answer both questions without being asked the second one. Monitor and note interesting answers and invite students to answer one of the questions each in front of the class.

Answers
Students' own answers

» TEST AND TRAIN: Exam Practice: Speaking Part 1

Speaking Part 2
Long turn (Unit 8, Unit 20)

Remind students of the format of Speaking Part 2 and refer them to the exam information and tips boxes. This part is also practised in the Student's Book on pages 49 and 115.

1 Ask students to read the question and look at the photos. Give students one minute to think of ideas and then give them three minutes to compare the photos in pairs. Ask one pair to perform their dialogue in front of the class.

Answers
Students' own answers

103 2 When students have listened to the recording, elicit the ideas the speaker gave and then ask pairs for any other ideas they had in Exercise 1 which weren't mentioned.

Answers
Students' own answers

» AUDIOSCRIPT TB PAGE 310

3 Encourage students to spend about 30 seconds describing and comparing the two photos and then to spend another 30 seconds answering the question. The student who isn't speaking can time the other student and tell them when 30 seconds have passed. When it is the second student's turn to speak, their partner can also time them to see if they can keep speaking for 30 seconds. Monitor and note useful phrases used.

Answers
Students' own answers

4 Before the students swap roles, tell the class some of the useful words and phrases you heard and encourage other students to use similar words and phrases. Students then carry out the exercise in the same way as Exercise 3.

Answers
Students' own answers

» TEST AND TRAIN: Exam Practice: Speaking Part 2

Speaking Part 3

Collaborative task (Unit 12, Unit 16)

Remind students of the format of Speaking Part 3 and refer them to the exam information and tips boxes. This part is also practised in the Student's Book on pages 71 and 93.

104 **1** Ask students to read the question and look at the points in the mind map. In pairs, students discuss which of the ideas they think would interest young people and which wouldn't. Elicit ideas and then play the recording. Elicit what Sara and Álvaro said and ask students if they agree with them.

Answer

They think that reading about history is too much like studying.

» **AUDIOSCRIPT TB PAGES 310–311**

105 **2** Play the recording and elicit what the task is and then ask the class which one they think would be the most interesting and why.

Answer

They have to choose the way of finding out about the history of an area which they think would be most interesting to young people.

» **AUDIOSCRIPT TB PAGE 311**

106 **3** When students have listened to the discussion, elicit the answer and then play the recording again for students to note down how the two students ask for and give opinions and agree and disagree. Elicit these and write them on the board to help weaker students.

Answer

Talking to people who have lived in the area for a long time.

» **AUDIOSCRIPT TB PAGE 311**

107 **4** Play the recording. As the students do the task, monitor and note interesting ideas and invite one or two pairs to act out their conversation in front of the class.

Answers

Students' own answers

» **AUDIOSCRIPT TB PAGE 311**

» **TEST AND TRAIN: Exam Practice: Speaking Part 3**

Speaking Part 4

Discussion (Unit 12, Unit 16)

Remind students of the format of Speaking Part 4 and refer them to the exam information and tips boxes. This is also practised in the Student's Book on pages 71 and 93.

108 **1** Ask students to read the questions and then put the them into six groups. Give each group one of the questions to discuss together and elicit what they think Sara and Álvaro might say. Elicit ideas and then play the recording. Elicit which questions they answered.

Answers

Do you think people should look to the future rather than the past? Why are people so interested in their own family's history? How can history lessons be made interesting at school?

108 **2** When students have listened again, put them into groups of three to discuss what they remember from the recording. Elicit ideas from different groups and ask the class which ideas they agree with and which they disagree with.

Answers

Álvaro thinks that people should study the past in order to learn from it. Sara says it's important not to worry too much about what's happened, but to learn from it and move on.
Sara says people like finding out about their family's history because it's more personal than learning about people we don't know. Álvaro says it's interesting to understand how people take after each other and that traditions are passed on between generations, which helps family members feel closer to each other.
Álvaro thinks that listening to people who are passionate about their subject is very interesting. Sara would like to take part in more discussions on the subject.

» **AUDIOSCRIPT TB PAGE 311**

3 Look at the example dialogue. Invite students to give their own answers to the same question and then put them in pairs to answer the other questions. Monitor and note interesting ideas and invite pairs to give their answers.

Answers

Students' own answers

» **TEST AND TRAIN: Exam Practice: Speaking Part 4**

» **TEST AND TRAIN: Practice Test: Speaking**

EXTRA ACTIVITIES

UNIT 4 PAGE 26 VOCABULARY

2 **Complete the sentences with the correct form of the phrasal verbs in Exercise 1. Then discuss the questions.**

0 What kinds of things *get* you *down*?
1 I felt really dizzy when I ________ after fainting.
2 Does it take you a long time to ________ arguments with good friends?
3 The smell of sour milk makes me want to ________. It's disgusting!
4 Have you ever ________ an illness because you've been outside in the cold for too long?
5 I eventually ________ after the argument, but I was really annoyed at the time.

3 **Ask and answer the questions with a partner.**

1 What kind of things get you down?
2 Have you ever come down with food poisoning?
3 Do you usually get over illness quickly?
4 Have you ever come round after fainting and wondered where you were?
5 Do you find it easy to calm down after an argument?
6 Have you ever thrown up on a long car journey?

UNIT 7 PAGE 44 VOCABULARY

3 **Complete the sentences about you. Then compare them with your partner.**

1 The year before last, I …
2 I haven't … for some time.
3 Before long, I'd like to learn how to …
4 I often … for hours on end.
5 I could learn to … in no time.

UNIT 8 PAGE 49 SPEAKING

PREPARE FOR THE EXAM

Speaking Part 2

5 **Work in pairs. The photographs show two cities at different times of year.**

Student B: Compare the two photographs. Say what the people might enjoy about living in the cities at these different times of year.
Student A: What time of year do you like best where you live? Why?

UNIT 9 PAGE 54 VOCABULARY

WHAT WAS YOUR SCORE?

All the statements are characteristics of optimistic people. Optimists have a belief that things will always turn out well. They believe they are in control of their future and when things go wrong, they tend to see others as the reason, rather than themselves. They look for new opportunities and see themselves as very able people in everything they do. They are goal-oriented and often determined to achieve their goals.

The more statements you agreed with, the more optimistic you are.

35–40: VERY OPTIMISTIC
You always look on the bright side of a situation. The positive attitude you bring to everything you do means your friends probably see you as someone whose presence cheers everyone up.

28–34: QUITE OPTIMISTIC
For the most part, you're someone who makes the most of things and looks forward to the future, but there is still a part of you that holds back. Perhaps a bit of realism is useful, though?

21–27: REALISTIC
For you, it's not about hoping for the best in situations or seeing the worst in people. It's about using reason to make decisions. You might not have the most exciting time, but your realism means you usually have a fairly accurate idea of what new experiences will be like.

14–20: QUITE PESSIMISTIC
You aren't a complete pessimist, but you tend to avoid new experiences, as generally speaking you think that something bad might happen.

8 (MINIMUM SCORE)–13: VERY PESSIMISTIC
If something can go wrong, your belief is that it will. And if you can blame yourself for the problem, you probably will too. Even if something good happens, you'll probably believe that it was only because of good fortune that things went well.

UNIT 9 PAGE 56 VOCABULARY

5 **Complete the questions using a form of the words in the box. Ask and answer the questions with a partner.**

driver enjoy personal recognise remark

1 What do you think are the advantages and disadvantages of ________ vehicles?
2 Who is the most ________ celebrity in your country?
3 What is the most ________ thing you have ever seen?
4 Are there any benefits to having a pessimistic ________?
5 What activities do you get the most ________ from?

UNIT 10 PAGE 60 VOCABULARY

4 **Ask and answer the questions with a partner.**

1 Do you know anyone who you would call 'an angel'?
2 When was the last time your parents or teacher grilled you about something?
3 Do you usually sail through things like exams or other challenges?
4 What lifts your mood when you're fed up?
5 Do you remember events clearly, or have you got a foggy memory?

UNIT 11 PAGE 66 VOCABULARY

3 **Ask and answer the questions with a partner.**

1 Are you a well-organised person?
2 Do you have many hi-tech gadgets?
3 Do you like to organise things well in advance, or do you prefer last-minute plans?
4 How important is it to get a well-paid job?
5 Do you eat a well-balanced diet?

UNIT 12 PAGE 70 VOCABULARY

4 **Read the speech bubbles aloud. Complete the sentences using *both*, *either of*, *either … or*, *neither of* or *neither … nor*.**

1
I'm really hungry!
I'm hungry too!
We're … !

2
I haven't got any money left.
I haven't got any either.
…

3
We don't have time to visit both museums. …

4
I'm so excited about our holiday! Poppy and Jake – are … ?

5
I'm not playing football today.
I'm not playing football today, either.
… Leroy … Heather is …

UNIT 19 PAGE 110 VOCABULARY

3 **Student A, read the sentences below. Student B will listen and say whether each sentence is correct or not. He/She will then correct the incorrect sentences.**

1 I've just heard some interesting new about Karl.
2 I love our school surrounding. They help me work hard.
3 I'm sure they'll serve some refreshments after the races.

Answers: **1** not correct – *news* **2** not correct – *surroundings* **3** correct

Now listen to Student B's sentences. Say whether each sentence is correct or incorrect. If the sentence is incorrect, say the sentence again, correcting the mistake.

EXTRA ACTIVITIES

UNIT 13 PAGE 76 VOCABULARY

WHAT WAS YOUR SCORE?

All the sentences are qualities of good leaders.

20–24: Wow! You're the kind of person that people look up to and you're on your way to becoming a great leader.

14–19: You're doing OK, but you probably have the potential to be even better. Look at the questions you scored the least on – is there anything you could do to improve your leadership skills?

8 (MINIMUM SCORE)–13: You're probably not a natural leader, but there's nothing wrong with that. All teams need good, positive team members!

UNIT 14 PAGE 82 VOCABULARY

4 **Take turns to read out the statements and report them using the correct form of the reporting verbs in the box.**

~~confess~~	enquire	forbid
insist	point out	recommend

0 'I stole the tablet from the technology lab,' she said.

She confessed that she had stolen the tablet from the technology lab.

1 'You are *not* allowed to go on your brother's motorbike. Not even for a short ride – absolutely not.'
My dad …
2 'You really must eat something,' my mum said.
My mum …
3 'You can't stop here – look, the sign says so,' Beth said to Charlie.
Beth …
4 'I suggest you park by the station,' the attendant said.
The attendant …
5 'Excuse me. Could you tell me where the nearest bus stop is?' asked the woman.
The woman …

UNIT 15 PAGE 88 VOCABULARY

3 **Work with a partner. Take turns to complete the sentences with your own ideas.**

1 I'm in favour of banning …
2 Many people think that … , but in actual fact …
3 When an exam is in progress, you shouldn't …
4 In the light of recent news about the acceleration of climate change, it's important that …
5 When working in groups, it's important to let everyone speak in turn, because …
6 In general I like … , but I'm not keen on …

UNIT 16 PAGE 92 VOCABULARY

3 **Ask and answer the questions with a partner.**

1 Do you eat a well-balanced diet?
2 At what age do you hope to become financially independent?
3 What do you do that is environmentally friendly?
4 Do you keep your social-media pages regularly updated?
5 Are any of your things made by globally recognised brands?

UNIT 18 PAGE 104 VOCABULARY

3 **Ask and answer the questions with a partner.**

1 What do you do to stop worries going round and round in your head?
2 Do you walk up and down while you're talking on the phone?
3 Have you got any dreams which are looking more and more unlikely?
4 Have you more or less decided on a career yet?
5 What activities do you only do now and then?

UNIT 19 PAGE 110 VOCABULARY

3 **Student B, listen to Student A's sentences. Say whether each sentence is correct or incorrect. If the sentence is incorrect, say the sentence again, correcting the mistake.**

Now read the sentences below. Student A will listen and say whether each sentence is correct or not. He/She will then correct the incorrect sentences.

4 The content is quite short, considering it's such a long book.
5 I love the lyrics of this song – they're so romantic.
6 My grandparents have just bought a flat on the outskirt of Paris.

Answers: **4** not correct – *contents* **5** correct **6** not correct – *outskirts*

UNIT 20 PAGE 115 SPEAKING

PREPARE FOR THE EXAM

Speaking Part 2

5 **Work in pairs. The photographs show people communicating with each other other using technology.**

Student A: Compare the two photographs. Say why the people might have decided to communicate with friends or family in these ways.
Student B: How do you prefer to communicate with friends? Why?

GRAMMAR REFERENCE AND PRACTICE ANSWER KEY

UNIT 1 SIMPLE, CONTINUOUS OR PERFECT

Present perfect, Past perfect, Past simple

1 **1** wanted, looked, had seen
2 was, 'd/had already started
3 've/have never seen, did you find

Present continuous, Past continuous

2 **1** d **2** f **3** b **4** e **5** a **6** c

3 **1** F **2** E **3** A **4** B **5** C **6** D

UNIT 2 PRESENT PERFECT SIMPLE AND CONTINUOUS

1 **1** Have you been waiting **2** haven't been listening, 've been telling **3** 's/has been mending **4** 've/have been walking **5** Have the children been playing **6** hasn't been living

2 **1** same **2** different (the first speaker has finished cleaning the car; in the second sentence we don't know if the job is finished or not) **3** same **4** different (the first speaker has finished cooking; in the second sentence we don't know if the lunch is ready or not) **5** different (the first speaker has never driven the car; the second speaker may have driven it in the past, but not recently)

3 **1** I've nearly finished **2** I've been designing **3** both **4** I've also visited **5** both **6** both

4 Possible answers

1 I've been living at my present address for ten years.
2 I've been studying English since I was eight.
3 Francis has been supporting that football team for six years.
4 I've been wearing these clothes since early this morning.

UNIT 3 THE GRAMMAR OF PHRASAL VERBS

1 **1** pay it back **2** make it up **3** looking forward to it

2 **1** broke down **2** come across **3** got me down **4** take up **5** get into **6** have gone by **7** think about **8** pass on

3 Possible answers

1 insults and violence. **2** upsetting them? **3** your own mistakes. **4** all kinds of people. **5** their parents' achievements.

UNIT 4 MODALS (1): NECESSITY, OBLIGATION, PROHIBITION AND ADVICE

Necessity, obligation, prohibition

1 **1** had to **2** didn't have to **3** have **4** have to **5** don't have **6** need **7** mustn't

Advice

2 **1** should I; ought I to **2** should I; ought I to **3** should I; should I; ought I to; ought I to

3 Possible answers

1 have a regular training programme. **2** eat junk food. **3** go to bed late very often.

4 Possible answers

1 you don't have to / you don't need to / you haven't got to.
2 should / ought to talk to your teacher.
3 mustn't bring food into the shop. **4** have to wear uniform.
5 Should I / Ought I to phone my brother?
6 You must let me help you.

UNIT 5 PRESENT AND PAST HABITS

1 **1** 're/are always advertising special offers.
2 was always handing her assignments in late.
3 's/is continually shouting at his children.
4 's/is constantly bringing mice into the house.
5 were always promising jobs for everyone.

2 **1** My dad would **regularly** have a snack in the afternoon.
2 I didn't **often** use to sleep more than six hours when I was young.
3 Do you **usually** get enough sleep during the week?
4 A doctor wouldn't **normally** prescribe sleeping tablets for someone as young as you.
5 The factory workers were **frequently** short of sleep and **sometimes** injured themselves as a result.
6 The students were **continually** yawning during lectures because they **never** went to sleep before midnight.
7 I **normally** sleep very soundly, but **from time to time** I have nightmares and wake up shouting. OR I have nightmares and wake up shouting **from time to time**.
8 Did you use to sleep in your parents' bed **all the time** when you were little?

3 **1** 'm walking **2** went / used to go **3** 're eating **4** Did [you] play / use to play

UNIT 6 BE/GET USED TO

1 **1** have got used to **2** weren't used to **3** were used to **4** wasn't used to **5** had been used to **6** am used to **7** can't get used to

2 **1** isn't used to doing the shopping OR hasn't got/become used to doing the shopping **2** 's/is used to staying up OR 's (has) got/become used to staying up **3** 's/is getting/becoming used to tidying **4** wasn't used to talking

UNIT 7 NARRATIVE TENSES

Past perfect simple v past perfect continuous

1 **1** had booked **2** had been raining / had rained **3** had been preparing **4** had already agreed **5** had texted **6** had been wanting / had wanted

Past perfect v past simple

2 **1** had been **2** had delayed **3** had been waiting **4** boarded **5** were **6** had already given **7** had moved **8** heard **9** went out **10** returned **11** got out **12** turned out **13** had caused **14** had been completed **15** were able to **16** had arrived **17** hadn't eaten **18** enjoyed **19** landed **20** cheered

UNIT 8 FUTURE (1): REVIEW

1 **A** **1** I'm meeting **2** we'll try **3** I'm about to start **4** begins **5** I won't be **6** comes **7** is the taxi picking **8** leaves **9** will be **10** is **11** won't hold **12** you arrive **13** I'll see

B **1** is about to start **2** have gone **3** I'll go **4** I'll get **5** I'll have **6** we're going to have **7** won't start **8** we're **9** we'll be (He might say 'we're going to be fine' but he can't really know for sure!)

UNIT 9 FUTURE (2): CONTINUOUS AND PERFECT

Future continuous

1 **1** will be closing; won't be opening **2** will be taking **3** Will he be playing; won't be playing

Future perfect and future perfect continuous

2 **1** 'll/will have spent **2** 'll/will have sunbathed OR 'll/will have been sunbathing **3** won't have eaten OR won't have been eating **4** 'll/will have danced OR 'll/will have been dancing **5** won't have missed us OR won't have been missing us **6** 'll/will have texted us

3 **1** 'll/will have been married for forty years. **2** 'll/will have lived / 'll/will have been living here for (over) ten years. **3** 'll/will have slept / will have been sleeping **4** 'll/will have tidied up (the kitchen). **5** 'll/will have been travelling

4 **1** ✓ **2** ✓ **3** ✗ **4** ✗ **5** ✓ **6** ✗ **7** ✓ **8** ✓ **9** ✗ **10** ✗ **11** ✓ **12** ✗

UNIT 10 MODALS (2): MODALS IN THE PAST

1 **1** shouldn't have shouted **2** wouldn't have looked **3** should have sent **4** should I have given **5** needn't have bothered **6** Shouldn't / Should you have given **7** needn't have worried **8** would have sent **9** didn't need to take **10** would you have chosen

2 Possible answers

1 have enjoyed it **2** have changed your plan / have come with us **3** have gone this time / have missed the concert **4** have bought it for me

UNIT 11 RELATIVE CLAUSES

1 **1** My sister, who is at university, can drive.

2 I followed the instructions (that/which) you gave me.

3 My phone, which is brand-new, has a broken screen.

4 I loved the DJ who played at your party.

5 I'm having dinner with my best friend, who I introduced you to last month.

6 She can tell you where to go shopping for a bargain.

2 **1** Have you ever visited the island that your grandparents came from? (no comma)

2 John's bicycle, ~~that~~ **which** was stolen last week, has turned up in the next street.

3 Is that the coat you wanted to buy ~~**it**~~?

4 This is the website ~~who~~ **(which/that)** I told you about.

5 The city where I went to university is a lively place. (no commas)

6 The singer who I like ~~**her**~~ most is from Argentina.

7 The friend I stayed with ~~**her**~~ in Geneva is a painter.

UNIT 12 THE PASSIVE (1): REVIEW

1 **1** was bought **2** had been resisted **3** was made **4** was included **5** have not been told **6** have been persuaded **7** will be given **8** will be put **9** are being sold **10** will be used

CAUSATIVE *HAVE/GET*

2 **1** got the shop to replace **2** 'm/am having / 'm/am going to have it cleaned **3** got / are getting my parents to pay **4** got my boss to call **5** had a bunch of flowers delivered

UNIT 13 THE PASSIVE (2): OTHER STRUCTURES

1 **1** to be amused **2** being told off **3** be given **4** to be served **5** to be awarded **6** being treated **7** to be called **8** be chosen **9** being hugged **10** to be asked **11** being involved **12** being stopped **13** to be used **14** to be delivered **15** being allowed

UNIT 14 REPORTED SPEECH

1 **1** they had seen Ahmed **2** (that) he hates shopping / to hate shopping **3** they went to Morocco **4** to see **5** where the ticket office is/was

2 **1** 'I'm enjoying the movie.'

2 'Where can I charge my phone?'

3 'What's/was the score?'

4 'I've been to the library a few times.'

5 'What do you need?'

6 'Did you see the film?'

3 **1** agreed **2** denies **3** praised **4** suggested **5** enquired **6** persuaded

UNIT 15 MODALS (3): DEDUCTION

1 **1** can't be **2** must know **3** may/might/could be **4** can't be **5** can't have **6** must be **7** may/might/could block OR may/might/could be blocking **8** may/might/could be

2 **1** e **2** c **3** a **4** f **5** b **6** d

3 **1** could have been **2** might have been **3** can't have been **4** could be **5** can't be **6** must be **7** must have been

UNIT 16 CONDITIONALS (1): REVIEW

Zero conditional

1 Possible answers

1 live **2** get **3** arrives/gets

First conditional

2 **1** b **2** a **3** d **4** c

Second conditional

3 **1** were/was you, I'd take a smaller suitcase.
2 check the weight limit if I were/was you.
3 walk along this road at night if I were/was you.
4 were/was you, I'd take a torch with me.

Third conditional

4 **1** have seen the band if she'd gone to the party. **2** have won the tournament if he hadn't entered it. **3** trained carefully, he wouldn't have felt fine at the end of the race.

5 **1** wouldn't have asked **2** find **3** don't give **4** would be **5** had **6** 'd remembered **7** wouldn't have got **8** didn't forget **9** would save

UNIT 17 CONDITIONALS (2): MIXED

Mixed conditional (present affected by past)

1 **1** hadn't eaten; wouldn't be **2** would/could go; hadn't started **3** had told; wouldn't repeat **4** would/could we play; hadn't installed **5** would/might get; 'd/had studied **6** 'd/had finished; could/would relax

Mixed conditional (past affected by present)

2 **1** would/might/could have gone; had **2** was/were; could/would have used **3** didn't exaggerate; might/would have believed **4** would/could your friends have stayed; didn't have **5** would/could/might have given; had

3 **1** hadn't worked / didn't work **2** wouldn't be **3** Would Rosa have **4** might/could/would have saved **5** could/would have **6** weren't **7** 'd/had brought **8** would be **9** had never existed **10** might/would/could have walked **11** would/might cities be

UNIT 18 USES OF VERB + *-ING*

Verbs + *-ing* after verbs

1 **Possible answers**
1 going to bed late. **2** going out for a meal?
3 being unhappy in a place like that. **4** helping you.
5 walking home.

Verb + *-ing* after prepositions and phrases

2 **1** after **2** without **3** by **4** when **5** spend time **6** have no difficulty **7** it's not worth **8** pass the time **9** get fed up with **10** Since **11** by

Participle clauses

3 **1** Sitting at the back of the hall, I couldn't see the show very well.
2 Not being interested in rugby, I didn't go to the match with my cousins.
3 My dad, wanting to know why I wasn't home, phoned the school office. / Wanting to know why I wasn't home, my dad phoned the school office.

UNIT 19 SUBJECT–VERB AGREEMENT

1 **1** correct
2 The city is very quiet because everybody **is** on holiday this week.
3 Revising for exams **was** preventing my brother from doing any sport.
4 correct
5 No one has come to see me for ages. I must have done something to upset **them**.
6 correct
7 A number of my friends **are** taking part in a riding competition on Saturday.
8 My phone's dead. **Has** anyone brought their charger with them?
9 The majority of people in this town **work** at the electronics factory.
10 The class **were** texting their friends as they came out of the exam.
11 correct (*The swimming club have put up their membership fees* would also be correct.)
12 Learning about other people **is** an important part of growing up.
13 Both of my parents **work** long hours, but we have plenty of fun together at weekends.
14 correct

UNIT 20 DETERMINERS

1 **1** a **2** the **3** the **4** The **5** the **6** several **7** – **8** Some **9** – **10** plenty of **11** – **12** a **13** The **14** lots of **15** the **16** the **17** a **18** few **19** very little **20** the **21** a **22** number of **23** – **24** much **25** a few **26** the

WORKBOOK ANSWER KEY AND AUDIOSCRIPTS

UNIT 1 Creative minds

VOCABULARY

1 **1** b **2** i **3** d **4** e **5** g **6** c **7** f **8** h **9** a **10** k **11** j

2 **1** shot **2** track, charts **3** piece **4** cast, appearance **5** bestseller, series **6** broadcast **7** classic **8** stream

READING

1 Students should underline:

1 too frightening, young **2** regaining, lost **3** funny **4** journey into the past **5** may be hiding something **6** film **7** not very sociable **8** series **9** another work **10** interested, magic and fun

2 **1** D **2** B **3** A **4** E **5** E **6** C **7** A **8** B **9** D **10** C

3 Students should underline:

1 (D) While it may be a bit much for pre-teens to deal with, more mature readers will keep turning the pages …

2 (B) … in order to get back the shadows from the thieves …

3 (A) … occasionally laugh-out-loud read …

4 (E) Young hero Sam is taken back 300 years …

5 (E) … Dick, who Sam suspects is not all he claims to be.

6 (C) In fact, the movie rights have already been sold to a family-friendly Hollywood production company, and it is due for release next year.

7 (A) she prefers to chat with animals, trees, plants and inanimate objects, rather than other human beings

8 (B) This is the second of six breathtaking adventures …

9 (D) … she was inspired to write her book by drawing on the *Inferno's* riches.

10 (C) Dark, the … magician king, Dark's love of playing tricks

4 **1** brings to mind **2** thrilling **3** gentle **4** breathtaking **5** drawing on

GRAMMAR

1 **1** have you seen, saw **2** go, 've never been **3** are you doing, 'm doing, did **4** Did you enjoy, had finished, was **5** were you doing, was reading, 'm reading, are you enjoying, love

2 **1** 'm/am writing **2** 's/is shining **3** come **4** 's/has been **5** moved **6** stay **7** saw **8** were walking **9** ran **10** started **11** happen **12** happened **13** were sitting **14** had just paid **15** were getting **16** came **17** started **18** didn't want **19** have just come **20** want

3 **1** I <u>have</u> taken so long to write to you because I have been busy.

2 Did you <u>have</u> a good time on your holiday?

3 ✓

4 By the time I arrived, he <u>had</u> disappeared.

5 Surfing <u>has been</u> my hobby since 2010.

6 ✓

VOCABULARY

1 **1** novelist **2** critic **3** producer **4** editor **5** programmer **6** TV presenter **7** comedian

WRITING

1–2 Students' own answers

3 **1** However **2** Most people agree **3** For instance **4** Furthermore

4 **1** relaxing **2** unrealistic ideas about the future, stop caring about schoolwork **3** harmless fun, another idea of your own **4** summary of the points made, your conclusion

5 Students' own answers

UNIT 2 Addicted to fashion

VOCABULARY

1

about	at	by
bothered, cautious, decisive, mean	hopeless	impressed
of	**to**	**with**
aware, critical, jealous	addicted, loyal	adventurous

2 **1** A **2** C **3** B **4** A **5** B **6** A **7** C **8** B

3 **1** addicted to **2** bothered about **3** adventurous with **4** jealous of **5** decisive about

READING

1 Students' own answers

2 **1** A **2** D **3** C **4** A **5** B **6** C **7** C **8** B

3 A

4 **1** twentieth **2** too expensive **3** hide their eyes **4** encourage the public to wear sunglasses **5** look good

5 **1** remarkable **2** desirable **3** generates **4** avoid **5** mass-produced

GRAMMAR

1 **1** been wearing **2** lost **3** been sunbathing **4** been studying **5** sold **6** been reading **7** eaten **8** been drinking

2 **1** 've/have been keeping **2** has been **3** 've/have been sitting **4** 've/have already had **5** have met **6** 've/have been **7** 've/have been doing **8** 've/have been applying **9** has been trying **10** haven't eaten

3 **1** The football team <u>played</u> badly last year.

2 ✓

3 Agustina <u>has been</u> my best friend since we met in school when we were three years old.

4 I <u>have been</u> playing classical guitar for three years.

5 Yesterday I <u>was hiking / hiked</u> for five hours.

6 ✓

VOCABULARY

1 **1** for **2** at **3** with **4** with **5** on **6** without **7** of

LISTENING

1–2 Students' own answers

3 **1** C **2** G **3** A **4** F **5** B

4 **1** (expresses negative attitude) enjoy shopping **2** into **3** look forward **4** treat **5** to like **6** (expresses negative attitude) like about it

5 Possible answers

1 Yes, I'm really into shopping. / No, I'm not really into shopping.

2 It's a treat to go out for the day. / I enjoy looking at new fashions. / I don't particularly like shopping centres.

3 My friends. / My brother/sister.

4 After school. / At the weekend.

5 Jeans and trainers. / Casual clothes for hanging out with friends.

01 **1**

F: To be honest, I don't particularly enjoy shopping for clothes, but I do like getting a good deal. That's why I only shop when there are sales on. I buy cheap clothes. There's something quite satisfying about paying less for an article than it would have cost originally. Some of my friends like to spend loads of money – I guess it makes them feel good. But I don't understand that at all. I like to get the nicest clothes I can, with as little money as possible. To me, that's what it's all about.

2

M: Well, like all my friends, I'm really into fashion. When we go shopping together, we really enjoy seeing all the new designs when they come out. We always look forward to the new collection each season, but it can be expensive to buy them there and then, so we usually wait for a few months and then try to get a bargain. But it's important to us to be fashionable. It makes us feel good about ourselves and I think it's important to look good, too. Like it or not, lots of people judge you by what you wear.

3

F: I work as an assistant at a fashion store at weekends, and I'm careful with my money. The main thing I like about shopping for clothes is that it's one of the few occasions when I can make up my own mind about things. I come from a small family, and it was usually my parents who bought my clothes for me, and it's only in the last year that I've been given the freedom to make my own choices. It's quite a treat for me. Part of growing up, I suppose. Of course, I get a discount at the store where I work, too, which is nice.

4

F: Clothes shopping? Yes! What's not to like? Shopping for bargains, spending money, looking at yourself in the mirror in an outfit you can't possibly afford. But most of all, it's a great way to spend time with friends. I never actually spend a lot, but we have a great laugh when we go out shopping together – going for coffee, trying on the latest fashions. We have a brilliant time, even if we come home empty-handed, which, believe it or not, does happen occasionally! Not a lot, I admit! At least one of us usually finds something they want to spend their money on.

5

M: Don't get me wrong – I like to look good when I go out, and most people think I dress pretty smartly. But I can't say I actually enjoy shopping. It's the whole thing about walking round all the shops, trying things on. Ten minutes of that, and I've had enough! Honestly, I don't know what people like about it. Have they got nothing better to do? I usually look online and pick out exactly what I want, then go to the store and get it. That way I never come back empty handed – that, to me, would be a complete waste of time!

02 **Narrator:** You'll hear five short extracts in which teenagers are talking about shopping for clothes. For speakers 1 to 5, choose from the list, A to H, what each speaker says about shopping for clothes. Use the letters only once. There are three extra letters which you do not need to use.

The rest of Track 02 is taken from Track 01. It is from Speaker 1, 'To be honest, I don't particularly enjoy shopping for clothes, …' to Speaker 5, … 'that, to me, would be a complete waste of time!'

UNIT 3 All in the mind

VOCABULARY

1 **1** i **2** b **3** g **4** f **5** d **6** h **7** c **8** a **9** e

2 **1** C **2** A **3** B **4** C **5** B **6** C **7** A **8** B

READING

1 The chimpanzees are grooming each other to show empathy and affection.

2 domestic pets, whales, bees, chimpanzees, monkeys

3 **A** It seemed to be willing to go hungry rather than see a fellow animal suffer.

B Empathy plays a role in that, as it allows us to understand our fellow humans better.

C This fear of strangers will, we believe, protect us from personal danger.

D Other research has shown animals displaying empathy towards other animals and towards humans.

E The usual effect of this kind of behaviour is that it stops crying, shouting and other signs of being upset.

F We assume that people are able to think themselves into the position of another person, even though they may not have personally experienced that person's circumstances.

G They communicate this requirement by crying for attention and to show pain.

4 **1** F **2** D **3** A **4** G **5** B **6** C

5 **2** other research = One study **3** it = the first monkey **4** they = the young of all animal species; this requirement = the need to be cared for **5** that = working together, it = Empathy **6** this = fear of unknown creatures or strangers

6 **1** alike **2** possessed **3** released **4** unfamiliar **5** dilemma

GRAMMAR

1 **without an object:** show off, break down **separable:** put off, let down **inseparable:** care for, deal with **inseparable three-part:** look forward to, get out of

2 **1** showing off **2** put it off **3** let you down **4** broke down **5** care for the cat **6** looking forward to the party **7** get out of it **8** deal with this problem

3 **1** Have I ever let you down?

2 She can't deal with pressure.

3 Can you turn the TV down? / Can you turn down the TV?

4 I'll clear up the mess in the kitchen. / I'll clear the mess in the kitchen up.

5 Mum is caring for her.

4 **1** It will show off how healthy the students are.

2 I hope it will live up to your expectations.

3 She has looked after me since my childhood.

4 The youngest people sometimes show off in front of their friends.

5 ✓

VOCABULARY

1 **1** focus **2** up **3** in **4** think **5** up to **6** back

2 **1** focus **2** get **3** face **4** mix **5** thinking **6** back

WRITING

1 **1** a Write soon. **2** b The thing is, . . .
3 k But don't forget that . . . **4** f To start with . . .
5 j It's lovely to hear from you. **6** d As far as I know, . . .
7 h Keep in touch. **8** c To be honest, I reckon . . .
9 i I'm very happy to . . . **10** e Take care.

2 three

3 Sentences 3 and 5 shouldn't be in the response.

4 What do you think about this? – 2, 6; Are pets popular in your country? – 1; If so, which kind? – 4

5–6 Students' own answers

UNIT 4 Take it easy

VOCABULARY

1 **1** mind **2** faint **3** feel **4** appetite **5** panic **6** upset **7** lose Word down: difficulty

2 **1** going over and over . . . in my mind **2** upset stomach **3** lost her temper **4** feel dizzy **5** get in a panic **6** fainted **7** difficulty sleeping **8** lose my appetite

3 Students' own answers

READING

1 Possible answers: recording music; might be pleasant

2 Yes

3 **1** a recording studio **2** because sounds mean that things are working **3** lights can make a noise **4** because of the noises of his body **5** his time was finished

4 **1** B (It isn't his family who annoy him, just noise) **2** A **3** C **4** B (I felt anxious for two reasons . . .) **5** A **6** C

5 **1** cope **2** broken the record **3** heartbeat **4** disturbed **5** savings

GRAMMAR

1 **1** A **2** B **3** C **4** C **5** B **6** A **7** A **8** C

2 **1** do not / don't have to get **2** said (that) we should spend **3** do not/don't have to go, needn't go **4** must be over eighteen to **5** must not miss **6** you ought to cut

3 **1** ✓
2 I suppose you will ~~must~~ have fun in New York.
3 ✓
4 I've been told to give my opinion about whether students should only study what they enjoy.
5 You only have one life, and you mustn't/shouldn't waste it.

VOCABULARY

1 **1** Calm down **2** getting over **3** came round **4** threw up **5** coming down with **6** gets . . . down

LISTENING

1 **1** E **2** D **3** B **4** A **5** C

2 **1** feeling calm after the run **2** learning from others by listening **3** being part of a team, with great people **4** earning money **5** the feeling when you can play a difficult piece

3 Speaker 1 F Speaker 2 C Speaker 3 E Speaker 4 D Speaker 5 G

03 **1:**

M: I go running every day, in the late afternoon usually. It's great after a hard day at college, with all the concentration and mental activity. I mean, sure, it keeps me fit – I've always been pretty sporty anyway – but the best thing is that however I feel at the beginning of the run, I'm always totally calm at the end of it. Ready to jump in the shower, change into my jeans, and have a nice chilled time at home, or maybe go out with friends. There's nothing like it!

2:

F: I've never really been into sports or hobbies of any kind, to be honest. When I'm stressed out about something, I like to talk about it with a friend. Yeah, I'm a talker – people say I should get a career in radio or something, but I'm not sure about that. I'm a believer in the power of conversation. You feel much better when you talk something through, and you can get a lot out of just listening to people. It's surprising how few people really listen to advice, when other people can be such a great source of wisdom and knowledge. That's what I really love about it.

3:

F: I joined the local rock choir last year during my exams because I felt I needed to do something to help me stop thinking about them. And it worked. It was the best decision I ever made. We're all amateurs – I don't think we'll ever be able to charge money for our performances – but there's a great sense of being part of a team. And you do really build a strong bond of friendship with your fellow singers. When you're singing, you're really 'in the moment', but it's the opportunity to be with such great people that really makes it special for me.

4:

M: The gym is where I go when I'm stressed out, which is nearly every day, I must admit! I've always been really into fitness – I've been a gym member since I was thirteen, and I know everyone there. If a new member comes along, I'm always the one to show them around the equipment. I do a bit of private training on the side, too, which is a useful source of income. In fact, I couldn't do without it now, so that's really why I spend so much time there. Besides, it's quite satisfying to see people improving their fitness week by week.

5:

F: Learning to play the piano was my dad's idea. I'd been under a lot of pressure and I needed something to take my mind off things. It turns out studying a musical instrument is something you can get completely absorbed in, so it did the job in that respect! I love it. It'd be great to make a living out of it, but that's a long way off. In the meantime, there's nothing like the feeling you get when you work your way successfully through a difficult piece without making any mistakes. That's what keeps me going!

04 **Narrator:** You'll hear five short extracts in which teenagers are talking about free-time activities. For speakers 1 to 5, choose from the list, A to H, what each speaker likes best about their activity. Use the letters only once. There are three extra letters which you do not need to use.

The rest of Track 04 is taken from Track 03. It is from Speaker 1, 'I go running every day . . .' to Speaker 5, 'That's what keeps me going!'.

UNIT 5 Past times

VOCABULARY

1 **1** century **2** myth **3** found **4** decade **5** citizen **6** inhabitant **7** ancestor **8** get the vote **9** tribe

2 **a** 1 **b** 5 **c** 8 **d** 7 **e** 2 **f** 4 **g** 6 **h** 9 **i** 3

3 **1** myths **2** decade **3** century **4** citizen **5** ancestors **6** got the vote **7** inhabitants **8** founded **9** tribe

READING

1 2 d 3 h 4 a 5 c 6 f 7 g 8 e

2 **1** was **2** down **3** in/of **4** will/might **5** it **6** The **7** lot **8** though

3 3 (Ancient Egyptians, Ancient Greeks and Romans)

4 **1** It **2** other **3** were **4** would **5** place **6** many **7** out **8** do

5 **1** Vespasian **2** people **3** sailors **4** people

6 **1** storey **2** severely **3** fairs **4** largely **5** massive

GRAMMAR

1 **1** used to **2** is eating **3** is constantly looking **4** would go **5** feel **6** used to **7** was always

2 **1** I would ride my tricycle every day **2** 'm/am sleeping on the sofa **3** used to hate shopping for clothes **4** I (always) go for a run / go running **5** 'm/am constantly forgetting **6** was always telling **7** used to run home from school

3 **1** b **2** a **3** a **4** a

VOCABULARY

1 **1** seldom **2** all the time **3** every once in a while, from time to time **4** often

2 **1** We go to a circus *every once in a while.*
 2 I *seldom* go to bed after midnight.
 3 My best friend and I meet for a chat *most weeks.*
 4 I read a newspaper *every day*.
 5 I visit an art gallery *from time to time*.
 6 I *rarely* listen to music.
 7 My family *almost never* eats in a restaurant.

3 Students' own answers

WRITING

1 See answers to exercise 3.

2 4, 3, 1, 2

3 Paragraph 2 says what the writer admires about him/her.
 Paragraph 3 says what questions the writer would ask him/her.
 Paragraph 4 concludes the article with a summary sentence or two.

4 *Fairly informal*: All in all …. Who doesn't want that? Believe me … ! Not only that …
 One of the most amazing things

5 Students' own answers

UNIT 6 Totally emotional

VOCABULARY

1 **1** h **2** f **3** b **4** c **5** e **6** g **7** a **8** d **9** i

2 **1** scared **2** furious **3** over the moon **4** fed up / furious **5** pessimistic **6** optimistic **7** relieved **8** depressed **9** content

3 **1** cheerful **2** concerned / anxious **3** irritated **4** bad-tempered **5** scared / petrified **6** down / depressed

4 **1** cheerful **2** concerned **3** fed up **4** concerned **5** furious

READING

1 **1** D **2** C **3** D **4** A **5** B **6** A **7** D **8** C

2 **1** True (… it may seem quite busy. Your brain is in Beta mode.)
 2 False (Everyone's brain activity changes all the time.)
 3 False (He spent many productive hours being bored …)
 4 Not given
 5 False (They even have special rooms for encouraging daydreaming …)
 6 False (If you are lucky enough … enjoy those moments of boredom.)

3 **1** boredom **2** daydream **3** curiosity **4** observe **5** device

GRAMMAR

1 **1** isn't used to **2** 'm not used to, 'll get used to **3** aren't used to **4** 'm not used to, 'm used to

2 **1** get used to **2** wasn't used to (doing), get used to, 'm not used to / haven't got used to **3** was used to, got used to, get used to

3 **1** used to **2** get used to **3** used to **4** am getting **5** are used to **6** isn't used to

4 **1** In Sofia there are subways and trains but people do not usually travel on them.
 2 ✓
 3 I can cook very well too, because I am used to doing it when my mother is not at home.
 4 I got used to dealing with people and cooking different kinds of dishes.

VOCABULARY

1 adverbs of time: last year, until tomorrow; frequency adverbs: seldom, from time to time; adverbs of certainty: definitely, probably; adverbs of manner: quickly, calmly; adverbs of place: outside, nearby; connecting adverbs: however, nevertheless

2 **1** ✓
 2 She enjoys going to the beach *from time to time*. / *From time to time*, she enjoys going to the beach.
 3 It *probably* won't take you long to get used to it.
 4 James *calmly* picked up the spider and took it outside.
 5 ✓
 6 That's a good computer. *However*, it's a bit expensive. / It's a bit expensive, *however*.

3 **1** I don't often drink coffee.
 2 I'll finish my project next week. / Next week, I'll finish my project.
 3 She plays the piano beautifully.
 4 The kids probably won't enjoy this film.

LISTENING

1 main topic 2, 6; speaker's feeling 1, 5; speaker's opinion 4; a detail in the situation 3, 8; a reason for something 7

2 Students should underline: **1** summer job, how feel **2** circus, what, invited **3** race, what, say **4** TV show, why, like **5** teaching football, how feeling **6** event, what, doing **7** rock climbing, why **8** problem, phone, what, do

3 **1** A **2** C **3** B **4** B **5** C **6** B **7** A **8** C

05 **1**

F: My parents couldn't afford to pay the full cost of my university fees, so I took a summer job in a clothes shop. I'd never worked in a shop before, but my parents were keen for me to earn some money, even though they thought I'd probably get bored. They couldn't have been more wrong! There was a lot to learn, and I wasn't sure I'd be any good at the beginning. But I learned quickly and ended up having a pretty fun time there. I made a fair bit of money, too, which has come in very handy. They've asked me to come back next summer.

2

M: Belleview Youth Circus has been giving shows daily in the Memorial Park all summer, entertaining young and old with their amazing acts. They have just celebrated their 10th anniversary, and to mark the occasion they're taking a break from performing to invite would-be circus acts, and anyone else interested, to come and learn about the company. Circus manager Bill Mayhew will be explaining the history of the group, and several of the performers will also be there. So here's your chance to meet and chat with the professionals. Come along to the big tent in the Memorial Park at 7.30 – refreshments will be provided!

3

F: It was a great feeling, but we'd driven for four hours to get to it, and then I had classes the next day. So almost as soon as I got my trophy, we jumped in the car, I flopped down exhausted into the front seat, and we started the journey back home. Of course, I was thrilled by the whole thing. Winning was just amazing … but there was no opportunity to enjoy my success afterwards with friends, which was a shame. I had to be up early for school the next day! Luckily I'm used to that.

4

M: Hmm … I guess my favourite TV show would have to be *The Family*. It's a classic, in my opinion. The cast is amazing – the characters are so brilliantly developed and the actors seem to fit the parts so well, and the situations they get themselves into really are out of the ordinary. I'm just in awe of it. I've seen every episode and I'm often in tears of laughter. You know, it's completely ridiculous, but at the same time very human. The relationships they have with each other – even when they're fighting, the affection shines through. You should definitely watch it.

5

F: So, you survived your first week as a football coach. How was it?

M: Nothing like I expected. I mean, I knew it'd be exhausting, but I was amazed how quickly the week passed. It was over in a flash!

F: What were the kids like?

M: Fine. Not actually as bad as I'd been led to expect. I'd been warned to stamp on any disruptive behaviour, but I didn't come up against any of that. I guess I was quite strict from the start. I wasn't sure how they'd take that – but thank goodness they got used to it very quickly, and they all did as they were told.

6

M: Are you coming to the school art show on Saturday, Jenny? I heard you were furious that your painting wasn't in the final selection, but it's up to the judges really, isn't it?

F: That didn't bother me, I was just a bit irritated that I found out about it by chance. They should have told me personally.

M: Well yes, I agree that was a mistake – but apart from that, they've got things right. Anyway, look, I'd really like you to come along. It'll be fun!

F: Aren't you just worried you won't have enough people helping?

M: No, honestly, there's no problem with numbers. I just think you'd enjoy the event.

7

F: I love rock climbing. I've done it since I was in my early teens, and now I try to go on a climb at least four times a year. I learned on a course with a group of about twenty, but nowadays I climb alone. There's no feeling like it when you finally get to the top of a mountain and you stand there, looking at the view all around and thinking 'I made it!' You have to dig deep sometimes – but you get a real sense of having beaten the mountain. The really hard bit is getting up and going to classes again the next day!

8

F: This phone isn't working properly. Photos don't come out at all well.

M: Which one is it – the B72? Yes, I think there's a problem with that. The B90s are much better. Why don't you get one of those?

F: Well, I'd like one, but they're expensive, aren't they?

M: Yeah, but good value. It's your birthday soon – maybe you could ask your parents for one?

F: No, they think I spent too much on the B72. Perhaps I could take it back to the shop.

M: Well, yes. If it doesn't work, they should change it or repair it really.

F: I think that's the law, isn't it? I'll see what the man in the shop says tomorrow.

UNIT 7 Telling stories

VOCABULARY

1 **1** lean **2** tap **3** rush **4** kneel **5** slap **6** swing **7** wander **8** mumble **9** whistle **10** sigh **11** whisper **12** tremble

2 **1** leant **2** tapped **3** whispered **4** whistling **5** swung **6** wandered **7** sighed **8** mumbled **9** rushed **10** trembling

READING

1 **1** A **2** D **3** D **4** B **5** C **6** B

2 Students should underline:

1 In the case of Emily Franklin, it is all of those things

2 they never believed it would be published. 'So you can imagine their reaction when I told them it had been accepted. . .'

3 they're not expecting Emily to be the new J. K. Rowling, she's not giving up school anytime soon

4 quite a few people contacted me asking for advice, but … it

5 the whole thing is crying out for the big-screen treatment

6 I want my readers to consider topics like freedom and identity.

3 **1** remarkably **2** regardless of **3** themes **4** literary **5** reaction

GRAMMAR

1 **1** b **2** a **3** h **4** f **5** d **6** g **7** c **8** e

2 **1** had been waiting **2** didn't believe, had passed **3** put on, picked up, left **4** had been training, were **5** had only been sitting, came, asked **6** had been running, began **7** had already started, got **8** had never met, recognised **9** had been writing, was, offered **10** had, had all sold

3 **1** The teacher was talking when the fire alarm rang.

2 Karen had been learning Spanish for two years when she moved to Argentina.

3 I left home, ran for the bus and arrived at school on time.

4 When we got home, Dad had finished preparing dinner.

4 **1** a **2** b **3** a **4** b

VOCABULARY

1 **1** for some time **2** before long **3** the week before last **4** for weeks on end **5** in no time

a before long **b** in no time **c** the week before last **d** for weeks on end **e** for some time

2 **1** in no time **2** before long **3** for some time **4** the week before last **5** for days on end

WRITING

1 Students' own answers

2 Yes, it does.

3 What was in the package? A key and another note.
What happened next? Examined the key, looked out of the window at the garden, opened the back door
How did you feel? Saw a motorbike and parents and felt very surprised

4 **1** picked **2** read **3** had left **4** took **5** put **6** opened **7** had written **8** was raining **9** didn't want

5 Students' own answers

UNIT 8 A great place to live

VOCABULARY

1 **Across: 1** urban **5** close **9** relaxed **11** trendy **12** rural
Down: 2 remote **3** affordable **4** residential **6** inner city **7** welcoming **8** industrial **10** diverse

2 **1** rural **2** industrial **3** diverse **4** remote **5** affordable **6** inner city

3 **1** residential **2** remote **3** diverse **4** trendy **5** industrial **6** inner, affordable **7** close **8** urban, rural

READING

1 **1** C **2** D **3** A **4** B **5** C **6** B **7** B **8** C **9** A **10** D

2 Students should underline:

1. I didn't sleep particularly well, however, as it was mid-summer and the air conditioning wasn't working properly.
2. I chose the tower, which turned out to be a shame because the weather was poor. Those who went to the Louvre said it was incredible
3. But I needn't have worried. We were so busy having fun that I didn't have time to miss anyone!
4. The food was amazing, and considering Lisbon is a capital city, surprisingly reasonable.
5. I'm going to convince my parents to book us on a trip there this winter.
6. the family we stayed with made us feel so at home and put us at ease immediately. I couldn't believe how lovely they were
7. I got pretty close to quite a few people I'd never spoken to much before, so that was a bonus.
8. The hostel we stayed in was quite unique. The rooms were decorated with graffiti and modern art – very hip and fashionable.
9. the thing that really struck me about London was the huge variety of people there from lots of different cultures.
10. I went with a few others on a bicycle tour of the city, which is definitely worth the money if you're ever in Paris with a few hours to spare.

3 **1** reputation **2** struck me **3** awkward **4** budget **5** bonus

GRAMMAR

1 **1** A **2** B/C **3** C **4** B **5** B **6** A **7** C **8** A

2 **1** 's going to snow **2** 'll answer **3** 've/have finished **4** 's about to / 's going to jump **5** might get, might get **6** departs

3
1. We will pick you up from the airport when you arrive.
2. I am sure you'll find lots of interesting things to do during your visit.
3. ✓
4. It's great that you're coming / going to come to London.
5. We will discuss it when you come home.
6. ✓

VOCABULARY

1
1. Yes, he's acting as if / as though he's won the lottery.
2. It looks as if / as though the bus is going to be late.
3. I feel as if / as though I haven't slept for days.
4. She sounded as if / as though she wasn't happy about something.
5. I felt as if / as though I'd never been away.
6. No, but she's acting as if / as though she knows us!

LISTENING

1 a game or sport 8; a geographical feature, place 3, 9; a task 4; an ability 6; a qualification 2; a type of media 10; a food item 5; a subject / topic 1, 7

2 a conservation project on which she was a volunteer

3–4 **1** animals **2** (university) degree **3** the beach **4** washing up **5** favourite cereal **6** data collection **7** sea life **8** card games **9** park **10** diary

06 **F:** Hi, and thanks for inviting me here tonight to tell you about the time I spent as a volunteer on a conservation project in Madagascar. I was looking for something to do in the year before I went to university – what they call a 'gap year'. There were various possibilities, and I had a lot of interests: ecology, sports, computer programming – but it was my long-standing love of animals which led me to become a volunteer on this conservation project.

It was a great opportunity to learn more about the wildlife of that part of the world. Not just the obvious cuddly mammals, but also fish – and even the reptiles were fascinating. It was all good background knowledge to prepare for my university degree, which I'm currently halfway through.

The project involved taking surveys of both land animals and ocean creatures. For this reason, we were based in different camps, depending on the type of data we were collecting. Mine was next to the beach, but most people slept in another camp in the forest. Conditions were pretty basic – the beds were small, and there were four of us in each tent – but they weren't actually as bad as I thought they'd be.

I had to do camp duty once every two weeks or so, which I didn't mind so much because it kept me busy. It was interesting having to cook dinner for about 30 people! The washing up wasn't exactly fun, but you just took your turn like everyone else.

The food was actually pretty good: simple and fresh, with a huge variety of seafood. Seriously, I ate some strange things. I still have no idea what they were! They have amazing chocolate there, too. The only thing I really would have liked for breakfast was my favourite cereal – I couldn't find it anywhere. But I got used to fruit and coffee every morning.

One of the things that made the experience so worthwhile was all the stuff I learned. I learned how to scuba dive – it's so great to get up close to marine wildlife. … I'm currently finishing a project at university on birds and the practice I got in data collection during my time in Madagascar has definitely helped me with that. In fact, the whole thing kept my brain working, which is handy if you're taking a gap year from studying!

If you decide to go on something like this, I'd definitely advise you to take a decent camera. It was hard trying to get photos of birds, as they'd fly away most of the time, and my camera didn't have a very good zoom lens. I only had a small compact one, but it was completely waterproof, so, although I got some reasonable shots of lizards and monkeys, the best ones were of sea life. I've had some prints made.

We didn't get much spare time, but sometimes, when the weather was bad, we didn't do much because the wildlife would be hiding. A few of the volunteers were into playing chess, but I wasn't much good at that, so I spent my spare time reading or taking part in card games with the others. On sunny days when we couldn't do surveys for one reason or another, we could sunbathe or go for a walk or a swim.

We got Saturdays off, and we got to go on trips to nearby places. I visited a local school, some nice villages, and of course the zoo in the capital. One town has a park where you can hold out bananas for monkeys and they jump on your shoulders to get them – another great experience.

Some of the volunteers kept video recordings of their time there. They said they were going to upload them, but I haven't seen any of them yet. Others updated their blogs. I recorded things the old-fashioned way – every night I'd update my diary with the events of the day. I got some copies made, and you can buy one for a pound after this talk, if you're interested. I might get round to turning it into a website one day!

UNIT 9 A bright future

VOCABULARY

1 **1** f **2** g **3** h/j **4** h/j **5** b **6** a/i/k **7** a/i/k **8** a/i/k **9** l **10** d/e **11** d/e **12** c

2 **1** looks bright **2** achieve … goals **3** take every opportunity **4** went wrong **5** made the best of **6** make a difference **7** had a go **8** see the best in **9** has strengths and weaknesses **10** make the most of **11** put an end to **12** sees the worst in

READING

1 He seems to be an optimist.

2 **2** F **3** D **4** B **5** A **6** G **7** C

3 **1** B **2** B **3** A **4** A **5** A

4 **1** thrill **2** fortune **3** landlord **4** features **5** script

GRAMMAR

1 **1** you'll have spent **2** I'll be sleeping **3** will have been going **4** I'll have finished **5** she'll be working **6** will have been living **7** we'll have travelled **8** he'll be studying

2 **1** 'll have been writing **2** won't have finished **3** 'll have been **4** 'll have read **5** 'll have been building **6** will have cooked **7** 'll have been waiting **8** 'll have arrived

3 **1** I'll have finished my exams in a couple of days and then I'm going to a small island.

2 When the concert has finished you can interview the conductor of the orchestra.

3 I will continue for four days and finish on Saturday.

4 ✓

VOCABULARY

1 **1** personality **2** relationship **3** satisfaction **4** active **5** beneficial **6** remarkable

2 **1** friendship(s) **2** responsibility **3** emotional **4** practical **5** encouragement **6** effective **7** competition **8** valuable

WRITING

1 **Adding a new point:** Furthermore, In addition
Comparing/contrasting: whereas, compared to/with, On the one/other hand
Concluding: On balance, To sum up

2 Students' own answers

3 **1** whereas **2** On the one hand **3** Furthermore / In addition **4** On the other hand **5** compared **6** Furthermore / In addition **7** To sum up **8** On balance

4–5 Students' own answers

UNIT 10 Surprise!

VOCABULARY

1 **1** by **2** in **3** out of **4** in **5** in **6** in **7** by **8** at **9** at **10** out of

2 **1** at fault for the fire **2** (on my screen) out of nowhere **3** by chance **4** in detail **5** in secret **6** out of character **7** at risk

3 Students' own answers

READING

1 A

2 **1** G **2** A **3** F **4** D **5** C **6** B

3 **1** astonishingly **2** unharmed **3** simultaneous **4** occurrences **5** sample

GRAMMAR

1 **1** shouldn't **2** should have **3** didn't need to take **4** should **5** needn't **6** would **7** needn't **8** shouldn't have

2 **1** shouldn't have eaten **2** should have remembered **3** shouldn't have bought **4** should have studied **5** shouldn't have played

3 **1** should have told me in **2** did not / didn't need to go **3** should not / shouldn't have shouted **4** should have stayed/kept in **5** needn't / need not have taken so/that/this **6** might/would have frightened

4 **1** It would have been better to stay in bed.

2 I wondered how it would have been if you hadn't been there.

3 It would have been OK if he really wanted to come.

4 I shouldn't have done this, because I failed the test.

5 ✓

6 We had mountain bikes, so we thought that it would be a great idea to visit the forest.

VOCABULARY

1 **1** d **2** g **3** a **4** f **5** c **6** e **7** b **8** h **9** k **10** l **11** i **12** j

2 **1** angel **2** foggy **3** grilled **4** boiling **5** flooded **6** hit **7** bright **8** froze **9** lifted **10** stormy **11** weighed **12** sailed

LISTENING

1 Students' own answers

2 A

3 Students should underline: *I love it* and *There's a lot of work and a lot of worry involved.*

4–5 **2** B **3** C **4** C **5** C **6** B **7** C

07 *Track 07 is taken from Track 08. It is from the Interviewer's line 'This evening in our series on Dream Jobs, …' to Rob's line 'it's a fun job, and even better if you enjoy the social aspects.'*

08 **Interviewer:** This evening in our series on Dream Jobs, our guest is Rob Mitchell, who is a professional party planner – someone who arranges big parties for other people. Hi Rob.

Rob: Hi.

Interviewer: Is your job as much fun as it sounds?

Rob: I love it – but that's not to say it's one big party. It's a business, and you have to please the client. Just because you're throwing a party doesn't mean it's party time for you! There's a lot of work and a lot of worry involved, and you really can't relax until the last guest has left, and the venue is cleaned up. But if you don't mind working long hours, then yes – it's a fun job, and even better if you enjoy the social aspects.

Interviewer: How did you get into the party planning business?

Rob: My mum's an interior designer and my dad's an architect, and what I do is kind of related to that. But to be honest, I almost fell into the business by accident. A friend of mine invited me to an art event which was arranged by her brother's party planning company. I got talking to him and we found we had a lot in common, and I ended up being offered a job there and then. That was three years ago. I have my own events company now, of course.

Interviewer: You arrange events for a lot of celebrities, don't you? What's that like?

Rob: You might expect celebrities to be hard work, but in fact it's the non-celebrity clients that can give you the biggest headaches. The non-celebrities have the money, but not the fame, and they still tend to try to knock my fees down. I find the famous ones are much more relaxed about things, and let me run with my own ideas. Some of them have become good friends, I'm happy to say.

Interviewer: Have you had any strange requests for party themes?

Rob: Yes, a client insisted they wanted live monkeys to hand out gifts to guests! I tried to talk them out of it: the expense alone was huge, and of course there were health and safety issues, but the clients didn't care how much they cost, and were insistent. On the day, it wasn't quite the disaster it could have been. The monkeys started throwing food around, and some of the guests complained – but at least nobody was injured!

Interviewer: Ha ha! What advice would you give to anyone throwing a party?

Rob: No monkeys! But seriously – don't be afraid to be creative. It helps if your room's the right size – not too big, or the place will look empty; not too small, or it'll be too crowded. But above all, and this is true no matter where the party is, make sure you invite the right guests. They can make or break a party – with the right crowd you could have fun at a bus stop!

Interviewer: What do you like most about your job?

Rob: The fact that when I go into the office in the morning, I never know for sure what the day's going to bring. Some days will be quiet, other days I'll have an email from a rock star wanting me to arrange a party with a budget of half a million pounds! Sure, it's nice to meet celebrities, and with big clients the money's always pretty good, but on a day-to-day basis, that's not what gets me out of bed in the morning.

Interviewer: So, what are your plans for the future?

Rob: Ha! I wish I had time to plan anything but the next party! The truth is, I'm so busy just now – word's got around the celebrity circuit, and I'm in demand. I want an assistant, actually – someone to take care of the practicalities, answering the phone, taking messages etc. – that's my most pressing need. I sometimes think about trying my hand at festival organising, which would be a new challenge for me. But I've got my hands full with the parties at the moment.

UNIT 11 We are family

VOCABULARY

1 **Across: 4** down **5** off **8** let **9** hit **10** take
Down: 1 look **2** finish **3** count **6** fall **7** stick

2 **1** stick together **2** look up to **3** take after **4** count on **5** let (you) down **6** look down on **7** fall out **8** hit (it) off **9** go off

READING

1 **1** course **2** have **3** which/whom **4** for **5** where **6** take **7** other **8** again/more

2 Elephants, sea lions, chimpanzees

3 **2** E **3** E, S **4** C **5** S **6** P, C

4 **1** well-being **2** upbringing **3** offspring **4** supervised **5** abandon

GRAMMAR

1 **1** ✓ **2** (that) **3** ✓ **4** (that) **5** ✓ **6** ✓

2 **1** who **2** which **3** (which) **4** who **5** (who) **6** which

3 **2** a Moscow is the city which is famous for the Kremlin.
3 b I'll never forget that time (when) we went to the seaside in the rain.
4 d This is the house where my grandfather was born / (which) my grandfather was born in.
5 f There aren't many taxi drivers who have never had an accident.
6 c There's that boy whose father teaches at my college.

4 **1** You are lucky because I've got the information (that/which) you need about the new art class.
2 You will go to the village, which has a little supermarket, and buy some food.
3 One morning we went to the beach, which was about 30 minutes from our campsite.
4 Tina had dreamed of winning a ballet contest since she was five years old, which was when she started her lessons.
5 She is the actress who is in the new *X-Men* movie!

VOCABULARY

1 **1** behaved **2** organised **3** tech **4** balanced **5** grown **6** confident

2 **1** well-built **2** long-distance **3** last-minute **4** middle-aged **5** well-paid **6** short-term

WRITING

1 Students' own answers

2 Yes
A - Where would it be?
B - What would it be like?
C - How is it different from where you currently live?

3 **1** cool, fantastic, awesome, OK
2 Moving to New York is a dream of mine.
3 The worst thing is, we don't have a spare room.

4 How cool would that be? Did I mention there would also be a balcony with a view over the rooftops of the city? Wouldn't that be awesome? So, although there are some OK places in my town which I would show you if you came to visit, you'd have to sleep on the sofa. If I were you, I'd wait until we move to New York!

4 Students' own answers

UNIT 12 Making a difference

VOCABULARY

1 **1** d **2** c **3** g **4** e **5** b **6** h **7** f **8** a

2 **1** amused **2** spread **3** cheer . . . up **4** reassure **5** stimulate **6** speak out **7** congratulate **8** highlight

3 Students' own answers

READING

1 **1** C **2** E **3** F **4** B **5** A

2 **1** A **2** C **3** C **4** D **5** C **6** A

3 **1** humanity **2** fade **3** divorced **4** beyond **5** random

GRAMMAR

1 **1** Flour is used to make bread.
2 Portuguese is spoken in Brazil.
3 People under 15 are not allowed to watch this film.
4 The power in this house is provided by sunlight.
5 I was bitten on the leg by the neighbour's cat.
6 Everything will be arranged by my brother.
7 You will be given instructions on arrival.
8 More is being spent on smartphones than ever before.

2 **1** Dad had been moved to an office in a different town.
2 I have often been described as shy.
3 I was being shown into the building.
4 'I've been given the job of making you feel welcome here.'
5 I was really impressed by her kindness that day.

3 **1** I like to wear clothes which <u>are made from</u> cotton.
2 My bicycle <u>was stolen</u> on the 10th of September.
3 I have a lot of friends, but my best friend <u>is called</u> Maria.
4 They eat special cakes which <u>are made</u> for the wedding.
5 ✓
6 The first restaurant <u>specialises</u> in seafood.

4 **1** having/getting, painted **2** get, to look **3** have/get, taken **4** got, to cut **5** have/get, cleaned **6** had, taken out (*had* is better here – slightly more formal) **7** had/got, delivered **8** are having/getting, built

5 Possible answers:
I'd have all my food delivered.
I'd get an assistant to check my texts.
I'd get all my clothes made.
I'd have fresh flowers delivered every day.
I'd get someone to check my homework for me before I hand it in.

VOCABULARY

1 **1** You can have either a cake or a biscuit.
2 I don't like either cats or dogs. / I like neither cats nor dogs.
3 The film was both funny and scary.
4 Neither Maria nor Donna has any time.
5 Either Greg or Dave is lying.
6 He speaks neither French nor Spanish. / He doesn't speak either French or Spanish.

2 Students' own answers

LISTENING

1 Her job as a media officer at Happy Planet.

2 an event 7; a job 2, 9; a topic 5; a type of media 6; a subject of study 1; a personal quality 10; a person/organisation 3, 8; a number 4

3–4 **1** French **2** youth leader **3** (best) friend **4** three **5** green tourism **6** social media **7** conference **8** companies **9** presenter **10** communication skills

09 **F:** Good evening, and thank you for asking me to talk to you about my job as media officer at the environmental charity Happy Planet.

What's important for my work? Well, we're an international organisation, so I think it helps that I speak several languages. I've recently learned Portuguese and my degree at university was in Spanish and French. Most media officer positions require experience in journalism, but my story is quite different.

When I left university, I worked as a teacher of English in Spain for a year, followed by a nine-month contract as a youth leader at a camp in Portugal. But I wasn't satisfied. Our planet is in trouble, and I felt that I really wanted to make a difference. So I went back to London and started looking for a job that would let me do that.

My dad has been in journalism for most of his life – and he was very supportive – but it was my best friend who told me that the environmental charity, Happy Planet, was looking for a content provider for their website. Just keeping their activities up to date on a daily basis by writing a blog, interviewing activists, that kind of thing.

It wasn't exactly challenging, but it was a start. Then the organisation's media officer left after working there for only six months, and I applied for her position. Incredibly, after only three months as a lowly content provider, I got the job. I think it was my enthusiasm that convinced them!

The leader of our charity has quite a high profile in the world of environmentalism. He's got a weekly vlog on the internet which he uploads to a famous video channel, and he also does a regular weekly column on green tourism in a Sunday newspaper. Occasionally, when he's busy, I actually help him out with that, which I enjoy.

One of the main things involved in my job is keeping an eye on how we are portrayed in the media. We do get a lot of attention – not all of it friendly. So I watch out for negative coverage of our activities and do my best to correct it. The mainstream press are usually OK – but I have to monitor social media closely. That's where a lot of silly stuff comes up – it can be very frustrating.

Luckily there's a lot of travel involved. But it's not all fun – having to give a talk to an audience of hundreds can take the fun out of a weekend on a beautiful Greek island! I look forward to assignments that send me away to places I've never been – even if it does involve work. I was in New York last month at a conference, for example, which was fantastic.

But what's really important to me about my job is that it's all about highlighting the importance of environmental issues. It's not just dealing with the press, and the public – I do a lot of outreach work to corporations, too, and for things other than fund-raising. It's important that we work together to save this planet – and it's quite a challenge to get companies on board, but that's a really satisfying part of my work for me.

I'm excited that the charity is expanding my role to cover a wider range of media. The director's videos are very popular, and he's encouraged me to have a go at being a presenter – something which I'm very keen to do. We might need to employ an assistant to take over the day-to-day press office tasks from me, so I'll be managing him, too. It's an exciting new direction for me.

So, what advice would I give to anyone wanting to be a media officer? Obviously, not everyone can follow the same path – some might start at journalism school, others might start with their own blogs and move on from there. But I'd say the most important thing is to have communication skills. There's a lot of competition for posts, but if you find the right company, you are in a great position to make that difference.

UNIT 13 Leading the way

VOCABULARY

1 noun: doubt, drive, self-esteem, target
adjective: bossy, conscientious, motivated, sympathetic
verb: doubt, drive, put your mind to, stand out, target
adverb: fairly

2 **1** doubt **2** sympathetic **3** fairly **4** stand out **5** target **6** conscientious **7** drive **8** self-esteem **9** put your mind to **10** bossy **11** motivated

3 **1** doubt **2** target **3** sympathetic **4** stand out **5** fairly **6** put your mind to **7** conscientious/motivated **8** self-esteem

4 Students' own answers

READING

1 **1** E **2** C **3** B **4** E **5** B **6** A **7** D **8** C **9** D **10** A

2 Students should underline:

1 it was put to the vote, and I won

2 a role I've always felt pretty comfortable in

3 some of them had good ideas of their own, which I did take on board – and I think the final production was better for that

4 because I'd set a strict schedule early on

5 we didn't always agree on the approach to take. I found that quite awkward at first

6 I loved the tension and excitement

7 The arguments that broke out about who was doing what were awful!

8 I always raise my own game up a level … if you show passion and enthusiasm … it rubs off on the team

9 if I'm asked to do anything like that again, I'll run a mile!

10 an ankle injury put me out of action for a season … I was approached … to take over as temporary coach

3 **1** assigned **2** coming up **3** thrived **4** took over **5** ultimately

GRAMMAR

1 **1** always being made to do the boring jobs **2** of being offered a leading role in a film **3** must be handed in by Friday **4** are thought (by most people) to be an improvement (by most people) **5** to be told about the prize **6** might not be allowed to go on the climbing trip

2 **1** be rewarded **2** being given **3** to be punished **4** being helped **5** to be told **6** being handed

3 **1** It will save a lot of electricity as solar energy <u>will be</u> used.

2 As <u>can be</u> seen, bikes are really very good: cheap, fast and healthy.

3 ✓

4 It will be <u>prepared</u> by our school cook.

VOCABULARY

1 **1** set **2** keep **3** make **4** came **5** lived **6** Speak **7** turned

2 **1** he made up the whole thing! / made the whole thing up!

2 It lived up to all my expectations.

3 it is hard to keep up with him.

4 they eventually turned up an hour late.

5 You'll have to speak up

6 The police officer came up to me

WRITING

1 **1** b **2** d **3** f **4** e **5** a **6** g **7** c **8** h

2 Students should underline: summer camp, children, sports leaders, kitchen helpers, drama class assistants, which job, why suitable

3 Yes

4 **1** Dear Sir / Madam **2** I would like to **3** I believe / I feel certain **4** Could you let me know **5** I feel certain / I believe **6** I would be grateful if you could **7** Yours sincerely / Yours faithfully

5 Students' own answers

UNIT 14 Getting there

VOCABULARY

1 **Across: 2** drive **6** pull **8** out **9** keep **10** hold **12** ran
Down: 1 break **3** into **4** speed **5** Slow **7** up **11** over

2 **1** pull up **2** break down **3** speed up **4** run into **5** run over **6** keep up (with) **7** pull over **8** pull into **9** drive off **10** pull out **11** slow down **12** hold up

3 **1** pull over **2** held up **3** ran into **4** Slow down **5** pulled up **6** run over **7** keep up **8** pulled into **9** drove off **10** speed up **11** breaks down **12** pulling out

READING

1 B

2 **1** D **2** C **3** E **4** B **5** F **6** A **7** G

3 **1** environmental damage **2** tourists and residents nearby **3** conservation projects and local communities **4** Ecotourism involves travel into remote areas where people have no experience of foreigners. **5** very difficult

4 **1** interacting **2** remote **3** welfare **4** donations **5** waste

GRAMMAR

1 **1** couldn't **2** is, has tried **3** are going **4** is, is served **5** hadn't been

2 **1** (that) he won't be going on holiday this year.

2 (had) wanted to come/go to Kenya with them.

3 (that) she has always supported the idea of responsible tourism.

4 (that) she was organising a trip to Japan.

5 (that) he could arrange the whole thing for us.

6 (that) fifty million tourists will be visiting Africa this year.

3 **1** b **2** b **3** a **4** a

4 **1** Air travel is going to get much more expensive.

2 I enjoyed my holiday in Nepal very much.

3 I've been trying to reduce my carbon footprint.

4 The best holidays aren't always the most expensive.

5 I'll never forget the week I spent in India.

6 You'll never have a better opportunity to study abroad.

VOCABULARY

1 **1** h **2** b **3** a **4** g **5** c **6** d **7** e **8** f

2 **1** agreed to slow down
2 that she had run into / to having run into / to running into
3 recommended/suggested/advised pulling over
4 insisted (that) he knew
5 pointed out that riding
6 persuaded my dad to drive

LISTENING

1 Possible answers: entertainers, cleaners, waiters and waitresses, photographers, office staff

2 Speaker 1 D

3 Students should underline: A major part of my job is to mix with the guests, and everyone knows me by the end of the week.

4–5 Speaker 2 E Speaker 3 G Speaker 4 B Speaker 5 C
A, F and H aren't needed.

10 **1**

F: I help with the entertainment in the resort, which covers the nightly stage shows, daily talks and exhibitions, and talent contests. Basically, I'm the person who has to make sure that everything runs smoothly, whether this means finding extra bottles of water for the bands or helping a guest to choose a costume for the talent show. It's impossible to have a daily routine because every day is different – I never get bored! And I seldom get a moment to myself. A major part of my job is to mix with the guests, and everyone knows me by the end of the week. If I'm not actually making announcements on stage, I'm chatting or dancing in the audience. It's all part of what I do.

11 **2**

M: I play a lot of sport at school, which is why I'm working in the fitness centre at the resort. I explain the facilities to new arrivals and invite them to join one of our programmes. Not all of them take up the offer, of course – some just want to relax. I give tennis lessons to the kids, as well, which is good fun. And, as I hope to train as a sports instructor, it also means I'm getting useful experience for the future. Sometimes I wish I only worked during the day, but as the centre stays open until 11 at night, I stay late two or three times a week.

3

F: I have a great job here – I'm a photographer. There are three of us, and we take photos of the guests in various places: at the swimming pool, in the gym, dancing at the parties, or just walking around. People usually love having their picture taken, and are quite willing to buy prints from us. By evening my memory card has hundreds of photos on it, so I have to transfer them to the computer and prepare them to display on the big screen in our office the next day. Some of the others get bored by that part of the job, but I like it, as I'm keen on photography.

4

M: I work in the office, doing everything from taking phone bookings and answering emails to helping out with the resort brochure for the following year. Some days it's a bit dull, especially when there's no one else around to chat to. But at the same time I'm lucky because I never have to work at the weekend or in the evenings, unlike most of the others who have summer jobs here. It's the first time I've ever had a real job, too. I have no idea at this point what career I'm going to end up with, but I guess this is all good experience!

5

F: This is my second summer working as a waiter at the resort. I'm enjoying it much more this year as it's less of a challenge. I know quite a few of the staff working here now, and we're a pretty sociable bunch of people, who see each other outside work. The hours are long, but they move us around the different restaurants from week to week, so there's plenty of variety. My favourite is the Japanese restaurant because I love the sushi there. We're able to eat whatever we like after the guests have left, and we get breakfast if we're working early, too.

UNIT 15 The bigger picture

VOCABULARY

1 **1 noun:** ban, **verb:** ban **2 noun:** collection, **verb:** collect **3 noun:** cooperation, **verb:** cooperate **4 noun:** criticism, **verb:** criticise **5 noun:** election, **verb:** elect **6 noun:** supporter/support, **verb:** support

2 **1** criticise **2** collect **3** elect **4** ban **5** cooperate **6** support

3 **1** collecting **2** supporters **3** banned **4** election **5** cooperate **6** criticism

READING

1 C

2 **1** C **2** B **3** D **4** A **5** B **6** C **7** D **8** C

3 Possible answers:
1 … they are more concerned with their own lives.
2 … smaller issues that affect them directly, often using social media to comment and express their thoughts.
3 … they can express their support through 'likes' and 'retweets'.
4 … it makes people less likely to donate financially.

4 **1** involvement **2** shortage **3** specific **4** generate **5** contribute

GRAMMAR

1 **1** must have trained **2** can't be **3** must have snowed / must be snowing **4** must be **5** must have hurt **6** can't have waited **7** must have been **8** can't have seen, must have been

2 **1** might not have known about the party. **2** could have forgotten to tell you about it. **3** can't be your bag. **4** may have met when they were on holiday. **5** must have seen this film before. **6** might have missed the early train. **7** can't have been the first time he's played tennis. **8** might still be in class.

3 **1** ✓
2 It might go wrong, but it might go right too, and if it does it was worth the effort.
3 We wouldn't be able to do 80 km on Saturday because in the mountains it is very difficult and we could/might get lost.
4 You must have confused me with someone else.
5 Obviously, it's wonderful to go to a zoo and see the animals from different countries all together, but it can't be very nice to be disturbed all day and to have no freedom.
6 There are great views throughout the ride, and there's an astonishing castle and also a butterfly farm that might/could turn out to be very interesting.

VOCABULARY

1 Across: **1** light **3** progress **4** turn **5** favour **6** actual
Down: **2** general

2 **1** In actual fact **2** in progress **3** in turn **4** in general **5** In the light of **6** in favour of

WRITING

1 **1** D **2** C **3** A **4** B

2 **1** which **2** Now **3** once **4** Even though **5** Provided

3 B

4 Paragraph 1 introduces the topic
Paragraph 2 gives details of arguments 'for'
Paragraph 3 gives details of arguments 'against'
Paragraph 4 summarises the two sides, possibly with a personal opinion

5 Students' own answers

UNIT 16 New and improved!

VOCABULARY

1 **1** b **2** d **3** e **4** a **5** h **6** c **7** g **8** f

2 **1** sponsor **2** product placement **3** aimed at **4** ad breaks **5** samples **6** launched

3 **1** appeal to **2** sample **3** product placement **4** consumers **5** sponsor **6** launching, aimed at

4 Students' own answers

READING

1–2 Students' own answers

3 generally positive

4 **1** finding **2** been **3** from/to **4** may/might **5** either **6** part **7** whatever **8** into

5 **1** Marketing is about finding information to inform the making of products; advertising is about selling them.
2 No, because you have to have selling in your soul.
3 You have to work hard, the hours are long and there's a lot of competition for jobs.
4 You need to have talent and a little luck.
5 Because it's illegal to make false statements and there are severe penalties for doing so.

6 **1** well-off **2** tough **3** modest **4** immoral **5** penalties

GRAMMAR

1 **1** hear **2** watch **3** 'll/will save **4** formed **5** melts **6** won **7** 'll/will have **8** hadn't played **9** banned **10** 'd/would have made

2 **1** … I hadn't loved the campaign, I wouldn't have bought the product.
2 … the skirt had been on offer, she would have bought it.
3 … have watched the film if I hadn't read a great review.
4 … have sponsored you if you had asked me.
5 … she hadn't asked all the right questions, she wouldn't have got the job.
6 … have sold their products if they had advertised.
7 … I hadn't needed to go shopping, I'd/would have gone to the library.
8 … have met you at the cinema if we'd/had known you were going.

3 **1** You can go to the beach if the weather <u>is</u> good.
2 I<u>'ll have</u> <u>a/the</u> chance to prove myself, if you employ me.
3 I would be very pleased if you came and <u>visited</u> me.
4 Probably, if nothing <u>had happened</u>, I would have lost anyway.

VOCABULARY

1 **1** conveniently **2** finely **3** environmentally **4** nicely/well **5** naturally **6** well **7** ridiculously **8** actively

2 **1** scientifically proved/proven **2** amazingly tasty **3** globally recognised **4** ecologically safe **5** financially independent **6** incredibly economical **7** regularly updated

LISTENING

1 working in an advertising agency

2 They are all nouns or noun phrases.

3–4 **1** social media **2** (course) tutor **3** (visual) CV **4** shadowing **5** campaign calendars **6** meetings **7** (office) culture **8** creative industry **9** networking **10** blog

12 M: Hello, my name's Tom Atkins. I'm a second-year media student, and I'm here to tell you about the time I spent last summer working for an advertising agency called Imageco. I've always been interested in a career in advertising. My dad is a businessman, and my mum is a great graphic designer – but it wasn't them who really influenced me. Social media has been a big part of my life – nothing unusual there – and anyone who spends time on that will notice the clever way advertising works in that medium. I find that fascinating, and that's what led to me to a media studies degree.

I decided to try to get some work experience in advertising last summer, but I wasn't sure where to start looking. My best friend at university had found work experience easily – his uncle works in broadcasting, but that wasn't quite what I was looking for. In the end I asked my course tutor, who luckily was able to give me some contacts in the advertising industry.

So I wrote a few application letters, asked my teacher to write a reference, and created a visual CV to show what I could do – basically composed of photos and a bit of video, as well as a list of my qualifications and interests. The interviewer who gave me the job said that was the thing that swung it for me. I was very pleased with it.

For the first week of the job I was given a mentor – a woman who had worked at the agency for years. She was great. I helped her with lots of things – including making coffee! – and basically watched what she did, accompanying her everywhere. This is what they call 'shadowing' and it's what they do with all new recruits. I learned a lot that way!

Eventually the agency let me do some actual work for them. They have several client accounts which require management of their social networks. As they knew that was my big interest, they put me in charge of creating campaign calendars for each of the clients to follow, so that they wouldn't forget to engage with their customers. That was fun.

But it wasn't all fun. I had to go on what they called the 'lunch run', where I took food orders from everyone and went out to fetch them. I didn't really mind that, to be honest. There were a lot of meetings too, which I couldn't take part in – I just watched. Sometimes they went on all day. Now that was a drag.

On the whole, though, it was a fantastic experience. The whole office culture thing was a real eye-opener for me. I can see why people spend their life in this business. It was so relaxed – music was always on, people chatted and laughed, there was even table tennis, which I became quite good at.

Working the summer at Imageco helped me think about what I wanted to do after university. Advertising is a lively world to be in, but it's not necessarily where I'll end up. Another creative industry could be equally appealing to me – broadcasting, publishing, web design. I know for sure I want to work in that general area.

For those of you who are specifically into advertising, I did ask around at Imageco what the best way to get into the business was. They said all the usual stuff – hard work, imagination. Energy is important. But the thing they emphasised was networking – in advertising more than anywhere it's who you know rather than what you know, or what qualifications you've got.

If you want to know more about Imageco as a company, they have a very good website – as you would expect. I've written up my experience this summer in a little booklet – I'll leave a pile here on the table – feel free to take one. And if you want to keep up with what I'm doing, I've got a blog you can follow – the address is in the booklet. Now, are there any questions?

UNIT 17 Making headlines

VOCABULARY

1 **1** c/f **2** c/f **3** h **4** a **5** b/g **6** b/g **7** d **8** e

2 **1** amused **2** making **3** commenting **4** celebrate **5** date **6** gossip **7** make **8** cover

3 Students' own answers

READING

1 Possible answers:

Good journalists are curious; they have to be honest; they have to be accurate.

2 **1** competition **2** traditional **3** financial **4** inexperienced **5** vacancies **6** employer **7** discouraged **8** effective

3 **1** C **2** A **3** B **4** C **5** D **6** A **7** B **8** D

4 **1** relevant **2** compromise **3** intense **4** meaningful **5** capture

GRAMMAR

1 **1** c **2** e **3** b **4** h **5** f **6** a **7** g **8** d

2 **1** If he had brought his mobile phone, he could call for help.

2 I could have applied for the teaching job if I had a degree.

3 would have come to the cinema with us if she enjoyed horror films.

4 If we hadn't lost the match, we wouldn't be / might not be unhappy now.

5 John might be married now if he had met the right person.

6 If I was/were good at cooking, I could/might have become a chef.

7 They might have gone on holiday in the summer if they didn't have a new baby.

8 You would/might have some pocket money left if you hadn't broken the kitchen window.

3 **1** If I hadn't got good grades at school, I wouldn't be studying medicine now.

2 I think that our way of life would be very different if the telephone hadn't been invented.

3 They told me that I could go on the school trip, if I asked my parents first.

4 I'd really like to know what would have happened if you hadn't been there.

5 ✓

VOCABULARY

1 **1** c **2** f **3** a **4** d **5** g **6** h **7** e **8** b

2 **1** getting (ideas) across **2** clear up **3** followed up **4** backed (me) up **5** looks into **6** left out **7** catch up on **8** brought up

WRITING

1 **1** a film about the news media **2** in a local magazine **3** readers of the magazine / local people **4** what the film was about, its good points, its bad points, and whether you'd recommend it

2 positive

3 C B D A

4 Yes

5 **1** highly original **2** really hilarious **3** quite witty **4** absolutely determined **5** totally crazy

6 Students' own answers

UNIT 18 Creative careers

VOCABULARY

1 **1** badly paid **2** working long hours **3** make a living **4** meet deadlines **5** rewarding **6** take time off **7** well-paid **8** working shifts

2 **1** working long hours **2** a living **3** meet deadlines **4** badly paid **5** rewarding **6** working shifts **7** take time off **8** well-paid

3 **1** rewarding **2** take time off **3** working shifts **4** well-paid **5** working long hours

READING

1 **1** C **2** A **3** D **4** B **5** D **6** C

2 **1** schemes **2** blow **3** breeding **4** turned out **5** indigestion

GRAMMAR

1 **1** writing **2** forgetting **3** using **4** correct **5** studying **6** planning **7** correct **8** being

2 **1** working **2** Applying **3** playing **4** trying **5** arriving **6** watching **7** moving **8** feeling **9** Waiting **10** doing

3 Students' own answers

4 **1** I am writing this letter to say thank you for your hospitality.

2 ✓

3 I don't mind working hard and I feel good when I use my time efficiently.

4 I would prefer to work with animals instead of helping in an office.

VOCABULARY

1 **1** more or less / more and more **2** round and round **3** more and more / more or less **4** sooner or later **5** now and then **6** one or two **7** up and down **8** over and over

2 **1** now and then **2** more or less **3** more and more **4** up and down **5** sooner or later **6** one or two **7** over and over **8** round and round

LISTENING

1 Students' own answers

2 **2** enjoy most about her work **3** does not enjoy her job **4** use a computer **5** gets her ideas **6** look for in a new employee **7** spare-time activity

3 **1** A

4 Students should underline: I had a low opinion of the advertising industry at that time – you know, it's the business of lying to people to persuade them to buy things they don't need.

5 for B: I'd just graduated with a degree in psychology; for C: there aren't many opportunities available in that field

6–7 **2** C **3** B **4** A **5** B **6** A **7** B

13 *Track 13 is taken from Track 14. It is from the Interviewer's line 'Today in our series about young entrepreneurs, ...' to Tina's line 'Yes, we've been incredibly lucky.'*

14 **Interviewer:** Today in our series about young entrepreneurs, we're talking to Tina Jakes, who, along with her friend Marcus, started up a new advertising agency when she left university. Good morning, Tina.

Tina: Good morning.

Interviewer: So, Tina, what made you want to start an advertising business?

Tina: I didn't, really! It was Marcus's idea. I'd just graduated with a degree in psychology, and there aren't many opportunities available in that field. To be honest, I had a low opinion of the advertising industry at that time – you know: it's the business of lying to people to persuade them to buy things they don't need. But Marcus is a brilliant graphic designer, and he was looking for a partner in his new adverting business, so I thought – why not? Try it!

Interviewer: And it really took off!

Tina: Yes, we've been incredibly lucky.

Interviewer: What do you like most about working in advertising?

Tina: I work with an interesting bunch of people – some of them very talented – so there's never a dull moment. And I appreciate the chance to be creative. But I suppose the main thing for me is just taking part in the process that makes another business become a success. You know, when a campaign goes well, you get a real sense of achievement – that you've made a difference.

Interviewer: Are there any down sides?

Tina: It's a bit intense. I often work long hours – especially if there's a deadline coming up. But I really don't mind that. Being our own boss means we can choose our clients, but occasionally we get a difficult one who doesn't really know what they want from a campaign – they have nothing to offer, and expect you to do it all. That can be annoying. I appreciate working for someone who knows what they want!

Interviewer: Do you have to have really good computer skills?

Tina: Well, I use a computer quite a lot. When I have to make a presentation, I usually pull a few images off the internet, or go out and take some digital photos, which I'll download and edit. But then I transfer everything onto paper for the final stages, and that's what I show to the client. I don't use the computer for that – I'm a bit old-fashioned that way. Nobody seems to mind.

Interviewer: How do you come up with ideas for campaigns?

Tina: Everyone you talk to will give you a different answer to that question. Some people spend a lot of time on the internet, which is an amazing source of inspiration. Others like to get together and bounce ideas off each other until something comes up. I prefer to concentrate on my own; have a good look at exactly what the aims of the campaign are. And usually there's a clue there as to what direction you should take. I always come up with something eventually.

Interviewer: As your business has grown, you've taken on several new people. What sort of things do you look for in a potential employee?

Tina: Well, we employ people from a lot of different backgrounds at our agency. This summer we took on graduates in English, history, business – and even physics! Advertising is very people-focused, so while we do value things like IT skills, maths and English, we're really looking for team players. They need to be able to work well in a social environment, and to deal diplomatically with awkward clients occasionally.

Interviewer: And what do you do when you're not running your business, Tina? How do you get away from it all?

Tina: Sometimes it's really hard to switch off, but the thing that works best for me is music. I play the saxophone in a five-piece jazz band most weekends. We're not well paid, but we don't do it for the money. As well as helping me forget the office, I think it actually helps me to recharge, and go back in on Monday with fresh ideas. To me, it's really valuable, professionally.

UNIT 19 Points of view

VOCABULARY

1 **1** b **2** f **3** k **4** c **5** g **6** d **7** l **8** a **9** e **10** i **11** h **12** j

2 **1** convinced **2** to my mind **3** isn't/is (totally) against **4** your view on **5** go along with **6** is no doubt **7** As far as I'm **8** keep an open mind **9** hard to deny **10** bear in mind **11** firmly believes in, suspect

3 Students' own answers

READING

1 c

2 **1** C **2** G **3** F **4** A **5** B **6** D

3 **1** be able to tell **2** approaches **3** long-term **4** leading **5** exploit

GRAMMAR

1 **1** have asked **2** is **3** are **4** contributes / is contributing **5** understands **6** is **7** plans / plan / is planning / are planning **8** is **9** is taking **10** look

2 **1** has **2** have **3** has **4** are **5** frightens **6** isn't/aren't **7** hasn't/haven't **8** arrives

3 **1** I don't think there is <u>much</u> athletics on TV today.
2 The food at both of the <u>restaurants is</u> different.
3 ✓
4 In some homes everybody <u>has</u> a computer.

VOCABULARY

1 **Across: 1** lyrics **2** belongings **3** surroundings **4** outskirts **5** refreshments **6** contents **7** savings **Down:** clothes

2 **1** surroundings **2** refreshments **3** lyrics **4** contents **5** outskirts **6** clothes **7** belongings **8** savings

WRITING

1 **Contrast**: although, despite; **Purpose**: in order that; **Reason**: For this reason, Since; **Result**: Consequently, Therefore

2 Students' own answers

3 **1** Consequently / Therefore / For this reason **2** in order that **3** Consequently / Therefore / For this reason **4** Despite

4–5 Students' own answers

UNIT 20 Speak up

VOCABULARY

1 **1** c/f **2** c/f **3** g **4** d/h **5** d/h **6** e **7** b **8** a

2 **1** being a pain **2** was a piece of cake **3** crossed my mind **4** break the ice **5** has an eye for **6** breaks my heart **7** took my/our breath away **8** lost track of time

3 **1** broke my heart **2** was a piece of cake **3** it ever crossed your mind **4** took my breath away **5** to break /of breaking the ice

READING

1 a newspaper / online news site

2 **1** recognition **2** annually **3** Attendance **4** response **5** political **6** unsuccessful **7** difficulty **8** literary

3 **1** had varying success **2** caused social problems **3** it lacks cultural depth **4** it has achieved a lot in a short time **5** people need to be educated about Esperanto

4 **1** widespread **2** delegates **3** challenged **4** shortage **5** breadth

GRAMMAR

1 **1** the, – **2** – , the, the **3** –, an **4** the, a, the **5** an, the **6** a, a **7** The, a **8** a, –/the , –/the

2 **1** Plenty of **2** a bit of **3** number **4** many **5** amount, little **6** a lot of **7** Several **8** a few **9** a lot of **10** Some

3 **1** little **2** few **3** a few **4** a little **5** few **6** little **7** a little **8** a few

4 **1** I hope you will have great fun / a lot of fun.

2 Can you imagine a school where you can study only the subjects you enjoy?

3 ✓

4 However, not many people like to read a book.

5 I was really happy to spend a few days with you.

VOCABULARY

1 **1** A **2** C **3** C **4** B **5** A **6** A **7** C **8** B **9** C **10** A **11** C **12** B

2 Students' own answers

LISTENING

1 Students should underline: **1** how feel **2** what both think **3** what complaining about **4** what explain **5** why worried holiday **6** what business **7** how feeling **8** what think about documentary

2 A

3 Students should underline: Oh, I wouldn't have missed it for the world.

4 **1** B **2** F **3** D **4** C **5** H **6** E **7** A **8** G

5 **2** A **3** A **4** B **5** C **6** A **7** C **8** B

15

F: So what did you think of your first rugby match? Impressed?

M: It was a bit confusing, actually. I still don't understand the rules.

F: So you didn't enjoy it? That's a shame.

M: Oh, I wouldn't have missed it for the world! I just lost track of what was going on, that's all. But the players are obviously very good at what they do.

F: So, would you come again?

M: Yes, but I'll be sure to eat before we go next time. I was starving for most of the game.

F: Sorry – it didn't cross my mind that you'd be hungry! Next time we'll have lunch at the clubhouse restaurant. It's very good.

16

1 *The first part of Track 16 is taken from Track 15. It is from the line 'So what did you think of your first rugby match? Impressed?' to 'It's very good'.*

2

F: Have you been to the new gym near the school yet?

M: Yeah, I went with Dan last Saturday. There were a lot a people there, but we had a good workout. Twenty pounds a month for membership seemed a bit dear, though.

F: I thought it wasn't too bad – it must have cost a lot to set up. What did you think of the equipment?

M: It was all nice and new, and well laid out – someone obviously put a lot of time into the planning. But I do think they should limit the number of people allowed in at one time.

F: I know what you mean! I'm only going at lunchtime from now on.

3

F: Well, that's definitely the last time I'm buying anything from that online store. I needed a new jacket for my holiday next week, and I saw what looked like the perfect one for me. So I ordered it, medium size, and paid extra for next day delivery. Their prices are pretty reasonable – you know I have an eye for a bargain – and it arrived when they said it would. But when I tried it on, the sleeves came down to my fingertips. Now I've sent it back and I have to wait another two days for the right one. It's such a pain!

4

M: I'd always been fascinated with movement, as far back as I can remember. My mother was a dance teacher – she owned her own school, in fact – but she never made it in the theatre and that was something she always regretted, I think. She used to take me to lots of shows, both classical and modern. The first show I saw took my breath away. I was hooked on both forms from the beginning! Of course, my mother's name opened a lot of doors for me when it came to getting parts, but I like to think my talent and enthusiasm had contributed more to my success.

5

M: So, Jen. Have you decided whether you're coming to France with my family next month? It won't cost you much.

F: Oh, I don't know, Tom. It's very generous of your parents, and money's not a problem, but two weeks is a long time to be away from the drama club.

M: You said the director of the play thinks you're great, so you can't be worried about losing your part.

F: No, it's not that. I don't think she'd mind. I'm just not sure what they'll do without me. We all need to practise, and I don't think they'll be able to do it very well while I'm away.

M: Jen, let go sometimes!

6

F: Have you always wanted to get into this business?

M: No, not really. It kind of grew naturally from what I used to do as a hobby – which was racing motorbikes.

F: How long have you been in business?

M: About five years. Dad helped me buy the garage first, then we got the bikes to rent out. It's a holiday resort, and we do quite well.

F: What do you have to spend money on now?

M: Well, there's the repair and maintenance costs – they're quite high. And we pay for advertising space in the local and national press in the summer, but that's worth every penny.

7

F: How was your first Esperanto class?

M: It was OK. Everyone in the class was new, so the teacher started with a mixing activity to break the ice.

F: Sounds fun.

M: No, I hate that kind of thing. It was just a one-off, thankfully. But there's an interesting mix of people – all different ages and abilities. Some of the older ones seemed quite fluent, so I felt a bit out of my depth.

F: Did that put you off?

M: Not at all. The teacher's really supportive, and the better students are quite willing to help us slow ones. I think I'll be fine.

F: So you'll go again?

M: Sure.

8

F: Having read Dan Horgan's book on the natural history of South Africa, I was really looking forward to the documentary based on it. Now that part one has been broadcast, I can report that it's as good as I'd hoped. In fact, I'd say it's an improvement on the written format because the rich possibilities of sight and sound really bring the work to life. The book was full of information, and the TV show seems to have lost some of that in favour of spectacular photography, but it's none the worse for it. Give it a go – you won't be disappointed.

17 *Track 17 is taken from Tracks 15 and 16. It is from the line 'So what did you think of your first rugby match? Impressed?' to 'Give it a go – you won't be disappointed.'*

STUDENT'S BOOK AUDIOSCRIPTS

02 Unit 1, Student's Book page 12

Speaker 1

Man: I aim to do at least four thousand words every day. It might not sound like a lot, but that's about six hours' work. The first draft of anything takes me at least two months. I haven't had any bestsellers yet, but there *is* a film version of one of my short stories.

Speaker 2

Woman: The majority of my work is related to TV, rather than films. Most days I get sent new shows – sometimes months before they're going to be released. I watch them, take notes on key scenes and the characters, and then write my review. Most of my stuff is published online but the occasional thing is printed in newspapers.

Speaker 3

Man: People often confuse my job with that of the director. Whereas he or she will spend some of the time behind the camera, telling the cast what to do, I spend less time on set, instead doing things like raising funding for projects, hiring production staff, and managing the film project from start to finish.

Speaker 4

Woman: I work very closely with the author of a book to get it ready for publication. A lot of people think we just correct spelling and grammar mistakes, but it's a lot more than that. I'm responsible for seeing a story through from the very first idea until the book is finally on the shelves, and hopefully a bestseller!

Speaker 5

Man: People think I have the easiest job in the world, but it's not true. The show I'm doing at the moment is live from seven in the morning. That means I have to be up at four, ready to leave home by four thirty and at the studio by five, not to mention being in bed by eight the previous evening to make sure I get enough sleep! Then, it's meetings, rehearsals and, of course, make-up. You have to look good if millions of people are watching!

03 Unit 2, Student's Book page 14

Emma: I'm aware of what's in fashion because I read fashion blogs. I never buy any of the stuff they feature though! I admit it, I'm easily impressed by designer labels. My favourite is Prada. I love looking at the window displays in their city centre shop, but I've never had the courage to go in. I couldn't afford any of it, for one thing. I get most of my stuff from department stores or online. You can usually get quite good versions of the 'real thing' for a fraction of the price. Even so, I think I dress really well. I'm pretty adventurous with my taste in clothes, but I'd never wear fur.

Ahmed: I'm addicted to shopping for clothes. I just can't stop. It's a bit of an obsession of mine. I do need to be cautious about spending too much though. Once I accidentally spent £200 on clothes. I'd been given some money for my birthday, and I went shopping with one of my friends. I'm absolutely hopeless at making decisions about clothes, so I bought loads. When I got home and added up how much they all cost, I couldn't believe it! It was a bit of a disaster really, and I had to return a lot of stuff.

Dan: I'm not all that bothered about what others think of my dress sense. I just wear whatever I like, mainly jeans and football shirts. You could say it's a bit conventional, but I believe in keeping things simple. Anyway, you shouldn't be critical of the way others dress. It's up to individuals to choose how they want to look. I've never been mean about a friend's dress sense. People can be very sensitive about their appearance.

Sara: People are obsessed with brands, I think. There's no point in being loyal to a particular brand. You should feel free to wear anything that looks good. And you should enjoy it for what it is, not for the label it's got on it. I certainly wouldn't be jealous of a friend just because they had an expensive brand of trainers or something like that. You're paying for the label most of the time, not the actual quality of the clothing. I know what clothes suit me and I'm fairly decisive about what to buy. I don't waste time worrying about what else might be available, worrying that there might be something slightly better in the next shop.

05 Unit 2, Student's Book page 17

Speaker 1

Girl: Some people say that wearing a school uniform restricts your creativity – how can you express your individual character if you all look the same? I don't see it that way. If there's nothing to distract us in class, like someone's jewellery or bright red jumper, it means we can all get on with what we're meant to be doing. It's kind of like a blank canvas. Not that I'm saying it makes us all the same – far from it. The school blouse I've got is not exactly the most comfortable thing to wear – it's a bit scratchy round the collar – but never mind.

06 Unit 2, Student's Book page 17

Speaker 2

Boy: Everyone in my country wears a school uniform. Some schools are strict about how students present themselves – they say the way students act on their way to and from school reflects on the school and its values. I guess that means that looking smart reflects well on the school. Fortunately, our headteacher doesn't insist on jackets and ties – we wear tracksuits instead. They aren't the coolest clothes I've got, but at least once they're on, I don't have to worry about anything being too tight or hot or whatever for the sake of looking good, compared with how I feel when I put my best stuff on to go out with my mates.

Speaker 3

Girl: I'm not a huge fan of my school uniform – the colour's horrible and the fabric's cheap-looking. But it means that nobody stands out or gets laughed at because of what they're wearing. There's just one supplier of our uniform in town, too, so we all get our stuff there. You can't turn round to someone and say, 'Wow! Your sweater's so cool!' because you've got the same one! And no one's ever left out. Our teachers think uniforms make us all feel part of a special community, but I'm not sure that this is true because there are lots of different friendship groups who wouldn't necessarily spend time with each other if they didn't go to the same school.

Speaker 4

Boy: Wearing the same thing day in, day out is a bit boring, but our school's fairly casual about our uniform in the sense that we all wear one, but there's a lot of choice – you can wear shorts in summer or trainers instead of shoes. We do have to wear the same colours, and we have bags with a school badge on so we can be identified when we're walking home or away from the school grounds – you know, in case we do something wrong. I can cope with that and you tend to think twice about messing about – like climbing trees or whatever!

Speaker 5

Girl: It's difficult to concentrate when you've got an itchy woollen jumper on or your new shoes are rubbing your feet, but I suppose we wear uniforms for a reason. I think the idea is that everyone's the same when they wear the same clothes – like, no one's better off than anyone else. I don't think there's much truth in that, but there are advantages to uniforms. It saves time in the morning trying to put an outfit together. I'd find it impossible to get out of the house if I was worrying about that! I probably don't look after my uniform the way I look after my other clothes though.

07 Unit 2, Student's Book page 17

Examiner: What's your name, and where are you from?

Miguel: My name's Miguel. I'm from Salamanca, in Spain.

Examiner: How long have you lived there?

Miguel: I was born in Salamanca and I've lived there all my life.

Examiner: What do you like most about your school?

Miguel: The atmosphere's quite relaxed and the teachers are good at motivating us. They keep a balance, though, and don't put too much pressure on us. I would say one of the best things is the extracurricular programme, which includes things like sailing and climbing. I wouldn't think of doing that myself, outside of school, but when it's organised and your friends are doing it, it's fun.

Examiner: Do you like shopping?

Miguel: I absolutely love shopping, especially for clothes and shoes! To tell the truth, I probably spend too much time shopping! I go into town every weekend, and probably spend two or three hours walking around the shops. I don't buy stuff all the time, but I'm always reading fashion blogs and window shopping.

Examiner: What else do you like doing in your free time?

Miguel: Let me think. … Well, I guess I spend quite a lot of time online, chatting and using social media, that kind of thing. I have a tablet at home and I tend to have it with me wherever I go. I spend a lot of time with friends, too. We don't always go out, but we maybe just hang out together and chat about things.

Examiner: Thank you, Miguel.

Examiner: What's your name, and where are you from?

Vika: My name's Vika. I'm from Moscow in Russia. But I'm living in Birmingham at the moment.

Examiner: How long have you lived here?

Vika: I've been living here for three months. My dad's got a one-year contract at Birmingham International. He's an engineer.

Examiner: What do you like most about your school?

Vika: Well, I'm new and it seems really friendly so far – I've made a couple of friends already. It's very sociable and there's lots to do after classes, which is really nice for someone who's new. The classes are interesting, too. I'm quite into science, and there's a good science department here. The teachers are all really friendly, and they're good at explaining things to students.

Examiner: Do you like shopping?

Vika: I do sort of like hanging out and going in computer and game shops, but, personally speaking, I'm not that bothered about clothes shopping. If I want something, I tend to buy it online rather than going into town. It's quicker that way, and often cheaper, too.

Examiner: What else do you like doing in your free time?

Vika: I spend loads of time playing games, and the brilliant thing about online games is that I can still play with my friends back in Russia. To be honest, I probably spend too much time in front of my computer … Movies are a big interest of mine, too. I always used to go to the cinema on Sundays in Russia, and I still do that now. I like having movie nights in with friends, too. We watch a movie and have pizza.

Examiner: Thank you, Vika.

08 Culture: The British fashion scene, Student's Book page 18

Man: Once a year, the British Fashion Council rolls out the red carpet for The Fashion Awards – a star-studded event to honour the nation's most talented and creative designers. The Council held its first awards ceremony in 1984 with the introduction of its *Designer of the Year* award. The first winner was a young designer named Katharine Hamnett. She made a name for herself with T-shirts that had bold, controversial slogans, such as 'Stop and Think' and 'Make Trade Fair'. Five years later, in 1989, the BFC decided to add more categories and The Fashion Awards were born.

Along with the year's best designer, the ceremony honours the best menswear and the best accessories, such as shoes, hats and jewellery. Kim Jones, the London-born designer, has won the award for Best Menswear Designer on four different occasions. Most recently, in 2018, he won the newly created Trailblazer Award which recognises innovators who are shaping the fashion industry. His look can be described as 'expensive luxury meets street style' and the result is that his designs are so popular, they fly out of the shops!

There are also awards for best fashion brands, which Victoria Beckham has picked up for her self-named company. Her clients include Selena Gomez, Cameron Diaz and Meghan Markle. Keeping fashion in the family, her husband, former footballer David Beckham, co-owns a menswear fashion label. He has recently been given a new role as Ambassadorial President of the BFC, to represent British fashion around the world.

Every year there is an Award for Outstanding Achievement to recognise designers who have made an impact on the global fashion industry. In 2018, this award went to Miuccia Prada for her talent in bringing together multiple creative disciplines including fashion, art and architecture. In the same year, the British stylist Clare Waight Keller won the award for Designer of the Year for her work with the luxury fashion house Givenchy.

The Fashion Awards also include Emerging Talent Awards for the most new and up-and-coming names in the fashion world, and an award for the year's best fashion model. Past winners of that include the English supermodels Kate Moss and Cara Delevingne. Cara's modelling career began when she was just ten years old, but it wasn't until nine years later that she made her first major appearance at London

Fashion Week. Since then she has gone on to become one of the world's most successful fashion models, and has also starred in hit movies such as *Suicide Squad* and *Valerian and the City of a Thousand Planets*.

11 Unit 3, Student's Book page 20

Clara: Have you listened to *The debate* yet this week, Yusuf?

Yusuf: No, but I've downloaded the podcast. Was it any good?

Clara: Yeah, fascinating actually. It was all about your genes and your environment – nature versus nurture – and they discussed what you need to achieve success in life.

Yusuf: Sounds interesting. So, what *do* you need?

Clara: Well, first you need the right genes! If you're going to be a great footballer or a brilliant scientist, you need the luck to be born with the right genes.

Yusuf: So, it's all down to nature then?

Clara: Well, not exactly. That was a common belief in the past, but it seems it's only part of it. As well as the right genes, you also need the right environment. Basically, the genes you have will only become active if you're brought up in the right environment.

Yusuf: So, you mean you could be born naturally athletic, or with the intelligence to be a great scientist, but if you're brought up in the wrong environment, you'll never achieve greatness?

Clara: That's right.

Yusuf: Hmm, so it seems you need more than just ambition to become a professional footballer or a brilliant scientist, then? I guess I'll probably have to accept that those things aren't for me.

Clara: Well, it seems there might be a bit of hope – when it comes to being a scientist anyway.

Yusuf: Really?

Clara: Yeah. The participants in the debate were in agreement that students who have the drive to study hard can actually become more intelligent – more academic – as they get older.

Yusuf: Oh?

Clara: Yeah. It seems that if you really try to improve your concentration, really push yourself, the development of different parts of your brain could then allow you to be more successful – like you can become better at problem-solving, for example.

Yusuf: Great! So, if it's true that you can improve how intelligent you are, maybe the same is true for your sporting ability. I'll give that some thought! Maybe there's still hope that I could be the next Messi!

13 Unit 4, Student's Book, page 24

1 **Woman:** Oh no! My flight leaves in just over an hour! I'll never make it in time! Oh, what am I going to do?

2 **Boy:** I don't know what to do. I've tried reading, listening to music, everything. I've been lying here since eleven and it's now after midnight. I have to get up at seven, too.

3 **Girl:** I keep thinking about my driving lesson. It was so scary. I almost lost control of the car. I saw the corner but I didn't slow down in time. The instructor had to use his controls to stop the car – and he grabbed the steering wheel! We only just avoided hitting a wall.

4 **Woman:** How dare they?! This is absolutely ridiculous! £100 to cancel my phone contract!

5 **Woman:** I don't think it's anything serious. I think I just stood up too quickly. I don't remember anything until I woke up lying on the floor. It didn't last for long, did it?

6 **Girl:** I had a sandwich for lunch at school but I just don't feel like anything now. Maybe it's because I'm a bit worried about tomorrow. I'll be OK, though. I'll probably feel like something later, but I'll make it myself. Don't worry.

7 **Woman:** Oh, my head feels funny. I think I need to sit down. I don't feel very well.

Man: Yes, you look very pale. You should probably sit down on that bench for a few minutes until you feel better.

8 **Girl:** I've felt like this since I woke up. Maybe it was those meatballs I had last night. I don't think I can go to college today.

15 Unit 4, Student's Book page 27

Speaker 1

Boy: It's not a big deal but I do get stressed – almost always before exams. The first thing that happens is I lose my appetite and partly because of that, I reckon, I get in a bit of a mood. I have a few tricks to keep the stress under control, though. I talk to my parents about whatever's worrying me, I avoid staying up late, I even go to a couple of intense exercise classes. Within a day or so I've usually got over whatever it is, and I feel OK again, ready to get on with my life! I try not to let things get me down in general.

16 Unit 4, Student's Book page 27

Speaker 2

Girl: I think people underestimate how stressful life can be for teenagers these days. We've always got loads of deadlines – essays, projects, tests, everything. I get in a panic, which isn't very nice, but I can't really say anything negative to the teacher. I always work hard and I know I put in more effort than some other students, but teachers never stop reminding us how important everything is, how much we need to study now in order to get a good job or go to university. That's what worries me the most. My brother's helpful whenever things get me down. He's at university, so he's already been through it all.

Speaker 3

Boy: I used to be much more sensitive about things and worry about friends, school, all the things that bother people my age. I'd have difficulty sleeping and end up getting really overtired. Then we were discussing stress one day in class. Our teacher suggested a variety of ways to deal with stress, including writing a diary. I must admit, I thought doing that sounded like hard work at the time. Then by coincidence someone gave me a cool notebook and I thought I'd have a go. I don't write a lot – and I don't even manage to do it every day, but it helps me to calm down and feel better.

Speaker 4

Girl: Once in a while – at weekends usually, when I've got a lot to do before Monday – I get a bit stressed. I end up watching TV or just wasting time online. I'll basically do anything to avoid doing the things I need to do! By the end of the day, I'm feeling worse than ever about the stuff I've put off. I end up being bad-tempered and that annoys me about myself. I'm sure running would be one of the best things I could do – that's what people say, anyway. I'm not into sport, though. Maybe I should go walking … you never know, perhaps I'll become more active one day!

Speaker 5

Boy: Sure I worry about things from time to time: when I'm late for something, especially school, or when I have to give a presentation in class. But everyone gets that, don't they? I rarely fall out with friends and ninety-five per cent of the time I get on fine with my parents. I'm not the highest achieving student in the world but I do my best. I might be a bit tired in the mornings from time to time, and even a bit grumpy occasionally. I'm not half as bad as my sister, though! You can barely speak to her until she's been up for an hour or two.

17 Unit 4, Student's Book page 27

Ben: Hi, Olivia. Everything OK?

Olivia: I can't miss band practice at eight and I have to finish an essay. And I *must* take some games back to Atif's tonight. He was really annoyed that I forgot to bring them in this morning!

Ben: I'm seeing Atif later. Shall I take the games for you?

Olivia: Are you sure? That'd be fantastic! Thanks, Ben.

Ben: OK. I'll text you when I leave here, if you like. It'll be about seven thirty.

Olivia: Thanks, but there's no need. I'll have left for practice by then. My parents will be in all evening, though. They can give you the games.

Ben: OK. Good luck with the essay!

18 Unit 4, Student's Book, page 27

Mum: I don't know how I'm going to manage tonight, Noah. Your dad isn't back until late, so I have to pick your sister up from the station. Then there's the online shopping which has to be done by eight, not to mention dinner. I haven't even thought about that.

Noah: Would you like me to pick Lisa up? I'll have to borrow your car, of course.

Mum: Um, it's OK, I can do it myself.

Noah: Let me do the sho…

Mum: The dinner? It'd be great if you could! Thanks! I think there's stuff in the fridge and you could get some more on the way home from school.

Noah: Actually, Mum, I was thinking of doing the shopping.

Mum: The shopping? No, don't worry. I can manage that. Thanks again, Noah. Back about seven. OK?

19 Life Skills: Time management, Student's Book, page 28

Man: Right, if you're all settled, it's time to make a start and in fact 'time' is the subject of our tutorial today. You've all only recently started your degree, so I'm sure you've begun to notice the increased freedom and responsibility that you have, especially compared to your school life, right?

Now, this morning we'll be talking about how to manage your time effectively here at university. I'm here to help by giving you some advice on how to stay on top of your studies.

Let's begin with one of the most crucial skills you'll learn during your degree: planning. Although you'll be spending some of your time in compulsory lectures and tutorials, you'll also have a lot of independent time, and creating a *study schedule* is a must. It should include all of your study commitments *and* personal commitments. And it can include both your current weekly plan and your long-term goals to help you look ahead.

Getting your schedule out of your head and onto paper – a wall chart, or a planning app is the key here. It will help you to establish a routine, meet assignment deadlines, make sure you have enough free time, and reduce stress in the process! Study plans change over time and can be flexible, but the fact is that you're much more likely to stick to a schedule if, when you're developing it, you consider your own habits.

Which brings me to my next piece of advice – improving your study patterns. A good place to start is by paying attention to your own unique rhythms. We all have different times of the day when we're more productive and work better. It's all about working out your optimum study methods. So try to do the most difficult tasks when you generally concentrate best. And, going back to my first point, if you can plan your schedule around when you study best, you'll really feel the difference! I'd also recommend having a designated study area – a space you always do your work in. And make sure you keep it tidy. It's difficult to feel organised with a messy desk. Lastly, experiment with your study patterns to find out what works for you. Most people need to take regular breaks and find that it helps to alternate between interesting tasks, and, well, less interesting tasks, so you don't get bored!

The last area I'd like to talk about today is prioritising. There's so much to do at university that it's normal for you to have frequent conflicts in your schedule. And what you need to do here is focus on what really matters the most to you at the time. You'll be balancing multiple demands: study, personal commitments, perhaps part-time work, and longer-term goals. It's a lot to process, so I always recommend using a time matrix to help. A time matrix is a simple and effective way to help you decide what you really want to spend your time on, categorising things from 1 to 4 according to their urgency and importance. Inevitably, you'll end up identifying tasks which are neither important nor urgent – basically just a waste of your time. And with the time you save by dropping those activities, you'll find it much easier to meet your commitments for the things that really do matter.

21 Unit 5, Student's Book page 32

1

Man: Well, man's earliest ancestors appeared about 200,000 years ago, in central Africa. Later, about 100,000 years ago, humans started to move out of Africa into the Middle East and then Asia. The first humans arrived in Europe around 40,000 years ago, and in the Americas only 12,000 years ago.

2

Man: Many cities have been renamed since they were first founded. London comes from the name 'Londinium', for example, which the Romans used – but they probably didn't just make the name up. Linguists think the name could come from Plowonida, a Celtic name, though there are other theories, too. New York was originally named New Amsterdam when Dutch people first settled there in 1609. As for Paris, well, that was known as Lutetia in Roman times.

3

Man: Well, you can read about the Amazons, Centaurs and Titans in Ancient Greek myths. According to these myths, the Amazons were a tribe of all-female soldiers, Centaurs were half-man, half-horse and the Titans were Greek gods. Of course, the Amazon River in South America was named after the Amazons. The river was given this name by the Spanish in the 1540s, because they were fighting against the indigenous people, including many brave women.

4

Man: Cars have been around for about 120 years. Lots of inventors were developing cars at the same time, including Gottlieb Daimler in Germany and Henry Ford in the United States. But it was a German inventor called Karl Benz who produced the world's first car in the 1890s, at the end of the 19th century. The great era of the car was the 20th century, but these days, the problem of climate change means transport will have to change.

5

Man: Well, all three of these are very big countries, but with very different population sizes. In 1900, Russia had 120 million citizens. India was more populated, with 270 million citizens, but China was the most populated country, with 415 million citizens. Today, 1.4 billion people live in China but India is catching up fast, with 1.3 billion citizens. The world's third largest country in terms of population is now the United States with more than 329 million citizens. Russia's population is about 140 million.

6

Man: Most of you probably know that Tokyo is the most populated city in the world now. The Tokyo-Yokohama region has more than 38 million inhabitants. By comparison, London's population is just over 8 million and New York City's population is about 19 million. However, in 1900, London had the most inhabitants, with a population of six and a half million people. New York had about three and a half million inhabitants at that time, and Tokyo had only one and a half million.

7

Man: It's difficult for us to imagine life without television, but in fact it has been around for only a few decades. There was a race amongst inventors in the UK, the USA and Germany to produce the first televisions and there is still some argument about who came first. But the first public broadcasts were in the 1930s. The first commercial TV stations in the 1930s showed pictures in black and white. Domestic colour TVs weren't available until the 1960s.

8

Man: In 1872, a movement to fight for the right of women to vote was set up in the UK. People who campaigned for women's rights were known as suffragettes, and in the early 1900s they were treated very badly because of the protests they organised. By 1918, however, they were making progress, and women over 30 were allowed to vote, though men could vote aged 21. It took until 1928 for all women over 21 to get the vote. Nowadays, any man or woman in the UK can vote from the age of 18.

23 Unit 6, Student's Book page 36

1 **Claudia:** My laptop is really annoying. The screen now stays like this for ages and you can't do anything. Even when it does eventually start up, it's so slow.

2 **Ben:** Come on! It's already quarter past! We've still got a bit of time before the film starts, but I'm worried there won't be any decent seats if we get there too late.

3 **Jade:** Oh, can I open it now? Great! No, no! I can't believe it! Thank you so much. It's exactly what I wanted!

4 **Olly:** Alex! Alex! I'm watching something here. Can you turn that awful noise down?! I don't know why you like that band so much.

5 **Jade:** I went on the ticket website at exactly nine, but it had already crashed. When I eventually got the page to load, they'd sold out. I just want to forget the whole thing. I wasted all morning on it.

6 **Claudia:** It's only a little one. Aw, it's quite sweet, really. Look at its little legs!

Olly: Just get it away from me! Seriously. Please, Claudia!

25 Unit 6, Student's Book, page 39

Narrator: 1. You hear a student talking about her degree in psychology.

Girl: I started my psychology degree three months ago. I didn't realise it'd be as tough as this, but I'm really enjoying it even so – I knew I would. There's a ton of reading but it's incredible – all the experiments that psychologists have done. I've probably spent more on books since I started than in the rest of my life put together, though! I haven't really thought beyond the next few years yet, but I'm happy I chose this course. The main thing for me is that I like what I'm studying. Other degrees, like law, may be more practical, but I didn't think I'd get into something like that as much.

Narrator: 2. You hear a boy telling his friend about losing his phone.

Boy: I've lost my phone.

Girl: On the school bus again? You're always leaving it there! It's a good job the driver keeps handing it in!

Boy: I walked everywhere today, actually. It's bound to be in one of the places I went to. I'll have to go round and track it down. It'll take ages and I'm supposed to be meeting Jack to go to the cinema. He's having a break from social media, so that's the only way I can get him. At least the phone's locked – there isn't much anyone'll be able to find out if they've picked it up… Will you come and help me look for it?

Girl: Sure.

Narrator: 3. You hear a girl leaving a voicemail for her friend about a history test.

Girl: Hi Alex. Where are you? I'm starting to get a bit stressed about tomorrow's history test. I know it isn't a big deal, but I want to do well in it. There's just so much to remember – I'm not used to learning all these dates. Isn't it more important to understand the events rather than exactly when they happened? Anyway, I think I've memorised everything now, but it'd be good to talk through our notes and then maybe practise testing each other. What do you think? Sorry to go on and on about *me* when you might be in the same situation. Can you give me a ring back, please?

Narrator: 4. You overhear two friends talking about a school project.

Girl: How are you getting on with your science project?

Boy: Not too bad. I've just looked up some more stuff on a bit I was having problems understanding.

Girl: Have you got it sorted now?

Boy: Fortunately. I showed our science teacher where I'm up to this morning. He seemed impressed. There's quite a bit more to do before I hand it in on Friday. I can't see there being a problem with that, though. By the way, have you done your maths homework, yet? I don't get it at all. And I've really tried.

Girl: Let's have a look. Oh, these calculations take ages. I'll help you if you like.

Boy: Yes, please!

Narrator: 5. You hear a father talking to his daughter on the phone.

Girl: Hi, Dad. It's me. This is Samantha's phone.

Father: Carly! We were wondering where you'd got to!

Girl: Sorry! My battery died and I lost track of time.

Father: I thought so. Your phone's been going straight to voicemail. You said you might need a lift home from Samantha's, so we weren't sure how to contact you – we don't have Samantha's number. We should make a note of it. Anyway, never mind. The main thing is I know where you are now. Let us know a bit sooner if it happens again though. I'll come and pick you up now – I'm not sure the buses are still running.

Girl: Thanks, Dad.

Father: No problem.

Narrator: 6. You hear a boy telling a friend about learning to ride a motorbike.

Girl: Hey! How are you enjoying your motorbike lessons?

Boy: I'm getting used to being on the bike. It felt a bit weird trying to balance at first – I'm definitely improving, though, thankfully. It certainly isn't something you can learn in a day. You've got to build experience of handling the bike before going out in traffic.

Girl: I'm sure.

Boy: Some stuff we're doing in lessons is quite challenging. Like, I've still got to master going round tight corners without wobbling, but that'll come in time my instructor says. But most of it's straightforward and makes sense. I can't wait till I can go out driving in the countryside!

Girl: I'll come as a passenger!

Narrator: 7. You hear a psychologist talking about being optimistic and pessimistic.

Woman: Positive thinking is something that we're always told by experts we should try to do. If you believe it's possible good things will happen, they will, as long as you're an optimist, they say! Being optimistic certainly improves well-being. But being pessimistic has its advantages, too. Pessimism doesn't just mean having a negative attitude. For example, some pessimists who believe things won't work out for the best tend to try harder to reach their goals, and they prepare themselves for things that may not go right. When things go wrong for optimists, it can affect their confidence more severely than for a pessimist in the same situation.

Narrator: 8. You hear two friends talking about a programme they have seen about phobias.

Boy: Did you see that TV programme about how to get over a phobia?

Girl: Yeah, it was fascinating. I wish I'd known about those self-help techniques when I was a kid and scared of going to sleep without my light on!

Boy: Some of them sounded complicated. The phobias they brought up were pretty common ones, though – hopefully that's helped a lot of people.

Girl: Apart from that woman who was scared of rabbits! They're such cute animals.

Boy: I've seen that guy presenting other programmes – he always seems quite a tough interviewer. He was much kinder in this programme.

Girl: I know – maybe 'cause he has a phobia himself. He did mention that.

26 Unit 6, Student's Book page 39

Harry: My best day is Saturday. What normally happens is I wake up about ten. The first thing I do is check my phone for messages – someone might have come up with a good plan for the day. Nine times out of ten my parents have already gone out, so I go into the kitchen, put on some loud music and make myself some breakfast. It's my favourite start to a day.

Elif: Virtually every Monday we have tests at school. So my worst day is often Sunday. I spend most of it revising and end up going to bed too late and feeling a bit tense. As a rule, I don't have difficulty in sleeping, with the exception of Sunday nights. Sometimes I lie awake for hours.

27 Unit 6, Student's Book page 39

Steffi: Generally speaking my best days are Wednesdays. It's a good day in terms of lessons – lots of science, um, no music! And over an hour of ICT. I get really into that. Then after school, I have football practice. Ninety per cent of the time, we all go for a snack or something afterwards. There's a great bond between the players on my team.

Antonio: No one likes Sunday nights, of course, especially if you haven't done your homework, but I make every effort to get it done on Friday or Saturday. For the most part I don't have bad days – although one exception is possibly Tuesdays. We do public speaking at school then, and from time to time I have to give a speech in front of the whole school. I'm always really nervous – though on the whole I'm actually quite good at it and it turns out fine.

28 Culture: Colours around the world, Student's Book page 40

Presenter: Hi there, everyone. For today's programme about colours and culture, our reporter, Sandra Connelly, went to Heathrow International Airport, here in London, to ask people about special colour meanings in their cultures. Here's what some of them had to say.

Sandra: Excuse me. Can I ask you some questions about colours?

Girl: Sure, what do you want to know?

Sandra: Well, first of all I should ask you, where do you come from?

Girl: I've come from Vietnam – my flight just arrived.

Sandra: No, sorry, I mean, where are you from?

Girl: Oh! I'm from China. I'm studying English here at university.

Sandra: Oh, perfect! And is there a special, lucky colour in China?

Girl: Yes, there is. It's red.

Sandra: Really! And why is red special?

Girl: Well, red is special because it symbolises fire, life, and good fortune. Red is also used in many happy festivals in China.

Sandra: For example?

Girl: Like during the New Year festival. People put up red decorations, and they also give each other presents or money, in red packages.

Sandra: How interesting! Thank you for answering.

Girl: No problem at all.

Sandra: Excuse me, sir. Can I ask you some questions about colours?

Man: Yes, why not?

Sandra: Thank you! My first question is where are you from?

Man: I'm from Brussels, in Belgium.

Sandra: Oh, that's quite close to the UK. So colours probably mean the same thing there as they do here, right?

Man: Yes, I think so. But I do remember something interesting from when our children were very young.

Sandra: Really? What?

Man: Well, I visited England a lot for work in the past and I had British friends who also had young children. I always thought it was funny that they dressed their baby girls in pink and baby boys in blue.

Sandra: Oh! And why was it funny?!

Man: Well, in Belgium it was the opposite. We bought light blue clothes for girls and we dressed baby boys in pink!

Sandra: And is that still the same now?

Man: No, now I think blue for boys and pink for girls is more common.

Sandra: That's interesting. Thanks very much!

Man: You're welcome.

Sandra: Hello, madam. Do you mind answering some questions about colours?

Woman: Of course. I have an hour before my plane leaves!

Sandra: Oh, good! Where are you from?

Woman: Me? I'm from São Paulo, in Brazil.

Sandra: Brazil! What a beautiful country. I've been to Peru. That's next to Brazil, isn't it?

Woman: Yes, it is. Peru is on the Pacific coast of South America.

Sandra: And compared to the UK, are there any colours that mean something different in Brazil?

Woman: Hmm ... something different? Oh, yes. Purple.

Sandra: Purple! And what does it mean there?

Woman: Well, it doesn't mean royalty, like it does here in the UK. For Brazilians, purple is a colour for sad occasions, like when someone dies.

Sandra: Oh, well that is very different. Here in the UK, we wear black when someone dies.

Woman: Oh, we do that in Brazil, too. But you also see purple.

Sandra: OK, well thanks for answering my questions. Have a nice flight!

Woman: Thank you!

Sandra: Excuse me. Can I ask you some questions about colours, sir?

Man: About colours? Yes, I suppose so.

Sandra: Thanks! Where are you from?

Man: Well, I live in Paris now, but I'm originally from Bangkok, in Thailand.

Sandra: Oh! I love Thailand! People often wear yellow there, don't they?

Man: Yes, they do. It's a very popular colour.

Sandra: And why is that?

Man: Well, Thailand is a Buddhist country, and yellow is a special colour for Buddhists. It symbolises the Earth. It's also our King's royal colour. He was born on a Monday, you know.

Sandra: On a Monday?

Man: Yes, and for Buddhists, yellow is the special colour for Monday. Many people wear yellow clothes on Mondays.

Sandra: How interesting! And does every day have a colour?

Man: Yes. Every day is different.

Sandra: How nice! Well, thanks very much for stopping!

Man: You're very welcome. Bye, bye.

30 Unit 7, Student's Book page 42

1 Woman: So, don't tell anyone, but I think the best thing to do would be to hide behind the sofa.

2 [Someone whistling]

3 [Someone sighing]

4 Man: Good afternoon, my name is James and I'm here to talk to you about our new software that's just come out ...

32 Unit 8, Student's Book page 46

David: I've just started my degree, I'm doing architecture at Bristol University. As part of my degree, I'm going to study at a university abroad in my second year. I have a massive long list of universities to choose from. It's so long I don't know where to start and I need a bit of help. I come from a small town in Devon, half an hour from the nearest city. My parents' place is in a quiet, residential neighbourhood and it's quite a close community, so everyone seems to know everyone else's business. On the one hand it's nice, but it's also very rural and a bit remote and I find it a bit dull. Bristol's much better. There are a lot of industrial estates in the suburbs, but the student areas have a really relaxed atmosphere and a lively social life. In terms of what I want from my year abroad, I'm looking for somewhere urban, that's trendy and culturally diverse, where the people are very welcoming – somewhere that's good for young people, basically. If you have any suggestions, please post them on my blog. It'd be great to hear from you!

34 Unit 8, Student's Book page 49

Anna: I just love skateboarding, but I live in a small town where, until recently, there were no facilities for it. But three years ago, my friends and I decided to convince our local community that we really needed a proper skate park. Most people were really supportive of our ideas and we soon formed an action group consisting of teenagers and adults – teachers, parents and other people – all led by a local restaurant owner called Stefano Russo. We were lucky to meet him.

Our leader was really helpful in getting things going, as he had good contacts with companies in the area. Fortunately, they began to offer financial help. Stefano also knew how to go about getting a government grant to develop the park, and he got involved in making that happen straightaway.

The next thing the action group had to do was to start raising serious money. We persuaded our teachers to let us organise a concert at our school and all the ticket money went towards the skate park fund. As well as this, my friends and I did different jobs to try and get the amount we needed. I washed cars, and others organised sales of second-hand books and DVDs, and stuff like that.

At the end of six months, there were funds of £185,000 available – local businesses had contributed money, too. That was slightly short of our target of £200,000, but more than enough to allow the building work to get started. In fact, within a year, we'd managed to raise nearly £300,000, which meant we were also able to afford lighting as well.

In the meantime, a woman called Janie Collinson, who lived in the area, was helping out with planning. This was an important stage of the project. She works as an architect in London and has close links with colleagues in the United States.

Through them, she discovered a specialist business in California called Xcite, which has won awards for their skate park designs. We all thought their website was pretty awesome, especially the video clips of similar parks they'd created. There was some interesting feedback posted on the website and it seemed that they had lots of satisfied clients in the USA.

The action group thought the guys behind the company were perfect for what we wanted. We organised a community meeting and held a vote to decide whether we should ask them to design our skate park. Almost everyone said yes. We celebrated the result with a small party.

Things moved pretty quickly after that. Janie asked three of us to join her in a few transatlantic discussions on Skype, where we explained what we wanted to achieve, not only for skateboarders like us, but for the BMX riders too. For example, the BMXers requested a great jump called a 'whale tail', which is principally made of steel, with thin strips of wood on top. Xcite came up with some very imaginative ideas for this, and did some rough designs for other features, which they emailed to us.

Then, the main designer from Xcite flew over for three days to show us his drawings. When we looked at them, we thought they were really cool. He got to know the layout of the area and talked with our group a lot about what we wanted, which helped him to improve his design.

We also took the designer to where the skate park was going to be built. The construction site was an empty piece of land that used to have a factory on it and which had been bought by the town council for us. Within the next few weeks, the skate park was built – it's brilliant and worth all the effort everyone went to!

35 Unit 8, Student's Book, page 49

Examiner: In this part of the test, I'm going to give each of you two photographs. I'd like you to talk about your photographs on your own for about a minute, and also to answer a short question about your partner's photographs. Thalía, it's your turn first. Here are your photographs. They show different kinds of village. I'd like you to compare the photographs and say what you think people might enjoy about living in these different villages. All right?

Thalía: Yes, thank you. Both of these places are small, rural villages. Neither place looks as though it's busy or industrial. Both seem quiet and peaceful, but as they're in the middle of nowhere there probably aren't many facilities like shops or youth clubs. And they probably aren't very culturally diverse, like a city is. In the photograph on the left there's some mountain scenery. It looks fresh and green, whereas the other village is in a hotter country. The hills are brown, dry and dusty, so it obviously doesn't rain that much. I think that the villages may have very different standards of living. While the village in the first photograph has quite large houses, the village in the second photograph has much smaller, simpler houses. I reckon that the people in the first village are probably quite wealthy, whereas the people in the second village probably have less money.

Examiner: Thank you. Oleg, how does your hometown differ from these villages?

Oleg: The main difference is the size. Both of these villages look tiny compared with St Petersburg. I assume that there isn't much to do, especially for young people, whereas where I live there are loads of facilities. On the other hand, I assume that the villages would have less crime and they'd have closer communities than in a big city. The weather and lifestyle in St Petersburg are closer to the village in the first photograph.

Examiner: Thank you. Now, Oleg, here are your photographs. They show …

36 Unit 8, Student's book, page 49

Oleg: The main difference is the size.

Thalía: Both of these places are small, rural villages.

Thalía: Neither place looks as though it's busy or industrial.

Thalía: It looks fresh and green, whereas the other village is in a hotter country.

Thalía: While the village in the first photograph has quite large houses, the village in the second photograph has much smaller, simpler houses.

Oleg: On the other hand, I assume that the villages would have less crime.

37 Life Skills: Creative writing, Student's Book page 50

Presenter: Welcome to the show, Zack. Now I know you've come in to talk to our listeners about some great ideas for creative writing. What have you got planned for us today?

Zack: Hi there. I've been running creative writing workshops for years now. Creative writing is something which many people see as a solitary pastime. But I'm going to talk about some of my favourite creative writing exercises for groups.

Presenter: Oh right! That isn't what I was expecting! Well, over to you, Zack.

Zack: Thanks! One of the exercises I always like to start with is a *Round Robin*. I get students into small groups of three or four and each person starts writing their own story for about five minutes. Then, when the time is up, students pass their story to the person sitting on their left. They all read what has been written so far and then have a few minutes to continue writing, developing the story with their own ideas. This continues until everyone in the group has written a part of each story, and then the finished products are shared as a group. I guarantee that this exercise will generate some surprising and often hilarious results!

Presenter: I bet! I can't wait to try that one!

Zack: Well, the next one is even more fun! It's called *Who on Earth is it?* and it works like this. I give each group a photo of a person, someone they don't know, so no celebrities! It might be a close-up, someone in the distance or someone doing something. I ask the group to talk about the person and decide on a name for them. From the name, I ask them to create a brief description of the person's background. They need to use their intuition – you know, the feeling that you know something without being able to explain why! Finally, they present and explain their ideas to the other groups. You'd be amazed at how creative they get in a short space of time!

Presenter: Brilliant! I'm going to try that one later with my friends. There are enough of us to make a couple of small groups!

Zack: Do it – you'll love it! Next, we've got *What's in a list?* This one can be done in groups of any size. Each group member creates a list of 15 things to be included in a story. These could be the names of characters, settings, specific adjectives, objects, things they want the characters to say … you get the idea! Put all the lists together, mix them up and give each person a list – making sure that no one gets their own list back. Everyone then has a time limit to create a new story that includes everything on the list. This activity also works really well for writing poems or scripts for plays – it can be quite a challenge though!

Presenter: It certainly sounds it! You need to really have your thinking cap on for that one.

Zack: Yes! *[Chuckling]* Now, here's an exercise that works really well for people who are interested in the lives of the rich and famous! It's called *Guess the celebrity!* Everyone has to think of a well-known person – someone that they are sure that everyone in their group will know – and they have to write a letter, email, social media post, or something similar from that person. The idea is to focus on the celebrity's individual experiences and to get across his or her personal perspective. Then they take it in turns to read out their piece and the others in the group need to guess who the celebrity is!

Presenter: Genius! My kids would love that one – they're all celebrity obsessed!

Zack: Well, writing can be an excellent way to enjoy expressing personal interests. I always encourage my groups to join or start a writing group of their own. It's their chance to build a community around their shared passion, connect to others and grow as writers through collaboration …

Presenter: Yes, that's great advice. Thanks so much for sharing all those brilliant ideas.

39 Unit 9, Student's Book page 54

Joseph: Hi, Naomi. What have you got there?

Naomi: Hi, Joseph. It's a quiz about how optimistic you are. Apparently, I'm very optimistic!

Joseph: Oh, yeah? Let's have a go.

Naomi: OK. So for each of these statements, you have to give yourself a score from one to five. One means you strongly disagree. Five means you strongly agree.

Joseph: OK. There aren't loads of questions, are there?

Naomi: No, just eight. Here's the first. 'I'm good at making the best of a bad situation.'

Joseph: Hmm, I'm a two on that one. I get in a bit of panic when things go wrong.

Naomi: OK. 'I think the future of mankind looks bright. For instance, one day, science will put an end to major diseases.'

Joseph: Well, yes, one day that might happen. But not for a long time, I reckon. And between now and then we'll have loads of problems to deal with. Some things though, especially technology, are just going to keep improving – getting faster, and so on. And not just stuff like smartphones and tablets. Important things. Things that might make a difference to the world.

Naomi: So …?

Joseph: I'd say I'm a three – I partly agree.

Naomi: OK. Question three. 'I'm always willing to have a go at something new. I always take opportunities that come my way, and I make the most of them.'

Joseph: You know the answer to that one! I'm pretty lazy, and I don't always take opportunities that come my way.

Naomi: So, a one or a two on the scale, then?

Joseph: Two would be too generous I think.

Naomi: OK. Question four, 'I rarely think it's my fault when things go wrong.' Actually, you're the least likely person to blame someone else, aren't you?

Joseph: Well, …

Naomi: You're always apologising, even when it's definitely not you. A *'one'* for your answer?

Joseph: Yes, sure. What's question five?

Naomi: 'I have more strengths than weaknesses.'

Joseph: That's pretty hard to answer. I guess I do. I mean, I don't spend a lot of time worrying about things I'm not very good at.

Naomi: Or your hairstyle, or the clothes you wear …

Joseph: Ha ha. Overall, I'm happy with myself – I'd give that one a four.

Naomi: That's almost a 'strongly agree'! Question six. 'I really think I'll be able to make a difference to the world one day.'

Joseph: Well, I might have some strengths, but I'm not Einstein or anything. But yes, I'd say another four. I won't be ending climate change, but I'm definitely going to try to do a job that's useful to the world.

Naomi: Like what?

Joseph: I don't know. Maybe I'll teach!

Naomi: Really? What would you teach?

Joseph: I don't know. I haven't thought about it that much. What are the last two questions?

Naomi: Seven. 'I hope I will achieve all my goals in life.'

Joseph: Hmm. I don't think I have any goals in life.

Naomi: Hold on! That's not true. You just told me one of them. You want to be a teacher, don't you?

Joseph: I only said 'maybe I'll teach'. I guess I do have some goals, though – or at least ideas about what I want. But will I actually achieve them? I don't know. I'm not completely confident. That'll be a three, I guess.

Naomi: Last question. 'I often see the best in people, rather than the worst.' This is definitely you. I've never heard you say anything bad about anyone … That's definitely a 'Strongly agree'. Your only one. OK. So, here's your result. You got a total of …

41 Unit 10, Student's Book page 58

Speaker 1

Woman: I couldn't believe it. There were only a few hundred people left at the venue. Most people had gone, but it had taken us ages to get our coats. It was only by chance that I glanced through the door and noticed him coming back onto the stage. He played another couple of songs, so the whole concert lasted over two hours in all. It was really special.

Speaker 2

Boy: Unfortunately, he found out about it in advance. I'd left an email open by accident, and he saw it when he borrowed my tablet. After that there was no point in trying to keep it secret. I don't think it mattered, though. I think he enjoyed himself on the night and almost everyone we'd invited turned up!

Speaker 3

Girl: He burst into my room out of nowhere and scared the life out of me! I was talking to a friend on my *brand new* phone and I nearly dropped it! Actually, it's not exactly out of character for my brother to turn up like that, but I was impressed that he'd made the effort to come home from university for one evening, just for my birthday.

Speaker 4

Man: United are now at risk of finishing the season without any trophies. They were expected to beat City easily, but instead the game ended two–all due to a last-minute effort from City's new Brazilian striker. United's goalkeeper was partly at fault for the goal when he …

Speaker 5

Man: … still talking about this week's surprise news from the singer Melissa Zane. She refused to speak in detail about the ceremony, but said that it had taken place in secret a couple of weeks ago. The singer's agent is expected to make a longer statement this evening. The announcement was particularly surprising after the very public break-up the couple went through a year ago.

43 Unit 10, Student's Book page 61

Interviewer: Hi, Amanda. Now we understand you've just had an interesting weekend, when your friends and family held a surprise party for you! Tell us all about it. Did you know something special was going to happen?

Amanda: Absolutely not. I had no idea anything was happening, especially as it isn't even my birthday until tomorrow. On Saturday, my best friend, Jenny, suggested seeing a film in the evening. We met at the cinema, but were a bit early, so Jenny suggested some new café she'd heard of where we could get a coffee. I remember being a bit confused. We usually just get something at the cinema.

44 Unit 10, Student's Book page 61

Interviewer: Hi, Amanda. Now we understand you've just had an interesting weekend, when your friends and family held a surprise party for you! Tell us all about it. Did you know something special was going to happen?

Amanda: Absolutely not. I had no idea anything was happening, especially as it isn't even my birthday until tomorrow. On Saturday, my best friend, Jenny, suggested seeing a film in the evening. We met at the cinema, but were a bit early, so Jenny suggested some new café she'd heard of where we could get a coffee. I remember being a bit confused. We usually just get something at the cinema.

Interviewer: But all your relatives and friends were waiting there?

Amanda: Yes, but a few things happened before that. The café turned out to be a restaurant, but they were happy for us to just have a drink. Then something strange happened. My uncle turned up! When he saw me, he looked like he was surprised and not exactly happy to see me. He mumbled something about being late to meet a friend. Obviously his friend wasn't there, and he came to sit with us. I guess he should've been at the party already, hiding with everyone else.

Interviewer: And then your friend Jenny got a text.

Amanda: Right. She suddenly stood up and said, 'Let's go and see what the downstairs bit of the café's like. I heard you can book it for parties – I'm having one soon.' I remember thinking, 'The film's starting in a few minutes. Have we really got time to start looking around?' But I saw it was getting busy where we were sitting, and wondered whether they needed the tables for people ordering food. I thought we could take a quick look downstairs and then leave for the cinema. So we started heading down the steps – I was first. At the bottom, there was a door. I pushed it open, but it was dark inside. I was about to turn round when the lights went on and I heard a huge 'Surprise!'

Interviewer: And what did you do when you saw the party?

Amanda: I just stood there with my mouth open! I was really shocked! My sister, typically, captured the exact moment on film. I looked like a fish! I immediately spotted my twin cousins. I hadn't seen them for months. They're at university in Scotland, so I definitely wasn't expecting to see them! They'd come home specially! Then everyone starting singing *Happy Birthday*. I was almost in tears.

Interviewer: So what happened next? Did your parents do anything?

Amanda: Well, my mum said a few words, which was unexpected 'cause she doesn't usually do that kind of thing. She didn't say much about me, fortunately – I'd have been embarrassed. My dad and his friends played some music – Dad sings in a band. He'd even rewritten the lyrics to a famous Beatles song so that it was about me. It was really funny. After about an hour, my parents said that the adults were leaving. I pretended I was a bit disappointed, but I don't think they believed me!

Interviewer: Did you enjoy the party?

Amanda: Well, some people like being the centre of attention – but it's not my thing. But knowing everyone had made the effort to get there just for *me* made me realise just how important my friendships are, and I think they've become stronger because of it. When people do things for *you*, you're more likely to do something nice for *them* in turn. And I did have fun.

Interviewer: Whose idea was the party?

Amanda: My sister's. Apparently, my parents weren't really sure about it at first. They were OK about holding a party, and they knew I would appreciate the whole thing, despite me being a bit shy. Their problem was that they thought it would involve more organisation than they'd have liked – doing it at home. So my sister promised to find a venue, – which they weren't too worried about paying for – and sort out the invitations. It was so lovely of all of them to do it!

45 Unit 10, Student's Book page 61

Zoe: Hey, Jared, do you remember that short story competition I entered?

Jared: Of course. It was a while ago, wasn't it? Don't tell me, you …

Zoe: No, not me! But Lisa Winters did. She won!

Jared: Did she? That's amazing! What was the prize again?

Zoe: The school gets some money and her story will be published online. The principal came into our English lesson to tell us. He was really pleased.

Jared: I bet he was. Wow! I'd never have guessed Lisa was a good writer.

Zoe: We sit next to each other in English once in a while. She's quiet, but really creative. … By the way, have you heard about Michael's bike?

Jared: No, what happened?

46 Unit 10, Student's Book page 61

Jared: Hi, Michael. Zoe told me what happened to your bike at the weekend. But, no lock? I mean, seriously?

Michael: I know, I know. I should have locked it. That's what my dad said. He was absolutely furious with me.

Jared: Was he? I'm not surprised to be honest. Did you report it?

Michael: Yes, and the police said there was no chance of getting it back. But get this! I got a call from them this morning. They found my bike!

Jared: Really?

Michael: Yeah. Someone – they didn't know who – took the bike back to the shop where I lost it.

Jared: You're kidding!

Michael: It was the last thing I expected, too. I'm going there after school to pick it up.

Jared: No way! That's so lucky! I wonder what happened. Do you think someone felt …

47 Culture: Perceptions of time, Student's Book page 62

Speaker 1

Man: Time matters to everyone, but not in the same way. You see, time is not black and white. It's not a simple concept that we can all agree on. Time is a grey area and different people and cultures see it very differently. First, we need to understand different perceptions of time. Cultures, or entire nations, can have different attitudes towards thinking more or less about the past, present or future. *Time orientation* affects how people value their time and feel they can control it. People in future-orientated cultures usually run their lives by the clock. The United States has a very time-conscious culture, with a fast and stressful pace of life. Visitors from other cultures can often feel very rushed when they visit. Western cultures in general see time as something linear and sequential, with a concrete beginning and end. Consequently, people in Western cultures feel that time is limited and so their lives need to be structured with objectives and deadlines. And not meeting these objectives or deadlines, or being late, is usually seen as something very negative.

Other cultures perceive time as something cyclical, like a big wheel. What's more important for these cultures is doing things well, while maintaining a positive relationship between everyone involved. Deadlines are seen as targets and these are often not as important as other priorities such as flexibility. For example, in India life is focused on traditions and customs. It's not strange for a train to be a few hours late, or even to arrive a day later than planned. And people accept this as normal and the wait doesn't cause them too much stress! It's important to keep these differences in mind when we visit other countries and cultures, so we accept them as they are and don't judge them in an unfair way.

Speaker 2

Woman: So what's your personal attitude towards time? I'm going to describe two possible profiles.

Profile one: you like to do things one at a time and you work best when you have specific deadlines and timetables. You prefer to be responsible for completing a task and for the results that are achieved. The relationships you form with other people are often practical and last for the time needed to complete the work or project.

Or maybe, this sounds more like you – Profile two: You like multi-tasking and focussing your attention on what's happening around you at that moment. You're serious about reaching goals and getting results, but what's most important for you is sharing experiences with people and forming strong relationships.

Now, you might not think that all the things in one profile describe you perfectly, but one of the two probably describes you quite well. So which one is it…?

Speaker 3

Man: Chronemics is the study of time, particularly in relation to non-verbal communication in cultures. There are two groups in chronemics: The first group is monochronic cultures. Time is viewed as something precious that can be spent, saved, shared, or wasted. Time is divided and managed in precise, small units. Timetables are very important for people from these cultures. Canada, Japan and South Korea are all examples.

The second group is polychronic cultures. Here time is more fluid. Clock time and calendars are less important, and the cycle of the seasons or the patterns of life within a community are more important. A person in this culture might not finish a job on time. But they will focus on doing what they think the other person needs. Even if that is not necessarily what the person asked for! Many African and Asian cultures fall into this category.

49 Unit 11, Student's Book page 64

Narrator: 1. Who is Olivia counting on to be on time?

Olivia: Hi, Xavi. Who are you waiting for?

Xavi: My dad. He's always late though.

Olivia: Oh. My dad's really reliable. He said he'd be here at six o'clock, and …

Dad: Hi, Olivia. Jump in!

Olivia: Do you want a lift, Xavi?

Xavi: No, I'd better wait, thanks.

Narrator: 2. Who does Carolina take after?

Carolina: My mom found all these old photos in a box the other day. Look at this – it's my mom when she was at college!

Jacob: Wow, Carolina! You don't look at all like her.

Carolina: I know, but look at my grandma, here, when she was my age.

Jacob: You're almost identical to her!

Carolina: I know. It's amazing, isn't it?

Narrator: 3. How well did Stephanie hit it off with Yvette's cousin?

Thomas: Hi, Stephanie. How was the evening at Yvette's?

Stephanie: It was OK, but it was a bit embarrassing at first. I got there early and Yvette's cousin was there.

Thomas: I've never met her, I don't think.

Stephanie: I'd never met her either. I didn't have anything to say to her and there were lots of awkward silences. We just didn't have anything in common. I was glad when everyone else turned up.

Narrator: 4. Who does Hans feel he has let down?

Pippa: How were your maths results, Hans?

Hans: Hmm, lower than last time. The maths teacher said he thinks I understand the material and he's sure I'll do better next time, but I know my parents will be really disappointed. I promised them I'd get a higher grade in this test.

Narrator: 5. Does Mateo's brother look *down* on him or look *up* to him?

Ella: What's up with your brother? He used to be so friendly.

Mateo: I know. It's since he's been at university. I think he thinks he's better than me.

Ella: Than 'us' you mean. He obviously can't be bothered to spend time with any of us!

Narrator: 6. Has Nicholas hit it off with his cousin or fallen out with him?

Tanya: Why does Nicholas always avoid his cousin? It's ridiculous. They've been friends since they were little.

Jennifer: I know. I heard they had a big argument. It's a pity.

51 Unit 12, Student's Book page 68

Photo A

Rosie: I love things like this. You see more and more of them these days. They're just supposed to amuse you, aren't they? I mean, they're not more serious than that.

James: Yeah, I guess they're there to cheer people up, really, just to help them to have a nice day. You could call it 'art.' There's no real message though: just 'love.'

Rosie: I do actually think that little things like this can improve your day, you know.

James: Yeah. They've made an effort to make people smile.

Photo B

James: You see these messages by the side of the road all the time. They're often there to congratulate people on their birthday.

Rosie: Or on passing their driving test or something maybe.

James: It's a nice thing to do, isn't it? I'd be pleased to see one for me.

Rosie: To be honest, I think they're a bit annoying and messy. Imagine if everyone's birthday was celebrated with these signs!

Photo C

Rosie: I really like this sort of street art. It looks like graffiti, but it's actually much more thoughtful than that.

James: Well, it highlights an issue of some kind, doesn't it? You know, about how little power the average person has over their lives – that sort of thing. The artist is obviously speaking out about something they feel strongly about. Especially by painting it on a wall. It's right there in the street, where everyone can see it.

Rosie: It's interesting, and it certainly stimulates you to think about things.

Photo D

James: This one's obviously there to promote a business.

Rosie: Maybe a second-hand clothes shop or an independent shop of some sort. I don't think a high street chain would advertise like this, it's too homemade.

James: True. It's humorous. I mean, it is quite funny! But it's also trying to persuade you to go along to the shop and take a look.

Rosie: Yes, at least it's funny. They've made an effort to get people to laugh.

53 Unit 12, Student's Book page 71

Amy: Hi, my name's Amy Linton and I want to tell you about something which happened to me one day on my way to work in London. It was a cold winter's morning and I was walking towards my local underground station. It was a journey I'd started making recently after switching from my job as freelance editor to journalist and I go into the newspaper's office most days. It was about half-past eight and I was surrounded by other people dashing to work: shop assistants, waiters, all the people who keep the busy city working.

Arriving at the station, I ran down the steps and into the ticket hall. That's when I realised I could hear the sounds of a violin playing and I wondered where it was coming from. I made my way through the automatic barriers and took the escalators down to the trains. The music got louder as I walked through the underground passages, and as I emerged onto the platform, I spotted a female violinist sitting beside the entrance.

The woman was playing a tune I recognised and her playing was exceptional – that's what made me stop and listen. Her eyes were closed and every time she drew the bow across the strings, she moved her head as well. Her whole body seemed to be filled with this wonderful music.

Usually when people play music like this in orchestras, they're all dressed up in smart evening dress, but this musician was wearing casual clothes. I had to smile at that because I felt uncomfortable in my own work clothes that day!

I stood absolutely still, just listening to her. By her feet next to her closed violin case was a cap with a few coins shining in the bottom. Every now and again, passers-by would throw one in, but nobody else stopped to listen.

Then a little boy came past, holding hands with his father. The man kept on walking, but the boy stopped and turned to look, so he stopped, too. The violinist seemed to sense that the boy was there, because she looked up. I thought she might've smiled or greeted the pair, but she was soon immersed in her playing again.

It was a very moving piece that I recognised from somewhere. I tried to think where. Was it the theme from a TV series perhaps, or used in a well-known advert? Then it came to me: I'd heard it recently on a radio programme. It was lovely. Busy commuters rushed past, and although some of them glanced at the musician, nobody else seemed to have the time to stop and listen.

The music ended and I clapped, impressed with the performance. I was surprised when the musician seemed a little embarrassed by the attention. I don't think she'd realised I was there. 'That was fantastic. You were amazing!' I said. Thanking me, she put her violin back into its case and we started to chat.

I'd thought the musician looked familiar and then I finally remembered who she was. I'd seen her playing in London three months earlier – not at a concert, as you might expect, but at a wedding I'd attended. I couldn't believe I hadn't recognised her earlier.

What was she doing here, I asked her? She explained that she had to practise somewhere and that she enjoyed playing in public places, because each location produced a slightly different sound quality and that interested her. Theatres and other music venues would always have good acoustics, she said. I promised to come and listen to her again and we said our goodbyes.

54 Unit 12, Student's Book page 71

Examiner: I'd like you to imagine that your school is starting a programme to help disabled children in the local community. Talk to each other about how each of these ideas could help disabled children in the local community.

Johann: Where shall we start?

Alexandra: Let's start with access to school. We could collect people on our way to the bus stop and help with getting on and off transport, and getting into school.

Johann: Yes, I agree.

Alexandra: How about computer gaming?

Johann: Again, depending on the disability, people might need help with actually playing games.

Alexandra: What exactly do you mean?

Johann: Well, pressing buttons and things like that.

Alexandra: I'm not so sure that would help. Computer games are all about our own reactions, so I think it would be annoying to be helped with that sort of thing.

Johann: Maybe you're right. How about going shopping?

Alexandra: Well, I think this is an obvious area where we could help quite a lot. Lots of shops have steps or are difficult to access, especially if you're in a wheelchair. I think we could definitely help.

Johann: I'd add that it should be boys helping boys and girls helping girls with the shopping, though.

Alexandra: Agreed! What about going out at the weekend, you know, to the cinema and things like that?

Johann: Again, as with shopping, we could easily help with this sort of thing. We could organise lifts for people and help them in and out of places. Anything else?

Alexandra: I was just going to say that we may be able to take them to places they or we don't normally get to.

Johann: True. Do you want to add anything?

Alexandra: I guess we'd have to match up people with similar interests.

Johann: Good point. Last of all, what about tidying up? Is that something we could help with?

Alexandra: It's really hard keeping places tidy, even if you tidy every day, so this is definitely an area people would appreciate help with.

Johann: Of course. And it would be easy to set up a timetable for something that is very regular.

Alexandra: Good point.

Examiner: Thank you. Now you have a minute to decide on one area you would both like to help with.

Johann: Right, well I can tell you what I wouldn't want to do: tidying up would be my least favourite.

Alexandra: Mine too. I'd also rule out computer gaming. I think we agreed that would be too complicated.

Johann: Yes, and it's probably not that helpful anyway.

Alexandra: I think access to school would be hard, too. I find it impossible to get up and out of the house in the mornings, and I think it would be really stressful if I had lots of things to do in the morning before school.

Johann: I agree. That leaves going out at the weekend and going shopping. Do you have a preference for either of these?

Alexandra: I think I'd go for the shopping.

Johann: Hmm. I'm not a great fan of shopping to be honest. But you could argue that going out at the weekend includes shopping.

Alexandra: That's a very good point.

Johann: Shall we agree that going out at the weekend is the area we'd both be happy to help with?

Alexandra: Definitely.

Examiner: Thank you.

55 Unit 12, Student's Book page 71

Track 55 is taken from Track 54. It is from Johann's line 'Where shall we start?' to 'True. Do you want to add anything?'.

56 Unit 12, Student's Book page 71

Examiner: I'd like you to talk about something together for about two minutes. Some people think it would be a good idea for students to spend time helping elderly people in their local community. Here are some things to think about and a question for you to discuss. First you have some time to look at the task. Now, talk to each other about whether it is a good idea for students to spend time helping elderly people in their local community.

57 Life Skills: Volunteering, Student's Book page 72

Woman: There are many organisations involved in running summer volunteer programmes abroad. Some of them are large international charities, while others can be smaller projects, organised by local communities. So, I guess you're wondering what kind of things you could get up to while spending a summer away from home!

Well, teaching languages or sports in another country is one option, if you like spending time with kids that is. Other programmes focus on conservation projects. These often involve protecting endangered marine species or wildlife. And then there are sustainable development projects which are also very popular – especially those involving farming or building community facilities. Or perhaps you'd like to spend the summer supporting disabled people with social activities? The list is endless.

There's one thing that all these volunteer opportunities have in common. They're a great way to build relationships and grow as a person. Now, if you aren't convinced about the idea of spending a few weeks away from home in a strange and unknown place, I can totally understand how you feel! However, there are many benefits. Experiences like this help boost your confidence and improve your ability to adapt to new situations. You see, by immersing yourself in a local community you'll develop your intercultural understanding and get a strong sense of social responsibility. It's also likely that your people skills, such as being tolerant and compassionate, will improve greatly. Along the way you'll pick up authentic language skills and you may also get the opportunity to obtain useful qualifications like a first-aid certificate.

Trying to choose a summer volunteer programme can be overwhelming because there's so much choice. Begin by making a list of projects that sound interesting, and investigate the organisers of each one. Try to find out if the projects are ethical – what long-term impacts do they have on their communities? Contact a representative from the organisation and don't be afraid to ask specific questions about the programmes. For example, asking about the support that staff provide to volunteers might make you feel more relaxed about volunteering. You should also try to find information from previous participants and search for reviews online.

So, let's talk about the money! I know you'd like to travel abroad for free, but very few programmes like that exist because of the costs involved in organising everything, travel, insurance, accommodation, visas, to name just a few! Working out your budget will be key here – it will determine when you can go and how long you can go for. If money is a big issue, there *are* less expensive volunteering opportunities, and there may also be financial assistance available in some cases too. Or, you could think about doing your own fundraising for your trip.

And when you've been accepted on a programme, the planning doesn't stop there! You'll need to get your travel documents in order and start practising your foreign language skills. It's a good idea to start writing a packing list and, of course, you should continue finding out more about the host country. There's so much to learn about each unique destination and the fun things you'll be doing when you're there.

59 Unit 13, Student's Book page 76

Phoebe: I think I lead more than I follow when I'm in a team situation. I try to treat people fairly, but actually I don't always work that well as part of a team. My problem is that I can't stand people who make excuses. 'I couldn't do it because I didn't have enough time.' 'I wasn't well.' 'I had too many other things to do.' Whatever. If you want to do something, and if you want to do it well, you will do it – like I do. I'm pretty conscientious and I haven't got time for people who don't want to do anything.

Mo: I just want to be part of the group. I hate standing out from the crowd and I think I'll always be this way. I'm generally happy to fit in with others' plans and it doesn't really bother me if a bossy person tells me what to do – it makes decisions easier for me! What I enjoy most is just spending time with my friends. I don't need to be the one in charge.

Nathan: I used to be much more cautious. I didn't want to look different. I just wanted to be the same as everyone else. But in the last year, I've changed a bit. One of our teachers has been really helpful. I'm not the best on the football team, but he made me captain a year ago. I'm so grateful he did that. I've really enjoyed the experience and I'm more confident in myself and what I can achieve now.

Ruby: I'm often the one in charge of things. I guess I like it that way. I set myself targets and if I put my mind to it, they'll all get done! My parents say I'm always telling them what a bad idea everything is – how someone should have done something, how I would have done it. I should try and stop that. It's just that I often say what I'm thinking a bit too quickly.

Unit 13, Student's Book page 76
60

Woman: Have you ever had an idea that might possibly change the world? Could you lead a team of people so that the idea becomes a reality? This is the challenge that Three Dot Dash sets for thirty teenagers every year. This charitable organisation, founded by the musician Nile Rodgers, supports teenagers who have had ideas about how to solve problems related to basic human needs – things such as food, health, shelter and education. The challenge starts with a conference in New York, where teenagers work with leading experts in relevant fields to develop their ideas. They then have one year to lead their project to success. In its short life, Three Dot Dash, and the projects it has sponsored, have already influenced the lives of millions of people all over the world.

Unit 14, Student's Book page 80
62

1 **Dad:** Sophie. I have to go. I'll be late!
Sophie: Just five minutes, Dad.
Dad: Sorry, Sophie. You've still got time to walk. I'm leaving now. Bye!

2 **Man:** We've been in this traffic jam for half an hour now. Something serious must have happened. We've already missed the beginning of the film.

3 **Woman:** Oh no! I thought they'd fixed the problem! We'd better call the repair man. Put the hazard lights on so people can see that we've stopped.

4 **Woman:** Want me to wait?
Man: No, go ahead. I just need a minute.

5 **Man:** We're lost. Let's ask someone for help. Look, there's someone. Just stop the car here and I'll ask her for directions.
Woman: Yes, how can I help?
Man: I'm looking for …

6 **Woman:** Watch out for that box in the middle of the road.
Man: Where? Too late! I guess we'd better stop and pick it up. Look – it's completely flat!

7 **Woman:** We are now approaching Waterloo Station. This train terminates here. Please make sure you take all your belongings and luggage with you.

8 **Woman:** Overtake that lorry – it's going so slowly.
Man: OK. Here we go!

Unit 14, Student's Book page 82
64

1 **Woman:** I know you were supposed to stay until the evening, but you really must go home now.
Man: Yes, there's a big storm coming this afternoon and you should get home before it starts.

2 **Man:** Yes, it's here. I always have it with me. Here you are.
Woman: Thank you, sir. Are you aware that this is out of date?
Man: What?

3 **Man:** I really wish you wouldn't drive like this. We're in no hurry.
Woman: Sorry! Yes, you're right. We don't need to go so fast. I'm just looking forward to getting there. Can you switch on some music? Maybe that'll help me relax.

4 **Man:** OK. A nice straight road. Now's the perfect opportunity. Go on! You'll never get a better chance! We don't want to be stuck behind this forever.
Woman: Here goes! Mirrors, indicators, and we're off.

5 **Woman:** If I were you, I'd wait until after seven before you leave. The buses are very crowded around six o'clock when everyone's coming home from work.
Man: OK. I'll wait till a bit later and leave at about seven then.

6 **Woman:** Is everything back on time or are there still delays on certain lines?
Man: I'm afraid there are still delays on some routes.

7 **Woman:** Good evening, sir. Do you have your licence on you?
Man: No, no, I don't, but I know I was going faster than I was supposed to back there. I'm sorry.

8 **Man:** After the party, make sure that you get the bus home with someone else.
Woman: You must *not* go by yourself, do you understand?

Unit 14, Student's Book page 83
65

Speaker 1

Girl: It was our first family holiday abroad. For me and my younger brother it was all a big adventure and we were so excited, but we nearly missed our flight. While we were waiting to be called to the gate, my brother suggested playing hide and seek. I thought it'd help pass the time, so I counted and he hid. The trouble was he hid a bit too well! Nobody could find him and we ended up almost missing the last call for our flight – totally his fault. We ran to the gate and just made it. My parents weren't amused at the time, but they think it's funny now.

Speaker 2

Boy: I went abroad for the first time at the age of seven and remember staying in this big hotel. Our room had an amazing balcony. Anyway, we'd barely left the hotel on the first day when I tripped on the pavement and broke my wrist. Mum thought I should have been more careful but I don't think she was right – the pavement was really rough and stony. I had to go to hospital, which meant we missed a day at the beach, but after that we had a good time, even though my arm was in plaster and I couldn't get it wet in the sea.

Speaker 3

Boy: We did an exchange with a French school a few years ago. You know, you visit them for a week and then they stay with you. I didn't know much about my exchange partner in advance. I couldn't find him online and I only had his parents' email. So, the first time we met was in France. He was really cool and we got on well! I was having a great time when I suddenly came down with some virus and spent the rest of the week in bed. It was such a shame and I missed out on some fun activities.

Speaker 4

Girl: Last summer, my parents said I could go to a music festival. Even better, my friend Lauren – she can already drive – persuaded her dad to lend us his car. We were really organised – we had tents, food, sleeping bags and stuff, and we set off in plenty of time. Halfway there, though, the car suddenly broke down! There we were in the middle of nowhere with no choice but to wait for Lauren's mum to come to our rescue. Anyway, once we finally got to the festival, we had an amazing time – we saw some brilliant bands and we're definitely going to go back again next year – on the train!

Speaker 5

Boy: Our trip to the cinema last night was eventful. We should've realised that we needed to leave a lot earlier than we did, but we thought we'd left enough time. We knew the local football team were playing at home that night and it's always busy near the stadium on those days. The police often close down several roads, which makes our journey to the cinema so much longer. Last night it took me well over an hour and by the time we arrived, everybody had already gone in and we'd missed half the film. We were a bit fed up about it!

66 Unit 14, Student's Book page 83

1 Anita: Yeah, I do. In fact, I'm learning to drive at the moment. The first time I got behind the wheel I felt pretty nervous, but I'm looking forward to the freedom it will give me once I've passed my test. Besides that, I'll be able to go to places I can't get to on public transport. It'll be more expensive running a car and paying for petrol, but it'll be worth it.

2 Marco: It's not bad. There are a few different options available like buses and local taxis, which are really cheap. The region I live in is really mountainous, so there aren't many train lines, which is a shame 'cause I love train travel. Anyway, I use the taxis a lot – you can stop them anywhere in the street and they're really cheap. The buses are usually used for longer journeys, like when you travel to another town or city.

3 Anita: Yes, a few times. I didn't know what to expect the first time I did it, but I loved looking down over the city as we took off, seeing lots of familiar places, as well as feeling all these new sensations in my body. I thought it'd be boring, but I watched a film and looked out of the window at the clouds. It was cool.

4 Marco: Well, I haven't had one since I was a kid, but I used to like riding round to friends' houses and following these tracks through the woods. A lot of people I know cycle to work or college. There are a lot of advantages, such as getting fit and not having to worry about being held up in traffic. It's cheap and better for the environment, too.

5 Anita: I like being a passenger in a car 'cause you can just relax and look at the landscape. But sometimes when I'm on a bus or a train, I just sit and watch people. I don't mean staring at them, but I love making up little stories about who the other passengers are, and where they're going. I'm probably wrong, but it's a fun way to pass the time!

6 Marco: It was when we went on a family holiday to Australia. It took about sixteen hours to get there by plane. It got pretty boring just sitting in a small space without being able to stretch my legs out. However, the in-flight entertainment was decent, and I watched a few films. In the future, if I was going to do something like that again, I'd take a few magazines or a good book as well.

7 Anita: Let me think … I went on a bus ride in the mountains of Morocco when I went backpacking with a few friends. That was pretty cool. I'd saved up some money from doing a part-time job during the year and thought travelling would be a great thing to do for a couple of weeks. But, as I was saying, the bus ride was fascinating – it wasn't that comfortable, but the countryside we drove through was gorgeous.

67 Culture: Gap years, Student's Book page 84

Man: I know that deciding whether or not to take a gap year after secondary school is a big decision. And hopefully I'll be able to help you a little. We're going to spend a while looking at the advantages and disadvantages of gap years. But of course, it's not all black and white because these things will depend on personal situations. You may need to take several things into consideration, or just one important factor might make the decision clear for you. For a start it's important that you remember that a year out isn't the best option for everyone.

Right then, let's start with the pros. Firstly, a gap year's a great opportunity to take a break from studying and to come back refreshed and ready for the challenges of university life! Taking a year to have new experiences, and possibly travelling at the same time, is what many people dream about … I know I do! And the great thing about taking a gap year now, at your age, is that you can do it without having any other responsibilities to think about. It's also a chance for you to start to become independent from your parents, and to learn important life skills, such as teamwork and making and managing your own money.

Gap year programmes are designed with your age group in mind. This means that often they don't have any entry requirements. In other words, anyone can join them. For most jobs, being young and inexperienced can be seen as something negative. But this is exactly what makes you the perfect candidate for a gap year job, because you're flexible and keen to learn new skills.

In addition, going to university can be expensive. Doing a degree is a major financial investment in your future. An extra year, if you spend it working of course, allows you to save money to help make your life at university more comfortable.

Whatever happens in a gap year, you can be sure that you'll get to know yourself better. You'll grow as a person and discover what makes you happy and motivates you. And of course, you'll learn lots of things that you can put into practice at university.

Well, as you can see, there are plenty of good reasons to take a gap year. Now we come to the possible cons.

Are you the type of person who needs deadlines to get things done? Would you be happy to lie in bed all day if no one told you to get up? Then a gap year might not be the best idea for you right now. You see, in order to make the most of a gap year, you have to be able to motivate yourself and be responsible for your own schedule.

A gap year also needs to be structured and carefully planned. So if you're disorganised, again it might not be a good choice for you. And a few students can find it hard to return to study after a year away. In the end, some people find that a year out became a distraction from their longer-term plans.

Also, I mentioned the financial investment of education earlier. Education can be expensive, and a gap year can be very costly too! Without careful budgeting, it's possible that you'll find yourself in a worse financial situation after your gap year.

Finally, some people, your parents for example, might not understand your choice and they might want you to go to university straight after school. Do your research and think carefully about how to explain your reasons well and justify your gap year plan to other people so that this isn't a big negative.

So, those were the pros and cons. Now I'm sure you have lots of questions, so just take a moment in pairs to write them down and then I'll do my best to answer them all.

69 Unit 15, Student's Book page 86

Speaker 1

Woman: A powerful tornado which passed through northern Oklahoma has destroyed thousands of properties and injured hundreds of people. Aid agencies are cooperating with the state government to get emergency supplies to the worst-affected areas. Unfortunately, cooperation between the two organisations hasn't worked out because of problems with cell phone coverage.

Speaker 2

Man: We've collected a hundred pounds for an anti-poverty charity called *Chance For All*. They do lots of work with long-term unemployed people and people on low wages. I think it's really important to help people in society who are less fortunate. Sometimes we organise a food collection for a local homeless hostel.

Speaker 3

Man: Vehicles in this city cause terrible congestion and cars are either standing still or going much too fast! The traffic and parking is dreadful. Cars should be banned from busy city streets. City centres should be quiet, safe environments for pedestrians and cyclists – and public transport. A ban on private cars would make a huge difference in the city centre.

Speaker 4

Woman: The local council has been criticised for not dealing with litter in the city. The number of people employed to pick up litter in the city has been reduced, and people are starting to complain about the amount of rubbish in the streets. There has been further criticism of the local council for closing down leisure facilities in the area.

Speaker 5

Woman: I just want to explain my position because I think we're in agreement here! To start with, you seem to think I don't support your views on animal rights. In fact, that's not true. I'm a great supporter of animal rights, and I certainly think we should do more to protect animals.

Speaker 6

Boy: It's great that Ann's been elected as leader of the school council. It means she'll be going to monthly meetings with the headteacher and the board of governors. The election was also for student representatives from the other years, and they'll be at the meetings with her. I can't believe it! It's a massive responsibility. I'm so proud of her for winning the election!

71 Unit 16, Student's Book page 90

Daniel: Can you turn the volume down, Jade? The ad breaks are boring.

Jade: Oh, I don't mind watching the adverts – some of them are quite cool.

Daniel: Well, we'll have to agree to disagree about that.

Jade: Hey, Daniel, I've got a great clip to show you on YouTube. Hang on …

Daniel: OK.

Jade: Oh, we'll just have to wait for this advert to play before the video starts.

Man: Have you ever dropped your phone and damaged it? Have you lost your phone or had one stolen? Can you afford not to have phone insurance? For a small sum every month, protect your phone against accidental damage, loss and theft. Free same-day replacement on most phones. Keep talking. Go to PhoneGuard.com.

Jade: Hmm. Boring.

Daniel: Well, I bet it's really expensive, but actually I could do with some kind of phone insurance. I'm always dropping mine and cracking the screen.

Daniel: Look, this advert's just popped up on my social media page. 'Download the GameTime gaming app and play your days away'. Cool advert – and the app's free. Sounds brilliant, doesn't it?

Jade: Well, it's not really aimed at me, but I guess it would appeal to gamers like you, yes. Are you going to give it a go?

Daniel: Yeah, maybe,

Daniel: Why do you like adverts so much, Jade?

Jade: It's not that I want to sit and watch them all day, it's just good to be informed, that's all. You know, about cool products and new brands – and sometimes you get free samples in magazine ads. I suppose it's like being interested in news about DJs or celebrities or current affairs. Or football transfers!

Daniel: Really?!

Jade: Well, adverts help you find out what's available. You'd never know what new products were on offer if they weren't promoted. Anyway, you like car ads, don't you? Look – is this a new one?

Woman: Take the path less travelled. Experience the freedom of the open road. Get home in time for dinner! Terms and conditions apply.

Daniel: Yeah, I didn't mind that one. And I didn't know they were launching a new model this year. I'd love a car like that.

Jade: See? You're a consumer just as much as me or anybody else. You can't avoid it. Everyone's a consumer – everyone buys stuff. It's just part of life!

Daniel: I think some people are more influenced by advertising than others. I'm not.

Jade: Hmm… Remember when you wanted some chocolate the other day when we were watching catch up? That's 'cause one of the characters was eating a *CHOCCO* bar! That's product placement – companies pay for their goods to appear in programmes and it's just another form of advertising! And you fell for it.

Daniel: Hmm… The football's back on.

Jade: Cool. Oh – see that logo?

Daniel: The bank logo? What about it?

Jade: That's another example of marketing.

Daniel: They're the sponsors. All football teams are sponsored by companies.

Jade: Exactly. And why do companies sponsor certain teams? Because having their logo at matches and on football shirts is good publicity.

Daniel: Yeah, OK. Maybe you're right.

73 Unit 16, Student's Book page 93

Sophia: My name's Sophia Spencer and I study at a girls' school. I'd like to tell you about an unusual advertising campaign I was involved in, thanks to a new role I've been given at school. As one of the oldest girls in the school, I was hoping for the position of Homework Leader, which involves helping students who find a particular subject hard. Instead, I was made Head Girl! This means that I represent students' points of view on the school council and so on.

Anyway, I got involved in advertising when I received a huge parcel one day at school. It was a laugh opening it with my friends. We assumed it was going to be publicity from a bookshop, but it turned out to be from a record company. Inside the parcel was a box full of cool stuff linked to a band called The Emissary. There was a poster that I liked and we decided to put it on the common room wall. What was particularly special, though, was the diary they sent because it had my name on it in gold. They also supplied a link to some free downloads which I shared with everyone.

From the internet, I found out that parcels like this one had been sent to 130 school students – all girls like me! The band's target audience is fifteen to nineteen-year-old girls, and *somehow* the recording label had decided *we*, these 130 schoolgirls, were *particularly* cool. If *we* liked The Emissary, others would like them too, was the theory. I wasn't so sure. I might have some influence on the twelve to fourteen-year-olds at school, but everyone in my year's fairly independent-minded. Though that's not how advertisers see things when it comes to teenage girls. For them, a recommendation – you know, via word of mouth – is often much more effective than an advert in a music publication, for example. And it's worth even more if that person is influential – like me, apparently!

Anyway, if they wanted to send me free stuff, I wasn't going to complain. I'm sure they believed their plan was brilliant, and, in my view, it was certainly smart. We played The Emissary in the common room quite a lot and we were becoming fans whether we liked it or not!

Next, I was sent a box of T-shirts to hand out because the promoters wanted to use them to launch the band's first album. They were quite cool, actually! They also sent five tickets for the band's next live tour. I kept one for myself and offered the other four on Twitter. Some of the gigs were held in concert halls in other parts of the country, but my tickets were for the band's show in my town, in a stadium.

The gig was unbelievable and the whole experience was fun. I didn't think about it too much until three weeks later, when I got a call from a publicity agency. They were based in London and had worked with The Emissary's record producer. They wanted to discuss a new campaign with me, to promote this clothing brand in secret.

What I had to do was recommend the brand to people I knew, but without telling them that I was doing some advertising. This is called 'undercover' advertising, which is very different from the more traditional campaign I'd taken part in before. Now I'm not sure what to do. Part of me feels it's dishonest. But then they're offering me a lot of money!

I was invited to a launch event in London. I went with my mum and it was great watching the famous models walking up and down – though getting to speak to them wasn't an option. I did manage to say hello to two or three famous journalists though, and I was thrilled! I must admit I'm tempted to take part in this new campaign. What would you do if you were offered money to work in the glamorous world of advertising at my age?

74 Unit 16, Student's Book page 93

Sun: Where shall we start?

Johann: Let's start with TV adverts. I imagine that they're the most expensive way to advertise. You have to make the ad, which means paying the actors and a film crew, a producer and an editor, plus the music and so on. Then you have to pay every time the advert's broadcast.

Sun: I agree, but TV ads can have a big impact. They can be very memorable.

Johann: Only if the audience watches TV! If you think about it, TV ads are either for really valuable products – like cars – or something that people will buy a lot of.

Sun: That's true. What do you reckon about posters in the street?

Johann: I assume that they're cheaper to produce than TV ads and the good thing about posters is they last for a long time. So a poster might stay in the street for a month or two, and every time you walk past it you're reminded of the product.

Sun: That's a good point. And a magazine advert's the same, because it seems to me that every time you flick through the magazine, you might see the ad. A magazine ad is quite permanent, and more personal too, because you have it in your hands or in your home.

Johann: What about online pop-up ads?

Sun: Well, as I see it, pop-up ads are a nuisance because they always appear when you're busy trying do something else.

Johann: Yes, I get that. Suddenly you hear a voice and you're like, what's that? Then you realise it's the audio on a pop-up ad!

Sun: Exactly. From the point of view of the company that's advertising, I guess they must work, otherwise they wouldn't exist. Maybe they're a cheap option for advertisers?

Johann: Maybe. What do you think of guerrilla marketing?

Sun: It depends. To be honest, I don't like the sound of underground marketing very much. I get the impression that it's fairly uncommon though.

Johann: Mmm. I reckon it's a bit scary! And frankly, body advertising sounds weird.

Sun: Yes, but viral ads are cool.

Johann: Yes, I guess a lot of videos you see on social media are viral ads of some kind. I don't care though. If I enjoy the video, it doesn't bother me if it's some kind of publicity.

Sun: Yes. I get the feeling that viral ads must be the best value for companies.

Johann: But only if the video or photo goes viral. If it doesn't, it could just be an expensive mistake.

75 Unit 16, Student's Book page 93

Johann: I imagine that they're the most expensive way to advertise.

Johann: If you think about it, TV commercials are either for really valuable products – like cars – or something that people will buy a lot of.

Johann: The good thing about posters is they last for a long time.

Sun: It seems to me that every time you flick through the magazine, you might see the ad.

Sun: Well, as I see it, pop-up ads are a nuisance …

Sun: From the point of view of the company that's advertising, I guess they must work …

Sun: I get the impression that it's fairly uncommon though.

Johann: I reckon it's a bit scary.

76 Life skills: Assessing advertising, Student's Book page 94

Woman: In today's day and age we are constantly exposed to advertising, whether it's in magazines, on TV, online, on billboards or in shops. You might think that adverts simply contain a few images and some information about their product in order to persuade us to buy it. However, there's a lot more to creating an effective advert than meets the eye, and it's actually a very calculated attempt to connect with our emotions on a subconscious level, without us noticing it. In this talk we're going to look at some of the common techniques advertisers use to influence us and get us to buy or do something.

The first technique is association. This is when advertisers use positive images in their ad, in the hope that we associate the positive feelings we have about the image with their product. For example, a clothing brand might show happy, attractive people in their TV adverts. The idea is that the viewer will associate being happy and attractive with the brand's clothes. Or a brand might use a country's flag in its advertising or packaging. The aim is the same though – to associate the positive feelings or opinions people have about the country with the product being advertised.

But advertisers don't just rely on using positive feelings to get us to buy things, they also make use of negative emotions like fear and embarrassment. That's the second technique we're going to cover. Brands target the worries and insecurities people have, and promote their products as solutions to these problems. This is especially common in beauty and hygiene products - for example, chewing gum adverts play on people's worry of having bad breath, and ads for skincare products aimed at teens draw on their insecurity about having spots or bad skin.

The third technique is celebrity endorsements. This is when brands hire a famous person to appear in their advert to say how much they love the product or how effective it is. Advertisers choose celebrities that their target audience trust and want to imitate. If a famous football player appears in an ad wearing a particular brand of trainers, people are likely to buy those trainers to try to be like him or her. It's worth remembering that the celebrity has agreed to appear in the ad because the company has paid them a large amount of money to do so, and he or she probably doesn't actually use the products being promoted in real life.

Have you ever seen an advert that says something like 'The number one film at cinemas across the country!'? This is an example of the next technique I'm going to talk about. It's called the bandwagon effect, and it's when advertisers imply that everyone is already using their product or seeing their film, for example, and try to make us feel like we're the only ones who aren't. They aim to make us feel anxious that we are missing out on something that everyone else is enjoying.

So, those are just a few of the techniques that advertisers use to influence us and get us to buy a product, use a service, or do something. Next time you see an ad, see if you can spot any of these techniques in action.

78 Unit 17, Student's Book page 98

1 **Man:** Let's look at the latest celebrity news. What are the tabloids saying?

Woman: Well, there's been a story going round on social media that Taylor Swift used to travel around in a suitcase to avoid the paparazzi, and singer Zayn Malik seems to have confirmed this theory.

2 **Man:** Oh, my goodness – have you read this joke about the Olympians at the 2020 games in Tokyo? It's hilarious!

3 **Man:** And the latest now from the Etihad, where Manchester City are still ahead of United by two goals to one, with ten minutes remaining.

4 **Woman:** And you can see here this amusing drawing of the politician. Some people say it's unkind, but many will understand it as the artist intended, which is a little joke about how tall he is.

5 **Woman:** Professor Stephen Hawking's signed PhD thesis, entitled 'Properties of the Expanding Universe' has sold at auction for an incredible £584,750.

6 **Man:** Carla Wiggins, what do you make of the scandal concerning politicians' salaries?

Woman: Well, in my opinion, it's as worrying as the press are suggesting it is. I mean, when you think about how little …

7 **Woman:** This week has seen the discovery of some fascinating cave art in France, dating back an amazing 12,000 years! Scientists have been very excited about finding the pictures of a horse and deer hidden beneath layers of graffiti on the cave walls.

8 **Man:** Now it's time to take a look at the top stories about global events this week.

80 Unit 18, Student's Book page 102

1 **Sofia:** I don't mind having to meet deadlines, but I want a balance between work and my social life, so working long hours wouldn't be for me. Life outside work will always be important – I don't want a job that means having to work shifts or anything that might mean I can never see my friends. I don't really see myself working in a boring office or anything like that. I'd like to have my own company one day, something to do with design, something creative, but that's also rewarding. I know those kinds of jobs can sometimes be badly paid, but that doesn't matter too much.

2 **Martin:** I'd like something that involves working with my hands. I don't mean something repetitive – I'd get bored very quickly doing the same thing over and over again. I definitely can't imagine doing lots of paperwork – I hate that kind of thing. And I don't want to feel stressed. I wouldn't enjoy anything that involved having to meet deadlines. That would start to stress me out. I'd also like to have a job where I can take lots of time off, and it would be great if I could make a decent living as well!

3 **Tara:** I really want something that challenges me, and I wouldn't have a problem with having to work long hours. So, my dream job needs to be demanding, something professional, you know, like a lawyer, a doctor or something like that. It needs to be well paid too. I'm a sociable person, so I think I'd be good at dealing with people, and sorting out their problems. That's the kind of stuff I'm good at. I'd also like a job where I could travel, too. That would be cool.

82 Unit 18, Student's Book page 105

Interviewer: Our guest today is Aiden Cass, the seventeen-year-old behind Unique Tees, an online T-shirt business that's made quite an impact in just a few years. So how did it all start, Aiden?

Aiden: Well, at fifteen, I desperately wanted a new computer – a pretty expensive one – so in order to save money for it, I started up a business collecting stuff from neighbours – things they were going to throw out – and then selling it online. There was no shortage of stuff, but one thing I noticed was that cool vintage T-shirts – you know, old ones you can't get any more – attracted a lot of interest and often sold for good prices. Chatting to my dad, I mentioned that if I could just sell T-shirts, I'd be earning a fortune. He agreed and offered to help.

Interviewer: But things didn't go according to plan did they? What sort of problems did you encounter?

Aiden: Well, at first I started advertising on social media for unwanted T-shirts. I soon had hundreds of them – at one point our garage at home was pretty full and we knew we would have to be careful about how many we collected. People tend to keep their favourite – and often coolest – T-shirts until they fall apart and are impossible to fix. And the majority were simply a bit boring, so I ended up with stuff I couldn't get rid of.

Interviewer: So you changed your approach? How does the business work now?

Aiden: Well, at first we tried importing old T-shirts from abroad. We had some success, but getting them delivered wasn't cheap. Then my brother pointed out that thousands of people are designing cool logos and putting them on the web for other people to use. So we thought, let's forget about the old T-shirts and create new ones with those logos instead. My brother's into design and he found some great sources online. I contacted various designers and they agreed, for a share of the profit, to let us use their work.

Interviewer: Does that involve a lot of paperwork?

Aiden: Sometimes. I used to spend every Friday night catching up with paperwork, preparing contracts and so on, and I found it challenging to do by myself, even though in reality, there wasn't actually loads of it. You do have to meet deadlines with some things, though. Nowadays my parents do a fair amount of it, especially with the financial side of the business, and that's a relief.

Interviewer: How do you balance your business with other priorities – school, for example?

Aiden: I attend an online school, which means I can take lessons at almost any time, even when I'm travelling. But I won't pretend that the business hasn't had an impact on my education. It has. Sometimes I've missed a few homework deadlines, just because I've been too tired or I haven't been able to get interested in the subject. It's more difficult to ignore work. If I do, I end up with hundreds of emails from dissatisfied customers!

Interviewer: How have people around you reacted to your success?

Aiden: My teachers are happy as long as my progress is OK. To be honest, I don't talk about it with my friends much. Those that know about it aren't actually that bothered about asking questions really, which surprised me at first 'cause they all love their T-shirts! They think it's just a hobby. Now that I have to work long hours, we can't spend as much time together, but they're understanding and never complain about it. My family are a different matter of course. They're always giving me helpful ideas.

Interviewer: Had you had any experience of business before you started your company? A summer job, for example?

Aiden: From a young age, I always had summer jobs. They weren't necessarily interesting and often involved a lot of effort, considering how badly paid they were! I was happy with anything then, though. But interacting with adults gave me a lot of useful skills, like communicating and getting on with others in a variety of situations. I was always persuading people to let me cut their lawn or clean their car. That kind of thing's been really useful with the business now.

83 Unit 18, Student's Book page 105

Conor: The best thing about working in a fast food restaurant is that you might get some free food!

Leila: I'm not sure about that! A friend of mine did it for a summer. She says that by the end of the first week, she didn't want to see another chip again in her life. And that her clothes always smelled of greasy fried food.

Conor: Ugh! That's horrible.

Leila: Stacking shelves is pretty repetitive, but you might be able to listen to music while you're doing it.

Conor: I bet they wouldn't let you do that. Personally, I can't really see the point of doing this kind of work. You often have to work shifts – in the middle of the night! And you're hardly learning anything.

Leila: I'm with you on that.

Conor: Working in a shop is probably quite well paid for a summer job and it isn't particularly demanding. One of the best jobs here, I reckon. What do you think?

Leila: I'm not convinced. Firstly, you'd have to dress smartly every day and you'd spend most of the day folding clothes.

Conor: And you'd have to look happy while you were doing it!

Leila: Yes!

Conor: To me, babysitting feels like the least demanding job. As long as you don't get disturbed by the children, you can just watch TV! What do you reckon?

Leila: Absolutely! The bad thing is, you'll usually be working in the evenings. And that means, no going out.

Conor: That's a good point.

Leila: I reckon that being a waiter is quite hard work, especially when the restaurant is busy. And you probably get difficult customers sometimes, which wouldn't be much fun.

Conor: I agree up to a point, but it's also good to get some experience of working under pressure.

Leila: Fair enough. I guess lots of us will have to deal with pressure at work at some stage, but I'd rather I didn't have to.

Conor: Right.

84 Culture: Fan culture, Student's Book page 106

Presenter: A very warm welcome to our guest today, Sam Gold. Sam is a Media Studies lecturer at City University and he's going to talk to us about … on second thoughts, I don't want to spoil it for you! Good morning, Sam.

Sam: Many thanks and good morning everyone. Now, imagine this scene: it's a normal day and you're online, scrolling through endless videos and memes. You're not paying much attention to what you're clicking on and then suddenly, a look of shock appears on your face! Yes, you've seen a spoiler! And now you know exactly how your favourite series ends. But of course, you didn't want to know that because you still have the whole of the final episode to watch! Yes, everyone hates spoilers, right?

Presenter: Yes, that happened to me this weekend in fact! It would be interesting to know how often our listeners see or hear spoilers.

Sam: Yes, it would. The question I ask my students is: why do some people love to ruin things for others? Well, it's most likely the feeling of exclusivity and superiority that some people get when they are the first to see a new film or read a new book. You see, it gives them a sense of power to potentially ruin your experience with just a few words or by posting an image that reveals important details or events in the story.

Presenter: So are spoilers a recent trend then?

Sam: No, they're not a new phenomenon at all. They've been there throughout history. Like when people shared the endings of old folk stories that were passed on from one generation to the next. Or the novel *Don Quixote*, which used spoilers in its chapter titles. And now we have movies like *Avengers: Infinity War* or *Aquaman* that have spoilers in their trailers! One thing is for sure, with social media, spoilers are definitely more common than before.

Presenter: I find it surprising that filmmakers would intentionally put spoilers in their trailers. Surely if you've seen a spoiler before watching, it will make a film less enjoyable?

Sam: Not necessarily I would say – it depends on the person. For people who work in the entertainment industry, spoilers in trailers are really just a marketing technique. They're designed to generate as much online discussion as possible, which in turn generates interest in the movie.

Presenter: Well, yes, they definitely do that!

Sam: But of course, the makers of some films and series do the opposite – they put a lot of time and energy into keeping things secret! Nowadays, it's not unusual to write and distribute fake versions of the script of a new film. The objective here is to confuse the media and any fans who love spoilers. And fandoms sometimes play an important role in fighting what's called 'spoiler culture'. For example, when the new *Fantastic Beasts: The Crimes of Grindelwald* film was released, there was a campaign on social media by the Fantastic Beasts fandom asking fans not to spoil the plot for others who hadn't yet seen the film.

Presenter: It certainly seems very divided. I'm wondering if some people actually enjoy spoilers?

Sam: Well, there hasn't been much research done to answer that question, but I can think of one study where participants read mystery stories. Some readers had stories with paragraphs which spoiled the plot by revealing the end, while other readers had stories, but without the spoilers. At the end, both groups were asked how much they had enjoyed reading the stories.

Presenter: And which group said they liked the stories the most?

Sam: It was the readers with the spoilers! You see, spoilers can change your reactions to a story, in many cases improving it for you. And in a way, knowing what will happen in the end can give you something to look forward to.

Presenter: You know I hadn't thought about it like that! I've always avoided spoilers, but next time I see a spoiler alert, I might take a look and see if I prefer knowing what's going to happen!

Sam: Yes, try it – you might be surprised!

86 Unit 19, Student's Book page 108

Conversation 1

Woman: I really think that professional sportspeople are paid too much.

Man: I'm not sure. You have to bear in mind that their careers are short. Only the very best are still involved at a competitive level by their mid-thirties.

Woman: I've never been convinced by that argument. I mean, at the top, many of them earn more in six months than most people earn in their life. They could, to my mind, easily get another job after playing. Lots of people change jobs in their thirties.

Conversation 2

Boy: I don't think students should be able to bring their mobile phones to school, do you?

Girl: I think you should keep an open mind about allowing mobile phones in school. A ban isn't necessarily the best thing.

Boy: I'm totally against students using their phones at school. Some people can't help checking them every five minutes. It can be really distracting for everyone.

Girl: I'd go along with that view. But I'm still not sure a ban is the answer.

Conversation 3

Girl: So what are your views on vegetarianism?

Boy: It's hard to deny that it must be better for you. Some meat products are unhealthy – they've got so much fat in them. What about you? What do you think?

Girl: As far as I'm concerned, people just need to eat less meat. Then their diets would be just as healthy.

Conversation 4

Boy: A lot of people say that being an adult is better than being a teenager.

Girl: I suspect this is true, to be honest. As you grow up, there's so much more freedom.

Boy: I agree up to a point. I mean, there's no doubt that you're more independent when you're older. But in many ways that means more responsibility, too. Work, money, things like that. I firmly believe in enjoying yourself while you've got the chance.

88 Unit 20, Student's Book page 112

1 **Man:** There was a tense atmosphere when I arrived for the rehearsal. No one likes being the first to talk, so I decided to tell a joke, which helped to break the ice. Soon, everyone was chatting quite happily.

2 **Girl:** Don't turn over to Channel Four!

Boy: Why not?

Girl: There's a documentary about the dairy industry, and I don't want to watch it. I saw the ad for it, and it broke my heart to see all the cows in little sheds.

Boy: But you aren't a vegan!

Girl: I know. But I still have feelings!

3 **Woman:** Our plane landed at ten pm in Zürich and from there we had a two-hour coach journey to Tirol. When I woke up the next morning, I opened the hotel window and the view really took my breath away. I'd never been to the Alps before, and I simply hadn't expected the landscape to be so perfect – so impressive and so beautiful!

4 **Boy:** Have you written your essay yet?

Girl : Do you mean the history homework?

Boy: Yes. Was it hard?

Girl: Not at all! It was a piece of cake. I did it in less than half an hour.

Boy: Wow! Will you help me with mine?

5 **Girl:** When I got home late on Friday, my mum asked me where I'd been and who I'd been with. I thought she was annoyed because I'm always late. Then I realised that she had tears in her eyes and she just held my hand and smiled. It had never crossed my mind that she was actually just worried. I felt really guilty and promised to keep in touch in future by texting more often.

6 **Boy:** How come you're so good at drawing? Have you had drawing classes or something?

Girl: No. I've always loved drawing though.

Boy: So this one, did you do it from memory or did you actually go down to the city centre with a notepad?

Girl: Well, I did a quick sketch while I was there. Then I filled in the rest from memory.

Boy: You have a very good eye for detail. There are so many little bits you've remembered, it's really amazing!

7 **Boy:** My best friend lives on the fifteenth floor. If I'm visiting, it can be a real pain if we need to pop out to the shops or something. One time we had to go out four times in one afternoon. Waiting for the lift every time drove me mad!

8 **Man:** When I'm on holiday, I love doing absolutely nothing. I can lie on a beach for days and days, and I never get bored. It's great to lose track of time and feel completely relaxed, in my own little world.

90 Unit 20, Student's Book page 115

Narrator: 1. You hear two friends talking about their college library.

Boy: I'm going to the library to renew my books.

Girl: You can renew them online.

Boy: Yes, but if you want to renew them for a third time, you have to take them in.

Girl: They probably want to make sure you haven't lost them. Also, if someone's waiting for a book, they might decide to give someone else the chance to borrow it instead!

Boy: Not helpful when you're in the middle of an essay. It'd be better if they had a few copies of each book, then you could have them for more time.

Girl: Maybe. But then there'd be loads of the same books – it's better to have a range.

Boy: I'm not sure ….

Narrator: 2. You hear a linguist talking about endangered languages.

Woman: Did you know half of the world's languages are endangered? There are currently around seven thousand languages spoken on the planet and, incredibly, we might lose three thousand or more by the end of this century. This is really worrying, because hardly anything's known about many of these languages. Does this matter? Yes. When there are no written records of a language, stories of a culture's past, which are handed down from generation to generation by word of mouth, also disappear. Even if you're talented at acquiring languages, it's virtually impossible to bring one back from extinction.

Narrator: 3. You hear two friends talking about a novel they have read.

Girl: I've finished *Kes*. Thanks for lending it to me!

Boy: What did you think?

Girl: The writing was brilliant, I thought.

Boy: You really think so? Not me, though I felt like I had a really good idea of what it must have been like to live in a northern English town sixty years ago.

Girl: It gave you a really clear picture of life in Barnsley in the 1960s, didn't it? And what about the main character? He was brilliant.

Boy: Billy? I don't know. Were kids really so different back then? I found it hard to believe in him.

Narrator: 4. You hear a teacher talking to her students about the school holidays.

Woman: At this time of year, of course you're all thinking about the holidays and looking forward to spending time with your families – and friends you may not have had the chance to see much of during term time. By all means, relax, and put thoughts of schoolwork to one side – that's what holidays are for. But I'd like to ask one thing of you. Please make an effort each week to note down a few interesting things you've been doing, so that you can share them with each other next term. I don't need to remind you to have a great time these holidays, but take care, and enjoy the break.

Narrator: 5. You hear two friends talking about speaking two languages.

Boy: I saw this interesting programme about being bilingual. You know, speaking two languages fluently.

Girl: Being bilingual must be cool, right? You can speak to more people around the world. And that helps you appreciate different cultures.

Boy: That may be true, but did you know that there may be benefits to being bi- or multi-lingual that people who just speak one language don't get?

Girl: What, like they can just keep acquiring more and more languages?

Boy: Actually, being bilingual seems to have an effect on the brain that has nothing to do with language. Bilingual people are great at solving problems and puzzles, and can plan and concentrate particularly well. It's quite surprising.

Narrator: 6. You hear a student advisor talking about young people starting university.

Man: It's always better for students starting out at university to be aware of what lies ahead. Hopefully you won't have too many concerns about your new place of study. The biggest change is the amount of research that students are expected to do on their own. That's something you'll really have to adjust to. Making time for regular breaks is crucial – the social element is just as important in some ways. In the early days you may feel it's a good idea to try and make millions of friends – this isn't actually the case. But do get involved in life outside your studies. I'm sure you'll all do very well and enjoy your new lives!

Narrator: 7. You hear two friends talking about a long-distance running race.

Boy: So, have you been training for Saturday?

Girl: Yes, I've been out every day after school, so I should be OK. I was a bit bothered that my shoes were rubbing, but I bought some new socks and they feel fine now. Imagine if I couldn't complete the race just because of my footwear!

Boy: That would be bad luck! So you're not too nervous then?

Girl: Well, I wouldn't say that! Actually, I think I'm more concerned about the people watching than the actual race. I mean, all my friends and family will be there, cheering and stuff. It adds a bit of pressure.

Boy: Well, it'll give you support!

Narrator: 8. You hear a boy telling a friend about a blog he writes.

Girl: How long have you been doing your blog?

Boy: It must be about five years now. It's incredible really, it doesn't feel that long. At first, I thought it'd be really hard thinking of something different to say each week, but in fact, I usually have more to say than I have space for – I mean, I try to limit each post to about five hundred words. That's the key thing, because if you write longer posts, people stop reading. I write stuff because I enjoy it, not just to try to keep my readers happy. But I've got over a thousand followers now and I'm getting more every week.

Girl: Cool!

91 Unit 20, Student's Book page 115

Andrea: There's a group of people sitting together. I'm not sure exactly what they're doing, but clearly they're communicating with each other. I'm not sure who the guy on the screen is. I get the impression that the man is their boss. It looks like a fairly informal situation but everyone in the group is paying attention to what's going on. It must be a meeting of some kind.

92 Unit 20, Student's Book page 115

Andrea: In the other photo, the people are sitting in a room. They seem to be learning or practising something, but it doesn't look as though it's a classroom. Maybe it's a language class. I get the impression that the woman in the yellow sweater is the teacher. I think they might be learning sign language. There are people of different ages in the class.

93 Life skills: Preparing for exams, Student's Book page 116

Tutor: OK, so thanks for coming both of you. I know that last year you found it quite difficult to cope with stress around exam time, so today I want to talk about that and hopefully find some ways for you to manage better this year and to feel happier with everything.

Marco: Sounds great!

Lucia: Perfect. I definitely need some help!

Tutor: Now, first things first, it's important to plan instead of panicking.

Marco: Hmm, but planning always takes so long. And I need as much time as I can get for studying!

Tutor: I know exactly what you mean, Marco. But prioritising and writing a study plan will save you lots of time in the long run. You'll know what you need to do each day, so it will feel much more realistic – and you'll be calmer.

Lucia: That's true. When I plan my revision, I feel more relaxed in general.

Tutor: That's good to hear, Lucia. And how do you feel just before an exam?

Lucia: A bit nervous, to be honest. Even if I've prepared well, I still worry about failing the exam.

Tutor: And that's perfectly normal! It's a good idea to sit down on your own before an exam and to write down anything that you're worried about. This simple step will make you feel more relaxed going into the exam.

Marco: Wow, really! I'll give that a try then.

Lucia: But if I still can't stop worrying?

Tutor: Well, then maybe you need to focus on creating a positive mindset for your studies.

Lucia: And what does that mean exactly?

Tutor: It means that instead of focusing on failure, you should believe that you can be successful! And don't be afraid to ask a friend, teacher or your parents for help. We all need advice sometimes.

Marco: Yep, my parents are full of good advice. In fact, I don't know why I don't ask them for help more often! They told me that when I'm getting stressed with my exams, I need to stop and think of a happy memory – something that makes me smile. Doing that produces chemicals in the brain that give us a sense of well-being. And feeling happier and less stressed will provide the motivation to spend a bit more time studying.

Tutor: What a great bit of advice! I'll recommend that to other students!

Marco: Haha! Glad I can help!

Tutor: Talking about parents, here's something my parents used to say to me when I was anxious about exams. They told me to focus on making progress and not on achieving perfection. In other words, they were saying: 'Don't be too hard on yourself'. It's important to recognise how you are improving and to celebrate any successes, like a good grade in a test, for example, or finally understanding something that was a complete mystery before!

Lucia: I think I definitely need to focus more on how I'm improving. I'm a total perfectionist sometimes and it really stresses me out.

Tutor: Well, I'm glad my parents' advice can help you too. There is one more thing I'd like to suggest. Exam preparation is a mental activity, but we mustn't forget that our mind is connected to our body. So, when you feel tension in your shoulders or neck, or your back or legs start to ache, you need to get up for ten minutes and do some stretches. Stretching your muscles and moving around will release tension in your body and, at the end of a long day of study, it will help you relax.

Marco: Yeah, my neck does get really stiff when I'm sitting at my desk for a long time.

Lucia: Shall we try a few stretches now, before we go back to class?

95 Prepare for the Exam, Student's Book page 131

Narrator: 1. You hear two friends discussing a novel.

Girl: I've just finished that novel you lent me. I'm really glad I read it, but I must admit I found the story a bit hard to follow at times.

Boy: Did you? That wasn't an issue for me. I'd read it again, actually. What about the main character, Jake? He was really true to life somehow, and I thought that was brilliant.

Girl: Good point. And his friends behaved just like we do at times, didn't they?

Boy: Right. I was less keen on the descriptions of Liverpool and Manchester. I mean, I've been to those cities and for me they didn't feel right.

Girl: Oh? That didn't bother me.

Narrator: Now listen again.

[The recording is repeated.]

96 Prepare for the Exam, Student's Book page 131

Narrator: 1. You hear two friends discussing a novel.

Girl: I've just finished that novel you lent me. I'm really glad I read it, but I must admit I found the story a bit hard to follow at times.

Boy: Did you? That wasn't an issue for me. I'd read it again, actually. What about the main character, Jake? He was really true to life somehow, and I thought that was brilliant.

Girl: Good point. And his friends behaved just like we do at times, didn't they?

Boy: Right. I was less keen on the descriptions of Liverpool and Manchester. I mean, I've been to those cities and for me they didn't feel right.

Girl: Oh? That didn't bother me.

Narrator: Now listen again.

[The recording is repeated.]

Narrator: 2. You hear a boy talking on the phone about some homework.

Boy: Hi, it's Harry here. I just wanted to have a quick chat about our geography homework. I'm getting a bit worried about it. I know there're a couple more days before it's due, so that's not what's bothering me. I've read the chapters we were told to read in the textbook loads of times, and I still can't come up with enough to say about the topic. We have to write two thousand words, don't we? How are you getting on with it? Do you think you could ring me back when you get a minute and help me out? Thanks!

Narrator: Now listen again.

[The recording is repeated.]

Narrator: 3. You hear two friends talking about social media.

Girl: You're always on social media! Why don't we just chat instead?

Boy: You're right! I'm just nosy – I want to know what everyone's been up to since I last saw them. But I guess I do waste quite a lot of time posting selfies.

Girl: I bet you've got thousands of friends online as well.

Boy: Actually, I'm pretty careful about who I invite to be a friend on my social media accounts, and I only accept friend requests from people I know.

Girl: Me, too. I don't go on my page much, but I like uploading photos so I can look back at them later.

Boy: Yeah, it stops you forgetting about what you've done. It's like keeping a diary, isn't it?

Girl: Exactly!

Narrator: Now listen again.

[The recording is repeated.]

Narrator: 4. You hear a girl telling her friend about moving house.

Boy: Didn't you move house with your family at the weekend?

Girl: Yeah. Everything went well and we've unpacked most of our stuff. I had to get rid of loads of old clothes and books 'cause my new bedroom's smaller than my old one. It makes such a difference looking out on fields instead of apartment blocks, though, and that's what matters to me. But I do feel a bit homesick! I keep wanting to go back to where we were – it's where I grew up. Anyway, we'll settle in soon and the house is near the stables, so I won't have a long train journey to get to my horse-riding lessons now.

Narrator: Now listen again.

[The recording is repeated.]

Narrator: 5. You hear a teacher talking to his class about being a good citizen.

Man: Today, we're going to look at what it means to be a good citizen. I'm not simply talking about not breaking the law or causing harm, but having consideration for others. Look at any online forum and you'll find people complaining that others don't hold doors open any more, or care about the community they're part of. I'd like us to think about what good citizens are – how do they behave? What projects do they get involved in which benefit others? But, I don't want it to stop there. Go and try some of these things out and report back next lesson. I can't wait to hear all about it.

Narrator: Now listen again.

[The recording is repeated.]

Narrator: Six. You hear an announcement at a railway station.

Woman: Good morning ladies and gentleman. As you are no doubt aware, the track work which has been going on for the last few weeks has now been completed. Unfortunately, there has been a mechanical failure reported near Northport this morning, which means that trains are not running between Stockden and Marsh Gate. Any customers wishing to travel to these stations should go to the front of the station, where a bus will be provided at no extra charge. You will need to show a valid ticket to the driver. We do not expect this to add further time to your journey. May we wish you a safe and pleasant journey.

Narrator: Now listen again.

[The recording is repeated.]

Narrator: 7. You hear a boy talking to his sister about climbing.

Boy: Hey! Are you coming to the climbing centre with me? They've got a new climbing wall and I want to have a go.

Girl: I don't know. What level is it? I thought they said it was for advanced climbers only – I don't think I'll be good enough.

Boy: Well, it might be a bit harder than you're used to. I can give you a hand, though. You know, guide you through it.

Girl: Well, OK. I'll come along and see how I feel.

Boy: I'm so glad you put our names down for next week's climbing trip. That won't be as tough. If you hadn't remembered, we wouldn't have got places on it.

Narrator: Now listen again.

[The recording is repeated.]

Narrator: 8. You hear two friends talking about the girl's temporary job.

Boy: Did you find a job for the school holidays?

Girl: Yeah – as you know, I'm saving up for a new bike and I managed to get a job at a supermarket. It's just putting stuff on shelves.

Boy: Boring!

Girl: Actually, I work with some great people and we have a laugh. It's quite late in the evenings, so not many customers are around then, even though the store's open. The thing that's a bit of a pain is how the shelving system works. Nothing's arranged logically, so you spend loads of time walking up and down the aisles in the store to find where stuff goes. Anyway, I should save up enough in no time.

Narrator: Now listen again.

[The recording is repeated.]

97 Prepare for the Exam, Student's Book page 132

Cristina: I'm Cristina and I'm going to tell you about a guy called Jamal Edwards who started his own online broadcast music channel, SBTV, a few years ago at the age of fifteen.

Jamal had been given a video camera as a present and took it outside to film around the houses and gardens of the area where he was living in London. He focused on some foxes and uploaded a short video of them online. Jamal couldn't believe it when he got tons of views for this single clip, and he decided to try filming something else.

Jamal loved music and at the time grime music, which is a unique mix of hip-hop and garage music, was just becoming really popular. You couldn't find it on the main TV channels, though, and Jamal immediately saw an opportunity to make this kind of music more widely available.

Jamal started out filming rappers doing their thing in London. He went backstage at gigs and even captured live music that musicians were playing in cars – everyone loved that setting 'cause it was so unusual. These performances were delivered straight to camera and without any editing, and were posted online within days. They became an instant hit on YouTube.

Because Jamal's videos were doing so well, he decided to invest in better equipment. At the time, while studying at college, he was a sales assistant in a clothes shop and people asked him why he was wasting his time doing that. But Jamal says you can save money no matter what kind of work you do – like working in a fast food restaurant or whatever.

Jamal posted his videos on YouTube under the name SBTV, and he started making thousands of pounds from advertising. After gaining over thirty-nine million hits, Jamal set up an SBTV website and quickly employed a team of twelve assistants, who went out filming the music scene in and around London and uploading their videos to the SBTV website.

The SBTV website has moved on from just posting videos of new talent. There are now loads of interviews with the latest musicians as well. In addition, there are news stories. I really enjoy reading those 'cause they're cool and interesting. There are articles, too. I haven't read any of those yet, but I'm sure they're just as fascinating.

I think Jamal's really inspirational because although he made mistakes when his business started to take off, he's learned from them and become really successful. He admits that finances weren't his strong point at first. Like, one thing he didn't do was keep receipts of things he bought, which are important for working out what you've spent on your business.

Another thing I found out about Jamal was that he used to be quite timid. When he took on his first staff members, he was scared of talking to them face to face. If something went wrong, he wouldn't sit down and have a conversation with them, so he used to email them instead!

I think Jamal's a really down-to-earth guy, and he gives great advice. I read an article about him where he said that confidence is the key to success. He says that's the main thing to work on – rather than practical skills. If you believe in yourself, you can do anything. It's something I'm definitely going to work on!

Loads of people have heard of Jamal now, but it wasn't always that way. In fact, it was his mum that people used to recognise. She's a singer and had been a contestant on *The X Factor* and was recognised everywhere afterwards. Jamal didn't really understand why everyone wanted photos of her. He didn't really like the idea of being famous and found it hard at first when it happened to him. I think he probably likes it a lot more now he's got used to it. Has anyone got any questions?

Narrator: Now you'll hear Part 2 again.

[The recording is repeated.]

98

Prepare for the Exam, Student's Book page 132

Speaker 1

Man: I was working in a rescue centre in South Africa for a month, looking after animals and birds that were hurt or young ones that'd been found wandering about alone – mainly monkeys. It was quite demanding work, with long days, but it was incredibly rewarding, especially when I realised that, without my efforts, the animal I was looking after would've died. It was tiring though. Luckily we all slept on site so we didn't have far to travel from the rescue centre to our accommodation at the end of the day. I barely noticed the landscapes because I was so absorbed in my work, but my photos show how pretty it was there.

99

Prepare for the Exam, Student's Book page 132

Speaker 1

Man: I was working in a rescue centre in South Africa for a month, looking after animals and birds that were hurt or young ones that'd been found wandering about alone – mainly monkeys. It was quite demanding work, with long days, but it was incredibly rewarding, especially when I realised that without my efforts, the animal I was looking after would've died. It was tiring though. Luckily we all slept on site, so we didn't have far to travel from the rescue centre to our accommodation at the end of the day. I barely noticed the landscapes because I was so absorbed in my work, but my photos show how pretty it was there.

Speaker 2

Woman: I'd always wanted to see Costa Rica so I was so happy to get the chance to volunteer on a research project there. My work involved trekking through the rainforest with a group of researchers, helping them as they gathered information on the various birds we came across. When they interviewed me, they'd made it clear that I'd need some understanding of local species – like being able to recognise different birds from their song – stuff like that. In the end, I spent three weeks with them. It was time well spent, because applying that knowledge was the highlight of the trip for me.

Speaker 3

Man: My trip to a Caribbean island was supposed to be a working holiday, but at the beginning it was all work and not much holiday! I wasn't prepared for that. I did everything from planting vegetables to repairing buildings, and ended up with a bad back as a result. Still, I made some nice friends, and when more volunteers arrived, we got more free time. That was the thing that made the trip for me – having time to take in the gorgeous scenery, even though I couldn't walk far from camp. We'd hoped to see several unusual species out in the rainforest. We didn't, but that didn't spoil it for us.

Speaker 4

Woman: I had a memorable time working in Mexico. I was on the Yucatan Peninsula, helping on a jaguar conservation project. Jaguars are a kind of big cat, and they're seriously endangered, so I knew I probably wouldn't actually see any during my stay. But as my job was to install and repair the remote cameras in the jungle, I did manage to capture them on video, and it was truly amazing to think they were somewhere nearby. Now I'm passionate about preventing this beautiful creature from dying out altogether and I'll be returning to the same camp as soon as I can afford it.

Speaker 5

Woman: I was involved in a project that protects the baby sea turtles born on the beaches of the Peloponnese region in Greece. The first two months are always the busiest, as that's when the eggs hatch. Every day, I had to do an early morning beach survey for the scientists, where I checked the nests and monitored the number of new baby turtles – by looking at the tracks in the sand leading from the nest down to the sea. It wasn't difficult to do, but I felt so proud to be in charge of such a key aspect of the project, because not everyone gets that kind of experience as a volunteer.

Narrator: Now you'll hear Part 3 again.

[The recording is repeated.]

100

Prepare for the Exam, Student's Book page 133

Interviewer: My studio guest today is seventeen-year-old Maria Smith, who's just carried out an internet survey on attitudes to the future among students her own age. Maria, this was a college project. Why did you decide on this topic area?

101

Prepare for the Exam, Student's Book page 133

Interviewer: My studio guest today is seventeen-year-old Maria Smith, who's just carried out an internet survey on attitudes to the future among students her own age. Maria, this was a college project. Why did you decide on this topic area?

Maria: Everyone at college is starting to think about what's going to happen after we finish. There are only two real options – continue in education or find work. Our teachers have suggested we give it some thought – we'll have to make up our minds about going on to higher education soon. My best friend's already got a clear idea about what she wants to do, but I haven't a clue and I wanted to see if everyone else feels as nervous as I do.

Interviewer: So, you put together a survey. What was the most challenging thing about doing this?

Maria: None of it was easy! I had to design the survey, making sure that my questions were clear and asked for the right information. That was the trickiest thing. In terms of finding enough people to take part, I had no trouble because of all my social media connections. Examining the results took a fair bit of time, though it was quite straightforward, really.

Interviewer: So, is your generation concerned about the future?

Maria: Yes. Typically, seventeen-year-olds like me are anxious about being able to find work that fits their particular set of skills. Additionally, a few participants expressed worries about the impact of the economy on their future way of life. A lower percentage are bothered that they won't get into the university they want to go to, and think this will affect their prospects.

Interviewer: Let's hope they're wrong. Now, you asked participants about attitudes to technology.

Maria: Right. We depend on technology far more than previous generations did, when it wasn't as advanced. We've always had the internet and apps and so on. We regard technology as central to our lives and I can't see that changing any time soon. Loads of participants expressed the idea that they'd prefer to be less dependent on it for their social lives – and eventually their professional lives, too. Personally, I wish I could take a break from the continual need to upgrade my devices.

Interviewer: What else did you ask participants about?

Maria: I wanted to know what they considered success to be. I expected a large number of answers to be focused on wealth, having a big house, and all that. I was astonished when people said that, although they saw those things as desirable, happiness was more important than things like getting ahead in their career. I'd have loved to chat with them and get a deeper understanding of their answers, but that wasn't possible.

Interviewer: Interesting. What are you going to do with the data you've gathered?

Maria: Ideally, I'd like to share it with others. I've got permission from the survey participants to make their answers public, though they'll be anonymous of course. I've got a blog but that probably isn't the right place for it. Instead, I'm putting a copy of the questions I asked and the results I've written up in the college library where everyone will have access to them. I think it'll help other people, so I'm going to suggest students at college take a look at it.

Interviewer: Did carrying out the survey change how you feel about the future?

Maria: Well, before I did the survey, I didn't fully understand what options were available. Now, after learning about other people's ideas, there are so many things to choose from. You might think that would make things even more challenging but someone wrote about following your heart – doing something that appeals rather than what you think you should do. That actually made things clearer and if I keep that in mind, I know I won't go wrong with what I choose to do. It's taken me a while to get to this point, but I'm more positive about my future now!

Interviewer: Thank you for talking to us, Maria.

Narrator: Now you'll hear Part 4 again.

[The recording is repeated.]

102 Prepare for the Exam, Student's Book page 134

1 **Sara:** I usually walk. I live fairly nearby and it gives me some exercise. If the weather's bad, my dad sometimes gives me a lift.

2 **Sara:** I'd love to be a singer-songwriter, and my brother plays the guitar, so when we're not at school, we'll be at home, composing stuff on the guitar. I like mountain biking as well, and there are some good places near where I live to do that with my friends.

3 **Sara:** Not often. I think you miss out on life when you're walking around staring at your screen. I see my friends a lot, and when I'm not with them, I don't feel I need to know what they're doing every minute of every day!

4 **Sara:** My grandparents live in a small village, so if I visit them, I'll take the bus. Otherwise, I hardly ever really use it, and there are no trains where I live.

103 Prepare for the Exam, Student's Book page 134

Examiner: Here are your photographs. They show young people doing different things in their free time. I'd like you to compare the photographs, and say what you think the people like about doing these activities.

Álvaro: Well, the girl in the first photo is relaxing in her bedroom. She looks as if she could be wearing her pyjamas. She has headphones round her neck, so she has probably been listening to music. I think she is enjoying being on her own at home and having time to herself. She's looking at her tablet and laughing, so perhaps she's enjoying catching up with her friends on social media. So, although she's alone, she's in contact with people.

The children in the second photo are at home too. They're sitting on cushions on the floor playing a game on their PlayStation or some other games console, and they're also wearing casual clothes. Although they are together, they aren't communicating with each other – they're concentrating on their game. But I think that, in spite of this, they like having each other for company. And the little girl probably is very pleased that the older children have allowed her to play with them.

Examiner: Thank you.

104 Prepare for the Exam, Student's Book page 136

Álvaro: OK, shall I start?

Sara: Sure, go ahead.

Álvaro: I think museums are OK but it depends on what they're like. Some can be pretty boring places, though the ones with interactive displays and so on are more interesting. Actually, I think watching films might be quite a good idea, not necessarily documentaries, but things based in a particular period of time. Do you agree?

Sara: Well, that could be interesting, especially if they were dramas. Everyone loves films. It might be difficult to find that sort of thing that's just about our area, though. Hmm. What about going to talks, then? Where would you do that?

Álvaro: I guess in a library or a college perhaps? That's quite a good idea I suppose.

Sara: Well, they could be interesting – depending on who's speaking, of course. Someone enthusiastic who has stuff to show you – like old photos or something – might be interesting.

Álvaro: Yeah, maybe. Let's think about reading now.

Sara: OK. Speaking personally, reading history books reminds me of being at school. There's nothing wrong with that but you need a change from feeling like you're in the classroom, don't you?

Álvaro: Yeah. You can find good stuff online but it still feels like studying.

Sara: Right!

Álvaro: And what about talking to people who've lived in the area for a long time? I guess that means older people. Actually, my grandparents have some good stories of what it was like growing up for their generation.

Sara: Yes, that would be a good way to find stuff out, wouldn't it?

105

Prepare for the Exam, Student's Book page 136

Examiner: Thank you. Now you have about a minute to decide which way of finding out about the history of an area would be the most interesting to young people.

106

Prepare for the Exam, Student's Book page 136

Álvaro: Well, let's see. Talks could be boring, I think, if the speakers or topics aren't appealing to our age group.

Sara: I can't imagine many people would want to sit through talks about pots and coins, but you never know!

Álvaro: Films are a good idea, especially if they were about our area, but I just think it would be difficult to find things like that.

Sara: Maybe, you'd have to watch more general stuff about a particular era, I think, which wouldn't be as interesting as something about where we live. What about visiting museums? They can have interesting displays and stuff.

Álvaro: True. I'm not sure I'd want to stand and read a load of information boards, though, to be honest.

Sara: Right – there would need to be photos and other exhibits, I think.

Álvaro: What about reading? There's loads of stuff online, though books you find in libraries do tend to be quite old, don't they?

Sara: Yeah, and it's like being at school! It seems like talking to people might be the most interesting way to find out about the history of our area. I love listening to older people's stories. It's a fun way to learn about history.

Álvaro: Yeah, they have a personal element to them which I like. OK, shall we say talking to people who've lived in the area for a long time, then?

Sara: Yeah, great.

107

Prepare for the Exam, Student's Book page 136

Examiner: Some young people would like to find out more about the history of the area where they live. Here are some ways they could find out about their area and a question for you to discuss. First you have some time to look at the task. Now, talk to each other about how interesting young people would find these ways of finding out about history.

108

Prepare for the Exam, Student's Book page 137

Examiner: Do you think people should look to the future rather than the past?

Álvaro: Well, I'm not sure about that. I think it's useful to study the past in order to learn from it and make progress as a society. Like, in the past there may have been wars or disagreements and it helps to look at why these occurred, with the aim of making sure they don't happen again.

Examiner: Do you agree?

Sara: Up to a point, yes, although I think it's also important not to worry too much about things that have happened that you can't do anything about now. I think it's better to try and learn from things and move on.

Examiner: Why are people so interested in their own family's history?

Sara: I suppose it's more personal, isn't it? I mean, you know these people, or know people who knew them. You can find out about who you're similar to, or who you look like. That's more relevant to you than learning about people you've never heard of.

Examiner: What do you think?

Álvaro: I agree with Sara. I love hearing my grandparents talk about life when they were young, and understanding how my parents have taken after them! I think we pass ideas and traditions on from generation to generation, which is nice because you feel like you belong to your own little group. That makes you closer as a family.

Examiner: How can history lessons be made interesting at school?

Álvaro: I think our classes are interesting. Our teacher has a lot of passion for the subject, and that makes everyone else interested. She brings history alive somehow. Sometimes all we do is listen to her talk. It feels like we're getting an easy class when that happens, but she's so interesting that you remember everything she says.

Sara: In my class, we do a lot of studying from books. That's fine, but it would be interesting to have more discussions about things – like why people acted the way they did and why history seems to keep repeating itself – like, people do the same things over and over hoping for a different result.

Examiner: Thank you.

Acknowledgements

The authors and publishers acknowledge the following sources of copyright material and are grateful for the permissions granted. While every effort has been made, it has not always been possible to identify the sources of all the material used, or to trace all copyright holders. If any omissions are brought to our notice, we will be happy to include the appropriate acknowledgements on reprinting and in the next update to the digital edition, as applicable.

Teacher's Book

Pg9: Alem Omerovic/EyeEm/Getty Images; loops7/DigitalVision Vectors/Getty Images; Thomas Söllner/EyeEm/Getty Images

All other texts, photographs and illustrations used are from the Student's Book.

Front cover photography by William King/The Image Bank/Getty Images Plus/Getty Images.

Videos

Key: C = Culture

Photography

The following photographs are sourced from Getty Images:

C1: FG Trade/Vetta; Deagreez/iStock/Getty Images Plus; PacoRomero/iStock/Getty Images Plus; FG Trade/Vetta; Image Source Ltd/Photodisc; Vetta; **C2:** 1971yes/iStock/Getty Images Plus; duncan1890/DigitalVision Vectors; KatarzynaBialasiewicz/iStock/Getty Images Plus; irina88w/iStock/Getty Images Plus; dit26978/iStock/Getty Images Plus; **C3:** AlonzoDesign/DigitalVision Vectors; Pixsooz/iStock/Getty Images Plus; **C5:** RetroAtelier/iStock/Getty Images Plus; Joshua_Kurz/iStock Editorial.

Video Clips

The following video clips are sourced from Getty Images:

C1: Borovikk/Creatas Video+; Hoptocopter/Vetta; BBC Motion Gallery Editorial/BBC News/BBC Editorial; Getty Images Entertainment Video; mrs_veronik/Creatas Video+; Image Source Ltd/Jupiterfootage; ISVID/Creatas Video+; Tolga TEZCAN/Creatas Video; thisnight/Creatas Video; hocus-focus/Creatas Video; Bronek Kaminski/one80: Signature; MichaelSapryhin/Creatas Video+; Sladic/Creatas Video; ReeldealHD Ltd./Verve+; Roy JAMES Shakespeare/Image Bank Film; Just One Film/Image Bank Film: Signature; halbergman/Creatas Video; tawattiw/Creatas Video; HQuality Video/Creatas Video+; **C2:** republica/Creatas Video+; Jordan Siemens/Image Bank Film: Signature; robausch/Creatas Video; Panasevich/Creatas Video+; Mattia Bicchi Photography/Moment Video RR; Rufous52/Creatas Video; Science Photo Library/Photolibrary Video; saicle/Creatas Video+; FotografiaBasica/Creatas Video+; PiXXL/Creatas Video; Science Photo Library/Image Bank Film; Science Photo Library/Image Bank Film; Thomas Barwick/Image Bank Film: Signature; South_agency/Creatas Video; Faithfulshot/Image Bank Film; American Rogue/Image Bank Film; Yellow Dog Productions Inc./Image Bank Film; Picture Palace/Image Bank Film; BSPC/Creatas Video; Daniil Rybkin/Creatas Video+; **C3:** warrengoldswain/Creatas Video+; gustavofrazao/Creatas Video+; peterhowell/Creatas Video+; Vetta; The Lighthouse Film Co, Inc./Lighthouse Films; Science Photo Library/Image Bank Film; WOWstockfootage/Iconica Video: Signature; Multi-bits/Image Bank Film; Fina Filmes/Image Bank Film; slavemotion/Creatas Video; thaiview/Creatas Video; LazyFocus/Creatas Video+; The Lighthouse Film Co, Inc./Lighthouse Films; wundervisuals/Creatas Video+; baddoggy/Vetta; GokhanApaydin/Creatas Video; russlann/Creatas Video+; FluxFactory/Vetta; STK Pictures/Image Bank Film: Signature; champja/Vetta; Science Photo Library/Image Bank Film; Tom Ang/Image Bank Film: Signature; gawrav/Vetta; The Lighthouse Film Co, Inc./Lighthouse Films; eastlight/Vetta; South_agency/Creatas Video; Thomas Barwick/Image Bank Film: Signature; **C4:** giddyuptimelapse/Creatas Video; gorodenkoff/Creatas Video+; Marc Romanelli/Image Bank Film: Signature; Ariel Skelley/Iconica Video: SignatureLaurence Dutton/Vetta; slavemotion/Creatas Video; ReflectFilms/Creatas Video; Vadim_Key/Creatas Video+; selected-takes/Creatas Video; Counter/Image Bank Film; FilippoBacci/Creatas Video; Robin Beckham/Vetta; Ariel Skelley/Iconica Video: Signature; SolStock/Vetta; MachineHeadz/Vetta; AleksandarNakic/Vetta; Ariel Skelley/Image Bank Film: Signature; tawattiw/Vetta; Ariel Skelley/Iconica Video: Signature; Dave168/Creatas Video; xavierarnau/Creatas Video; watcharakorn malithong/Creatas Video+; Samuel Cockedey/one80; Mike Mackinven/Moment Video RF; GoodSport.Video/Image Bank Film; MediaProduction/Vetta; Aerial Filmworks; BBC Universal/BBC Creative; SolStock/Creatas Video; BBC Universal/BBC Creative; DeRepente/Creatas Video+; **C5:** selected-takes/Vetta; Auuu/Vetta; Petrified Films/Archive Films: Creative; Petrified Films/Archive Films: Creative; Dick Clark Productions Inc./Archive Films: Creative; Archive Films/Archive Films: Creative; The Lighthouse Film Co, Inc./Lighthouse Films; Dick Clark Productions Inc./Archive Films: Creative; Archive Films/Archive Films: Creative; shironosov/Creatas Video+; BBC Universal/BBC Creative; Bill Bennett/Corbis Video; T-Bone Films/Image Bank Film: Signature; gl0ck/Creatas Video+; stepporido/Creatas Video+; Дмитрий Ларичев/Creatas Video+; U%C4%9Fur Karamuk/Creatas Video; Guido Mieth/DigitalVision; thaiview/Creatas Video; Robin Beckham/Vetta; The Lighthouse Film Co, Inc./Lighthouse Films; prpicturesproduction/Creatas Video+; selected-takes/Creatas Video; AzmanL/Creatas Video.

Audio

The following music clips are sourced from Getty Images:

Intro: LP_MUSIC/SoundExpress; **C1:** TimTaj/SoundExpress; **C2:** DirtyProductions/SoundExpress; **C3:** Inspirational Audio/SoundExpress; **C4:** TOY INVENTION/SoundExpress; **C5:** LFO62/SoundExpress; mitja mithans/SoundExpress.

The publishers are grateful to the following contributors: author of *Prepare!* Level 7 Teacher's Book first edition: Louis Rogers; cover design and design concept: restless; typesetting: Mouse Life S.L; author of Culture videos: Anna Whitcher; videos in units 1, 2, 7, 8, 10, 11, 14, 15, 17 and 18 produced by Purple Door Media Ltd.